# THE OFFICIAL (ISC)²® SSCP® CBK® REVIEW SEMINAR

## STUDENT HANDBOOK

Version 10.0

(ISC)²®

SECURITY TRANSCENDS TECHNOLOGY℠

*World Headquarters*
Jones & Bartlett Learning
5 Wall Street
Burlington, MA 01803
978-443-5000
info@jblearning.com
www.jblearning.com

Jones & Bartlett Learning Canada
6339 Ormindale Way
Mississauga, Ontario L5V 1J2
Canada

Jones & Bartlett Learning International
Barb House, Barb Mews
London W6 7PA
United Kingdom

Jones & Bartlett Learning books and products are available through most bookstores and online booksellers. To contact Jones & Bartlett Learning directly, call 800-832-0034, fax 978-443-8000, or visit our website, www.jblearning.com.

Substantial discounts on bulk quantities of Jones & Bartlett Learning publications are available to corporations, professional associations, and other qualified organizations. For details and specific discount information, contact the special sales department at Jones & Bartlett Learning via the above contact information or send an email to specialsales@jblearning.com.



**Production Credits**
Chief Executive Officer: Ty Field
President: James Homer
SVP, Chief Operating Officer: Don Jones, Jr.
SVP, Chief Technology Officer: Dean Fossella
SVP, Chief Marketing Officer: Alison M. Pendergast
SVP, Chief Financial Officer: Ruth Siporin
SVP, Curriculum Solutions: Christopher Will
VP, Manufacturing and Inventory Control: Therese Connell
Editorial Management: High Stakes Writing, LLC, Editor and Publisher: Lawrence J. Goodrich
Copyeditor: Katherine Dillin
Reprints and Special Projects Manager: Susan Schultz
Composition: Richard B. Whiteman, Pixel Works
Cover Image: © the International Information Systems Security Certification Consortium, Inc. (ISC)².
Printing and Binding: Lightning Source
Cover Printing: Lightning Source

ISBN: 978-1-4496-3734-7

6048
Printed in the United States of America
15 14 13 12 11 10 9 8 7 6 5 4 3 2 1

# Table of Contents

Dear Seminar Participant,

We are pleased that you have chosen to take advantage of (ISC)$^2$'s Official Systems Security Certified Practitioner (SSCP®) CBK® Review Seminar in anticipation of becoming a certified member of our organization. This comprehensive course will both review and deepen your knowledge of information security. Your efforts this week will go a long way toward attaining the SSCP certification.

Information security is one of the most rapidly advancing fields in the world and becoming certified is a great step toward securing your future in this exciting industry. The SSCP is ideal for hands-on practitioners who implement the plans and policies designed by the CISO, CSO or equivalent on a daily basis. It is also useful for professionals in non-security disciplines, such as IT, whose positions require an understanding of basic security principles.

In addition to receiving recognition from employers and their peers in the industry, our certified members enjoy many career, professional education, and networking opportunities beyond certification, most of which are offered at no additional cost. (ISC)$^2$ members are provided with the latest news and trends in the field via our quarterly digital magazine, *InfoSecurity Professional* and bi-monthly *(ISC)$^2$ Journal*. They also have access to virtual and real-world continuing education and networking opportunities, as well as community awareness programs such as Safe and Secure Online, aimed at spreading cyber security awareness to children, to name a few.

By leveraging the course material provided with the expertise of your qualified (ISC)$^2$ instructor and your own review initiatives, you are constructing the ideal preparation model for the SSCP examination. This Review Seminar includes materials based on the latest version of the (ISC)$^2$ CBK, contributions from (ISC)$^2$-authorized instructors and subject matter experts, as well as a post-seminar self-assessment.

The time you invest in studying for the exam is worth the outcome when you receive that certificate stating that you're now an elite member of the top information security certification organization in the world. I wish you the best of luck this week and on the challenging examination!

Sincerely,

W. Hord Tipton, CISSP-ISSEP, CAP, CISA
Executive Director
(ISC)$^2$

33920 US Highway 19 North, Suite 205 Palm Harbor, Florida 34684 United States of America
PH: 1+727.785.0189 FX: 1+727.786.2989 www.isc2.org

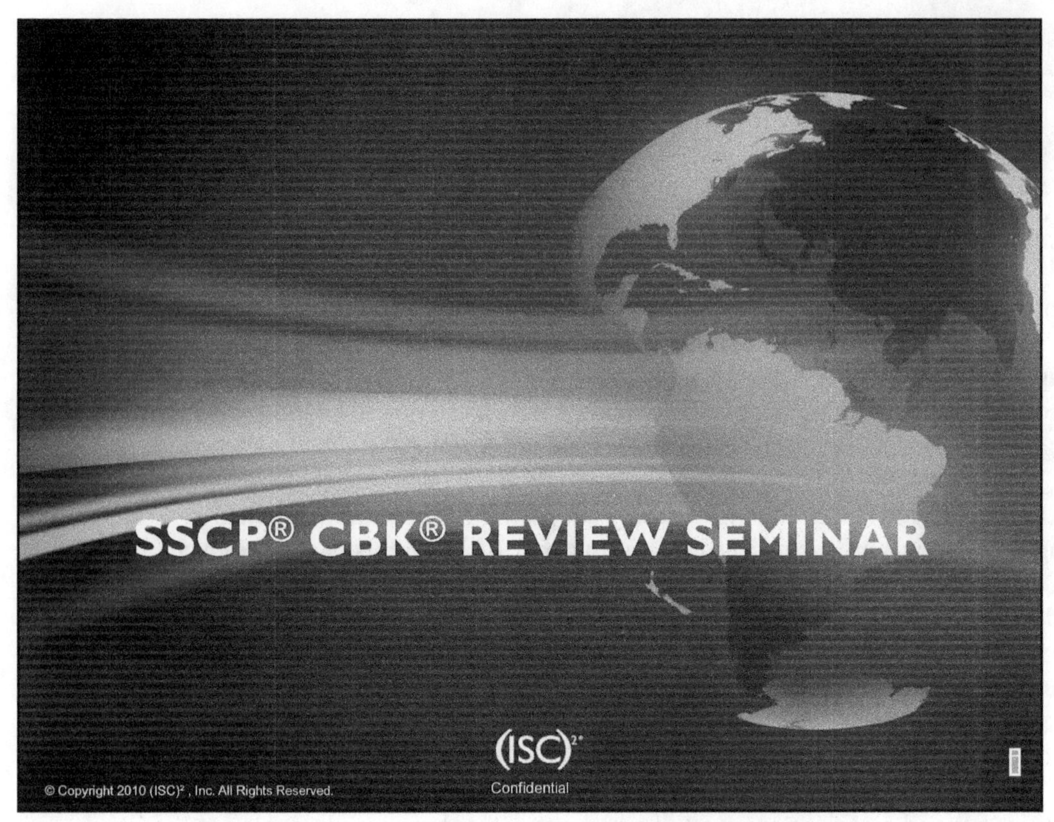
SSCP® CBK® REVIEW SEMINAR
(ISC)²
© Copyright 2010 (ISC)², Inc. All Rights Reserved.
Confidential
i

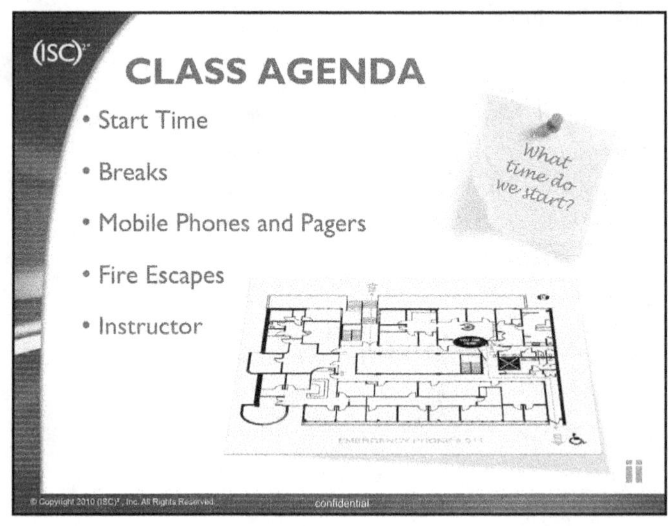
(ISC)²
CLASS AGENDA
• Start Time
• Breaks
• Mobile Phones and Pagers
• Fire Escapes
• Instructor
What time do we start?
ii

(ISC)²
WHO IS (ISC)²®?
▪ The global, not-for-profit, leader in educating and certifying information security professionals throughout their careers.
▪ Based in Palm Harbor, FL
➢Offices in London; Tokyo; Hong Kong; Vienna & Virginia
▪ Worldwide affiliates
▪ Over 70,000 certified professionals in 135 countries
(ISC)² EMEA
(ISC)² AMERICAS
(ISC)² JAPAN
(ISC)² ASIA-PACIFIC
confidential
iii

PATH TO (ISC)²® MEMBERSHIP
1. Examination
Sign up for the exam
Submit the examination fee
Assert professional experience
2. Certification
Pass the SSCP exam
3. Endorsement
Get endorsed by an active (ISC)² member in good standing; one that can attest to your professional experience
4. Background Verification
Employment
Certifications
Degree
iv

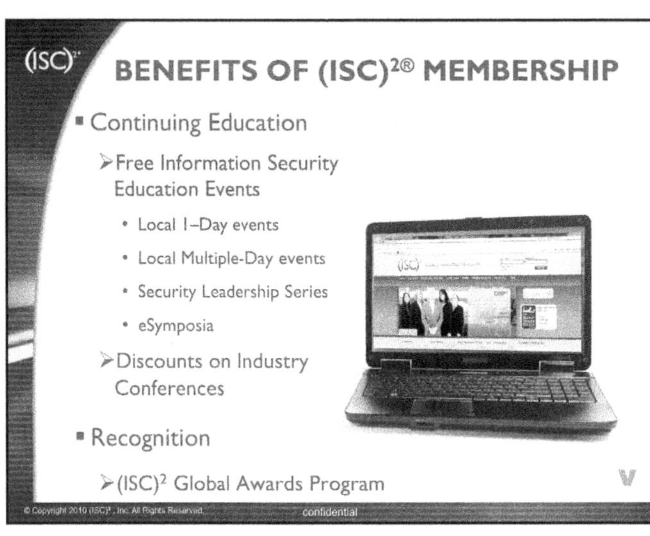
BENEFITS OF (ISC)²® MEMBERSHIP
Continuing Education
Free Information Security Education Events
Local 1–Day events
Local Multiple-Day events
Security Leadership Series
eSymposia
Discounts on Industry Conferences
Recognition
(ISC)² Global Awards Program
v

BENEFITS OF (ISC)²® MEMBERSHIP
Publication/Tools
The (ISC)² Journal
(ISC)² Magazine
Global Resource Guide for Today's Information Security Professional
SecurityTALK
Safe and Secure Online
Credential Verification
Additional benefits
www.isc2.org/industry-resources
InfoSecurity
Journal
Safe and Secure Online
vi

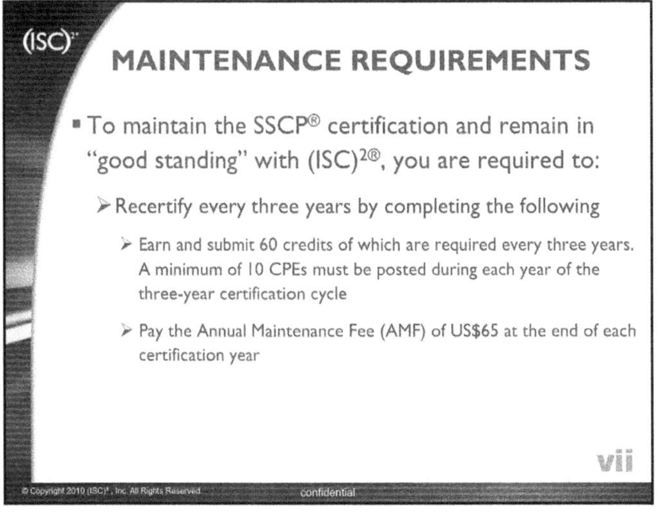
MAINTENANCE REQUIREMENTS
To maintain the SSCP® certification and remain in "good standing" with (ISC)²®, you are required to:
Recertify every three years by completing the following
Earn and submit 60 credits of which are required every three years. A minimum of 10 CPEs must be posted during each year of the three-year certification cycle
Pay the Annual Maintenance Fee (AMF) of US$65 at the end of each certification year
vii

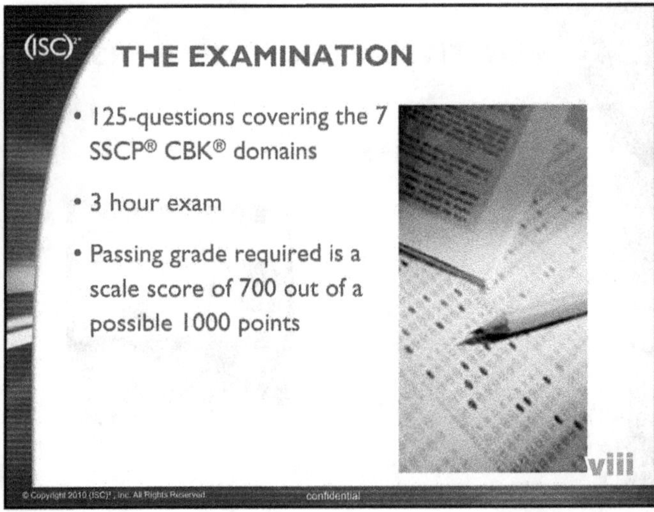
(ISC)²
THE EXAMINATION
• 125-questions covering the 7 SSCP® CBK® domains
• 3 hour exam
• Passing grade required is a scale score of 700 out of a possible 1000 points
viii

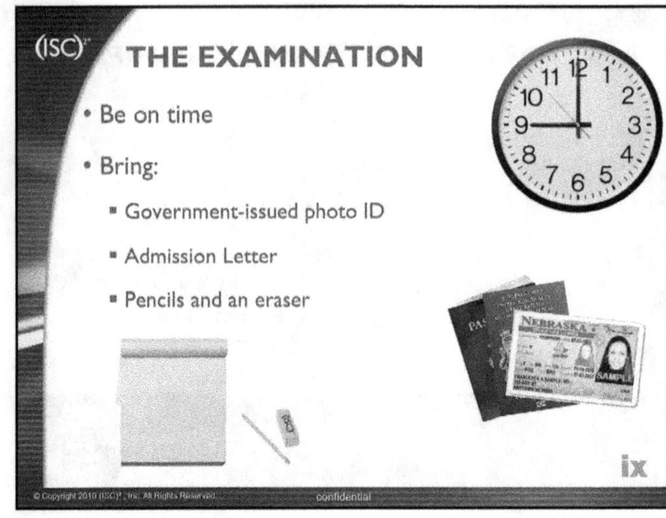
(ISC)²
THE EXAMINATION
• Be on time
• Bring:
▪ Government-issued photo ID
▪ Admission Letter
▪ Pencils and an eraser
ix

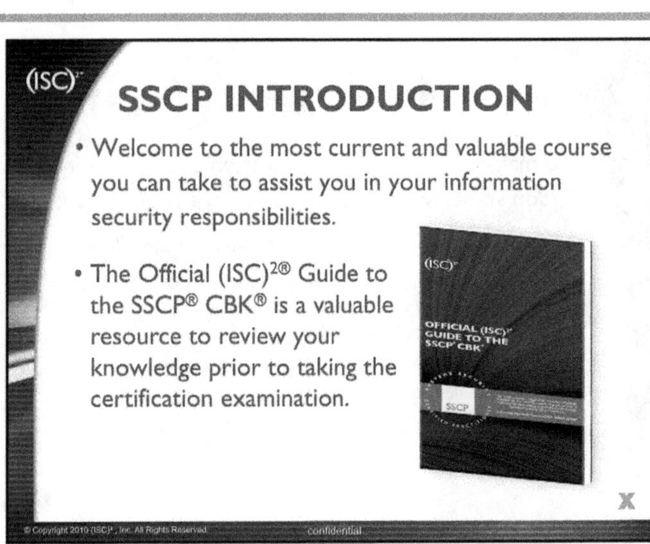
(ISC)²
SSCP INTRODUCTION
• Welcome to the most current and valuable course you can take to assist you in your information security responsibilities.
• The Official (ISC)²® Guide to the SSCP® CBK® is a valuable resource to review your knowledge prior to taking the certification examination.
x

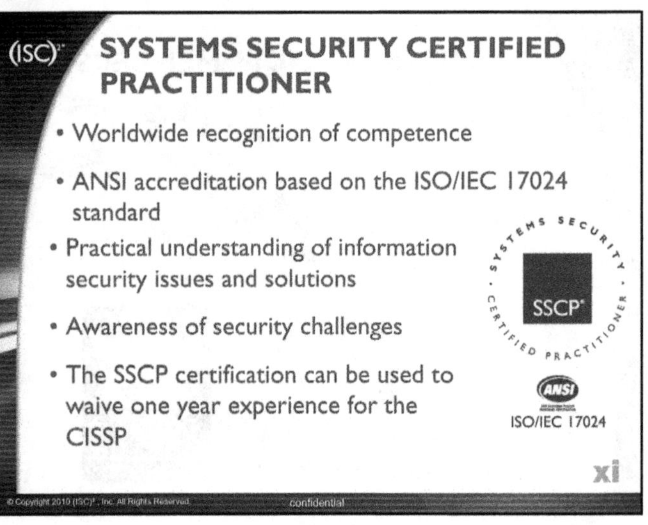
(ISC)²
SYSTEMS SECURITY CERTIFIED PRACTITIONER
• Worldwide recognition of competence
• ANSI accreditation based on the ISO/IEC 17024 standard
• Practical understanding of information security issues and solutions
• Awareness of security challenges
• The SSCP certification can be used to waive one year experience for the CISSP
SSCP®
ISO/IEC 17024
xi

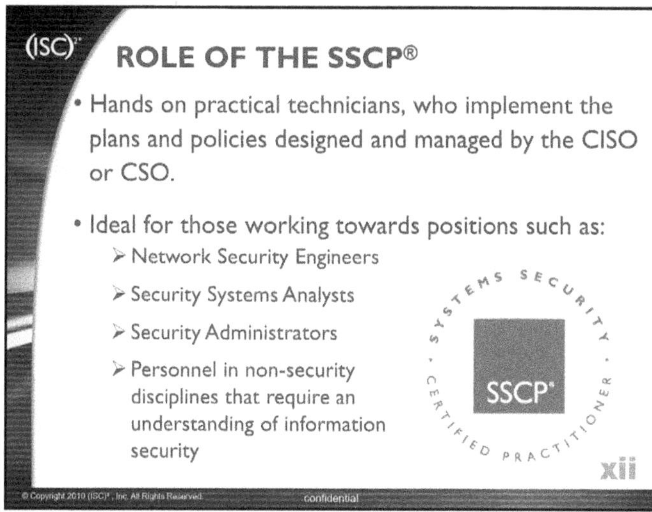
(ISC)²
ROLE OF THE SSCP®
• Hands on practical technicians, who implement the plans and policies designed and managed by the CISO or CSO.
• Ideal for those working towards positions such as:
➢ Network Security Engineers
➢ Security Systems Analysts
➢ Security Administrators
➢ Personnel in non-security disciplines that require an understanding of information security
SYSTEMS SECURITY CERTIFIED PRACTITIONER
SSCP®
xii
© Copyright 2010 (ISC)², Inc. All Rights Reserved.
confidential

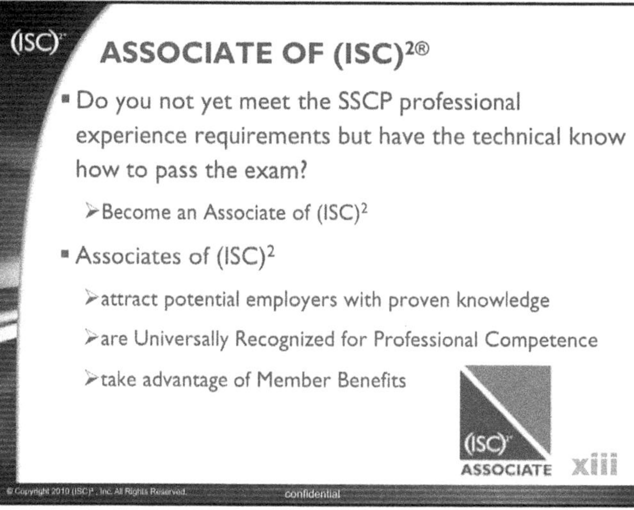
(ISC)²
ASSOCIATE OF (ISC)²®
▪ Do you not yet meet the SSCP professional experience requirements but have the technical know how to pass the exam?
➢Become an Associate of (ISC)²
▪ Associates of (ISC)²
➢attract potential employers with proven knowledge
➢are Universally Recognized for Professional Competence
➢take advantage of Member Benefits
(ISC)²
ASSOCIATE
xiii
© Copyright 2010 (ISC)², Inc. All Rights Reserved.
confidential

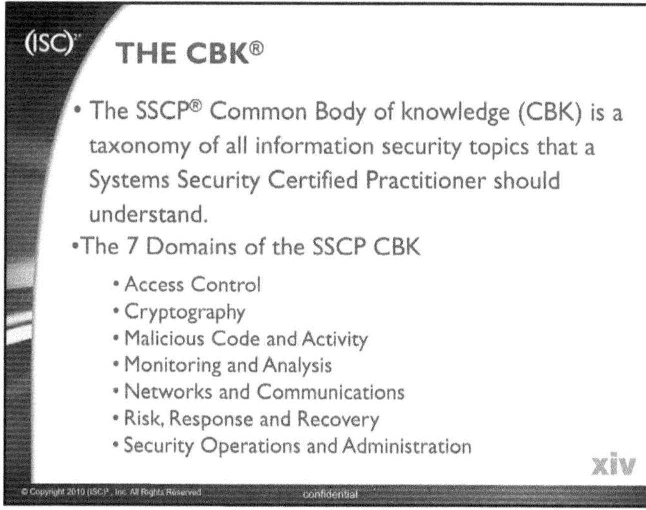
(ISC)²
THE CBK®
• The SSCP® Common Body of knowledge (CBK) is a taxonomy of all information security topics that a Systems Security Certified Practitioner should understand.
•The 7 Domains of the SSCP CBK
• Access Control
• Cryptography
• Malicious Code and Activity
• Monitoring and Analysis
• Networks and Communications
• Risk, Response and Recovery
• Security Operations and Administration
xiv
© Copyright 2010 (ISC)², Inc. All Rights Reserved.
confidential

"SECURITY TRANSCENDS TECHNOLOGY"
(ISC)²
Confidential
XV
© Copyright 2010 (ISC)², Inc. All Rights Reserved.

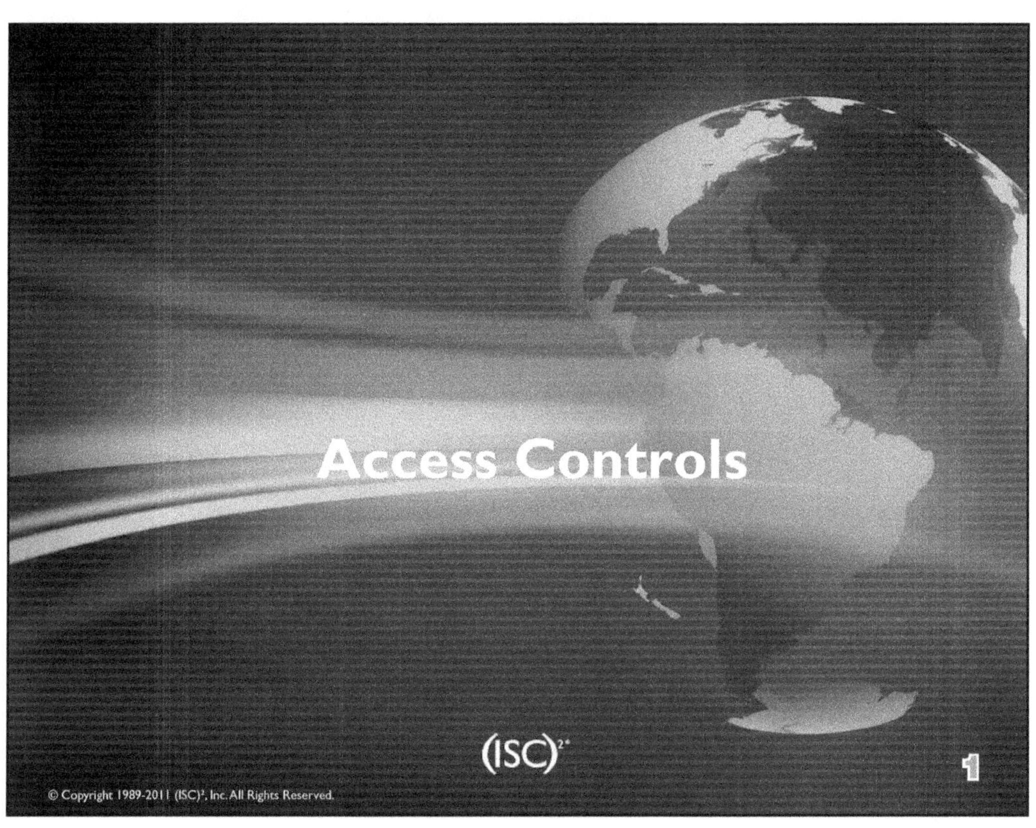
Access Controls
(ISC)²
1
© Copyright 1989-2011 (ISC)², Inc. All Rights Reserved.

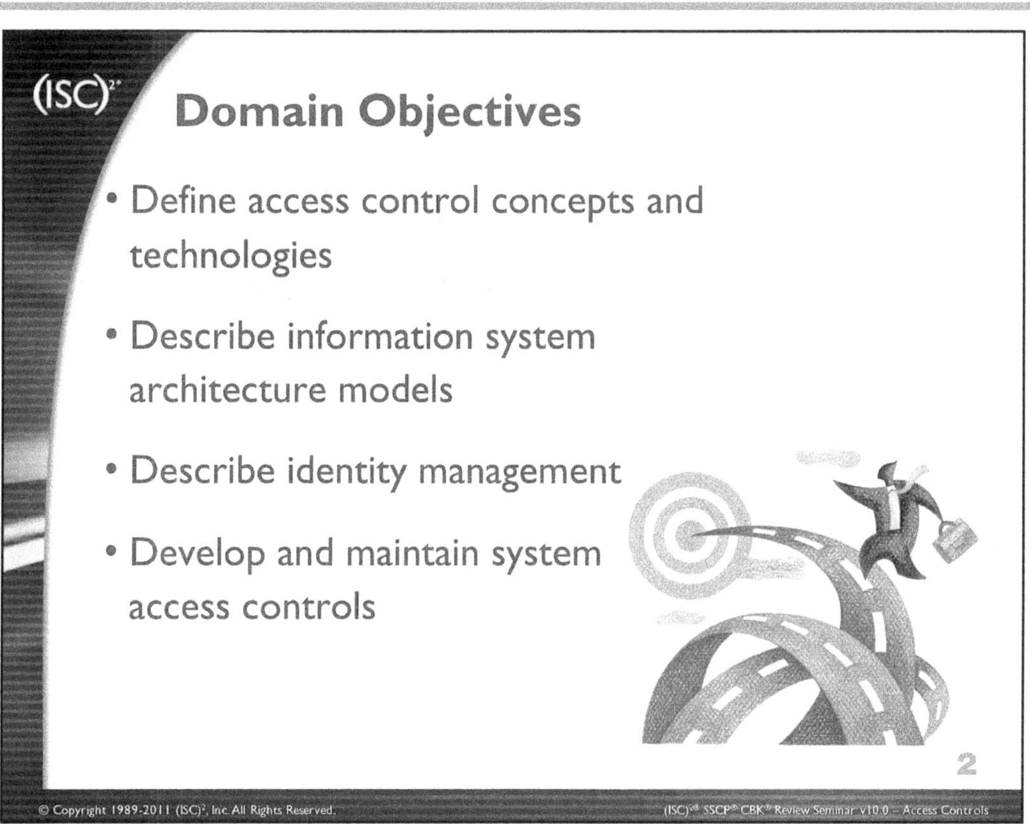
(ISC)²
Domain Objectives
• Define access control concepts and technologies
• Describe information system architecture models
• Describe identity management
• Develop and maintain system access controls
2
© Copyright 1989-2011 (ISC)², Inc. All Rights Reserved.
(ISC)²® SSCP® CBK® Review Seminar v10.0 – Access Controls

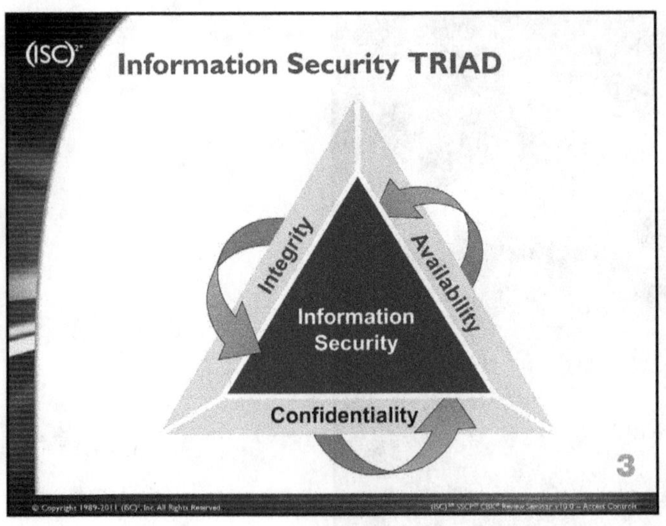


- **INFORMATION SECURITY TRIAD –** Access control impacts all of the legs of the triad with a nearly equal emphasis on each leg, ensuring that:
  - Data and systems are available to the people who need them (Availability).
  - Data is not changed in an unauthorized manner and systems process transactions correctly (Integrity).
  - Data is not disclosed to unauthorized people or locations (Confidentiality).

---

**REFERENCE:**

"Integrity in Automated Information Systems," National Computer Security Center Technical Report 79-91, September 1991.

(ISC)²

### Definition: Access Control

- Allowing only authorized users, programs, or processes the right to use resources
- Operations/procedures managed by hardware, software, or people to control the use of resources
- Includes monitoring and identifying requests, logging requests, and granting or denying permissions based on a security model

4

- **DEFINITION: ACCESS CONTROL –**
  - Access control is the mediation or enforcement of restrictions concerning who, or what, will have permission to execute a certain activity, whether on a computer, in a building, or other facility.
  - Access control includes assertion of identity (identification), proof of that assertion (authentication), control over what a user or process can or cannot access (authorization), and creation or maintenance of appropriate audit trails for later investigative purposes (accounting).

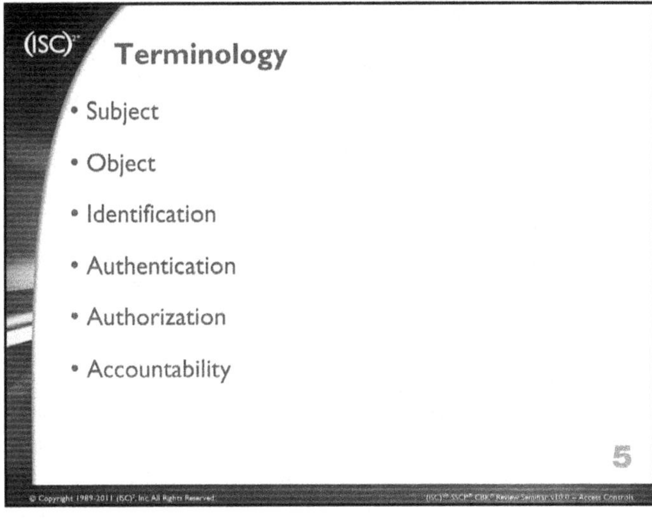


- **SUBJECT –** Any entity (e.g., users, programs, and processes) requesting permission to access objects.
- **OBJECT –** Any item to which access should be controlled (e.g., files, programs, instructions, data, or hardware).
- **IDENTIFICATION –** The process of claiming the identity to gain access to a resource, generally employing unique machine-readable names, that enables recognition of users or resources as identical to those previously described to the computer system.
- **AUTHENTICATION –** The process of proving the claimed identity. Verification, validation, or proof of the professed identification of a person or node.
- **AUTHORIZATION –** Specifies what a user is permitted to do (e.g. read, write, execute, delete, etc.) after being successfully identified and authenticated by the system.
- **ACCOUNTABILITY –** The ability to be able to hold individuals responsible for their activities on a system. Accountability requires positive identification and an effective audit trail.

---

**REFERENCE:**

Official Guide to the CISSP Exam, Auerbach, 2004.

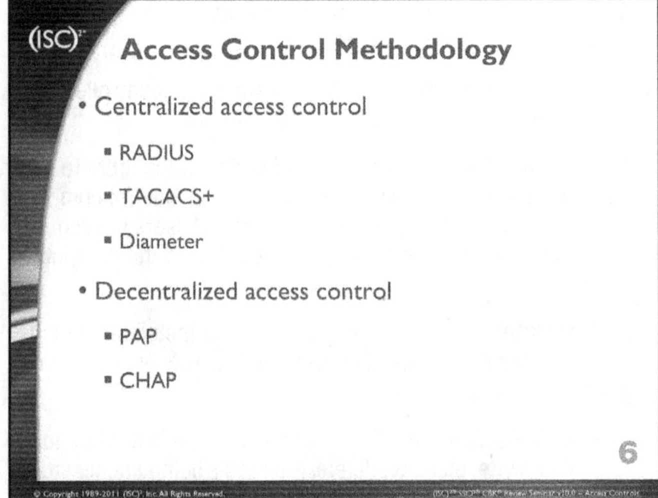

(ISC)²
Access Control Methodology
• Centralized access control
▪ RADIUS
▪ TACACS+
▪ Diameter
• Decentralized access control
▪ PAP
▪ CHAP
6


- **CENTRALIZED ACCESS CONTROL –** Where a common, single entity (e.g., individual, department, device, etc.) makes system and network access decisions about who is authorized to gain access to those systems and networks. The access controls are managed centrally rather than at the local level. Owners decide what users can access which specific objects and the central administration supports these directives. Centralized authentication services are implemented through the use of authentication, authorization, and accounting (AAA) servers.
  - Examples of AAA servers include remote authentication dial in user service (RADIUS), terminal access controller access-control system plus (TACACS+), and Diameter. The benefits of using AAA servers include:
    - Lower user administration time because user accounts are maintained on a single host.
    - A reduction in configuration errors because different access devices will have similar formats.
    - A reduction in security administrator training needs, as there is only one system to learn.
    - Compliance auditing is better and easier because all access requests are handled by one system.
    - A reduction in help desk calls because of the consistent user interface.
  - The authentication process is separated from the communications process thereby enabling the consolidation of user authentication data on a centralized database.
  - **RADIUS –** Remote authentication dial-in user service. The most popular AAA service uses two configuration files: A client configuration file, which contains client address and the shared secret for transaction authentication; and the user file, which contains the user identification and authentication data as well as the connection and authorization information. A network access server (NAS) completes several authentication steps. The NAS:
    - decrypts the user's user datagram protocol (UDP) access request.
    - authenticates the source.
    - validates the request against the user file.
    - responds by allowing or rejecting access, or by requesting more information.
  - **TACACS+ –** Terminal access controller access-control system plus. An Internet Engineering Task Force (IETF) standard that uses a single configuration file to control server operations, define users and attribute/value pairs, and control authentication and authorization procedures. An options section contains operation settings, the shared secret key, and the accounting file name. To implement the authentication steps, the client using the transmission control protocol (TCP):
    - sends a service request with the header in cleartext and an encrypted body containing UserID, password, and shared key.
    - the reply contains a permit/deny, as well as attribute/value pairs for connection configuration, as required.
  - **DIAMETER –** Although based on RADIUS, Diameter has been enhanced in order to overcome the inherent limitation of RADIUS that restricts its use for a highly fluid or mobile workforce. Diameter consists of a base protocol and extensions. The base protocol defines the message format, transport, error reporting, and security used by all extensions. The extensions conduct specific types of authentication, authorization, or accounting transactions. Diameter also uses UDP but in a peer-to-peer rather than client/server mode. This allows servers to initiate requests and handle transmission errors locally, which reduces latency and improves performance.
    - The user sends an authorization request containing the request command, a session ID, and the user's UserID and password, etc., to the NAS (network authentication server).
    - The server validates the user's credentials and if the validation is successful, returns an answer packet containing attribute/value pairs for the service requested.
    - The session ID uniquely identifies the connection and resolves the RADIUS problem with duplicate connection identifiers in high-density installations. One other advantage of Diameter is that a secure connection virtual private network (VPN) can be pre-established, which protects transactions using IPsec (Internet protocol security) or TLS (transport layer security).
    - The drawback to centralized access is that it is a central point of failure. If the AAA service is not available, subjects cannot access objects.
- **DECENTRALIZED ACCESS CONTROL –** The access control decision and administration is administered locally. Access control is, therefore, in the hands of the people such as department managers who are closest to the users of the system. Access requests do not get processed by one centralized entity. On the one hand, decentralized access control often results in confusion because it can lead to non-standardization and to overlapping rights which may cause gaps in the access control configuration. On the other hand, a decentralized approach eliminates the "single point of failure" problem, or the perception that a central controlling body is unable to respond effectively to local conditions. The two most common examples of decentralized access control are:
  - **PAP –** Password authentication protocol (PAP) uses cleartext usernames and passwords.
  - **CHAP –** Challenge-handshake authentication protocol (CHAP) hashes the password with a one-time challenge number in order to defeat eavesdropping-based replay attacks.

---

**REFERENCE:**

"Centralized Authentication Services (RADIUS, TACACS, DIAMETER)," Stackpole, Data Security Management, Auerbach, 2000.

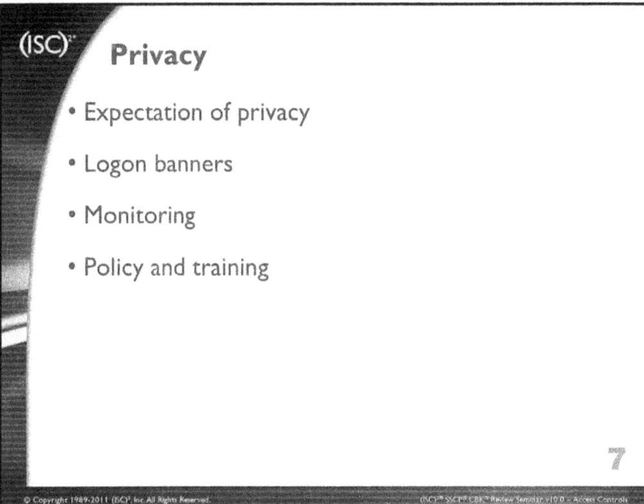


- **PRIVACY –** Concerns about liability in harassment suits, skyrocketing losses from employee theft, and productivity losses from employees shopping or peeping at pornography from their cubicles have led to companies conducting various forms of electronic monitoring. This electronic monitoring leads to issues of privacy within the workplace. Depending on the country or jurisdiction, the amount of monitoring of employees permitted may vary widely.
- **EXPECTATION OF PRIVACY –**
  - Current thinking is that for a person to establish a reasonable expectation of privacy, he or she must establish two things: that he or she has a subjective expectation of privacy, and that the subjective expectation of privacy is reasonable. If either element is missing, no protected interest is established. This means that if an employee is led to expect that something (e.g., email communications) is private, the company cannot legally violate that privacy. If the company informs its employees that email sent over the company's network is monitored, however, the employee can no longer claim to have an "expectation of privacy." In other words, once the company stakes its claim over its cyber-dominion, its employees have no right to privacy there.
  - The key for successfully managing the balancing act between privacy and security is for companies to make clear to their employees what the organization's policy on acceptable usage and monitoring is. In many cases, it may be accurate to state that an employee has no expectation of privacy while using corporate systems.
- **LOGON BANNERS –** "Logon banners" are messages that provide notice of legal rights to users of the device. These should be used on your systems and devices. Logon banners are used to gain employee:
  - Consent to monitoring.
  - Awareness of potential disciplinary action in the event of misuse of the account.
  - Consent to the retrieval of stored files and records.
  - In summary, logon banners are used to legally eliminate any expectation of privacy for employees using corporate systems.
- **MONITORING –** An American Management Association (AMA) survey of "Workplace Monitoring & Surveillance" found that in 2001, "more than three-quarters of major U.S. firms (77.7%) record[ed] and review[ed] employee communications and activities on the job, including their phone calls, e-mail, Internet connections, and computer files."
  - Monitoring in the workplace includes but is not limited to:
    - Opening mail or email.
    - Use of automated software to check email.
    - Checking phone logs or recording phone calls.
    - Checking logs of websites visited.
    - Getting information from credit reference agencies.
    - Collecting information through "point of sale" terminals.
    - Recording activities on closed circuit television (CCTV).
  - Employers monitor their staff, in one way or another, as a way to check the quality and quantity of their employees' work. As employers are very often liable for the actions of their employees, they also need to be sure that their employees are behaving properly.
- **POLICY AND TRAINING –** To ensure that monitoring is understood by all employees, employers should have a code of conduct or policy that covers workplace monitoring. The activities monitored can be the subject of disciplinary action if employees are using workplace equipment in ways that are not permitted.
  - Policies alone do not suffice. Employers are expected clearly to communicate to staff what they can and cannot do. The best way to do this is through training. If and when systems change, the policy should be updated and employees informed.

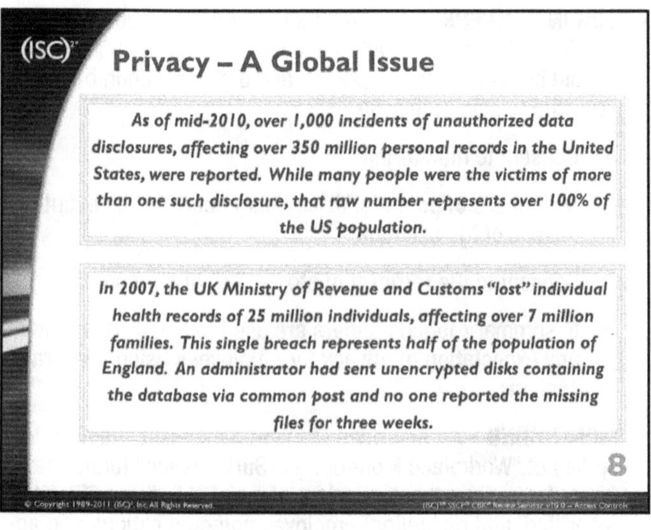

(ISC)²
Privacy – A Global Issue
As of mid-2010, over 1,000 incidents of unauthorized data disclosures, affecting over 350 million personal records in the United States, were reported. While many people were the victims of more than one such disclosure, that raw number represents over 100% of the US population.
In 2007, the UK Ministry of Revenue and Customs "lost" individual health records of 25 million individuals, affecting over 7 million families. This single breach represents half of the population of England. An administrator had sent unencrypted disks containing the database via common post and no one reported the missing files for three weeks.
8


- **PRIVACY – A GLOBAL ISSUE –** This slide highlights the basic issue security professionals face with regard to access control over individual identity records. This is an international issue.
- The Organization for Economic Cooperation and Development (OECD) has published an international guide to privacy protection (www.oecd.org) and actively promotes national initiatives worldwide.
- An interesting reference on US data breaches mentioned is available at: http://www.privacyrights.org/ar/ChronDataBreaches.htm.
- See http://news.cnet.com/U.K.-government-reveals-its-biggest-privacy-disaster/2100-1029_3-6219772.html for more on UK Ministry of Revenue and Customs data breach.
- Also, see http://wiki.openrightsgroup.org/wiki/UK_Privacy_Debacles.
- Accenture publishes an international summary of global privacy issues at: https://microsite.accenture.com/dataprivacyreport/Documents/Accenture_Data_Privacy_Report.pdf.

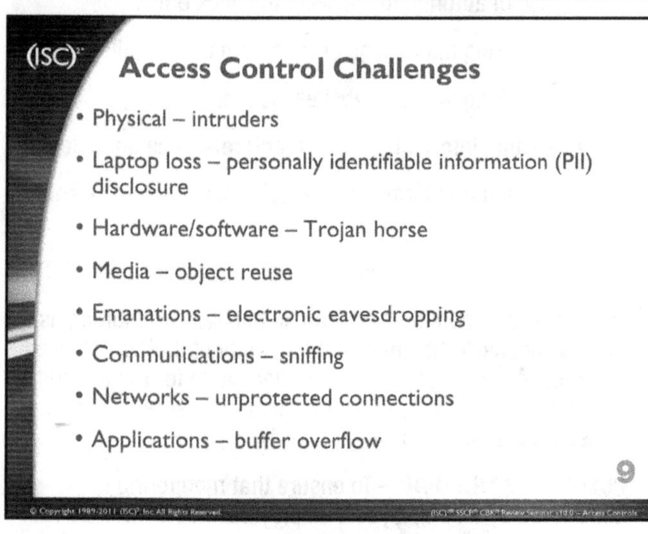


- **PHYSICAL – INTRUDERS –** If you give an intruder physical access, your data is no longer your own. Booting to alternate media allows access to your data with nothing blocking the way, at which point it becomes trivial to copy the data to a portable drive or even to an Internet server. The only limitation on the intruder is time.
- **LAPTOP LOSS – PERSONALLY IDENTIFIABLE INFORMATION (PII) DISCLOSURE –** A lost laptop poses many of the same problems posed by physical access – except that in this case, the intruder (or thief) will have an indefinite amount of time to attack and access the data. In addition, laptops can offer much in the way of PII or even access passwords to corporate sites. PII is the subject of many legislative initiatives around the world.
- **HARDWARE/SOFTWARE – TROJAN HORSE –** The unauthorized programs installed on a system by an attacker are under the control of the attacker, and can permit access without the network administrator or workstation owner being aware of the breach.
- **MEDIA – OBJECT REUSE –** Do not simply discard media at the end of its life. Even if erased or reformatted, the data that it held can be recovered. While it is possible to permanently erase data, the time and cost is usually greater than the value of the media. Shredding or other physical destruction is a safe and inexpensive choice.
- **EMANATION – ELECTRONIC EAVESDROPPING –** A technique such as wiretapping of network cabling is a well-known, time-tested attack. While some media are more resistant than others (fiber is safer than copper, for example), none is immune. The widespread introduction of wireless access points (WAPs) in recent years has significantly increased this risk.
- **COMMUNICATIONS – SNIFFING –** Another variation of eavesdropping is the physical interception of communications called "sniffing." Sniffing can be accomplished by attaching to the network media and listening to the traffic as it goes by, or by relaying the data as in a "man-in-the-middle attack."
- **NETWORKS – UNPROTECTED CONNECTIONS –** Many organizations build their networks with more "drops," or open connectors (i.e., jacks), at wall plates than they need in order to provide for future growth. These unused connection points are often active connections that could be used to gain access to the network by visitors or intruders.
- **APPLICATIONS – BUFFER OVERFLOW –** Countless programs and modules (such as dynamic link libraries (DLLs)) have been discovered to have a common programming weakness known as "buffer overflow." By entering more characters than expected into an input field, an attacker can cause an application to execute malicious code.
- This list can never be complete. New challenges evolve constantly. As this is being written, the security community is discussing a newly discovered peer-to-peer risk in which P2P users inadvertently share their "My Documents" folder thereby exposing sensitive company documents.

## Effects of Access Control Breaches

- Disclosure of confidential information
- Corruption of data
- Loss of business intelligence
- Danger to facilities, personnel, and systems
- Damage to equipment
- Failure of systems and business processes
- Denial of service (DOS)

10



- **EFFECTS OF ACCESS CONTROL BREACHES –** Failure in maintaining access control can give advantage to the opposition, whether the opponent is a military force or a business interested in competitive intelligence. This list, while not complete, is suggestive of the kinds of losses that can occur.
- Not all incidents have the same effect or carry the same weight, nor are some as easy to detect as others. For example, losses due to disclosure of business secrets (including business intelligence) will typically go unnoticed in the short term. Losses due to corruption of data, especially if the corruption is done slowly over time, might make a database and all its backups useless by the time the corruption is discovered. Such data corruption can easily cause systems and business processes to fail or give erroneous results.
- Some kinds of denial of service (DoS) attacks are short lived and are as easily noticed as a network outage. Other kinds take longer to evolve but result in a business being unable to support the needs of its customers, forcing the business to turn them away – possibly to competitors – thus creating a more severe, long-lasting outcome.

## Responses to Access Control Violations

- The impact of security breaches often leads to:
  - Loss of confidence by customers
  - Loss of business opportunities
  - New legislation and regulation
  - Negative publicity
  - Increased oversight
  - Financial penalties

11



- **RESPONSES TO ACCESS CONTROL VIOLATIONS –** This slide lists a few of the potential negative effects that can occur if an organization has access control violations.
- Here is an example: Egghead software voluntarily reported a breach in the summer of 2000 and was widely praised in the trade press. They also went out of business within a year of the disclosure. Customers were reluctant to use credit cards when transacting business with a company that had admitted that it didn't secure credit card information properly. With that result in the collective memory of corporate executives, violations were seldom made public until legislation was enacted that required it.
- In 2003, California passed a mandatory disclosure law that affects all companies that do business in California or with that state's residents – thereby including virtually every non-local business in the United States and in many non-US countries. The law covers disclosure of personally identifiable information (PII) that might be used to commit identify fraud. Note that it does not cover other intrusions, such as theft of intellectual property.
- A US-centric, state by state summary of similar disclosure laws can be found at: http://www.csoonline.com/article/221322/CSO_Disclosure_Series_Data_Breach_Notification_Laws_State_By_State?source=nlt_csoupdate.

**REFERENCE:**

California Security Breach Information Act (SB-1386), 2003.

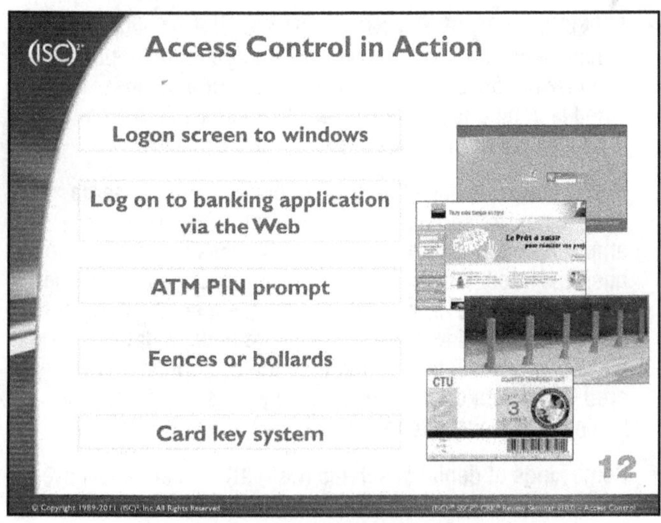


- **ACCESS CONTROL TAKES MANY FORMS, SUCH AS:**
  - Logical
    - Logon screens.
    - Log on to banking application through the Web.
    - ATM personal identification number (PIN) prompt.
  - Physical
    - Fences or bollards.
    - Card key system (as most hotels use).
- In all of these examples, some subject seeks access to some object. Access control mediates this request.

**IMAGES:**
https://logitelnet.socgen.com/
http://www.plasticprinters.com/accesscards/accesscard11.jpg

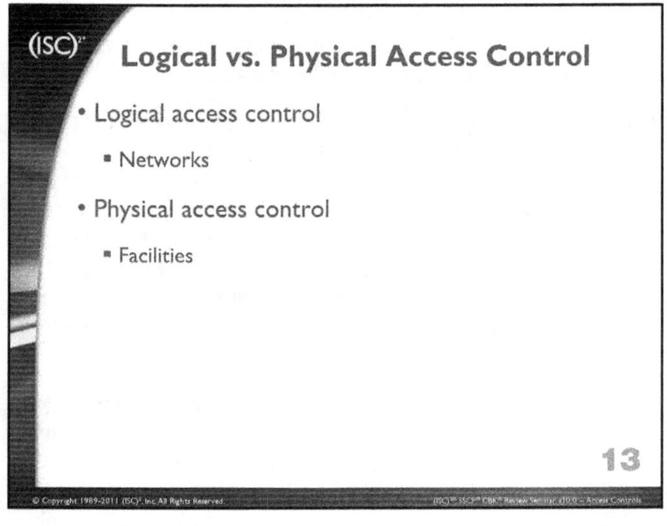


- **LOGICAL ACCESS CONTROL –** Activities such as logging into a network typically require purely logical access controls. Some combination of username, password, token, smart card, or biometrics is presented and the user is authorized or denied access by the system.
- **PHYSICAL ACCESS CONTROL –**
  - Gaining access to the computer on which one can log on is a function of physical access. Physical access controls start with simple things such as limiting access via guards and gates, then practicing defense in depth by using proximity cards for access to secure areas or locking cables to prevent theft. More complex physical access controls employ biometrics or certificates (on smart cards or tokens).
  - A particular access control method, such as biometrics, can be an example of either logical access control (when used to authenticate) or physical access control (when used to identify and authenticate).

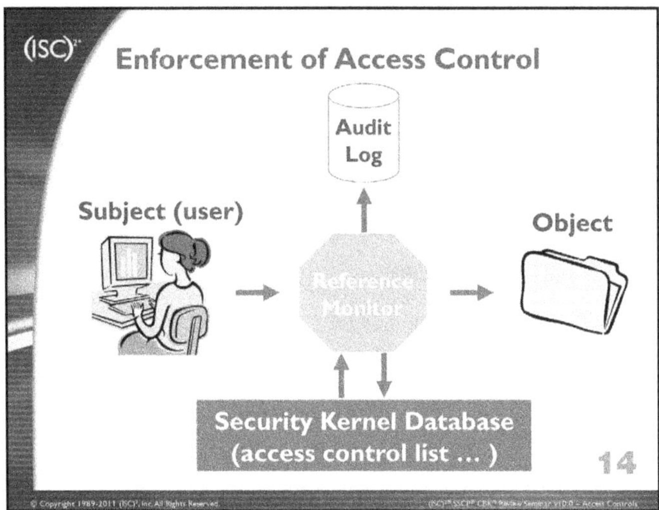


- **ENFORCEMENT OF ACCESS CONTROL –** The enforcement of access control with respect to computer systems is performed by the security kernel. The security kernel implements the concept of the reference monitor. The reference monitor is the concept of mediating all access requests and permitting access only when the appropriate rules or conditions are met.
- **THE FUNDAMENTAL PRINCIPLES CENTRAL TO A REFERENCE MONITOR ARE:**
  - Tamperproof.
  - Complete mediation of all access (always invoked).
  - Compact/small enough to permit full analysis to prove correctness.
- **THIS WORKS AS FOLLOWS:**
  - The subject requests access to a particular object and the request is intercepted by the security kernel.
  - The security kernel refers to its rules base to determine access rights according to the policies in place.
  - The security kernel then allows or denies access.
  - All access requests handled by the system are logged for later tracking and analysis.
- The slide shows a request for access coming from the subject, "user," to a particular object (in this case a file). The access request is intercepted by the reference monitor and the access granted according to the rules in the security kernel database.
  - The security kernel checks its rules base, also known as the "security kernel database," to determine whether the subject should have access to the object. This rule base may be an ACL (access control list), directory, or other repository of access permissions. If the rules permit the access request, the reference monitor will permit access and create a log entry.
  - Access is based on authorization levels specified in the security rules (read/write/execute).
    - A READ operation is permitted only if there is a need-to-know.
    - A WRITE is permitted only if the result does not compromise the security level of the object or later permit an unauthorized access.
    - An EXECUTE privilege is limited to specific subject permissions, generally based on least privilege and separation of duties.

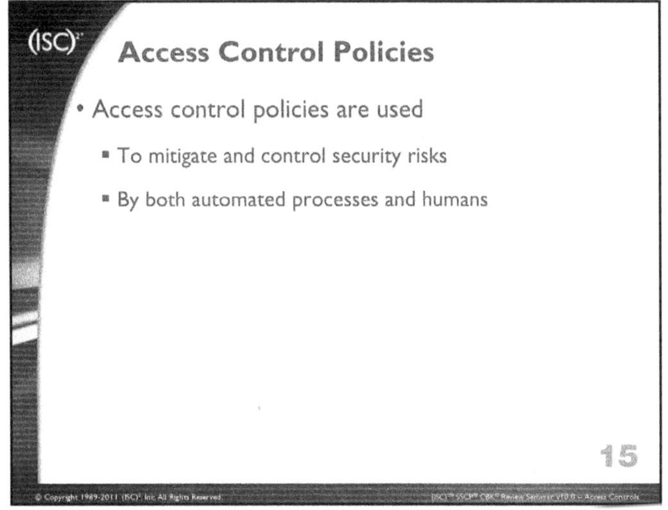

Access Control Policies
• Access control policies are used
▪ To mitigate and control security risks
▪ By both automated processes and humans
15


- An access control policy authorizes a specific group of users to perform a particular set of actions on a particular set of resources. Users will not have access to functions in the system unless authorized via access control policies.
- In order to manage/administer access control policies, you must understand four central elements of access: users, actions, resources, and relationships:
  - "Users" are the people who use the system.
  - "Resources" are the protected objects in the system that only authorized subjects should be permitted to access, and then only in authorized manners.
  - "Actions" are the activities that authorized users are able to perform on the resources.
  - "Relationships" are optional conditions that exist between users and resources. They are permissions granted to an authorized user, such as Read/Write/Execute, etc. See the descriptions from the previous page.
- Access control policies state the overall objective and ownership of access control, such as least privilege, discretionary, or mandatory access control.

## Type of Access Control

- Preventive: Protect vulnerabilities from being exploited
- Deterrent: Discourage unlawful or unauthorized activities with warnings
- Detective: Provide information about a past or present attack
- Corrective/recovery: Countermeasures taken to reduce a risk or minimize impact after a vulnerability has been successfully exploited or an event has occurred

16

 (ISC)² SSCP® CBK® Review Seminar v10.0 – Access Controls

- **PREVENTIVE –** Preventive controls pre-empt a potential incident from occurring by applying restrictions to activities. The concept of "least privilege" is based on this idea – subjects are given access to resources only when they need to have them. Applying appropriate permissions to subjects ensures that assets will be protected from unwanted exposure.
- **DETERRENT –** Deterrent controls are designed to discourage unlawful or unauthorized behavior by posting rules or warnings. Examples might include "no trespassing" signs, acceptable use policies for Internet access, etc.
- **DETECTIVE –** Detective controls are used to provide information about things that have happened (e.g., forensic analysis of past activities) or that are happening at that moment (e.g., real-time alerts of inappropriate activities). Real-time access alerting can be related to intrusion detection systems, antivirus systems, network monitoring, and other security management tools. These tools provide visibility into the operational environment, monitor for unauthorized activities, and log events for after-the-fact analysis.
- **CORRECTIVE/RECOVERY –**
  - Corrective – Corrective controls enact countermeasures to address a threat to, or incident on, the system. Examples include changes in access control lists on network devices, changing encryption schemes, or adding new security techniques to improve access control. Dispatching security guards to investigate an alarm, or activating automatic sprinkler systems after fire detection, are other examples of corrective controls.
  - Recovery – Recovery controls are designed to prescribe actions taken after an event to restore normal operations, and can be automatic (system restart capability) or manual (disaster recovery procedures).
- Most individual controls cannot provide complete protection, and are often combined as a "system of controls" to increase the overall depth of security. Some controls are interdependent and rely on or interact with other controls, such as intrusion detection systems (IDS) sensors (detective) sending alarms to intrusion prevention system (IPS) systems (preventive/corrective) to block harmful traffic.

## Access Control Policy Implementation

- Administrative
- Logical/technical
  - Hardware
  - Software
    - Operating systems/file systems
    - Applications and security protocols
- Physical

17

 (ISC)² SSCP® CBK® Review Seminar v10.0 – Access Controls

- **ACCESS CONTROL POLICY IMPLEMENTATION –** Access controls can be implemented in various forms, levels of restriction, and at different levels within the computing environment. A combination of access controls can provide a system with layered, "defense-in-depth" protection.
- **ADMINISTRATIVE –** Policies written by management and passed down to staff. Administrative policies are a first line of defense that inform users of their responsibilities (e.g., written policies regarding password length).
- **LOGICAL/TECHNICAL –** Policies are controlled and enforced via automated methods, thereby reducing human error (e.g., the automated enforcement of password policies such as a minimum number of characters in a password).
  - **HARDWARE –** A hardware component that enforces successful identification and validation. Hardware controls include things such as media access control (MAC) filtering on network devices, smart card implementation for two-factor authentication, and security tokens such as radio frequency identification (RFID) tags.
  - **SOFTWARE –** Include controls within the operating system and applications such as NTFS permissions, user accounts requiring logon, and rules restricting services or protocol types. These items are often part of the identification and validation phase that ensure proper access to resources.
- **PHYSICAL –** Include controls/systems/procedures such as security guards, ID badges, fences, door locks, etc., that mediate physical access.

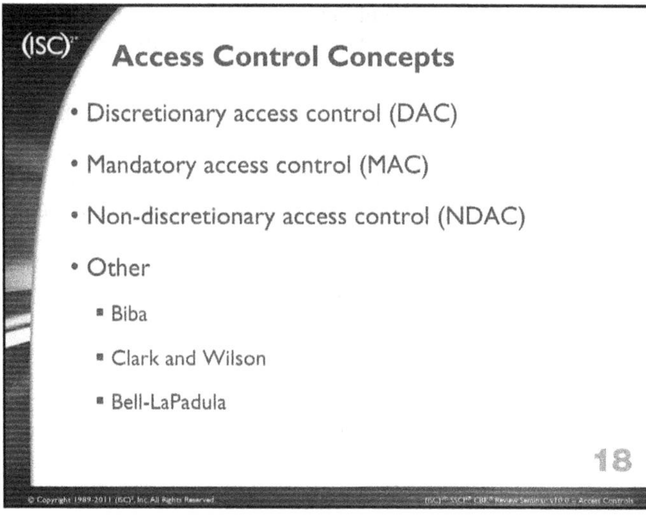

(ISC)²
Access Control Concepts
• Discretionary access control (DAC)
• Mandatory access control (MAC)
• Non-discretionary access control (NDAC)
• Other
▪ Biba
▪ Clark and Wilson
▪ Bell-LaPadula
18


- **DISCRETIONARY ACCESS CONTROL (DAC) –** The owner of the resource determines the access and changes permissions as needed. Note that subjects with certain access permissions are able to pass on access permission to other subjects.
- **MANDATORY ACCESS CONTROL (MAC) –** Systems enforce access decisions based on classification levels that are determined by the object owner. Stronger than DAC because only a central administrator can change the permission – i.e., access permissions cannot be passed along by anyone other than the original owner.
- **NON-DISCRETIONARY ACCESS CONTROL (NDAC) –** In non-discretionary access controls, access controls are closely monitored and managed by the security administrator (not the system administrator).
- **OTHER –** Other models are based on the work of Biba, Clark/Wilson, and Bell-LaPadula. These traditional models describe the operations of access controls and permissions to preserve confidentiality or integrity requirements.

(ISC)²

Discretionary Access Control (DAC)

- DAC
  - Access determined by the identity of subjects and/or groups to which the subjects belong
  - Owner of object determines access and can pass along this right
- Operating system-based
  - Rule-based
  - Role-based
- Application program-based
  - Constrained interface (aka view-based)

19

- **DAC –** As defined in the Orange Book (Trusted Computer Security Evaluation Criteria (TCSEC)), DAC is "a means of restricting access to objects based on the identity of subjects and/or groups to which they belong. The controls are discretionary in the sense that a subject with a certain access permission is capable of passing that permission (perhaps indirectly) on to any other subject." The Orange Book also notes that "security policies defined for systems … used to process classified or other sensitive information must include provisions for the enforcement of discretionary access control rules. That is, they must include a consistent set of rules for controlling and limiting access based on identified individuals who have been determined to have a need-to-know for the information." Note that these definitions apply equally to both public and private sector organizations processing sensitive information.
- **OPERATING SYSTEM-BASED –** Operating systems are responsible for controlling access to system resources such as files, memory, and applications. Note, however, that many servers work by having the operating system give them full control and, therefore, provide/restrict access control at the server level.
  - When operating system-based, access control lists (ACLs) contain entries for individual entities/users (rule-based) or for users based on common parameters, such as job function, location, common tasks, etc. (role-based). In role-based access control (RBAC) mechanisms, the restriction or permission is assigned to the group rather than to individual entities/users.
  - **PERIODIC REVIEW –** Over time, users often legitimately obtain special permissions in order to accomplish a particular project or perform some special function. These permissions need to be reviewed from time to time to ensure that they are revoked when no longer needed. This enforces policy compliance to ensure that people can only gain access to required areas.
  - **NEW USER REGISTRATION –** When a new user joins a department or organization, his or her user account must be created or updated. This process can be time-consuming, but because lack of access can prevent the employee from performing his or her job role, it must be done quickly. In order to maintain a secure environment, this user registration process must be standardized, efficient, and accurate.
- **APPLICATION PROGRAM-BASED –** These involve constrained interfaces. Constrained interfaces can be context-based or content dependent. With constrained interfaces, access is limited by the functionality of the interface (e.g., ATM machine menus) or by restricting interaction (by graying out menu options, or making them entirely unavailable/invisible).
  - In a context-based system, access is based on user privileges as defined in users' personal data records. This is usually granted to persons acting in a certain job role or function.
  - In a content-dependent system, access is based on the value or sensitivity of data items in a table. This would check the content of the data being accessed and only allow a manager of Department A to see employee records for personnel that contain an A in the Department field and not allow access to records containing any other value in that field.

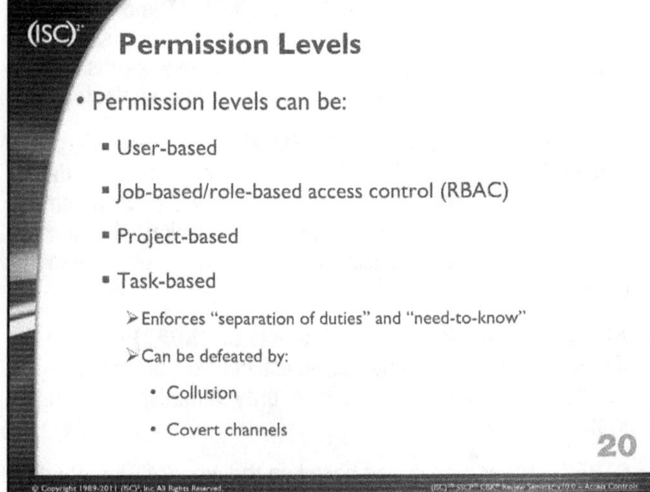


- **PERMISSION LEVELS –** Indicate a subject's rights to a system, application, network, etc. Permission levels can be:
  - **USER-BASED –** The permissions granted to a user are often individual to that user. In these cases, the rules are set according to a UserID or other unique identifier.
  - **JOB-BASED/ROLE-BASED ACCESS CONTROL (RBAC) –** Permissions are based on a common set of permissions for all people in the same or similar job roles.
  - **PROJECT-BASED –** When a group of people (e.g., a project team) are working on a project, then they are often granted access to documents and data related specifically to that project.
  - **TASK-BASED –** Task-based access control limits a person to executing certain functions and often enforces mutual exclusivity – in other words, if a person executes one part of a task, he or she might not be allowed to execute another, related part of the task. This is based on the concept of "separation of duties" and "need-to-know."
    - **SEPARATION OF DUTIES –** Is the business rule that separates a task into a series of separate activities performed by different individuals, each of whom is only allowed to execute one segment of the overall task. This principle prevents a person from both inputting and approving his/her work (for example), and can be a valuable tool in preventing fraud or errors by requiring the cooperation of another person in order to complete a task.
      - **DUAL CONTROL –** Is an example of separation of duties. Examples include a safe with two combination locks on the door, or a missile control system that requires simultaneous turning of keys in consoles too far apart for one person to manage.
    - **NEED-TO-KNOW –** Is the concept of preventing people from gaining access to information that they do not require to carry out their duties. This can reduce the likelihood of improper handling of data or the improper release of information.
  - Separation of duties and need-to-know can be defeated by:
    - **COLLUSION –** Employees working together (i.e., colluding) to circumvent the controls and assist each other in performing unauthorized tasks. This risk can be reduced through job rotation.
    - **COVERT CHANNELS –** Hidden (i.e., covert) methods of passing information in violation of organizational policy. There are two main types of covert channels: timing (signaling from one system to another) and storage (the storing of data in an unprotected or inappropriate place).

## Mandatory Access Control (MAC)

- The strictest level of control - used when consequences of disclosure are very high
- Owner sets sensitivity classification labels
  - Security administrator sets clearances in accordance with policy
- Managed by administrators - not users
- Difficult to configure and manage
- System enforces both classification labels and clearances in combination with need to know

21

- **MANDATORY ACCESS CONTROL (MAC) –** As defined in the Orange Book (TCSEC), MAC is a "means of restricting access to objects based on the sensitivity (as represented by a classification label) of the information contained in the objects and the formal authorization (i.e., clearance) of subjects to access information of such sensitivity." The Orange Book also notes that "security policies defined for systems that are used to process classified or other specifically categorized sensitive information must include provisions for the enforcement of mandatory access control rules. That is, they must include a set of rules for controlling access based directly on a comparison of the individual's clearance or authorization for the information and the classification or sensitivity designation of the information being sought, and indirectly on considerations of physical and other environmental factors of control."
- As with Discretionary Access Control, the Orange Book definitions fit the needs of both public and private sector organizations that need to protect sensitive information.
- How it works: The system and the owner jointly participate in the decision to allow access. The owner provides the "need-to-know" element to authorize access (because not all people with a privilege or clearance level for sensitive material need access to all sensitive information, irrespective of clearance) and the system compares the subject and object labels in accordance with the specifications of the Bell-LaPadula confidentiality model (covered in the next section) to decide whether to allow access. Remember:
  - Sensitivity labels, or classifications, are applied to all objects.
  - Privilege, or clearance-level labels, are assigned to all subjects.

**REFERENCES:**

"DoD Trusted Computer System Evaluation Criteria," DoD Computer Security Center, 1983.

"Content-dependent Protection," Martin, Security, Accuracy, and Privacy in Computer Systems, Prentice-Hall, 1973.

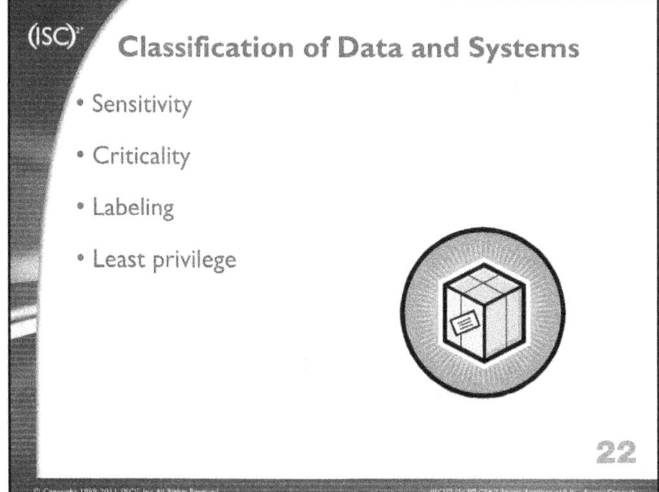
(ISC)²
Classification of Data and Systems
• Sensitivity
• Criticality
• Labeling
• Least privilege
22

- **CLASSIFICATION OF DATA AND SYSTEMS –** In order to protect data and systems from unauthorized access or modification, it is important to give them a classification.
- **SENSITIVITY –** Data or systems that contain sensitive data (such as privacy related information, trade secrets, marketing plans, financial data, etc.) need to be labeled or marked so that authorized users know how to handle such data properly, and so that the system can control user access according to access rules. This is enforcement of information classification policies and a critical part of regulatory compliance.
- **CRITICALITY –** Some systems and data are critical to the successful operation of the business process or organization. These systems must be identified so that protective measures (e.g., redundancy, controls over tests, maintenance, etc.) can be provided.
- **LABELING –** A classification scheme must have some form of labeling so that the classification of a system or of the data can easily be identified by the system or user.
- **LEAST PRIVILEGE –** Similar to need-to-know, the concept of "least privilege" ensures that a user or process is restricted to only performing the minimum, or least invasive, actions required for the user/system to do its job. For example, if "read-only" access is sufficient, the user should not have authority to "write" or "execute."

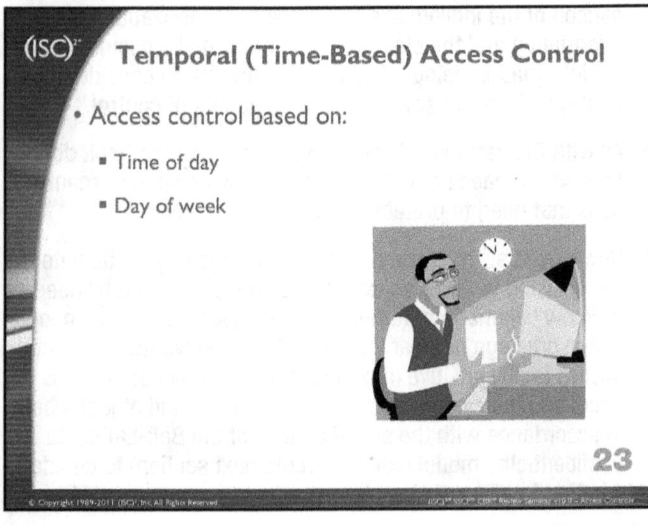


- **TEMPORAL (TIME-BASED) ACCESS CONTROL –** Often referred to as time-based access control, this technique provides a physical method of exercising a pseudo mandatory access control by labeling the classification (sensitivity) level of objects and then setting up the system to process a particular sensitivity level only during a specified period of time (e.g., time of day or day of week). Often used in combination with role-based access control, wherein users are only allowed access at specified times.

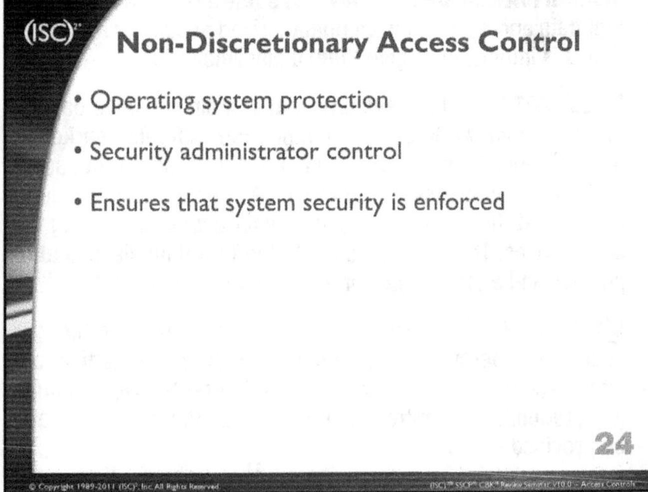


- **NON-DISCRETIONARY ACCESS CONTROL –** In non-discretionary access control (NDAC), access rules are closely managed by the security administrator rather than by the system owner or by ordinary users for their own files.
- **OPERATING SYSTEM PROTECTION –** Non-discretionary access control can be installed on many operating systems. This will result in stronger security than that available from discretionary access control because the system doesn't rely only on users' compliance with organization policy. For example, even if users try to comply and implement well-defined file protection, a Trojan horse program could change the protection to allow uncontrolled access. This kind of exposure isn't possible under non-discretionary access control.
- **SECURITY ADMINISTRATOR CONTROL –** Security administrators have sufficient control to ensure that sensitive/critical files are write-protected for integrity and readable only by authorized users for confidentiality. Because users can execute only those programs for which they are specifically authorized, the system is protected against executing untrustworthy programs.
- **ENSURES THAT SYSTEM SECURITY IS ENFORCED –** Non-discretionary access control is able to assist in ensuring that the system security mechanisms are enforced and tamperproof. As a result, organizations that process highly sensitive information should seriously consider implementing non-discretionary access control. Non-discretionary access control does a better job of protecting confidentiality and integrity than DAC because the data owner (who is often the user) does not make access decisions. In this respect, it takes on some of the benefits of MAC without the additional administrative overhead.

**REFERENCE:**

Operating System Security: Adding to the Arsenal of Security Techniques, Ferraiolo & Mell, Computer Security Division, Information Technology Laboratory, NIST, 2006.

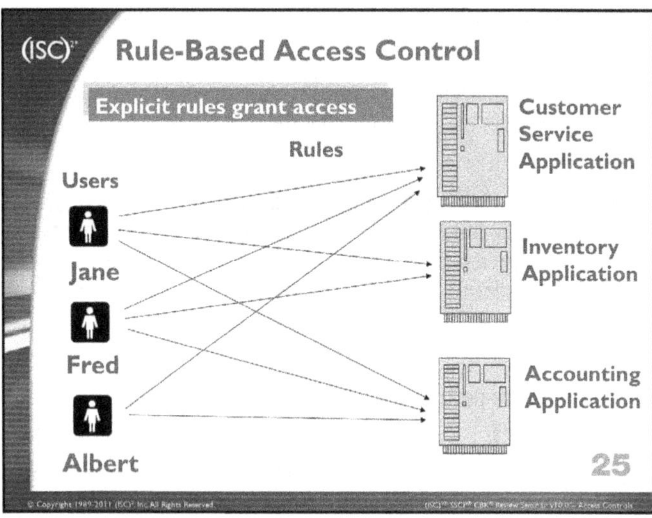


- **RULE-BASED ACCESS CONTROL –** In a rule-based system, access is based on a list of rules that determine what access is to be granted. The rules are created or authorized by data owners and specify the privileges granted to users (i.e., "read," "write," "execute," etc.).
- In the graphic on the slide, rule-based access control demonstrates that each individual's permissions on the respective systems are controlled by individual rules.

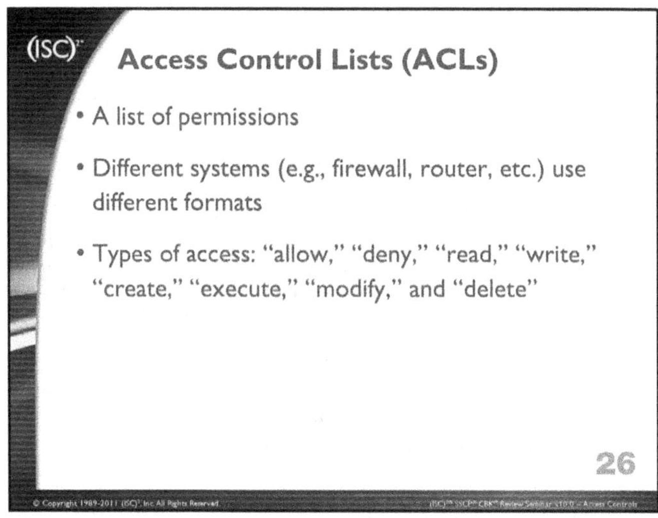


- **ACCESS CONTROL LISTS (ACLS) –** ACLs are a very common implementation of access control and provide an easy method of specifying the users allowed access to each object.
- ACL-based mechanisms can be used to provide access to particular objects by specifically defined groups or individual users. ACLs work in coordination with access-control matrices. The ACL implements the access control matrix by representing the columns as lists of users attached to the protected objects. (See next slide.)

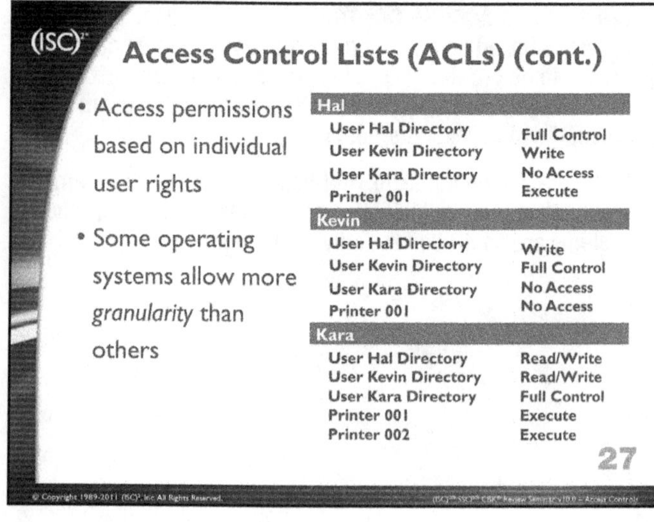

(ISC)²
Access Control Lists (ACLs) (cont.)
• Access permissions based on individual user rights
• Some operating systems allow more granularity than others
Hal
User Hal Directory Full Control
User Kevin Directory Write
User Kara Directory No Access
Printer 001 Execute
Kevin
User Hal Directory Write
User Kevin Directory Full Control
User Kara Directory No Access
Printer 001 No Access
Kara
User Hal Directory Read/Write
User Kevin Directory Read/Write
User Kara Directory Full Control
Printer 001 Execute
Printer 002 Execute
27


- Different operating systems provide different ACL-enabling options; for example:
  - Linux and Apple Macs have "read," "write," and "execute." These can be applied to file owners, groups, or global users.
  - Windows has both share permissions and security permissions, both of which are ACL-enabling. Share permissions are used for accessing resources via a network share; security permissions are used for accessing resources when the user is logged on locally. Available permissions are as follows:
    - Share permissions: "full," "change," "read," and "deny."
    - Security permissions: "full," "modify," "list folder contents," "read-execute," "read," "write," "special," and "deny."
    - In both share and security permissions, "deny" overrides every other permission.
  - Because of the greater number of choices, Windows ACLs are said to be more granular.

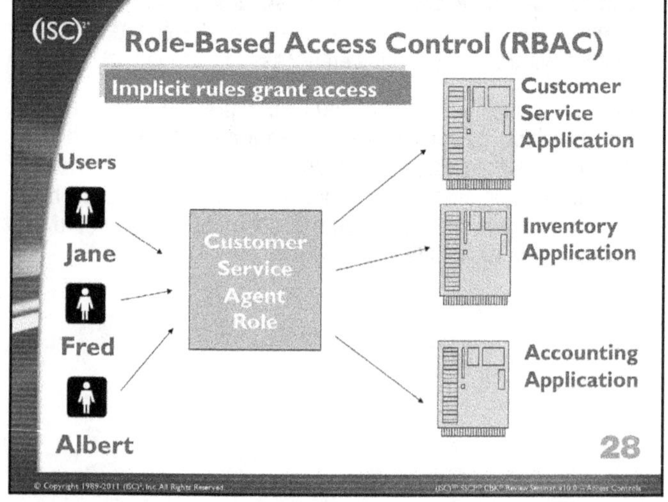


- **ROLE-BASED ACCESS CONTROL (RBAC) –** A RBAC policy bases the access control authorizations on the job functions that the user is assigned to perform within an organization. Other parameters might include location codes, department codes, etc. Determination of what roles have access to a particular file is at the file owner's discretion.
  - Role engineering, a required initial procedure, is the process of determining roles, authorizations, role hierarchies, and constraints. The real benefit of RBAC over the other access control methods lies in its capability to represent the structure of the organization and force compliance with control policies throughout the enterprise.
- Note: Consider the issue of "need-to-know" for Albert (see the earlier slide on rule-based access control). According to that slide, Albert did not have access to the inventory application as the others did. Perhaps Albert was in a junior position. When a decision is made to create roles, it may be prudent to use one role for everyone rather than set up different roles, and then explicitly exclude or add special permissions to an individual. Windows' "deny" permission makes it possible to create a rule that overrides the role, thus fixing Albert's "excessive" permission.
  - This is a decision made dependent on risk, wherein a person may be enrolled in a role with similar privileges and granted access above his or her need-to-know in order to reduce administrative overhead.
  - RBAC might also facilitate periodic reviews (audits) of permissions, and separation of duties can be enforced more efficiently (manager roles versus user roles).

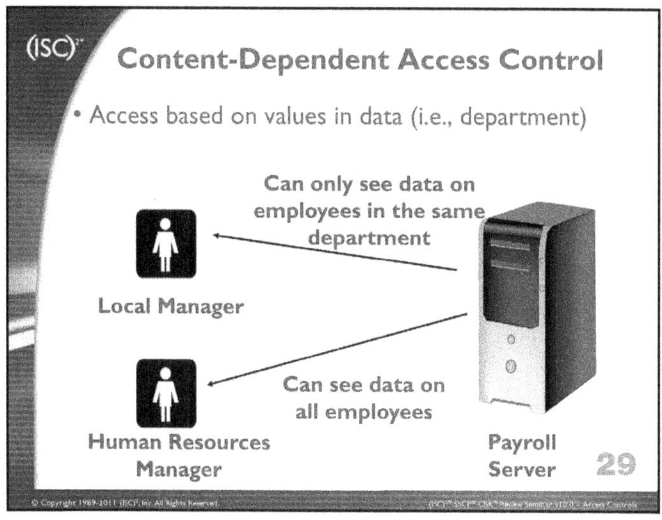


- **CONTENT-DEPENDENT ACCESS CONTROL** – This form of access control is based on the content of the data. It requires the access-control mechanism (the arbiter program, which is part of the application – not the operating system) to actually look at the data in order to make the access decision. The result is better granularity (because access is controlled to the record level in a file rather than simply to the file level) but requires more processing overhead because of the need to run the arbiter program. The arbiter program uses information in the object being accessed (i.e., the content of a record) and the format of the question (usually a simple "if-then" question, such as if "high-security-flag" equals "yes" then check security level of user) as the basis for its authorization decision. For example, managers in an organization may have access to the payroll database to review data pertaining to their specific employees, but not to the data pertinent to employees of other managers.

**REFERENCE:**

"Content-dependent Protection," Martin, Security, Accuracy, and Privacy in Computer Systems, Prentice-Hall, 1973.

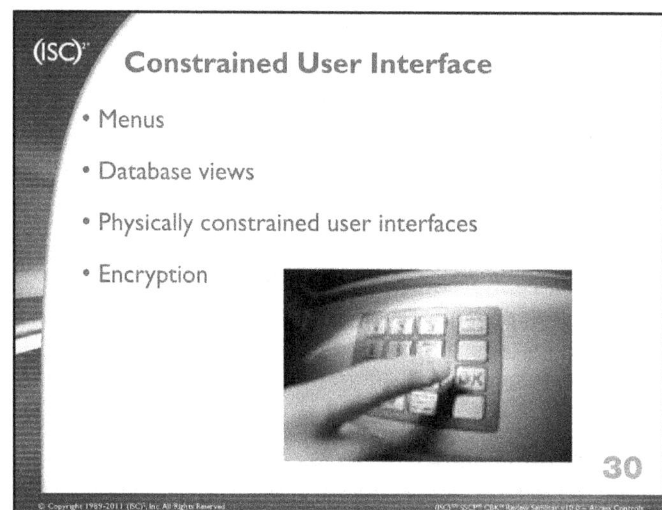


- **CONSTRAINED USER INTERFACE** – A user's ability to interface with, or access, certain system resources can be inhibited not only by the user's rights and permissions, but also by the limitations of the device or program providing the interface. When a device (such as an automated teller machine (ATM)) or software (such as on a public access kiosk browser) is in place, it can allow access only to specific functions, files, or other resources by restricting the user's ability to even request access to unauthorized resources. As an example, some systems grey out icons that are not available for use in the current mode of operation. Several methods of constraining users are described in the following paragraphs.
- **MENUS** – A widely used form of constrained user interface occurs when a user logs on to a system and is presented with one or more menus linked to processes, or the parts of the system resources that have been approved for use by that user. The user theoretically has no knowledge of the parts of the system that he or she is not authorized to use.
- **DATABASE VIEWS** – Also called view-based access control (VBAC), this constrained user interface is used when dealing with relational databases. VBAC views can be preset to an established process the user would use, or can be dynamically created for each user upon logon and allow access to certain job-related parts of the database.
- **PHYSICALLY CONSTRAINED USER INTERFACES** – The user interface mechanism presents the user with a limited number of options. For example, an ATM machine only offers a certain number of buttons to push.
- **ENCRYPTION** – Constrains users by requiring them to have the decryption key in order to access (or read) information stored on the system, or masks information such as credit card details so that the user cannot see sensitive information.

**REFERENCE:**

NIST SP 800-12, "An Introduction to Computer Security: The NIST Handbook," 1995.

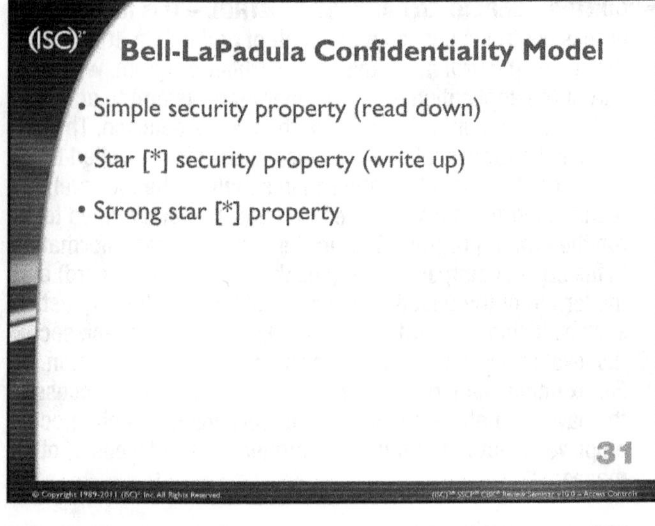
(ISC)²
Bell-LaPadula Confidentiality Model
• Simple security property (read down)
• Star [*] security property (write up)
• Strong star [*] property
31

- **BELL-LAPADULA CONFIDENTIALITY MODEL –** The first formal state-machine model to address confidentiality protection in multi-level computer systems was based on a hierarchical lattice of protection levels defined by David Bell and Leonard LaPadula in 1977. The Bell-LaPadula model distinguishes subjects from objects and controls disclosure of sensitive (classified) information through labeling. Bell-LaPadula's confidentiality policy consists of three parts, or properties.
- **SIMPLE SECURITY PROPERTY (READ DOWN) –** The first property specifies that a subject cannot READ objects that have a higher level of sensitivity than the subject's permission level.
- **STAR [*] SECURITY PROPERTY (WRITE UP) –** The second property specifies that a subject cannot WRITE (disclose) information from objects that have a high level of sensitivity to objects protected at a lower level.
- **STRONG STAR [*] PROPERTY –** The third property specifies that if a subject is granted READ/WRITE permissions, no access is allowed to other levels of protection. This is sometimes referred to as the discretionary security property and uses an access matrix to define the access control.

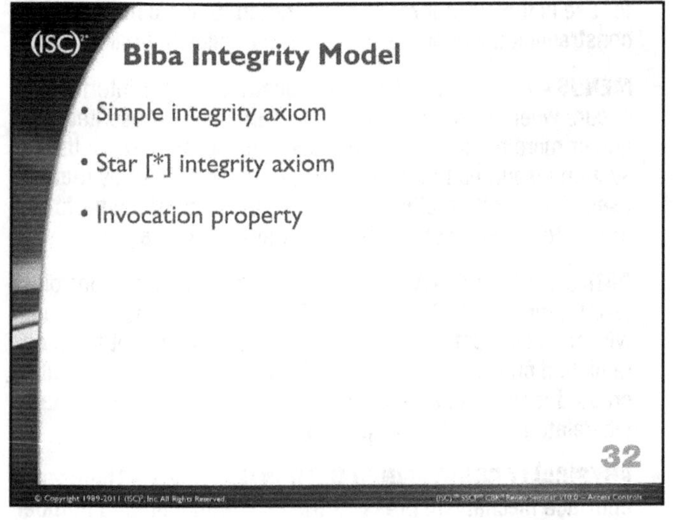
(ISC)²
Biba Integrity Model
• Simple integrity axiom
• Star [*] integrity axiom
• Invocation property
32

- **BIBA INTEGRITY MODEL –** The first model to address integrity in computer systems was based on a hierarchical lattice of integrity levels defined by Biba in 1977. The Biba integrity model is similar to the Bell-LaPadula model for confidentiality in that it uses subjects and objects, but whereas Bell-LaPadula controls disclosure, Biba controls object modification. Biba's integrity policy consists of three parts.
- **SIMPLE INTEGRITY AXIOM –** The first part specifies that a subject cannot read objects that have a lower level of integrity than the subject.
- **STAR [*] INTEGRITY AXIOM –** The second part specifies that a subject cannot modify objects that have a higher level of integrity.
- **INVOCATION PROPERTY –** The third part specifies that a subject may not request service from subjects that have a higher integrity level.

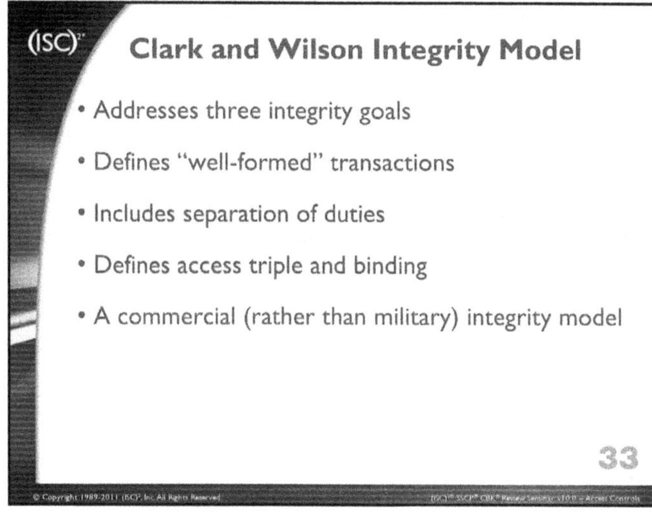
(ISC)²
Clark and Wilson Integrity Model
• Addresses three integrity goals
• Defines "well-formed" transactions
• Includes separation of duties
• Defines access triple and binding
• A commercial (rather than military) integrity model
33

- **CLARK AND WILSON INTEGRITY MODEL –** Published in 1987 by David Clark and David Wilson, the Clark and Wilson model focuses on authorized users' unauthorized acts and internal integrity threats, both of which were missing from Biba's model. A major internal integrity issue that this model addresses is whether the software does what it is supposed to do.
- **ADDRESSES THREE INTEGRITY GOALS –**
  - Preventing unauthorized users from making modifications. (Biba addressed only this integrity goal.)
  - Preventing authorized users from making improper modifications.
  - Maintaining internal and external consistency.
- **DEFINES "WELL-FORMED" TRANSACTIONS –** A transaction where the user is unable to manipulate data arbitrarily, but only in constrained (limited) ways that preserve or ensure the integrity of the data. For example, a commercial accounting system should require offsetting debit or credit transactions to complete an accounting entry.
  - Preserves internal consistency. Internal consistency ensures that the system operates as expected every time.
  - Preserves external consistency through range and validity checks on data (data values must be valid according to business logic rules to ensure values reflect the real world logic of the transaction).
- **INCLUDES SEPARATION OF DUTIES –**
  - Operation is divided into subparts.
  - Different entity executes each part.
  - Helps ensure external consistency .
  - Prevents authorized users from unauthorized modifications.
- **DEFINES ACCESS TRIPLE AND BINDING –** A subject's access is controlled by the authorization to execute the program (well-formed transaction). Therefore, unauthorized users cannot execute program (first integrity rule) and authorized users could each access different programs that allow each to make specific, unique changes (separation of duties).
  - **ACCESS TRIPLE –** Subject - Program - Object.
  - **INTEGRITY IS ENFORCED BY BINDING –** Integrity is enforced by subject/user-to-program and program-to-object/data binding, which creates separation of duties and ensures that only authorized transactions can be performed.
- **A COMMERCIAL (RATHER THAN MILITARY) INTEGRITY MODEL –** Unlike the earlier models, this model was designed for commercial rather than military applications.

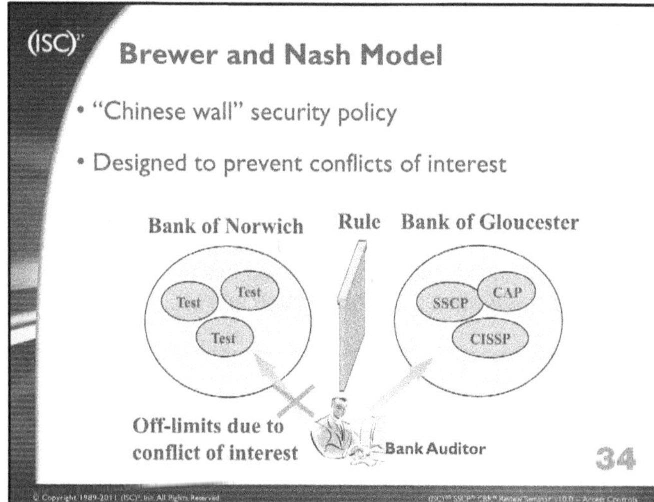
(ISC)²
Brewer and Nash Model
• "Chinese wall" security policy
• Designed to prevent conflicts of interest
Bank of Norwich
Rule
Bank of Gloucester
Test
Test
Test
SSCP
CAP
CISSP
Off-limits due to conflict of interest
Bank Auditor
34

- **BREWER AND NASH MODEL –** A mathematical theory published in 1989 to ensure fair competition and used to implement dynamically changing access permissions. It is a way of separating competitors' data within the same integrated database to ensure that users do not make fraudulent modifications to objects that belong to a competing organization, and to prevent taking advantage of data in situations in which the user or client has a conflict of interest.
- **"CHINESE WALL" SECURITY POLICY –** Defines a wall, or barrier, and develops a set of rules that ensure that no subject will be able to access objects on the other side of the wall.
- **DESIGNED TO PREVENT CONFLICTS OF INTEREST –** Ensures that conflicts of interest are recognized and that people are prevented from taking advantage of data to which they should not have access. (Controls can't "prevent" conflicts of interest – conflicts of interest have to do with individuals' positions, not with the data.) For example, if a user accesses one company's data, the data belonging to competitors can automatically be deemed "off-limits."
- An example of a Chinese Wall in action is the way an audit company handles audits for competing companies. An auditor who has accessed data related to Bank of Gloucester would be prohibited from accessing any data belonging to Bank of Norwich. Even though the auditor worked for a company that performed the audits for both banks, internal controls at the audit company would restrict access between areas that would be in a conflict of interest.

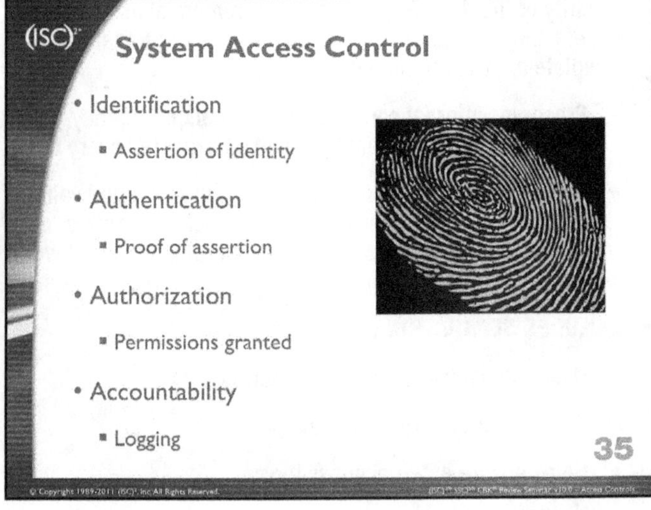
(ISC)²
System Access Control
• Identification
▪ Assertion of identity
• Authentication
▪ Proof of assertion
• Authorization
▪ Permissions granted
• Accountability
▪ Logging
35

- **IDENTIFICATION –** Who or what is requesting access.
- **AUTHENTICATION –** How to prove that only the correct person is using that proffered ID.
- **AUTHORIZATION –** What rights the user has once authenticated (e.g., read, write, execute, etc.).
- **ACCOUNTABILITY –** Is being able to hold a user accountable for what he or she does on the system. It is accomplished by a combination of the identification and audit trail.

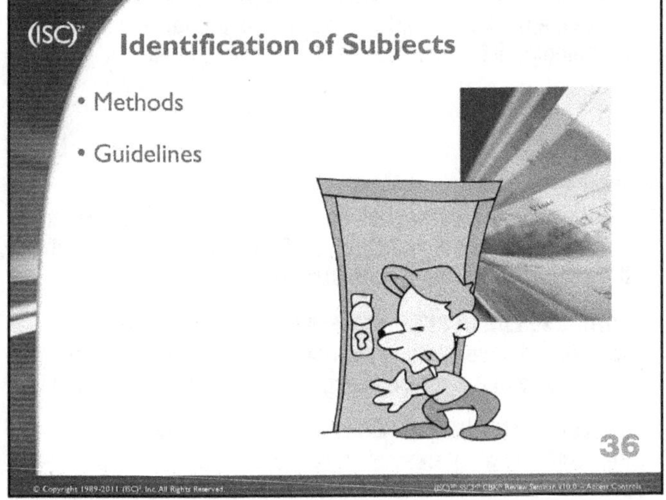
(ISC)²
Identification of Subjects
• Methods
• Guidelines
36

- **IDENTIFICATION OF SUBJECTS –** This is the method used by subjects – whether a user, process, or other entity – requesting access to the system to identify themselves to the system.
- **METHODS –** Most common identification systems use a user name (in the form of a UserID, account number, or PIN (personal identification number)) for system access control, and badges for physical access control. Biometrics are often used for identification in physical access control and normally for authentication in logical (system) access control.
- **GUIDELINES –** Identifiers must be unique for each user so as to ensure accountability (unless anonymity is an important factor (i.e., in some library systems)). Identification data should be monitored and kept current. IDs of users who leave the organization or that are inactive for a prolonged period of time should be disabled. Standard naming conventions should be applied and should not relate to job functions. The process for issuing IDs should be documented and secure.

**REFERENCE:**

NIST Pub 800-14, "Generally Accepted Principles and Practices for Securing Information Technology Systems," 1996.

(ISC)²

## Authentication Types

- Something you know – passwords, PIN, pass phrases, mother's maiden name, etc.
- Something you have – tokens, proximity cards, keys, badges, passports, certificates, etc.
- Something you are – fingerprint, retina, signatures, facial, etc.
- Multi-factor recommendation – use two of the three types for better security

37

- **AUTHENTICATION TYPES –** Authentication is the validation or proof that the subject requesting access is legitimately allowed to use that identification (ID). There are three types of authentication. Systems containing sensitive or critical information should be protected by using at least two of the three factors for access.
- **SOMETHING YOU KNOW –** Knowledge – Something you know, such as a password, pass phrase, or PIN.
- **SOMETHING YOU HAVE –** Ownership - Tokens and smart cards are examples of something you have.
- **SOMETHING YOU ARE –** Characteristics/biometrics - Digitized representations of physical features such as fingerprints, or physical actions such as signatures.
- **MULTI-FACTOR RECOMMENDATION –** The use of two or more of these techniques (often called two-factor authentication) can provide a higher level of assurance. This is often accomplished by using a token or smart card in conjunction with a PIN or password in order to prevent the misuse of the physical object.
    - Note that a username and a password is not two-factor; it is single factor. The username is an identifier, verified via the password.
    - Remember as well that all of these access controls can be compromised fairly easily. This is why single-factor authentication is considered to be inadequate.

**REFERENCES:**

NIST Pub. 800-14, "Generally Accepted Principles and Practices for Securing Information Technology Systems," 1996.

Secrets and Lies, Schneier; John Wiley & Sons, 2000.

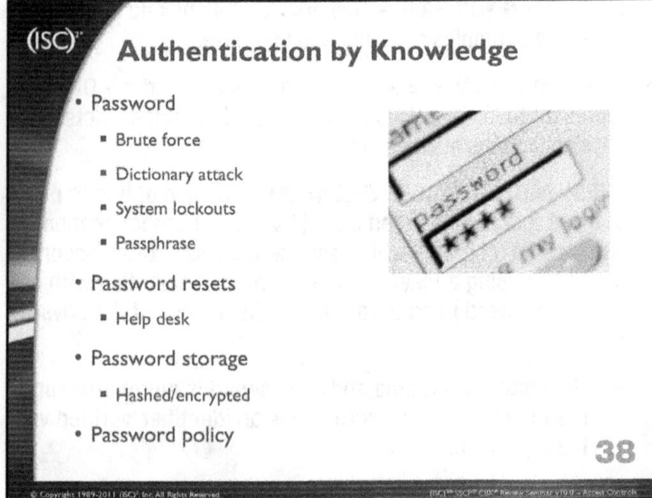

(ISC)²
Authentication by Knowledge
• Password
▪ Brute force
▪ Dictionary attack
▪ System lockouts
▪ Passphrase
• Password resets
▪ Help desk
• Password storage
▪ Hashed/encrypted
• Password policy
38


- **PASSWORD –** Static passwords are the oldest and most-used method of authentication for computer systems and currently the weakest. (Static passwords refer to passwords that are seldom, if ever, changed. Even a 30-day password is considered static in today's environments.) With the high-powered systems available today, it is trivial for hackers to discover a reusable password via either a brute force or dictionary attack.
  - **BRUTE FORCE –** Involves trying every combination of characters possible. Modern password crackers don't try every combination of letters, numbers, and special characters in alphabetic order. Rather, they measure the entropy (a measure of randomness) and test low entropy words first, then medium, then high.
  - **DICTIONARY ATTACK –** Works by hashing all of the words in a dictionary (often supplemented with suffixes such as 01, 02, 4u, and so on and comparing the hashed value to the system password file to discover a match). Hackers are also on to all the usual tricks, such as spelling a name backward or simple substitution of characters, such as "3" for "e," "0" for "o," "$" for "s," etc.
  - **SYSTEM LOCKOUTS –** Systems can be programmed to disable a UserID after a certain number of consecutive failed logon attempts (typically less than three or five). This level is referred to as the "threshold." The user may be locked out for a few minutes, hours, or until reset by a security officer. Although this helps guard against the kinds of attacks described above, it also enables an intruder to lock out several users – a form of denial of service attack – by entering groups of incorrect passwords.
  - **PASSPHRASE –**
    - A series of words selected by and easily remembered by a user. It is a way to get users to choose higher entropy passwords while still being able to remember them. The user can convert the passphrase manually to a password or the system can be programmed to do it automatically in accordance with an algorithm. Stronger than a password because it won't be found in a dictionary, but a little longer to enter! Although still static, passphrases are not as susceptible to a brute force attack as passwords.
- **PASSWORD RESETS –** All user and system passwords should be forcibly reset on a regular basis. This will prevent the continued misuse of a password that has been compromised. The time period that a password should remain valid will vary according to the privilege level associated with the password.
  - **HELP DESK –** When a user forgets a password or the password must be reset by the help desk, the new password should only be good for a single login and must expire within a short period of time (typically <48 hours). Unless the process has been automated, password resets are often the most common call received by a help desk.
- **PASSWORD STORAGE –**
  - **HASHED/ENCRYPTED –** Passwords should never be stored or transmitted in cleartext. Transmission and storage should only be done with a hash of the password. (Note that some systems encrypt these hashes in order to slow down brute force attacks.) The password file must be protected from unauthorized access.
  - Since most systems store a hash of the password (hashes are described in detail in the Cryptography domain), attackers will pre-compute these dictionary words and build a table, then look up the stored, hashed version of the password in the table in order to discover the "word" that generated it. These tables are known as "rainbow tables" and are widely available. For example, a forensic investigator's tool called FTK by AccessData Corp. comes with a million-word rainbow table. According to its website, the table will resolve 28% of user passwords.
- **PASSWORD POLICY –** Often set at some degree of complexity/entropy. SSCPs should teach users how to create secure but memorable passwords.

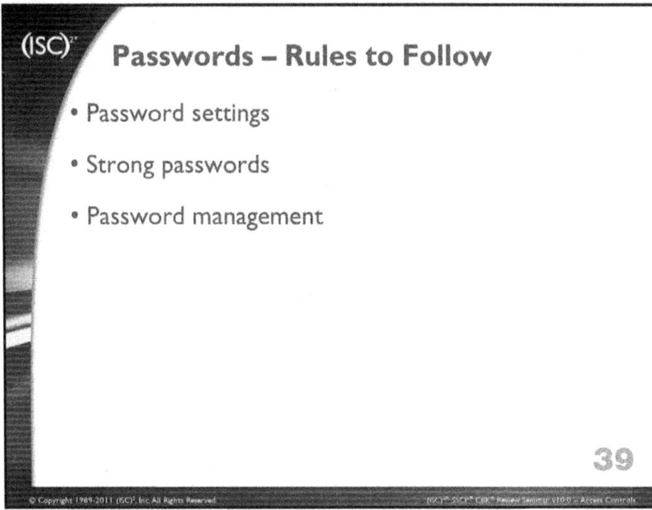
(ISC)²
Passwords – Rules to Follow
• Password settings
• Strong passwords
• Password management
39

- **PASSWORD SETTINGS –**
  - Always use strong passwords. Note that certain easily guessed words are commonly used as (poor) passwords, e.g., "guest," "password," "secret," etc. Words such as these should never be used as passwords.
  - Only store a written copy of the password (and then only if absolutely necessary) in a secure place and destroy the copy when it is no longer needed.
  - Never share passwords with anyone.
  - Use different passwords for different user accounts. Using a single password is the equivalent of using a single key for your car, house, mailbox, and safety deposit box – if a user loses the key, he or she will have given an attacker access to everything. If a user's password is compromised on one system, having different passwords on different systems will help prevent intruders from gaining access to accounts and data on these other systems. Similarly, multiple passwords should not be trivially derivable once one is known.
  - Change passwords immediately if you believe that the password has been compromised.
  - Be careful about where passwords are saved on computers. Some dialog boxes (such as those for remote access and other telephone connections) present an option to save or remember a password. Selecting this option poses a potential security threat.
  - Choose passwords that are hard to guess. Passwords should not be based on personal information easily obtained from the net. Remember that hackers have easy access to very powerful password-cracking tools that incorporate extensive word and name dictionaries. More secure passwords are those which are based on passphrases and/or non-dictionary words (including "nonsense" words), combined with obscure character substitutions. These can be extremely difficult to guess or crack. Remember that cracking tools will also check for simple tricks such as words spelled backward, or simple substitutions of certain characters (i.e., "mouse" becomes "m0us3").
- **STRONG PASSWORDS –** Are generally agreed to be ones that:
  - Are at least eight characters long (http://www.owasp.org/index.php/Password_length_&_complexity).
  - Do not contain the user's username, real name, or company name.
  - Do not contain a complete dictionary word.
  - Are significantly different from previous passwords. Passwords that increment (e.g., Password1, Password2, Password3 ... ) are not strong.
  - Contain characters from each of the following four groups: uppercase, lowercase, numeric, and special characters.
  - Test password (try http://www.testyourpassword.com/).
- **PASSWORD MANAGEMENT –** It is important to define password policy so that all users are obliged to follow best practices. This can be done by choosing password-policy settings such that users:
  - Must choose passwords with a specified minimum number of characters.
  - Are unable to use the same password when the original password expires.
  - Are required to change passwords as often as necessary for the environment (typically every 30 to 90 days). With this policy setting, if an attacker cracks a password, he or she will only have access to the network until the password expires.
  - Cannot change their passwords until they are more than a certain number of days old. This policy setting works in combination with the "Enforce password history" policy setting. If a minimum password age is defined, users cannot repeatedly change their passwords to get around the "Enforce password history" policy setting and then immediately re-use their original password.
  - Must meet certain complexity requirements. (This is enforced with the "validate that the password meet complexity requirements" policy setting.) This policy setting checks all new passwords to ensure that they meet basic strong password requirements.
  - **ACCOUNT LOCKOUT POLICIES –** Be cautious when defining account lockout policy. Account lockout policy should not be applied haphazardly. While you increase the probability of thwarting an unauthorized attack on your organization with a stringent account lockout policy, you can also unintentionally lock out authorized users, which can be costly for the organization. If you decide to apply an account lockout policy, set the account lockout threshold policy to a high enough number that authorized users are not locked out of their user accounts simply because they mistype a password.
  - **AUDITING LOGON EVENTS –** Auditing logon events will give you a record of when every user logs on or off of a computer. If an unauthorized person steals a user's password and logs on to a computer, you can determine when the breach of security occurred. If you decide to audit failure events in the logon event category, you can see whether unauthorized users or attackers are trying to log on to a computer. Although this can be helpful for intrusion detection, it also increases the possibility of a denial-of-service attack. If you have failure auditing enabled in these event categories, users from outside of your organization can fill the security log or cause events to be overwritten by continuously attempting to log on to your network with incorrect usernames or passwords.

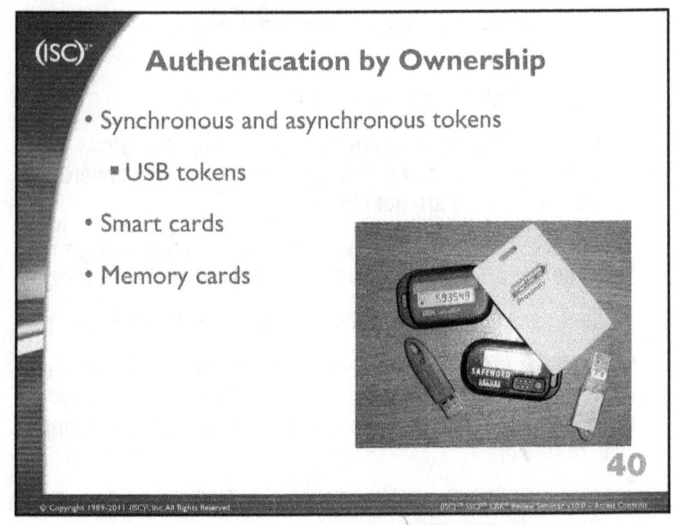

(ISC)²
Authentication by Ownership
Synchronous and asynchronous tokens
USB tokens
Smart cards
Memory cards
40


- **AUTHENTICATION BY OWNERSHIP –** This is the formal description of the second factor, "something you have."
- **SYNCHRONOUS AND ASYNCHRONOUS TOKENS –** There are two types of token-based devices:
    - The synchronous version uses an algorithm that calculates a number at both the authentication server and the device and displays the number on the device's screen. The user enters this number as a login authenticator (as with a password).
    - The asynchronous version resembles a credit card-sized calculator. The authentication server issues a challenge number which the user enters. The token computes a response to the value provided by the authentication server. The user replies to the server with the value displayed on the token. Most of these systems also protect the token from misuse by requiring the user to enter a PIN along with the initial challenge value.
    - **USB TOKENS –** USB tokens use PKI technology (i.e., a certificate signed by a trusted certification authority) and don't provide one-time passwords. The presence of the digital signature on the token is enough to provide proof of possession (something you have).
- **SMART CARDS –** Credit card-shaped tokens that contain one or more microprocessor chips that accept, store, and send information through a reader. These can be either contact or contactless. The information contained in the smart card provides authentication.
- **MEMORY CARDS –** Several varieties of magnetic stripe cards provide identification/authentication applications, usually oriented toward physical access control to restricted areas such as sensitive facilities or parking areas.

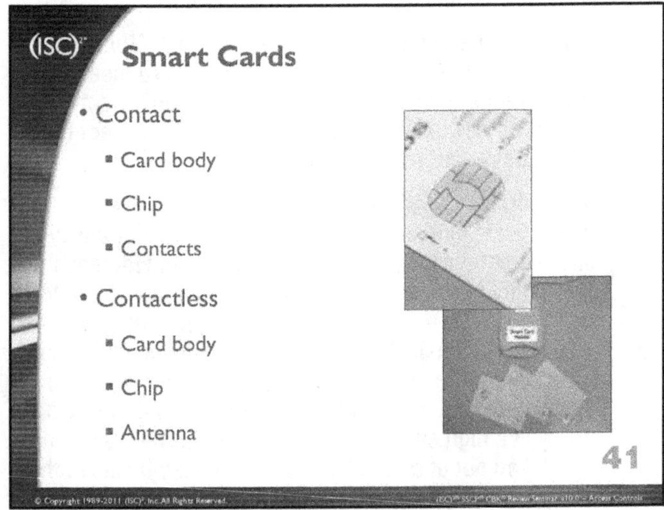


- **SMART CARDS –** There are two main categories of smart cards: contact and contactless.
- **CONTACT –** As an access control device for authentication, these need a reader to provide power to the embedded microprocessor and to communicate with the reader. The card is inserted into the reader to establish communication. A significant disadvantage to the use of contact smart cards is the propensity of some users to leave the smart card inserted in an unattended reader.
- **CONTACTLESS –** To communicate with the readers or other devices, these contain an embedded RF transceiver that can work in close proximity to the reader.
- A significant advantage of the use of smart cards is that the user-authentication process is completed at the user location between the smart card and the reader. This avoids the "trusted path" problem, since IDs and authentication data are not transmitted to a remote server, thereby potentially exposing sensitive information to sniffers or tappers. Instead, the reader maintains a handshake with the authentication server and directly vouches for the authentication. A trusted path in accordance with "Trusted Computer System Evaluation Criteria" is used when a positive system-to-user connection is required (i.e., logon, etc.).
- OATH (Open AuTHentication) is an initiative begun to encourage the use of standards-based two-factor authentication for Internet applications, such as banking. Documented as RFC 4226 by the IETF, and sponsored by OpenAuthentication.org, is based on use of HMAC and one-time password capable systems.

**REFERENCES:**

"DoD Trusted Computer Evaluation Criteria," DoD Computer Security Center, 1983.

http://www.openauthentication.org/news/060215

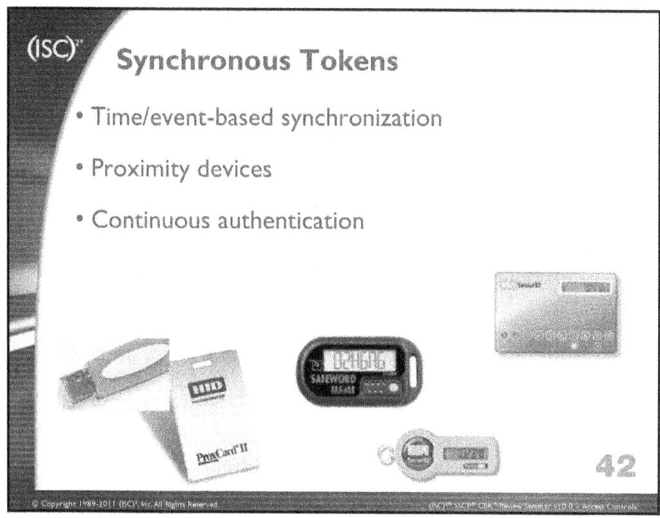
Synchronous Tokens
• Time/event-based synchronization
• Proximity devices
• Continuous authentication
42

- **TIME/EVENT-BASED SYNCHRONIZATION –**
  - **TIME-BASED SYNCHRONIZATION –** In this system, the current time is used as the input value. The token generates a new dynamic password (usually every minute) that is displayed in the window of the token. The password is entered with the user's PIN at the workstation to gain access. No token keyboard is required. This system requires that the clock in the token remains in sync with the clock in the authentication server. If the clocks drift out of sync, the server can search three or four minutes on each side of the time to detect an offset. If the difference becomes too great, a resynchronization operation is required.
  - **EVENT-BASED SYNCHRONIZATION –** Avoids the time-synchronization problem by incrementing a counter with each use. The counter is the input value. Here, a button is pressed to generate a one-time password which is then entered with the user's PIN at the workstation to gain access. If a password is created using the token but not used to log on, the counter in the server and the counter in the token go out of sync.
- **PROXIMITY DEVICES –** Synchronous tokens can be implemented in proximity devices that cause both the PIN and the password to be entered automatically.
- **CONTINUOUS AUTHENTICATION –** Used by systems that are continuously validating the authentication of the user. This is often done via proximity cards or other devices that are continuously communicating with the access control system. If the user were to walk away from the desktop, the system would lock the desktop as soon as the user was outside of the range of the access control detector.

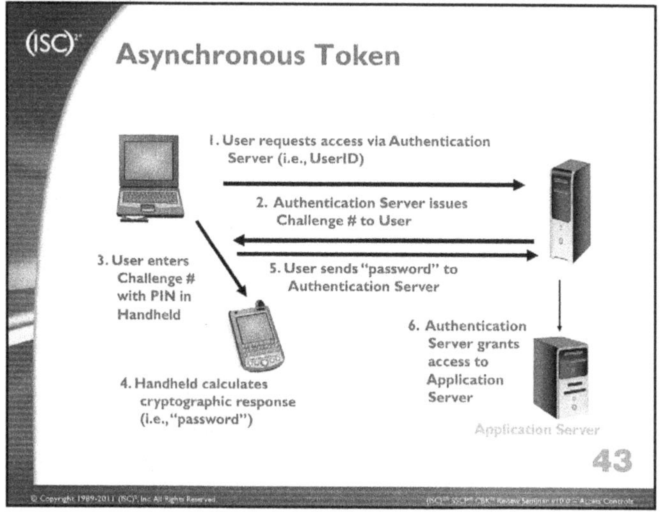
Asynchronous Token
1. User requests access via Authentication Server (i.e., UserID)
2. Authentication Server issues Challenge # to User
3. User enters Challenge # with PIN in Handheld
4. Handheld calculates cryptographic response (i.e., "password")
5. User sends "password" to Authentication Server
6. Authentication Server grants access to Application Server
Application Server
43

- **ASYNCHRONOUS TOKEN –** Uses challenge-response technology involving dialogue between the authentication service and the remote entity trying to authenticate. Requires a numeric keyboard. The process is as follows:
  - **STEPS 1 AND 2 –** The user initiates a logon request and the authentication server provides a challenge (a random number that is the input value) to the remote entity.
  - **STEP 3 –** The user enters the challenge received from the server and secret PIN known only to the user into the calculation device (a credit card-sized calculator or a software program on a personal computer (PC) or personal digital assistant (PDA)).
  - **STEP 4 –** The token (or program) generates the response (the password) to the challenge, which appears in the window of the token.
  - **STEPS 5 AND 6 –** The password is then provided to the authentication server by the user and access is granted. Without the asynchronous token device and the correct PIN, a correct answer to the challenge cannot be generated.

(ISC)²

## Authentication by Characteristic

- Biometrics
  - Physiological (i.e., static) characteristics
  - Behavioral (i.e., dynamic) characteristics
  - Concerns
  - Advantages
  - Disadvantages
  - Privacy issues

44

 (ISC)² SSCP® CBK® Review Seminar v10.0 – Access Controls

- **BIOMETRICS –** Can be used for both identification (physical biometrics) and authentication (logical biometrics) and consist of measuring various unique parts of a person's anatomy or physical activities. Biometrics can be broken into two different categories, physiological and behavioral.
- **PHYSIOLOGICAL (I.E., STATIC) CHARACTERISTICS –** "What you are." Physiological biometrics include such things as recognizing fingerprints, iris granularity, retina blood vessels, facial looks, hand geometry, etc.
  - **FINGERPRINT/PALM PRINT –** A fingerprint is the pattern of breaks and forks on the tip of a finger. A palm print is the physical structure of the palm. Both are considered to be highly accurate for authentication purposes. The system reaction time is five-to-seven seconds and user acceptability is generally good.
  - **HAND GEOMETRY –** A camera takes a picture of the palm side of the hand and (via 45 degree mirror) the side of the hand. Decisions are made using the length, width, thickness, and contour of the fingers. Highly accurate for authentication purposes. System response time is one-to-three seconds and user acceptability is good. This system was used to identify athletes at the Olympic village in the 1996 Atlanta event.
  - **RETINA SCAN –** Analyzes the blood vessel pattern of the inside rear portion of the eyeball area (the retina) using a low-level light source and a camera. Very accurate for identification and authentication, although susceptible to variations in a person's physical condition, such as those caused by diabetes, pregnancy, heart attacks, etc., conditions which would require a re-enrollment procedure. Not well accepted by users because of the feelings of intrusion, lack of sanitation, and potential privacy issues if medical information is compromised. Response time averages four-to-seven seconds.
  - **IRIS SCAN –** Records unique patterns in the colored portion of the eye (the iris) caused by striations, pits, freckles, rifts, fibers, etc., using a small video recorder. Very accurate for identification and authentication and provides the capability for continuous motoring to prevent session hijacking. Response time is one-to-two seconds and is well accepted by users.
  - **FACIAL RECOGNITION –** Video cameras are used to measure certain features of the face, such as the distance between the eyes, the shape of chin and jaw, the length and width of the nose, shape of cheek bones and eye sockets, etc. Fourteen or so features are selected from the (approximately) 80 that can be measured to create a facial database. Accurate for authentication because face angle can be controlled, but less accurate for identification in a moving crowd. Because it is passive and non-intrusive, it can be used to provide continuous authentication.
- **BEHAVIORAL (I.E., DYNAMIC) CHARACTERISTICS –** "What you do." Behavioral biometrics include such things as voice inflections, keyboard strokes, signature motions, etc.
  - **VOICE PATTERN –** Audio recorders and other sensors capture as many as seven parameters of nasal tones, larynx and throat vibrations, and air pressure from the voice. Not considered to be very accurate for authentication and accuracy can be further diminished by background noise. Well accepted by users. Response time varies up to 10-14 seconds.
  - **KEYSTROKE DYNAMICS –** Consists of recording a reference template by measuring the "dwell time" (how long a key is held down) and "flight time" (the amount of time between keystrokes) when typing a selected phrase. Considered to be very accurate for authentication and lends itself well to two-factor authentication because of the ease of using the technology for the logon process (something you know plus something you do). Very well accepted and can provide continuous authentication.
  - **SIGNATURE DYNAMICS –** Sensors in the pen, stylus, or writing tablet are used to record pen stroke speed, direction, and pressure. Accurate for authentication and well accepted by users.
- **CONCERNS –**
  - **ACCURACY –** There is a trade-off between the "false reject rate" and the "false accept rate." The point at which the two rates are equal is called the "crossover error rate" (CER). The CER is the measure of accuracy of the system expressed as a percentage. Note that high security systems will be willing to accept a high level of false rejects, whereas lower security requirements will be willing to allow potentially unauthorized personnel to have access so as not to excessively slow down access.
  - **ACCEPTABILITY –** Certain biometric measurements such as retinal scans are more objectionable to some users than others, such as signature dynamics. If users are not comfortable using the system, problems can occur. See above with respect to tolerance depending on need for security.
  - **REACTION TIME –** This is the amount of time required for the system to read input and provide output.
  - **INABILITY TO CHANGE PARAMETER –** Once compromised (say a fingerprint image is captured and used for replay), it is extremely difficult if not impossible to change (unlike changing passwords or card systems).
- **ADVANTAGES –**
  - A person must be physically present in order to authenticate.
  - Convenience: There is nothing to remember.
  - Fraud reduction: Biometrics are hard to fake.

- Eliminate problems caused by lost IDs or forgotten passwords.

- **DISADVANTAGES –**
  - Physical characteristics may change.
  - Physically disabled users may have difficulty with authentication systems based on fingerprints, hand geometry, or signatures.
  - Not all techniques are equally effective, and it is often hard to determine which technique is the most suitable for a given application.
  - Time-consuming and expensive. Particularly with methods that require significant lengths of time to authenticate, the organization will have to provide a potentially large number of authentication devices so as not to cause significant bottlenecks at points of entry/access.

- **PRIVACY ISSUES –**
  - Biometric technologies don't just involve collecting information about the person, but rather information intrinsic to them. Every person must submit to an examination which is then digitally recorded and stored. Unauthorized access to this information could lead to misuse.
  - Biometrics can be used for monitoring people's movements and actions.
  - Recorded and replayed identification data may be used to masquerade as someone else, thus creating a risk for identity theft.

**REFERENCES:**

Information Security Management Handbook, Tipton & Krause, Auerbach, 2007.

Enhancing Security through Biometric Technology, Stephen D. Fried, CISSP.

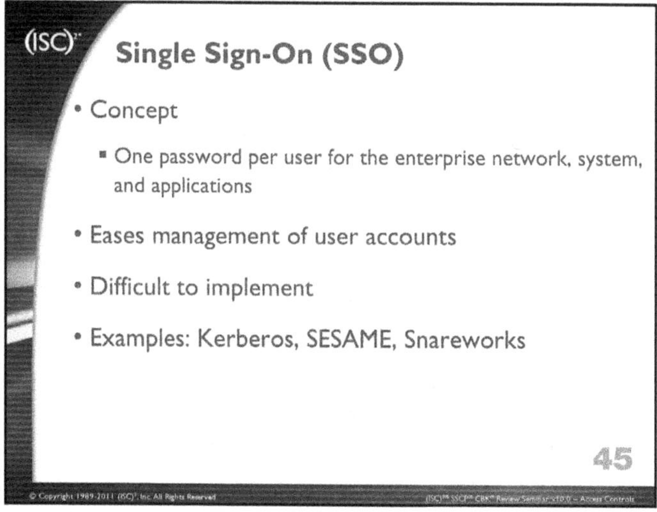


- **CONCEPT –** The concept behind SSO is that the user authenticates once to a central server and then transparently to the user, authenticates to the other network services. This maintains the security domain relationships that have been defined within the organization without burdening the user with remembering and maintaining authentication credentials for each of those services.
- **EASES MANAGEMENT OF USER ACCOUNTS –** SSO is designed to ease the management issues associated with issues and maintaining multiple passwords.
- **DIFFICULT TO IMPLEMENT –** Without proper awareness, training, and education, SSO can be difficult to implement successfully within a complex enterprise environment.
- **EXAMPLES –** The most common solution implemented today is Kerberos. Secure European System for Applications in a Multi-Vendor Environment (SESAME) is a European alternative to Kerberos designed to enhance some of the shortfalls.
- The use of single sign-on (SSO) has several advantages, and disadvantages, as seen on the next slide. But one challenge with the implementation of SSO is often to integrate all the legacy applications together. This makes it somewhat difficult to implement entirely in some organizations.

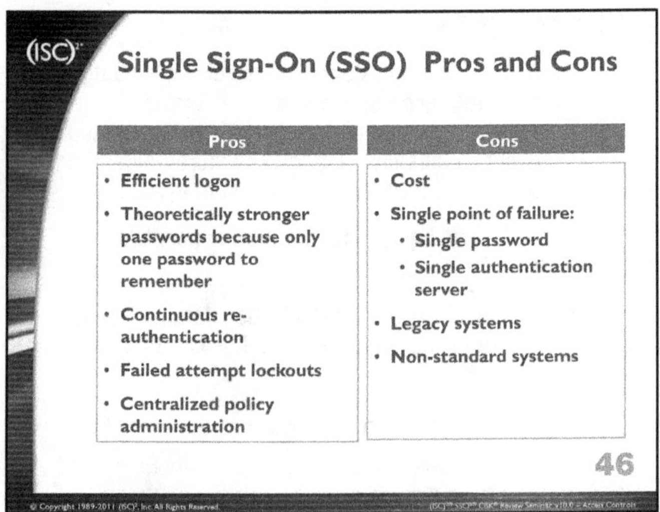

(ISC)²
Single Sign-On (SSO) Pros and Cons
Pros
• Efficient logon
• Theoretically stronger passwords because only one password to remember
• Continuous re-authentication
• Failed attempt lockouts
• Centralized policy administration
Cons
• Cost
• Single point of failure:
• Single password
• Single authentication server
• Legacy systems
• Non-standard systems
46


- **PROS –**
  - **EFFICIENT LOGON PROCESS –** The user only has to log on once.
  - **THEORETICALLY STRONGER PASSWORDS –** With only one password to remember, users may be willing to use better passwords.
  - **CONTINUOUS, TRANSPARENT RE-AUTHENTICATION –** The SSO server will keep in contact with the workstation and will monitor it for network activity. This enables timeout thresholds that can be enforced consistently throughout the system near the user entry point. Timeouts due to inactivity at a workstation for a certain period of time are used to protect against a user being away from his or her workstation while leaving it available to an unauthenticated person who could masquerade as the original user. When the timeout period is reached, the workstation is disconnected.
  - **ATTEMPT THRESHOLDS AND LOCKOUTS –** The attempt threshold refers to failed logon attempts. This is used to protect against an intruder attempting to obtain an authentic UserID and password combination by brute force.
  - **CENTRALIZED ADMINISTRATION –** Ensures consistent application of policy and procedures.
- **CONS –**
  - Static passwords provide very limited security. It is strongly recommended that two-factor authentication or, at least, one-time (dynamic) passwords be required for SSO.
  - A compromised password allows the intruder into all authorized resources available to the password owner. This problem can be mitigated by employment of dynamic passwords and/or two-factor authentication.
  - Inclusion of unique computers or legacy systems in the network may be difficult.
  - Except for the use of scripting, which is an administrative headache, unusual types of computers may not interface well with SSO software.
  - The authentication server poses the risk of becoming a single point of failure for system access.

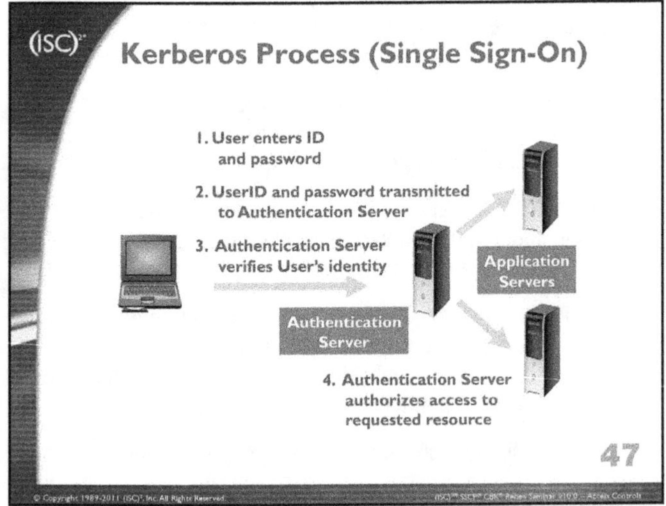


- **KERBEROS PROCESS (SINGLE SIGN-ON) –** All keys used to encrypt each step in the process are symmetric. Every user shares a unique secret key based on the user's password with the Kerberos key distribution center (KDC), and each available service (object) in the system shares a different key with the KDC.
- **THE PROCESS WORKS AS FOLLOWS:**
  - **STEPS 1 AND 2 –** To get started, the user sends his or her ID and access request through the Kerberos client software on the workstation to the KDC.
  - **STEPS 3 AND 4 –** The authentication server of the KDC verifies that the user and the requested service are in the KDC database and sends a ticket for the requested service to the user encrypted with the key shared with the user.
  - Initial authentication can also be performed using a smart card. Included in the ticket are the UserID and the session key, as well as the ticket for the object encrypted with the object's key shared with the KDC.

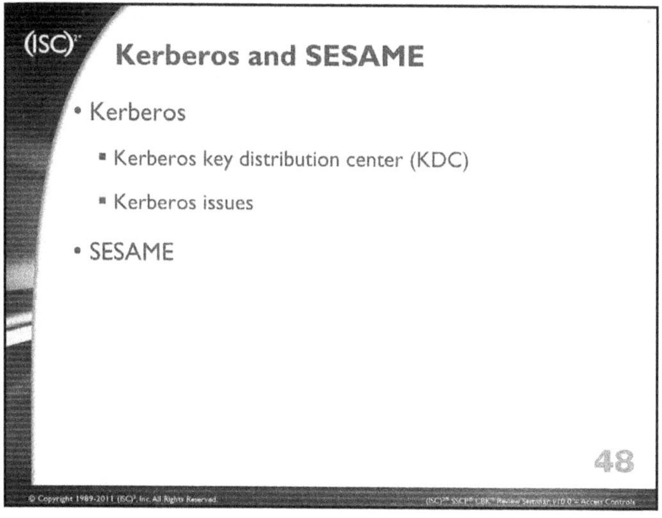


- **KERBEROS –**
  - **KERBEROS KEY DISTRIBUTION CENTER (KDC) –** The Kerberos KDC (KDC) serves two functions:
    - An authentication server (AS), which authenticates a user via a pre-exchanged secret key based on the user's password. This is the symmetric key that is shared with the KDC and stored in the KDC database. After receiving a request for service from the user, all further transmissions with the user workstation are encrypted using this shared key. The user's password is not transmitted to the KDC during the authentication process. Instead, the authentication occurs at the time the Kerberos software on the user's workstation requests the password to create the shared key to decrypt the ticket from the authentication server. The ticket contains the session key for use in communicating with the desired application server, so if the wrong password is supplied, the ticket can't be decrypted and the access attempt fails.
    - The ticket granting server (TGS) provides a means to obtain additional tickets for the same or other applications after authentication by the authentication server so that step doesn't need to be repeated several times during a day. Tickets usually expire on a daily basis or less.
  - **KERBEROS ISSUES –** Security depends on careful implementation and maintenance. Lifetimes for authentication credentials should be as short as feasible using time stamps to minimize the threat of replayed credentials. The KDC must be physically secured because it, and particularly the authentication server, is a potential single point of failure. Redundant authentication servers are strongly recommended. The KDC should be hardened and should not allow any non-Kerberos network activity. Kerberos secrets are also potentially vulnerable to dictionary attacks.
- **SESAME –** The Secure European System for Applications in a Multi-Vendor Environment (SESAME) is a European research and development project funded by the European Commission and developed to address some of the Kerberos weaknesses. It supports SSO and, unlike Kerberos, it improves key management by using both symmetric and asymmetric keys for protection of interchanged data. It is essentially an extension of Kerberos, offering public key cryptography and role-based access control capabilities. SESAME v.3 can be implemented in a distributed environment across multiple platforms. (See http://www.cosic.esat.kuleuven.be/sesame/.)

---

**REFERENCE:**

http://www.ntsecurity.nu/toolbox/kerbcrack/.

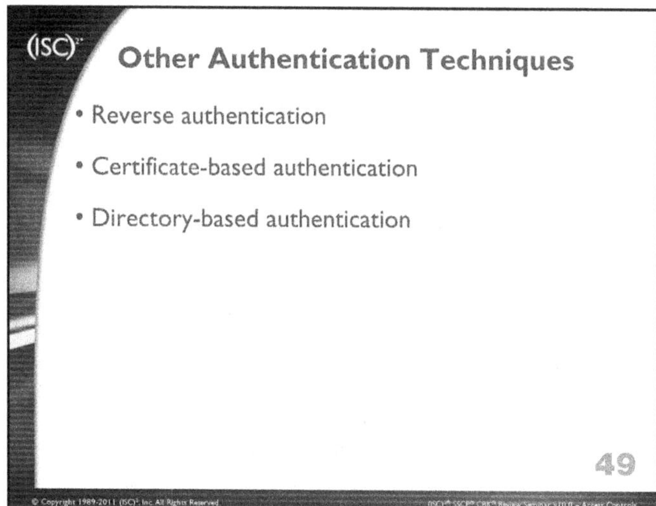


- **REVERSE AUTHENTICATION –** In normal authentication, you enter a password and the website verifies you are the correct user. In reverse authentication, the website gives YOU a password or passphrase (chosen by you) so you verify you are at the correct website.
  - When you set a reverse authentication passphrase, PasswordUser.com will show you this passphrase after you enter your username and password, but before you enter your encryption key, each time you log on. This verifies that you have reached the authentic PasswordUser.com website. If you were somehow misled to another website which looked similar to PasswordUser.com the impersonating website would not be able to give you the correct reverse authentication passphrase, set by you. This protects you, your encryption key, and your passwords.
  - A reverse authentication passphrase can be anything you want: a word, a phrase, a positive message, or something silly.
- **CERTIFICATE-BASED AUTHENTICATION –** Based on public key infrastructure (PKI) standards, this methodology complements a PKI enabled infrastructure. Certificates are presented to the authentication server and verified with the certificate server (or CA).
- **DIRECTORY-BASED AUTHENTICATION –** Use of standard directory databases (e.g., X.500, lightweight directory access protocol (LDAP), domain name system (DNS), etc.) to authenticate and map resources is common in client-server environments (such as Microsoft's Active Directory).

(ISC)²

## Accountability/Auditing (Logging)

- Logging is an essential component of secure access control
- Tracks subject's activities such as logon, privilege escalation, etc.
- Review of audit logs for suspicious activities should be done on a regular basis
- Protect access to logging facilities and log entries to prevent alteration or destruction.

50



(ISC)² SSCP® CBK® Review Seminar v10.0 – Access Controls

- **ACCOUNTABILITY/AUDITING (LOGGING) –** The final component of access control is creating and maintaining log files in order to account for the use of a system.
- In the early days of computing, logs were used for billing on time-share systems, and even later when companies like CompuServe and AOL billed by the hour. Mobile phone use is a current example of fee-based usage.
- Logging is now often used as a detective, preventative, or monitoring tool to validate and verify access control.
- The standard format for logs is SYSLOG, which produces an output suitable for integrating into a consolidated or correlated record of events from a variety of sources (see RFC 5424).
- From a forensic perspective, SYSLOG records and other logging data can become evidence in an incident investigation, and must be secured/controlled accordingly to prevent alteration, contamination, or destruction.

(ISC)²

## Media Disposal

- Ensure that media that you are disposing of does not contain data that can be read
- Degaussing
- Overwriting
- Destruction

51



(ISC)² SSCP® CBK® Review Seminar v10.0 – Access Controls

- **MEDIA DISPOSAL –** These requirements are to protect files, memory, and other objects in a trusted system from being accessed by unauthorized subjects. Media can be re-used providing that the above has been complied with and the data originally stored was not of excessive sensitivity.
- **DEGAUSSING –** A degausser is a device that can generate a magnetic field for erasing magnetic storage media. Degaussing leaves the domains in random patterns with no preference to orientation, thereby rendering previous data unrecoverable. Note that there may be some sections of the media where the magnetic alignment is not sufficiently randomized after degaussing. Proper degaussing will ensure that there is insufficient magnetic remenance to reconstruct the data. However, for media that has contained very sensitive data, it is usually necessary to physically destroy the media.
- **OVERWRITING –** Overwriting is the act of writing random characters over the data enough times to ensure the data is not recoverable. In general, overwriting storage is feasible if the amount of storage to be overwritten is relatively small, and the overwriting is relatively fast.
- **DESTRUCTION –** Examples of destruction include shredding, burning, or grinding of CD-ROMS.

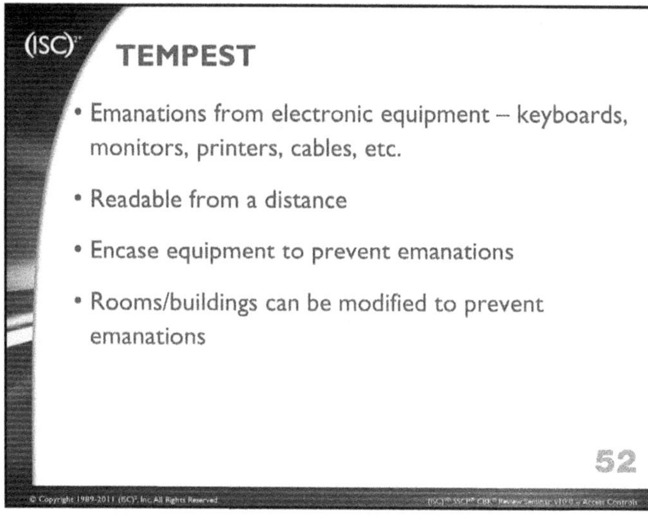


- **EMANATIONS FROM ELECTRONIC EQUIPMENT –** keyboards, monitors, printers, cables, etc. – Some computer and telecommunications devices emit electromagnetic radiation (EMR) in a manner that can be used to reconstruct intelligible data.
- **READABLE FROM A DISTANCE –** The range in which an eavesdropper can monitor emanations varies tremendously according to conditions. In most cases, the emanations can be picked up with proper equipment from a distance of around 200-300 meters. However, in some cases where a signal has been captured by a conductive medium (such as a power line), monitoring can occur over a distance of many kilometers.
- **ENCASE EQUIPMENT TO PREVENT EMANATIONS –** Shielding of devices from EMR is achieved by a number of methods. The most sophisticated devices use advanced micro-components that have been designed from scratch to minimize TEMPEST emanations. Generally, shielding involves encompassing the device in a "Faraday cage" that does not permit stray emanations, along with making special modifications to the power source. This usually involves a heavy metal case around an object.
- **ROOMS/BUILDINGS CAN BE MODIFIED TO PREVENT EMANATIONS –** TEMPEST shielding can also involve such issues as specially designing a room and carefully placing equipment within it so as to ensure that no information can escape.

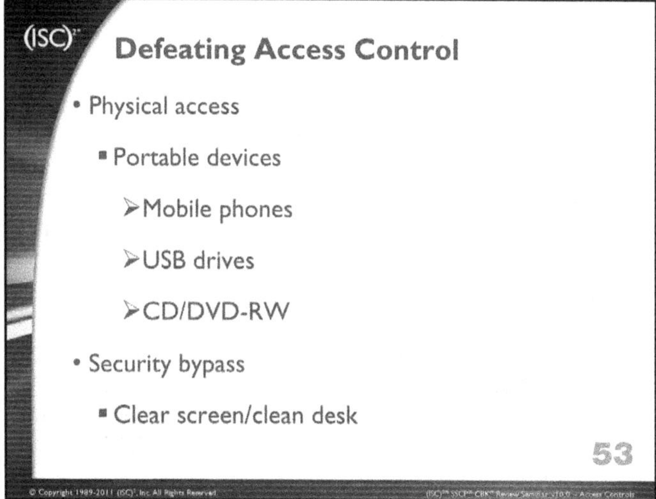


- **PHYSICAL ACCESS –** If an intruder has physical access to a device, logical access control is worthless. Data can be copied or stolen outright.
  - **PORTABLE DEVICES –** Small removable media such as writable CDs, DVD media, USB memory sticks or hard drives make copying data and surreptitiously removing it a relatively easy task. Mobile phones typically have cameras and many have voice recording capability.
- **SECURITY BYPASS –** All forms of access to data must be mediated. While developers may think about access via one method (e.g., via a website), the information-security team must consider alternate access paths such as attackers being able to map a drive, or logging in directly via the server's keyboard.
  - **CLEAR SCREEN/CLEAN DESK –** An often overlooked form of security bypass is eavesdropping by observation. Data visible on papers on an authorized user's desk or screen can provide unauthorized access. Proper policy and procedures should be implemented to prevent this kind of data leakage.

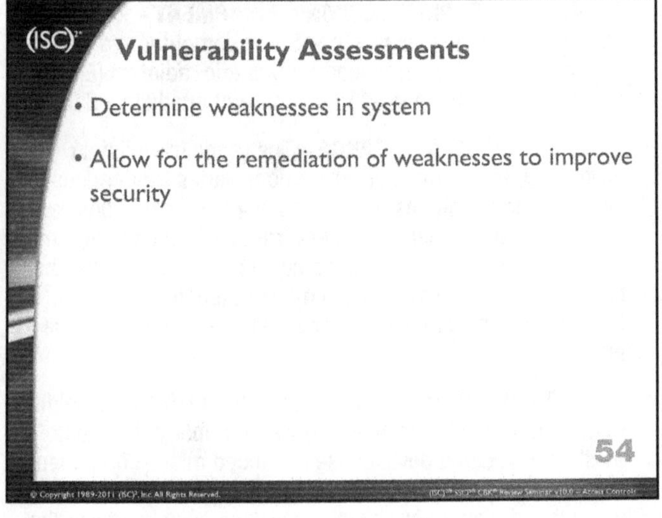

(ISC)²
Vulnerability Assessments
• Determine weaknesses in system
• Allow for the remediation of weaknesses to improve security
54


- **VULNERABILITY ASSESSMENTS –** A vulnerability assessment is the process of identifying, quantifying, and prioritizing the vulnerabilities in a system.
- **DETERMINE WEAKNESSES IN SYSTEM –** Assessments are typically performed by doing the following:
  - Cataloging assets and capabilities (resources) in a system.
  - Assigning quantifiable values and importance to those resources.
  - Identifying the vulnerabilities of, or potential threats to, each resource.
  - Mitigating or eliminating the most serious vulnerabilities for the most valuable resources.
- **ALLOW FOR REMEDIATION OF WEAKNESSES TO IMPROVE SECURITY –** Assessments should be performed at scheduled intervals because vulnerabilities can occur at any time. Corrective actions should be planned and implemented based on assessment findings.

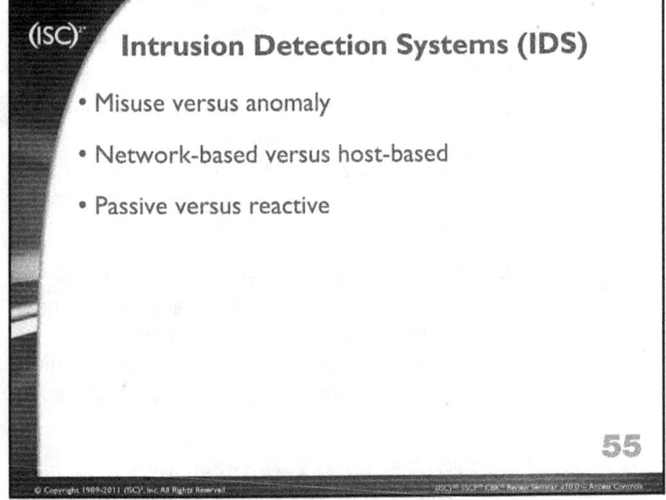


- **INTRUSION DETECTION SYSTEMS (IDS) –** An IDS inspects all inbound and outbound network activity and identifies suspicious patterns that may indicate a network or system attack from someone attempting to break into or compromise a system. There are several ways to categorize an IDS:
- **MISUSE VERSUS ANOMALY –**
  - In misuse detection, the IDS analyzes the information it gathers and compares it with large databases of attack signatures. Essentially, the IDS looks for a specific attack that has already been documented. Misuse detection software is only as good as the database of attack signatures that it uses to compare packets against.
  - In anomaly detection, the system administrator defines the baseline, or normal, state of the network's traffic load, breakdown, protocol, and typical packet size and the anomaly detector monitors network segments to compare their state with the normal baseline and look for anomalies.
- **NETWORK-BASED VERSUS HOST-BASED –**
  - In a network-based intrusion detection system, or NIDS, the individual packets flowing through a network are analyzed. The NIDS can detect malicious packets that are designed to be overlooked by a firewall's simplistic filtering rules.
  - In a host-based intrusion detection system, the IDS examines the activity on each individual system.
- **PASSIVE VERSUS REACTIVE –**
  - Passive IDS: The IDS detects a potential security event, logs the information, and signals an alert.
  - Reactive IDS: The IDS responds to the suspicious activity by taking some form of action. These actions vary from product to product.

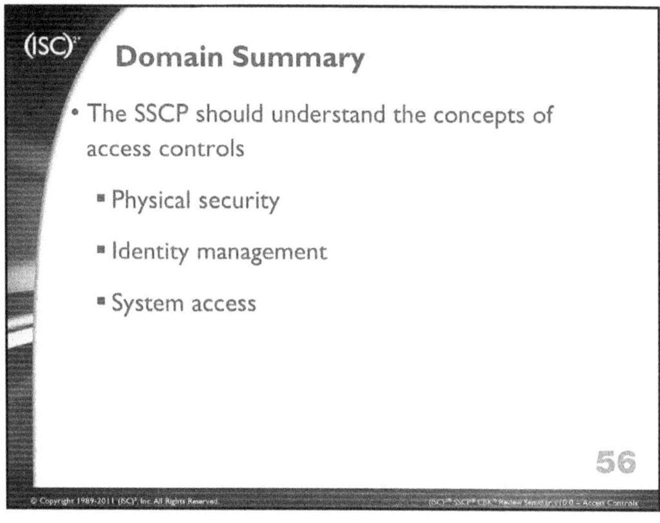

Domain Summary
The SSCP should understand the concepts of access controls
Physical security
Identity management
System access
56


- The SSCP should have a thorough understanding of access control concepts and techniques. Security controls include administrative, physical, and logical (technical) activities designed to provide protection of assets.
- Administrative controls are the foundation to managing security, and include policies, standards, and procedures created to document and enforce security. Also included are elements such as acceptable use policies which define what is and is not allowed in the use of systems.
- Physical security includes practices and techniques designed to restrict access to authorized personnel, such as perimeter controls (fences, bollards, locks, etc.), and to enable continuous monitoring of activities (things such as camera systems). Tests of these controls, through assessments, ensure they are working properly.
- Logical or technical controls include automated security processes and programmed actions taken to restrict, monitor, and enforce access to systems and data.
- Identity management is essential in determining WHO should be allowed access and to defining clearly those permissions which are to be granted to individuals. It also documents the relationships that need to be administered and managed among a variety of constituents.
- System access relies upon a variety of solutions which are integrated to protect availability, integrity, and confidentiality of critical systems and the data they contain. A number of common concepts and models are used to implement these controls, and the SSCP should have a good understanding of what they are, how they operate, and how to maintain them.

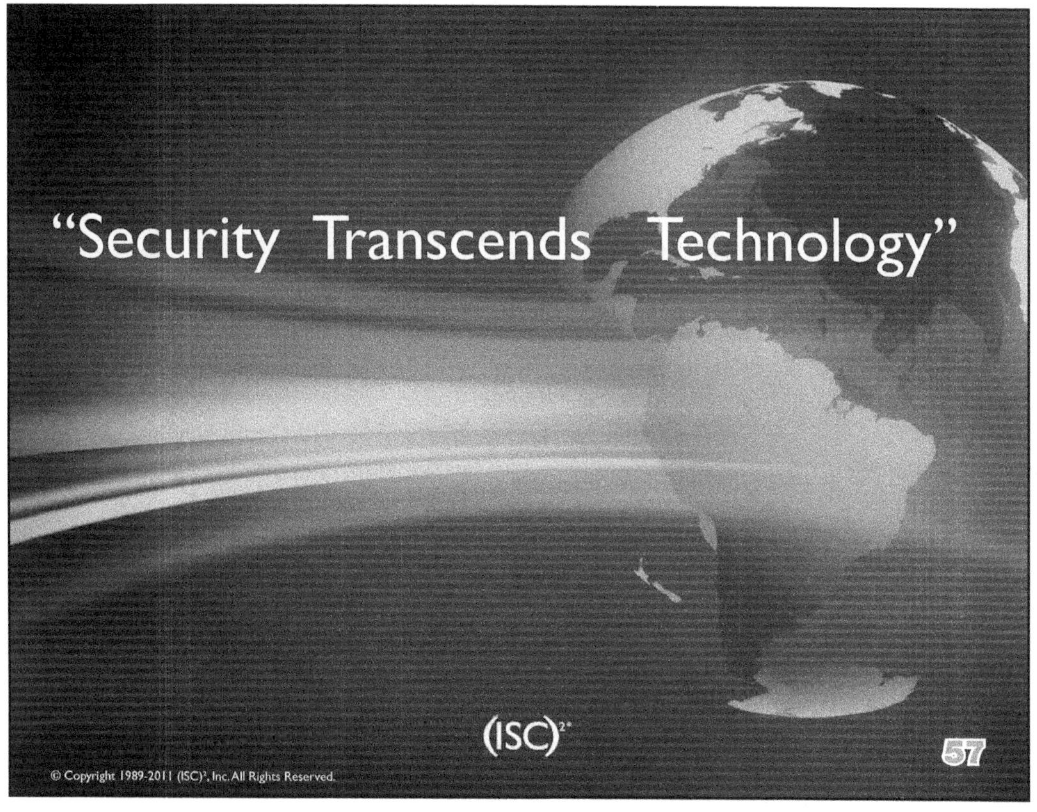

# Review Questions

## ACCESS CONTROL

1. **The three types of access controls are administrative, technical, and**
   a. preventive.
   b. deterrent.
   c. physical.
   d. discretionary.

2. **Access control assurance is provided by**
   a. incident response handling.
   b. penetration testing.
   c. the reference monitor.
   d. vulnerability mapping and scanning.

3. **Integrity pertains to the system and the**
   a. data.
   b. process.
   c. information.
   d. transaction.

4. **The BEST control to prevent collusion is**
   a. supervision.
   b. need to know.
   c. rotation of duties.
   d. awareness training.

5. **A one-time password is a**
   a. password given only once to an employee to ensure no impersonation or stealing.
   b. password that cannot change.
   c. password which is difficult to remember.
   d. password used for only a single session.

6. **In discretionary access control (DAC), who determines access permissions?**
   a. The data owner.
   b. The data owner, in conjunction with the operating system.
   c. The operating system.
   d. The security administrator.

7. **What is an authoritative system of records (ASOR)?**
   a. A hierarchical end system that contains users, accounts, and authorizations for that system.
   b. An active directory (AD), where all users are created and managed.
   c. A hierarchical parent system that tracks users, accounts, and authorization chains.
   d. A lightweight directory access protocol (LDAP) directory, where all users are created and managed.

8. **What is an advantage of legacy single sign on (SSO)?**
   a. It provides a single system where all authentication information is stored.
   b. It allows integration of old, non-interoperable systems into the SSO process.
   c. It provides a single technology allowing all systems to authenticate the users once using the same technology.
   d. It allows users to authenticate once – no matter how many different systems they wish to access.

9. **TEMPEST controls are used to provide what type of security?**
   a. Physical security
   b. Access control
   c. Cryptographic security
   d. Emanations security

10. **Secure European System for Applications in a Multi-vendor Environment (SESAME) is**
    a. an alternative authentication system used in single sign-on.
    b. an asymmetric cryptographic system.
    c. an emanations security control.
    d. a type of mantrap.

11. **In mandatory access control (MAC), the need-to-know element is defined for each asset by the**
    a. operating system.
    b. information owner.
    c. security administrator.
    d. system administrator.

**12. In content dependent access control, the key element that determines the effective access authorization is the**

a. arbiter program.
b. system administrator.
c. data owner.
d. security administrator.

**13. A compensating control is**

a. a control used by the executive compensation committee to align salaries to assigned duties.
b. an alternate control used when another control fails.
c. a control that compensates for the weaknesses built into automated risk management programs.
d. a control that compensates for vulnerabilities that may be present in commercial software.

**14. How can an attacker cause an intrusion prevention system (IPS) to become an attack tool?**

a. By directly attacking the IPS and embedding it with a RAT (remote access trojan).
b. By switching it into detection mode, as opposed to prevention mode.
c. By implementing a buffer-overflow attack against it.
d. By generating a false attack causing the IPS to block legitimate traffic.

**15. How can attackers exploit password security guidelines to their advantage?**

a. By intentionally performing failed authentication for many users causing them to lock-out of the system.
b. By using brute-force password cracking tools to expose weak passwords.
c. They cannot. Implementing password security guidelines ensures passwords cannot be exploited.
d. By being able to assume what type of passwords will be used, thus making password guessing a lot easier.

**16. Why are passphrases considered to be more secure than passwords?**

a. Passphrases use more complex characters than passwords.
b. Passphrases are made of a series of passwords, making them harder to apply a brute-force attack.
c. Passphrases are used to protect access to encryption keys, which are far more secure than passwords.
d. Passphrases are comprised of easy to remember sentences, thus allowing users to remember them better than they can remember meaningless passwords.

**17. What is a major disadvantage of token-based authentication versus password-based authentication?**

a. It is easier to compromise a system if it is protected by passwords.
b. Tokens require more administrative overhead.
c. Tokens cannot be replaced as easily as passwords.
d. Passwords are simpler to use than tokens.

**18. What is a major advantage of smart cards versus memory cards?**

a. Smart cards use stronger encryption to protect the information on them than the encryption used by memory cards.
b. Memory cards are sensitive to electro-magnetic interference (EMI), which can erase the card content.
c. Smart cards are less secure than memory cards.
d. Authentication occurs locally between the smart card and the reader as opposed to over the network like a memory card.

**19. In mandatory access control (MAC), how are access and privileges determined?**

a. The owner determines who has access and what privileges they have with particular files.
b. The owner determines the classification level of the data.
c. The owner determines the classification level of the data and the system determines access based on classification and clearances.
d. The security administrator determines who has access and what privileges they have with particular files.

**20. Access control decisions which are based upon job function describes which type of access control?**

a. Role-based
b. Rule-based
c. Content-based
d. Non-discretionary

# Notes

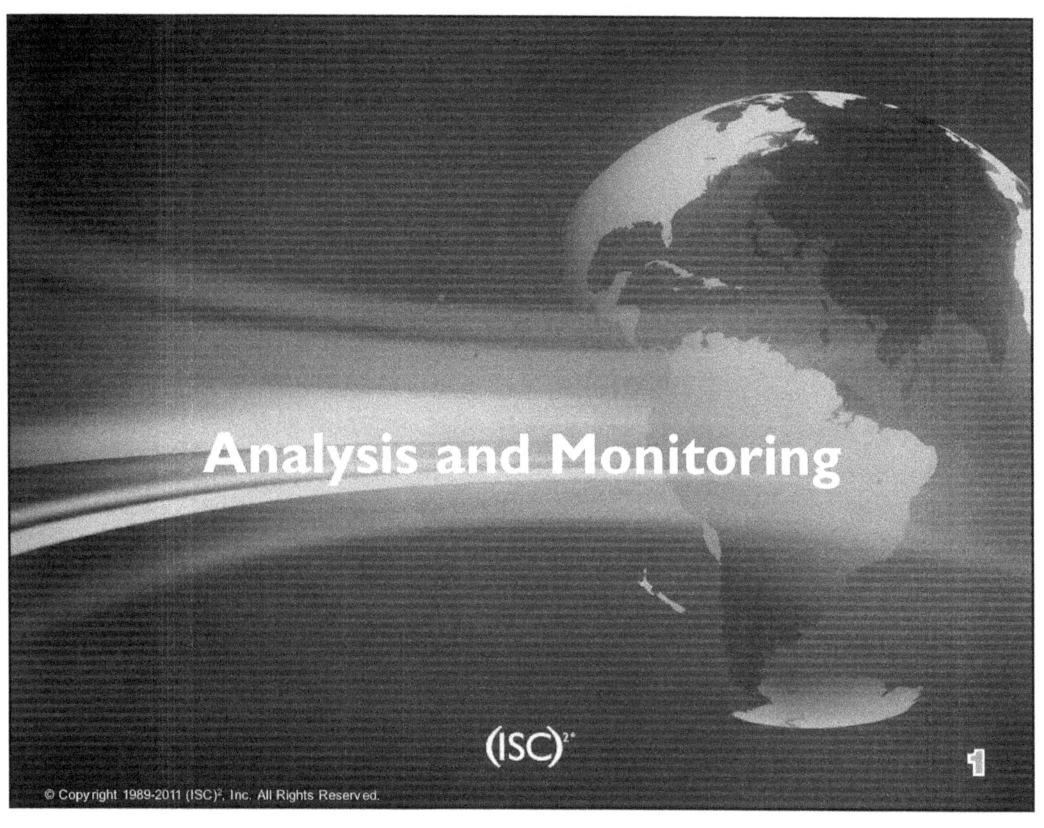

Analysis and Monitoring
(ISC)²
1
© Copyright 1989-2011 (ISC)², Inc. All Rights Reserved.


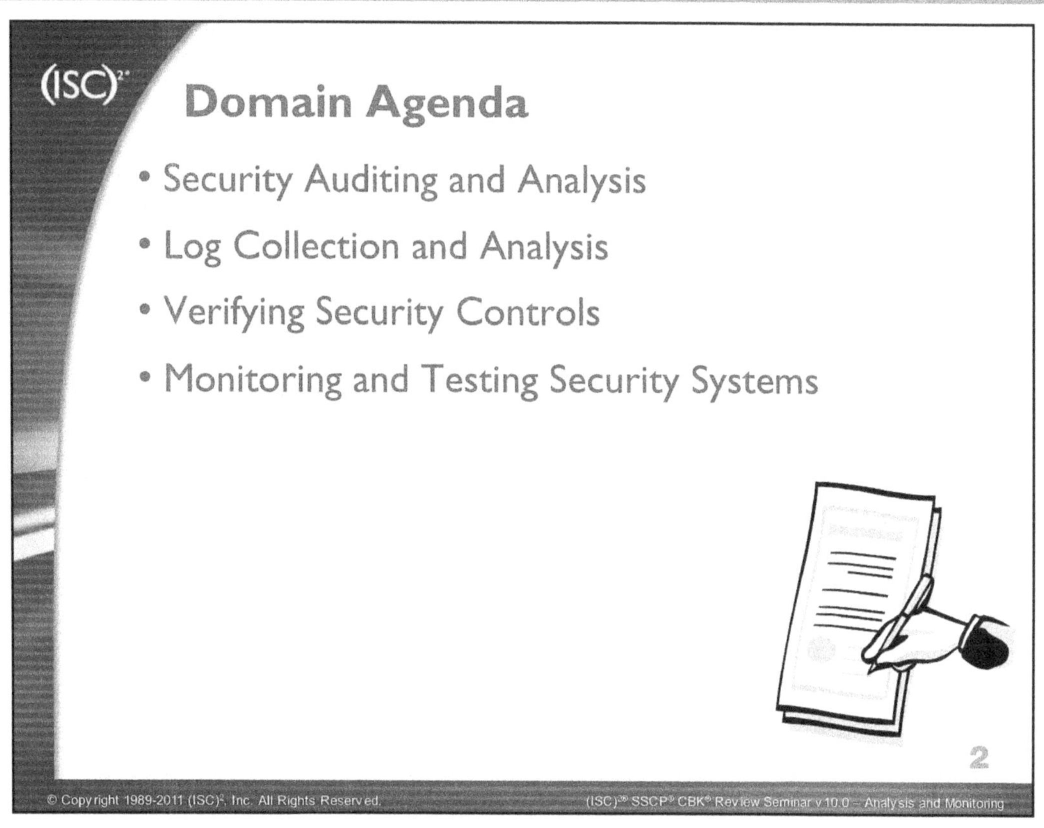

(ISC)²
Domain Agenda
• Security Auditing and Analysis
• Log Collection and Analysis
• Verifying Security Controls
• Monitoring and Testing Security Systems
2
© Copyright 1989-2011 (ISC)², Inc. All Rights Reserved.
(ISC)²® SSCP® CBK® Review Seminar v.10.0 – Analysis and Monitoring

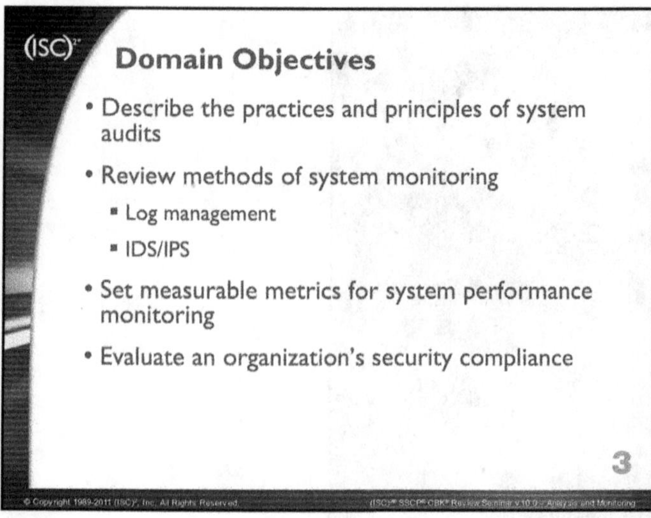


- **DOMAIN OBJECTIVES –** This is a list of the primary domain objectives.
- **DESCRIBE THE PRACTICES AND PRINCIPLES OF SYSTEM AUDITS –** We will identify some of the main methods of audit, along with some example regulatory requirements.
- **REVIEW METHODS OF SYSTEM MONITORING –** Discuss methods of log management, such as clipping levels, log roll-up, and SIEM tools.
- **SET MEASURABLE METRICS FOR SYSTEM PERFORMANCE MONITORING –** Discuss key performance indicators (KPIs) of effective log management and measurement techniques.
- **EVALUATE AN ORGANIZATION'S SECURITY COMPLIANCE –** Differentiate between compliance and vulnerability containment.

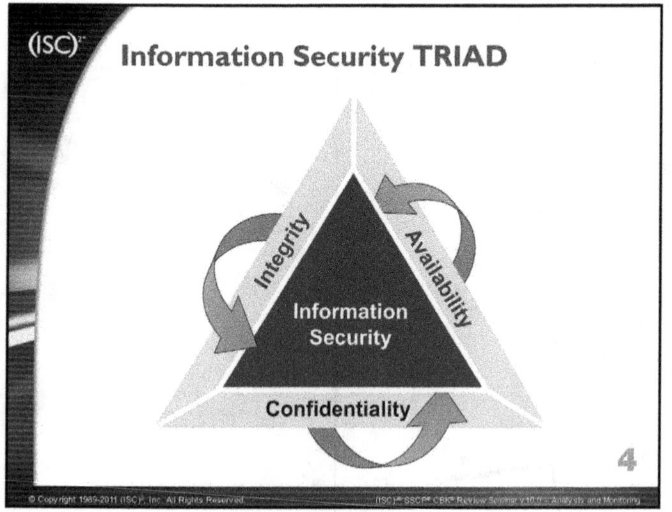


- The Analysis and Monitoring domain is concerned with the availability of logs and tracking information; the integrity of changes to systems; the accuracy of access permissions granted to users, systems, and processes; and the confidentiality of system processes, workflows, and user sensitive data.

# Domain Agenda

- **Security Auditing and Analysis**
- Log Collection and Analysis
- Verifying Security Controls
- Monitoring and Testing Security Systems

5

 (ISC)²® SSCP® CBK® Review Seminar v.10.0 – Analysis and Monitoring

## Security Auditing Overview

- Security reviewers check for the following at a high level:
  - The existence of sound security policies appropriate for the business or activity
  - The existence of controls supporting organizational policies
  - The effective implementation and upkeep of controls
  - Measurement of controls and their effectiveness

6

 (ISC)²® SSCP® CBK® Review Seminar v.10.0 – Analysis and Monitoring

- **SECURITY AUDITING OVERVIEW –** The purpose of a security audit is to ensure that the security program is effective and achieving the desired results.
- **THE EXISTENCE OF SOUND SECURITY POLICIES APPROPRIATE FOR THE BUSINESS OR ACTIVITY –** Security is not a means unto itself - its purpose is to support the business mission and reflect the risk appetite of the organization. An organization's policies and supporting documents (e.g., procedures, standards, baselines, etc.) will define the mission and risk appetite. Auditing is a comparative function. It asks the question, "Are the policies followed and understood?" The audit function does not set new policies, though the auditors might make recommendations based on experience or awareness of new regulations.
- **THE EXISTENCE OF CONTROLS SUPPORTING ORGANIZATIONAL POLICIES –** Are the controls aligned correctly with the strategies and mission of the organization? Do the controls support the policies and culture of the organization? A control that cannot be justified as a direct result of, or response to, a policy is a candidate for removal. Whenever a control is explained as "for security" with no other explanation given, it should be withdrawn. "Security" is not a profit center and should never grow for its own sake. It is a support department, the purpose of which is to protect the company's assets and income stream.
- **THE EFFECTIVE IMPLEMENTATION AND UPKEEP OF CONTROLS –** As the business evolves and threats mature, it is important to ensure that the controls continue to effectively address the risks the business faces.
- **MEASUREMENT OF CONTROLS AND THEIR EFFECTIVENESS –** What types of metrics should be used to measure control effectiveness? Metrics such as false positives, help desk trouble call resolution times, and trouble call escalation percentage can be used to help monitor and adjust controls to the appropriate levels.

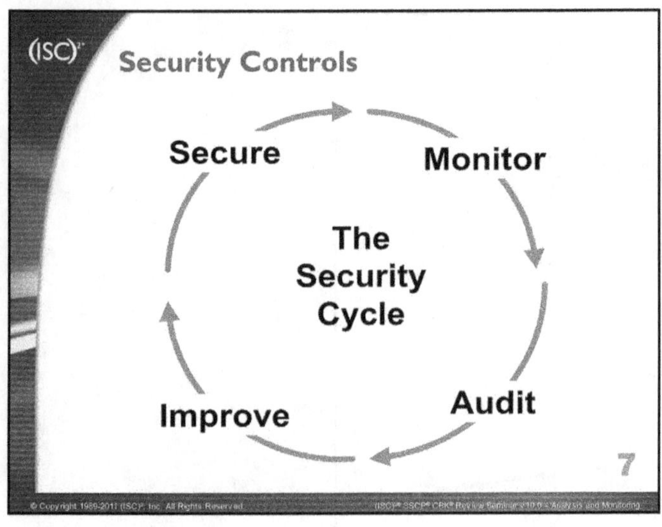


- **CONTROLS ADDRESS RISK –** Controls place limitations on activities that might pose a risk to the organization (fuller discussion in the Risk, Response, Recovery domain). The security of the organization must be reviewed on a regular basis to determine that the security controls continue to keep pace with the security cycle.
- **THE SECURITY CYCLE –**
  - **MONITOR –** All controls need to be reviewed and measured to capture the actions and changes on the system.
  - **AUDIT –** This is the review of the logs and overall environment with the purpose of providing independent analysis of the effectiveness of the security policy and controls.
  - **IMPROVE –** The results of an audit should include recommendations on how to improve the security program and controls - whether they are technical, physical, or administrative in nature. The "improve" step implements the recommended changes as accepted by management.
  - **SECURE –** The controls are operational and maintained to provide the level of security intended.

- **DETERMINING WHAT IS ACCEPTABLE –**
- **ACCEPTABLE AND UNACCEPTABLE ACTIVITY –**
  - Acceptable and unacceptable transactions should be defined by policy.
  - Organizations may create their own standards from policy guidelines produced by standards bodies.
  - How do we determine what is acceptable?
- **ACCEPTABLE SYSTEM ACTIVITY –**
  - Acceptable system activity is defined as communications within acceptable bounds and of an acceptable type and are stated in a policy document.
  - How do we determine what is unacceptable?
- **UNACCEPTABLE SYSTEM ACTIVITY –**
  - Unacceptable system activity is defined as communications specifically disallowed in a security policy or something that might cause damage to a system's integrity, reveal confidential information, or make the system unavailable, even if the communication is not specifically banned by policy.
  - Unacceptable system activity may be defined as everything that is not recognized as acceptable.
- Note: Creation of policies and their supporting documents is covered in the Security Architecture domain.

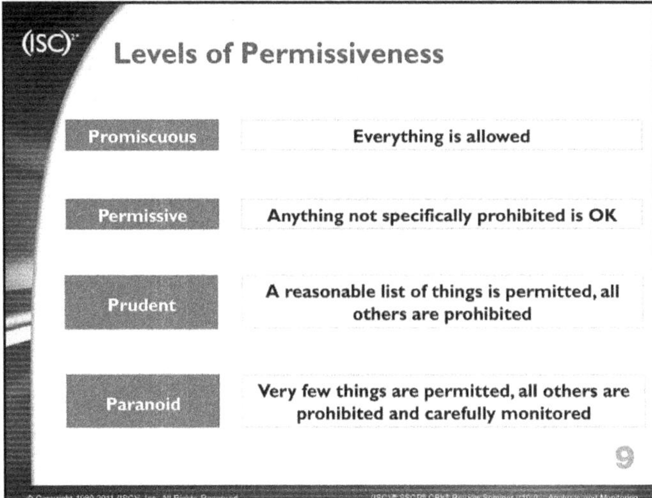


- **LEVELS OF PERMISSIVENESS –** The right level of permissiveness depends on the organization, its needs, and its policies. Matching the permissiveness level of a business with the security structure is essential. Failure to do so will cause loss of data (and reputation) or will cause users to bypass security controls.
- **PROMISCUOUS –** Universities and most home users.
- **PERMISSIVE –** Most public Internet sites, some schools and libraries, many training centers.
- **PRUDENT –** Many businesses.
- **PARANOID –** Secure facilities.

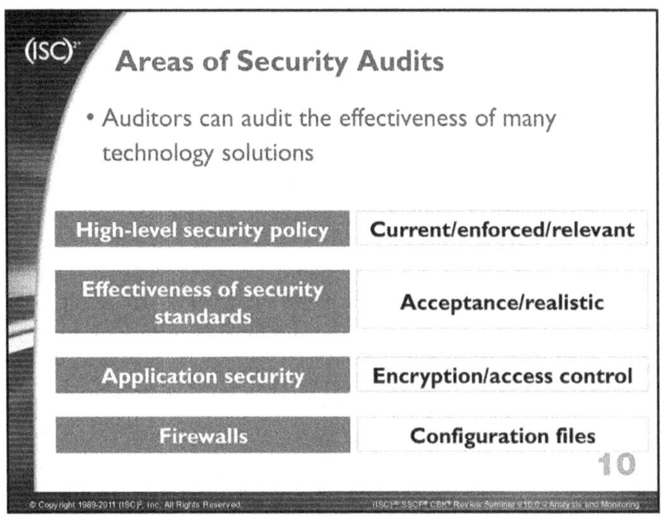


- **AREAS OF SECURITY AUDITS –** Audits can be very large in scope, taking in entire departments or business functions, or they can be very narrow and look only at one system or control. The purpose of an audit is to provide management with an independent assessment of the effectiveness and appropriateness of the controls in order to address the risks to the organization.
- **HIGH-LEVEL SECURITY POLICY –** Is the review of policy to ensure it is communicated, up to date, relevant, enforced, and that it reflects the culture of the organization.
- **EFFECTIVENESS OF SECURITY STANDARDS –** Audits may test whether the users or customers are accepting the controls or whether they are attempting to bypass controls that they feel are unrealistic.
- **APPLICATION SECURITY –** The audit will test the protection of the data being processed by an application and whether the application is limiting access to authorized people only and hiding (encrypting) data that is confidential.
- **FIREWALLS –** Firewalls need to be audited to ensure that they are functioning as intended and that oonfigurations are set according to policy. Audits will often test the technologies themselves in order to see whether the firewall, router, or IDS is functioning according to policy, that the rules are up to date, documented, subject to change control procedures, etc.

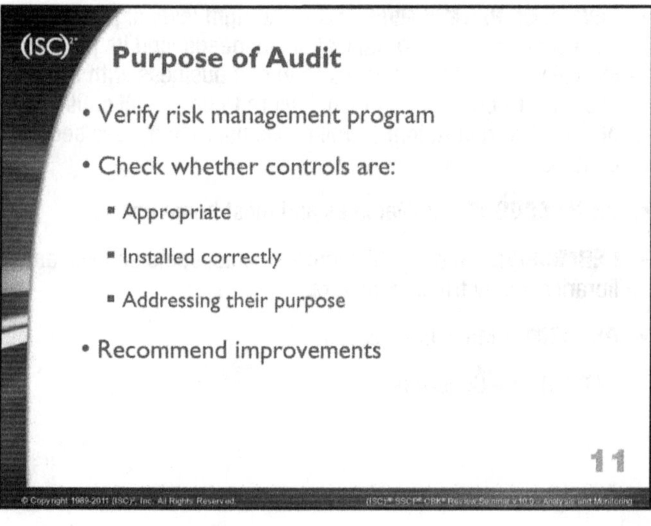
(ISC)²
Purpose of Audit
Verify risk management program
Check whether controls are:
Appropriate
Installed correctly
Addressing their purpose
Recommend improvements
11

- **VERIFY RISK MANAGEMENT PROGRAM –** The audit will review the risk-management program to validate whether the program has correctly identified and mitigated or otherwise addressed the risks to the mission of the organization.
- **CHECK WHETHER CONTROLS ARE:**
  - **APPROPRIATE –** Is the level of control commensurate with the risk the control is designed to mitigate?
  - **INSTALLED CORRECTLY –** Is the control in the right place and working effectively?
  - **ADDRESSING THEIR PURPOSE –** Is the control effective in reducing the risk it was designed to mitigate?
- **RECOMMEND IMPROVEMENTS –** Through the findings of the audit, the audit report should recommend improvements or changes to the organization's processes, infrastructure, or other controls as needed.

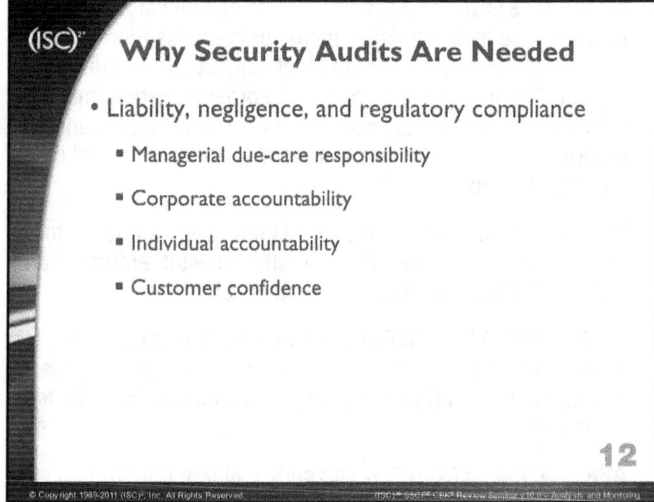
(ISC)²
Why Security Audits Are Needed
Liability, negligence, and regulatory compliance
Managerial due-care responsibility
Corporate accountability
Individual accountability
Customer confidence
12

- **LIABILITY, NEGLIGENCE, AND REGULATORY COMPLIANCE –** Audits are required by law in many jurisdictions. Laws in some places require all companies over a certain size, or perhaps all companies in a certain industry (e.g., financial services), to have both an internal and external audit function.
  - **MANAGERIAL DUE-CARE RESPONSIBILITY –** To demonstrate that management has exercised the principles of due care to protect the assets of the organization through an identification of risks and an implementation of reasonable controls.
  - **CORPORATE ACCOUNTABILITY –** Is a large issue today with many organizations being subject to stricter accounting and reporting laws, such as SOX or HIPAA (US) or PIPEDA (Canada).
  - **INDIVIDUAL ACCOUNTABILITY –** The audits may identify a lack of trained and skilled staff, or a lack of sufficient oversight of protection programs and asset management. This may even lead to recommendations for training or providing educational programs for staff. Many regulations are also increasing the level of individual (rather than corporate) accountability for fraud or mismanagement of corporate assets.
  - **CUSTOMER CONFIDENCE –** The trust and confidence of customers is often a key factor in the buying decision. The attestation or verification of an organization through an audit may increase a customer's confidence in sharing personally identifiable information or financial information with an organization.
- SOX: Sarbanes-Oxley, US Corporate Accountability Law.
- HIPAA: Health Insurance Portability and Accountability Act, US Healthcare Privacy Legislation with regard to personally identifiable healthcare information.
- PIPEDA: Personal Information Protection and Electronic Documents Act, Canadian law that protects how personal information is collected, used, or disclosed, with special attention to e-commerce transactions.

(ISC)²

## The Security Function and Audit

- Security team supports audit process
- Provides accurate and timely response to audit's questions
- Security team may resolve issues uncovered by the audit process

13

 (ISC)² SSCP® CBK® Review Seminar v10.0 – Analysis and Monitoring

- **THE SECURITY FUNCTION AND AUDIT –** The security team must support the periodic audit process. It is critical that the security team provide accurate and timely responses to the audit team's inquiries. The end result of the audit process helps the security team resolve uncovered issues discovered by the audit process.

(ISC)²

## Defining the Audit Plan

- Define the audit objectives
- Understand the audit objectives
- Understand the personnel resources
- Review previous audits
  - Verify previous audit comments addressed
  - Save repeated work
  - Don't be influenced or biased in review

14

 (ISC)² SSCP® CBK® Review Seminar v10.0 – Analysis and Monitoring

- **DEFINE THE AUDIT OBJECTIVES –** Organizational policy is key to defining the audit objectives in order to ensure they support the organization's mission and contribute to the overall improvement of the security policy and program.
- **UNDERSTAND THE AUDIT OBJECTIVES –** An auditor should know what the objectives are for the audit, what systems or business processes will be reviewed, and the areas of assurance that will be addressed.
- **UNDERSTAND THE PERSONNEL RESOURCES –** An auditor will need to know which personnel from his or her own team and from the organization being audited will be involved. These people will help gather and synthesize information and move the audit along. The auditor must be sure that all staff has the skills to perform the audit.
- **REVIEW PREVIOUS AUDITS –** An auditor may wish to review previous similar audit results to become familiar with past issues. Some auditors, however, may not want to be prejudiced by previous conclusions.

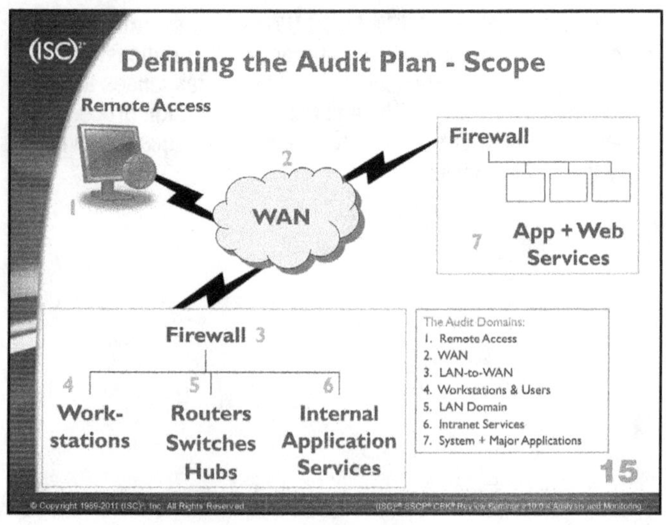
(ISC)²
Defining the Audit Plan - Scope
Remote Access
1
2
WAN
Firewall
7
App + Web
Services
Firewall 3
4
5
6
Work-
stations
Routers
Switches
Hubs
Internal
Application
Services
The Audit Domains:
1. Remote Access
2. WAN
3. LAN-to-WAN
4. Workstations & Users
5. LAN Domain
6. Intranet Services
7. System + Major Applications
15

- **DEFINING THE AUDIT PLAN - SCOPE –** One of the critical parts of an effective security review is to ensure that the boundaries of the review are defined at the beginning of the project. It is, therefore, critical to determine which areas will be reviewed and which areas are out of scope. Ensure, however, that the areas determined to be out of scope are subject to another review and that responsibility for those areas is established. There should not be a system or a network that does not have a clearly designated "owner."
- Another issue to be decided at this point is who to tell that an audit is under way. If it is possible that staff will change the way they work (for example, follow rules they often ignore), then making those people aware of an ongoing audit is going to generate false results. On the other hand, performing an audit without notification will make the auditor's work more difficult and might limit the auditor's access to critical information needed to do a proper assessment. This is a trade-off that has to be considered on a case-by-case basis.

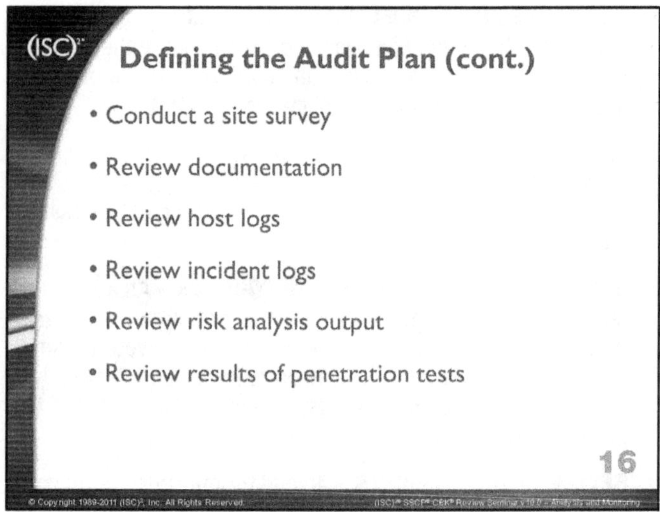
(ISC)²
Defining the Audit Plan (cont.)
• Conduct a site survey
• Review documentation
• Review host logs
• Review incident logs
• Review risk analysis output
• Review results of penetration tests
16

- **CONDUCT A SITE SURVEY –** An auditor will want to understand the environment and the interconnections between systems.
- **REVIEW DOCUMENTATION –** An auditor will want to review system documentation and configurations.
- **REVIEW HOST LOGS –** An auditor may ask to examine system logs looking for changes to programs, permissions, or configurations.
- **REVIEW INCIDENT LOGS –** An auditor may ask to review security incident logs to get a feel for problem trends.
- **REVIEW RISK ANALYSIS OUTPUT –** An auditor will want to understand system criticality ratings that are a product of risk analysis studies. This helps rank systems in the appropriate order for mitigation in the reporting phase.
- **REVIEW RESULTS OF PENETRATION TESTS –** When an organization conducts penetration tests, the tester prepares a report listing weaknesses and vulnerabilities found. The auditor needs to review this report and make sure that all items are addressed.

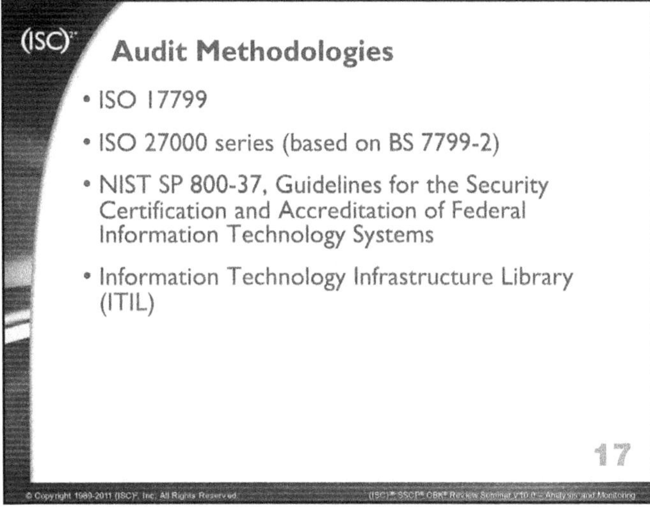

(ISC)²
Audit Methodologies
• ISO 17799
• ISO 27000 series (based on BS 7799-2)
• NIST SP 800-37, Guidelines for the Security Certification and Accreditation of Federal Information Technology Systems
• Information Technology Infrastructure Library (ITIL)
17


- **AUDIT METHODOLOGIES –** These are some examples of common methodologies used to audit or review systems, business processes, or security controls.
- All of these are "best practices" and are often used as guidelines for auditing a business or business process. If one of them has been formally adopted by your management (which might be the result of regulation or legislation, especially for government entities), that will be the method that directs the course of the audit. Otherwise, the methodology will be set by the auditor, with senior management approval.
- **ISO 17799 –** Is a best practices document, which provides good guidelines for information security management. However, in order for an organization to claim compliance, an audit needs to be done.
- **ISO 27000 SERIES (BASED ON BS 7799-2) –** Is the audit standard. The :2005 nomenclature is a reference to the current version.
- **NIST SP 800-37 –** Is a standard published by the US government specifically for federal (government owned/operated) computer systems. It has both best practices and audit sections.
    - NIST SP 800 is a series of best practices. The website is organized newest first, but lower numbered items might still be current, as revisions don't change the number.
- **ITIL –** Is the Information Technology Infrastructure Library, a set of concepts and policies for managing information technology (IT) infrastructure, development, and operations.
    - ITIL is published in a series of books, each of which covers an IT management topic. ITIL gives a detailed description of a number of important IT practices with comprehensive checklists, tasks, and procedures that any IT organization can tailor to its needs.

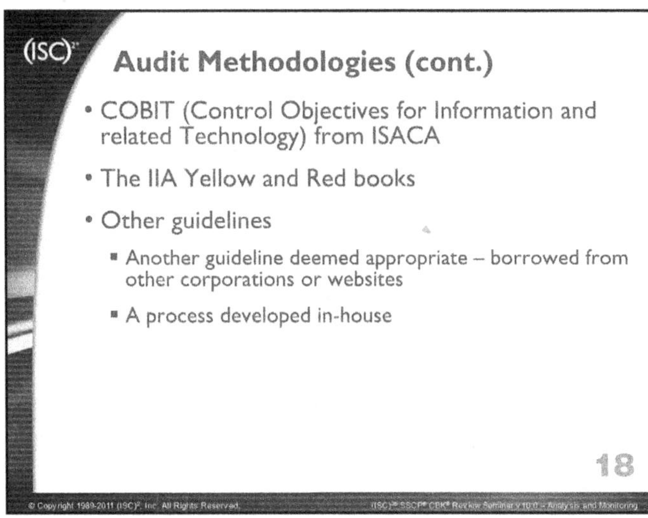

(ISC)²
Audit Methodologies (cont.)
• COBIT (Control Objectives for Information and related Technology) from ISACA
• The IIA Yellow and Red books
• Other guidelines
▪ Another guideline deemed appropriate – borrowed from other corporations or websites
▪ A process developed in-house
18


- **AUDIT METHODOLOGIES (CONT.) –** Other commonly used audit guidelines from other organizations, ISACA, and The Institute of Internal Auditors. Organizations may develop a guideline in-house or customize an audit plan used elsewhere.
- **COBIT (CONTROL OBJECTIVES FOR INFORMATION AND TECHNOLOGY) –** The Control Objectives for Information and related Technology (COBIT) is a set of best practices (framework) for information technology (IT) management created by the Information Systems Audit and Control Association (ISACA), and the IT Governance Institute (ITGI) in 1996. COBIT provides managers, auditors, and IT users with a set of generally accepted measures, indicators, processes, and best practices to assist them in maximizing the benefits derived through the use of information technology and developing appropriate IT governance and control in a company.
- **IIA YELLOW AND RED BOOKS –** IIA is Institute of Internal Auditors. The IIA and the US GAO (General Accountability Office) have created a series of books dealing with government auditing. The Yellow and Red books apply to information systems and IS networks.
- **OTHER GUIDELINES –** Unless there is a law or regulation to the contrary, businesses are free to choose whatever audit methods make the most business sense. A method might be one of the published documents mentioned on this or the previous page; it might be a guideline from another organization or trade group; it might be a document developed in-house over time.

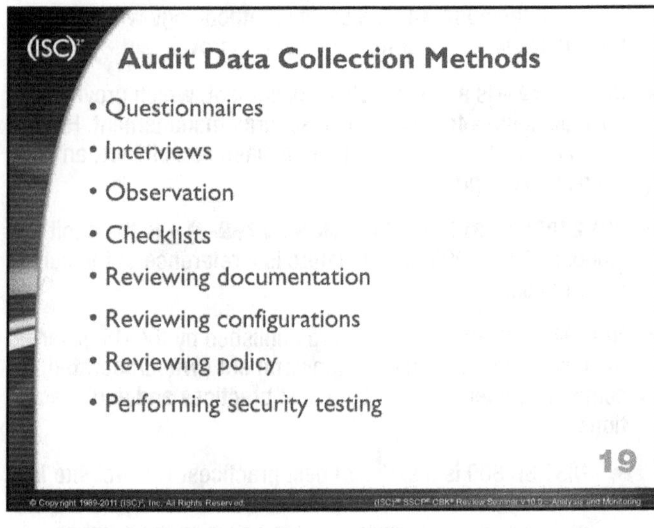


- **QUESTIONNAIRES –** Should be prepared and administered to both managers and users.
- **INTERVIEWS –** Are designed to gather insight from all parties into the operations and often prove to be a valuable source of information and recommendations.
- **OBSERVATION –** To differentiate between "paper procedures" and how the job "is really done."
- **CHECKLISTS –** Ensure that all areas are covered in the information gathering process.
- **REVIEWING DOCUMENTATION –** For currency, adherence, and completeness.
- **REVIEWING CONFIGURATIONS –** Including the change-control procedures and the appropriateness of controls, rules, and layout.
- **REVIEWING POLICY –** For senior management signature, relevance, and currency, as well as completeness.
- **PERFORMING SECURITY TESTING (VULNERABILITY ANALYSIS AND PENETRATION TESTING) –** Technical information gathering to determine whether there are vulnerabilities in the security components, networks, or applications.

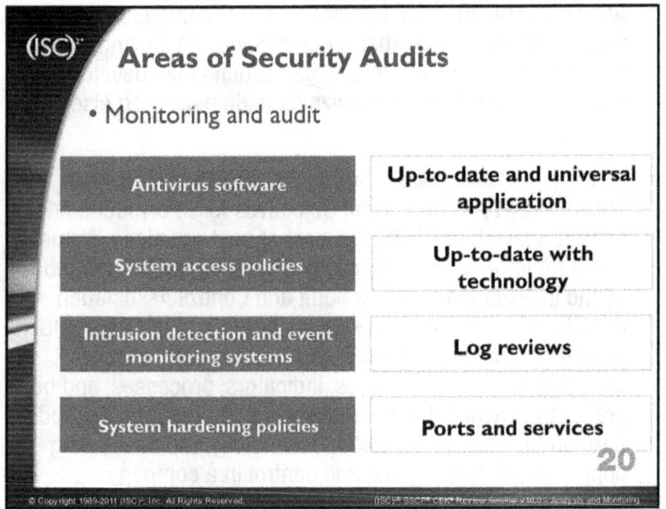

(ISC)²
Audit Data Collection Methods
Areas of Security Audits
• Monitoring and audit
Antivirus software
Up-to-date and universal application
System access policies
Up-to-date with technology
Intrusion detection and event monitoring systems
Log reviews
System hardening policies
Ports and services
20


- **AREAS OF SECURITY AUDITS –** This is a partial but critical list of areas that must be included in a security audit.
  - Auditors will check to see that there are policy statements in existence for key areas and will mention any shortfalls. After that, they check to see if policies, procedures, and standards are being followed.
- Many organizations have a "password policy." This is a misnomer. There should be a policy on access control that says something on the order of "Authorized users should be able to do only that which is authorized, and unauthorized users should be prohibited from doing anything." In support of that policy there will be a password standard (defining minimum characters and complexity, for those systems that use passwords) and a password procedure (how to set, change, and reset passwords). As companies change to tokens or smart cards or biometrics for authentication, passwords are falling into disuse. A password policy will become impossible to follow, and having policies that aren't followed is a recipe for security failures.

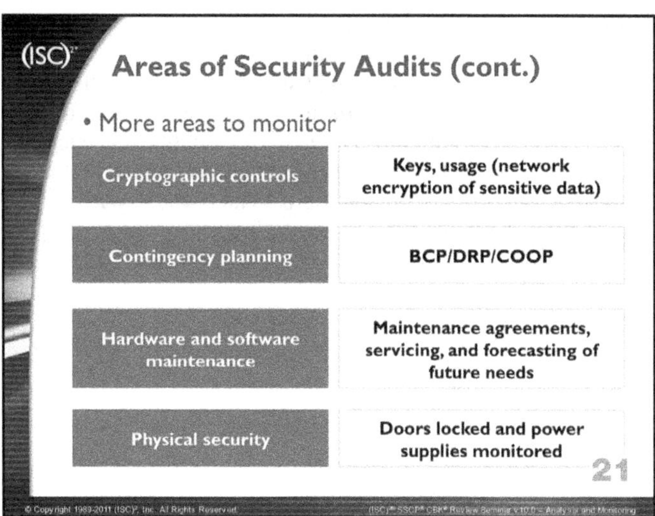


- **AREAS OF SECURITY AUDITS (CONT.) –** These are areas that need to be addressed in a security audit.

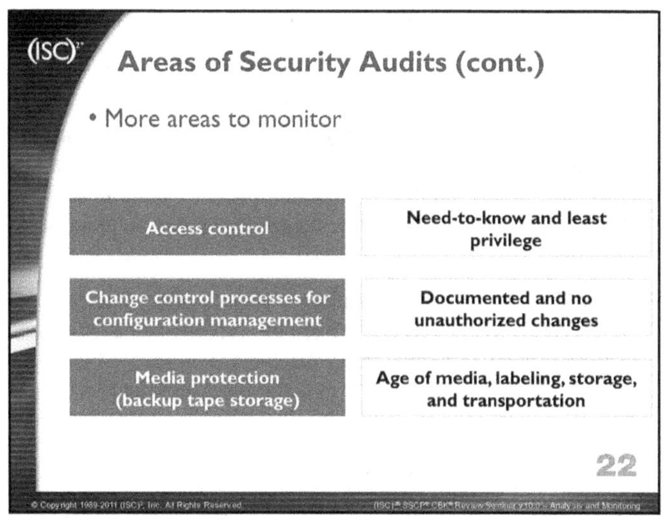


- **AREAS OF SECURITY AUDITS (CONT.) –** These are important areas that must be addressed in a security audit.

(ISC)²

**Control Checks – Identity Management**

- Effectiveness of identification and authorization systems
  - Approval process – who
  - ID format
  - Password policy and enforcement
  - Monitor for unauthorized access
  - Screensavers – password protected
  - Remote access systems
    - Needed
    - Multifactor

23





- **CONTROL CHECKS –** Identity Management – This next section deals with the important task of ensuring that our security controls are functioning reliably and as intended. Without monitoring and review, we have no assurance that our information security program is effective, or that due diligence is being exercised. When auditing an identity management system, the areas listed above are some of the key areas on which the audit will focus.

(ISC)²

**Post-Audit Activities**

- Exit interviews
- Analyze the data
- Produce audit findings
  - Findings according to policy/best practices
  - Recommendations:
    - Criticality and follow-up

24





- **EXIT INTERVIEWS –** After an audit is performed, an exit interview will alert personnel to glaring issues and recommendations that will be listed in the audit report. This allows management to respond to the recommendations and act on serious issues immediately. Aside from these preliminary alerts, auditors should not give detailed verbal assessments that may falsely set the expectation level of the organization with respect to their security preparedness in the area audited.
- **ANALYZE THE DATA –** An auditor will likely perform data analysis and synthesis away from the organizational site. This stage allows the auditor to review everything learned and present his/her observations in a standard reporting format.
- **PRODUCE AUDIT FINDINGS –** An auditor will produce audit findings for presentation to the organization.
  - **FINDINGS ACCORDING TO POLICY/BEST PRACTICES –** Are often listed by level of compliance to the standard benchmark. The comparison of audit findings to stated policy and/or industry "good" practices produces a picture of what must be improved.
  - **RECOMMENDATIONS –** Findings often include recommendations for mitigation or correction of documented risks as well as instances of non-compliance with policy or processes. Those issues which are deemed most critical should be addressed first.
    - **FOLLOW-UP –** A follow-up audit is scheduled to review the implementation of the recommendations of the audit.

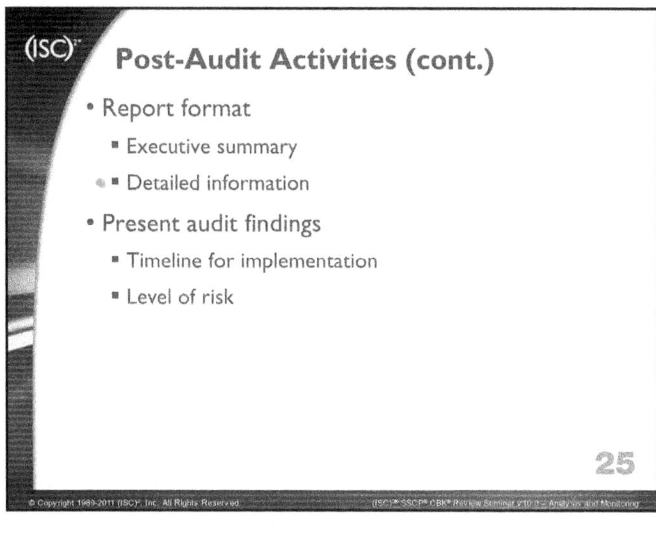

(ISC)²
Post-Audit Activities (cont.)
• Report format
▪ Executive summary
▪ Detailed information
• Present audit findings
▪ Timeline for implementation
▪ Level of risk
25


- **REPORT FORMAT –**
  - **EXECUTIVE SUMMARY –** An audit report often begins with an executive summary followed by detailed information.
  - **DETAILED INFORMATION –** For most organizations and government agencies, the executive summary is public information and must be carefully written so as not to detail possible security vulnerabilities.
- **PRESENT AUDIT FINDINGS –** Audit findings and the audit report are typically presented to management. The findings may lead to mitigation activities based on an available budget.
  - **TIMELINE FOR IMPLEMENTATION –** The manager responsible for the area being audited should provide a timeline for the implementation of the responses to the audit recommendations.
  - **LEVEL OF RISK –** The audit should indicate the level of risk to the organization related to each finding.

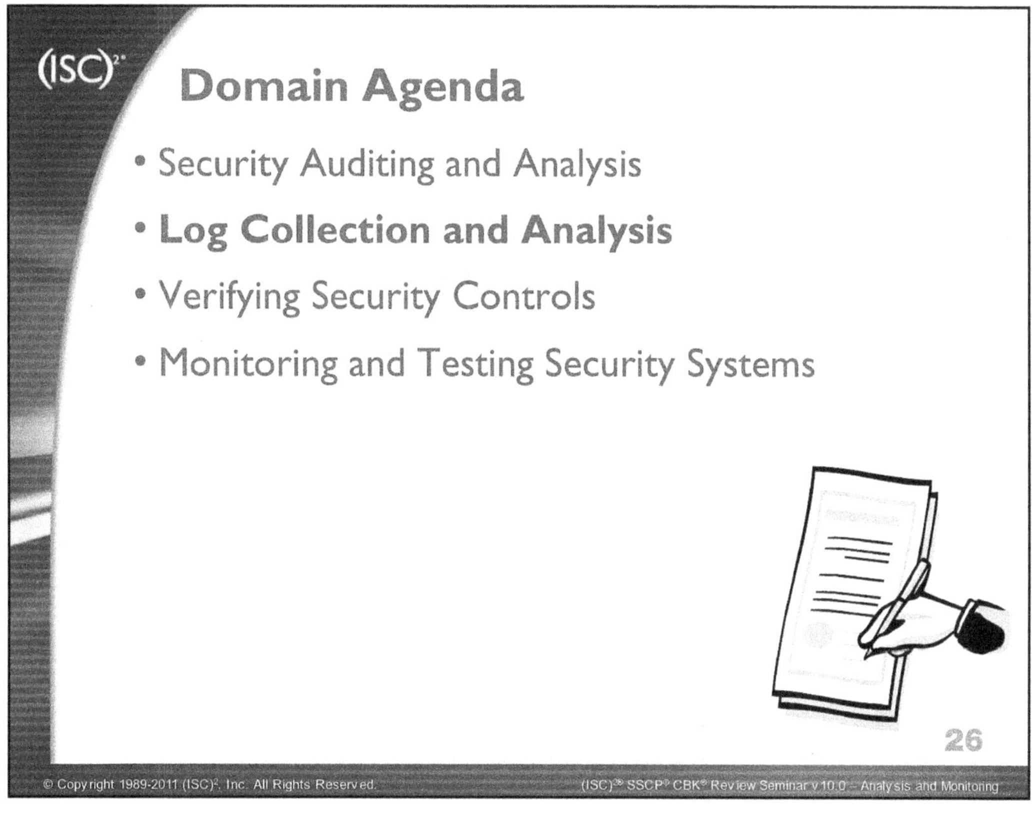

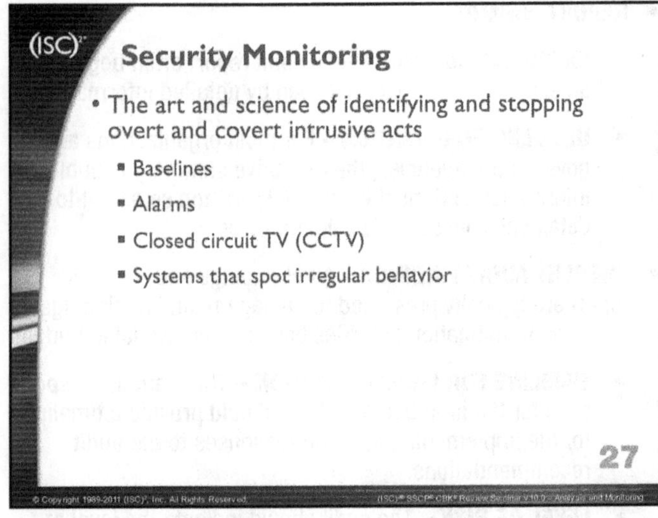


- **SECURITY MONITORING –** A security program must be tuned to detect abnormal behavior. These systems may be technical such as an IDS, or they may be administrative such as observing employee or customer behavior (monitoring closed circuit TV in a casino, for example).
- **THE ART AND SCIENCE OF IDENTIFYING AND STOPPING OVERT AND COVERT INTRUSIVE ACTS –** Improper actions may be overt (obvious and intentional) or covert (hidden and secret) depending on the attitude and intention of the perpetrator. Security must be obvious enough to discourage improper or unwanted actions and yet, in most cases, careful not to be overbearing. Some of the tools and techniques that we can use for security monitoring include:
  - **BASELINES –** In order to recognize something as abnormal, one first has to know what normal looks like. Seeing a report that disk space is at 80% used tells you nothing unless you know what it was yesterday and last week. A system that has been using an additional 1% of disk every week and just tipped the alarm is very different from one that was at 40% last week and each week for the preceding month, but just doubled in usage. Baselines are essential in security monitoring.
  - **ALARMS –** Will notify personnel of a possible security incident (door open alarm or fire alarm). One risk associated with alarms is the tendency of personnel to become desensitized to repeated alarms and not respond to a real incident when there have been several false alarms previously. (Think about what happens when your neighbor's car alarm goes off.)
  - **CLOSED CIRCUIT TV (CCTV) –** Requires monitoring and recording. Where security personnel are watching the behavior of people, they must be trained in the types of actions to watch for. Some jurisdictions prohibit profiling on particular factors (such as race); some have no such prohibitions. It is important to know the local laws.
  - **SYSTEMS THAT SPOT IRREGULAR BEHAVIOR –** Such as an IDS or honeypot (a trap set out to capture information about improper activity on a network).

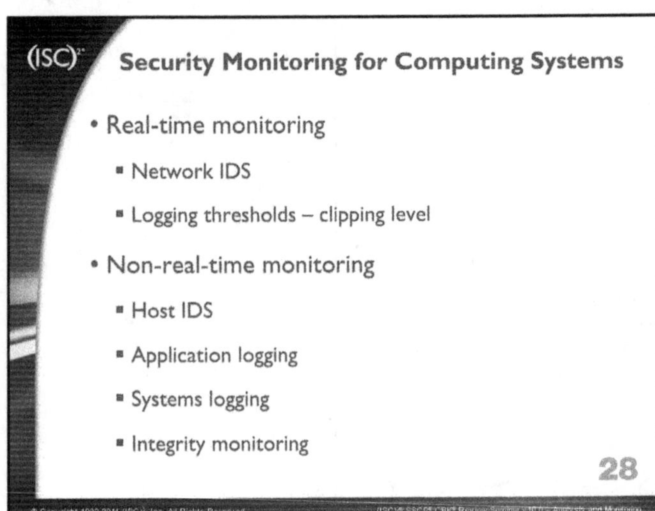

(ISC)²
Security Monitoring for Computing Systems
Real-time monitoring
Network IDS
Logging thresholds – clipping level
Non-real-time monitoring
Host IDS
Application logging
Systems logging
Integrity monitoring
28


- **REAL-TIME MONITORING –** To contain incidents and ensure the preservation of business operations, it is important to be able to detect and respond to incidents in real-time.
  - **NETWORK IDS –** A network IDS is a valuable tool for monitoring and capturing network traffic in real time.
- **NON-REAL-TIME MONITORING –**
  - **HOST IDS –** A host IDS is excellent for "noticing" changes in near-time to a host or system.
  - **APPLICATION LOGGING –** All applications that access or modify sensitive data should have logs that record who accessed or changed the data. This allows for proof of compliance with privacy regulations, investigation of errors or problems with records, and tracking of transactions. When coupled with a host IDS, it is often called an AIDS.
  - **SYSTEMS LOGGING –** Provides a record of who accessed the system and the activities on the system.
  - **INTEGRITY MONITORING –** Error reports should be handled carefully and edit checks performed on all incoming data and job completions to ensure that errors are not introduced into the system – or that processing is not generating unexpected results.

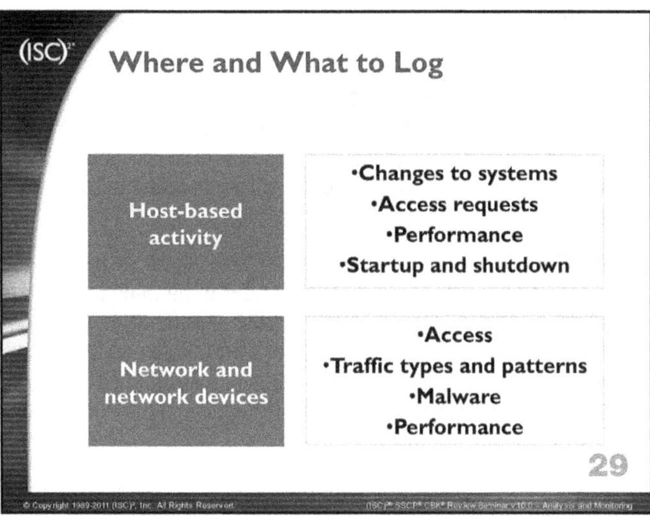


- **WHERE AND WHAT TO LOG –** This is a short list of some activities that should be logged.

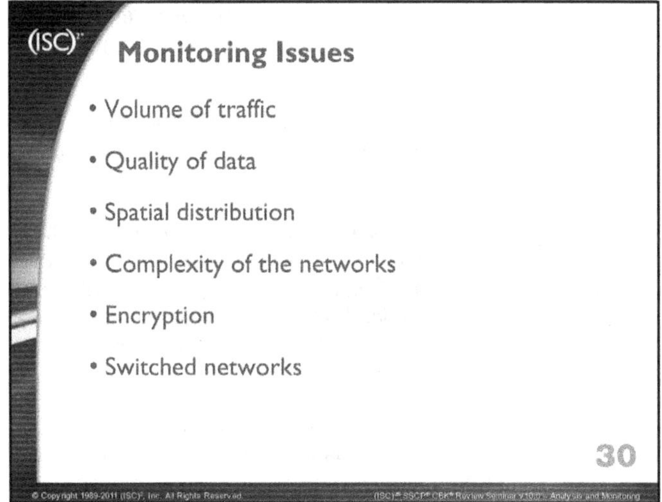


- **VOLUME OF TRAFFIC –** Many organizations tend to turn off logs due to the sheer volume of information they may be capturing. If there isn't enough staff to review the logs, there's little point in continuing to gather unused information.
- **QUALITY OF DATA –** When this staffing problem is added to other challenges such as poor-quality log data, the complexity of attacks, and the other issues listed, it is challenging to see the value in allocating personnel to performing extensive log analysis.
- **SPATIAL DISTRIBUTION –** The use of distributed networks and the attack approach of spreading the attack over geographically disbursed systems that may be managed by different administrators makes the monitoring of a widespread attack difficult.
- **ENCRYPTION –** Data can be encrypted at various levels:
  - Link layer encryption (wireless WEP and WPA) encrypts everything above the link layer.
  - Network layer encryption (IPSEC and some other tunneling protocols) encrypts everything above the network layer.
  - Application layer encryption (SSL and SSH and others) encrypts above the transport layer.
  - The non-encrypted parts can be logged, but the rest is virtually invisible. (Note: The Networks and Communications domain covers many of the details referenced in the above bullets.)
  - All organizations should be monitoring to see whether sensitive data is being transmitted through the network unencrypted.
- **SWITCHED NETWORKS –** It can be harder to capture traffic on networks that are very segmented through the use of switches and virtual LANs.

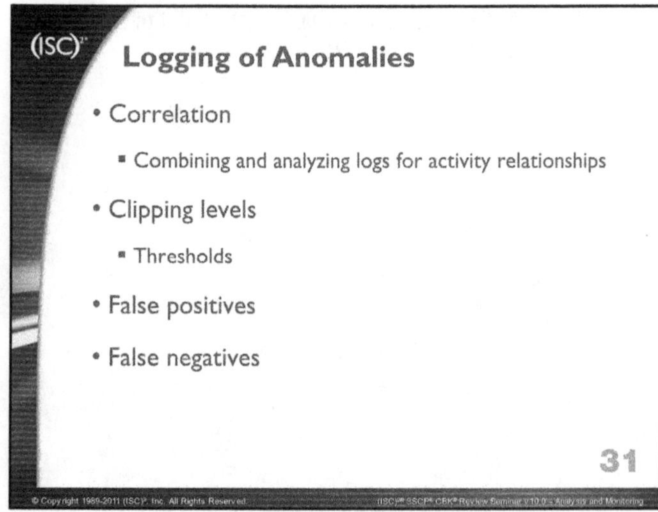


- **LOGGING OF ANOMALIES –** One of an administrator's important tasks is to differentiate between real attacks or log entries, and attacks and entries that are merely noise or minor events.

- **CORRELATION –** Is the art of gathering and discovering related activity that may indicate a larger attack.
- **CLIPPING LEVELS –** The administrator may decide not to record infrequent or human-error "attacks." This is done by establishing clipping levels that will ignore an event unless it happens with a certain frequency or meets some other predefined criteria.
- **FALSE POSITIVES –** (Also known as false reject, or type I errors.) These are the alerts that appear to be malicious and yet are not a real security event – false alarms that cause distraction and waste administrator effort. False positives can desensitize the administrator to attacks resembling those giving false positives and ultimately into ignoring an alarm that may actually be serious.
- **FALSE NEGATIVES –** (Also known as false accept or type II errors.) False negatives are the failure of the alarm system to detect a serious event. The alarm may not have noticed an event, or it may have been fooled into thinking an event was not serious when in fact it was.

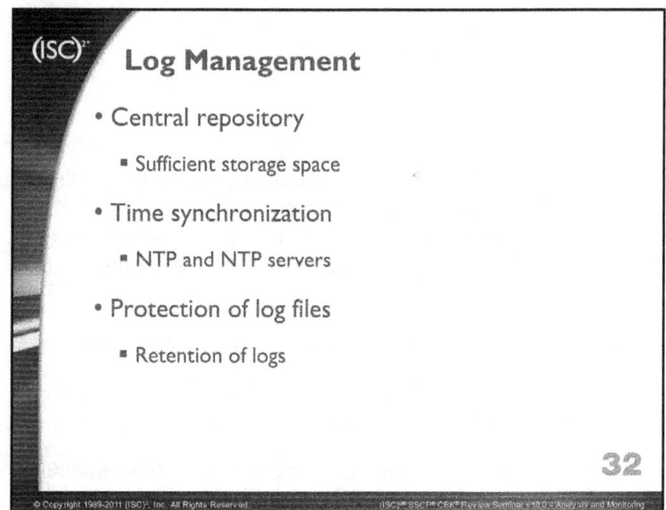


- **LOG MANAGEMENT –** The security and systems administrator must take several things into consideration with respect to the retention and protection of logs.
- **CENTRAL REPOSITORY –** It might be best to keep logs in a central location for the purposes of protection and more thorough analysis.
    - **SUFFICIENT STORAGE SPACE –** When log files fill, administrators are faced with three bad choices:
        - Stop logging.
        - Overwrite the oldest entries.
        - Stop processing (controlled or crash).
    - Attackers sometimes purposely fill a log in order to cause one of these failures. The log file must be large enough to prevent this.

- **TIME SYNCHRONIZATION –** In order to associate traffic between various systems and logs, the systems must maintain synchronized clocks.
    - **NTP AND NTP SERVERS –** Network Time Protocol (NTP) will sync time for all devices that support it. (Most modern routers and servers do this.) International government-run NTP servers provide an unbiased third party to supply the time.
    - A list of NTP servers can be found in MS Knowledge-base article number 262680, found here: http://support.microsoft.com/kb/262680.
- **PROTECTION OF LOG FILES –** To prevent overwriting or modification, some systems will write logs to a CD WORM or other read-only device. Logs often contain confidential information about users, or information that may be needed for investigations. Log files must therefore be protected from unauthorized access, deletion, or modification.
    - **RETENTION OF LOGS –** Is the decision of how long to keep logs. This may be mandated by regulation, policy, or log volume.
    - If a log file is subject to litigation, it must be retained until the case is completed.
    - If litigation is not already under way, a company is allowed to make its own decisions about log quantity and retention. (There may be exceptions based on laws or regulations.) Once litigation begins, providing the data in those logs is a costly process that the company must bear. Litigation costs can be reduced by reducing the quantity collected to only that which is needed and keeping it only for as long as it is likely to be useful.

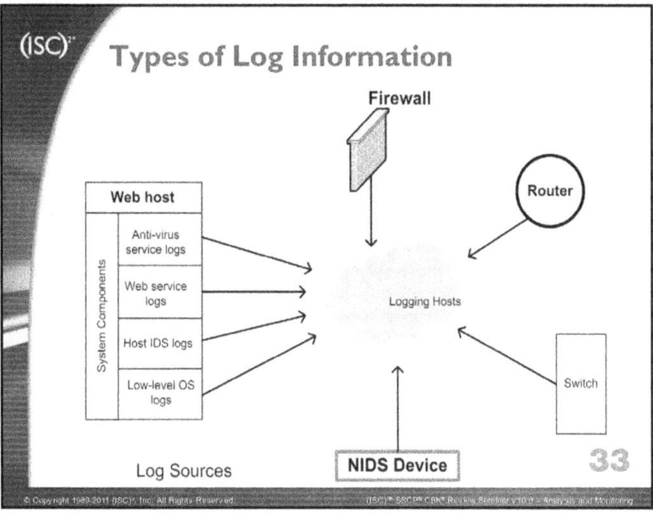


- **TYPES OF LOG INFORMATION –** There are a large number of logs that may be needed to provide a record of the activity on systems, networks, and applications. All suspicious activity, errors, unauthorized access attempts, and access to sensitive information should be recorded. This will enable the tracking of incidents, and the accountability of users. The security incident and event manager (SIEM) compiles and analyzes the data from the various logs and is a valuable tool for log analysis.

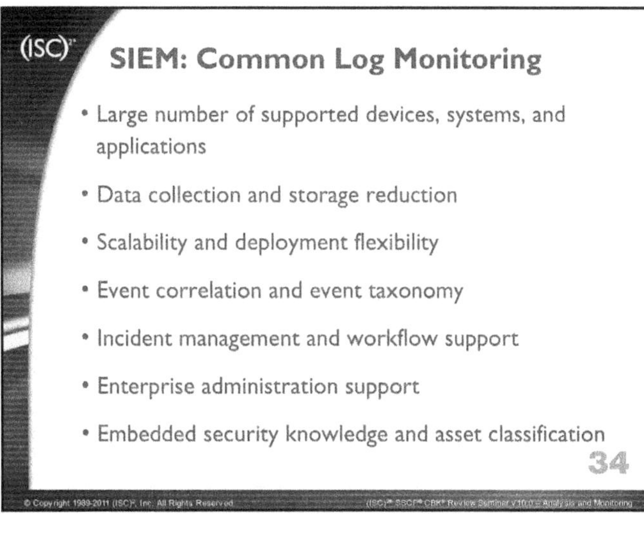


- **SIEM: COMMON LOG MONITORING –** The number of different logs being created on systems has led to the development of a common platform for capturing and analyzing the log entries. These are called security information and event management systems or SIEM. SIEM system's benefits are described on the slide.
- **LARGE NUMBER OF SUPPORTED DEVICES, SYSTEMS, AND APPLICATIONS**
- **DATA COLLECTION AND STORAGE REDUCTION –** SIEMs have the ability to "roll-up" log information, and provide detailed reports for recent activity as well as summary reports for historical events and incidents. This helps save storage space.
- **SCALABILITY AND DEPLOYMENT FLEXIBILITY –** Able to support both small and large deployments.
- **EVENT CORRELATION AND EVENT TAXONOMY –** Analysis of isolated events to determine the root cause of a security incident.
- **INCIDENT MANAGEMENT AND WORKFLOW SUPPORT –** Can support trouble ticket creation, and resolution process.
- **ENTERPRISE ADMINISTRATION SUPPORT –** Can support user provisioning and rights management.
- **EMBEDDED SECURITY KNOWLEDGE AND ASSET CLASSIFICATION –** Systems are able to automatically assign security controls to certain data assets.
- Organizations collect log data from a variety of sources such as firewalls, IDSs/IPSs, Web/SQL servers, and specialized devices such as LDAP and Kerberos servers. In addition, many organizations have multiple brands or versions of these logging devices.
- SIEM collection and analysis devices take the log data in whatever format it is created, from whatever device creates it, and normalizes (standardizes) it into a database. It can then run SIEM-vendor supplied reports or custom reports against those databases.
- As companies change products (upgrade a firewall, perhaps using a different vendor, for example), the new log files can be merged into the same database without limiting the ability to produce reports that cover the before-and-after time period.

(ISC)²

## SIEM: Capabilities

- Data repository (cost-effective, long-term storage)
- Analysis of historical data
- Reporting customizable to fit organizations
- Collection and correlation in near real-time
- Multiple collection protocols
- Security optimized console environment

35

 (ISC)² SSCP® CBK® Review Seminar v10.0 – Analysis and Monitoring

- **SIEM: CAPABILITIES –** SIEM systems provide both storage of log data and tools with which to analyze them.

(ISC)²

## SIEM: Regulatory Compliance

- Support to monitor user activity from systems, applications, and object access log
- Integration with identity management
- Ability to express and track compliance with user-specific policies

36

 (ISC)² SSCP® CBK® Review Seminar v10.0 – Analysis and Monitoring

- **SIEM: REGULATORY COMPLIANCE –** Because SIEM systems can monitor user activity and make certain that users are acting in accordance with policy, they are a valuable method for ensuring regulatory compliance. They can also integrate with identity management schemes to ensure that only current user accounts are active on the system.
- Many organizations face demands from laws and regulations (e.g., FISMA, GLBA, HIPAA, ISO/IEC 27002:2005, JSOX, NERC, NIST 800-53, PCI DSS, and Sarbanes-Oxley (SOX)). Not all of them ask for the same thing, or ask for it in the same way. Modern SIEM products can add modules that provide reports to meet the mandates of various govenment or trade organizations.
- Many organizations acquire identity and access control software (IAM) to manage user account policy compliance. However, the wide variety of platforms (e.g., PC, MAC, Linux, Unix, Mainframe, etc.) coupled with a wide variety of versions of each make this process virtually impossible for individual administrators. SIEM identity management products do the same for IAM software as the basic SIEM products do for log file consolidation.

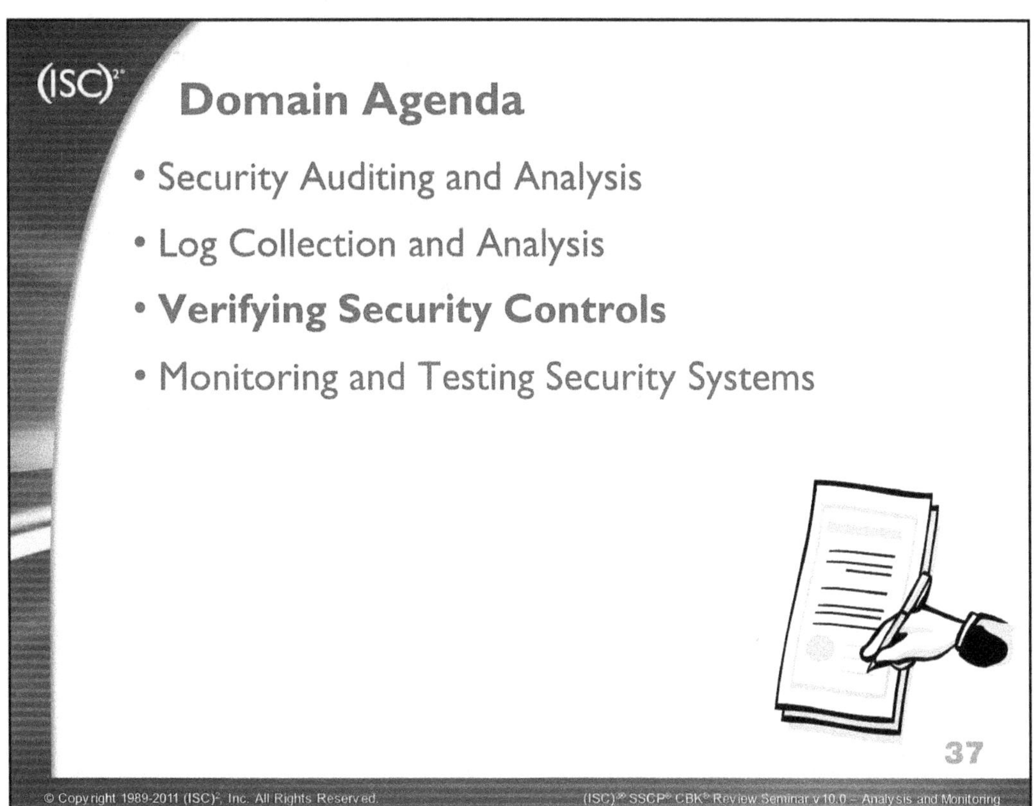


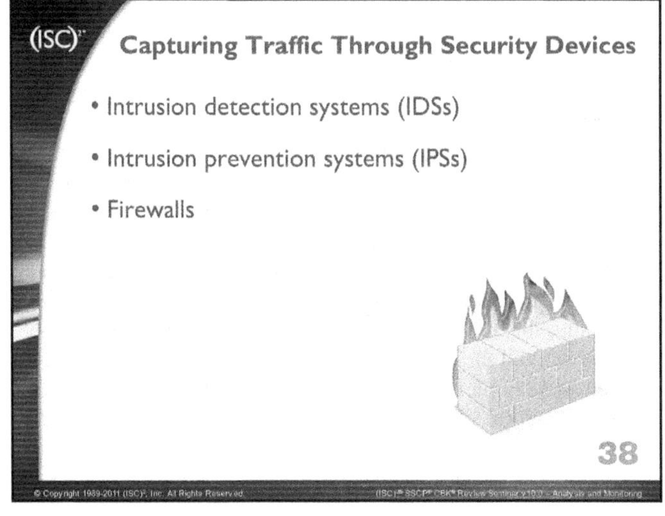

(ISC)²
Capturing Traffic Through Security Devices
• Intrusion detection systems (IDSs)
• Intrusion prevention systems (IPSs)
• Firewalls
38


- **CAPTURING TRAFFIC THROUGH SECURITY DEVICES –** Each of these technologies will be looked at in more detail in the next few slides.

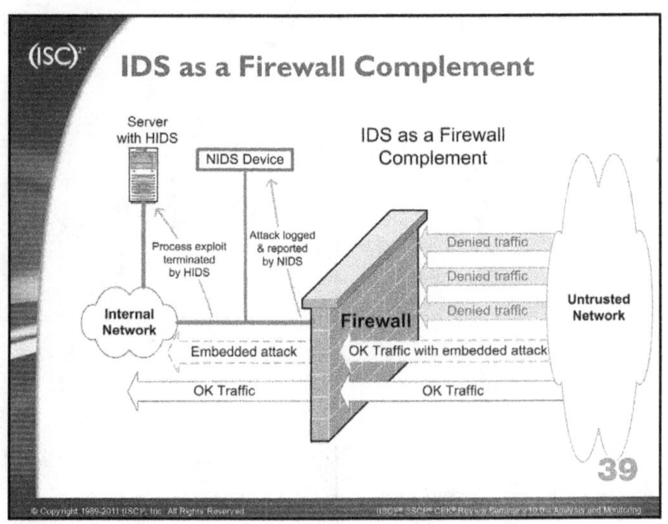


- **IDS AS A FIREWALL COMPLEMENT –** Layered defense necessitates the use of multiple controls to prevent an attack. One of the most common layered defense mechanisms is to place an IDS behind a firewall in order to provide increased security. The network–based intrusion detection system (NIDS) will detect traffic that gets through the firewall (sometimes intentionally, such as Web traffic aimed at a public Web server; and sometimes unintentionally in that the attacker's packets may have fooled the firewall and successfully entered the network). It will capture and report the incident, while the host-based intrusion detection system (HIDS) will do the same for traffic aimed at a particular device. Because the HIDS will see a narrower view, it can be more carefully tuned. Unlike the NIDS, it will also see traffic that originates inside the perimeter.

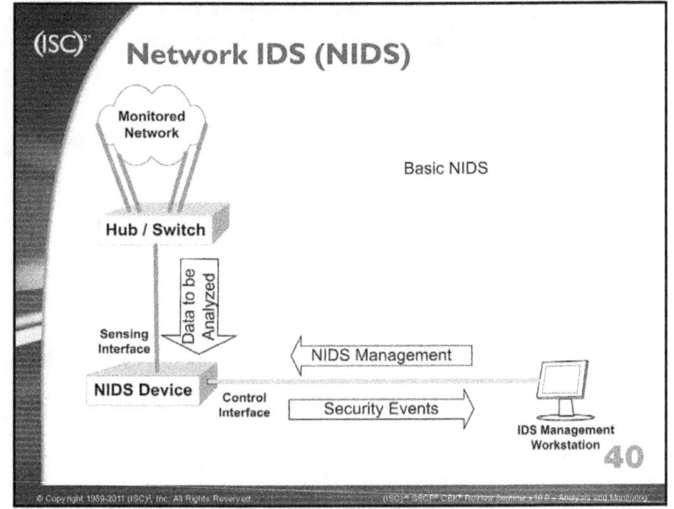


- Network IDS (NIDS) - A Network IDS can be connected to a switch or hub as shown above. The IDS will then capture all traffic on the switch and analyze it to detect unauthorized activity. There are several ways that the analysis can be done, depending on the type of engine in the IDS. The IDS is connected to a management console that allows the administrator to monitor and manage it. Ideally, the IDS will not be detectable from the network and hackers will, therefore, not be able to determine where the IDS is positioned on the network. The administration port on the IDS is not accessible from the network, which prevents a hacker from altering the configuration of the IDS. (It is quite common to configure the NIDS without an IP address on its monitoring port. That makes it impossible for the outsider to send packets to or otherwise directly address the NIDS. Administrators access the device via another interface, which should be on a different subnet.)

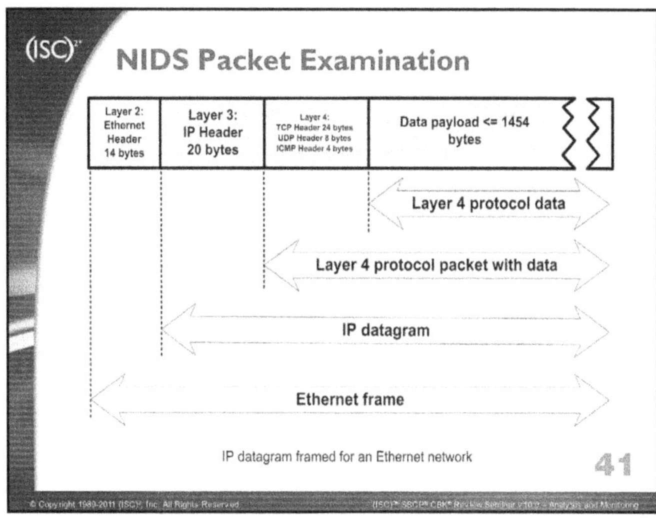


- **NIDS PACKET EXAMINATION –** A packet traveling through the network will have a series of headers and the data payload itself. The type of IDS or firewall being used will determine how intensely the packet will be examined. Some devices will only examine the Layer 3 header information, while others will look more closely at the Layer 4 header or even at the data itself.

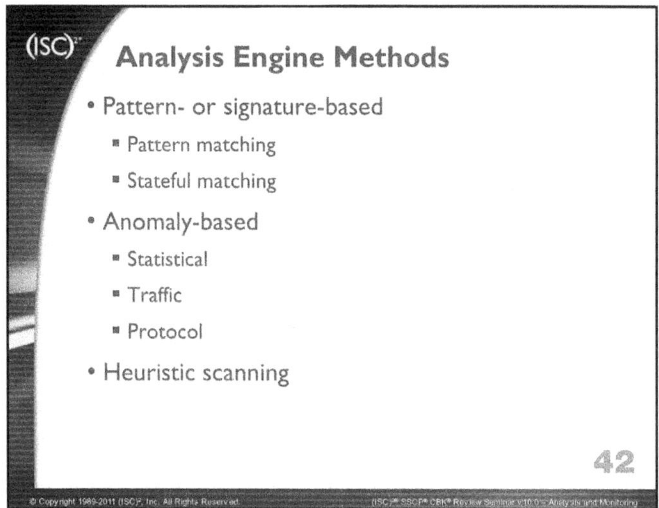


- **ANALYSIS ENGINE METHODS –** While each of these analysis engine methods is described separately, it is important to understand that vendor devices perform a combination of some or all of these techniques, to provide a more complete scanning environment.
- **PATTERN- OR SIGNATURE-BASED –** The IDS compares current traffic with known activity patterns (signatures) that are consistent with that of a previously discovered attack. Note, however, that known attacks are often modified in an attempt to escape detection.
  - **PATTERN MATCHING –** Pattern matching systems scan packets to determine whether specific byte sequences, known as "signatures," match the signature of known attacks. Often, the patterns are related to a certain service and port (e.g., source or destination). Frequent updates of the signature files to identify new attacks are required to maintain accuracy. Since these systems will report close matches, false positives may occur, particularly if the pattern lacks granularity (i.e., is not unique).
  - **STATEFUL MATCHING –** Improves on simple pattern matching by looking for specific sequences appearing across several packets in a traffic stream rather than just in individual packets. Although more granular than pattern matching, it can still result in false positives. As with pattern matching, it can only detect known attacks and requires frequent signature updates.
- **ANOMALY-BASED –** Sometimes called profile-based systems, these compare current activity with stored profiles of normal (expected) activity. These are only as accurate as the determination of what is normal.
  - **STATISTICAL –** Develop baselines of normal traffic and throughput activity. Deviations from these norms result in alerts. These can catch unknown attacks. Because of the challenge of precisely identifying normal activity, false positives often occur.
  - **TRAFFIC –** Identifies any unacceptable deviation from expected behavior based on traffic and signals an alert. Can also detect unknown attacks and floods.
  - **PROTOCOL –** Protocol standards are provided by requests for comment (RFCs). Deviations from protocols can identify attacks without a signature. This works for well-defined protocols, but results in false positives for those that are not well defined.
- **HEURISTIC SCANNING –** Heuristic scanning methods vary depending on the specific vendor technology utilized. Some allow emulation of the file's activities in a virtual sandbox, while others scan the file more intensively, searching line by line for any offending sequences of code. Heuristics are designed to detect previously unknown virus threats – viruses that are newly released into the wild for which antivirus vendors have no specific definition files with which to address the threat. Unfortunately, heuristics are not tremendously successful in catching newly released threats. This is a result of consumer demand for unobtrusive scanners. To minimize the risks of false positives, some vendors cut back on the level of heuristics employed, or give users configurable options to lessen or increase heuristics as desired. As a result, traditional antivirus scanners, even those with heuristics, are more adept at detecting and disinfecting known viruses only.

**REFERENCE:**

Information Security Management Handbook, 5th edition, Tipton & Krause, Auerbach, 2004, page 1601.

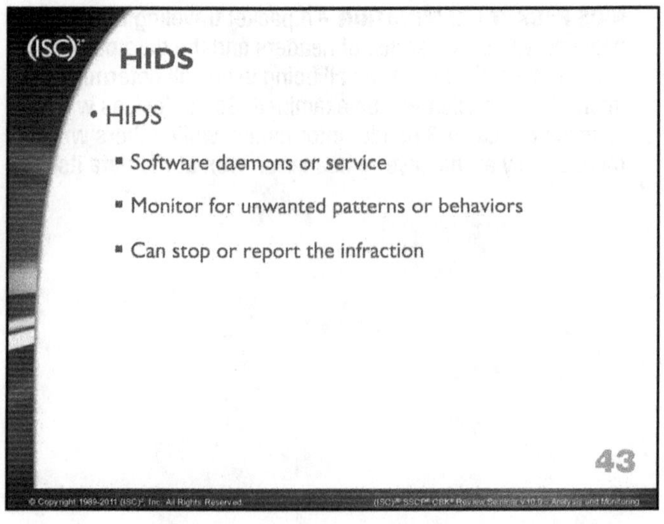


- **HIDS –** Host-based intrusion detection (HIDS) technology adds to your entire system's protection by keeping watch on sensitive processes inside of a host. HIDS generally have the following qualities:
  - **SOFTWARE DAEMONS OR SERVICE –** HIDS systems are usually software daemons or services that are designed to run on hosts.
  - **MONITOR FOR UNWANTED PATTERNS OR BEHAVIORS –** They intercept and examine system calls or specific processes (database and Web servers, for example) for patterns or behaviors that should not normally be allowed.
  - **CAN STOP OR REPORT THE INFRACTION –** HIDS daemons can take a predefined action such as stopping or reporting the infraction.
- HIDS also have a different point of view than the NIDS. They can, therefore:
  - Detect inappropriate traffic that originates inside the network.
  - Recognize an anomaly that is specific to a particular machine or user. For example, a single user on a high volume mail server might be originating 10 times the normal number of messages for a user in any day (or hour). The HIDS can notice and alert on this, but a NIDS would not notice a reportable event.

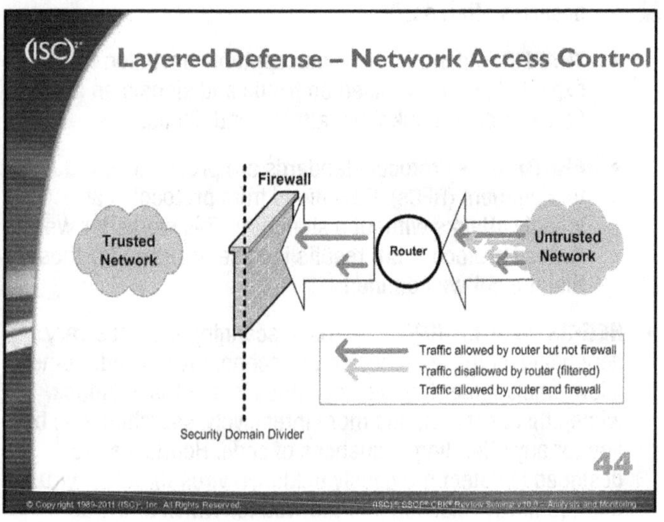


- **LAYERED DEFENSE –** Network Access Control – This concept diagram shows how network devices try to prevent an attack on the internal protected network. The router will detect and filter out some traffic and the firewall will disallow traffic that it is designed to detect and prevent.

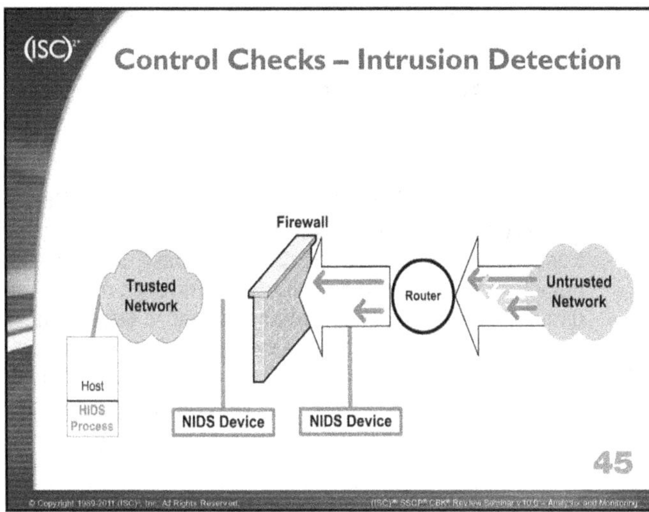


- **CONTROL CHECKS –** Intrusion Detection – As shown in this diagram, network-based intrusion detection systems (NIDSs) can be used to monitor outside attacks as well as insider misuse of networks. The NIDS outside of the network will provide some idea of the types of attacks faced by the firewall. The internal NIDS will detect the types of attacks that may be penetrating the firewall. This device may also be installed as an IPS. The host-based IDS (HIDS) will see the types of activity being attempted on the host itself.

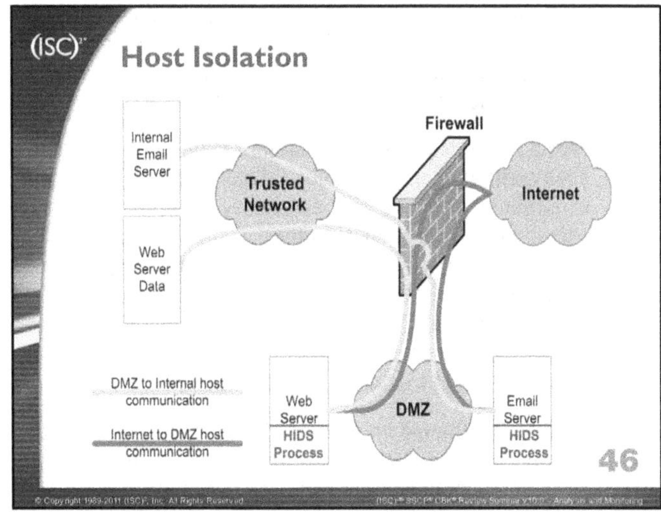


- **HOST ISOLATION –** Is the isolation of internal networks and the establishment of a demilitarized zone (DMZ). Outside traffic from the untrusted Internet will only be allowed into the DMZ where it can access certain company services. The Web applications in the DMZ will then access the trusted internal network – but prevent the outside user from obtaining direct access to the internal network.

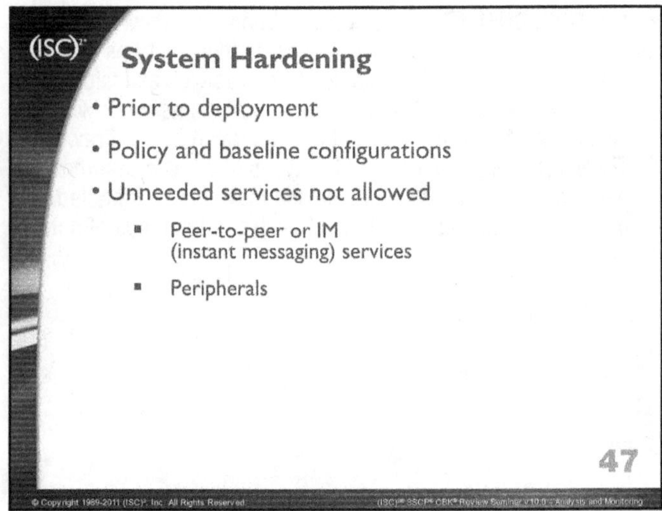

System Hardening
• Prior to deployment
• Policy and baseline configurations
• Unneeded services not allowed
Peer-to-peer or IM (instant messaging) services
Peripherals
47

- **SYSTEM HARDENING –** A "hardened configuration" is a system that has turned off or disabled unnecessary services. The security patch levels for the system should be up to date and the processes secured from unauthorized modification.
- **PRIOR TO DEPLOYMENT –** All systems should be hardened prior to being implemented. Failure to harden the system before it is put into production will almost certainly result in compromise of the system.
- **POLICY AND BASELINE CONFIGURATIONS –** The baseline configuration for systems should be determined in order to ensure that security is consistent between the various systems.
- **UNNEEDED SERVICES NOT ALLOWED –** A decision should be made as to whether certain services or applications should be allowed on the system such as:
    - **PEER-TO-PEER OR IM (INSTANT MESSAGING) SERVICES –** Consider disallowing or put policy in place to protect from misuse. IM can provide useful business convenience, but at the risk of confidentiality. IM traffic does not go directly from one party to another. Instead, it goes from sender to server to recipient. External IM servers such as those maintained by Microsoft, AOL, and others are able to see all messages, including files, sent between stations.
        - Good policy will limit or prohibit IM attachments.
        - Similarly, IM-based video can disclose unintended information and, at a minimum, use excessive bandwidth. Good policy controls these issues.
    - **PERIPHERALS –** Consider deactivation of CD ROMs or USB ports.
        - At minimum, disable Autorun, which launches programs as soon as a CD or USB drive is detected.
        - Software that limits USB to human interface devices such as mice, keyboards, or presentation pointers can be used to protect against unauthorized copying and transporting of data.

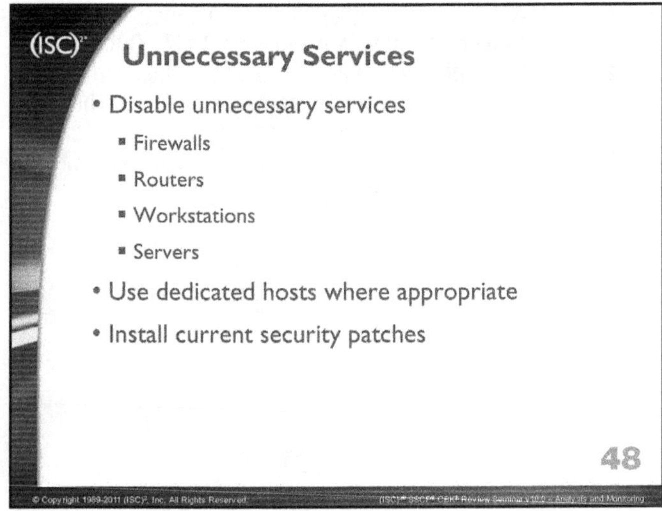

Unnecessary Services
• Disable unnecessary services
Firewalls
Routers
Workstations
Servers
• Use dedicated hosts where appropriate
• Install current security patches
48

- **DISABLE UNNECESSARY SERVICES –**
    - **FIREWALLS –** Unneeded ports should be closed and certain services (such as mobile code, Telnet, UDP) may be restricted. Firewalls should be configured to deny that which is not specifically allowed. By doing so, many new and unexpected services cannot be surreptitiously introduced.
    - **ROUTERS –** Should be hardened, including protection from unauthorized administrator access and changes to router tables. Routers come with no passwords configured. These should be added and like all passwords, should be complex and changed regularly. Changes to router configurations must be logged (with the UserID of the administrator making the changes) and the logs must be examined on a regular basis, perhaps by a security incident and event manager (SIEM) implementation.
    - **WORKSTATIONS –** Need a standard configuration and access controls. Companies should have a basic image that is hardened (removal of unnecessary services, addition of security products such as antivirus and personal firewalls). The image should also contain company standard software such as the word processor, spreadsheet, and browser plugins. That image should then be restored to all new desktops and laptops in order to ensure security compliance and to reduce maintenance time.
    - **SERVERS –** Should be physically protected (e.g., behind locked doors) as well as have all patches up to date. Third party patch management software can be used to track patches issued by all vendors of all products installed on a company's servers. Some products have automatic "phone-home" patch management, but many do not. This covers that gap.
- **USE DEDICATED HOSTS WHERE APPROPRIATE –** In many cases, the best solution is to ensure that a server that hosts vulnerable services, such as the Web server, is not used for any other purpose.
- **INSTALL CURRENT SECURITY PATCHES –** It's imperative that vendor supplied security updates and patches be first tested and installed with regularity. Additional controls should be considered to protect vulnerable systems during the update window (the period from patch announcement to deployment).

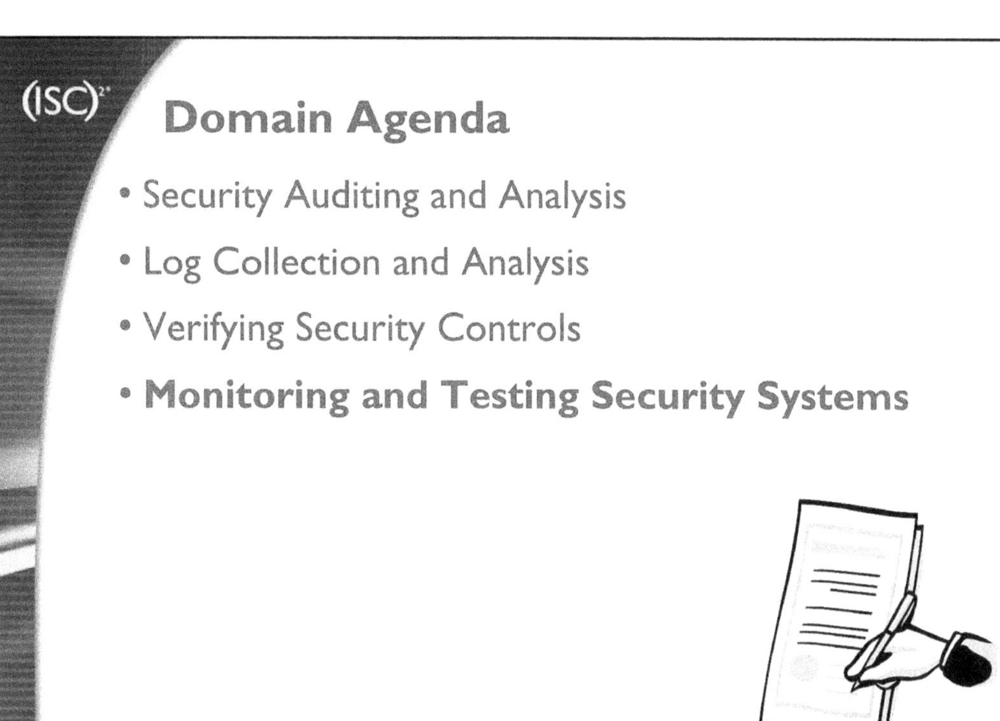

(ISC)²
Domain Agenda
• Security Auditing and Analysis
• Log Collection and Analysis
• Verifying Security Controls
• Monitoring and Testing Security Systems
49
© Copyright 1989-2011 (ISC)², Inc. All Rights Reserved.
(ISC)²® SSCP® CBK® Review Seminar v 10.0 – Analysis and Monitoring

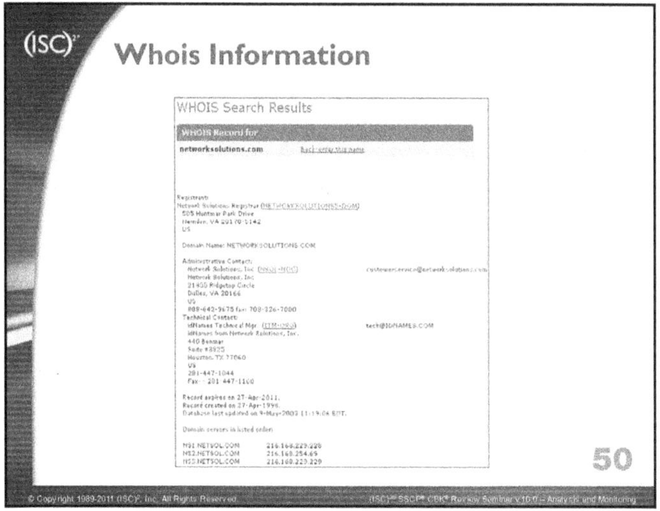

(ISC)²
Whois Information
WHOIS Search Results
50

- **WHOIS INFORMATION –** Can sometimes provide information about an organization such as administrator names and phone numbers. It is also important for an organization to ensure that its domain name registration does not lapse and lead to the loss of the domain name.

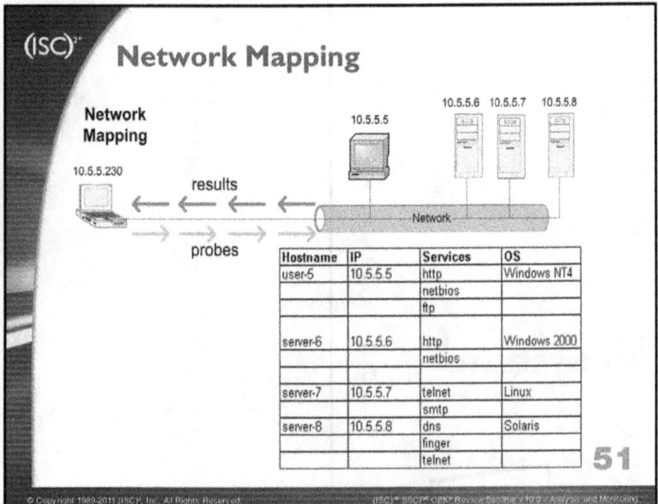


| Hostname | IP | Services | OS |
|---|---|---|---|
| user-5 | 10.5.5.5 | http | Windows NT4 |
| | | netbios | |
| | | ftp | |
| | | | |
| server-6 | 10.5.5.6 | http | Windows 2000 |
| | | netbios | |
| | | | |
| server-7 | 10.5.5.7 | telnet | Linux |
| | | smtp | |
| server-8 | 10.5.5.8 | dns | Solaris |
| | | finger | |
| | | telnet | |

- **NETWORK MAPPING –** Network mapping is the discovery of the details about a network, including the hosts and the host addresses on the network, as well as the various services available on the network.

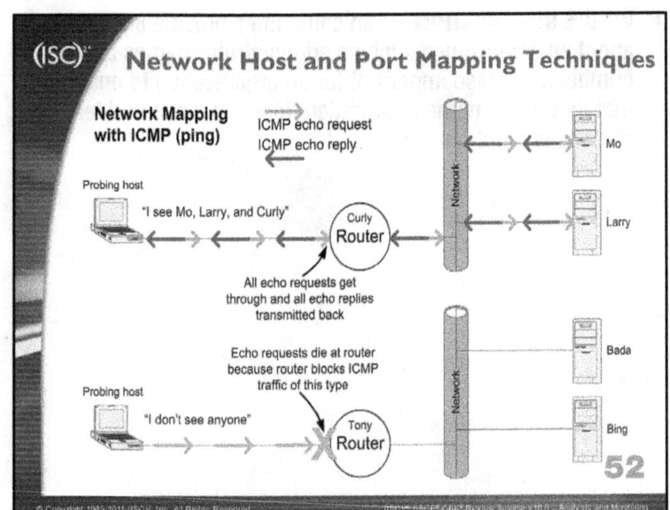


- **NETWORK HOST AND PORT MAPPING TECHNIQUES –** The use of Internet control message protocol (ICMP) "ping" packets to discover a network layout can give an attacker a real advantage in setting up an attack. The blocking of ping packets as seen with the "Tony" router can prevent the attacker from learning about the network, although it also prevents the administrator from being able to use this valuable tool for network troubleshooting.

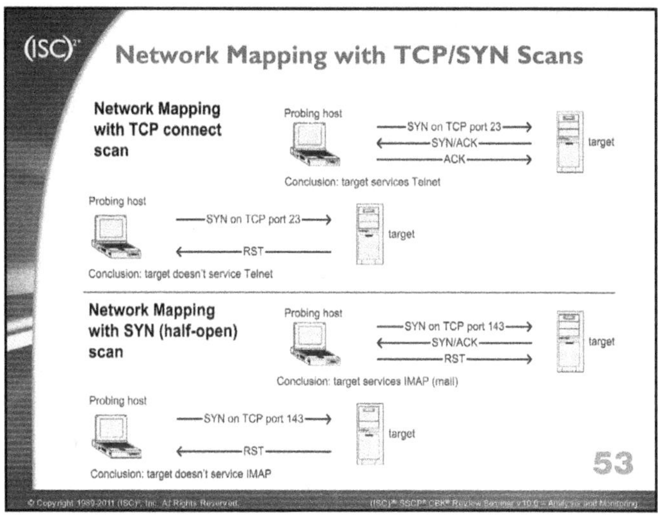


- **NETWORK MAPPING WITH TCP/SYN SCANS –** This diagram shows how an attacker can discover the services that are available on a target host. The attacker sends packets to common ports and can determine from the response whether the host is accepting these services.

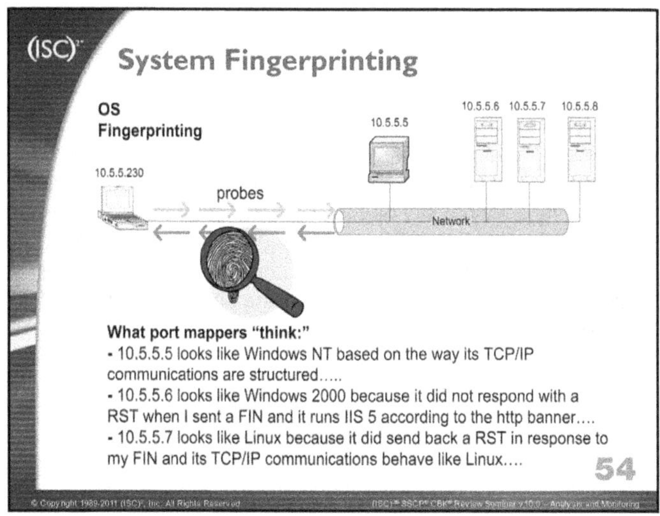


- **SYSTEM FINGERPRINTING –** An attacker can learn what operating systems are installed on a host through port mapping. This can assist an attacker in discovering hosts that may be vulnerable through a lack of patches or through known exploits.

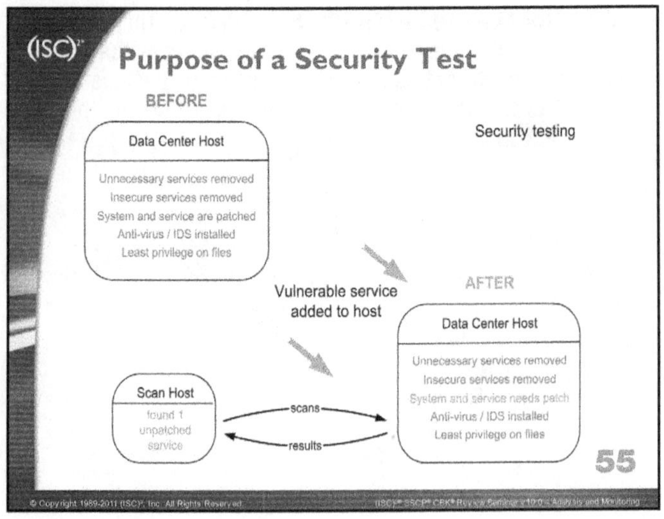


- **PURPOSE OF A SECURITY TEST –** Is to find new or undiscovered vulnerabilities on a system. Although a system may have been secured previously, a new service or application added to the system may have made the system vulnerable. The scan is intended to discover the new vulnerability so that it can be mitigated.

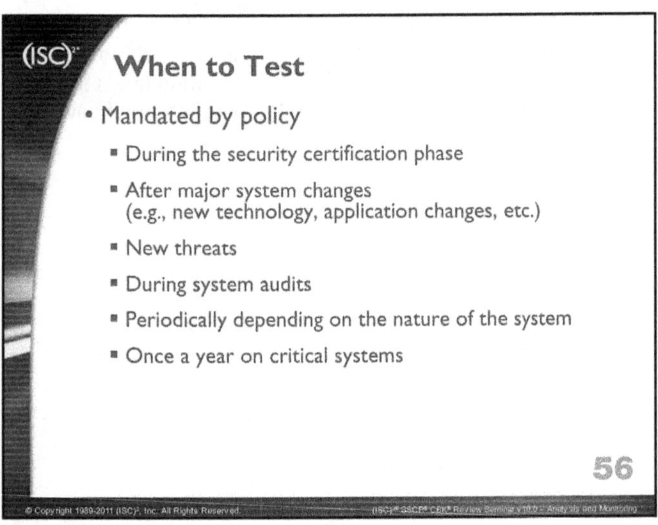


- **WHEN TO TEST –** How often to test often depends on several factors such as the volatility (rate of changes) of the system and the sensitivity or criticality of the system.
- **MANDATED BY POLICY –** Often the tests are mandated by policy or regulation. A few of the most common test-schedule trigger points are shown here. The bottom bullet "once a year" is merely a way to say that if one of the other items on the list doesn't trigger a test, then a maximum time limit should be in place as a safety trigger. Some companies might choose shorter or longer durations, depending on the results of a risk analysis for that system.

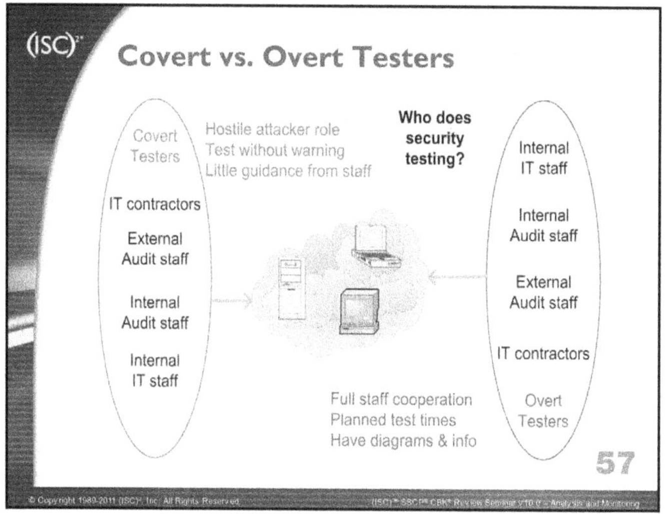


- **COVERT VS. OVERT TESTERS** – The tests may be done by internal (overt) or external (covert) staff. This may be mandated by regulation or may be a decision based on the skill level of internal staff.
  - White box testing: Done by internal staff. Cheaper but more likely to miss problems. (The in-house staff will have protected against all of the threats they know about and will then test against those same threats. The unknown threats will go uncorrected and untested.)
  - Black box testing: Done by outside experts. Much more expensive, but also much more thorough. They simulate an attack done by an unknown hacker who only knows the name or IP address of the company he or she wishes to attack.
  - Grey box testing: A compromise between the two. Often done by large organizations where the staff from one division will take on the outside-consultant role against another division.
  - No matter who does the testing, certain things must be coordinated in advance:
    - Potential for harm. Some tests might crash a system, while others are usually safe. Agreements must be made as to which tests are allowed. Plans must be made to recover if the tests, even the safe tests, crash a system.
    - Time of day/day of week. While testing in the low volume times is tempting because it won't affect as many users, it might not be realistic enough to trust. An alternative is to do more dangerous tests during off times, but others during high-volume hours.

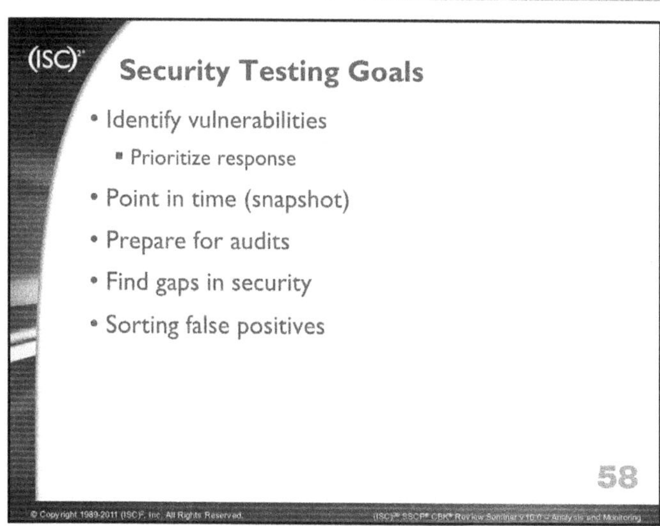


- **IDENTIFY VULNERABILITIES** – And rank them for mitigation based on system criticality.
- **POINT IN TIME (SNAPSHOT)** – Document as a "point-in-time" test for comparison with other time periods.
- **PREPARE FOR AUDITS** – Enables IT staff to tune and test their own procedures using vulnerability analysis in preparation for "real" audits.
- **FIND GAPS IN SECURITY** – Enables covert testers to determine the likelihood of system compromise and intrusion detection.
- **SORTING FALSE POSITIVES** – Allows security staff to focus on actual potential issues.

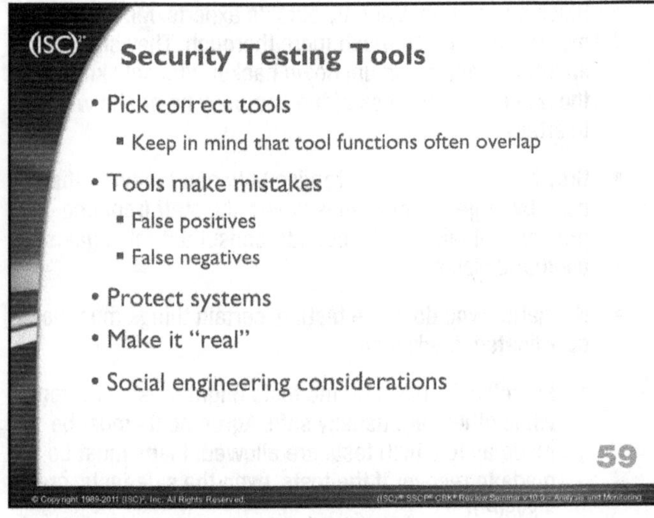


- **PICK CORRECT TOOLS –** According to what is to be tested and the test plan.
  - **KEEP IN MIND THAT TOOL FUNCTIONS OFTEN OVERLAP.**
- **TOOLS MAKE MISTAKES –** Preliminary results should be seen as circumstantial.
  - Watch for false positives or false negatives. Tool results can vary because detection methods are often inconsistent.
- **PROTECT SYSTEMS –** Running tools at the wrong time or in the wrong way can negatively affect systems.
- **MAKE IT "REAL" –** The tests should be as "real life" as possible and run against production networks and systems as much as possible – without impairing system operations.
  - It is common to run a series of tests that are not likely to crash or significantly impact a system first, then fix the uncovered vulnerabilities. After that, tests that might crash a system are often run with the timing set so that a crash will have the minimum negative impact possible.
  - On the most critical systems, these tests can be run in conjunction with business continuity plan testing (e.g., test at the alternate site or test at the primary after the full interruption test has been run successfully, but while still operating at the alternate site).
- **SOCIAL ENGINEERING CONSIDERATIONS –** Another important consideration is whether to include social engineering as part of the penetration test. The tester and management will decide if the test should be limited to technical (remote) means or if the tester should try to take advantage of human behavior in order to get access.

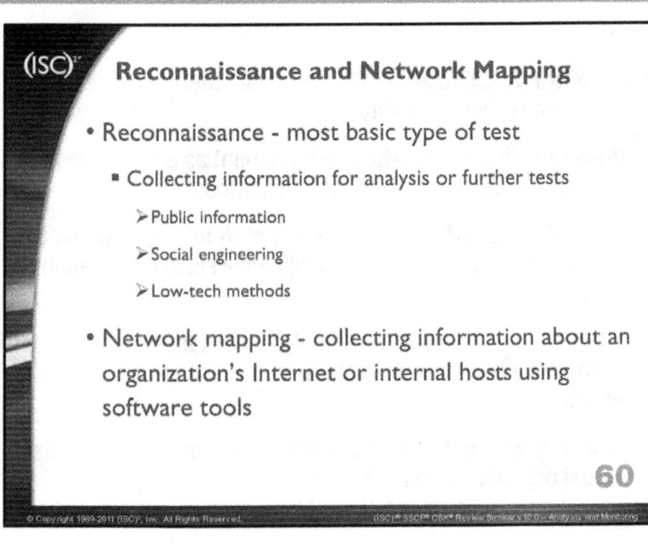


- **RECONNAISSANCE –** This is the first phase of many tests and is primarily concerned with gathering information through techniques such as social engineering or website research.
- **NETWORK MAPPING –** Is the practice of discovering the layout of an organization's network. This may allow the identification of certain types of systems, applications, services, and configurations that may be vulnerable to attack.

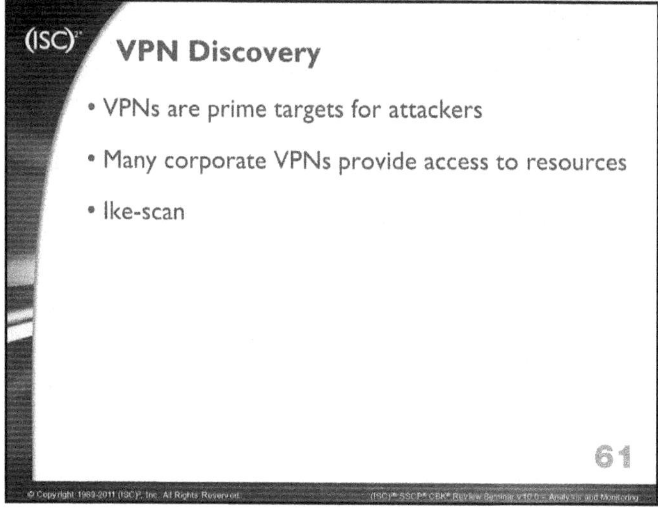


- **VPNS ARE PRIME TARGETS FOR ATTACKERS –** VPN systems often provide full access to the internal network which makes them tempting targets to an attacker.
- **MANY CORPORATE VPNS PROVIDE ACCESS TO RESOURCES –**
  - In addition, many people assume that their VPN servers are invisible and impenetrable which is a dangerous assumption given that research at NTA, the maker of several scanning tools, shows that IPSec VPN systems can be discovered and the manufacturer identified.
  - When this potential for discovery and identification is combined with the fact that several VPN vulnerabilities have been reported in the past few months, it would seem to be only a matter of time before hackers start to target VPN systems.
- **IKE-SCAN –** One of the more common tools that can be used to discover and fingerprint remote VPNs is called "ike-scan" which looks for IPSec Internet key exchange (IKE) packets that are waiting for acknowledgments.

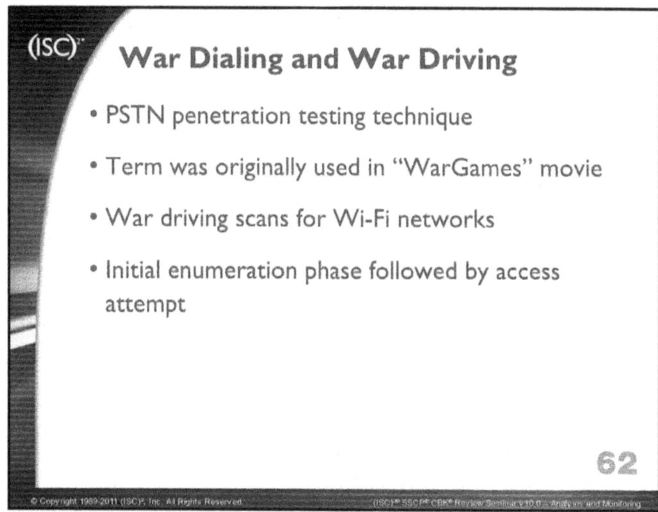


- **WAR DIALING –** War dialing is a technique of using a modem to automatically scan a list of telephone numbers, usually dialing every number in a local area code to search for computers, bulletin board systems, and fax machines. Hackers use the resulting lists for various purposes, hobbyists for exploration, and crackers (i.e., hackers who specialize in computer security) for password guessing. A single war dialing call would involve calling an unknown number, and waiting for one or two rings, since answering computers usually pick up on the first ring. If the phone rings twice, the modem hangs up and tries the next number. If a modem or fax machine answers, the war dialer program makes a note of the number. If a human or answering machine answers, the war dialer program hangs up. Depending on the time of day, war dialing 10,000 numbers in a given area code might annoy dozens or hundreds of people, some who attempt and fail to answer a phone in two rings, and some who succeed, only to hear the war dialing modem's carrier tone and hang up. The repeated incoming calls are especially annoying to businesses that have many consecutively numbered lines in the exchange, such as used with a Centrex telephone system.
- **WAR DRIVING –** Many war drivers use global positioning satellite (GPS) devices to measure the location of the network and log it on a website to form maps of the network neighborhood. A popular Web-based tool today is WiGLE. One of the pioneering mapping applications was StumbVerter, which used Microsoft MapPoint automation to draw found networks. For better range, antennas are built or bought, and vary from omnidirectional to highly directional.
  - The maps of known network IDs can then be used as a geolocation system — an alternative to GPS — by triangulating the current position from the signal strengths of known network IDs. Examples include Place Lab by Intel, Skyhook, Navizon by Cyril Houri, and SeekerLocate from Seeker Wireless.
  - In December 2004, a class of 100 undergraduates worked to map the city of Seattle, Washington, over several weeks. They found 5,225 access points; 44% were secured with WEP encryption, 52% were open, and 3% were pay-for-access. They noticed trends in the frequency and security of the networks depending on location. Many of the open networks were clearly intended to be used by the general public, with network names like "Open to share, no porn please" or "Free access, be nice." The information was collected into high-resolution maps, which were published online.

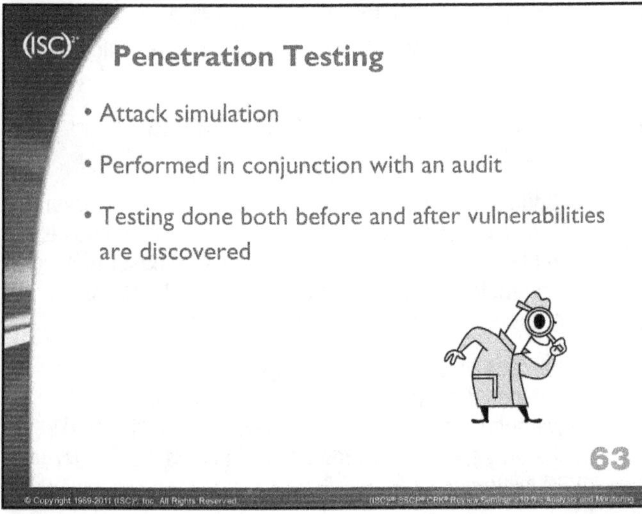

(ISC)²
Penetration Testing
• Attack simulation
• Performed in conjunction with an audit
• Testing done both before and after vulnerabilities are discovered
63


- **PENETRATION TESTING –** A penetration test (i.e., pentest) is a method of evaluating the security of a computer system or network by simulating an attack from a malicious source, known as a black hat hacker, or cracker. The process involves an active analysis of the system for any potential vulnerabilities that could result from poor or improper system configuration, both known and unknown hardware or software flaws, or operational weaknesses in process or technical countermeasures. This analysis is carried out from the position of a potential attacker and can involve active exploitation of security vulnerabilities. Any security issues that are found will be presented to the system owner, together with an assessment of their impact, and often with a proposal for mitigation or a technical solution. The intent of a penetration test is to determine the feasibility of an attack and the amount of business impact of a successful exploit, if discovered.

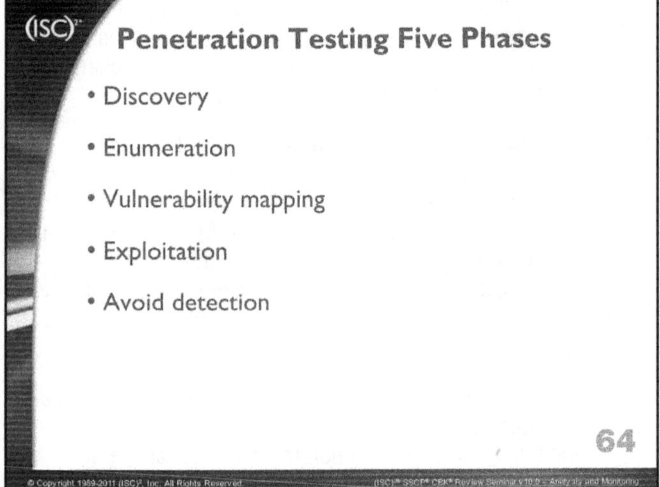

(ISC)²
Penetration Testing Five Phases
• Discovery
• Enumeration
• Vulnerability mapping
• Exploitation
• Avoid detection
64


- **DISCOVERY –** Pen testers perform thorough searches of the various whois databases, scan tools, etc., to obtain as much information as possible about the target organization. These searches often reveal many more Internet connections than the organizations expect. It is also important to leverage Usenet postings and social engineering tactics (if in scope) – many organizations are amazed by how willing their employees are to divulge information that is useful to an attacker.

- **ENUMERATION –** Once specific domain names, networks, and systems have been identified through discovery, the penetration tester will gain as much information as possible about each one. The key difference between discovery and enumeration is the level of intrusiveness. Enumeration involves actively trying to obtain user names, network share information, and application version information of running services, limited only by agreed-upon rules of engagement and scope.

- **VULNERABILITY MAPPING –** Vulnerability mapping, one of the most important phases of penetration testing, occurs when security practitioners map the profile of the environment to publicly known, or in some cases unknown vulnerabilities.

- **EXPLOITATION –** The exploitation phase begins once the target system's vulnerabilities are mapped. The penetration tester will attempt to gain privileged access to a target system by exploiting the identified vulnerabilities. The key to this phase is manual testing. No automated tool can duplicate the testing of an experienced penetration tester who is skilled in the art.

- **AVOID DETECTION –** Attackers will do their best to avoid leaving any trace of their activities.

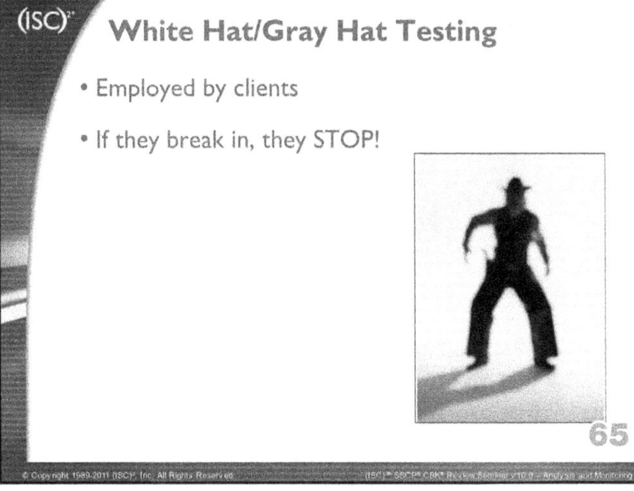
(ISC)²
White Hat/Gray Hat Testing
• Employed by clients
• If they break in, they STOP!
65

- White hat hackers are computer security experts, who specialize in penetration testing, and other testing methodologies, to ensure that a company's information systems are secure. Such people are employed by companies where these professionals are sometimes called "sneakers." Groups of these people are often called tiger teams or red teams. These security experts may utilize a variety of methods to carry out their tests, including social engineering tactics, use of hacking tools, and attempts to evade security to gain entry into secured areas.

(ISC)²

## Domain Summary

- This domain reviewed the importance of security monitoring and determining the appropriate response with respect to:
  - Security policy compliance
  - Compliance monitoring techniques
  - Audits: techniques, documentation, logs, and log reviews
  - Security control testing
  - Response to incidents

66

(ISC)²® SSCP® CBK® Review Seminar v.10.0 – Analysis and Monitoring

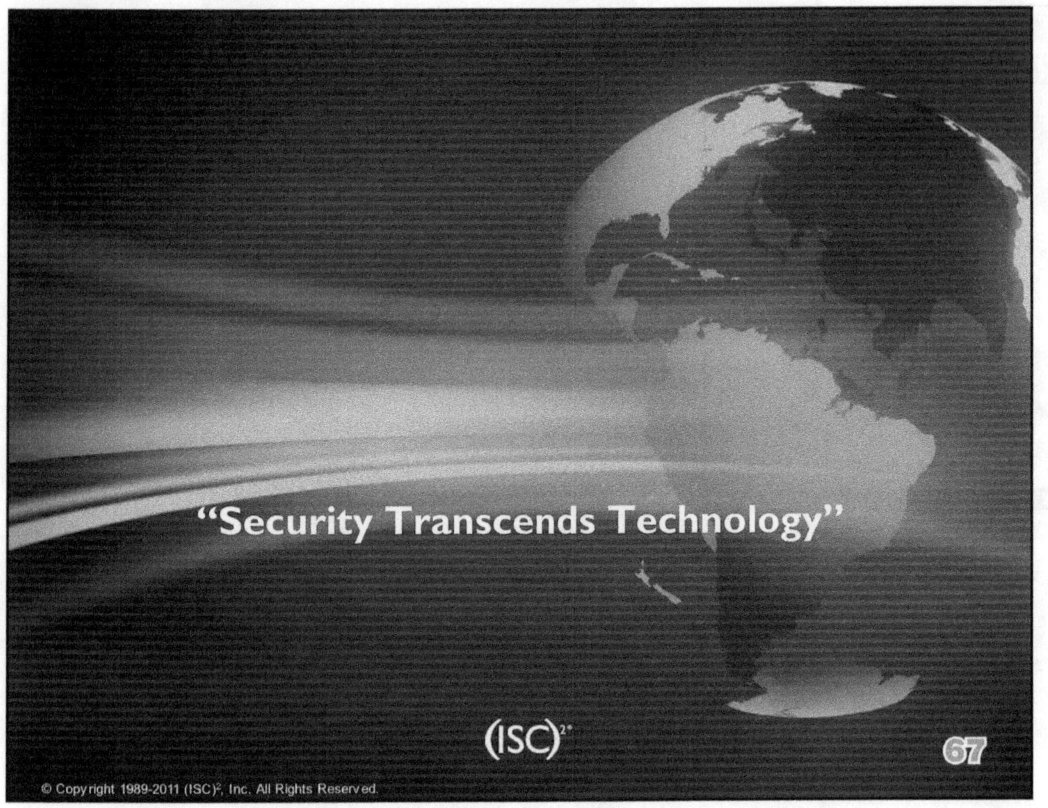
"Security Transcends Technology"
(ISC)²
67
© Copyright 1989-2011 (ISC)², Inc. All Rights Reserved.

# Review Questions

## ANALYSIS AND MONITORING

**1. Services that are designed to "assure" management that the information systems supporting a security framework are in place and working properly are called**

a. intrusion detection systems.
b. access controls.
c. network administration.
d. security auditing.

**2. As a security practitioner, what is the BEST way to interact with auditors?**

a. Remember they are your enemy – provide only as little information as possible when asked.
b. Give your information to the auditors and cooperate.
c. IT practitioners and auditors are not both participants in audits.
d. Cooperation is not necessary for full utilization and good practice in analyzed data.

**3. A chance to initiate face-to-face dialogue with stakeholders, system owners, and system operators is provided by**

a. interviews.
b. observations.
c. checklists.
d. policy reviews.

**4. The collection of potential vulnerability information is involved in what?**

a. Security testing
b. Observation
c. Policy review
d. Configuration review

**5. Which development to aid the security framework defines the minimum required parameters to achieve a consistent level of security for a system of business process?**

a. Standards
b. Baselines
c. Procedures
d. Guidelines

**6. What is the correct order of the security cycle?**

a. Secure , audit, monitor, and improve
b. Secure, monitor, audit, and improve
c. Monitor, improve, secure, and audit
d. Audit, secure, monitor, and improve

**7. Anti-virus (malicious code) detection for workstations and hosts is an example of which type of control?**

a. Access control
b. Administrative control
c. Physical control
d. Technical control

**8. Since reducing all risks usually costs more than the budget allows, it is better to do which of the following?**

a. Reduce all risks regardless.
b. Request a larger budget estimated to fit the costs.
c. Reduce only a small number of risks to save money.
d. Reduce risk on an overall, acceptable level within the budget.

**9. Which of the following describes using low-tech methods to gather information?**

a. Reconnaissance
b. Network mapping
c. Vulnerability testing
d. Penetration testing

**10. Which of the following terms is used to describe carrying out an attack?**

a. Reconnaissance
b. Network mapping
c. Vulnerability testing
d. Penetration testing

**11. "Googling" a target refers to which type of activity?**

a. Reconnaissance
b. Network mapping
c. Vulnerability testing
d. Penetration testing

**12. An intrusion detection system (IDS) recognizing an event correctly is a definition of a**

a. false positive.
b. false negative.
c. true positive.
d. true negative.

**13. When an attacker sends massive amounts of communications to different targets, but is only after one of the targets, it is called**

a. network flooding.
b. system overloading.
c. packet flooding.
d. data overloading.

**14. What does obfuscation mean?**

a. Illegal entry or penetration of the target.
b. Hidden objective or hidden intent.
c. Unannounced or spontaneous testing.
d. Any use of a low-tech method to penetrate a network.

**15. An attacker can wipe out the record of system changes or make it appear as if an innocent party was responsible by using what technique?**

a. Reconnaissance
b. Log alteration
c. Obfuscation
d. Record obfuscation

**16. A network intrusion detection system (NIDS) which resets the connection (with a TCP reset) between an attacker and the host being attacked is what type of action?**

a. Practical
b. Passive
c. Active
d. Responsive

**17. Activities that are outside the normal baseline are called**

a. system errors.
b. anomalies.
c. crashes.
d. fault.

**18. Which of the following defines the intent of a system security policy?**

a. A description of the settings that will provide the highest level of security.
b. A brief, high-level statement defining what is and is not permitted in the operation of the system.
c. A definition of those items that must be denied on the system.
d. A listing of tools and applications that will be used to protect the system.

**19. What would be the BEST tool to deal with a distributed port scan?**

a. Penetration test
b. Event log
c. Network intrusion detection system (NIDS)
d. Host intrusion detection system (HIDS)

**20. Which of the following network technologies would be best suited to operate in an error-prone environment?**

a. Frame relay
b. Asynchronous transfer mode
c. X.25
d. Ethernet

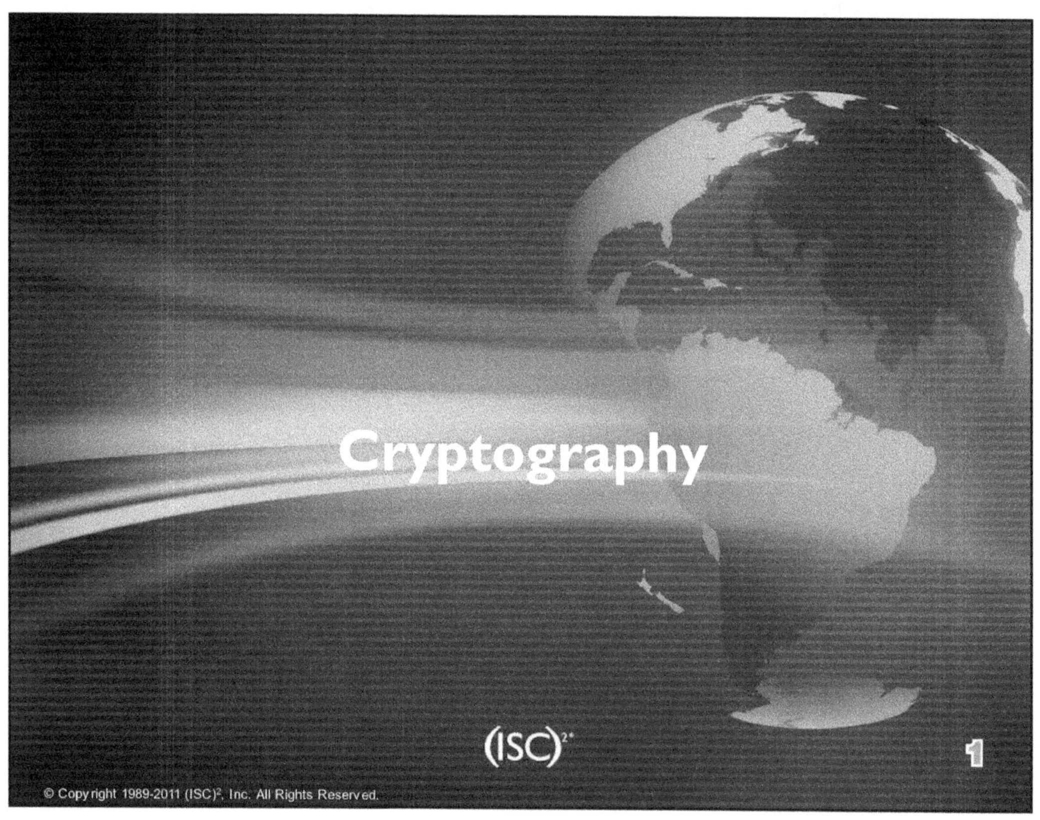


## Domain Objectives

- Define the basic concepts of cryptography
- Describe symmetric, asymmetric, and hashing algorithms
- Examine the uses of cryptography
- Understand the challenges of cryptographic implementations
- Define certificate management

2

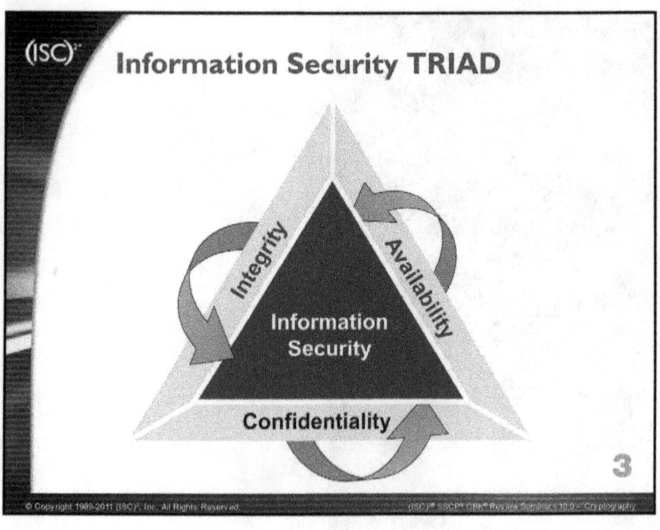


- **CONFIDENTIALITY –** The most obvious aspect of cryptography: A message is made confidential through encrypting it.
- **INTEGRITY –** Part of cryptography involves hashing, which is a traditional technique used to identify accidental changes to data. Cryptographic hashing techniques combined with a key can also be used to identify intentional changes.
- **AVAILABILITY –** Key management and distribution is a major issue in the realm of cryptography. A missing or lost key leads to loss of availability.

(ISC)²

## Domain Agenda

- **Cryptography Definitions**
- Stream and Block Ciphers
- Algorithms
  - Symmetric
  - Asymmetric
  - Strengths and Weaknesses
- Integrity Checking
- Key Management
- Cryptographic Attacks

4



(ISC)² SSCP® CBK® Review Seminar v 10.0 – Cryptography

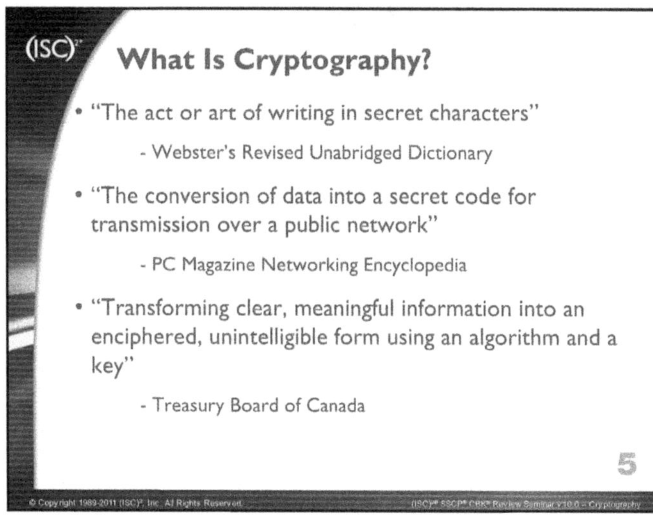


- There are dozens of definitions of cryptography. This is just a tiny sample. For a much more complete list, fire up Google and use this search term: define: cryptography.
  - This is a good technique for any unfamiliar term you come across!
- Several of the essential terms having to do with cryptography are documented on the following pages.

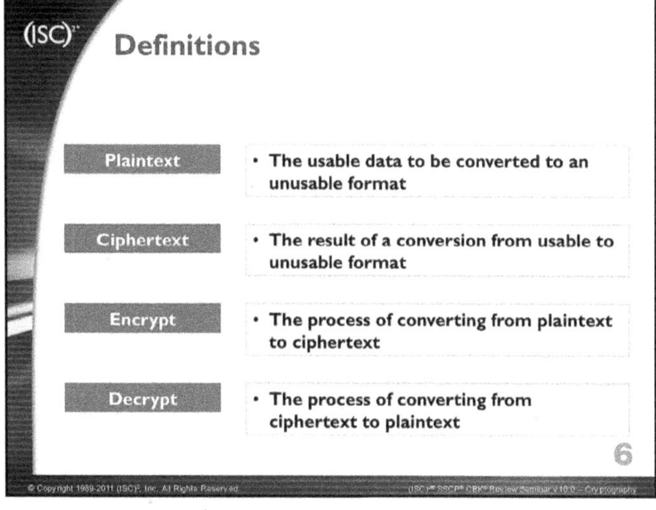


- **PLAINTEXT (PT) –** Its name comes from the original practice of only converting human-language based messages, but the term now applies to any kind of source file to be converted.
- **CIPHERTEXT (CT) –** Ciphertext may be stored, stored then transmitted, or transmitted only.
- **ENCRYPT (E) –** The abbreviation "E" is typically symbolized inside a circle.
- **DECRYPT (D) –** The abbreviation "D" is typically symbolized inside a circle.

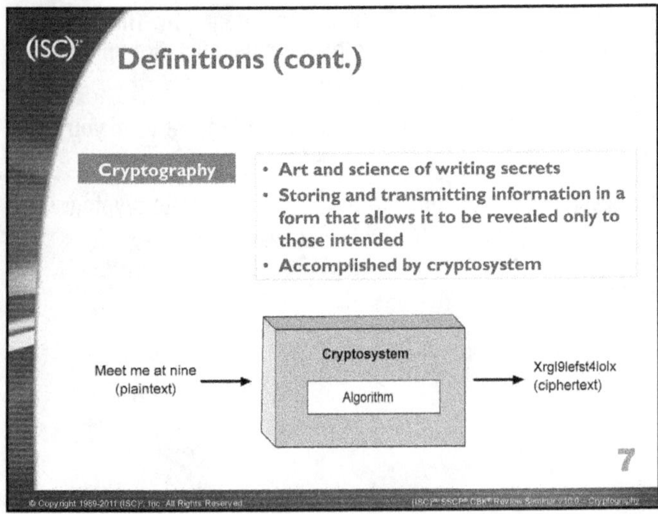


- **PLAINTEXT/CLEARTEXT –** The message in its natural form.
- **CIPHERTEXT/CRYPTOGRAM –** The scrambled message.

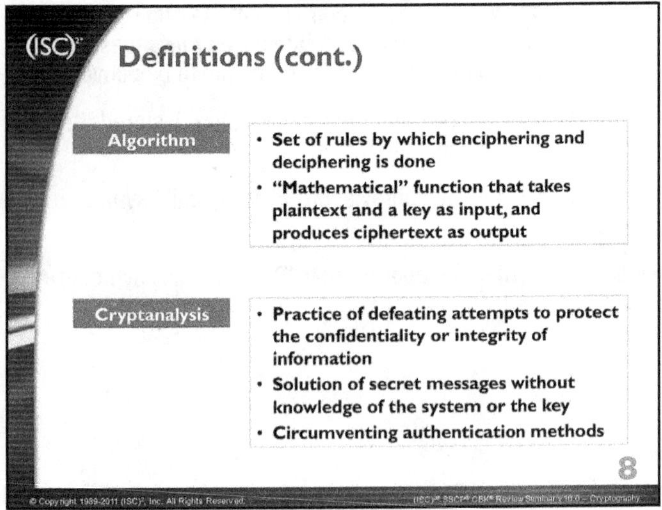


- **ALGORITHM –** The 'mathematical' rules used by the cryptosystem to perform the encryption or decryption.

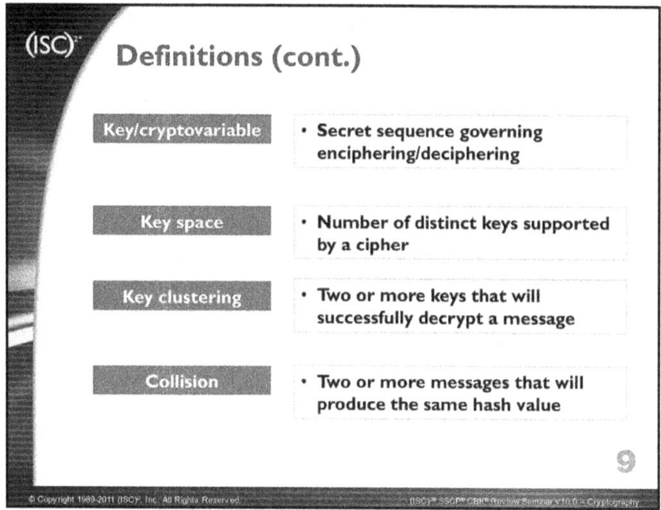

(ISC)²
Definitions (cont.)
Key/cryptovariable
• Secret sequence governing enciphering/deciphering
Key space
• Number of distinct keys supported by a cipher
Key clustering
• Two or more keys that will successfully decrypt a message
Collision
• Two or more messages that will produce the same hash value
9


- **KEY/CRYPTOVARIABLE –** The unique value used that causes the cryptosystem and algorithm to operate in a predictable, repeatable manner.
- **KEY SPACE –** Key size is expressed as a number of bits. For symmetric systems, this represents the number of possible keys. When the key is in a binary format, the number of keys is (2^keysize). Some systems allow hex values in the key. A common example of a key is a bank card PIN code. A four-digits PIN would have a key space of 10,000 (10^4) values.
- **KEY CLUSTERING –** A brute force attack tries to determine the key used to decrypt a message by trying all possible keys, therefore, it takes longer to try all the keys for an algorithm with long (more) keys than it does to try those for an algorithm using shorter keys. However, if the algorithm has a weakness that would allow several different keys to operate in the same way, it is subject to a flaw known as key clustering. When several keys would work to decrypt the message, the amount of effort needed by the attacker to guess the correct key is much less.
  - DES has a few well-known keys for which this is true (example, alternating 010101). There is also a pair of special keys for which the ciphertext is the same as the plaintext. Proper implementation of DES calls for software that disallows usage of these special keys. For more information, go to: http://csrc.nist.gov/publications/nistpubs/800-67/SP800-67.pdf.
- **COLLISION –** A weakness with a hash function that would allow an attacker to find two messages that create the same hash value thus undermining the ability to have confidence in the authentication of the message.

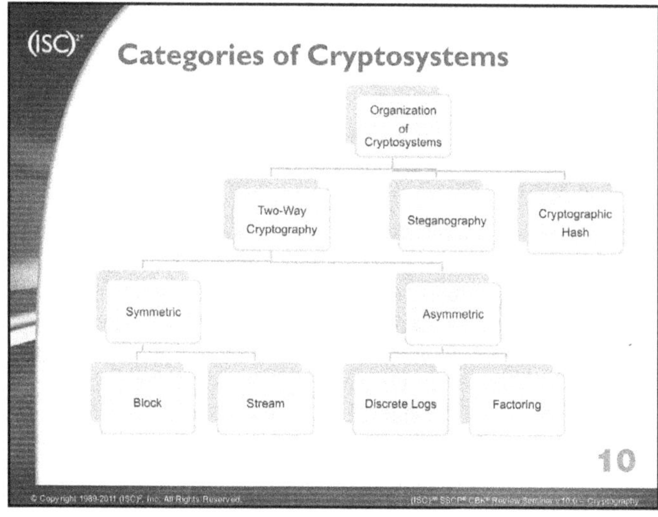

(ISC)²

## Steganography

- Art of hiding communications
  - Deny message exists
- Data hidden in picture files, sound files, slack space on floppies
  - Example - the least significant bits of bitmap image can be used to hide messages, usually without material change to the original file

11



(ISC)² SSCP® CBK® Review Seminar v10.0 – Cryptography

- **ART OF HIDING COMMUNICATIONS –** Unlike encryption, which uses an algorithm and a "seed value" (a random value or nonce) to scramble or encode a message to make it unreadable, steganography makes the communication invisible. Steganography simply takes one piece of information and hides it within another. For example, this can be accomplished by "stealing" the least significant bit from every byte in a picture and using it to contain the message data. This results in a small change to the picture but only through a direct, visual comparison of the original and processed image could this be noticed. Typically, however, the original will not be available to an analyst and the presence of a hidden message will be unnoticed.
- **DATA HIDDEN IN PICTURE FILES, SOUND FILES, SLACK SPACE ON FLOPPIES –** A variation of this is to use a null cipher, which is a simple and very ancient form of steganography. In this case, the recipient will know to read (for example) every fifth word or the first letter in each new sentence, or some other similar pattern, in order to sift the secret message out of the apparently benign plaintext.

(ISC)²

## Traditional and Modern Cryptography

- Cryptography originally used for secrecy
- Modern cryptography, however, offers many solutions such as the ability to:
  - Prevent unauthorized disclosure of information
  - Prevent unauthorized access to information, computers, websites, applications, etc.
  - Detect tampering
  - Detect injection of false data
  - Detect deletion of data
  - Prevent repudiation
  - Forge coded signals

12



(ISC)² SSCP® CBK® Review Seminar v10.0 – Cryptography

- Ancient cryptographic techniques only dealt with secrecy. Over time, and especially as techniques became automated, other functions became available. For example, modern crypto techniques allow for non-repudiation, which means that by using crypto, a receiver can be certain who sent a message – and the sender will not be able to deny (or "repudiate") that he or she was the source of the message.
- Some of the benefits realized from modern-day cryptography include the ability to provide greater control over access to information (through hash functions and PKI); the ability to detect any accidental or intentional tampering of a message, whether in storage or in transit; the ability to establish links between a person or process and an action (especially in e-commerce); and the ability for an imposter posing as a trusted source through creation of false messages or altering genuine messages.

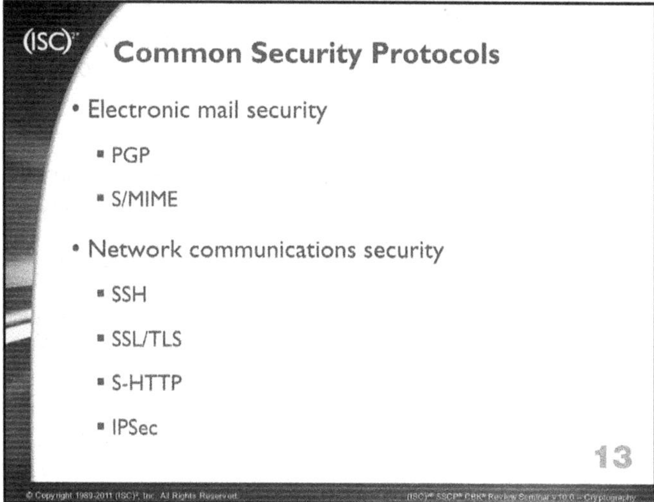

(ISC)²
Common Security Protocols
Electronic mail security
PGP
S/MIME
Network communications security
SSH
SSL/TLS
S-HTTP
IPSec
13


- **COMMON SECURITY PROTOCOLS –** There have been a number of standards developed for security over the years. Since standard applications often provide little or no security or privacy protection, there have been a number of efforts intended to address the deficiencies. Most have focused on providing message integrity and encryption services, but some have also addressed key management and non-repudiation.
- **ELECTRONIC MAIL SECURITY –** Two of the more common email security enhancements include PGP and S/MIME:
  - **PGP –** Pretty good privacy. While not intended solely for email, PGP has commonly been used to provide message confidentiality and integrity. Like privacy enhanced mail (PEM), it is a hybrid cryptosystem that uses both symmetric and asymmetric key cryptography. Messages are encrypted using a randomly chosen symmetric session key and a copy of the session key encrypted using the recipient's public key (thus ensuring that only the holder of the related private key can decrypt it). PGP is extremely flexible with the use of cryptographic algorithms – it has, for example, been able to use RSA, Diffie-Hellman, and Elgamal for asymmetric key cryptography. It can also provide message integrity through the use of a standard hash function and digital signatures (typically through the use of the digital signatures standard (DSS)). It has the ability to work with standard X.509 public key certificates as well as its own proprietary certificate format, and has been known to work with both a certificate authority (CA)-based trust model as well as its traditional web of trust. With the advent of multipurpose Internet mail extensions (MIME), PGP has since also been redeveloped as an alternative extension to S/MIME or MOSS as PGP/MIME.
  - **S/MIME –** Secure multipurpose Internet mail extensions. Originally developed by RSA, S/MIME was heavily backed by most early Internet developers, which may explain some of its success and why it has become the de facto standard for email privacy and authentication services. Building from PEM and MOSS, it is based on public key cryptography standards (PKCS) and focuses strictly on a hierarchical trust model based on certification authorities, although self-signed certificates can be supported. Most commercial implementations use RSA for asymmetric key cryptography, Triple DES for symmetric key, and SHA-1 for hashing. Some will also support other algorithms (for example, Diffie-Hellman for asymmetric and digital signature standard (DSS) for signature services). Many implementations are available as plug-ins to common email client software.
- **NETWORK COMMUNICATIONS SECURITY –** Today businesses make extensive use of network and internet communications, and one or more of the following protocols are commonly used to provide security services:
  - **SSH –** Secure shell. Most early implementations of remote access were designed for trusted networks. Protocols/programs, such as TELNET, RSH, and rlogin, consequently transmit without encryption, which allows traffic to be easily intercepted. Secure shell (SSH) was designed as an alternative to these insecure protocols and allows users to securely access resources on remote computers over an encrypted tunnel. SSH's services include remote logon, file transfer, and command execution. It also supports port forwarding, which redirects other protocols through an encrypted SSH tunnel. There are two incompatible versions of the protocol: SSH-1 and SSH-2, though many servers support both versions. SSH-2 has improved integrity checks (SSH-1 is vulnerable to an insertion attack due to weak CRC-32 integrity checking) and supports local extensions and additional types of digital certificates, such as Open PGP. SSH was originally designed for UNIX, but there are now implementations for other operating systems including, Windows, Macintosh, and OpenVMS.
  - **SSL/TLS –** SSL virtual private networks (VPNs) are a client-server approach to remote access that creates a secure tunnel between two applications (such as a Web browser and Web server). Remote users can then exchange sensitive information with the server. Even though users employ Web browsers, SSL VPNs are not restricted to applications that use the HTTPS protocol. With the aid of plug-ins such as Java, users can access back-end databases and other non Web-based applications.
  - **TLS –** Transport layer security, a protocol that guarantees privacy and data integrity between client/server applications communicating over the Internet. TLS is application protocol-independent. Higher-level protocols can layer on top of the TLS protocol transparently. Based on Netscape's SSL 3.0, TLS supersedes and is an extension of SSL, providing both client and server authentication. TLS and SSL are not interoperable.
  - **S-HTTP –** Secure HTTP. Another protocol for transmitting data securely over the World Wide Web. Whereas SSL creates a secure connection between a client and a server over which any amount of data can be sent securely, S-HTTP is designed to transmit individual messages securely.
  - **IPSEC –** Internet protocol security is a set of protocols developed by the IETF to support secure exchange of packets at the IP layer. IPSec has been deployed widely to implement virtual private networks (VPNs). IPSec supports two encryption modes: transport and tunnel. Transport mode, designed for end-to-end security, encrypts only the data portion (payload) of each packet, but leaves the header untouched. The more secure tunnel mode encrypts both the header and the payload and was designed primarily for gateway to gateway connections. On the receiving side, an IPSec-compliant device decrypts each packet. For IPSec to work, the sending and receiving devices must share a public key. This is accomplished through a protocol known as Internet security association and key management protocol/Oakley (ISAKMP/Oakley), which allows the receiver to obtain a public key and authenticate the sender using digital certificates. The two security services offered are authentication header (AH), which provides integrity and replay protection as well as source authentication, and encapsulating security protocol (ESP), which adds confidentiality through encryption.

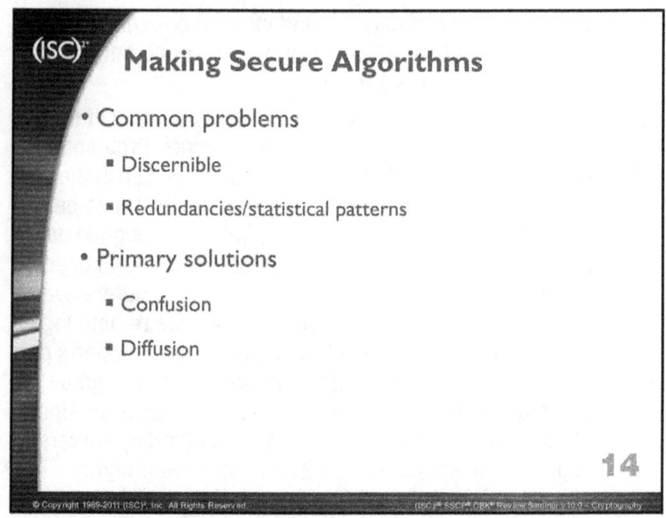


- **MAKING SECURE ALGORITHMS –** Claude Shannon was one of the fathers of modern information theory. In his 1949 paper "Communication Theory of Secrecy Systems," he explained that the biggest problems with making a truly secure secrecy system lay with the redundancy of natural language typical to the plaintext and the fact that (apart from ideal OTP schemes) the keys being used are smaller than the plaintext and may be reused.
- **COMMON PROBLEMS –**
  - **DISCERNIBLE –** Simple cryptosystems are not very secure. Knowing the language that was used in the plaintext, statistical analysis allows the cryptanalyst to attempt "frequency analysis" attacks against the system, using common patterns in language, until he or she finds the right plaintext. The goal of a secure cryptographic algorithm then, should be to make it extremely difficult for the cryptanalyst to get to the single, correct answer, by *providing as many equally probable options as possible.*

    The assumption is that the "enemy cryptanalyst" knows which cryptographic algorithm is being used, and that his or her task lies solely with identifying the most probable plaintext from a given ciphertext without knowing which key was chosen.
  - **REDUNDANCIES/STATISTICAL PATTERNS –** Redundancy tends to make the cryptanalyst's job easier. It may be thought of as the tendency for plaintext to provide more information than is strictly necessary to communicate one's message. For example, the "u" after "q" in the English language is essentially redundant. These redundancies allow the cryptanalyst to test available keys to find out which ones are the most probable, since they would allow the cryptanalyst to quickly test their keys to see if they generate improbable plaintext. For example, if a potential key being used to crack a ciphertext message results in an English plaintext message that has a "q" followed by any character other than "u," it is not a probable key.
- **PRIMARY SOLUTIONS –**
  - **CONFUSION –** Is the principle of hiding patterns in the plaintext by substitution. This makes it more difficult for the cryptanalyst to directly relate ciphertext sequences with plaintext words. A perfect cryptosystem would allow a character in ciphertext to decrypt as any possible plaintext character.
  - **DIFFUSION –** Is the property of transposing the input plaintext throughout the ciphertext so that a character in the ciphertext would not line up directly in the same position in the plaintext.

**REFERENCES:**

Shannon, Claude, "Communication Theory of Secrecy Systems," Bell System Technical Journal, vol.28(4), page 656–715, 1949.

csrc.nist.gov/archive/aes/round1/conf2/papers/massey.pdf

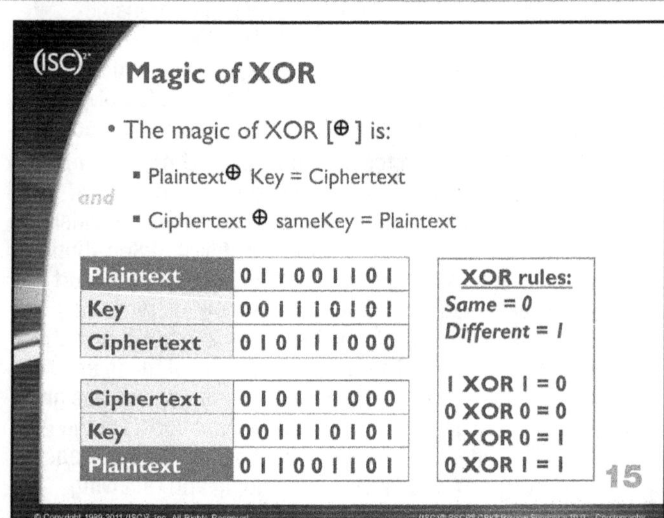


- The XOR operation is represented by the symbol shown on the slide.
- When a stream-based crypto system operates, it produces a continuous stream of 1s and 0s (called a keystream) that are XOR'd against the plaintext to produce ciphertext. The recipient merely needs to generate the same keystream, XOR it against the ciphertext, and thus recover the plaintext.
- Another way to express XOR rules is "add without carry."
  - Thus 1+0 = 1,
  - And 0+1 = 1,
  - 0+0 = 0,
  - And 1+1 = 0
- Therefore, when the plaintext bit and the keystream bit are the same, the output ciphertext will be a 0. However, when the plaintext bit and the keystream bit are different, the output ciphertext will be a 1.

(ISC)²

## Domain Agenda

- Cryptography Definitions
- **Stream and Block Ciphers**
- Algorithms
  - Symmetric
  - Asymmetric
  - Strengths and Weaknesses
- Integrity Checking
- Key Management
- Cryptographic Attacks

16



(ISC)²® SSCP® CBK® Review Seminar v10.0 – Cryptography

- Symmetric ciphers come in two classes: stream ciphers and block ciphers.

(ISC)²

## Stream Ciphers

- Operate as 1s and 0s on continuous streams of plaintext
- Usually implemented in hardware
- Well suited for serial communications such as streaming audio, video, and telephone

17



(ISC)²® SSCP® CBK® Review Seminar v10.0 – Cryptography

- **STREAM CIPHERS –**
  - Encrypt a single bit of plaintext at a time.
  - Use a process known as Exclusive-Or (XOR) (described on the next slide).
  - Are well suited to serial (streaming) communications because they operate on, and transmit, each bit individually.
  - Stream ciphers are generally faster than block ciphers; however, as real-time solutions, they may not provide the same level of protection as block ciphers, which are generally more complex.
- For a fascinating look at a stream cipher that can be done with a simple deck of playing cards, look up "Solitaire Cipher." It was created by Bruce Schneier (author of AES contenders Blowfish and Twofish) and used in a book called *Cryptonomicon* by Neil Stephenson.

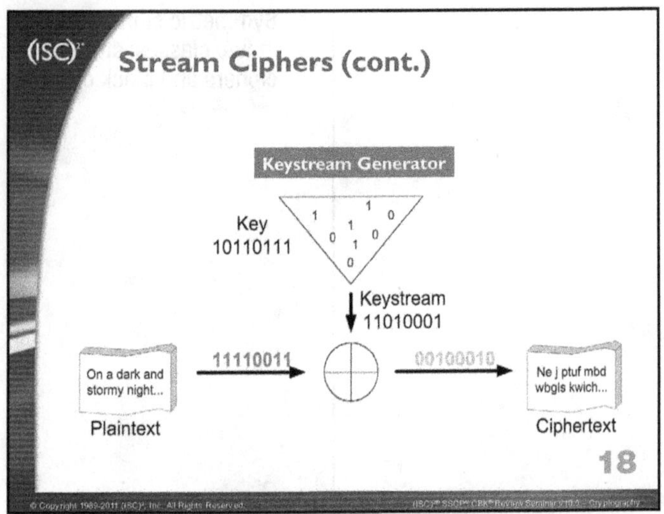


- **STREAM CIPHERS (CONT.)** – This slide describes how a stream cipher works. The cryptosystem generates a keystream (a pseudo-random series of 1s and 0s) based on the unique key used.
- The keystream will usually repeat at some point but it must be as long a period of non-repeating values as possible, and approximately evenly balanced between 1s and 0s.
    - The keystream is generated and combined with the plaintext to create the ciphertext. Using the exclusive, or XOR process, each bit of the input data is XOR'd with the corresponding bit in the keystream.
    - Stream ciphers are usually much faster than any block cipher.
- The keystream generator takes a starting key and uses it to generate the keystream.
    - An oversimplification of a keystream generator would be this formula:
        - Choose a 64-bit random number as the starting key.
        - Square the key (Product = key * key).
        - Use the rightmost 32 bits of the product for the keystream.
        - Use the leftmost 32 bits as the next key.
    - While this is mathematically flawed (it isn't balanced) and dangerous (a series of 0s creates problems when squared), it does show that an algorithm can use a portion of the output of one step to start the process for a latter step–in other words, it can act recursively.

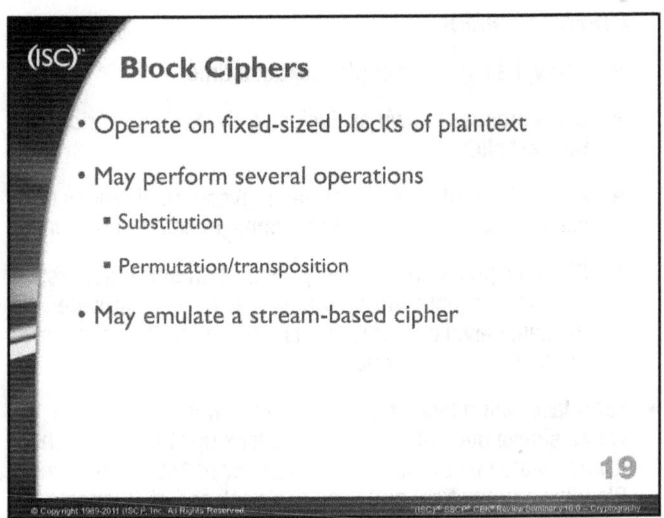


- **BLOCK CIPHERS** – The other form of symmetric ciphers is block ciphers.
- **OPERATE ON FIXED-SIZED BLOCKS OF PLAINTEXT** – Traditionally, block ciphers operate on fixed-sized blocks of plaintext to generate the same sized blocks of ciphertext, but it is also possible to use block ciphers to generate a keystream and use that keystream to encrypt the message as a stream rather than as a true block cipher. In other words, the block cipher algorithm is used as a keystream generator which is then used to encrypt the data as a stream operation rather than using the algorithm to directly encrypt the data in a block operation.
- **MAY PERFORM SEVERAL OPERATIONS** – In either mode, at least three operations are performed: XORing, substitution, and permutation (or transposition).
    - **SUBSTITUTION** – The value of the byte is changed, but not its position.
    - **PERMUTATION/TRANSPOSITION** – The position is changed, but not the value.
- Block ciphers operate in rounds. A block of plaintext goes through substitution, permutation, and XOR to produce an interim result and the interim result is then fed back through those three steps to produce a second interim result. This process is repeated a number of times. (The data encryption standard (DES) has 16 rounds, the advanced encryption standard (AES) has 10, and other block ciphers all operate with a certain number of rounds.) After the last round, the result is saved as the ciphertext. Decrypting takes the same number of rounds. A block of ciphertext is sent through the steps creating an interim, the process is repeated as prescribed, and the result is plaintext.
- To understand why rounds are needed, think of a new deck of playing cards. They're in a well-known suit and value sequence. Shuffling them once changes the order, but looking at them will make it clear that it is a new deck that has been shuffled once. Shuffle again and again (perhaps 16 times) and the sequence of the result will obscure the sequence of the original. Keep in mind that the result of the shuffling is only the result of permutation. The block algorithms add in XOR and substitution as well.

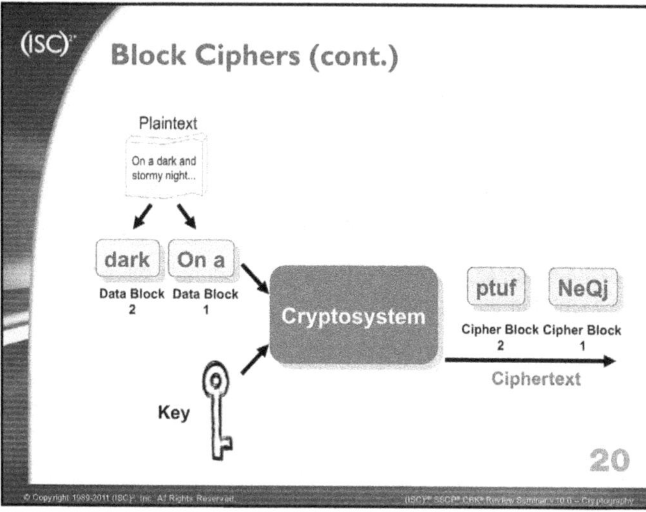


- **BLOCK CIPHERS (CONT.) –**
- The data to be encrypted is broken up into data blocks (DB1, DB2, etc.) of proper size.
- Each block is sent into the cryptosystem along with the key.
- The data block is modified and scrambled (substitution and permutation) and XOR'd or otherwise changed to produce the cipher block.
- Some systems also modify the key in much the same manner. (This is called Key Scheduling.)
- Some algorithms also use an IV (Initialization Vector) as described on the next slide.

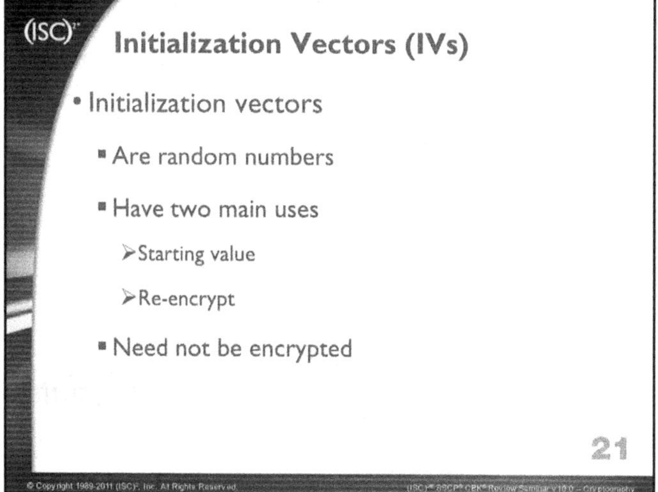


- **HAVE TWO MAIN USES –** Block ciphers use an initialization vector (IV) for two main purposes:
  - **STARTING VALUE:**
    - Since many messages to be encrypted will have a similar layout (such as the format of a memo or letter), the cryptanalysts have a distinct advantage when attempting to decrypt a message. They know that they have the correct key when the decryption starts to generate plaintext in the correct format. To avoid this, the algorithm selects a random value called an initialization vector that it exclusive ors (XORs) with the first block of plaintext to be encrypted. This random value will cause the algorithm to generate completely different versions of plaintext every time it is used.
    - To decrypt, the recipient needs to know the IV. It can be transmitted in the clear, however, because it is just as useless to an eavesdropper as the encrypted data (which can also be intercepted by the eavesdropper). For files in storage, such as an encrypted file on a hard drive, the IV must be saved as the first block of the file.
  - **RE-ENCRYPT –** The other main use of IVs is to re-encrypt (or encrypt the same plaintext twice) and wind up with different ciphertexts. If, for example, an eavesdropper were to see the same message being sent to many destinations (e.g., from an admiralty to ships at sea), the eavesdropper would be able to draw the inference that all recipients were receiving the same orders even without being able to decode the message. To thwart this kind of inference attack, each message will use a different IV, thus a different "block zero," and the result will be completely different ciphertexts, even when everyone is using the same key.

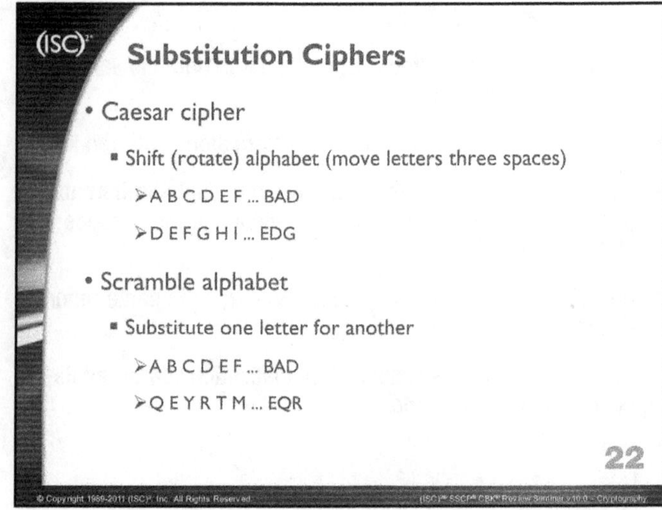


- **CAESAR CIPHER –** A classic example of a cipher based solely on substitution is the Caesar cipher. It simply shifts the letters by some fixed offset (the example here uses a shift of three). Substitution ciphers retain the position of each letter in the ciphertext; they simply change values.
  - Rotational ciphers are known by names that indicate the number of characters to rotate. ROT-3 is the Caesar cipher shown above. Rotational ciphers are still used today. As an example:
    - If you have a Windows machine handy, look for the Userassist key in the registry. Its "Count" subkey is encoded using ROT-13.
    - That key is a change log useful for troubleshooting and sometimes for computer forensics.
- **SCRAMBLE ALPHABET –** The second example involves scrambling the alphabet.
- Neither is difficult to break using frequency analysis, since statistics are available to show the most frequently used characters in a particular language. A first step used by the cryptanalyst would be to substitute the letters in the ciphertext with the statistically correct letters in the language. For instance, in English the most frequent letter is "e," so it would be logical to substitute an "e" for the letter that appears most frequently in the ciphertext. If the next most frequently used letter were "t," it would be substituted for the second most frequently used letter in the ciphertext, and so on. Also, well-known pairs of letters such as "th" or "ly" give further clues. If the text were still unreadable, the cryptanalyst would make other logical substitutions until enough translation was available to crack the code.

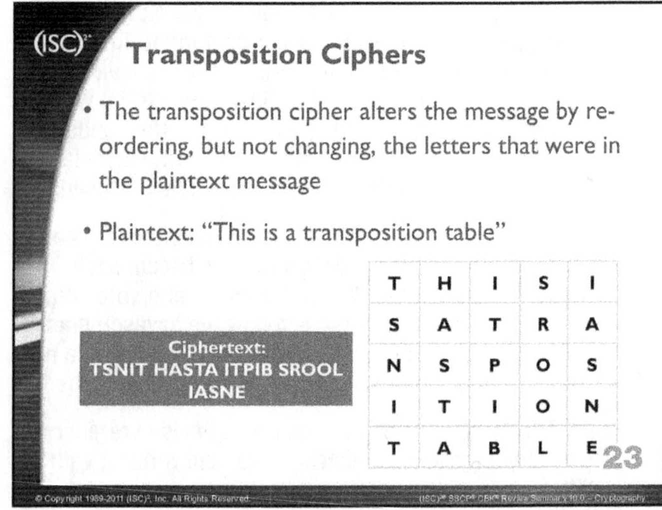


- **TRANSPOSITION CIPHER –** The transposition cipher is based on rearranging the characters in a message, but not changing their values. (An "A" remains an "A," it just changes position). The key is the technique used to rearrange letters, whether done manually or mathematically (using a computer).
- In this example, there are two secrets:
  - One is the size of the box (5 x 5).
  - The other is the sequence for encoding: The ciphertext is found by reading the columns in the table top to bottom, left to right.
- A different ciphertext could be found by encoding on the diagonals from the bottom left going up, thus making TIANT BSSIL TAPOE HTONI RSSAI.

(ISC)²

## Domain Agenda

- Cryptography Definitions
- Stream and Block Ciphers
- **Algorithms**
  - **Symmetric**
  - Asymmetric
  - Strengths and Weaknesses
- Integrity Checking
- Key Management
- Cryptographic Attacks

24



(ISC)²® SSCP® CBK® Review Seminar v10.0 – Cryptography

(ISC)²

## Symmetric Key Cryptography

- Also referred to as single key/secret key
- The sender and receiver use the SAME key to encrypt/decrypt the message
- Symmetric encryption is the fastest encryption technique available
- Requires secure key distribution

25



(ISC)²® SSCP® CBK® Review Seminar v10.0 – Cryptography

- **SYMMETRIC KEY CRYPTOGRAPHY/SINGLE KEY CRYPTOGRAPHY/SECRET KEY CRYPTOGRAPHY –** Also called shared key, private key, session key, and same key cryptography.
- **SYMMETRIC MEANS** "the same as." A symmetric cipher uses the same key in both the encryption and decryption process.
- **ASYMMETRIC MEANS** "not the same as." An asymmetric cipher uses a pair of related keys (a key pair) to encrypt and decrypt. The keys must be used as a pair, and, therefore, the key used to encrypt cannot be the same one used to decrypt.
- The biggest difficulty with symmetric key crypto is the distribution of the secret keys, since the key distribution method requires authentication and confidentiality.

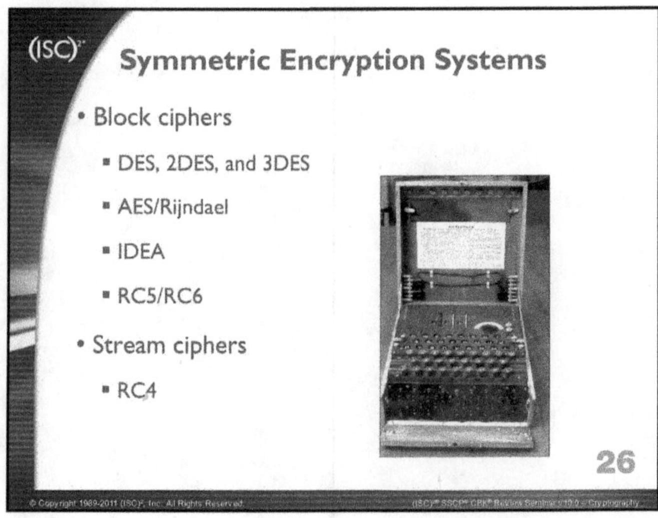


- **SYMMETRIC ENCRYPTION SYSTEMS –** These are well-known examples of symmetric systems.
- **RC4 –** Is a stream-based cipher. All of the others are block-based. RC4's most common use is in wireless encryption (WEP and WPA, but not WPA2). RC4 is also used in PPTP and Windows PWL files as well as being the most commonly implemented cipher in SSL.
- (The machine shown in the diagram is the German Enigma machine – a symmetric electro-mechanical device used in the World War II. Photo courtesy of the NSA Cryptographic Museum, Fort Meade, Maryland.)

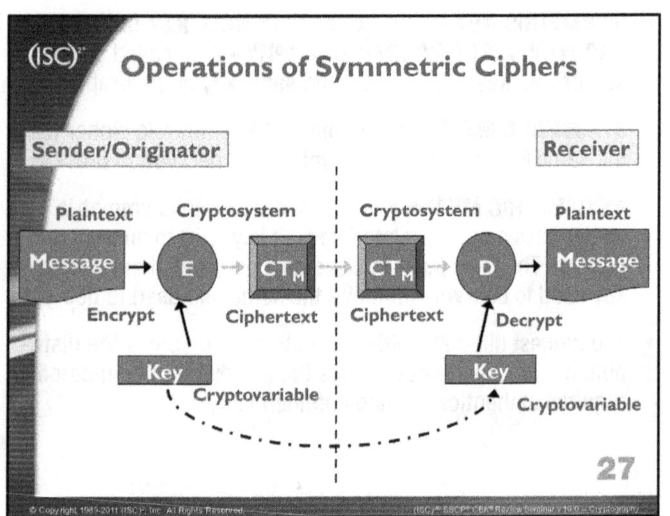


- This graphic shows the encryption and decryption operations of a symmetric cipher. Please note that, since the receiver needs the same key to decrypt as the originator used to encrypt the message, the key must be shared securely between the two parties. The key will often need to be sent through a different channel than the encrypted data. This is referred to as "out of band" distribution.

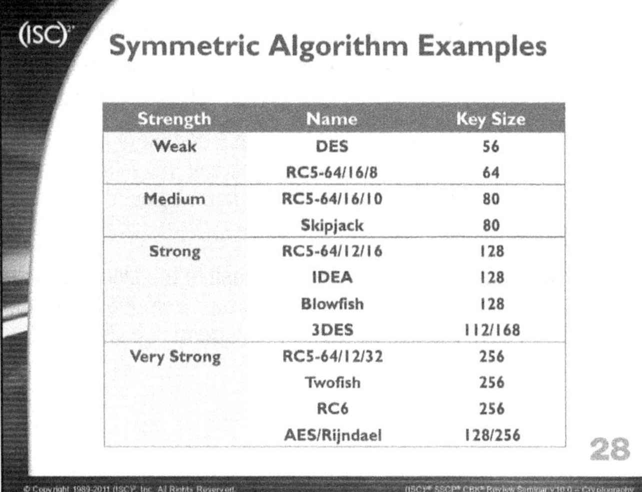
Symmetric Algorithm Examples

| Strength | Name | Key Size |
|---|---|---|
| Weak | DES | 56 |
| | RC5-64/16/8 | 64 |
| Medium | RC5-64/16/10 | 80 |
| | Skipjack | 80 |
| Strong | RC5-64/12/16 | 128 |
| | IDEA | 128 |
| | Blowfish | 128 |
| | 3DES | 112/168 |
| Very Strong | RC5-64/12/32 | 256 |
| | Twofish | 256 |
| | RC6 | 256 |
| | AES/Rijndael | 128/256 |

28



(ISC)²® SSCP® CBK® Review Seminar v10.0 – Cryptography

- **NOTE THAT RC5 IS A "PARAMETERIZED" ALGORITHM –** The first parameter refers to the block size in bits, the second parameter refers to the number of iterations during the scrambling, and the last refers to the key length in BYTES (i.e., 8 = 64 bits). This allows it to be used at various strengths. The larger the parameters, the stronger (but slower) the encryption. Obviously, the sender and the receiver must agree upon the parameters to be used.
- **3DES –** (Or TDES, the official NIST term – SP800-67) has an effective key strength of 112 using two independent keys (EDE2), or 168 using three independent keys, both of which protect against "meet-in-the-middle" attack. This attack was possible against Double DES.
- **SKIPJACK** is now widely deprecated due to its government key-escrow feature. Used primarily in the US government's Fortezza smart cards and Defense Messaging System (DMS) and currently being abandoned in favor of industry standard S/MIME-based secure messaging systems.
    - Key escrow is the storage of private keys with a trusted agency. In the case of Skipjack, this meant that a government agency would have the private key for users of the Clipper chip. They could only use the key with appropriate legal permission (a search warrant, for example). It failed to gain support in the United States and UK (among other countries) because corporations didn't want to trust governments with keys that protected intellectual property, and governments had no assurance that the key on deposit with the escrow agency was in fact the key being used to encrypt the data.

## Domain Agenda

- Cryptography Definitions
- Stream and Block Ciphers
- **Algorithms**
    - Symmetric
    - **Asymmetric**
    - Strengths and Weaknesses
- Integrity Checking
- Key Management
- Cryptographic Attacks

29



(ISC)²® SSCP® CBK® Review Seminar v10.0 – Cryptography

## Asymmetric Key Cryptography

- Instead of a single key, there is a "key pair"
  - The two keys are related to each other mathematically
  - One of the keys is kept secret (private key)
  - The other is made available to everyone (public key)
  - It is "computationally infeasible" to derive the private key from the public key

30

- **ASYMMETRIC KEY CRYPTOGRAPHY**, also known as public key cryptography, first became generally known due to the work of Diffie and Hellman in 1976. This type of algorithm uses two keys that are mathematically related as a key pair.
  - The keys work together to perform a complete cryptographic operation. If one half of the key pair is used to encrypt a message, the other half must be used in the decryption process.
  - Because it is computationally infeasible to calculate the value of the private half of the key pair from the other (the public key), the public key can confidently be shared.

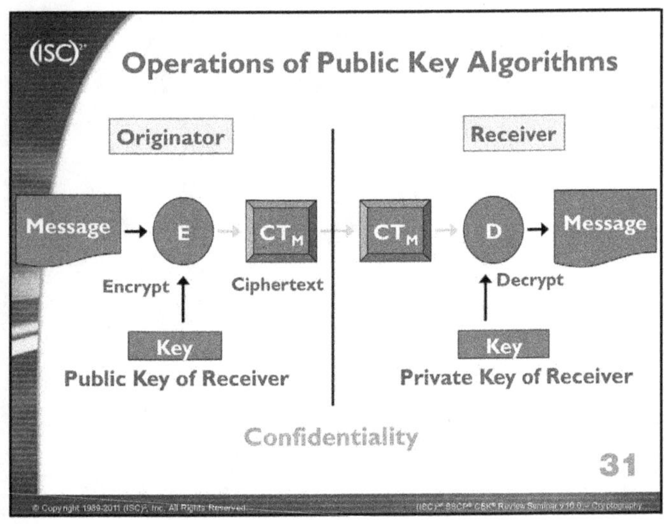


- **OPERATIONS OF PUBLIC KEY ALGORITHMS –** This slide describes a secure message format.
  - **CONFIDENTIALITY –** This slide shows the operations of an asymmetric algorithm that provides for the confidential encryption of a message. Encrypting a message with a public key will prohibit any who does not have the correct private key from viewing (decrypting) it.
  - The shortcoming of this mechanism is that anyone with the receiver's public key can send a message claiming to be anyone. The receiver has no assurance that the purported sender is the actual sender.

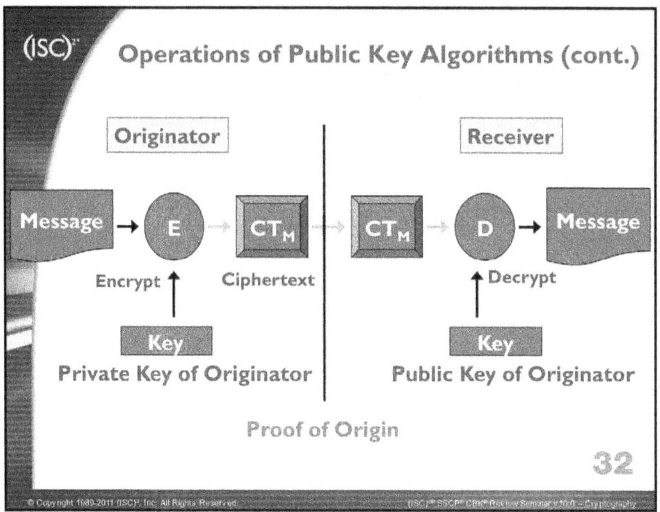


- **OPERATIONS OF PUBLIC KEY ALGORITHMS (CONT.) –** This Slide describes an open message format.
  - **PROOF OF ORIGIN –** If a message is encrypted with the private key of the sender, it can only be opened with the corresponding public key half of the key pair. This assures the receiver that the message did indeed originate with the holder of the private key.
  - The shortcoming here is that anyone who intercepts the message can decrypt it using the sender's public key.

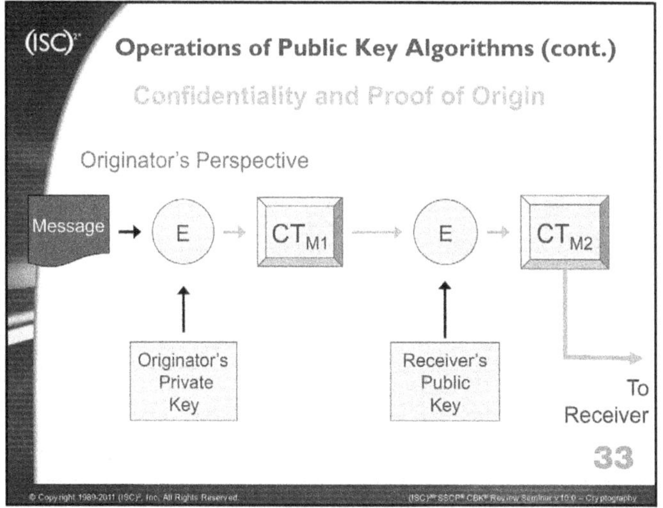


- **CONFIDENTIALITY AND PROOF OF ORIGIN –** Confidentiality and proof of origin – When both confidentiality and proof of origin are needed, use double encryption.
- First encrypt the message with the private key of the sender and then again with the public key of the receiver. This will provide both confidentiality and proof of origin.
- The operations are always done in this order. If they are done in the opposite order, an eavesdropper on the communications link would be able to use the originator's public key to partially decrypt the message. More importantly, the decryption sequence must be the reverse of the encryption sequence, so having a common order of operations makes the system work.

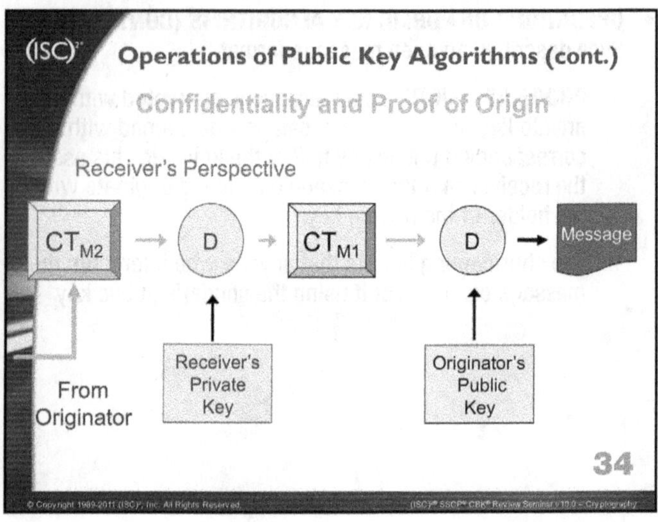


- When the receiver receives the message, he or she must decrypt it in the reverse order that it was encrypted in; first with the private key and then with the public key of the sender.

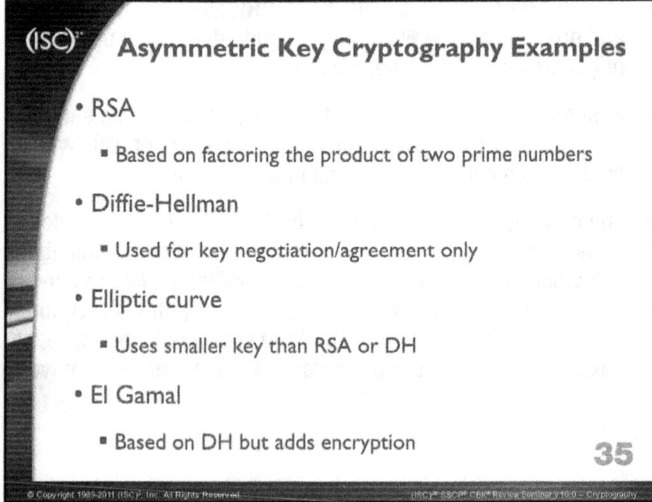


- **ASYMMETRIC KEY CRYPTOGRAPHY EXAMPLES –** These are examples of some of the most common asymmetric key algorithms.
- **RSA –** (Rivest, Shamir, Adleman) is the only asymmetric algorithm based on factoring the product of two large prime numbers. All of the others are based on discrete logs in a finite field.
- **DIFFIE-HELLMAN –** Was the first asymmetric key available that was based on the paper "New Directions in Cryptography." This algorithm is only effective for symmetric key negotiation and cannot be used for data or message encryption. It is frequently called the "Key Agreement Protocol."
- **ELLIPTIC CURVE –** Is the algorithm based on the points on an elliptic curve. It provides very strong cryptographic protection despite having a much smaller key than RSA or DH.
- **EL GAMAL –** An improvement on Diffie-Hellman in that it adds encryption functionality. Unlike the others, it is not patent protected.

## Domain Agenda

- Cryptography Definitions
- Stream and Block Ciphers
- **Algorithms**
  - Symmetric
  - Asymmetric
  - **Strengths and Weaknesses**
- Integrity Checking
- Key Management
- Cryptographic Attacks

36

 (ISC)²® SSCP® CBK® Review Seminar v 10.0 – Cryptography

## Asymmetric Key Cryptography Strengths

- Provides:
  - Encryption (confidentiality)
    - Efficient symmetric key distribution
  - Digital signature services (non-repudiation)
  - Integrity
  - Access control
  - Authentication (proof of origin)

37

 (ISC)²® SSCP® CBK® Review Seminar v 10.0 – Cryptography

- **PROVIDES –** Five elements of security:
- **ENCRYPTION (CONFIDENTIALITY) –** Since a message that has been encrypted with a public key can only be opened with the corresponding private key, the message is, therefore, confidential.
  - **EFFICIENT SYMMETRIC KEY DISTRIBUTION –** One party can generate a symmetric key, encrypt it with the other party's public key, and then transmit it over an insecure medium. An eavesdropper will not be able to discover the key, but the intended recipient will be able to decrypt it easily.
- **DIGITAL SIGNATURE SERVICES (NON-REPUDIATION) –** If the sender uses his or her private key to "sign" a message or creates a digital signature by encrypting a hash of the message with the private key, the receiver has proof of origin, or non-repudiation of the message. Since the message was encrypted with the sender's private key (that only the sender knows), the sender cannot deny (repudiate) sending it.
- **INTEGRITY –** Most asymmetric algorithms have built-in functionality to validate message integrity. Quite often this is done by a message digest, a hash, or the creation of digital signatures. Comparing the hash sent by the sender with a hash of the received message verifies whether the message sent was the same as the one received.
- **ACCESS CONTROL –** We can be sure that only the people intended are able to read a message because they are the only ones who have the necessary private key.
- **AUTHENTICATION (PROOF OF ORIGIN) –** The identity of the sender is verified when he or she uses his or her private key to encrypt the data or a hash of the data because only his or her public key will be able to decrypt it.

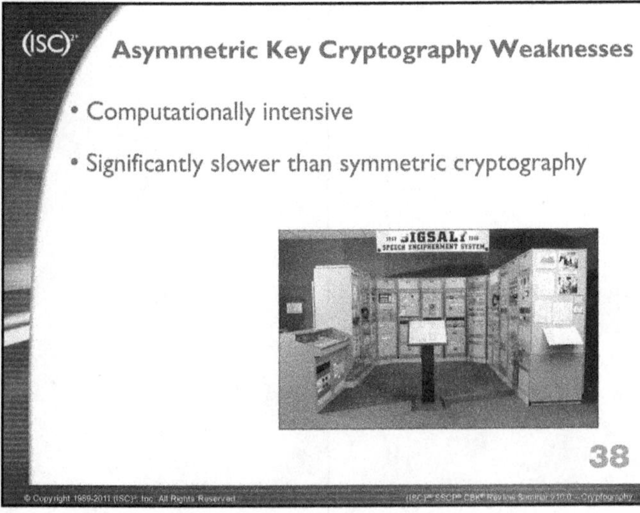

(ISC)²
Asymmetric Key Cryptography Weaknesses
• Computationally intensive
• Significantly slower than symmetric cryptography
SIGSALY
38


- **ASYMMETRIC KEY CRYPTOGRAPHY WEAKNESSES –** Because of the heavy mathematical requirements, asymmetric key cryptography is very slow.
- The device shown in this slide is one of the earliest devices used for secure (encrypted) voice communications. Courtesy of the NSA Cryptographic Museum, Fort Meade, Maryland.

(ISC)²

## Symmetric Key Cryptography Strengths

- Very fast - allows large amounts of data to be encrypted in a relatively short time
- Very difficult - to break the confidentiality of data encrypted with large keys
- Availability - algorithms and tools used for symmetric encryption are freely available

39

- **SYMMETRIC KEY CRYPTOGRAPHY STRENGTHS –** The speed advantage is relative to asymmetric cryptography. Using any cryptography is obviously slower than not using any at all.

(ISC)²

## Symmetric Key Cryptography Weaknesses

- Scalability
  - Sender and receiver must have a confidential and authenticated method for distributing keys
  - Since a unique symmetric key must be used between the sender and each recipient, the number of keys grows exponentially with the number of users: n (n-1)/2 (where n is the number of users)
    - ➢ 10 users = 45 keys
    - ➢ 1,000 users = 499,500 keys

40

 (ISC)² SSCP® CBK® Review Seminar v10.0 – Cryptography

- **SCALABILITY –** Is the ability to change a solution to meet the size of the problem. In the case of symmetric algorithms, this is a serious problem, since the problem of key management grows rapidly as the number of users increases.
  - Since each person needs a secret key to talk confidentially to each party, the number of keys required is determined as follows: n(n-1)/2, where n is equal to the number of users.

(ISC)²

## Symmetric Key Cryptography Weaknesses (cont.)

- Limited security
  - Only encrypt and restrict access to data
  - Do not provide proof of origin or non-repudiation

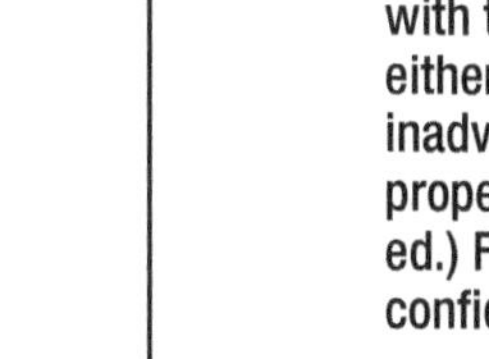

41

 (ISC)² SSCP® CBK® Review Seminar v10.0 – Cryptography

- **SYMMETRIC KEY CRYPTOGRAPHY WEAKNESSES (CONT.) –**
  - **ONLY ENCRYPT AND RESTRICT ACCESS TO DATA –** Although symmetric encryption provides both confidentiality and integrity (when used as CBC-MAC), any person with the key is able to change and re-encrypt a message either en route or after it has been received. (A message inadvertently corrupted while in transit would not decrypt properly and loss of integrity would, therefore, be detected.) Furthermore, if the key is compromised, you lose both confidentiality and integrity.
  - **DO NOT PROVIDE PROOF OF ORIGIN OR NON-REPUDIATION –** Because all parties in a communication share the same key, there is no non-repudiation possible. A symmetric algorithm restricts access to the key holders, but it does not provide any tracking of who among the individuals with the same key was the last one to access the file. This restricts the ability to hold any one key holder responsible for changes to the stored file.
- The photo shown is "The Bombe," which was the device used by the Allies to attack Enigma messages in the World War II. Photo courtesy of the National Security Agency (NSA) Cryptographic Museum, Fort Meade, Maryland.

(ISC)²

## Hybrid Systems

- Symmetric algorithms
  - Fast and strong (given sufficiently long keys)
  - But poor at key management
- Asymmetric algorithms
  - Good at key management
  - But terribly slow

42

 (ISC)² SSCP® CBK® Review Seminar v 10.0 – Cryptography

- **HYBRID SYSTEMS –** As we have seen, we have symmetric key cryptography algorithms that are very fast and strong (given sufficiently long keys) but are really bad at key management, and we have asymmetric key algorithms that are really good at key management, but are terribly slow. Real-world systems are usually hybrids that use the strengths of each technology.
- **SYMMETRIC ALGORITHMS –**
  - The data (message) is encrypted with the symmetric key for the sake of speed, and the symmetric key is sent to the receiver by encrypting it with the receiver's public key.
  - Since the receiver's public key is used to encrypt the symmetric key, the receiver is the only person who can decrypt it because the receiver's private key is the only one that can decrypt anything encrypted using the receiver's public key.
- **ASYMMETRIC ALGORITHMS –**
  - Even though asymmetric encryption is slow, the relatively small amount of data to be encrypted (keys are a few dozen to a few hundred bits) does not create a performance problem.
  - Digital signatures also provide for non-repudiation. Some national governments (and also some states in the United States) have passed legislation making digital signatures the equivalent of notarization.

(ISC)²

## Hybrid Systems (cont.)

- Hybrids will use each technology where it is best suited
  - Symmetric key algorithm for bulk data encryption
  - Asymmetric key algorithm for automated key distribution

43

 (ISC)² SSCP® CBK® Review Seminar v 10.0 – Cryptography

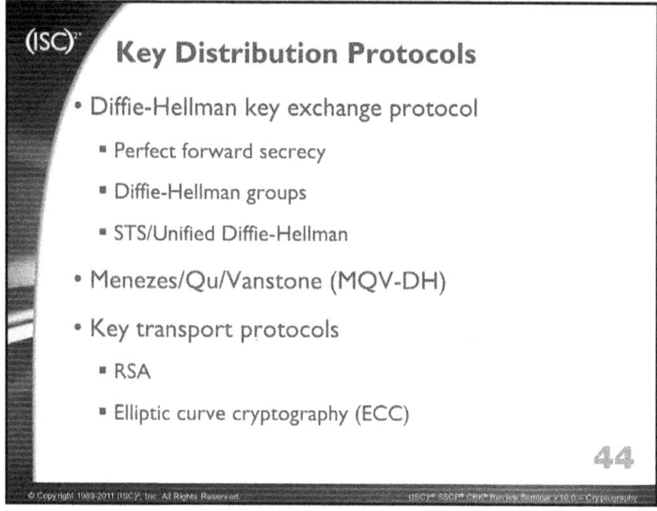

(ISC)²
Key Distribution Protocols
Diffie-Hellman key exchange protocol
Perfect forward secrecy
Diffie-Hellman groups
STS/Unified Diffie-Hellman
Menezes/Qu/Vanstone (MQV-DH)
Key transport protocols
RSA
Elliptic curve cryptography (ECC)
44


- **DIFFIE-HELLMAN KEY EXCHANGE PROTOCOL –** The first public-key cryptosystem (1976). It allows two entities to negotiate a session key that can be used to exchange secret information, without ever revealing their private keys. The patent expired in 1997.
  - **PERFECT FORWARD SECRECY –** Often called forward secrecy, PFS is the principle used in D-H that even if two private keys are used in negotiating a secret value (shared secret) as in Diffie-Hellman, and one of those private keys is later compromised, it will not be possible to determine either the secret key or the other private key from the knowledge of the compromised private key.
  - **DIFFIE-HELLMAN GROUPS –** D-H groups determine the length of the base prime numbers that will be used in calculating the key pairs. This is important to ensure a strong implementation of D-H for TLS, IKE, and S/MIME, since a longer key is much stronger than a short key.
  - **STS/UNIFIED DIFFIE-HELLMAN –** One weakness with D-H was the man-in-the-middle attack, where a person could impersonate either of the two end parties and intercept their communications. This led to the development of the station to station key agreement protocol (STS) by Diffie, Van Oorscht, and Weiner in 1992. This used public key certificates to authenticate the end parties. This is known as Unified Diffie-Hellmann.
- **MENEZES/QU/VANSTONE (MQV-DH) –** MQV is an enhancement to Diffie-Hellman and can provide AUTHENTICATED key agreement. The principle of MQV is to use trusted public keys (by exchanging digital certificates) to authenticate prior to initiating the key exchange process.
- **KEY TRANSPORT PROTOCOLS –** When using RSA or elliptic curve cryptography (ECC) for key negotiation, the symmetric (session) key is encrypted using the receiver's PUBLIC key. Once received, the receiver decrypts and installs the session key using its PRIVATE RSA or ECC key. ECC is much more efficient than RSA and is becoming the de facto standard (it was released as part of NSA's Suite B Crypto Modernization initiative in 2005).

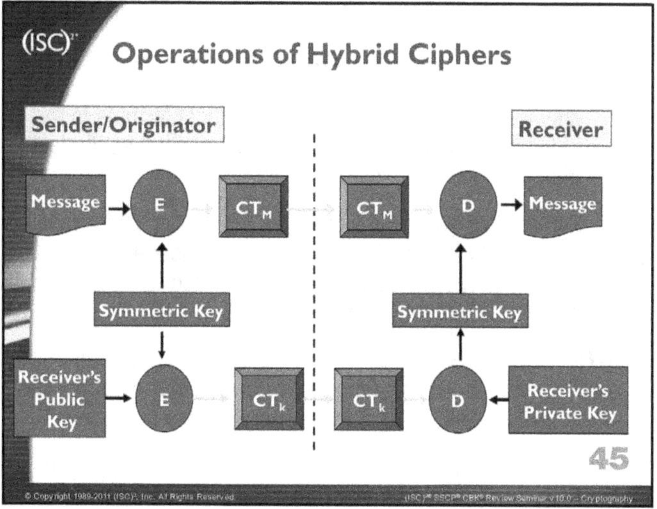


- **OPERATIONS OF HYBRID CIPHERS –** Encrypt the message with the symmetric key and use the receiver's public key to encrypt and send the symmetric key.
- The receiver needs the same key to decrypt the message. In our earlier example, we discussed passing the symmetric key to the receiver via "out of band" messaging, but we can use the advantages of asymmetric cryptography to send the symmetric key (which we would probably call a session key in this example) to the recipient.

(ISC)²

## Domain Agenda

- Cryptography Definitions
- Stream and Block Ciphers
- Algorithms
  - Symmetric
  - Asymmetric
  - Strengths and Weaknesses
- **Integrity Checking**
- Key Management
- Cryptographic Attacks

46



(ISC)² SSCP® CBK® Review Seminar v.10.0 – Cryptography

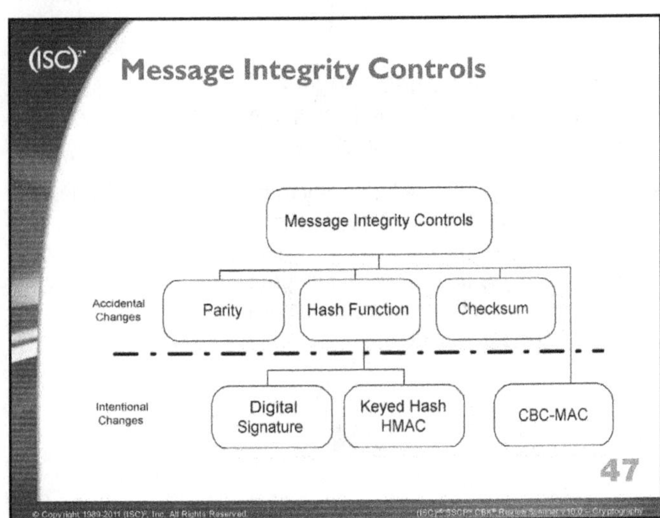


- **MESSAGE INTEGRITY CONTROLS –** This is a diagram illustrating a variety of integrity functions to show where the cryptographic functions fit in.
- **ACCIDENTAL ERRORS –** There are three basic examples of integrity controls (parity, checksum, hash) which can protect against accidental errors (i.e., a bit flipped in a network transmission) but that are unable to prevent a determined attacker from altering both the message and the integrity control.
  - **PARITY –** Is based on adding an extra bit to a single byte. (An eight bit is typically added to seven data bits.) The last bit will be a 1 or a 0 depending on whether the total number of 1s in the byte is even (for even parity) or odd (for odd parity). If the receiver calculates the parity and it is wrong (e.g., an odd number of 1s in an even parity system) then the receiver will know that the byte was not transmitted correctly. Note that double-bit errors (such as transposition of two bits) cannot be detected via parity.
  - **CHECKSUM –** Is more complex and can detect transposition and coding errors. (Credit card numbers all have a checksum.) Banks apply a mathematical formula to the individual digits and record part of the result as the last digit or digits of the card number.
  - **HASH FUNCTION –** Is a complex mathematical formula that results in a relatively long result. There are several different popular hashing formulas in use today (see next slide) with lengths ranging from 128 to 512 bits.
- **INTENTIONAL CHANGES –** To protect against an intentional integrity attack, use one of the three choices in the bottom row. The hash is protected by adding encryption to the process.
  - **DIGITAL SIGNATURE –** Uses asymmetric encryption to "sign" (encrypt) the hash/digest of the message, using the signer's PRIVATE key.
  - **KEYED HASH HMAC –** HMAC (hash message authentication code) often uses a symmetric key as secret input to a standard cryptographic hash and appends the hash to each frame of a message in transit.
  - **CBC-MAC –** Cipher Block Chaining Message Authentication Code uses symmetric encryption to encrypt a MAC (or hash) but is slower than an HMAC.

**REFERENCE**

Cryptography Decrypted, by H. X. Mel, RFC 2828, and Applied Cryptography by Bruce Schneier.

(ISC)²

## Hash Function

- Condenses a message of any length into a digest, or fixed-sized value that represents the message
- Any alteration to the original message will cause a dramatic change in the digest value, thus providing message integrity

48



(ISC)² SSCP® CBK® Review Seminar v10.0 – Cryptography

- **HASH FUNCTION –** The primary purpose of a hashing algorithm is to prove whether a message has been altered.
    - The hashed message can be of any length.
    - Two common uses of hashes are to store passwords (short), and to verify that a disk drive has not changed since it was acquired in order for it to be admissible in court (very large).
- Hashing algorithms by themselves only show accidental changes, such as a bit lost in transit. Checking for intentional changes involve other solutions in which hashing is just one of several steps involved.
- The math behind these algorithms is well beyond the scope of the SSCP. However, an important characteristic of a properly designed hashing algorithm is that even a single bit change in the message will result in at least 40% of the bits in the hash changing.

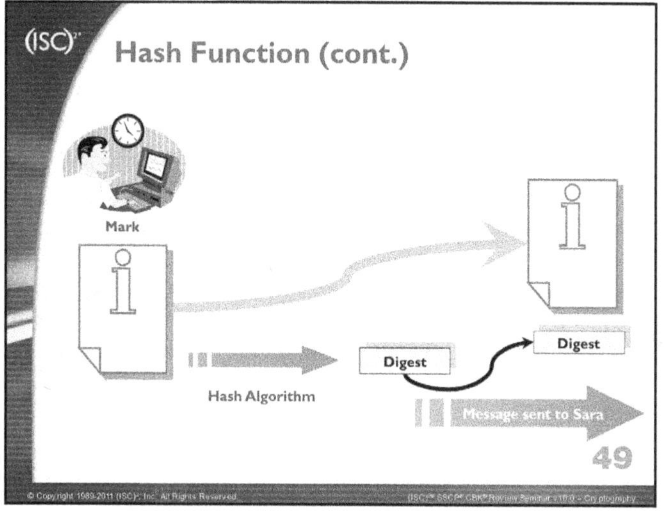


- **HASH FUNCTION (CONT.) –** The word "hash" is a verb or adverb. The result of an algorithm that hashes is the noun "message digest," often shortened to "digest."
- In its most basic form, a digest is created for a message and the pair are then sent to a recipient.

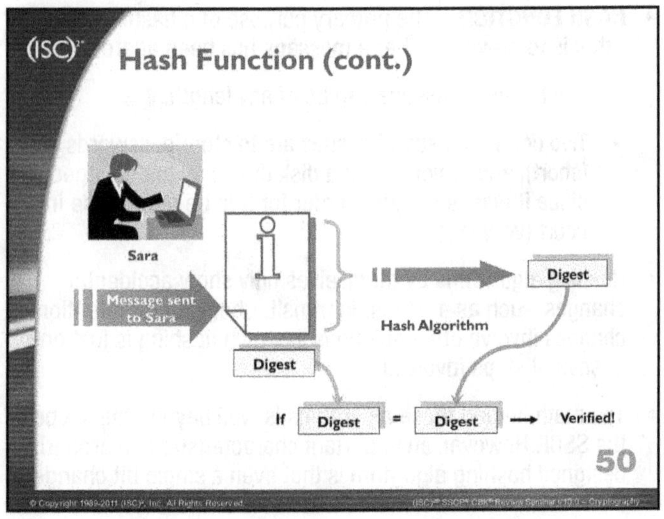


- **HASH FUNCTION (CONT.) –** The receiver calculates a digest from the message received. If the digest corresponds to the message digest sent along with the message (which was calculated from the original message), the receiver can be assured that there were no accidental changes to the message.
- Hashing has nothing to do with the confidentiality of the message. The message can be sent as plaintext or as ciphertext, depending on the needs of the situation.
- When confidentiality is desired, the hash is calculated on the plaintext and then the message is encrypted. The receiver will decrypt before hashing the resulting plaintext and comparing hashes.

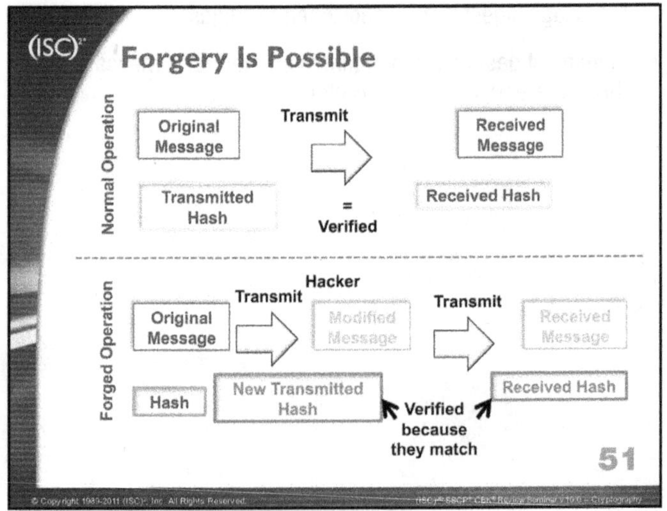


- **NORMAL OPERATION –** A message is created and hashed. The message and its digest are transmitted to a recipient who calculates a hash on the received message and compares it with the received hash. If they match, the recipient assumes that the message is unchanged.
- **FORGED OPERATION –** A message is created and hashed. An intruder anywhere along the path to the recipient intercepts the message, modifies it, and creates a new hash based on the modified content. The recipient calculates a hash on the received message and compares it with the received hash. If they match, the recipient assumes that the message is unchanged.
  - It is also possible for the recipient to change the message and create a new hash, and then falsely claim that the stored message on his or her machine is the original.
  - HMAC uses a hash function together with a secret key value shared between the sender and receiver. The use of the secret value means that the hacker in the middle cannot create a new hash value that will be the same as the hash value of the modified message when combined with the secret key at the far end.

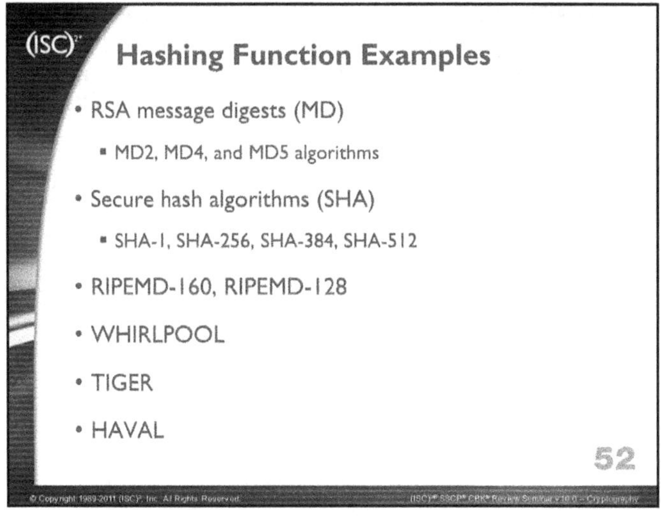


- **RSA MESSAGE DIGESTS (MD) –** were developed by Ron Rivest of RSA Security.
  - **MD2, MD4, AND MD5 ALGORITHMS –**
• RIPEMD-160, RIPEMD-128
    - **MD2** and **MD5** both produce fixed-length digests of 128 bits. MD2 is the slowest.
    - **MESSAGE DIGEST 5 (MD5)** replaced **MD4**, which was compromised. (Some partially successful cryptoanalytic attacks on MD4 were reported.) There are weaknesses in the current MD5. A short-term replacement is **HMAC-MD5**. HMAC is an enhanced method for calculating hashed message authentication codes that greatly increases the crypto strength of the underlying algorithm.
- **SECURE HASH ALGORITHMS (SHA) –** SHA-1 is one of four standard hashing algorithms in FIPS 180-2, and at 160 bits it is considered too short. It has been replaced with SHA-256, -384, and -512.
  - **SHA-256, SHA-384**, and **SHA-512** were created to resist birthday attacks. To defeat a birthday attack, hash functions need to use a message digest length twice that of the matching symmetric key function. SHA-256 was, therefore, created to be a partner for AES-128. Birthday attacks are discussed in more detail in the cryptanalysis section later in this domain.
  - US NIST is running another competition (much like the competition for AES) to develop and certify a new hash standard (SHA-3). Completion is expected by the end of the decade.
- **RIPEMD –** RACE integrity primitives evaluation message digest. Developed in Belgium in the 1990s. Like HAVAL, RIPEMD is available in a variety of hash lengths (128-bit, 160-bit, 256-bit, 320-bit). The original RIPEMD sets were fashioned after the traditional MD4 algorithm. Later versions of RIPEMD (such as RIPEMD-160) are generally recognized as being stronger functions than their predecessors but are still not as widely used as SHA.
- **WHIRLPOOL –** Adopted by the ISO and IEC standards' bodies after its development in 2000 for the NESSIE (New European Schemes for Signatures, Integrity and Encryption) project. It has since undergone two revisions that have strengthened the algorithm. The WHIRLPOOL function returns a 128-bit hexadecimal hash.
- **TIGER –** Created in 1996 and designed for speed on 64-bit machines. Tiger and Tiger 2 outputs are represented as 48-bit hexadecimal hashes. The Tiger algorithm uses 24 rounds and incorporates intricate functions of rotations, S-Box lookups, operation mixing with XOR, and addition/subtraction. The full 24-round function currently has no known/published weaknesses or collisions.
- **HAVAL –** Created in 1992. HAVAL differs from most widely-accepted hash algorithms in that it can produce a variety of hash output lengths (128 bits, 160 bits, 192 bits, 224 bits, and 256 bits) and allows users to specify the number of rounds (3, 4, or 5) used to generate the hash. Note that some vulnerabilities (collisions) have been found in the 128-bit, 3-round version of HAVAL.

**REFERENCE:**

NIST, and Practical Cryptography, by Ferguson & Schneier.

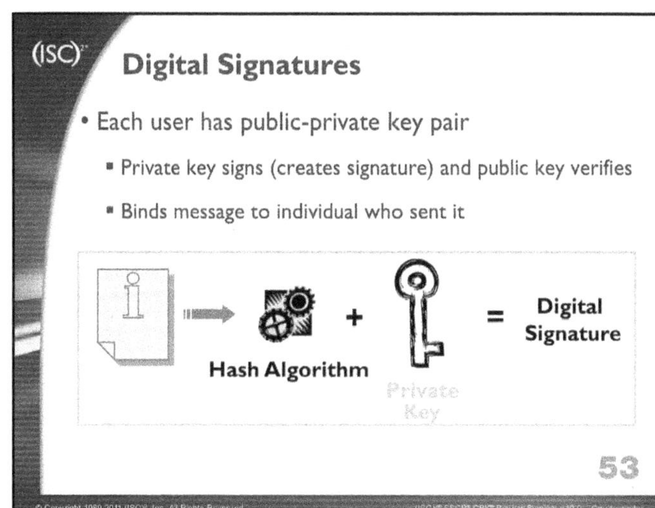

(ISC)²
Hashing Function Examples
Digital Signatures
• Each user has public-private key pair
▪ Private key signs (creates signature) and public key verifies
▪ Binds message to individual who sent it
Hash Algorithm
+
=
Digital Signature
Private Key
53


- **DIGITAL SIGNATURES –** A digital signature is created by encrypting a hash of a message with the private digital signature key of the sender. An eavesdropper or intruder might be able to read the message if it were not encrypted, but would not be able to modify the message and then recreate the digital signature.
- Because only the matching public key can decrypt (validate the digital signature), the recipient can prove that the message received is the same as the one the sender transmitted. This is the digital equivalent of a notary public.

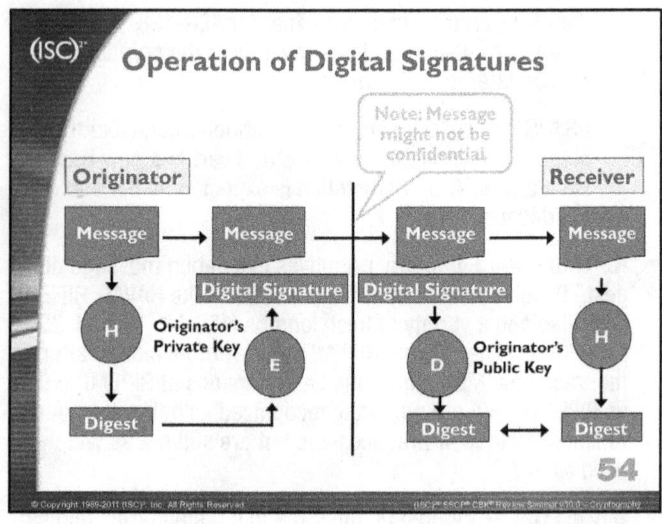


- **OPERATION OF DIGITAL SIGNATURES –** The recipient verifies the digital signature by opening it with the sender's public key. This allows the recipient to compare the digest embedded in the digital signature with a new digest that is created from the received message.
- This provides both non-repudiation (since we know that the message must have been sent by the holder of the private key) and message authentication (since any change in the message would have been made obvious by mismatched digest values).

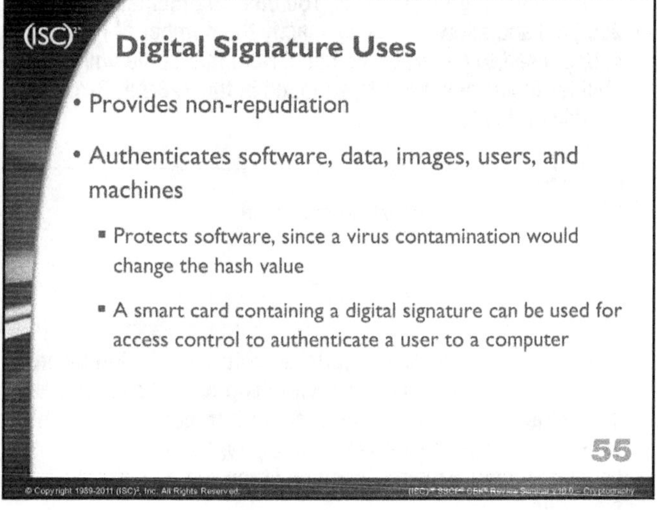


- **PROVIDES NON-REPUDIATION –** In paper-based systems, transactions are recorded in ink on non-erasable documents. Special papers have been developed that display certain indicators if they are modified. To prevent an individual from denying having engaged in a paper-based transaction, procedures have been established to verify individual signatures, keep duplicate copies of transactions, and entrust third parties with the adjudication of disputes. Digital signatures move this concept to the digital age.

(ISC)²

# Domain Agenda

- Cryptography Definitions
- Stream and Block Ciphers
- Algorithms
  - Symmetric
  - Asymmetric
  - Strengths and Weaknesses
- Integrity Checking
- **Key Management**
- Cryptographic Attacks

56



(ISC)²® SSCP® CBK® Review Seminar v10.0 – Cryptography

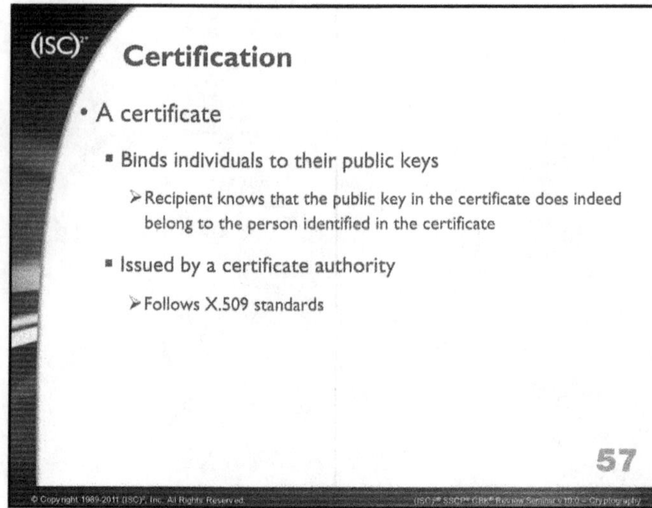

Certification
• A certificate
▪ Binds individuals to their public keys
➢ Recipient knows that the public key in the certificate does indeed belong to the person identified in the certificate
▪ Issued by a certificate authority
➢ Follows X.509 standards
57


- **CERTIFICATION –** There are Web servers on the Internet called "key ring servers." Perhaps the most famous is at MIT and is used for pretty good privacy (PGP – and now GNU-PGP) keys. Anyone can submit a public key to that server. The problem for other users is verifying that the key that purports to belong to an individual really does belong to that person.
  - The key might be an intentional forgery.
  - Because the key is issued in the applicant's name, the public key could belong to anyone of that name. For example, the author of this page lives in Pennsylvania, and is aware of a dentist in Arkansas with the same name. Both of us could legitimately add a public key to the MIT server and no one would be sure to which of us a particular key belonged.
- **BINDS INDIVIDUALS TO THEIR PUBLIC KEYS –** To solve this problem, independent third party companies were formed that tie a particular individual to a particular key. They are known as certification authorities (CA) and they produce (naturally!) certificates.
- **ISSUED BY A CERTIFICATE AUTHORITY –** It is also possible for companies to create their own CA and use it internally. This has the advantage of saving on the fees charged by the public CAs and, more importantly, allows the creation of certificates that only authorized users within that company are able to obtain.
  - The difficulty: We need to be sure that the public key we obtain for an individual really does belong to that individual. If it doesn't, an intruder could substitute his or her public key for that of the intended receiver, digitally sign a forged message purportedly from an authorized person (i.e., someone able to place a large order), which would be verified using the imposter's public key. The intruder (man-in-the-middle) could read the message (violating confidentiality), change it (violating integrity), and forward it on to the intended recipient using the intended recipient's public key.
  - Certification is the process by which some person or entity recognized to be in a position of trust (i.e., the certification authority) uses its own private key to sign a small digital record called the certificate, which couples an individual's public key to the individual's name. Each certificate contains: the name of the certification authority, the public key being certified, the name of the owner of the public key, a unique serial number for this certificate as assigned by the certification authority, and the beginning and ending dates for which this certificate is valid. The recipient of a digitally signed electronic document relies upon the digital certificate to confirm the relationship between the public key and the identity of the party who has digitally signed the electronic document.
  - The concept of a certification authority is specified in the International Telecommunications Union (ITU) X.509 portion of the X.500 (directory) standard, which is an internationally recognized format that defines public-key certificates. New certificates are issued as version 4, but most sites will continue to use their existing version 3 certificates until they have to be renewed.

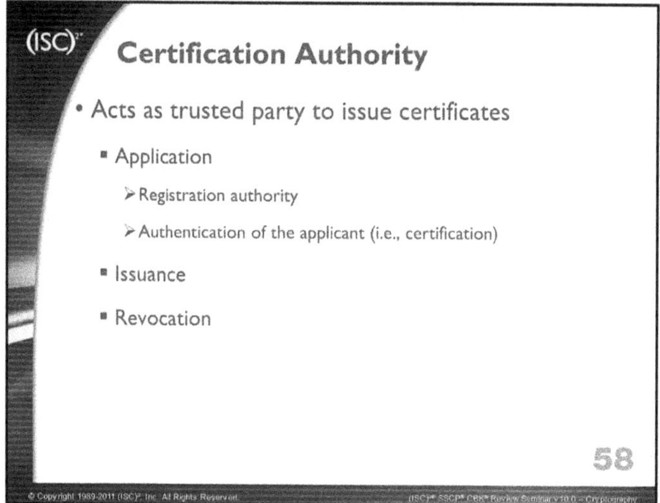


- **CERTIFICATION AUTHORITY –** A certification authority (CA) is a trusted entity or third party, the central responsibility of which is certifying the authenticity of users, much like a passport-issuing office in a government. A passport is a citizen's secure document, issued by an appropriate authority, that certifies that the citizen is who he/she claims to be. Any country trusting the authority of the first country's government's passport office will trust the citizen's passport. This is a good example of "third party trust." Third party trust refers to a situation in which two entities or individuals implicitly trust each other, even though they have not previously established a business or personal relationship. In this situation, the two parties implicitly trust each other because they share a relationship with a common third party, and that third party vouches for the trustworthiness of the first two parties.
  - A certificate then, is a network user's electronic equivalent of a passport. It contains information that can be used to verify the identity of the owner. A critical piece of information contained in a user's certificate is the owner's public key.
- **APPLICATION –** A CA manages digital certificate application, certification (authentication of the applicant), issuance, and revocation. In this role, it is often known as a registration authority (RA).
- **ISSUANCE –** A CA needs to validate an applicant's identity before issuing a digital certificate. Suppose our applicant is Mark. Once the CA has identified Mark's identity, the CA will issue a certificate containing Mark's public key. The digital certificate is like a traditional letter of introduction; it effectively says, 'I, the CA, hereby identify Mark and assert that this is really Mark's public key.'
- **REVOCATION –** Revocation is required when the user loses exclusive possession of the private key (compromised) or leaves the organization (trust is no longer desired). Certificate revocation is done by placing invalid certificates on a certificate revocation list (CRL). This list can be checked to see if the certificate provided by a website or user is still valid.

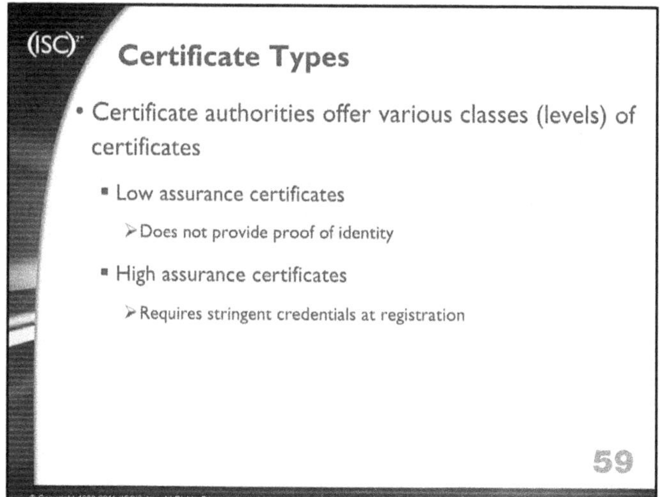


- **CERTIFICATE AUTHORITIES OFFER VARIOUS CLASSES (LEVELS) OF CERTIFICATES –** Most CAs offer various classes of digital certificates depending on the certifying documents the applicant submits, the amount of verification the CA does to prove the identity of the applicant, and the fee paid to the CA.
  - Certificates are issued by classes:
    - Class 1 is for individuals, generally for email.
    - Class 2 is for organizations where the purpose is to prove the identity of the organization (via trusted third party).
    - Class 3 is for software signing (these do not expire) or for servers where proof of identity is required.
    - Class 4 is for e-commerce (both consumer-to-business and business-to-business).
    - Class 5 is for governments and multinational organizations.

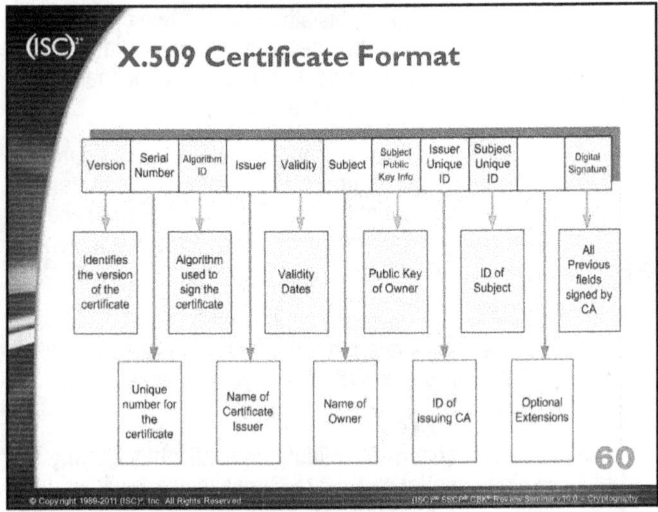


- **X.509 CERTIFICATE FORMAT –** Shows the usual contents of a digital certificate. Note that the certificate is protected from modification by being signed with the digital signature of the CA.

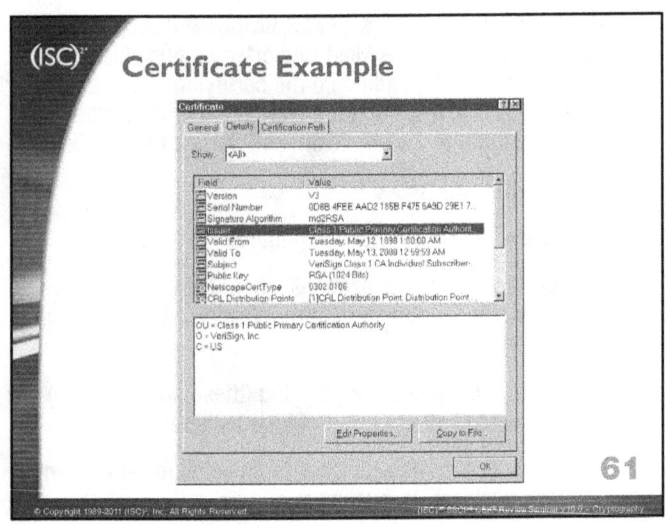


- **CERTIFICATE EXAMPLE –** Actual example of a digital certificate. You can see these by clicking on the "lock" icon on a secure webpage. The digital certificate allows the user to verify that he or she is at the correct site rather than at a phishing site pretending to be the genuine site.
- All of today's browsers do a certain amount of checking of validity dates, digital signatures, and domain names. However, it is still rare to find that people check to see if a certificate has been revoked.

(ISC)²

## Public Key Infrastructure (PKI)

- A security infrastructure the services of which are delivered and implemented using public key concepts
- Provides the foundation necessary for secure e–business through the use of cryptographic keys and digital certificates
  - Enables secure electronic transactions
  - Enables the exchange of sensitive information

62

 (ISC)² SSCP® CBK® Review Seminar v10.0 – Cryptography

- **PUBLIC KEY INFRASTRUCTURE (PKI) –** Doing business electronically allows for new revenue-generating services and lowers the cost of doing business. The same security must be provided for electronic services as are provided in the paper-based world. Security must provide five important capabilities, discussed on the next Slide.
- The most common infrastructure using PKI today is SSL (secure sockets layer). Other PKIs operate within companies and agencies to provide access control (e.g., common access cards (CACs) for U.S. Department of Defense workers).

(ISC)²

## Public Key Infrastructure (PKI) (cont.)

- For electronic business transactions, PKI provides:
  - Confidentiality
  - Access control
  - Integrity
  - Authentication
  - Non-repudiation services

63

 (ISC)² SSCP® CBK® Review Seminar v10.0 – Cryptography

- Use of cryptography (e.g., asymmetric, symmetric, and hashing algorithms) provides all of these features. However, secure key distribution is a complex problem. The various PKI solutions all provide alternatives to this difficulty.

(ISC)²

## Key Management Activities

- Key generation
  - Should be automated
    - For key discipline and secrecy
  - Closed and trusted process
  - Choose keys randomly from entire key space
    - Pattern can be exploited by attacker to reduce effort

64



(ISC)² SSCP® CBK® Review Seminar v10.0 – Cryptography

- **KEY MANAGEMENT ACTIVITIES –** The security of a cryptographic algorithm depends on the security of the key, not on the secrecy of the algorithm (Kerkoff's Principle).
- **KEY GENERATION –**
  - **SHOULD BE AUTOMATED –** Because users often generate keys from predictable values (i.e., birthdays).
  - **CLOSED AND TRUSTED PROCESS –** To ensure that others cannot learn the key and to prevent "man-in-the-middle" attacks.
  - **CHOOSE KEYS RANDOMLY FROM THE ENTIRE KEY SPACE –** To prevent the guessing of keys by exploiting patterns or the brute forcing of a small number of possible keys.

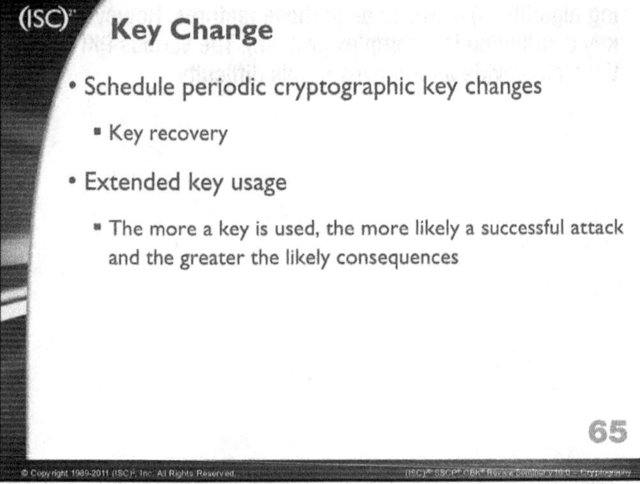

(ISC)²
Key Change
Schedule periodic cryptographic key changes
Key recovery
Extended key usage
The more a key is used, the more likely a successful attack and the greater the likely consequences
65


- **SCHEDULE PERIODIC CRYPTOGRAPHIC KEY CHANGES –** Keys should be changed frequently so that an attacker who learns a key will not be able to continue to read messages.
  - **KEY RECOVERY –** A lost key means lost data. Key escrow (i.e., keeping a copy of the key with a trusted party) is, therefore, a good practice. Companies should insist that all keys be available in case (for example) an employee is injured, and the company needs access to the employee's account. Companies cannot depend on employees to consistently, voluntarily follow this rule. They must deploy automated systems that record keys in a secure location whenever they are changed.
- **EXTENDED KEY USAGE –** The more a key is used, the more susceptible it becomes to attack. Keys should, therefore, be used cautiously and digital signature keys or keys used to encrypt very sensitive data should not be used for other purposes.

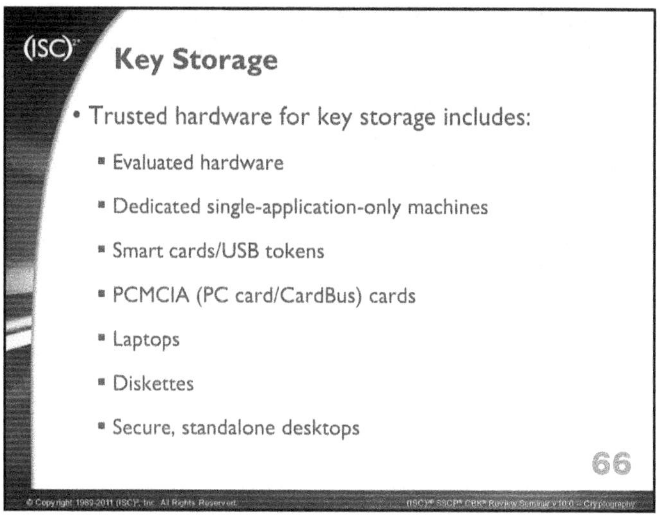


- **KEY STORAGE –** Key storage hardware is listed in decreasing order of trust/preference.
  - **EVALUATED HARDWARE –** Many third parties (such as Common Criteria evaluation labs) will have examined the hardware on which the key is stored and will certify that it performs as promised.
  - **DEDICATED SINGLE-APPLICATION-ONLY MACHINES –** Such as those from Atalla, BBN, Cylink, and Zergo. As a general rule, the use of multiuser systems is discouraged for key storage except for storing keys that are the property of the system owner or manager (i.e., the payroll manager key). As the number of users who can legitimately access a machine increases, the security of the data stored on that machine decreases. The best case is a machine that is dedicated to one task and is only accessible by those who are performing that task.
  - **SMART CARDS/USB TOKENS –** Keys can be stored on these devices in such a way as to prevent extraction. In addition, most or all of the encryption can be done on the smart card CPU.
  - **PCMCIA (PC CARD/CARDBUS) CARDS –** Are similar to smart cards in that they can be made such that it is almost impossible to remove the keys. The difference is that these have no CPU.
  - **LAPTOPS –** Laptops can store keys, and with proper precautions it is not easy for an intruder to extract the key. This is not as good an alternative as the previous examples though.
  - **DISKETTES –** Diskettes are easily portable and stolen, which makes key storage on diskettes risky. Diskettes can, however, be stored in a secure container, such as a safe, and thus used to back up keys.
  - **STANDALONE DESKTOPS –** These have all of the shortcomings of a laptop without the benefit of easy secure container storage.

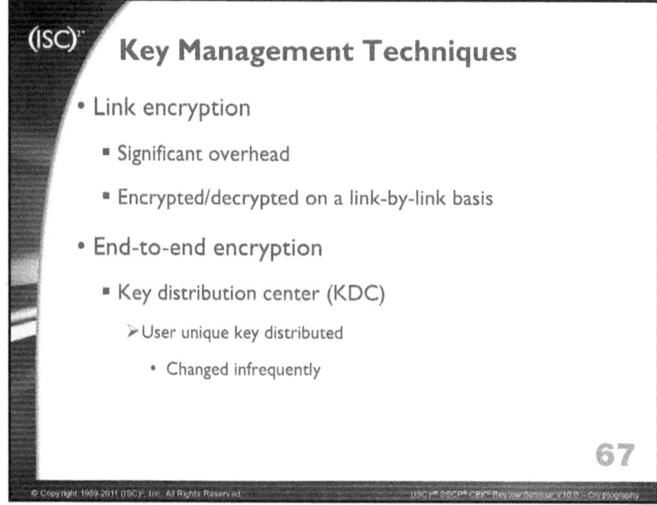


- **KEY MANAGEMENT TECHNIQUES –** These key management techniques are appropriate for symmetric key systems, usually for networks with many nodes.
- **LINK ENCRYPTION –** Each user has only one key, which is used for communicating with a local network node. Each node has a key in common with each neighboring node. The message is decrypted and re-encrypted as it passes through each successive node using the key common to the two nodes. Note, however, that the compromise of any node on the network will result in the compromise of all messages passing through it. In military networks where each node is a physically secure facility staffed by cleared personnel, link encryption is an attractive solution to the key distribution problem. It is much less attractive for a commercial network with a smaller budget whose nodes may be unmanned. Some commercial networks even place nodes on their customer's property in cities where they have no facilities of their own, but in this sort of an arrangement, link encryption would provide little protection.
  - The most common uses of link encryption today are wireless security methods such as WEP, WPA, etc.
  - Link encryption operates at the data-link layer and can, therefore, hide the network layer addressing information.
- **END-TO-END ENCRYPTION –** The protection of information passed in a telecommunications system by cryptographic means from the point of origin to the point of destination. This requires a session key for use between the origin and the destination and a key distribution center (KDC) to provide the session key to both parties.
  - The KDC shares a unique key with each user.
  - Network-layer data must remain unencrypted with end-to-end encryption so that Layer 3 devices (routers) can make appropriate forwarding decisions.

(ISC)²

## Schneier's 10 Risks of PKI

1. Who do we trust, and for what?
2. Who is using my key?
3. How secure is the verifying computer?
4. Which John Robinson is he?
5. Is the CA [certificate authority] an authority?
6. Is the user part of the security design?
7. Was it one CA or a CA plus a registration authority [RA]?
8. How did the CA identify the certificate holder?
9. How secure are the certificate practices?
10. Why are we using the CA process, anyway?

68




- **SCHNEIER'S 10 RISKS OF PKI –** A good list of the concerns related to public key infrastructure (PKI) from a world-renowned expert in the field of cryptography and author of several excellent books on security and cryptography *(Applied Cryptography, Secrets and Lies, Beyond Fear)*, the creator of the TwoFish and Blowfish algorithms, and the author of the monthly "Crypto Gram" newsletter.

**REFERENCE:**

http://www.schneier.com

(ISC)²

## Domain Agenda

- Cryptography Definitions
- Stream and Block Ciphers
- Algorithms
  - Symmetric
  - Asymmetric
  - Strengths and Weaknesses
- Integrity Checking
- Key Management
- **Cryptographic Attacks**

69

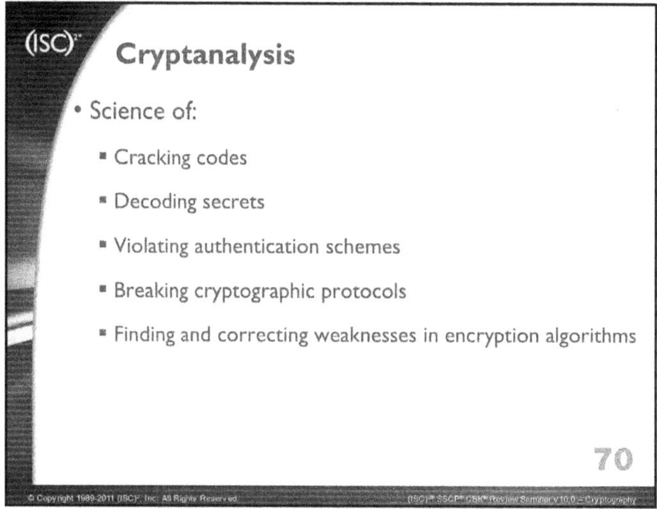


- **CRYPTANALYSIS –** Cryptanalysis is often used in information-warfare applications, for example, when forging encrypted signals. Competitors that learn the key used by another organization may use this to their advantage. They can decrypt messages to gain information or even use the key to send "authenticated" messages to the compromised organization in order to access confidential data. They might also pretend to be the source in order to send bogus information to others.
- While the techniques shown will be discussed generally over the next several slides, these are the overall objectives of cryptanalytic activities:
  - Cracking codes or decoding secrets might be accomplished by brute force to obtain keys or through analysis of the behavior of the algorithm.
  - Attacks such as man-in-the-middle could be employed to compromise an otherwise authenticated communication session between two parties. Birthday attacks could be used to discover or create counterfeit values that could be used to replace valid data and thus violate the authenticity of messages or transactions.
  - In some cases, the protocols using cryptographic processes are incorrectly developed or configured and can be exploited to compromise security schemes.
  - One typical use of cryptanalysis is for quality assurance and enhancement of cryptographic strength. Many standardized algorithms are subjected to stringent testing and evaluation before publication as approved technologies.

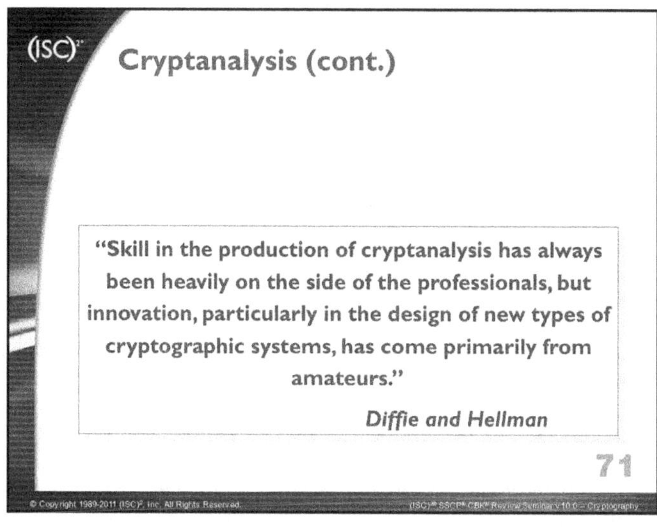


- While this has been true historically (the Caesar cipher, the Mary, Queen of Scotts cipher, and others), it is less likely to remain true as the power of supercomputers used to crack codes exceeds the capabilities of humans operating without sophisticated computers to invent and test them.

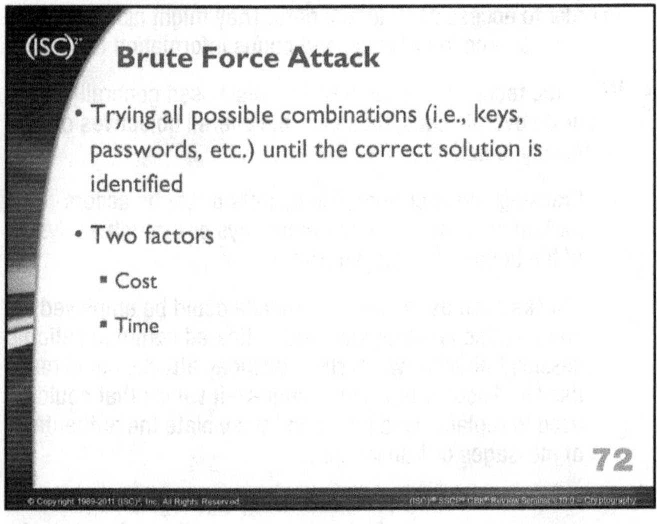


- **BRUTE FORCE ATTACK –** A brute force attack involves trying all possible keys until hitting on the one that results in cleartext. It can involve significant costs related to the amount of processing required to try quadrillions (in the case of the data encryption standard (DES)) of keys. The time required is a factor of how many keys can be tried per unit time – but, it is not limited to a single machine. Many cracking systems tie hundreds or even thousands of PCs in parallel.
- All of the cryptographic attacks described later in this section are attempts to derive the key or message in less time than a brute force attack would take.
  - The phrase "computationally infeasible" means that a brute force attack would be faster than trying to factor or otherwise reverse the math that generated the key.
  - The only kind of encryption that can be mathematically proven to be unbreakable is a one-time pad. All others will fall to brute force.

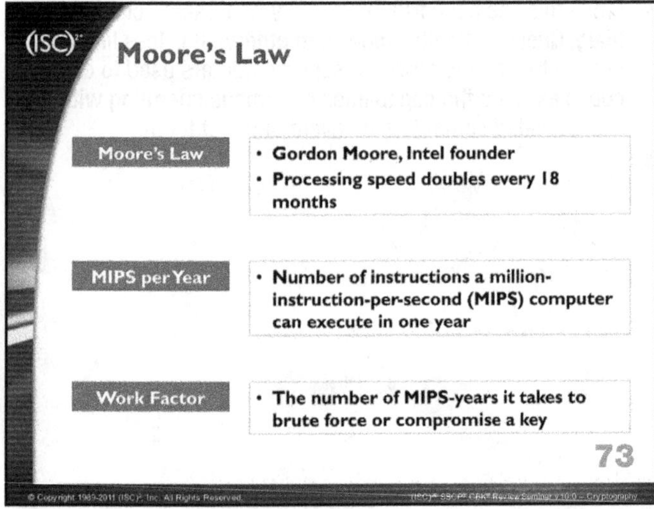


- **MOORE'S LAW –** Moore actually said that the density of transistors on a printed circuit doubles every 18 months and that as a result, processing power doubles along with it. The technology part of that statement ,"density of transistors" – was far less interesting to reporters and Powerpoint Slide authors than the implications of processing power doubling. This means that the time taken to try all possible keys or perform complex calculations will halve every 18 months as well. A cipher that was secure three years ago is down to a quarter of its relative strength today.
- When the data encryption standard (DES) was first created by IBM, its authors said it would take a hundred years to break it. That was true using the mainframe on which the developers worked (a 500Khz – that's kilohertz!) computer. As time went by and machines got thousands of times faster, their statement went into a special quotation archive along with others like "no one will ever need more than 640K" or "We [at IBM] only expect to sell a dozen of these [computers]."
- **MIPS PER YEAR –** To avoid future embarrassment and to provide a way to assess the relative strengths of various key lengths and algorithms, the MIPS-year term was invented. To convert to calendar years, just divide the number of MIPS-years the brute force attack will take by the number of MIPS-years work that can be accomplished in one calendar year. As computers get faster, the denominator grows, but the numerator stays the same.
- **WORK FACTOR** is the term used to describe the number of MIPS-years it will take to brute force or compromise a key. It has nothing to do with the effort it takes to encrypt or decrypt a message.

**Time Required for Brute Force Attack**

| Bits | Number of keys | Brute Force Attack Time |
|---|---|---|
| 56 | $7.2 \times 10^{16}$ | 20 hours |
| 80 | $1.2 \times 10^{24}$ | 54,800 years |
| 128 | $3.4 \times 10^{38}$ | $1.5 \times 10^{19}$ years |
| 256 | $1.15 \times 10^{77}$ | $5.2 \times 10^{57}$ years |

74

- **TIME REQUIRED FOR BRUTE FORCE ATTACK –** The table gives times required for a brute force attack on the key lengths using "Deep Crack" technology. Deep Crack technology was developed in 1998 by the EFF (Electronic Frontier Foundation) that built a machine (called the Deep Crack) capable of trying a million data encryption standard (DES) keys per microsecond against a readable ASCII string challenge phrase (the RSA DES Challenge). Even at this prodigious rate, it takes about 20 hours to try all possible keys. This machine cost about $250,000 to design and build, and in theory it makes DES worthless. In practice, by using Cipher Block Chaining (CBC), doing any initial scrambling of the data and/or doing it three times in a row (triple DES), it can still be fairly difficult to crack.
- Obviously, as the key length grows beyond 100 or so, the number of keys quickly becomes astronomically large. Note that if the brute force approach is possible, there is no real defense against it. The only hope is to have so many possible keys that it is not feasible to try them all in a reasonable amount of time. To put this in perspective, the Big Bang happened nearly 15 billion years ago – on the order of 15x10^9 years.
- The new advanced encryption standard (AES) standard, Rijndael, which is replacing DES, supports 128- and 256-bit keys. Even taking into account the staggering advances in computing power and cryptanalysis, 128-bit keys should be safe for virtually any of today's secrets. In other words, the useful life of a 128-bit AES key exceeds the useful life of any secret.

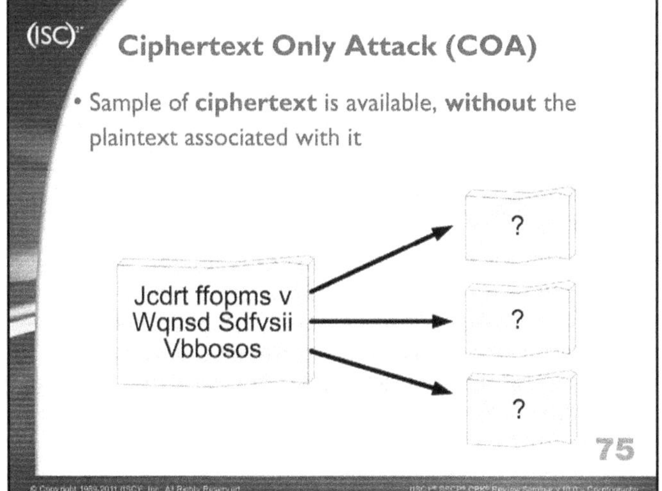

(ISC)²
Ciphertext Only Attack (COA)
• Sample of ciphertext is available, without the plaintext associated with it
Jcdrt ffopms v
Wqnsd Sdfvsii
Vbbosos
?
?
?
75


- Note that cryptanalytic attacks can be mounted not only against encryption algorithms, but also against digital signature algorithms, MACing algorithms, and pseudo-random number generators.
- **CIPHERTEXT ONLY ATTACK (COA) –** The case where only the encrypted message is available for attack. Sometimes the contents of the message are known to be a human language so a frequency analysis could be attempted, making it easier to crack. The situation where the attacker does not know anything about the contents of the message and must work from ciphertext only is much more difficult.
- The goal of this attack is to retrieve the plaintext message.

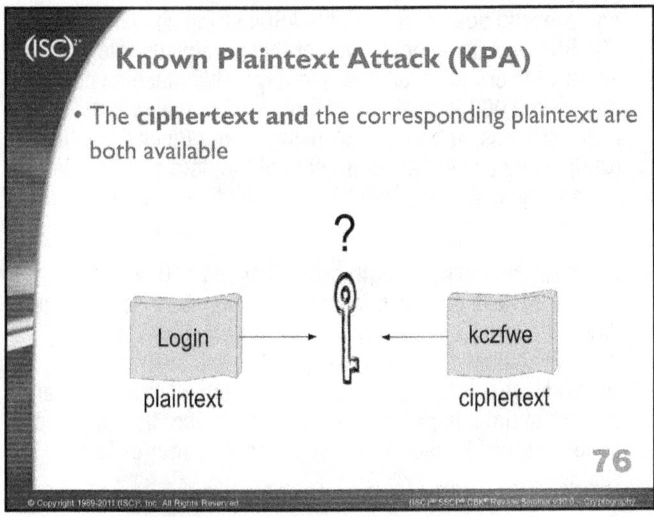

Known Plaintext Attack (KPA)
• The ciphertext and the corresponding plaintext are both available
?
Login
plaintext
kczfwe
ciphertext
76


- **KNOWN PLAINTEXT ATTACK (KPA) –** The case where both plaintext and matching ciphertext are available to the cryptanalyst, who can then discover the key. The purpose of this attack is to learn the key so that subsequent messages can be decrypted.

**Chosen Plaintext Attacks**

- Chosen plaintext attack (CPA)
  - Crypto device loaded with a hidden key is available; the attacker can input a selected plaintext and obtain the output from the device
- Adaptive chosen plaintext attack (ACPA)
  - Same as above except you are able to choose plaintext samples dynamically, and alter your choice based on the results of previous encryptions

77

- **CHOSEN PLAINTEXT ATTACK (CPA) –** The situation where the cryptanalyst has access to the crypto device containing the key and can use it to encrypt chosen text in an effort to discover the key. (Note that to dismantle the crypto device to find the key would cause the device to self-destruct.) This is often called the "lunch-time" attack, since it is often facilitated by an attacker gaining unauthorized access when the crypto device is temporarily unattended.
- **ADAPTIVE CHOSEN PLAINTEXT ATTACK (ACPA) –** When the cryptanalyst can choose the plaintext that is encrypted, but can also modify the choice based on the results of the previous encryptions. This usually requires unrestricted access to the device and is consequently often called the "midnight attack."

## Chosen Ciphertext Attack (CCA)

- Cryptanalyst may choose a piece of ciphertext and obtain the corresponding decrypted plaintext
- Generally applicable to attacks against public key cryptosystems

78



- **CHOSEN CIPHERTEXT ATTACK (CCA) –** The cryptanalyst can choose a ciphertext to be decrypted and has access to the decrypted plaintext. When the attacker has a message encrypted with the sender's private key, the attacker can decrypt using the public key. This gives access to the decrypted plaintext and is an attack on the private key.

## Adaptive Chosen Ciphertext Attack (ACCA)

- Adaptive version of a CCA
- Cryptanalysts can mount an attack of this type when they have free use of a piece of decryption hardware, but are unable to extract the decryption key

79



- **ADAPTIVE CHOSEN CIPHERTEXT ATTACK (ACCA) –** Not only can the cryptanalyst choose the ciphertext, but he or she can also modify his or her choice based on the results of previous operations.
- An ACCA is most often mounted when the decrypting hardware is captured but the key is embedded and not removable. The analyst can make some progress, then make modifications to the ciphertext, or choose a different ciphertext and view/compare the results.

(ISC)²

## Man-in-the-Middle Attack

- Cryptographic communications and **key exchange** protocols are susceptible to this attack
- Attacker is **between** parties on a communication line

80



(ISC)² SSCP® CBK® Review Seminar v10.0 – Cryptography

- **MAN-IN-THE-MIDDLE ATTACK –** This is an eavesdropping attack that takes place when two parties are exchanging keys for secure communications. The attacker places himself or herself between the parties on the communication line and performs separate key exchanges with each party. Both parties will think they have set up a secure channel. The attacker is then able to decrypt a communication from one party, re-encrypt it with the other key, and then transmit to the other party. Detecting man-in-the-middle attacks is possible if both sides compute a cryptographic hash function of the key exchange, sign it using a digital signature algorithm, and send the signature to the other side. The recipient can then verify that the hash matches the locally computed hash and that the signature came from the other party.

(ISC)²

## Side Channel Attacks

- Timing and power attacks
  - Continually measuring exact execution times of modular exponentiation operations
  - Relevant to most encryption methods including: RSA, Diffie-Hellman, DSS, ECC
  - Example: differential power analysis (DPA) attack

81



(ISC)² SSCP® CBK® Review Seminar v10.0 – Cryptography

- **SIDE CHANNEL ATTACKS –** According to Schneier, side channel attacks are a family of attacks that attack implementation details such as timing, power, radiation emissions, and other faults. By carefully measuring the amount of time required to perform private key operations, attackers may be able to find fixed Diffie-Hellman exponents, factor RSA keys, or break other cryptosystems. The attack is computationally inexpensive against a vulnerable system and often requires only a piece of known ciphertext. Systems are at risk (including cryptographic tokens, network-based cryptosystems, and other applications) when attackers can make reasonably accurate timing measurements.
- **EXAMPLE: DIFFERENTIAL POWER ANALYSIS (DPA) ATTACK –** Describes a new class of attacks against smart cards and secure cryptographic tokens. Discovered by researchers at Cryptography Research in San Francisco, DPA attacks exploit characteristic behaviors of transistor logic gates and software running on today's smart cards and other cryptographic devices. The attacks are performed by monitoring the electrical activity of a device, then using advanced statistical methods to determine secret information (such as secret keys and user PINs) in the device.

**REFERENCES:**

http://www.cryptography.com/timingattack

http://www.cryptography.com/dpa/qa

## Birthday Attack

- A class of brute force attacks used against hashing functions
- Birthday Paradox: Probability that two or more people in a group of 23 share the same birthday is greater than 50 percent
  - Collisions

82




- **BIRTHDAY ATTACK –** A message is deemed authentic when the calculated digest matches the received digest. If an intruder modifies a message, the digests should not match. One of the questions a cryptanalyst will ask is how many different messages share the same digest? The cryptanalyst might also ask whether or not it is possible to modify a message in such a way so as to generate the same digest before and after modification.
- **COLLISIONS –** The term for matching digests is a "collision." Over time, more than one message will inevitably generate the same digest. If these collisions are unknown to each other, there is no risk. When they can be forced, however, the hashing no longer guarantees integrity. Surprisingly, it takes far fewer messages to find a collision than one might guess. The **BIRTHDAY ATTACK** takes advantage of this fact. The defense is to make the pool of messages in which a collision is likely too large to be feasible.
- The math is fairly simple. To be safe, the number of bits in the digest should be at least twice the number of bits in the key.

## Birthday Attack (cont.)

- A hash function gives a set value for a message; a strong hash function must resist the birthday attack
- It is easier for an attacker to find two messages with the same digest value than to match a specific value
- A hash needs to be twice the length of the key to withstand a birthday attack

83




- **BIRTHDAY ATTACK (CONT.) –** You would expect that a 128-bit hash function would force the attacker to try 2^128 inputs to find a match to a specific source document, but the birthday paradox implies that the attacker will be able to find two ARBITRARY documents that hash to the same value in only 2^64 steps for a 128-bit hash function.

## Attacks on Symmetric Block Ciphers

- Four types
  - Differential cryptanalysis
  - Linear cryptanalysis
  - Differential linear cryptanalysis
  - Algebraic attacks

84

- **ATTACKS ON SYMMETRIC BLOCK CIPHERS –** These are the non-brute force attacks normally used against symmetric block ciphers such as DES, RC5, etc. These attacks include:
  - Differential cryptanalysis
  - Linear cryptanalysis
  - Combination of the above two (differential linear cryptanalysis)
  - Algebraic attacks
- More details are on the following slides.

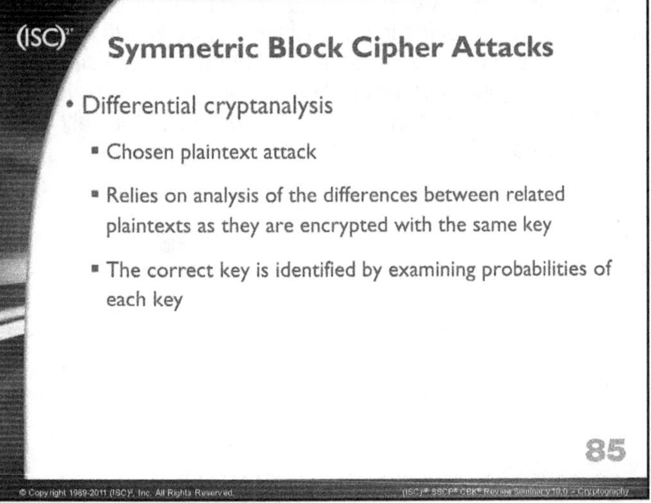

(ISC)²
Symmetric Block Cipher Attacks
• Differential cryptanalysis
▪ Chosen plaintext attack
▪ Relies on analysis of the differences between related plaintexts as they are encrypted with the same key
▪ The correct key is identified by examining probabilities of each key
85


- **DIFFERENTIAL CRYPTANALYSIS –** This attack is facilitated when the attacker can gain access to the cryptographic device and create several pieces of ciphertexts from related plaintexts. By observing the differences between them, the attacker may be able to gain statistical data about the key being used.

## Symmetric Block Cipher Attacks (cont.)

- Linear cryptanalysis
  - Known plaintext attack
  - Uses linear approximation to describe behavior of the block cipher
  - Given sufficient pairs of plaintext and corresponding ciphertext, bits of information about the key can be obtained

86



- **LINEAR CRYPTANALYSIS –** When the attacker has many copies of plaintexts and ciphertexts created from them, he or she may be able to find patterns in the way in which the algorithm is operating, or ways in which the pieces of ciphertext are similar. This may lead to an analysis of the key.

## Other Attacks

- Differential linear cryptanalysis
  - Combination of differential and linear cryptanalysis
- Algebraic attacks
  - Analysis of vulnerabilities in the mathematics of the algorithm

87



- **ALGEBRAIC ATTACKS –** Are the mathematical analysis of the algorithm to find weaknesses in the way in which it computes the cryptographic operation.

## Other Types of Cryptographic Attacks

(ISC)²
Other Types of Cryptographic Attacks
• Analytic
▪ Using algorithm and algebraic manipulation weakness to reduce complexity
➢RSA factoring attack
➢Double DES attack
• Statistical
▪ Using statistical weakness in design
➢More 1s than 0s in the keystream
88





(ISC)²® SSCP® CBK® Review Seminar v.10.0 – Cryptography

- **OTHER TYPES OF CRYPTOGRAPHIC ATTACKS –** This and the next chart address the other three types of attacks: analytic, statistical, and implementation. It would be beyond this course to go into details of each of these, but suffice it to say that the algorithm must be very strong (some vendor algorithms are not), the keystream needs to be without any bias (i.e., random – no patterns), and the implementation must be in accordance with good crypto concepts. Examples of each type of attack are provided.

## Other Types of Cryptographic Attacks (cont.)
▪ '95 attack of Netscape key
➢Deficient key randomization





(ISC)²® SSCP® CBK® Review Seminar v.10.0 – Cryptography

▪ Static WEP

- **IMPLEMENTATION –** In many cases, the problem with a cryptographic system is not with the algorithm, but in the way that it was implemented. For example, the Netscape vulnerability was related to a poor random number generator (RNG) which was dependent on time of day. The wireless equivalent privacy (WEP) key was vulnerable due to a short initialization vector (IV), which made it predictable.

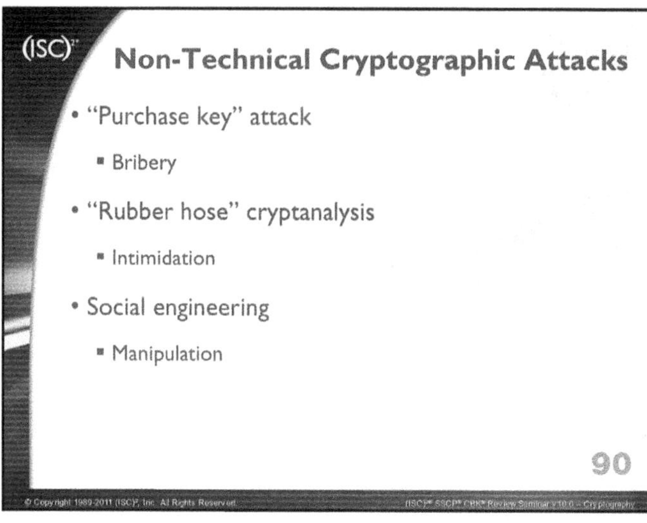

(ISC)²
Non-Technical Cryptographic Attacks
"Purchase key" attack
Bribery
"Rubber hose" cryptanalysis
Intimidation
Social engineering
Manipulation
90


- **NON-TECHNICAL CRYPTOGRAPHIC ATTACKS –** From Bruce Schneier's *Applied Cryptography and Secrets and Lies.* Note that these are often the most successful attacks. These attacks are against the users and operators of cryptosystems, who through bribery, intimidation, or manipulation may disclose secret keys or other sensitive data to an attacker.

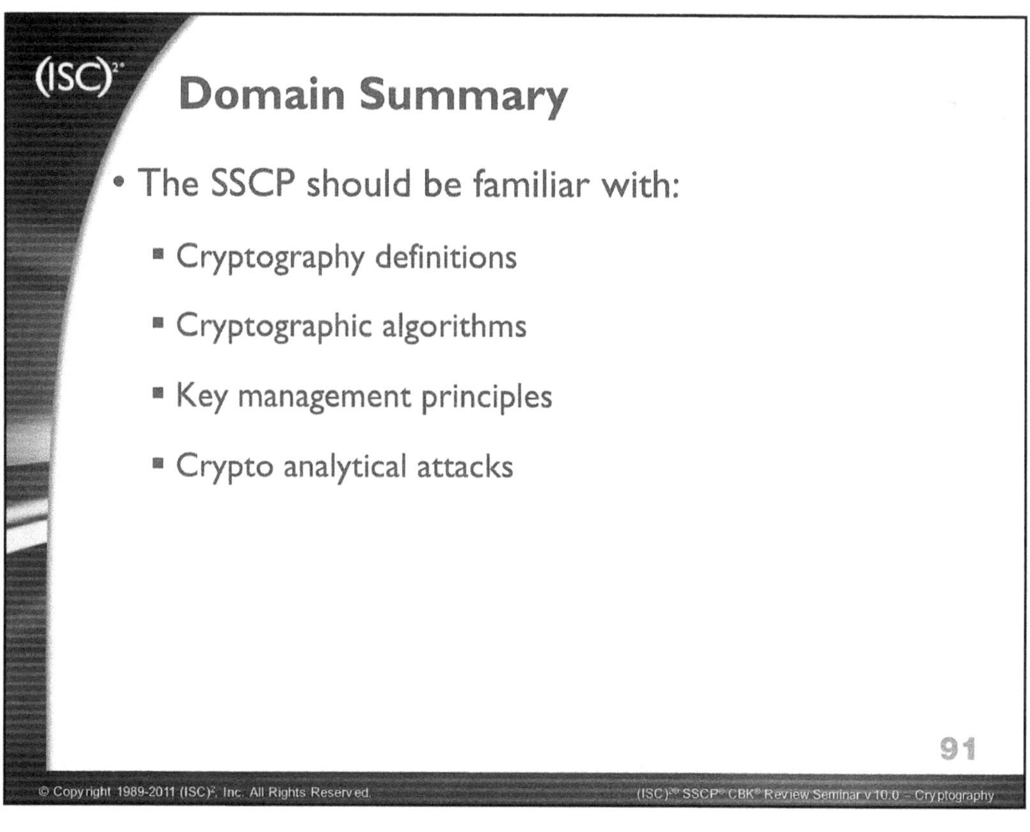

Crypto analytical attacks

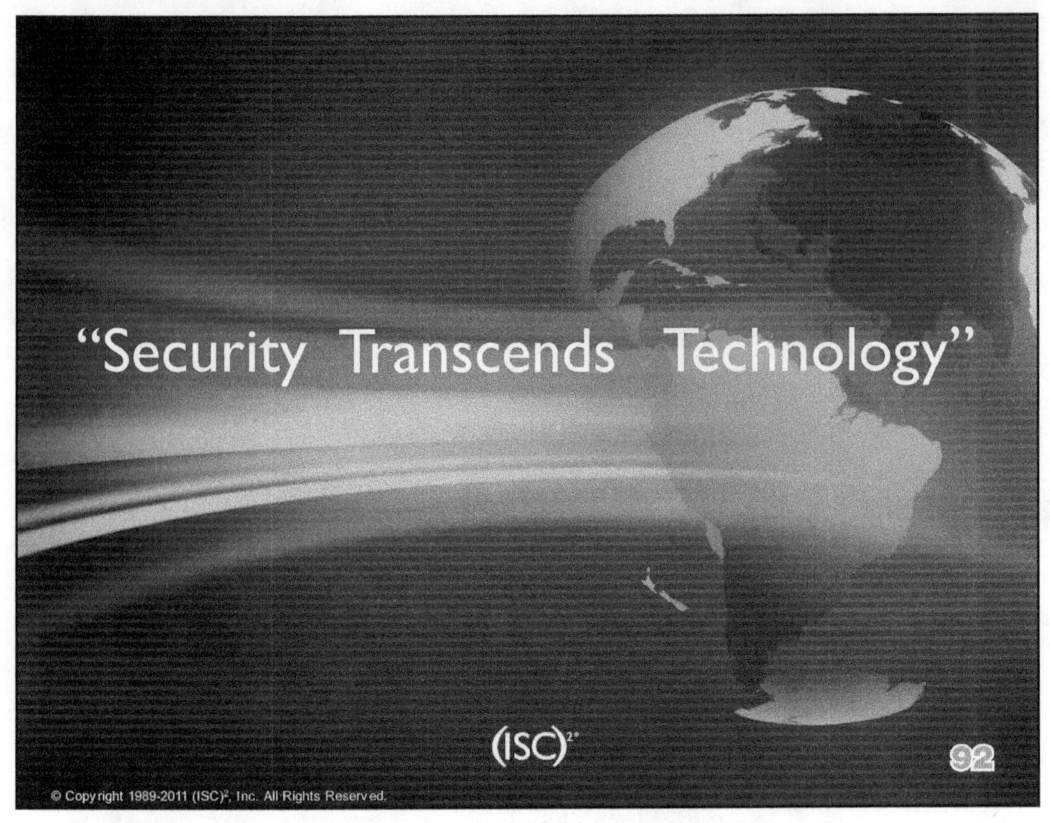
"Security Transcends Technology"
(ISC)²
92
© Copyright 1989-2011 (ISC)², Inc. All Rights Reserved.

# Review Questions

## CRYPTOGRAPHY

1. **In which type of cryptanalytic attack is a cryptosystem's work factor MOST relevant?**
   a. Differential cryptanalysis
   b. Chosen plaintext attacks
   c. Linear-differential cryptanalysis
   d. Brute force attacks

2. **What is the relationship between the RC4 and RC5 algorithms?**
   a. They are related symmetric key cryptographic algorithms - although RC5 was designed to accommodate larger key sizes.
   b. They both employ repeated substitution and permutation transformations on each plaintext block.
   c. They are unrelated symmetric key cryptographic algorithms -although they were created by the same individual.
   d. They both address the need for message integrity controls that resist intentional changes.

3. **Which of the following is the MOST common attack against message digests used to determine the original plaintext?**
   a. Cipher text only attack
   b. Dictionary attack
   c. Known plaintext attack
   d. Linear cryptanalysis attack

4. **If a cryptographic algorithm is found to be highly susceptible to chosen ciphertext attacks, it may allow the attacker to**
   a. take advantage of the algorithm's malleability.
   b. use differential power analysis to determine how many rounds are being used during the encryption sequence.
   c. encrypt any desired plaintext to achieve a desired ciphertext.
   d. simplify exhaustive search through all possible keys supported by the algorithm.

5. **The process of hiding information in photos, music, and videos in such a way as to make the alteration invisible to casual observers is called**
   a. steganography.
   b. optimal asymmetric encryption padding (OAEP).
   c. a null cipher.
   d. expansion.

6. **Which of the following is typically used to help two parties agree on a session key without exchanging secret information?**
   a. Initialization vectors (IVs)
   b. Exclusive-or (XOR) operations
   c. Rivest-Shamir-Adleman (RSA) algorithm
   d. Diffie-Hellman key exchange

7. **Keyed hashes and digital signatures differ in what way?**
   a. Keyed hashes employ symmetric keys alone while digital signatures employ symmetric keys and hash functions.
   b. Keyed hashes combine a hash function with a shared symmetric key while digital signatures combine a hash function with an asymmetric key.
   c. Keyed hashes provide for message integrity while digital signatures provide for message confidentiality.
   d. Keyed hashes are intended to detect accidental changes while digital signatures are intended to detect intentional changes.

8. **What is the MOST significant advantage that the advanced encryption standard (AES) offers over the data encryption standard (DES)?**
   a. Larger key space due to larger key sizes.
   b. More efficient operation when used in general-purpose computing devices.
   c. Smaller key sizes with greater strength per bit than DES.
   d. More block cipher modes are supported.

9. **The output of a one-way algorithm is referred to as a**
   a. Plaintext
   b. Ciphertext
   c. Hash
   d. Private Key

10. **What is the BEST way to verify that a digital signature is valid?**
   a. Verify the digital signature through a manual comparison of the hash value.
   b. Obtain the public key from the partner and verify the digital signature.
   c. Obtain a public key certificate from a trusted certification authority and verify the digital signature using that key.
   d. Use a hash algorithm to determine if the message has been altered.

11. **What is a hash collision?**
    a. The failure of a given cryptographic hash function to complete successfully.
    b. Repetitions within a message digest that indicate weaknesses in the hash algorithm.
    c. Matching message digests found during the verification of a digital signature.
    d. Two different input messages that result in the same message digest value.

12. **What would likely be the FIRST step in the establishment of an encrypted session using hybrid encryption systems, such as secure socket layer (SSL) or Internet protocol security (IPSEC)?**
    a. Key negotiation and exchange of symmetric keys.
    b. Exchange of public keys.
    c. Determination of a suitable hash function.
    d. Out-of-band communications to negotiate which cryptographic algorithms and settings will be used.

13. **When used in cryptographic applications, what function does certification perform?**
    a. It provides the ability to verify the authenticity of public keys.
    b. It ensures that a secure process is being used to generate and store keys.
    c. It is used to verify the integrity and authenticity of received messages.
    d. It provides evidence that security controls were implemented as designed.

14. **When should a certification authority place a certificate on a certificate revocation list (CRL)?**
    a. The certificate has not been used for an extended period of time.
    b. The session key has been compromised.
    c. The certificate has expired.
    d. The private key of the certificate owner has been compromised.

15. **An application developer wants an application to be able to encrypt sensitive data when it is stored on user laptops. What would be the BEST option to address the needs?**
    a. Develop a set of secure algorithms for the application based upon the latest industry standards.
    b. Provide an evaluated hardware cryptosystem that can be used to encrypt bulk data efficiently.
    c. Use an industry-standard software-based cryptosystem that can be accessed through a series of documented application programming interfaces (APIs).
    d. Recommend that all users be authenticated using unique digital certificates.

**Questions 16-18 apply to the following scenario:**

An information systems security professional who works for a large bank has been asked to evaluate a variety of cryptographic algorithms that are being considered as candidates for a proprietary electronic funds transfer (EFT) application.

The bank has three funds transfer offices, one each in New York City, London, and Tokyo. Several funds transfer agents work in each office and can send funds to any of the other offices. Each transaction must be identified as authentic and the agent who sent it must be verifiable. The quantity of data per transaction is small.

**Please answer the following three questions.**

16. **What is the best way to identify the agent who initiated a particular transaction?**
    a. By having the agent encrypt the message with the agent's private key.
    b. By having the agent encrypt the hash with the agent's private key.
    c. By having the agent encrypt the message with the agent's symmetric key.
    d. By having the agent encrypt the hash with the agent's public key.

17. **Confidentiality is a requirement for the transactions. The BEST way to accomplished this is by**
    a. using a one way hash as the cryptographic algorithm to provide the necessary confidentiality.
    b. Digitally signing all transactions before they are transmitted over an unsafe network.
    c. signing the transfer order with the sender's private key.
    d. encrypting the transfer order with the recipient's public key.

18. **The organization is already digitally signing and encrypting each message. Message acknowledgement is also a requirement. The BEST course of action is to**
    a. instruct the receiver to digitally sign and return the message.
    b. instruct the receiver to digitally sign and return the message hash.
    c. implement an automatic receipt of message function in the application.
    d. have the in-house certification authority digitally countersign each message and its timestamp.

**19. A trusted entity or third party that has the central responsibility of certifying the authenticity of digital certificate users is called a**

a. certificate revocation list.
b. certification authority.
c. authorizing official.
d. key distribution center.

**20. Keyspace size is BEST defined as**

a. the space available for holding keys.
b. the number of sets that require a combination.
c. the total number of key combinations you can use.
d. the amount of time it will take on average to guess all combinations.

# Notes

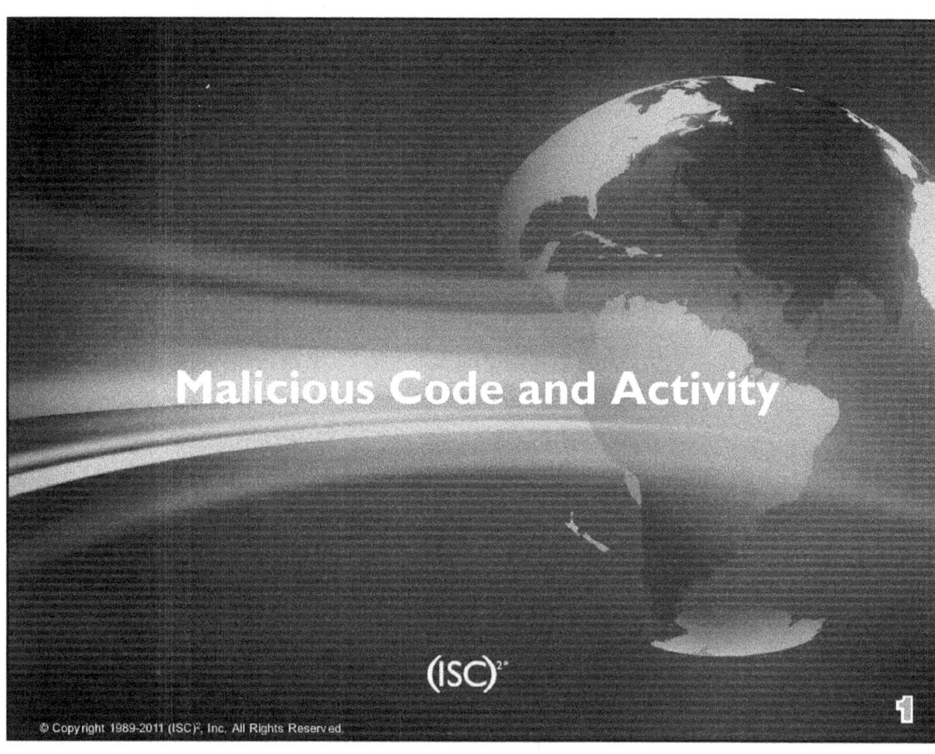


- The SSCP should become familiar with software vulnerabilities in order to ensure that adequate controls and safeguards are in place. While many of the topics covered in this domain are traditional, and many are not as prevalent today as they have been in the past, they comprise many of the basic concepts necessary to understand the more current exploits. Traditional controls have focused on identifying and remediating exploits.
- The emerging approach is to BUILD the security into software at the outset so that fewer opportunities for exploitation exist.
- Special reference to current industry initiatives should be included in the SSCP's knowledge base. These include OWASP, OSVDB, CWE, and "Build Security In." Regular visits to the following websites should be made a part of the SSCP's professional development:
- http://www.owasp.org
- http://www.osvdb.org
- http://www.cwe.org
- https://buildsecurityin.us-cert.gov/

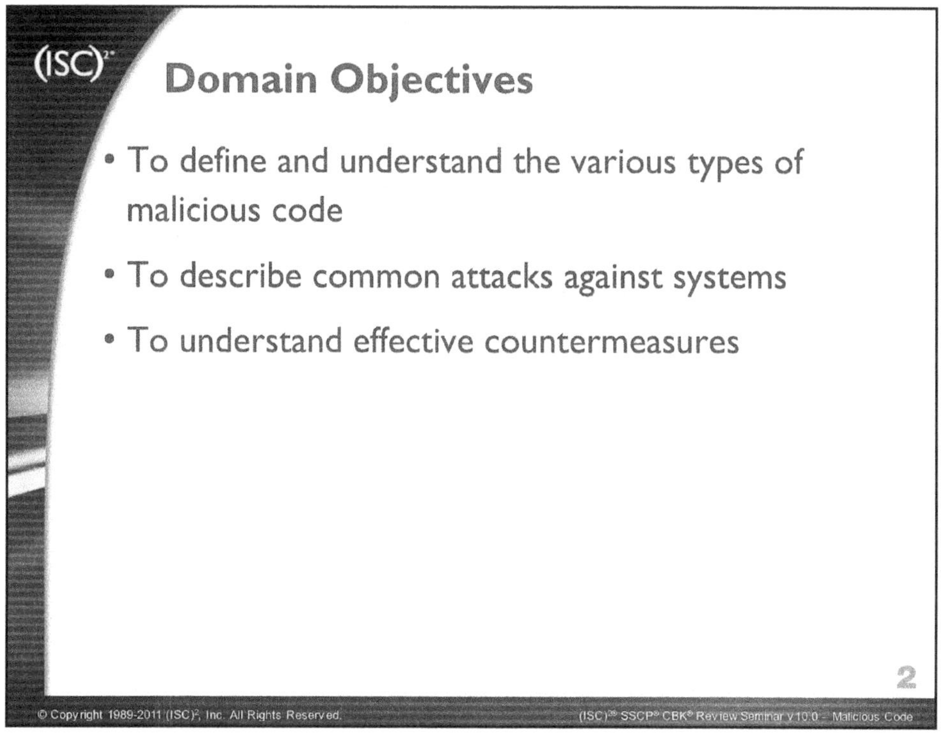

(ISC)²
Domain Objectives
• To define and understand the various types of malicious code
• To describe common attacks against systems
• To understand effective countermeasures
2
© Copyright 1989-2011 (ISC)², Inc. All Rights Reserved.
(ISC)²® SSCP® CBK® Review Seminar v10.0 – Malicious Code

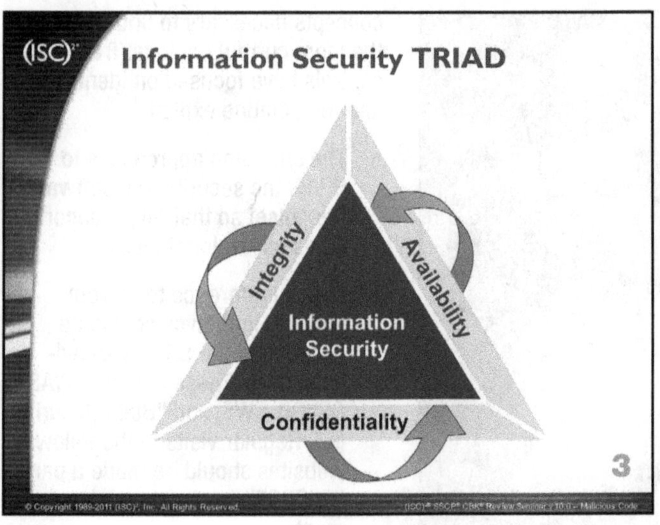


- **INFORMATION SECURITY TRIAD –** Malicious code attacks all three information security vectors.
- **AVAILABILITY –** Malware has often erased or overwritten files or caused considerable damage to storage media. Denial of service (DoS) can result from system files being overwritten, erased, or corrupted.
- **INTEGRITY –** Malware such as data diddlers modify records in databases over a period of time. By the time it becomes clear that integrity has been lost, backups will have become corrupted as well. Even a suspected breach means that all data must be integrity checked, often at considerable cost.
  - Malware often acts by using spoofed sender data, causing victims to falsely accuse the apparent attacker. (See "joe job": http://en.wikipedia.org/wiki/Joe_job).
- **CONFIDENTIALITY –** Spyware and Trojans can send company proprietary information to unauthorized destinations either as a deliberate attack, or as a side effect of another function.

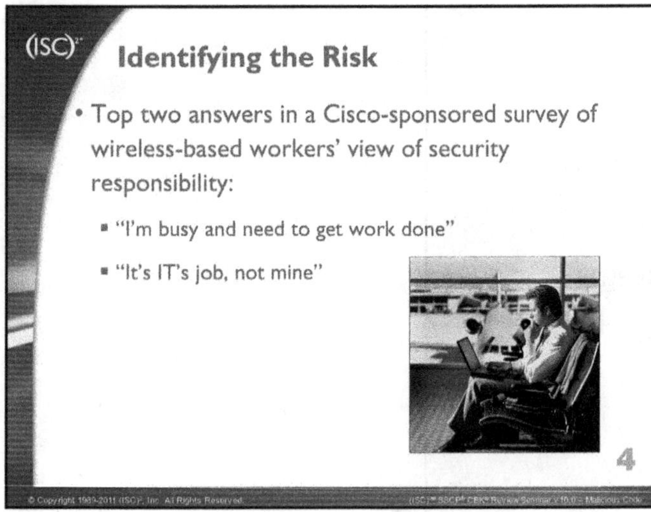


- We keep insisting that security is everyone's responsibility, but our job is far from done; workers continue to believe that security is "IT's job," and in fact consider it a roadblock to accomplishing their own work. Although we need to work hard to persuade people otherwise, in the short term, we need to put policies, procedures, and technologies aimed at preventing malware attacks into place.
- Malware makes the implementation of security much more difficult, since the security of the SSCP's network and devices will be affected by the security (or lack of security) of other devices. An infected system may be the source of a denial of service attack or even a flood of copies of a virus that poses a risk to the system the SSCP is trying to protect. A well-meaning user who circumvents security measures or installs unauthorized equipment may put the entire organization at risk.

**REFERENCE:**

http://www.informationweek.com/news/showArticle.jhtml?articleID=201801429

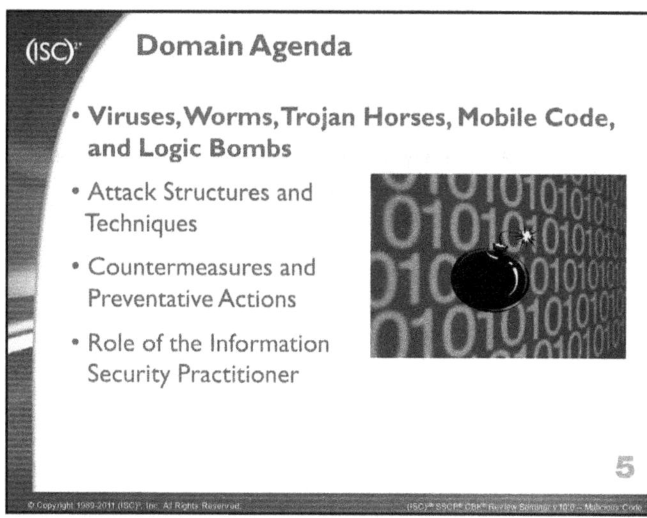


- **VIRUSES, WORMS, TROJAN HORSES, MOBILE CODE, AND LOGIC BOMBS –** In this domain, we will address the questions of "Who, What, Why, and How" regarding threats to organizations from malicious software code. This first section will provide some background and context, as well as describing the overall business impact of these threats.
  - We will address the motivations of people who intentionally or unintentionally engage in hostile code attacks and describe and compare popular terms such as "hackers," "crackers," and "script-kiddies," etc. People design and execute malicious code attacks for various reasons; understanding what these reasons are and recognizing the resultant patterns help prevent and control these attacks.
  - Hostile codes are characterized and categorized depending on their underlying coding structure (architecture) and the way in which the most common attacks are executed. All malicious code must be executed in some manner, either as a real-time interactive session or as a pre-programmed automatic process. We will compare viruses, worms, Trojans, and other forms of hostile code and explore in more detail how they are propagated and executed. We will discuss the popular classification schemes of malicious or hostile code and understand how classification depends on the construction of the code and how it behaves.
  - We will address countermeasures used to detect, mitigate, and recover from the damage or business interruptions caused by malicious code attacks and understand that these countermeasures are only effective as long as the users and others responsible for implementing them and maintaining a safe computing environment fully understand the risks and the needs for the controls.
  - Finally, we will note that the IT security practitioner has an ongoing responsibility to participate actively in the implementation of safe practices and to maintain awareness of emerging threats and the countermeasures and best-practices being deployed to address them. This domain concludes with recommendations to help practitioners meet this responsibility. We will also note that students are expected to have completed or have access to the other knowledge domains for more in-depth coverage of a number of related topics such as specific countermeasures and security practices.

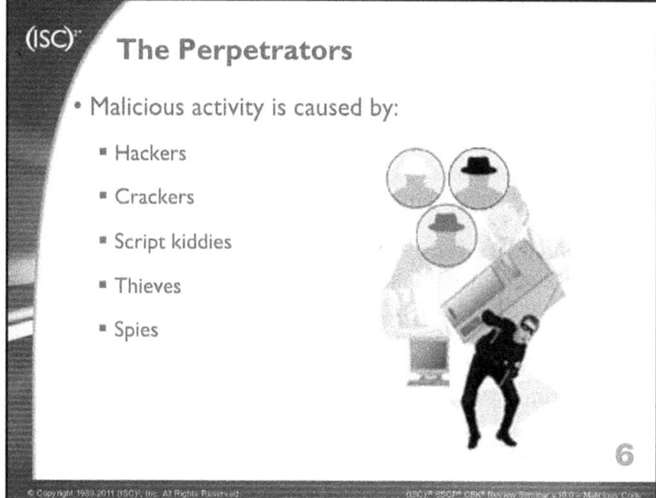


- **THE PERPETRATORS –** There are several types of attackers, ranging from the inexperienced and unskilled to the very sophisticated and knowledgeable.
  - **HACKERS –** There are also various types of hackers from ethical "white hat" penetration testers to "black hat" (malicious) intruders. "Grey hat" refers to hackers of questionable or indeterminate motives.
  - **CRACKERS –** "Cracker" is sometimes used to indicate a black hat, but is also used in a more specialized sense to mean someone who breaks software protection in order to make commercial software available for copying.
  - **SCRIPT KIDDIES –** Hackers have varying levels of sophistication. Least skilled are script kiddies, black hats who simply run scripts and applications that they have downloaded from various sources and often don't understand. While their chance of success is low, their large numbers potentially make them a hazard to system administrators.
  - **THIEVES/SPIES –** Of much more importance today are the thieves and corporate spies who attempt to penetrate an organization's networks for profit, or to gather trade secrets or competitive information.

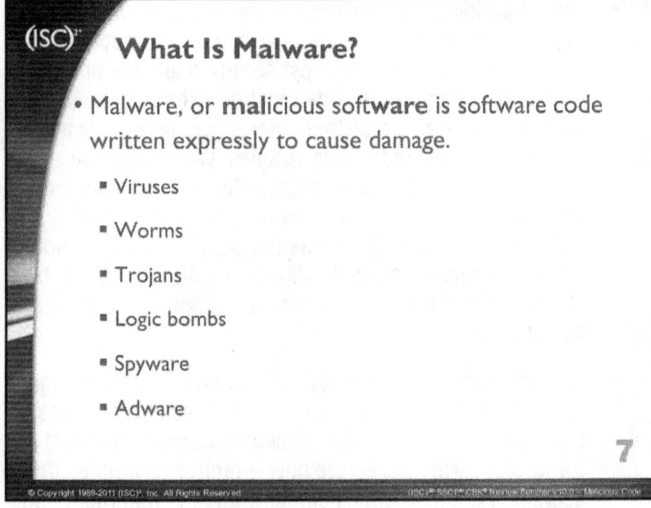

(ISC)²
What Is Malware?
• Malware, or malicious software is software code written expressly to cause damage.
▪ Viruses
▪ Worms
▪ Trojans
▪ Logic bombs
▪ Spyware
▪ Adware
7


- **WHAT IS MALWARE? –** The term malicious code has several meanings. In the broadest sense, malicious code is any set of instructions that can be executed on a computer system and perform operations that are not intended or desired.
  - What we generally understand as malware are discrete, executable software routines (programs) that are specifically designed to produce a hostile result and are transmitted directly to a target system through physical media or via a communications process. Some of these programs execute when an unsuspecting user performs a particular action (such as opening an infected document), while others execute by exploiting a vulnerability in an operating system or other utility. This kind of malware includes viruses, worms, and Trojan programs.
  - Commercial or custom utility programs developed for one purpose but capable of being used in a hostile manner are not generally seen as malware by researchers, but the scanning and intrusion activities should, nonetheless, be of concern for the security practitioner. Most remote administration tools and security probes fit this description, including SATAN, Back Orifice, and nMap. These tools are often used by network and security administrators to test a network for vulnerabilities, but these same features also permit hostile attackers to discover and exploit weaknesses in the network.

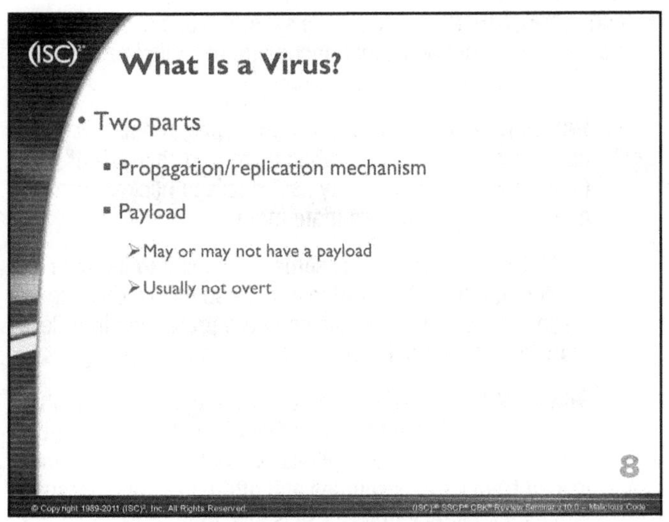

(ISC)²
What Is a Virus?
• Two parts
▪ Propagation/replication mechanism
▪ Payload
➢ May or may not have a payload
➢ Usually not overt
8


- **WHAT IS A VIRUS? –** Viruses are often considered to be damaging, or to carry some problematic payload. Most viruses with an obvious or damaging payload get noticed and, therefore, eliminated.
  - **PROPAGATION/REPLICATION MECHANISM –** The primary characteristic of a virus is replication, generally involving user action in some way.
  - **PAYLOAD –** Not all viruses have a payload. Some are just an annoyance or focus on replicating. The payload may be hidden and install a backdoor that may not be noticed by the victim, or the virus may have a very visible overt payload that causes immediate, noticeable damage to the victim.

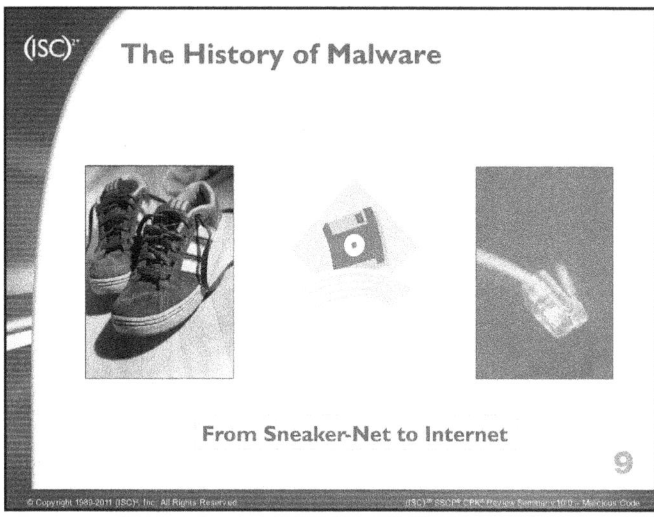
(ISC)²
The History of Malware
From Sneaker-Net to Internet
9

- **THE HISTORY OF MALWARE –** In the early days, malware spread via diskettes that were carried from machine to machine. This was often referred to as "sneaker net." This meant that a virus could take months to spread across the globe. Today's viral infections spread via networks and can cross the globe in a matter of minutes.
- As the virus-writing community evolved, more and more sophisticated viruses began to emerge – ones that could spread in multiple ways, and others that could spread via email, mobile code, or macros.

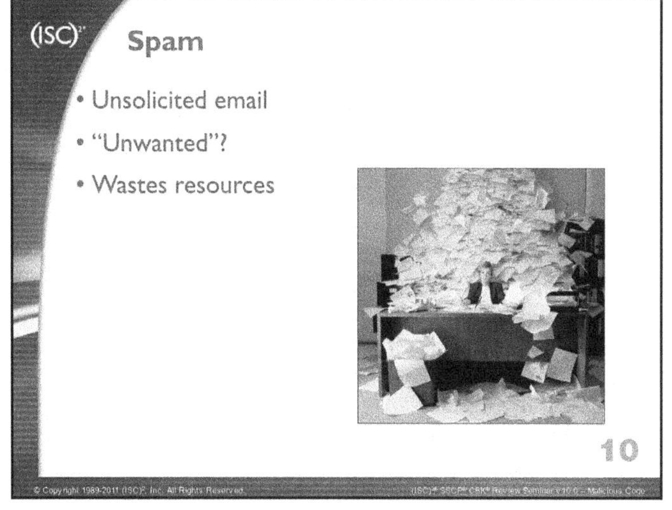
(ISC)²
Spam
• Unsolicited email
• "Unwanted"?
• Wastes resources
10

- **SPAM –** Spam is one of the most bothersome challenges faced by network administrators today. Not only does spam often contain viruses or other malicious code, but it congests networks and email servers, and can waste a lot of user time, impacting productivity.
- Many viruses now carry software to make an infected computer part of a spam botnet. These spam botnets are used to send out new versions of viruses.
- Most antispam vendors estimate spam at 70-90% of all email traffic. Theoretically, spam is any unwanted email. However, many users will open unsolicited email, attracted by the promise of jobs, lottery winnings, or reduced prices on products. This makes it hard to classify the email as strictly "unwanted."
- Note: SPAM™ (all uppercase) is a trademark of Hormel foods. In mixed or lowercase, it refers to unsolicited commercial email.

---

**REFERENCE:**

http://www.commtouch.com/documents/Commtouch_2007_Q1_Spam_Trends.pdf

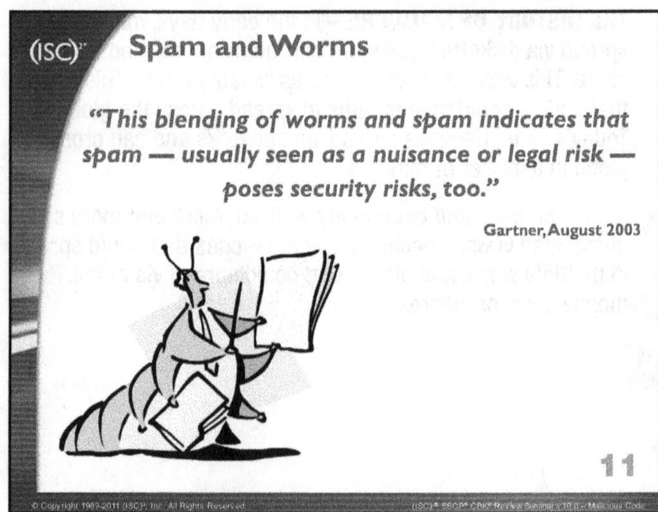

(ISC)²
Spam and Worms
"This blending of worms and spam indicates that spam — usually seen as a nuisance or legal risk — poses security risks, too."
Gartner, August 2003
11


- **SPAM AND WORMS –** Spam or "unwanted emails" are becoming a major problem for enterprises. Spam uses bandwidth needed to operate a business and wastes employees' time. It is also a "breeding ground/vehicle" for viruses and worms. If they are offensive and considered to create a hostile workplace, they can expose the enterprise to financial liability. Fortunately, there are automated tools available to assist the security administrator in eliminating these emails.

**REFERENCE:**

http://secureflorida.org/clientuploads/C-SAFE/CSAFEcybersecuritymanual.pdf

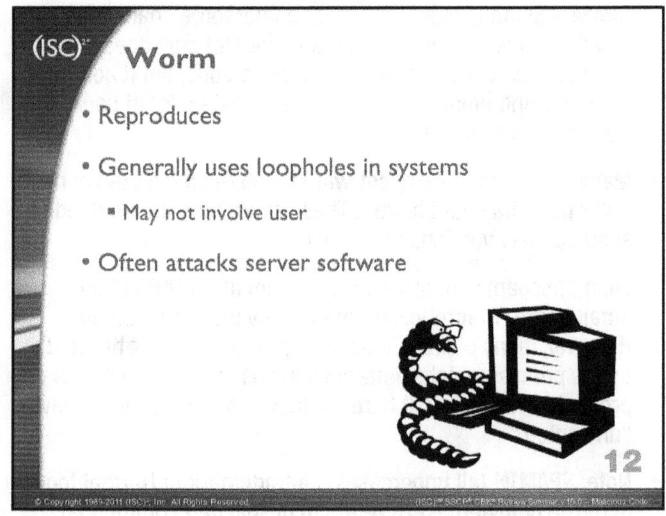


- **REPRODUCES –** A worm reproduces and spreads, like a virus and unlike other forms of malware. Originally, the distinction was made that worms used networks and communications links to spread, and that a worm, unlike a virus, did not directly attach to an executable file. The origin of the term "worm program" matched that of modern distributed processing experiments: a program with "segments" working on different computers, all communicating over a network (Shoch and Hupp, 1982).
- **GENERALLY USES LOOPHOLES IN SYSTEMS –** A worm will usually directly probe network-attached computers to exploit a specific weakness or loophole. Generally, worms look for a specific piece of server or utility software that will respond to network queries or activity. Examples of worms are the Internet/Morris Worm of 1988, and more recently Code Red and a number of Linux worms like Lion. (Nimda is an example of a worm, but it also spreads in a number of other ways, so it could be considered to be an email virus and multipartite as well.)
  - **MAY NOT INVOLVE USER –** A worm may spread rapidly without requiring any action by the user.
- **OFTEN ATTACKS SERVER SOFTWARE –** This is because many who write worms know that the servers are turned on all the time. This allows the worm to spread at a faster rate. Blaster is possibly one of the most successful worms, due to the fact that the function it used (DCOM) is available on all versions of Windows, desktop as well as server.

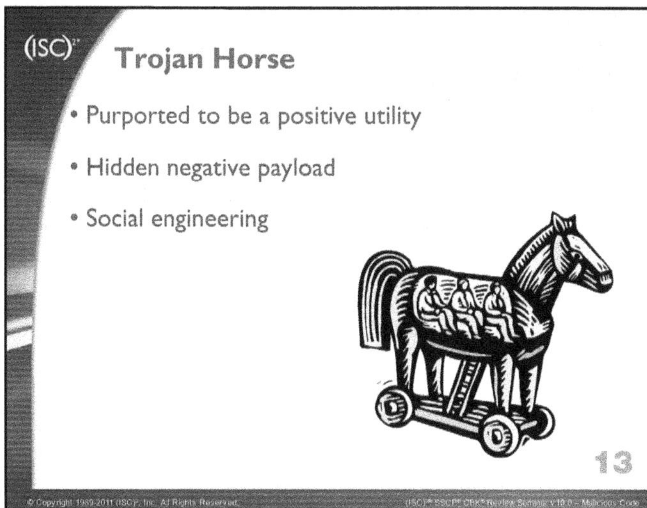


- **TROJAN HORSE –** Trojans, or Trojan horse programs, are the largest class of malware. However, the term is subject to much confusion, particularly in relation to computer viruses.
- **PURPORTED TO BE A POSITIVE UTILITY –** A Trojan is a program that pretends to do one thing while performing another, unwanted action.
- **HIDDEN NEGATIVE PAYLOAD –** The extent of the "pretense" may vary greatly. Many of the early PC Trojans relied merely on the filename and a description on a bulletin board. "Login" Trojans, popular among university student mainframe users, mimicked the screen display and the prompts of the normal login program and could, in fact, pass the username and password along to the valid login program at the same time as they stole the user data. Some Trojans may contain actual code that does what it is supposed to be doing while performing additional nasty acts that it does not tell you about.
- **SOCIAL ENGINEERING –** A major component of Trojan design is the social engineering component. Trojan programs are advertised (in some sense) as having some positive component. The term positive can be in some dispute, since a great many Trojans promise pornography or access to pornography, and this still seems to be depressingly effective. However, other promises can be made as well. A recent email virus, in generating its messages, carried a list of a huge variety of subject lines, promising pornography, humor, virus information, an antivirus program, and information about abuse of the recipient's account. Sometimes the message is simply vague, and relies on curiosity.
- An additional confusion with viruses involves Trojan horse programs that may be spread by email. In years past, a Trojan program had to be posted on an electronic bulletin board system or a file archive site. Because of the static posting, a malicious program would soon be identified and eliminated. More recently, Trojan programs have been distributed by mass email campaigns, by posting on Usenet newsgroup discussion groups, or through automated distribution agents (bots) on Internet relay chat (IRC) channels. Since source identification in these communications channels can be easily hidden, Trojan programs can be redistributed in a number of disguises, and specific identification of a malicious program has become much more difficult.
- Some data security writers consider that a virus is simply a specific example of the class of Trojan horse programs. There is some validity to this usage, since a virus is an unknown quantity that is hidden and transmitted along with a legitimate disk or program, and any program can be turned into a Trojan by infecting it with a virus. However, the term virus more properly refers to the added, infectious code rather than the virus/target combination. Therefore, the term Trojan refers to a deliberately misleading or modified program that does not reproduce itself.

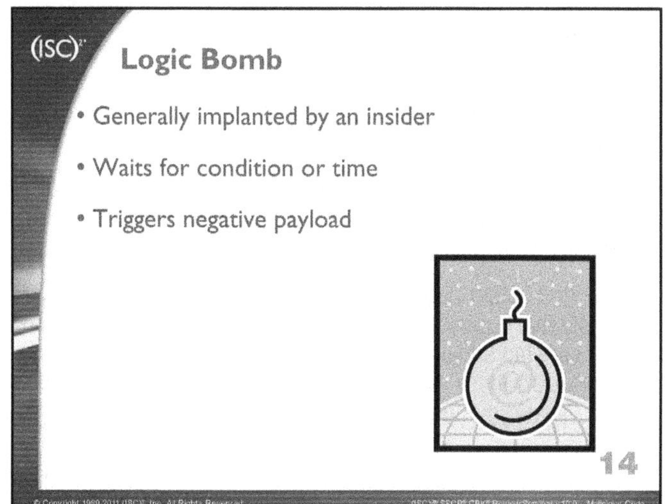


- **GENERALLY IMPLANTED BY AN INSIDER –** A logic bomb is generally implanted in or coded as part of an application under development or maintenance. Unlike a remote administration Trojan (RAT) or Trojan, it is difficult to implant a logic bomb after the fact, unless it is during program maintenance. A Trojan or a virus may contain a logic bomb as part of the payload. A logic bomb involves no reproduction, no social engineering.
- **WAITS FOR CONDITION OR TIME –** This is sometimes a date or event such as deleting a certain file.
- **TRIGGERS NEGATIVE PAYLOAD –** The payload can be almost anything that can be inserted into the system.

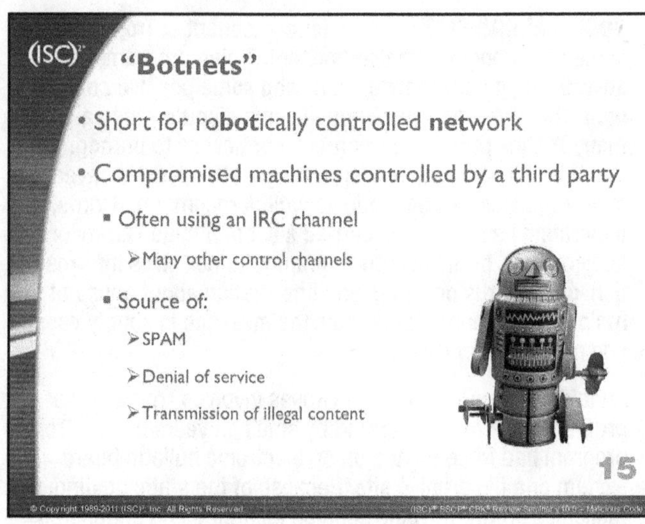

(ISC)²
“Botnets”
• Short for robotically controlled network
• Compromised machines controlled by a third party
▪ Often using an IRC channel
➢ Many other control channels
▪ Source of:
➢ SPAM
➢ Denial of service
➢ Transmission of illegal content
15


- **“BOTNETS” –** Botnets are established by hacking groups that infect vulnerable machines with agents that will perform various functions at the command of the “botherder” or controller. Typically, a botnet is controlled using IRC channels to communicate with the members of the botnet. Botnets can be used to distribute malware, spam, and launch denial of service attacks against organizations or even countries. They are a real threat to systems today, and thousands of botnets have been established.
- **OFTEN USING AN IRC CHANNEL –** IRC (internet relay chat): A protocol that enables text conversations over the Internet.

(ISC)²

**Denial of Service Attacks**

Today [June 13, 2007] the Department of Justice and FBI announced the results of an ongoing cyber crime initiative to disrupt and dismantle “botherders” and elevate the public’s cyber security awareness of botnets. OPERATION BOT ROAST is a national initiative and ongoing investigations have identified over 1 million victim computer IP addresses.

http://www.fbi.gov/pressrel/pressrel07/botnet061307.htm

16

- **DENIAL OF SERVICE ATTACKS –** Botnets are the main source of distributed denial of service (DDoS) attacks and of spam. (Note that a “botherder” is a hacker who operates a botnet.)
- While the report excerpted on the Slide is heartening, botnet creation and operation is ongoing. Botnets are extremely resistant to takedown with modern methods of command and control and fat-flux technologies.
- During 2007, the Storm botnet was estimated to be the second most powerful supercomputer in the world. During 2008, however, it was superseded by even larger botnets.
- Many organizations do not address the problem of denial of service (DoS) attacks during the testing and development phase of systems development and network testing.
- Note that botnet DoS attacks are growing and spreading so rapidly that descriptions such as this one cannot keep up. F-Secure (an antivirus/personal-FW/personal-IDS vendor) has a series of videos and always interesting updates on YouTube: http://www.youtube.com/fslabs.

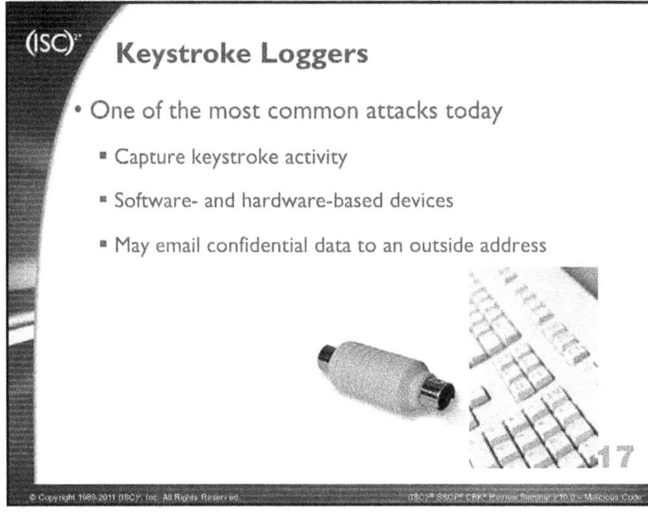


- **KEYSTROKE LOGGERS** – Are insidious and dangerous tools in the hands of an attacker. Whether software- or hardware-based, a keystroke logger captures "keystrokes" or user entries (some loggers can also capture entries on a touch screen) and forwards that information to the attacker. The attacker may thereby capture login information, banking information, and other sensitive data.
- To combat keyloggers, some people turned to onscreen virtual keyboards. In response, "black hat" groups of malicious hackers started distributing malware that would take snapshots of small areas of the screen around the area "clicked" by the mouse, and so the battle between security and hackers progresses as each side continues to develop new threats and new solutions.

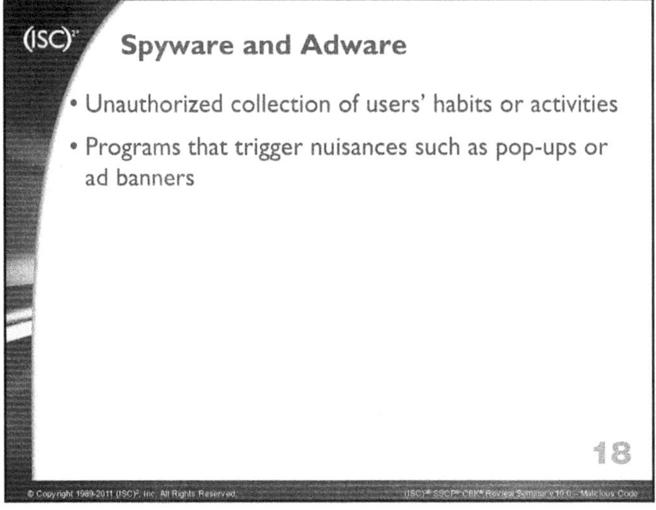


- **SPYWARE** – Is any unsolicited background process that is installed on a user's computer and collects information about the user's browsing habits and activities when he or she visits a website. These programs usually impact privacy and confidentiality and are usually installed when users download freeware or shareware programs.
- **ADWARE** – Programs which trigger such nuisances as pop-up ad pages and banners when users visit certain websites, impact productivity, and may also be combined with active background activities such as homepage hijacking code. Also, adware collects and tracks information about application, website, and Internet activity.
- The most problematic issue with spyware and adware is to distinguish between legitimate and illicit activities. Spyware and adware companies have taken full advantage of this, often suing antispyware companies for labelling their programs as spyware.

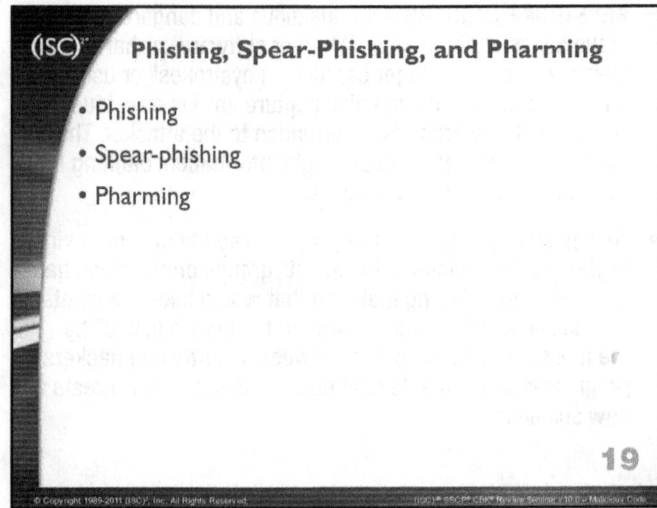
(ISC)²
Phishing, Spear-Phishing, and Pharming
• Phishing
• Spear-phishing
• Pharming
19

- **PHISHING –** An attack that tricks users into providing login information on what appears to be the account's legitimate website but is in fact a website set up by an attacker for this purpose. If the attacker can obtain login information for financial institutions, he or she may be able to steal from the victim. Very sophisticated technologies have been used to make such sites appear legitimate, including the use of frameless overlays to modify "browser chrome," such as the security locks.
- **SPEAR-PHISHING –** In order to increase the success rate of a phishing attack, the attacker will supply information about the victim that appears to come from the legitimate company. This information can be obtained in many ways, including guessing, sifting through trash (dumpster diving), or by sending bogus surveys.
- **PHARMING –** Pharming is the exploitation of a vulnerability in the DNS server software that allows a "cracker" to acquire the domain name for a site, and to (for example) redirect that website's traffic to another website. DNS servers are the machines responsible for resolving Internet domain names into their real IP addresses. The term pharming is derived from the term phishing, the use of a social engineering attack to obtain access credentials such as usernames and passwords.
    - Every host on the Internet has an IP address which consists of four numbers, each between 0 and 255. These numbers are separated by "." (dots), for example, "192.0.2.213." These IP addresses are comparable to the telephone numbers on a telephone system. As it would be very difficult to remember these numbers, websites usually also have a domain name, for example, "wikipedia.org." The domain name server acts as a "phone book" to associate the domain name of a website with its IP address ("resolving the domain name").
    - If the website receiving the traffic is a fake website, such as a copy of a bank's website, it can be used to "phish" or steal a computer user's passwords, PIN number, or account number. Note that this is only possible when the original site is not SSL protected, or when the user is ignoring warnings about invalid server certificates. For example, in January 2005, the domain name for a large New York ISP, Panix, was hijacked to a site in Australia. Secure email provider Hushmail was also caught by this attack on 24 April 2005, when the attacker rang up the domain registrar and gained enough information to redirect users to a defaced webpage.

(ISC)²

**Hoaxes and Myths**

"There is a virus going around called the AIDS Virus. It will attach itself inside your computer and eat away at your memory. This memory is irreplaceable. Then when it's finished with memory it infects your mouse or pointing device. Then it goes to your keyboard and the letters you type will not register on the screen. Before it self terminates it eats 15 MB of hard drive space and it will delete all programs on it and it can shut down sound cards rendering your speakers useless. It will come in e-mail called "Open: Very Cool!" Delete it right away. This virus will basically render your computer useless. Please alert all of your friends and colleagues to the potentially devastating problem!!"

20

- **HOAXES AND MYTHS –** Virus hoaxes are not always malicious. In some cases, the originator is not intending harm, only to amuse. However, the unwitting propagation of unverified warnings and bogus patches can lead to new vulnerabilities. Users can be unnecessarily worried, and IT help desks can be overwhelmed with support requests, slowing legitimate response to actual problems. The creator's objective is often merely to observe how widely the ruse can be propagated. This is a new version of the old chain letter attack where a person was sent a letter promising good luck or happiness if he or she forwarded the message to a dozen people.
- Here are some guidelines for recognizing hoaxes, especially virus hoaxes:
    - Did a legitimate entity (computer security expert, vendor, etc.) send the alert? Inspect any validation certificates or at least the source URL of the advisory.
    - Is there a request to forward the alert to others? No legitimate virus or security alert will suggest that the recipient forward the advisory.
    - Are there detailed-sounding explanations and terminology in the alert? Hoaxes generally use very complex, arcane, and confusing terms to intimidate the user into believing its validity. A legitimate advisory will typically omit any details and simply refer the recipient to a legitimate website for details. The website will also typically provide a suggestion for protection activities.
    - Does the alert follow the generic format of a chain letter?
        - Hook – A catchy or dramatic opening or subject line to catch attention.
        - Threat – A technical-sounding warning of serious vulnerabilities or damage.
        - Request – A plea to distribute or a suggestion to take some immediate action (download a patch, for instance, from a linked website).

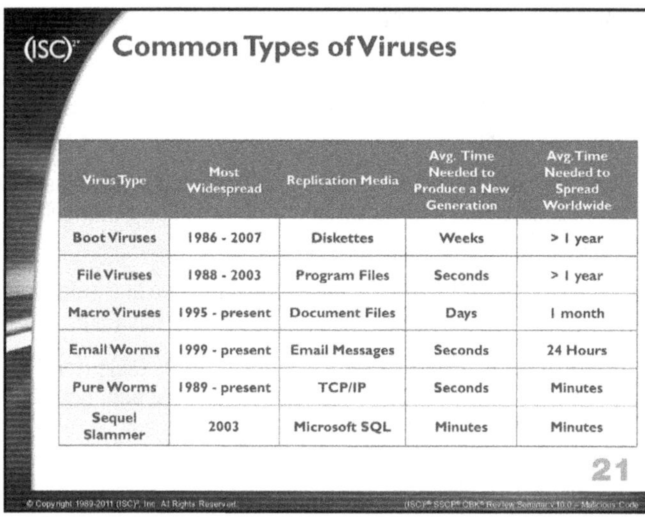

## Common Types of Viruses

| Virus Type | Most Widespread | Replication Media | Avg. Time Needed to Produce a New Generation | Avg. Time Needed to Spread Worldwide |
|---|---|---|---|---|
| Boot Viruses | 1986 - 2007 | Diskettes | Weeks | > 1 year |
| File Viruses | 1988 - 2003 | Program Files | Seconds | > 1 year |
| Macro Viruses | 1995 - present | Document Files | Days | 1 month |
| Email Worms | 1999 - present | Email Messages | Seconds | 24 Hours |
| Pure Worms | 1989 - present | TCP/IP | Seconds | Minutes |
| Sequel Slammer | 2003 | Microsoft SQL | Minutes | Minutes |

21



(ISC)²® SSCP® CBK® Review Seminar v10.0 – Malicious Code

- **COMMON TYPES OF VIRUSES –** There are a number of specific classifications of hostile code, each of which generally reflects the method of replication or distribution. All hostile codes represent executable programming that performs some form of malicious activity, whether or not economic damage or loss results. These activities may occur interactively in real-time sessions between an attacker and the target, or they may be stored processes (embedded through infection) that are triggered at some predetermined time or upon some predictable event. They may initiate a destructive action or may simply become passive observers and collectors of information.

## Domain Agenda

- Viruses, Worms, Trojan Horses, and Logic Bombs
- **Attack Structures and Techniques**
- Countermeasures and Preventative Actions
- Role of the Information Security Practitioner

22



(ISC)²® SSCP® CBK® Review Seminar v10.0 – Malicious Code

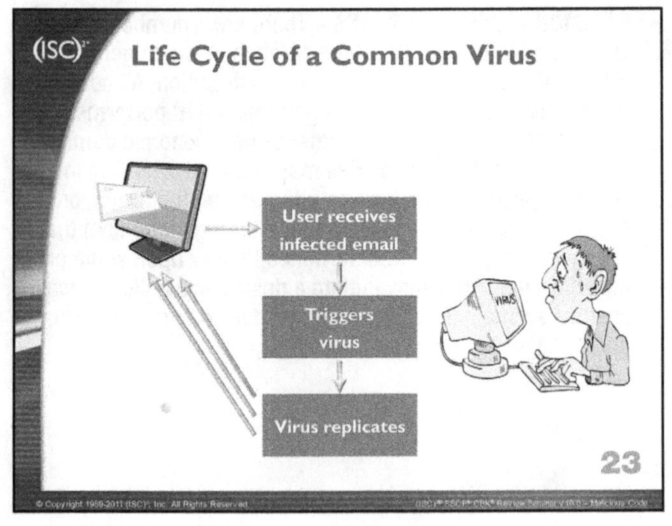


- **LIFE CYCLE OF A COMMON VIRUS –** Viruses are, by definition, executable programs that replicate and attach to (infect) other executable objects. Some viruses also perform destructive or discrete activities (payload) after having replicated and infected a system.
- There are several types of viruses, and although each type has been observed in several variations, they can be generically classified by the entity they infect.
    - **SYSTEM INFECTORS –** Target the hardware and software components involved in computer startup functions.
    - **FILE INFECTORS –** Attack and modify executable programs (such as DOS ".com" and ".exe" files and more recently, other executable 32-bit files (.sys and .dll files)).
    - **MACRO VIRUSES –** Attack document files containing embedded macro programming capabilities.

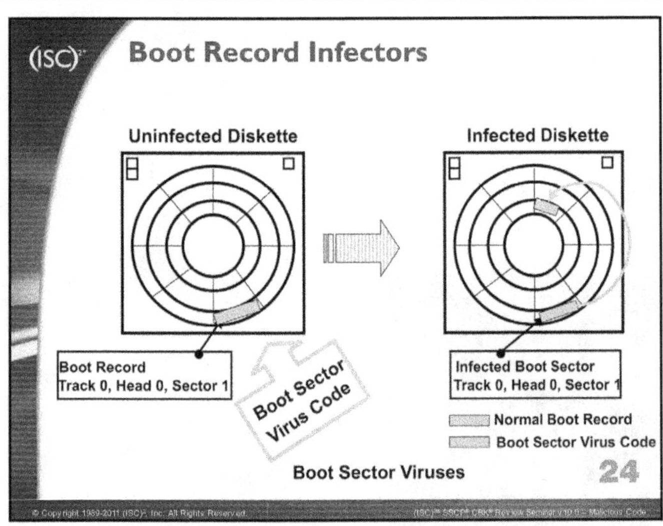


- **BOOT RECORD INFECTORS –** System infectors include a family of viruses targeting key hardware and system software components in a computing platform. The infected components usually attack during the system startup processes, allowing the virus to take control and execute before most software protective measures are able to detect their existence. The most prevalent types of system infectors include floppy boot record infectors and hard drive master boot record infectors. These viruses are transmitted predominantly through exchange of media (typically USB memory drives) or are "dropped" as a special payload from a file infector virus.
- The diagram is showing the basic architecture of boot records contained on a floppy diskette. A normal boot record location is overwritten by a virus, which causes the virus to execute upon system startup. Any subsequent startup will initialize the virus, and execute any payload it contains.

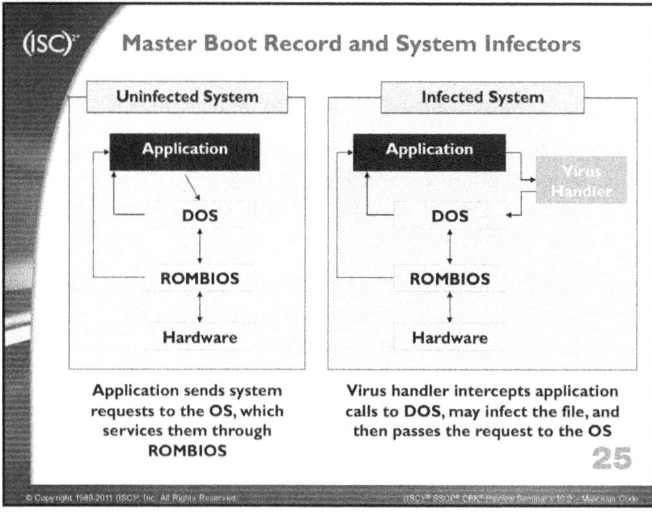


- **MASTER BOOT RECORD AND SYSTEM INFECTORS –** A master boot record infector moves or destroys the original master boot record and replaces it with viral code. It can then wrest control from the bootstrap program and perform its hostile mission. Typical master boot record infectors perform most of their tasks and then return control to the legitimate master boot record or the active partition boot record in order to mask their existence.
- Both types of boot record infectors typically load a viral proxy for the ROM-based system service provider process, thereby intercepting all normal application and operating system hardware requests. These requests include functions such as opening and closing files and file directory services, and the virus is, therefore, able to execute other types of malicious code routines and cover its tracks.
- A virus with dual-action capability that can infect multiple types of entities is called a multipartite virus and can execute file infection codes as well. Modern multipartites such as Nimda can infect five or more types of objects.

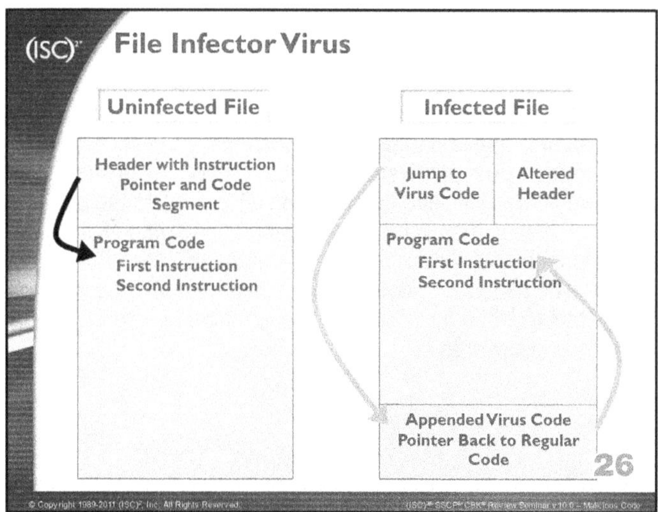


- **FILE INFECTOR VIRUS –** File infector viruses exhibit the classic "replicate and attach" behavior. They typically attack DOS program files with "COM" or "EXE" file extensions. In the MS Windows environment, there are over 150 executable file extensions; newer 32-bit virus strains are designed to work with "SYS" and many other file types as well.
- The objective of this virus type is to attach itself to the original program file in such a manner that it can control the execution of that file until it can replicate and infect other files and possibly deliver a payload.
  - One derivative file infector, called a companion virus, is really a separate program file that does not need to be attached to the original host program. Instead, the virus creates a new (companion) program with a matching file name but a higher precedent extension in the same directory path as the real program. The companion file with a higher precedent extension will execute first; for example, DOS will always execute COM files before EXE files, so issuing the Run command (or clicking the program icon) will cause the virus rather than the legitimate program to execute (for example, if the virus had created a companion file named "Format.com" and the user tried to run the "Format" utility, the virus file named "Format.com" would execute before the true file "Format.exe"). After the virus activity completes, the illicit program simply executes the command to start the original program.

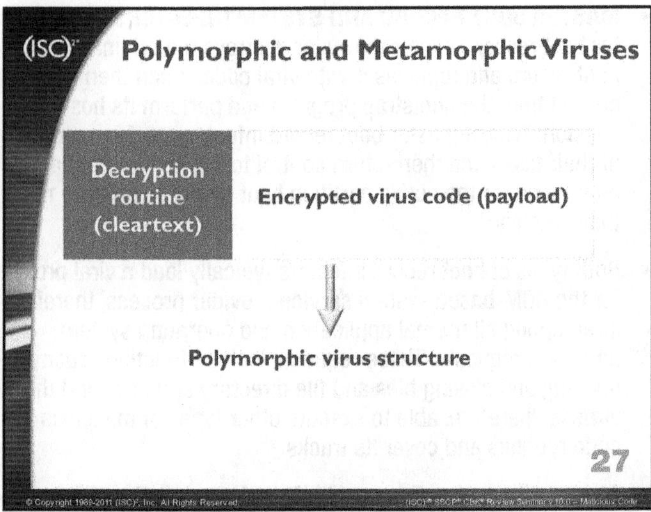


- **POLYMORPHIC VIRUS –** Literally meaning "many shapes," this technology refers to the virus' ability to change some aspect of itself as it replicates. This can be done through the modular design of the virus, or the inclusion of files from the infected computer. For example one email virus would randomly grab files from the "My Documents" library on an infected machine and attach them to itself before sending itself to the people in the infected person's address list. This was a very serious virus, since it sent many people's confidential information to others. By changing its subject line or characteristics it made itself slightly more difficult to detect than a virus that just remained the same and had a readily recognizable subject line such as "I Love You." Other viruses would try to hide their identity by self-encryption.
- Self-encrypting, polymorphic viruses duplicate the main body of the virus, and include a separate encryption engine that stores the virus body in encrypted format. Only the decryption routine itself is exposed for detection by antivirus software. The control portion of the virus is embedded in this decryption routine, which seizes control of the target system and decrypts the main body of the virus so that it can execute.
    - Highly polymorphic viruses use an additional mutation engine to vary the decryption process for each iteration, making this portion of the code even more difficult to identify.
    - Bugbear.B is a very complex polymorphic virus that spreads through both email and network shares. The worm sends emails with a range of different content. It uses a known vulnerability to execute the attachment automatically when the email is opened.
- While polymorphic viruses encrypt their functional code to avoid pattern recognition, such a virus will still need to decipher the code – unmodified from infection to infection – in order to execute.
- **METAMORPHIC VIRUSES –** A subcategory of polymorphism, change their code to an equivalent one (i.e., a code doing essentially the same thing), so that a mutated virus never has the same executable code in memory (not even at runtime) as the original virus that constructed the mutation. Metamorphic code is usually more effective than polymorphic code. Unlike with polymorphic viruses, antivirus products may not simply use emulation techniques to defeat metamorphism, since metamorphic code may never reveal code that remains constant from infection to infection.
- In computer virus terms, metamorphic code is code that can reprogram itself. Often, it does this by translating its own code into a temporary representation, editing the temporary representation of itself, and then writing itself back to normal code again. This procedure is done with the virus itself, and thus also the metamorphic engine itself undergoes changes. This is used by some viruses when they are about to infect new files, and the result is that the "children" will never look like their "parents." The computer viruses that use this technique do this in order to avoid the pattern recognition of antivirus software: The actual algorithm does not change, but everything else might.
- Polymorphic viruses also use a technique called self-modifying code. This is code that alters its own instructions while it is executing – usually to reduce the instruction path length and improve performance or simply to reduce otherwise repetitively similar code, thus simplifying maintenance. Self-modification is an alternative to the method of "flag setting" and conditional program branching, used primarily to reduce the number of times a condition needs to be tested for. Malicious coders have borrowed this technique to further try and keep their malware from being discovered.

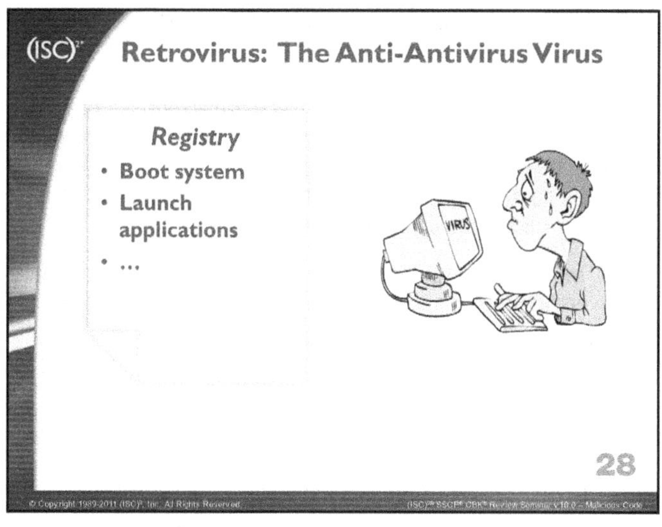


- **RETROVIRUS: THE ANTI-ANTIVIRUS VIRUS –** Retroviruses, also known as anti-antivirus viruses, are specifically designed to disable or infect countermeasures such as antivirus (AV) signature files or integrity databases in order to avoid detection. The virus searches for and deletes or alters these data files, thereby, crippling the AV software's ability to function properly. Other viruses, especially boot viruses (which gain control of the target system at startup) modify Windows Registry keys and other key files to disable any AV, firewall, and IDS software it finds. Examples of these viruses include:
  - "Cpw," which will delete SCAN.EXE.
  - "Zarma" is a memory-resident encrypted, stealth, COM, and EXE infector. It was discovered in France in May 1995. Zarma intercepts interrupt functions to mask its presence on an infected system. The virus hooks Int 3 to its own decryption routine which enables it to decrypt a second decryptor on the stack. Zarma can deactivate VSAFE, VDEFEND, and VWATCH.
  - Around 1990, the resident portion of Central Point Anti-Virus could be disabled with a mere 14 bytes of code. This code became widely integrated into variant viruses of the time, and was used, for a while, as a generic virus detection signature.

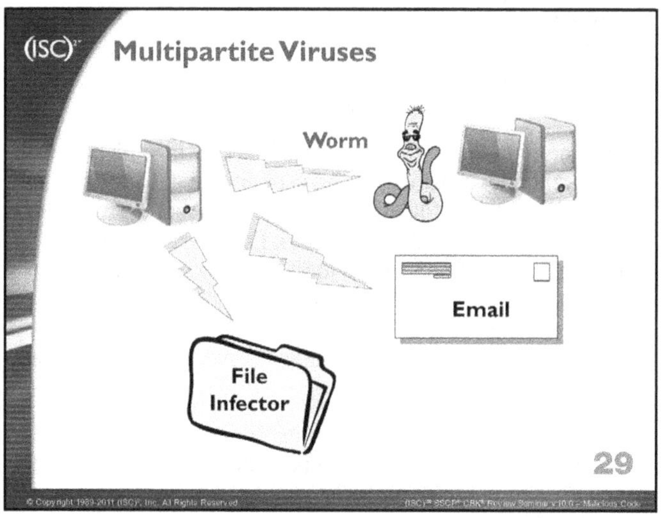


- **MULTIPARTITE VIRUSES –** Multipartite viruses are hybrids that exhibit multiple behaviors. Such viruses may be file infectors within an application and that spawn an MBR infection upon execution which will then infect other files when the system is restarted.
  - Nimda, for instance, infects as a worm, an email virus, and a file infector as it spreads through network shares. It contains its own SMTP engine to execute email propagation, and it searches for and uses backdoors (Trojans) left on IIS servers by Code Red to propagate to other servers. It can also search local network resources for file shares and propagate to local servers or end stations.
  - Some multipartite viruses, such as the one-half virus isolated in 1994, may also exhibit both stealth and polymorphic characteristics.
  - Multipartite viruses should not be confused with "blended" threats that combine the characteristics of viruses, worms, and Trojans to cause infections, exploit vulnerabilities, and spread.

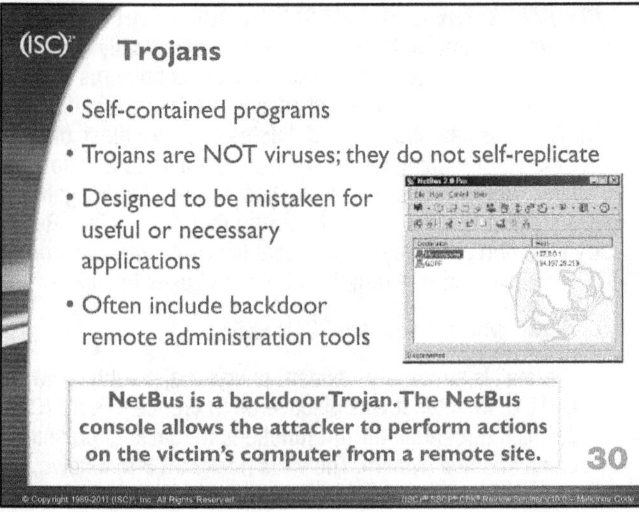

(ISC)²
Trojans
• Self-contained programs
• Trojans are NOT viruses; they do not self-replicate
• Designed to be mistaken for useful or necessary applications
• Often include backdoor remote administration tools
NetBus is a backdoor Trojan. The NetBus console allows the attacker to perform actions on the victim's computer from a remote site.
30


- **TROJANS –** Trojans are self-contained programs designed to be mistaken for useful or necessary applications. Trojans are not viruses; they do not propagate by self-replication. They may be introduced, or "dropped" as the payload of a classic virus, or may be accidentally introduced when users download files, open documents containing macros, open (or even read) emails containing malicious code, execute companion virus files, or click links displayed on webpages.
  - Trojans are also introduced directly by attackers who have compromised and penetrated a computer's defenses and gained administrative (root) access to the system.
  - The most common modern Trojan programs include back-door remote administration tools designed to permit undetected system access and potentially hostile activity, as well as keystroke and password sniffers that can capture login and authorization information for future attacks.

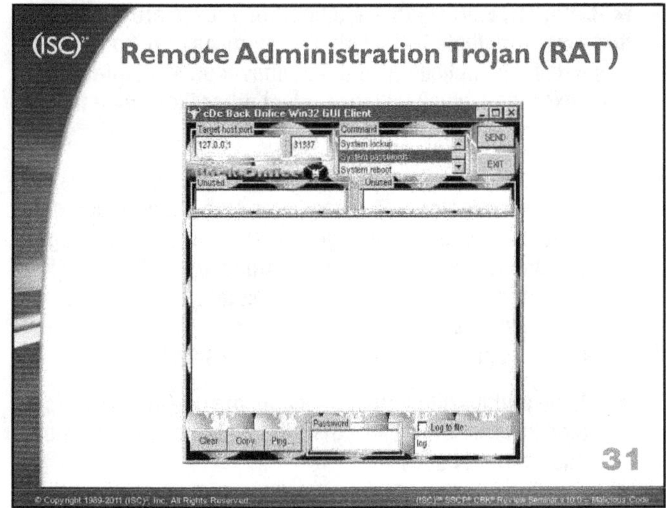


- **REMOTE ADMINISTRATION TROJAN –** A remote administration Trojan, or RAT, is a Trojan that allows an attacker to remotely control a machine via a "client" in the attacker's machine and a "server" in the victim's machine.
- The server in the victim's machine "serves" incoming connections and runs invisibly with no user interface. The client is a GUI front-end that the attacker uses to connect to victim servers and "manage" those machines. Examples include Back Orifice, NetBus, SubSeven, and Hack'a'tack. What happens when a server is installed in a victim's machine depends on the capabilities of the Trojan, the interests of the attacker, and whether or not control of the server is ever gained by another attacker.
- Infections by remote administration Trojans on Windows machines are becoming as frequent as viruses. One common source is through file and print sharing. Another common method of installation is for the attacker to simply email the Trojan to the user along with a social engineering hack (compelling message) that convinces the user to run it.

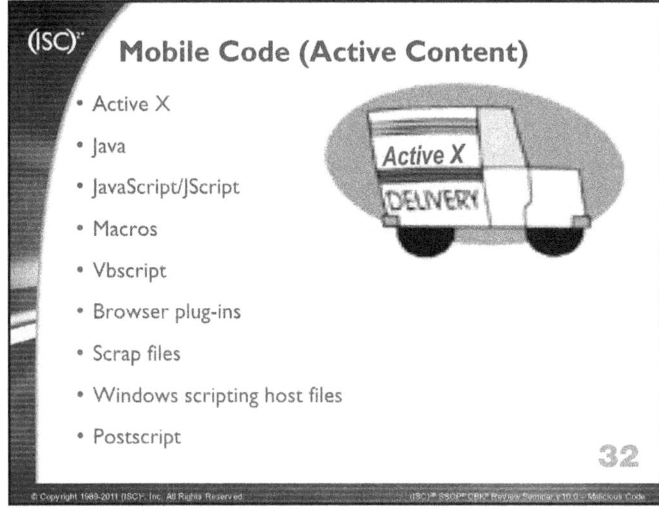
(ISC)²
Mobile Code (Active Content)
• Active X
• Java
• JavaScript/JScript
• Macros
• Vbscript
• Browser plug-ins
• Scrap files
• Windows scripting host files
• Postscript
Active X
DELIVERY
32

- **MOBILE CODE (ACTIVE CONTENT) –** The term "active content" includes ActiveX, Java, JavaScript/JScript, Macros, VBscript, browser plug-ins, scrap files, Windows scripting host files, and Postscript. This code runs as the user signed on to a PC and can do everything that the user can do.
  - Active content threats, including ActiveX, Java, and JavaScript code in HTTP data streams, are often referred to as "mobile code" because the programs are written to be sent from the remote host but run on your computer platform. Key points to consider regarding active code:
    - Java applets are considered untrusted code and are run within a virtual machine that uses a sandbox (a safe isolated area that can allow the program to execute but not affect the primary system) to restrict or prevent inappropriate actions on users' computers.
    - Java code can trigger (or spawn) the execution of OS functions that do not have the sandbox restriction, or that have loopholes such as those prevalent in Microsoft Internet Explorer implementations.
    - ActiveX is widely considered to be the greater threat because it is essentially a compact version of Microsoft's OLE (object linking and embedding) which permits direct access to native Windows calls and links them to system functions.
    - ActiveX has no built-in language restrictions controlling code behavior.
    - ActiveX controls can be built utilizing many different programming languages.
  - Many Internet websites now rely on Java applets and ActiveX controls to create their look and feel. For these schemes to operate properly, these bits of mobile code are downloaded to the user's PC, where they gain access to the local host and can then spawn malicious activity (viral infections, worm behavior, or Trojan functions).

(ISC)²

**Evidence of Active Code Attacks**

- Changes to homepage or browser settings
- Poor system performance reading email
- Increased antivirus or IDS sensor alarm activity during periods of Internet activity
- Unexpected new software installation messages (usually at startup after a reset)
- Unusual system activity after Internet sessions or after reboot following periods of Internet browsing

33

- Please be aware that these symptoms may be caused by things other than malware, and the root cause must be investigated carefully before remediation is performed. More information on detecting evidence of attacks can be found at: http://www.cert.org/security- improvement/implementations/i042.07.html.

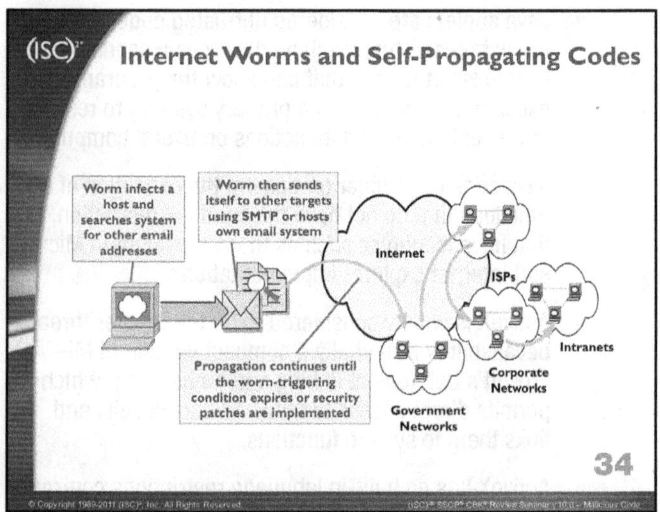
(ISC)²
Internet Worms and Self-Propagating Codes
Worm infects a host and searches system for other email addresses
Worm then sends itself to other targets using SMTP or hosts own email system
Internet
ISPs
Intranets
Corporate Networks
Government Networks
Propagation continues until the worm-triggering condition expires or security patches are implemented
34

- **INTERNET WORMS AND SELF-PROPAGATING CODES –** Worms are self-contained programs designed to propagate from one host machine to another, using the host's own network communication protocols. Unlike viruses, classic worms do not require any user action (such as opening infected files or sending infected attachments) to execute their routines.
  - The primary job of a worm is to make copies of itself and send them into the world by any means possible. They bog down networks by sending out hundreds or thousands of copies of themselves, thereby clogging up communications between computer systems on the Internet. Multipartite viruses can also contain components that behave in the same manner.

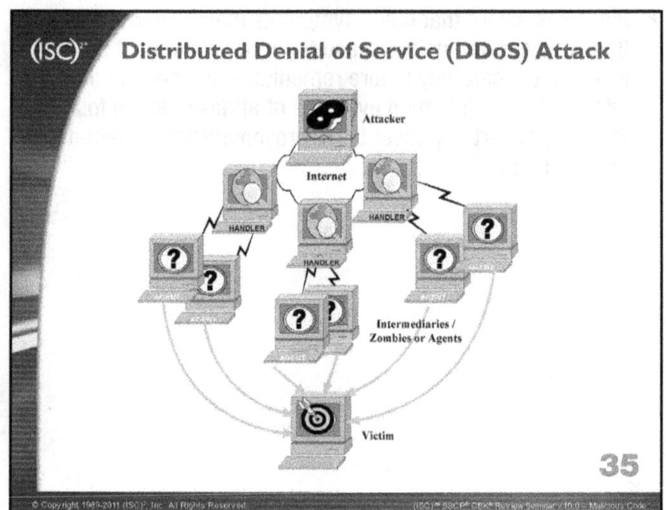
(ISC)²
Distributed Denial of Service (DDoS) Attack
Attacker
Internet
HANDLER
HANDLER
HANDLER
Intermediaries / Zombies or Agents
Victim
35

- **DISTRIBUTED DENIAL OF SERVICE (DDOS) ATTACK –** Unsuspecting hosts, or "zombies," act as intermediaries to conduct an attack. Zombies are compromised systems on which Trojan handler programs are installed, which then act as agents to execute a coordinated attack on a target system or network. The attacker controls one or more "master" handler servers, each of which can control many agents or "daemons." The agents are instructed to coordinate a packet-based attack against one or more victim systems. There are three parties in these attacks: the attacker, the intermediaries (handlers and agents), and the victim(s). Even though the intermediary is not the intended victim, the intermediary can also be victimized by suffering the same types of problems that the "victim" experiences such as DoS.

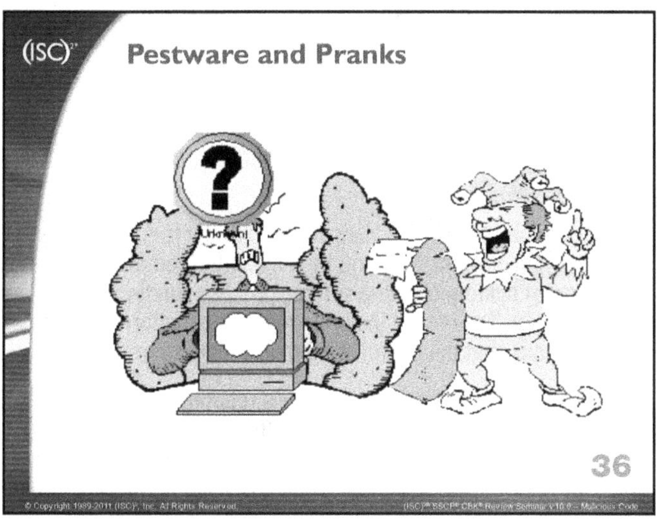
(ISC)²
Pestware and Pranks
36

- **A PEST** is an undesired process or code that can appear on a PC or network after freeware applications are downloaded from an Internet site. Pests are generally nuisances but can also include Trojans, spyware, remote administration tools, hacker tool kits, and more. **PESTWARE** in the form of tracking cookies is sometimes employed by commercial websites as a means of tracking a user's Internet browsing habits, or as pop-up or pop-under webpages that push unsolicited offers to a user who visits a competitive website. Pestware can threaten confidentiality and privacy and impact productivity.
- **PRANKS,** on the other hand, are often used by adventurous "script kiddies" or other internal or external users. Pranks can be malicious by damaging a system, or a nuisance by just executing unwanted activity (such as changing colors) on the victim's system.
- For further information, visit: www.scumware.com/wm2.html.

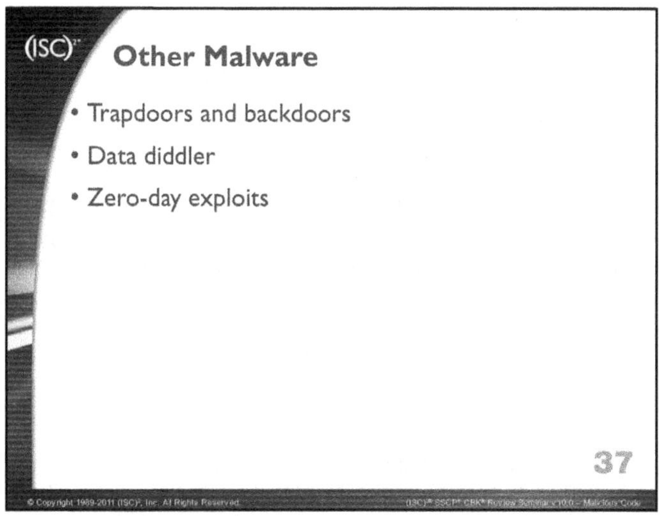
(ISC)²
Other Malware
• Trapdoors and backdoors
• Data diddler
• Zero-day exploits
37

- **TRAPDOORS AND BACKDOORS –** Backdoors or trapdoors are mechanisms that can be used to bypass normal security controls, particularly for access control. These are frequently (and legitimately) used while software is in development or implementation, where they are known as maintenance hooks. When such a mechanism is left in place once the system is in production, it becomes a security problem.
- **DATA DIDDLER –** A data diddler is a malicious program or payload that corrupts data files, by incremental small amounts, over a period of time. Although rare, we have recently seen instances that indicate a resurgence of interest in the technology.
- **ZERO-DAY EXPLOITS –** "Zero-day" attacks are based on the hacker finding a vulnerability and developing an exploit before anyone else is aware of the flaw and has time to react or patch the vulnerability. This would allow the hacker to compromise a system with no prior warning to the system administrators. In reality there are few of these types of attacks and usually the software companies and antivirus vendors release patches before a new attack can be launched.

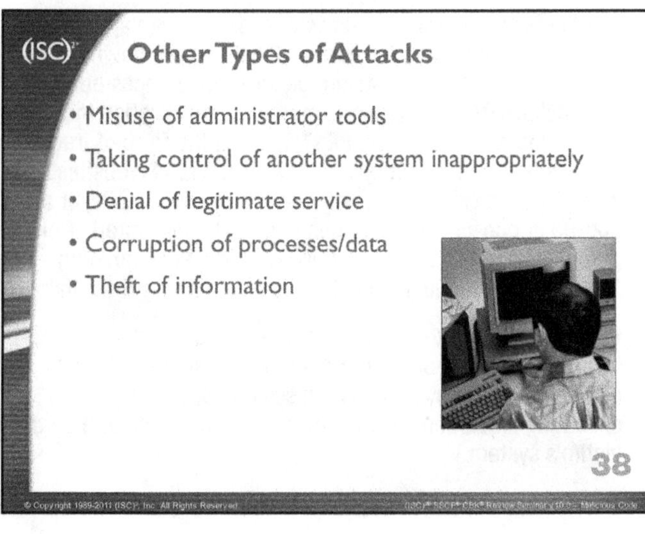

(ISC)²
Other Types of Attacks
• Misuse of administrator tools
• Taking control of another system inappropriately
• Denial of legitimate service
• Corruption of processes/data
• Theft of information
38


- **OTHER TYPES OF ATTACKS –** While not included within the normal definition of malicious code, there are other methods of conducting software-based network attacks. These include:
    - Interactive commands performed on a target system after an intruder has gained administrative control of the system.
    - Commands that are transmitted directly to a target system, misinterpreted, and then executed remotely on the target system or some service process running on that system. These may include unicode or malformed data attacks that could fool an antivirus system or firewall.
    - It is the IT security practitioner's responsibility to understand the kinds of malicious software threats that can present themselves in any of these formats in order to develop reasonable countermeasures to protect the organization.
    - Denial of service refers not to any actual breaches, but to any act that prevents the use for which a system is legitimately intended.
    - Corruption is, of course, any violation of integrity, and theft of information is the most common violation of confidentiality.

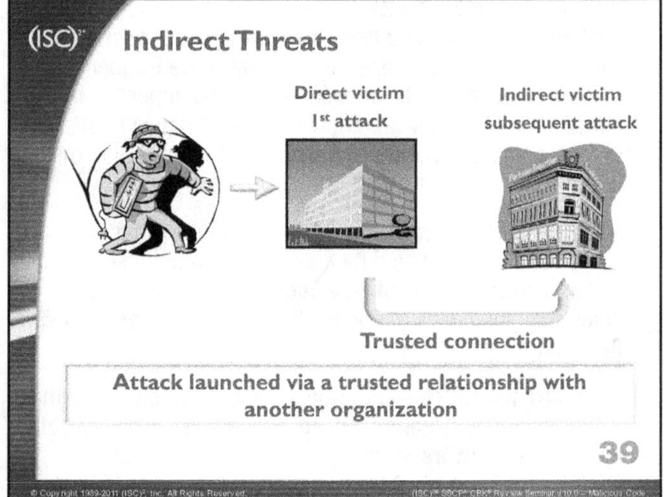


- **INDIRECT THREATS –** Another category of threat sources involves external but interdependent relationships that may pose unintended dangers to an organization.
- Indirect threats can come from Extranet trading partners (suppliers and customers) who may inadvertently compromise even the most sophisticated security measures through their own weaknesses and failures in information technology (IT) security. Once a partner network is compromised, malicious activity may easily extend through the same portals created to facilitate electronic data interchange (EDI) and virtual private network (VPN) communications between partners. This is traditionally referred to as a "trusted source" issue. Defenses require putting additional emphasis on the validation of traffic and data exchanged between companies.
- Because most organizations must rely upon Internet service providers to achieve connectivity to the Internet, IT security practitioners must also become knowledgeable about the service provider's potential security vulnerabilities, particularly regarding the outsourcing of hosted services. Availability is an additional consideration in designing redundancy into a network infrastructure, since an organization that relies on Internet service for critical operations must ensure that its connections are not easily affected by denial of service (DoS) attacks or problems from a customer or client.

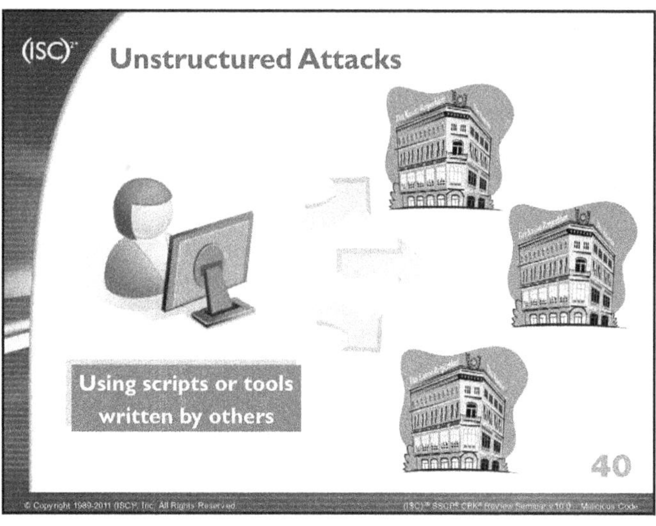

(ISC)²
Unstructured Attacks
Using scripts or tools written by others
40


- **UNSTRUCTURED ATTACKS –** Uncoordinated (or unstructured) attacks against network resources are generally perpetrated by minimally or moderately skilled persons such as script kiddies and cyberpunks. Script kiddies and cyberpunks are often motivated by personal gratification or the thrill of the challenge in achieving illegal access to a network or target system and frequently have no other real purpose in mind. Any level of success, however, may lead to further exploration and more malicious activity such as defacements (and the resulting embarrassment of having a webpage defaced) or crashing systems. All such activity is of concern to information technology security practitioners as it represents a compromise of defensive measures.
- Note that unstructured attacks occasionally expose an unintended vulnerability or target and the attacker may then continue with a more methodical approach. This is sometimes called rat dancing, shaking doors, or rattling locks.

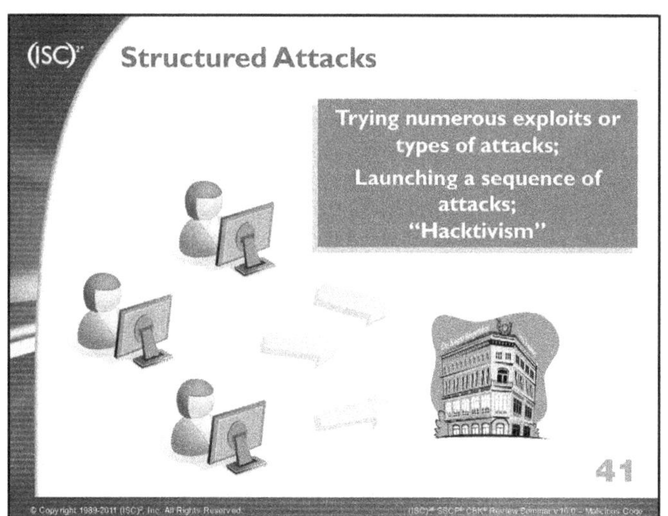

(ISC)²
Structured Attacks
Trying numerous exploits or types of attacks;
Launching a sequence of attacks;
"Hacktivism"
41


- **STRUCTURED ATTACKS –** Coordinated, preplanned, structured attacks are usually conducted by highly motivated and technically skilled crackers using complex tools and focused efforts. Attacks are usually conducted in phases, and may be aimed at a specific organization or a specific technology (such as an operating system (OS) version). Structured attacks are usually conducted in phases, after an overall goal is established.
- These attackers may act alone or in groups, and they understand, develop, and use sophisticated hacking techniques to locate, identify, penetrate, probe, and then carry out malicious activities. Crackers' motives may include money, anger, destruction, or political objectives. Irrespective of their motivation, crackers can, and do, inflict serious business damage on networks. In some cases, the purpose of the attack may be to make a social statement and attack an organization in order to protest the activities of the organization or government. This is sometimes called 'hacktivism.'

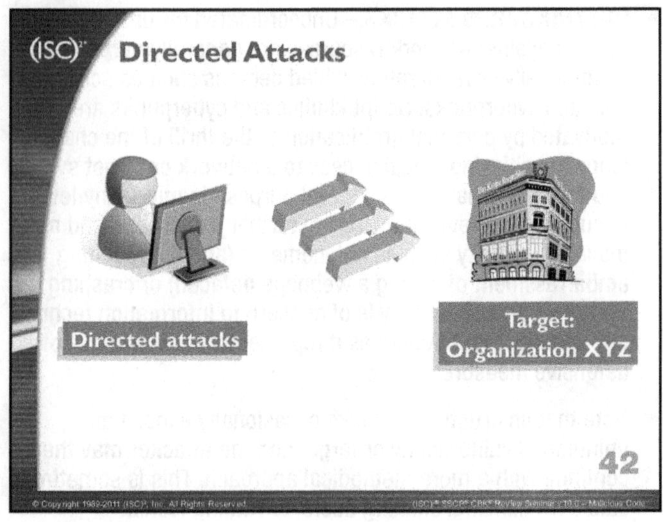


- **DIRECTED ATTACKS –** Directed attacks against specific targets (e.g., specific organizations) or target classes (e.g., networks that are using certain hardware, operating system versions, or services) are often conducted as interactive sessions using predefined exploits. An example might be an IIS unicode attack against specific Web servers in an organization.
- These exploits may be uncoordinated or unstructured, as when a script kiddie uses well-known hacker tools to discover vulnerable sites and then conducts random exploits to rat dance around the compromised network through trial and error.
- They may also be conducted as coordinated or preplanned attacks by individual crackers or by coordinated cyberterrorist groups, in which case they will likely work methodically and in phases to achieve their desired goals.

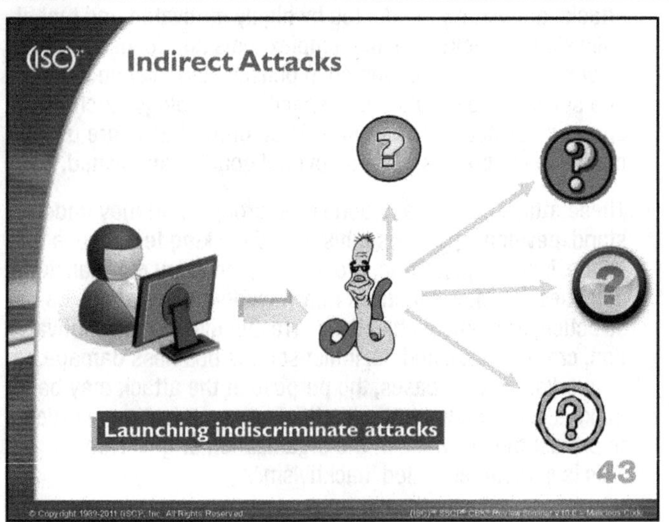


- **INDIRECT ATTACKS –** Indirect attacks occur as a natural result of preprogrammed hostile code exploits such as Internet worms or viruses. These attacks are unleashed indiscriminately and are designed to propagate rapidly and widely. While the worm or virus itself may be written to exploit a specific system or application vulnerability, the replication and transmission components of the code may damage communications or systems not originally intended.
- Note that the goal of a directed attack against a specific target might be to establish a starting point for an indirect attack against a more widely disbursed population. For example, an attacker might compromise a single Web server so as to install an email worm as a denial of service (DoS) exploit.

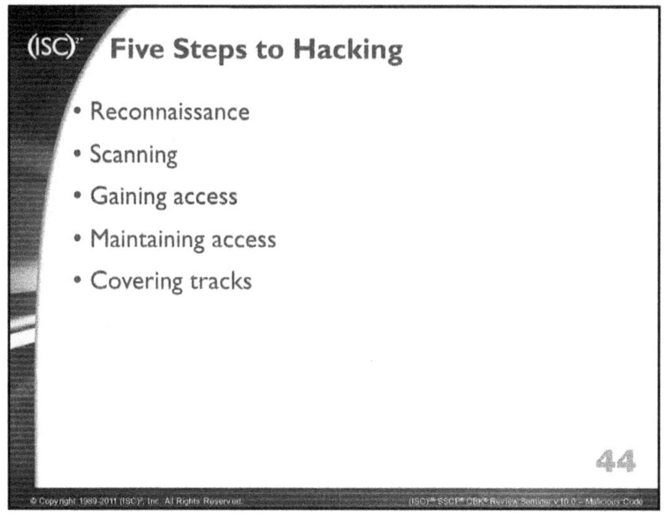
(ISC)²
Five Steps to Hacking
• Reconnaissance
• Scanning
• Gaining access
• Maintaining access
• Covering tracks
44

- Hackers work in stages. The best hackers work slowly, probing and testing and generally avoiding having their work logged when possible or minimizing and deleting logs of their work when not. They divide their work into five stages.
- **RECONNAISSANCE –** This is often passive (no contact with the target). It involves searching online databases such as Internet registries (to get domain information), using search engines and their cached pages to see content without visiting actual websites, and researching corporate officers via public records (such as the "Edgar" database maintained by the US Security and Exchange Commission). It might involve low-level active inquiries such as normal Web browsing.
- **SCANNING –** In this step, the attacker looks for machines operating on the victim's network. The attacker might start with "horizontal" scanning, which uses techniques such as pinging all addresses in a range to see which machines respond. He or she would then switch to "vertical" scanning to determine the operating system type and services running for each active machine found. There is a special case called "distributed" scanning that involves searching across a wide range of machines (horizontal) but looking only for a particular service (vertical) such as an SQL database, or Web server.
- **GAINING ACCESS –** Once the attacker has determined which operating system and services are being used and has found an unpatched version of either, he or she will use an "exploit" to gain access. The exploit might start at a normal user level, but the attacker will then attempt to gain privileged access, often through the use of other exploits. (This is known as "privilege escalation".) Using two or more exploits in series is known as a "chained exploit."
- **MAINTAINING ACCESS –** Having successfully attacked a machine, the hacker will often attempt to create a method allowing access in the future without having to hack the system/machine. This might mean creating a privileged user account or installing a Trojan or other remote access malware.
- **COVERING TRACKS –** To avoid being caught or even having the system cleaned, the attacker will try to cover his or her tracks. This usually involves deleting or altering log files. In some cases, attackers will patch the system so that other attackers won't use the same exploit, which would cause a slowdown and increase the likelihood of the administrator noticing the infection and cleaning the system. Patching will also often cause the owner to think that the system is secure and thus further decrease the chance of cleaning.

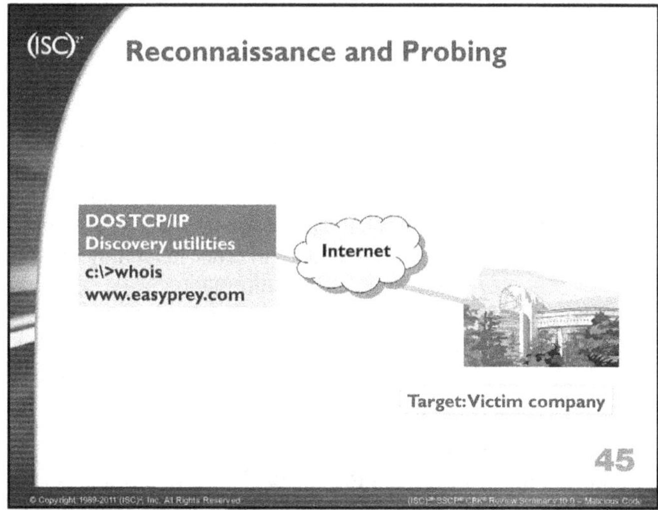
(ISC)²
Reconnaissance and Probing
DOS TCP/IP
Discovery utilities
c:\>whois
www.easyprey.com
Internet
Target: Victim company
45

- **RECONNAISSANCE AND PROBING –** Once the attacker's overall goal or objective is clear, the attacker will probe the target network and identify points of possible entry (the vulnerabilities). This phase may involve the use of tools that are readily available on the Internet, or are part of the underlying protocol suite, or are custom developed to exploit specific or potential targets. The tools can be used independently or as a coordinated suite of activities designed to provide a complete understanding of a targeted network (i.e., what protocols and operating system are used, what the server platforms are, what services/ports are open, what actual or probable network addressing and naming is being used, etc.).
- Methods can include:
  - Use of domain name system (DNS) and Internet control message protocol (ICMP) tools within the TCP/IP protocol suite.
  - Use of standard and customized simple network management protocol (SNMP) tools.
  - Using port scanners and mappers to locate potential target services.
  - Dissemination of spyware Trojans to collect reconnaissance data.

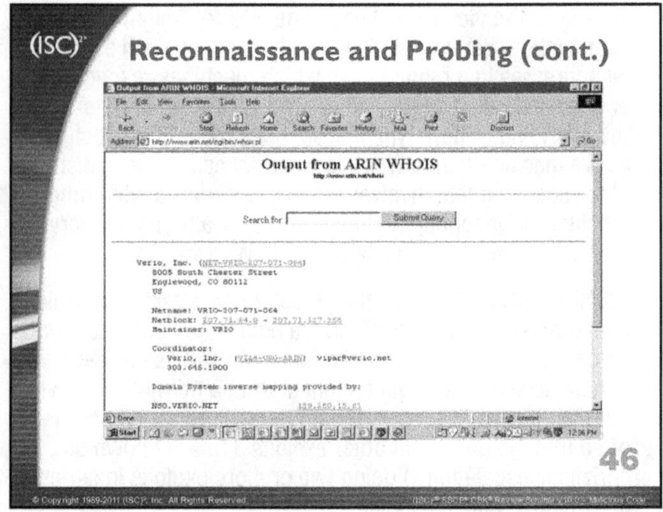


- Domain Name System (DNS) is a hierarchy of servers that provides an Internet-wide mapping (cross-reference) of the symbolic name (fully qualified domain name) to IP address or hosts connected to the Internet. Publicly available information on registered addresses is obtainable through a number of searchable websites. Discovery tools that are built into TCP/IP such as **WHOIS** (see above) and **FINGER** can also be used to gather preliminary information in profiling a target site.
- **REVERSE DNS LOOKUP** or **NSLOOKUP** are additional utility commands that will also interrogate DNS information and provide cross-referencing. These services are often provided for free on the Internet and can be located simply by searching on the command name itself.
- The example above is from http://www.arin.net/whois/, which can be used to locate the IP address of a potential target network. Note that ARIN WHOIS will not locate any domain-related information or any information relating to military networks.
- Many operating systems provide a WHOIS utility. To conduct a query from the command line, the format generally is: Whois-h hostname identifier (i.e., whois-h whois.arin.net<query string>).

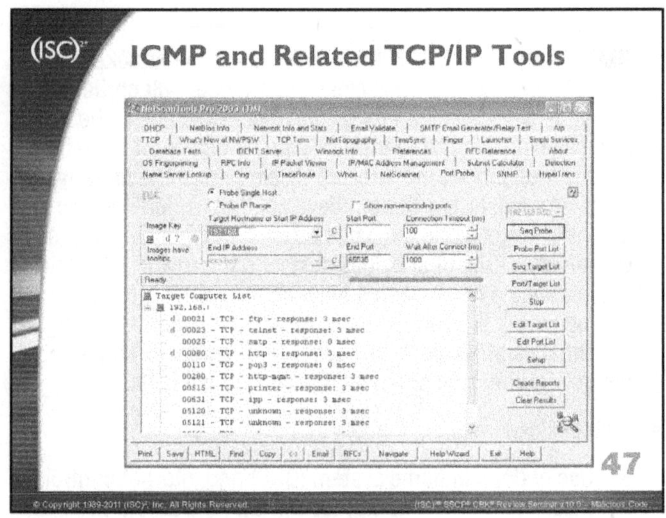

(ISC)²
ICMP and Related TCP/IP Tools
47


- **ICMP AND RELATED TCP/IP TOOLS –** The Internet control message protocol (ICMP) **PING** command and several closely related tools are available on most operating systems and are a key profiling tool in verifying that target systems are reachable. The **PING** command can be used with a number of extension flags to test direct reachability between hosts, or as part of the actual attack plan (see Ping of Death attacks).
- After a target network has been located, attackers may perform a **PING SWEEP** of the IP addresses (or a range of them) within the major network or subnet in order to identify other hosts that may be accessible. This information alone can sometimes expose the likely network size and topology and because many networks use a structured numbering scheme, it may also point to likely server and network device locations.
- If gaining access is one of the objectives, a simple **TELNET** login attempt might be performed first in order to test the softness of perimeter controls. **RPCINFO** could also be used to determine if this service is active for remote command execution.

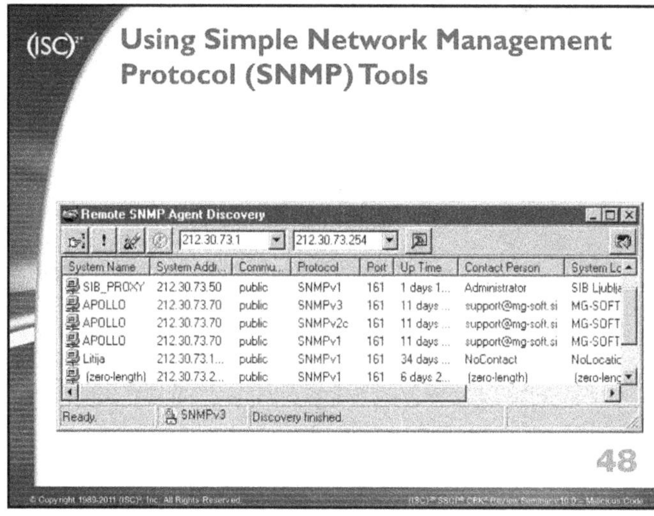


- **USING SIMPLE NETWORK MANAGEMENT PROTOCOL (SNMP) TOOLS –** Remote SNMP Agent Discovery utilities let you discover responsive SNMP agents running on network devices. This example reflects, for instance, a server ("APOLLO"), located at 212.30.73.70, which is responding to SNMP queries and can now be probed or scanned for other open service ports. Early versions of SNMP used cleartext community strings or passwords to allow remote access to equipment.
- SNMP is an application-layer protocol that facilitates the exchange of management information between network devices. It is part of the TCP/IP (transmission control protocol/ Internet protocol) suite. SNMP enables network administrators to manage network performance, find and solve network problems, and plan for network growth.
- Many of the more popular network management software suites, such as HP OpenView, SunNet Manager, and AIX NetView, are SNMP compliant and offer full support for managed devices, agents, and network-management systems. In addition, there are many utility programs that can be used to gather network device information, including platform, operating system version, and capabilities. Poorly configured network-management facilities will allow even moderately skilled attackers to gather significant attack profile information.

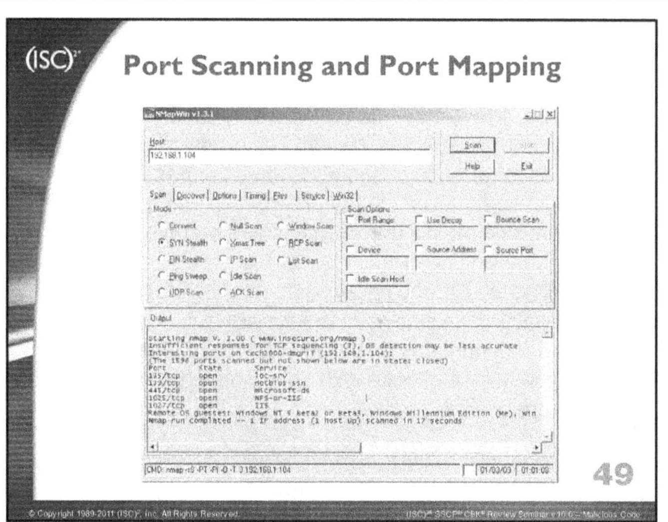


- **PORT SCANNING AND PORT MAPPING –** After the attacker identifies a target network, he or she may choose to explore what systems and services are accessible. This is done by "port scanning." There are several popular port scanning applications available, including **NMAP** (available for UNIX and Windows), and **MINGSWEEPER** (a network reconnaissance tool for Windows NT/2000, designed to facilitate large address space, high-speed node discovery, and identification). These tools permit an attacker to discover and identify hosts by performing ping sweeps, to probe for open TCP and UDP service ports, and to identify operating systems and vulnerable applications that might be running.

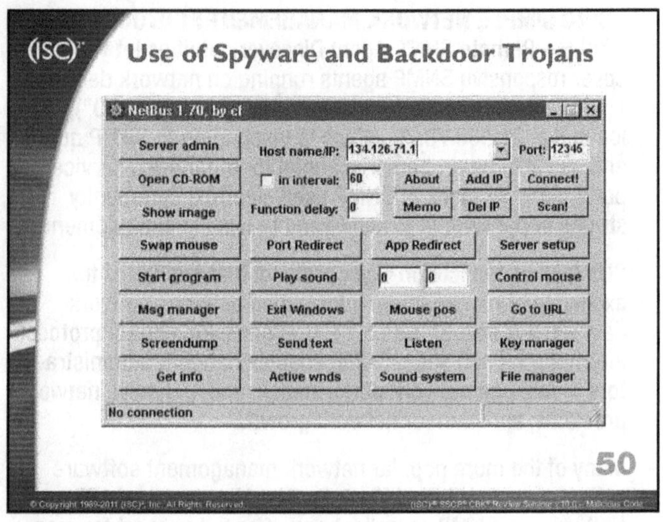


- **USE OF SPYWARE AND BACKDOOR TROJANS –** This is the administrator screen for **NETBUS**, a popular remote administration tool, which can be installed as a Trojan server process on an unsuspecting host machine and then be accessed and controlled through client software.
- **SPYWARE** is a term for Trojan software that employs a user's Internet connection in the background (the so-called "back-channel") without the user's knowledge or explicit permission. Spyware exists as an independent, executable program on a system and can monitor keystrokes, arbitrarily scan files on a hard drive, snoop other applications such as word processors and chat programs, read cookies, change the default homepage, interface with the default Web browser to determine what websites are visited, monitor other user behavior, and transmit this information back to the spyware author.

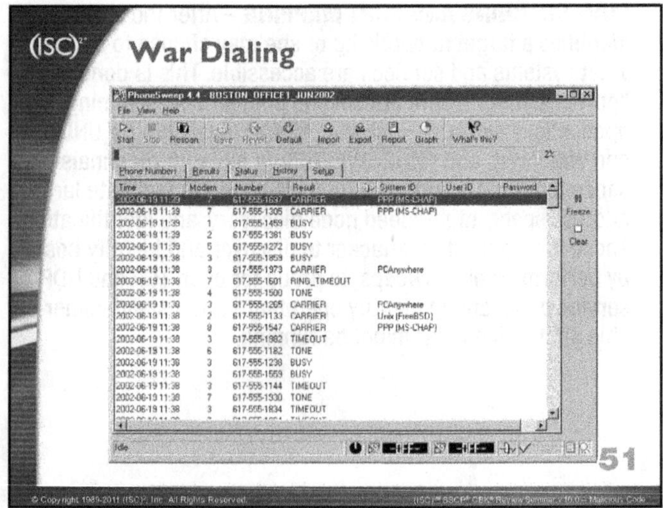


- **WAR DIALING –** A war dialer, usually obtained as freeware, is a computer program (such as PhoneSweep 4.4, above) typically used by a hacker to identify potential targets by identifying phone numbers that can successfully make a connection with a computer modem. The program automatically dials a defined range of phone numbers, and the results are logged into a database. Some programs can also identify the operating system and may also conduct automated penetration testing. In such cases, the war dialer will run through a predetermined list of common user names and passwords in an attempt to gain access to the system. If the program does not provide automated penetration testing, the intruder may attempt to hack a modem with an unprotected login or easily cracked password.
- Commercial war dialers, also known as modem scanners, are also used by system administrators in order to identify unauthorized modems on their own networks. Unauthorized modems can provide easy access to a company's network, and, in addition to having policy to prohibit them, the security administrator should periodically test for their presence.

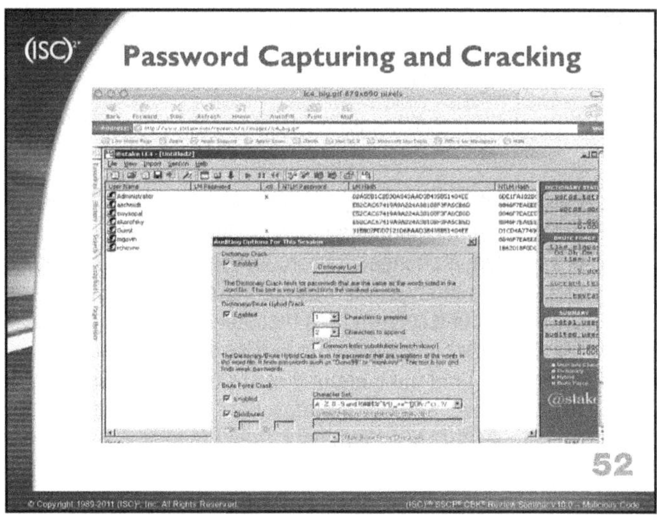


- **PASSWORD CAPTURING AND CRACKING –** Screenshot from **LOPHTCRACK** performing a brute force attack against a host's passwords. A password logger may be installed as a backdoor Trojan on a target machine in order to monitor the protocol and program activity associated with remote login processes. If login strings are captured remotely, a program such as LophtCrack (http://www.atstake.com/research/lc/download.html) can be used to quickly decrypt and compromise administrator and user passwords.
- There are other tools available for UNIX systems such as John the Ripper; and a common type of attack today uses rainbow tables of preidentified password hash values.

- **ADWARE/TRACKWARE –** Many adware applications install Trojan advertising components on your system that download ads and waste system resources even if you are not using the software that installed them. These advertising Trojans make clandestine connections to ad servers behind your back, consuming precious network bandwidth and potentially compromising the security of your data.
- **TRACKING COOKIES –** A "cookie" is a token that stores information about a browser session. The server side of a user connection to a Web server can place certain information (such as the user's interactions with that site) in the cookie and then give that cookie to the user's browser. While the user is on a webpage, or navigating through a website, the server can ask the browser for the cookie and retrieve this information. This becomes useful in any intelligent interaction between browser and website because the connection between a browser and server is not persistent.
- **CROSS-SITE TRACKING COOKIES**, or **SPYWARE**, are cookies that are shared across sites rather than being used only on a single site. Some cookies are persistent, and can be stored on your hard drive indefinitely without your permission. They can reveal private information which has been collected by tracking use across multiple sites.

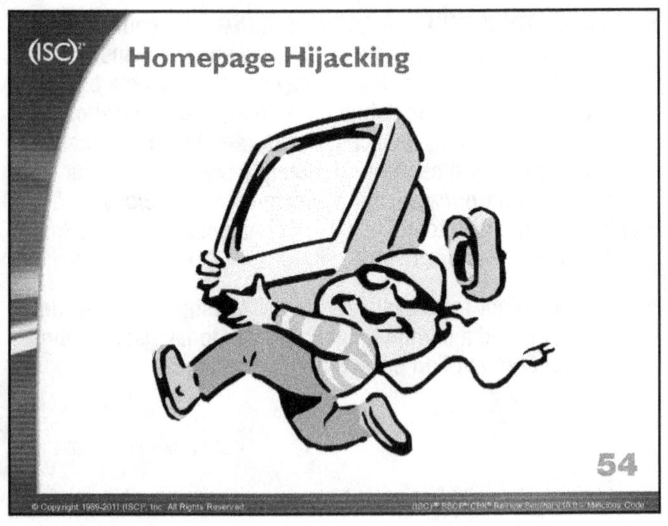


- **HOMEPAGE HIJACKING –** The purpose of these attacks is to change a browser's homepage to point to the attacker's site. There are two forms of hijacking:
    - Exploiting an IE vulnerability to automatically reset the homepage.
    - Covert installation of a browser helper object (BHO) Trojan program, which contains the hijacking code. After a BHO is executed, it changes (or forces) the browser's homepage back to the hijacker's desired site. Typically, hijacker programs put a reference to themselves into the Windows StartUp folder or registry run key, so that the hijacker runs every time the computer is started. If the user tries to change any of these settings, the hijacker program repeatedly changes them back until the hijacking software is found and removed.

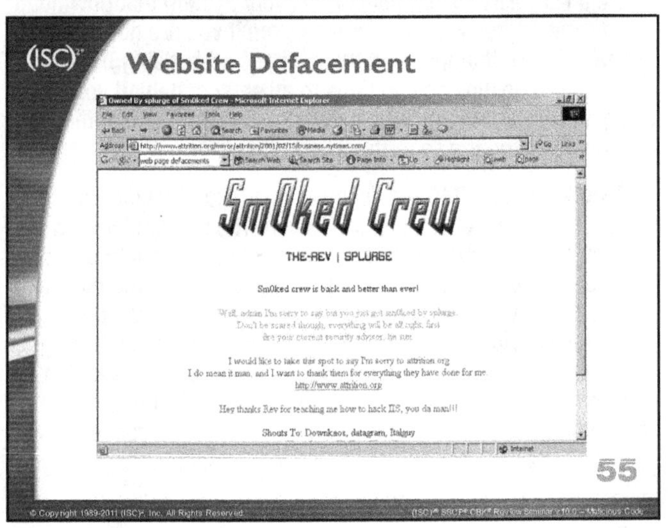


- **WEBSITE DEFACEMENT –** The terms "Web defacement" or "Web graffiti" refer to a situation in which an attacker gains unauthorized access to a Web server and alters its index page. The attacker typically exploits vulnerabilities in the target Web server in order to gain administrative access. Once in control, the html page will be replaced with altered versions.
- The defacement is typically akin to graffiti and is no more than a nuisance, but it can also embed more malicious active content code (such as viruses or Trojans) into the website. Code Red, for instance, includes payload that installs a backdoor Trojan that allows remote access to an infected IIS server that can be used to deface the front page of the Web server.
- To minimize risks, make sure that software versions are current, security patches are installed, and that websites are actively monitored.

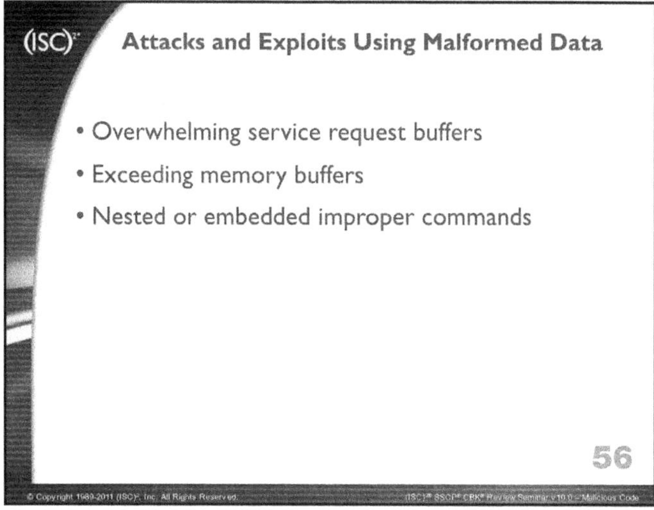

(ISC)²
Attacks and Exploits Using Malformed Data
• Overwhelming service request buffers
• Exceeding memory buffers
• Nested or embedded improper commands
56


- **ATTACKS AND EXPLOITS USING MALFORMED DATA –** Whether performed as an interactive (real-time) malicious exercise or built into the architecture of a virus or worm (i.e., Slammer and SQL, Code Red and IIS), this kind of attack exploits loopholes in various application processes (Web servers, databases, etc.) in an attempt to compromise the integrity of the running process and gain privileged access and control. If successful, the attacker or his or her malicious payload will be able to execute additional code routines such as the insertion of Trojan programs, viral infection of systems or files, and propagation to subsequent processes or hosts.
  - Malformed data attacks can fall into several types:
    - Denial of service (DoS) exploits: overwhelming the predefined capacity of these services to handle new requests.
    - Data that is outside the normal program parameters (i.e., larger than the program code is expecting), which can result in buffer overflows and other error conditions, thereby opening points of entry to the process.
    - Embedding data into other data structures so that it is not inspected by security processes and is subsequently executed by the service application.
    - Data that contains improperly constructed syntax that causes error conditions.
    - Any other data element (string) that takes advantage of normal program responses to special characters (e.g., escape characters), resulting in unexpected and potentially compromising behavior by the host system.
  - Server applications in general operate within some defined set of protocols or program specifications that define the normal or expected parameters of operation of the related service. Exploitation of the sometimes inflexible boundaries of these parameters has been a popular target for years. As an example, there are two major unicode vulnerabilities: the IIS/PWS extended unicode directory traversal vulnerability and the IIS/PWS escaped character decoding command execution vulnerability. Many current worms, including the Code Red variants and Nimda, have exploited these two unicode vulnerabilities in IIS. Other more recent worms have used buffer overflow conditions to gain service control of a target platform.

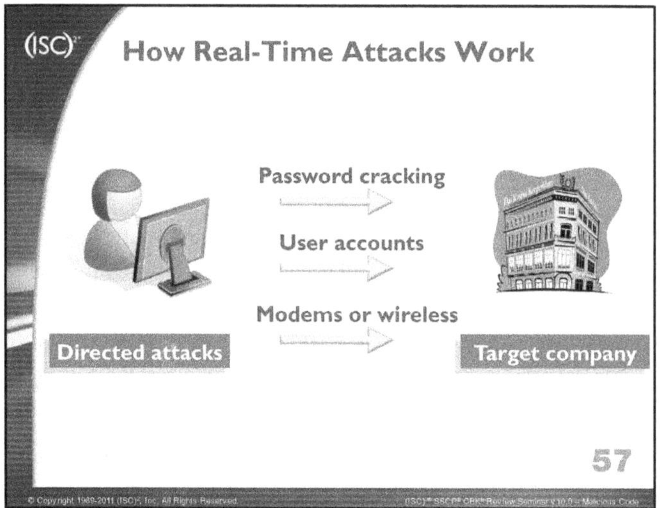


- **HOW REAL-TIME ATTACKS WORK –** The typical real-time directed attack is performed either by accessing a target system through remote login exploits (password guessing or session hijacking) or by exploiting a known vulnerability in the target operating system (such as a unicode vulnerability or active content vulnerability).
- The key characteristic is that the attack is being carried out in real time. Depending upon the sophistication of the attacker, the final objective may simply be to deface a website, or it may be a prelude to more malicious structured attacks. If the attacker can first locate and compromise a poorly protected target system, then it may be possible to use that as a launching pad to implant Trojan programs to further exploit other resources (files or systems) within the compromised network.

## Domain Agenda

- Viruses, Worms, Trojan Horses, and Logic Bombs
- Attack Structures and Techniques
- **Countermeasures and Preventative Actions**
- Role of the Information Security Practitioner

58



(ISC)² SSCP® CBK® Review Seminar v.10.0 – Malicious Code

## Antivirus (AV) Solutions

- Stay up to date!
- Signature-based
- Generic decryption (GD)
- Activity monitoring and heuristic scanners
- Integrity checkers

59



(ISC)² SSCP® CBK® Review Seminar v.10.0 – Malicious Code

- **ANTIVIRUS (AV) SOLUTIONS** – First generation antivirus scanners used brute force to analyze every byte of data in boot records and files in order to find patterns and strings known to be associated with virus activity. This method was obviously time-consuming and, as the number of viruses increased, has been supplemented by more intelligent algorithms that search the specific portions of files where virus code typically resides. While scanning approaches are still used today, other more efficient techniques such as algorithmic code entry-point scanning are now used to combat newer forms of viral code such as polymorphic strains. Note that most new viral codes (even of the polymorphic variety) are generally iterations or enhancements of previous-generation viral code.
- **STAY UP TO DATE!** – Because new viruses are discovered every day, antivirus software can only be really effective if it is updated regularly with the latest profiles.
- **SIGNATURE-BASED** – There are a variety of antivirus software packages that operate in many different ways, depending on how vendors choose to implement their software. Differences notwithstanding, all AV packages look for vendor-provided patterns (also known as virus profiles, or **"SIGNATURES"**) in the computer's files or memory, that suggest the presence of a known virus.
- **GENERIC DECRYPTION (GD)** – Is a newer technique wherein a virtual machine – i.e., an isolated and controlled environment – is used to trick a polymorphic virus into decrypting itself and exposing recognizable viral code components. As long as at least enough of the malicious code executes in the virtual environment so that the code successfully decrypts and transfers control to the resulting virus instructions, GD-based systems can usually detect it.
- **ACTIVITY MONITORING AND HEURISTIC SCANNERS** – Operate by looking for telltale signs or patterns of behavior consistent with known virus activity, logging it, and alerting the user of its presence. This allows the user to make the final decision about eradication. There are also schemes called "behavior blocking" that monitor system calls and other signs of activity that might indicate the presence of viral code. Many of these schemes will isolate the offending code and prompt the user to make a decision, or link to additional descriptive information on the AV vendor's website. Heuristic scanners perform activity monitoring on static code.
- **INTEGRITY CHECKERS** – Integrity checkers detect file modification by comparing a current checksum with the checksum when installed. (If the checksums don't match, the file has been altered.) Some integrity checkers are able to identify the virus that modified a file, while others simply alert the user to the changes. Note that integrity checkers are not only useful for detecting possible infections, but also helping detect intruders by noticing unexpected changes to files or programs.

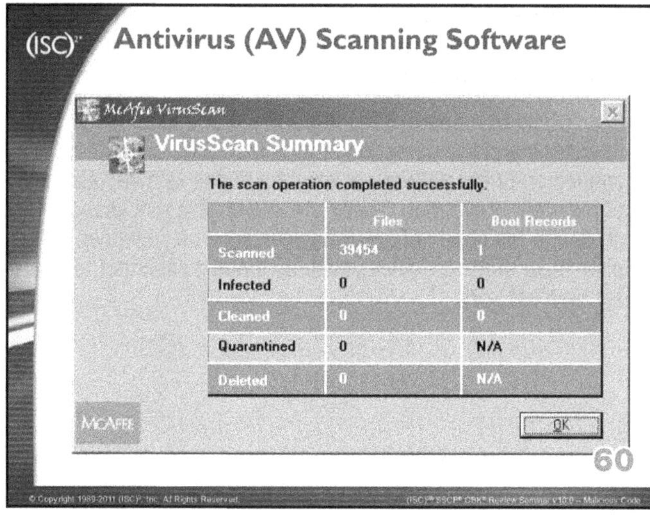


- **ANTIVIRUS (AV) SCANNING SOFTWARE –** Most PC users today use some form of virus protection to detect and prevent infection. Just as intrusion detection can be layered at the host and network levels, antivirus protection should be deployed on all devices that support AV programs.
- Network-based antivirus software permits screening of files and email traffic at the servers and proves remote scanning and inoculation of clients on a consistent basis.
- The key vulnerabilities to host-based antivirus software are:
  - Failure to keep every host system updated to the most current virus definition files.
  - The potential compromise of AV protection because of unsafe user practices such as installing unlicensed or unauthorized software, or indiscriminately exchanging infected email or document files.

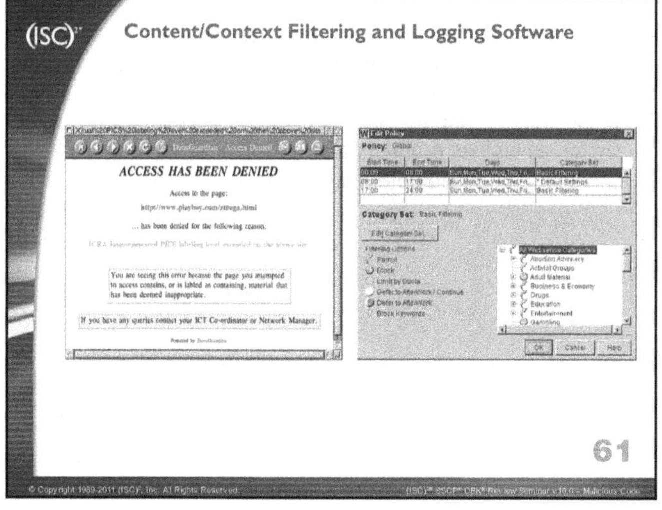


- **CONTENT/CONTEXT FILTERING AND LOGGING SOFTWARE –** The screen shot on the left is a message displayed as a result of a rules-set violation on "WebSense," and the screen shot on the right is an administrator configuration page that permits definition of Internet usage policies.
- Privacy and security must be balanced when implementing countermeasures designed to screen content. Content screening in combination with a clear corporate policy on acceptable use, however, is an additional layer of defense against malicious code. One of the more popular countermeasures in this category today is WebSense, which allows management to control Internet use.
- Plug-ins that screen email attachments, as well as content- and context-based filtering (access control lists) on network routers, offer additional layers of security and protection. Content-based filtering includes analyzing network traffic for active code (Java, Active-X) components and the administrative disabling of script processing on Web browser software. Context-based filtering involves comparing patterns of activity with baseline standards so that unusual changes in network behavior can be evaluated for possible malicious activity.

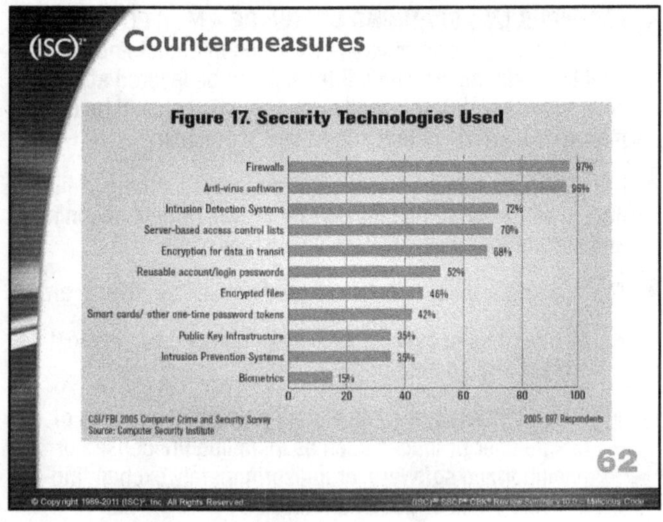


- **COUNTERMEASURES –** This Slide shows some of the most common countermeasures in use by organizations today to combat the threat of malware or other security risks.
- It is critical to recognize the importance of endpoint security measures and the detection of new machines or devices connected to the network or existing nodes as a key element of malware prevention. There is considerable risk associated with the ability of small devices such as advanced cell phones, or storage devices such as iPods, to connect to and act on a network.

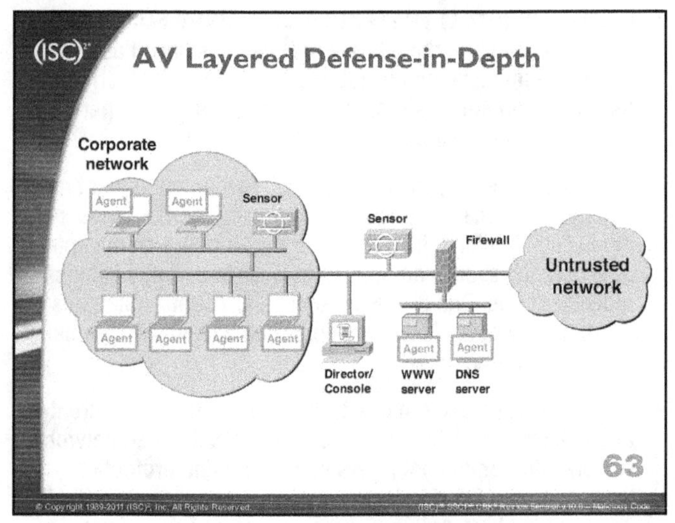


- **AV LAYERED DEFENSE-IN-DEPTH –** Defense-in-depth is the practice of "layering" defenses into defensive zones to increase protection and provide more reaction time to respond to incidents. A layered defense-in-depth antivirus approach will include both network-based and host-based intrusion detection as well as products that permit both signature-based and anomaly-based detection.

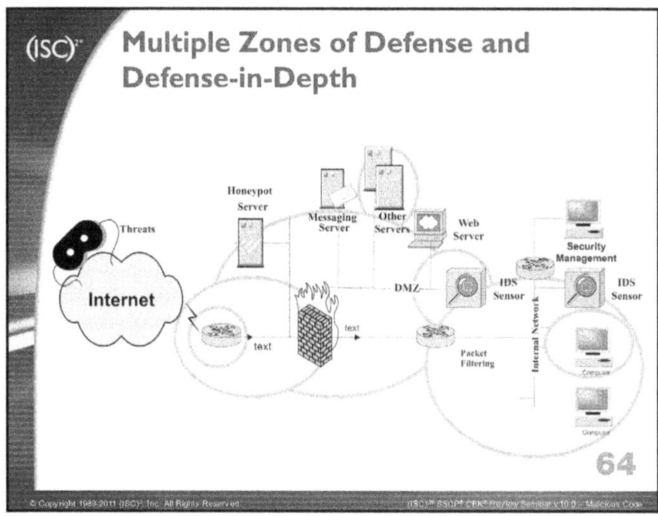


- **MULTIPLE ZONES OF DEFENSE –** This graphic depicts a number of countermeasures that might be deployed to create multiple zones of defense. Countermeasures include techniques such as screening routers, firewalls, intrusion detection, antivirus protection, and other measures that add layers of protection.
- One such measure is using a honeypot, or honeynet. A honeypot is a system which has been intentionally exposed to an untrusted network. It may or may not be using antivirus, or other protection techniques. Its purpose is to attract attackers to nonvital systems, and potentially monitor their attack methodology. Honeypots and honeynets are also used to confuse and misdirect attackers.
- **DEFENSE-IN-DEPTH –** Defenses should be designed so that a failure in one safeguard is covered by another. Layering defenses includes combining the capabilities of people, operations, and security technologies to establish multiple layers of protection, eliminating single lines of defense and effectively raising the cost of an attack. By treating individual countermeasures as part of an integrated suite of protective measures, the IT security practitioner is able to ensure that all vulnerabilities are addressed. Managers must strengthen these defenses at critical locations and then be able to monitor attacks and react to them quickly.
- With respect to malicious code threats, these layers of protection extend to specific critical defensive zones:
- Application defenses.
- Operating system defenses.
- Network infrastructure defenses.

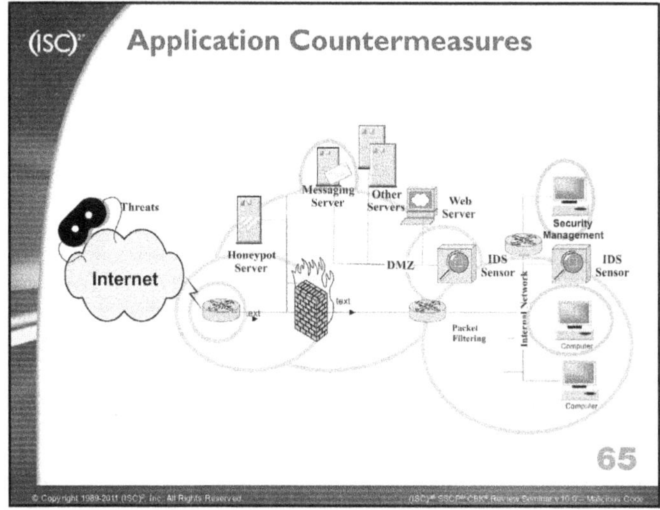


- **APPLICATION COUNTERMEASURES –** Application countermeasures include things such as hardening of applications, antivirus and IDS protection on hosts and servers, host-based intrusion detection, and network security monitors.
  - Educate users on malware in general and implement acceptable use policies.
  - Implement regular antivirus screening on all host systems and network servers and ensure that virus definition files are kept up to date.
  - Require scanning of all removable media and email (especially attachments).
  - Consider installation of personal firewall and IDS software on hosts as an additional security layer.
  - Deploy change-detection/integrity-checking software and maintain logs.
  - Implement email usage controls and ensure that email attachments are scanned.
  - Deploy specialized antimalware software and email filters to detect and block unwanted traffic (antispam filters, etc.).
  - Establish a clear policy regarding new software development/engineering practices, installations, and upgrades.
  - Ensure only trusted sources are used when obtaining, installing, and upgrading software, through digital signatures (authenticode and other validations).

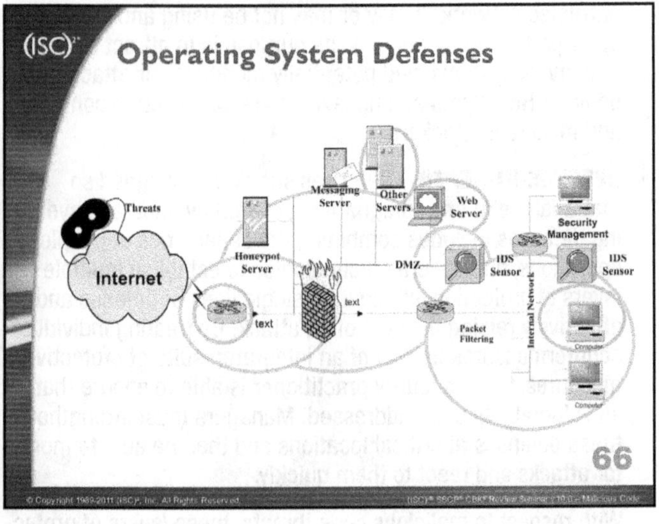


- **OPERATING SYSTEM DEFENSES –** Operating system countermeasures such as hardening operating systems and all devices involved in network communications, including routers, switches, servers, and hosts. The security specialist should regularly check to ensure that the latest security patches are deployed.
  - Deploy change-detection software and integrity-checking software and maintain logs.
  - Deploy or enable change-detection and integrity-checking software on all servers.
  - Ensure that all operating systems are consistent and have been patched with the latest updates from vendors.
  - Ensure only trusted sources are used when installing and upgrading OS code.
  - Disable any unnecessary OS services and processes that could pose a security vulnerability.

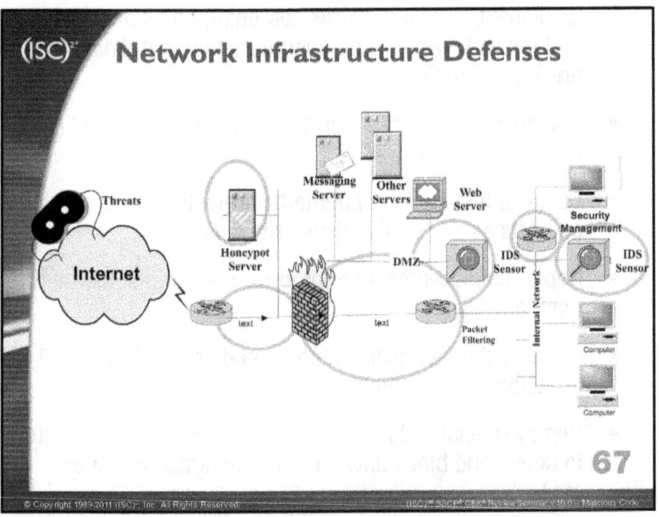


- **NETWORK INFRASTRUCTURE DEFENSES –** Network infrastructure defenses involve identifying where the traffic patterns are and where to deploy various countermeasures. The red circles indicate some of these locations as well as the devices that can provide elements of protection. Make sure to:
  - Create chokepoints in the network.
  - Use proxy services and bastion hosts to protect critical services.
  - Use content filtering at chokepoints to screen traffic and make sure that you screen outgoing as well as incoming traffic.
  - Ensure that only trusted sources are used when installing and upgrading OS code.
  - Disable any unnecessary network services and processes that may pose a security vulnerability.
  - Maintain up-to-date IDS signature databases.
  - Apply security patches to network devices to ensure protection against new threats and to reduce vulnerabilities.

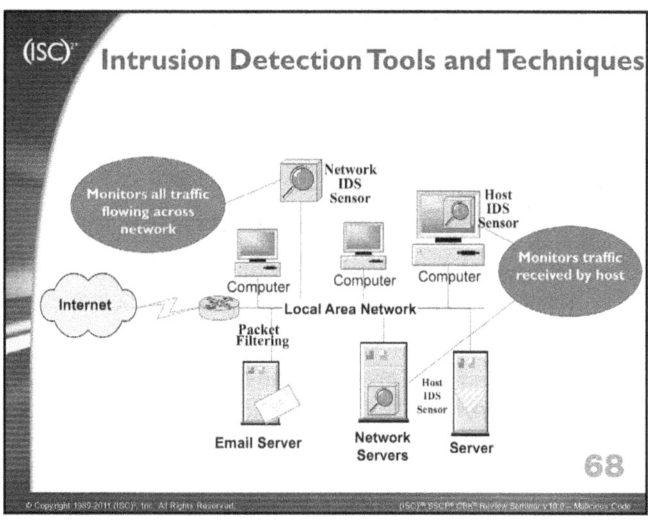


- **INTRUSION DETECTION TOOLS AND TECHNIQUES –** Intrusion detection tools are an integral component of defense–in-depth and should be deployed in critical areas of the network as an early warning system. There are a variety of implementations and each has features that provide unique capabilities to protect networks and hosts from malicious activity. Intrusion detection is designed to recognize a security event as soon as possible (malicious code attack, denial-of-service attack, network reconnaissance attack, etc.) so that immediate countermeasures can be executed to isolate and react to the event.
- Intrusion detection can be deployed on separate appliances/sensors that are managed by a security server, or they can be deployed as software on the hosts within the network. Each type has advantages and disadvantages.

(ISC)²

## Domain Agenda

- Viruses, Worms, Trojan Horses, and Logic Bombs
- Attack Structures and Techniques
- Countermeasures and Preventative Actions
- **Role of the Information Security Practitioner**

69



(ISC)²® SSCP® CBK® Review Seminar v.10.0 – Malicious Code

(ISC)²

## Safe Recovery Tools and Practices

- Store OS and data file backup images on CD-ROM
- Back up all critical configuration files
- Scan for viruses before installation/re-installation of software
- Protect systems during restoration

70



- **SAFE RECOVERY TOOLS AND PRACTICES –** Attacks are inevitable. Here are some solutions to make recovery easier and faster.
  - Back up all data.
    - Require company data to be stored on a server.
    - Install automated workstation backup solutions.
  - All incoming traffic (mail, attachments, etc.) needs to be scanned on a bastion or noncritical machine before acceptance.
  - Time to corrupt is less than time to restore. Consider this sequence of events.
    1. Reinstall XP.
    2. Visit windowsupdate to download SP2.
    3. Install SP2.
    4. Visit windowsupdate again for all post-SP2 patches.
    5. Install them.
    6. Your system will be found and taken over by attackers before step 2 completes. Therefore, it is important to store copies of operating systems, patches, and programs so that they can be re-installed without being subject to another attack during the recovery process.

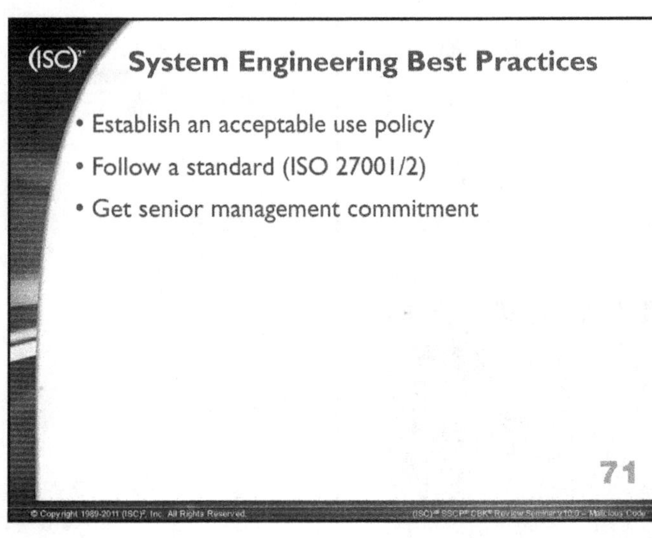

(ISC)²
System Engineering Best Practices
• Establish an acceptable use policy
• Follow a standard (ISO 27001/2)
• Get senior management commitment
71


- **SYSTEM ENGINEERING BEST PRACTICES –** The organization should adopt an acceptable use policy for network services and resources. This would include prohibitions against certain network activities, PC user habits regarding software licensing and installation, and procedures for transmitting files and media.
  - Adopt standardized software so that patches and upgrades can be controlled to ensure vulnerabilities are addressed.
  - Consider implementing an ISO 27001/2 compliant security policy. ISO 27001/2 is one of the most widely recognized security guidelines. Adoption of ISO/IEC 27001/2 (or indeed any detailed security practice) as an internal standard can be a challenging effort, even for the most security conscious organizations. Security practitioners should evaluate the practices to ensure that they make business sense to the organization and remember that policies need senior management commitment to be effective.

## Maintaining Sterile/Safe Computing Environment

- Use peer-to-peer products responsibly
- Always scan incoming and outgoing files
- Always scan media before and after use
- Do not accept files and media from untrusted sources
- Establish an "acceptable use policy" for users
- Prohibit unauthorized devices

72




- **MAINTAINING STERILE/SAFE COMPUTING ENVIRONMENT –** This Slide lists several suggested guidelines for maintaining a safe computing environment.
- **PROHIBIT UNAUTHORIZED DEVICES –** A common security flaw is caused by users or administrators connecting un-authorized equipment to the network or workstations. This can include the installation of USB drives, communications devices, wireless, and PDAs. These devices can propagate viruses, steal corporate data, misuse bandwidth or processing power, and provide backdoors into the system. Compliance software should be used that will scan the network for rogue devices, or the organization may disable USB ports.

## Domain Summary

- The SSCP should be familiar with the various types of attacks and the types of malicious code that can be used against systems.
- The SSCP should understand the countermeasures available to prevent malicious attacks from succeeding.

73

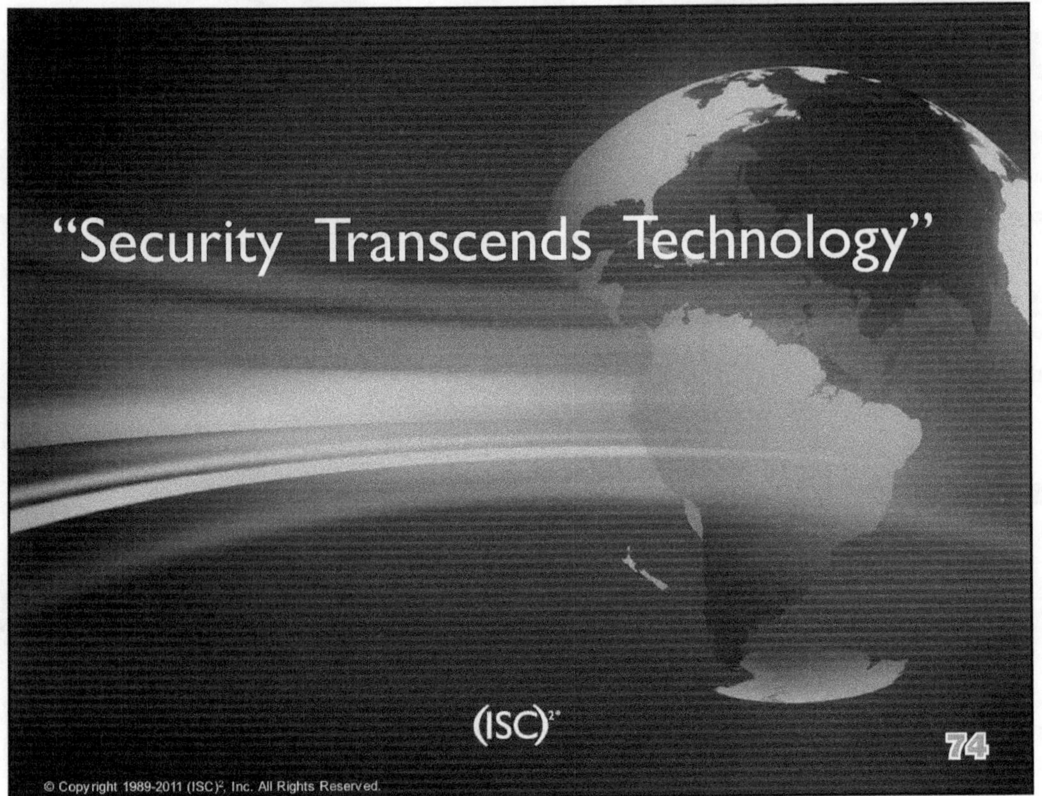
"Security Transcends Technology"
(ISC)²
74

# Review Questions

## MALICIOUS CODE AND ACTVITY

1. **What is an example of an "attack against productivity and performance"?**
   a) Unauthorized manipulation of sensitive data.
   b) Computer infected by a virus.
   c) Spyware
   d) Denial of service

2. **What does a boot sector virus do?**
   a) Attacks executable files.
   b) Opens a backdoor for hackers.
   c) Attacks disks and memory.
   d) Replaces the initial sector on a disk.

3. **Which of the following characterizes a common internal security threat?**
   a) Downloading unauthorized software or opening email attachments.
   b) Creation and release of viruses into the internal network.
   c) Denial of service attacks against department computing resources.
   d) Playing computer games while at work.

4. **An example of malicious code would include**
   a) a virus that does not contain a malicious payload.
   b) a software bug that impacts system integrity.
   c) an audit log containing sensitive information.
   d) a middleware application that permits uncontrolled access to applications.

5. **Individuals who obtain unauthorized access into telecommunications networks to exploit and illegally use the telecommunication provider's services are referred to as**
   a) system crackers.
   b) phreakers.
   c) white hat hackers.
   d) black hat hackers.

6. **Pop-up pages and banners, promoting company products and services, that appear when users visit web sites are caused by**
   a) spyware.
   b) adware.
   c) SPAM.
   d) viruses.

7. **After being closed for the weekend, on Monday morning an organization finds that its servers are running slow. The central processing unit (CPU) utilizations are showing 100%. Network traffic is also near maximum. On the close of business on Friday, all systems were behaving normally. Closer examination is likely to reveal which of the following infestations?**
   a) Data diddler
   b) Distributed denial of service (DDoS)
   c) Virus
   d) Worm

8. **A screen saver that opens an encrypted tunnel to a website under malicious control with the purpose of allowing attackers access to the infected machine is an example of which of the following versions of malware?**
   a) Logic bomb
   b) Trojan horse
   c) Virtual private network
   d) Spyware

9. **Information security professionals who often engage in hacking and cracking activities to research and improve security are know as**
   a) phreakers.
   b) script kiddies/click kiddies.
   c) black hat hackers.
   d) white hat hackers.

10. **Any unsolicited background process that is installed on a user's computer and collects information about the user's browsing habits is known as**
    a) adware.
    b) spyware.
    c) SPAM.
    d) a trojan password sniffer.

11. **Technically skilled individuals who break commercial software protection schemes and often post the "cracks" on Internet sites are known as**
    a) phreakers.
    b) script kiddies/click kiddies.
    c) black hat hackers.
    d) white hat hackers.

**12. What is the term used for scanning a network for accessible hosts?**

a) Ping
b) Ping sweep
c) MingSweeper
d) Network mapper

**13. A program that searches for available modem connections and sometimes tries penetration testing is referred to as a**

a) war dialer.
b) worm.
c) virus.
d) backdoor trojan.

**14. A remote administration tool (RAT)**

a) connects to and manages other computers.
b) changes settings of the host computer.
c) monitors data transmissions.
d) gathers administrative data about the network.

**15. In which phase of an attack does a hacker employ domain name system (DNS) tools, Internet control message protocol (ICMP) tools, port scanners, and mappers?**

a) Exploitation
b) Access and privilege escalation
c) Reconnaissance
d) Eavesdropping and data collection and theft

**16. A transmission control protocol (TCP) SYN flood attack is designed to**

a) gain access to a server by getting it to respond to at least one SYN request.
b) create many half open connections which prevent a server from responding to legitimate requests.
c) probe for open user datagram protocol (UDP) ports which might be accessible.
d) capture passwords and keystrokes that a user enters via keyboard.

**17. A virus which infects files with an encrypted copy of itself which is decoded by a decryption module and modifies the decryption module on each infection is known as a**

a) macro virus.
b) polymorphic virus.
c) companion virus.
d) file Infector virus.

**18. A worm most frequently spreads via**

a) user misuse.
b) vulnerabilities in software.
c) mobile code attacks.
d) infected USB drives and wireless access points.

**19. Spoofing is defined as**

a) eavesdropping on communications between persons or processes.
b) a person or process emulating another person or process.
c) a hostile or unexpected entity concealed within another entity.
d) the testing of all possibilities to obtain information.

**20. The predictable virus pattern of making an exact replica of itself before infecting a file, boot sector, or document is referred to in anti-virus software as**

a) replication.
b) prepending.
c) a signature.
d) behavior.

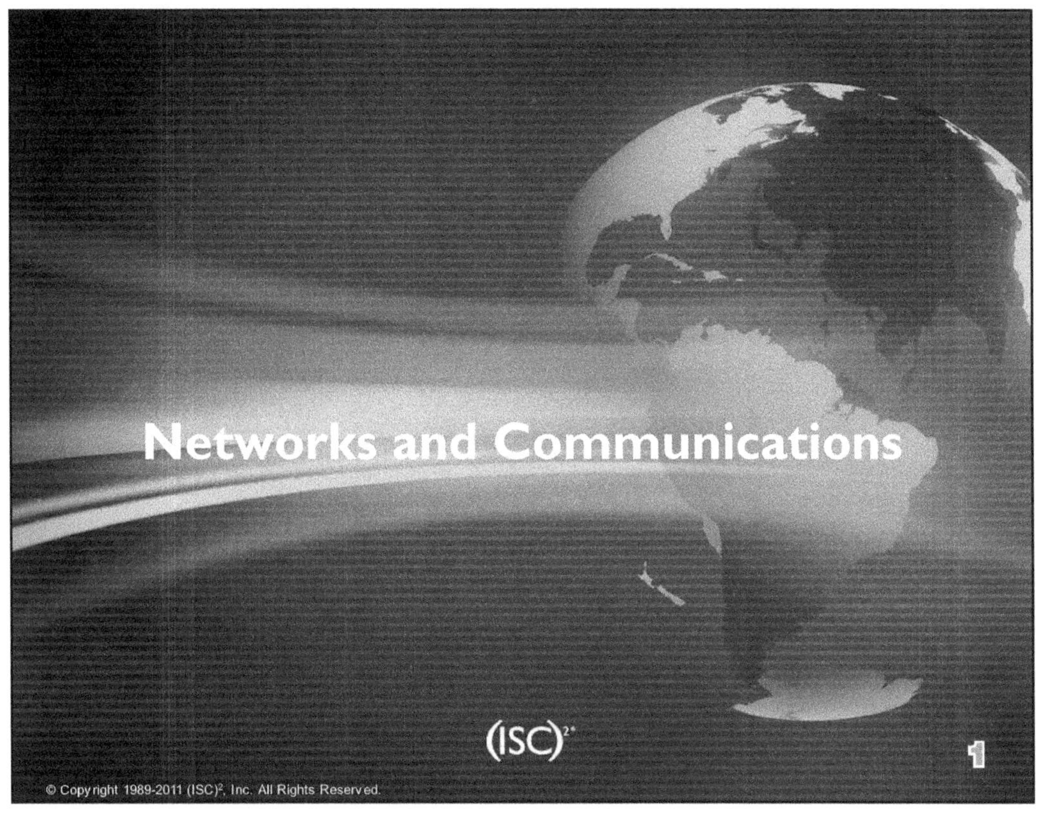


## Domain Objectives

- Understand network and telecommunications security concepts
- Understand network models and components
- Describe network topologies and layouts
- Describe network protocols
- Understand network security protocols and protection techniques
- Understand wireless telecommunications security
- Understand network service reliability and quality

2

 (ISC)²® SSCP® CBK® Review Seminar v.10.0 – Network and Communications

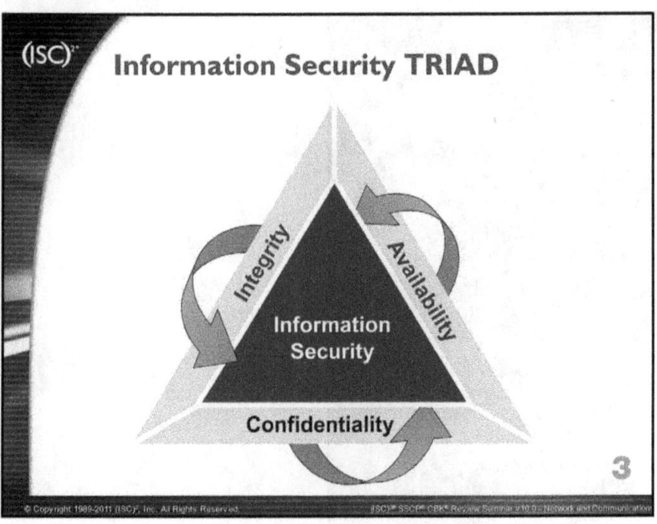


- **INFORMATION SECURITY TRIAD –** Most businesses and organizations today rely on their networks and communications as a critical part of their business's infrastructure. Many organizations could not continue operations if their network were unavailable or prone to errors. "Network security" means that the business' needs for availability, integrity, and confidentiality have been satisfied. The data transmitted through the network is protected from modification (either accidental or intentional), cannot be read by unauthorized parties, and its source and destination can be verified (non-repudiation). Business and security requirements are:
  - Access Control
  - Network stability and reliability
    - Integrity
    - Availability
    - Confidentiality/Non-repudiation.

(ISC)²

**Information Security Activities**

- Establishing a network security policy
- Sound network design (e.g., no single points of failure, defense in depth, etc.)
- Risk assessments and regular network scans
- Secure configuration
- Change and configuration management
- Security awareness and training

4

- The primary benefit of a network is its availability to the business to support today's global activities. The SSCP should have a good foundation in how networks are designed, managed, and secured.
- **ESTABLISHING A NETWORK SECURITY POLICY –** The main purpose of a security policy is to inform users, staff, and managers of their requirements for protecting technology and information assets. The policy will specify the mechanisms through which these requirements are to be met.
  - Another purpose of a security policy is to provide a baseline when acquiring, configuring, and auditing computer systems and networks in order to ensure that all of these comply with desired policy. Attempting to use a set of security tools in the absence of a security policy (or at the very least, an implied security policy) is therefore ineffective.
- **SOUND NETWORK DESIGN –** Ensure that IT services are available, yet secure. Security should be implemented in layers (i.e., defense in depth), and no single points of failure should be allowed unless alternate means are available to ensure continuity.
- **RISK ASSESSMENTS AND REGULAR NETWORK SCANS –** Network management involves ongoing security activities devoted to maintaining availability, integrity, and privacy of resources in order to support business requirements. Upper management must be persuaded to perform regular risk assessments and apply a cost-benefit approach to the security-policy development process. The network should be continuously monitored and tested to confirm that security practices remain effective.
- **SECURE CONFIGURATIONS –** Software and hardware configurations should permit security features to be included as transparently as possible, and changes to systems and configurations should follow best practices to ensure that no undocumented weaknesses are introduced.
- **SECURITY AWARENESS AND TRAINING –** As important as any technical or physical control is a high level of commitment to security by the people who will rely on IT. Regular security awareness and skills training will ensure that everyone from senior management to users has the knowledge needed to support information security.

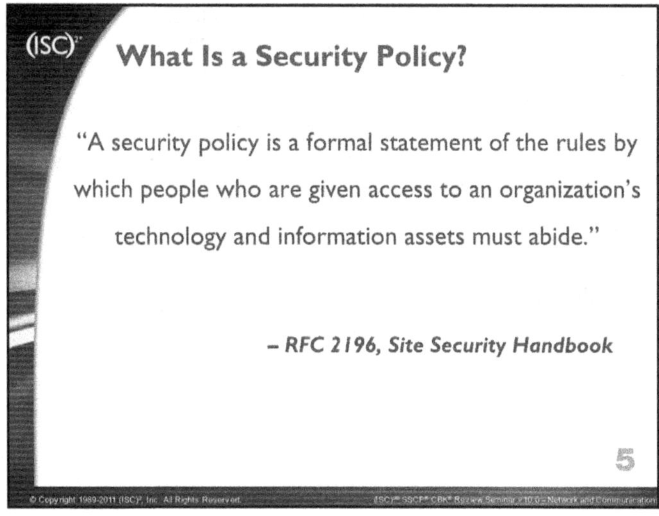

(ISC)²
What Is a Security Policy?
"A security policy is a formal statement of the rules by which people who are given access to an organization's technology and information assets must abide."
– RFC 2196, Site Security Handbook
5


- **PURPOSE –** Security policies are documents that record a company's security goals and implementations. Policies must be communicated to all affected people through a set of security rules.
- You cannot make good decisions about security without first determining your security goals. Until you determine these security goals, you cannot make effective use of any collection of security tools because you simply will not know what to check for and what restrictions to impose.
- Your goals will be largely determined by the following key tradeoffs:
  - Services offered versus security provided: Every service available to users carries its own security risks. In some cases, the risks will outweigh the benefits of the service and the administrator may choose to eliminate rather than try to secure it.
  - Ease of use versus security: The easiest system to use would allow access to any user and require no passwords. This offers no security. Requiring passwords makes the system a little less convenient, but somewhat secure. Requiring device-generated one-time passwords makes the system even more difficult to use, but even more secure.
  - Cost of security versus risk of loss: There are many different costs to security: monetary (i.e., the cost of purchasing security hardware and software such as firewalls and one-time password generators), performance (i.e., the time required for encryption and decryption), and ease of use (as mentioned above).
- There are also many levels of risk: loss of privacy (i.e., unauthorized individuals being able to read information that they should not), loss of data (i.e., the corruption or erasure of information), and loss of service (i.e., the filling of data storage space, usage of computational resources, and denial of network access. Each cost must be weighed against the associated loss.

**REFERENCE:**

http://www.ietf.org/rfc/rfc2196.txt

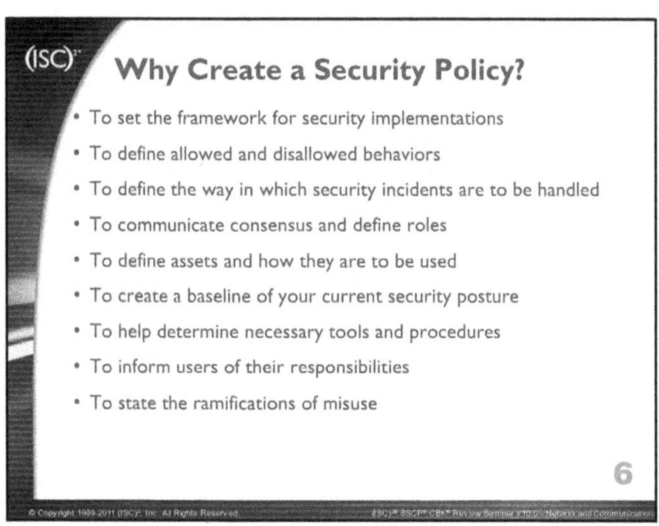

(ISC)²
Why Create a Security Policy?
To set the framework for security implementations
To define allowed and disallowed behaviors
To define the way in which security incidents are to be handled
To communicate consensus and define roles
To define assets and how they are to be used
To create a baseline of your current security posture
To help determine necessary tools and procedures
To inform users of their responsibilities
To state the ramifications of misuse
6


- **WHY CREATE A SECURITY POLICY? –** While the main purpose of a security policy is to inform users, staff, and managers of their requirements for protecting technology and information assets, the policy specifies the mechanisms through which these requirements are to be met.

## What Should the Security Policy Contain?

- Statement of authority and scope
- Acceptable use policy (AUP)
- Identification and authentication policy
- Internet use policy
- Campus access policy
- Remote access policy
- Incident handling procedure

7



- One of the most common security policy components is an acceptable use policy (AUP). This component defines what users may and may not do on the various components of the system, including the type of traffic allowed on the networks. The AUP should be as explicit as possible to avoid ambiguity or misunderstanding. For example, an AUP might list any prohibited USENET newsgroups.
- The security policy should have the acceptance and support of all levels of employees in the organization. Representatives of all key stakeholders and affected management should be involved in creating and revising the security policy.

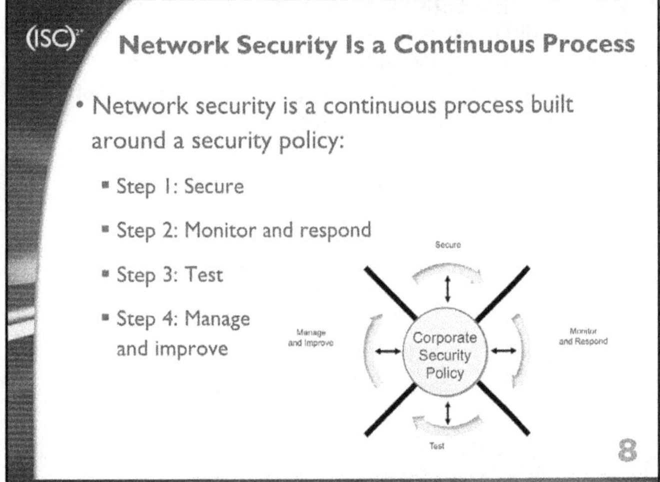

(ISC)²
Network Security Is a Continuous Process
Network security is a continuous process built around a security policy:
Step 1: Secure
Step 2: Monitor and respond
Step 3: Test
Step 4: Manage and improve
Secure
Manage and Improve
Corporate Security Policy
Monitor and Respond
Test
8


- Just as threats and vulnerabilities change, so also must the policies of the organization be reviewed and improved on a regular basis. A policy is a type of control, and once implemented it must be reviewed to ensure it provides the expected results. When it is found that the policy is not effective or not being complied with, steps must be taken to review the requirements and improve the policy.

(ISC)²

## Domain Agenda

- **Network Components and Topologies**
- Wide Area and Remote Access Networks
- Standard Network Protocols
- Network Security Protocols
- Wireless Network Configuration and Protection
- Managing Service Reliability and Quality

9



(ISC)²® SSCP® CBK® Review Seminar v 10.0 – Network and Communications

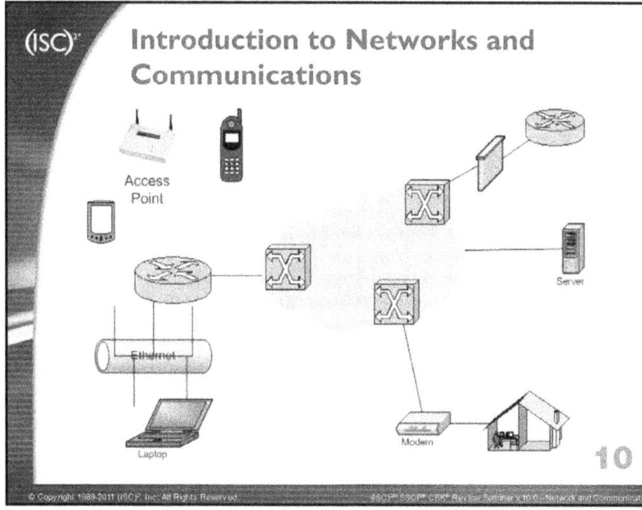


- **INTRODUCTION TO NETWORKS AND COMMUNICATIONS –** This domain examines the subject of networks and communications from the perspective of security. It looks at all of the elements of a network to see what the security concerns are, and how the various types of networking components do (or do not) address it.
- The SSCP will need to understand the following elements of the networks and telecommunications world:
  - OSI model
  - Network topology
  - Network devices
  - Network access methods

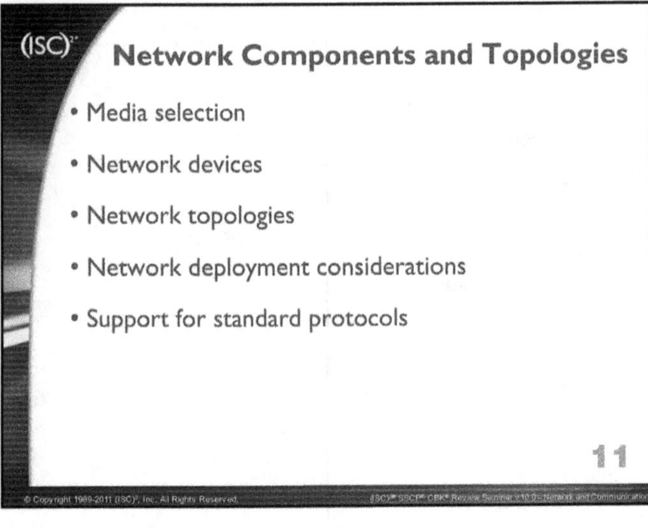


- These are items to be examined more closely in the next few slides.

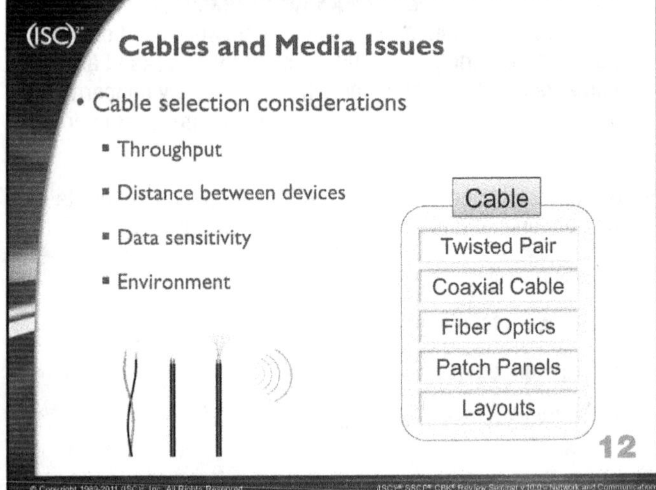


- **CABLE – THE SECURITY LIMITATIONS OF PHYSICAL MEDIA** – Physical media can be a cause of network insecurity. Each of the physical media types that we use has its own level of security risks and benefits.
  - Digital communication, for example, has a very predictable method of transmission. Certain combinations of pulses represent certain transmitted characters. Depending on the type of physical media selected for the network, attackers may be able to take advantage of this predictability.
  - Network cables and unused connectors must be protected. An intruder who gains access to network cables or a network port can cause a great deal of damage either by gaining access to the network or by disabling it by cutting cables. Consider the ease with which someone might be able to walk into a building, even if there are guards and card scanners.
  - For a high-security site, the cable conduits may need to be sealed.
- **CABLE SELECTION CONSIDERATIONS** – Here are some parameters that should be considered when selecting cables:
  - **THROUGHPUT** – The rate at which data will be transmitted. Certain cables, such as fiber optic, are designed for hauling an incredible amount of data at once.
  - **DISTANCE BETWEEN DEVICES** – The degradation or loss of a signal (attenuation) in long cable runs is a perennial problem, especially if the signal is operating at a high frequency. The time required for a signal to travel through the media (propagation delay) may also be a factor. A bus topology that uses collision detection may not operate correctly if the cable is too long.
  - **DATA SENSITIVITY** – What is the risk of someone intercepting the data in the cables? Fiber optics, for example, make data interception very difficult, but it is rather simple to intercept or monitor data transmission in other media types.
  - **ENVIRONMENT** – It's a cable-unfriendly world. Cables may have to be bent when installing. If there is a lot of electromagnetic interference in the environment, the best solutions may be to use shielded cable or fiber optic cable.

---

**REFERENCE:**

Computer Security Basics by Deborah Russell and G.T. Gangemi Sr.

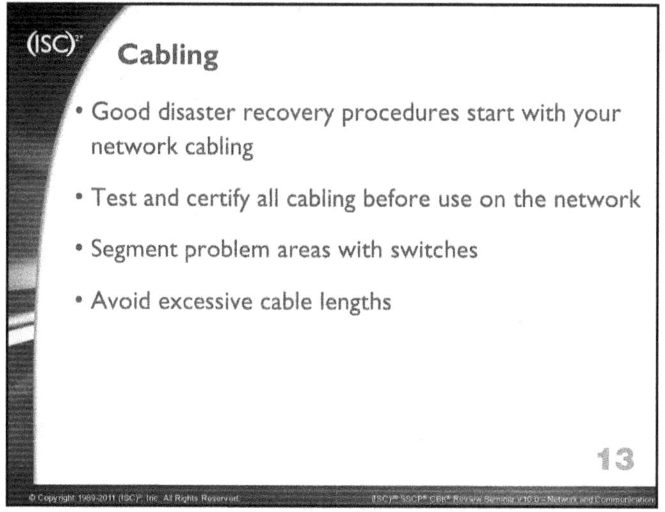
(ISC)²
Cabling
• Good disaster recovery procedures start with your network cabling
• Test and certify all cabling before use on the network
• Segment problem areas with switches
• Avoid excessive cable lengths
13

- **GOOD DISASTER RECOVERY PROCEDURES START WITH YOUR NETWORK CABLING –** The cabling you choose will go a long way toward determining how resilient your network will be in case of failure. Since your cabling is the medium that carries all of your network communications, a failure at this level can be devastating.
  - **THINNET AND THICKNET –** This type of cabling dates back to the original Ethernet specifications of the 70's. Both cable specs allow multiple systems to be attached to the same logical segment of cable. This provides a central point of failure, because if any portion of this length of cable becomes faulty, no system attached to it will be able to communicate. One of the biggest improvements you can make to network availability is to replace thinnet and thicknet cabling with a more modern solution.
  - **TWISTED PAIR –** Category 5e (or higher) cabling is the current cabling choice (standard) for most network installations. While this will eventually be replaced with fiber due to increasing bandwidth requirements, the wide installation base of Cat5 cable will guarantee that it will continue to be included in topology specs for a least a few more years. The problem arises from the amount of Cat3 cabling that is still in use, as well as the number of cabling installations that have only been tested for 10Mb operations. Cat5e does not guarantee a 100Mb or faster operation; it only provides the ability to support these speeds.
- **TEST AND CERTIFY ALL CABLING BEFORE USE ON THE NETWORK –** Problems typically do not occur until a heavy load is placed on the network– which means (by definition) that you have many users relying on network services. Problems due to poor cabling can take the form of slow network performance, frequent packet retransmissions due to errors, or even disconnection of users from services. Your best preventive method for avoiding twisted-pair cabling problems is to test and certify your cables before use.
- **SEGMENT PROBLEM AREAS WITH SWITCHES –** You can also consider segmenting problem areas with switches that are able to trap packet errors and to isolate transmissions into multiple collision domains. While this will not fix the errors, it will limit the scope of the effect that your cable problems have on the rest of your network.
- **AVOID EXCESSIVE CABLE LENGTHS –** Every logical topology has specs that identify the maximum cable lengths you can use. For example, 10mb and 100mb Ethernet both specify that twisted-pair cable runs cannot exceed 100 meters. These rules exist to ensure that a system at one end of the cable run can properly detect the transmissions of a system located at the opposite end. Exceeding these topology specs for cable length can produce intermittent failures due to low signal strength and also slow down communications along the entire segment due to an increase in collisions. Since these problems will tend to cause intermittent errors, they can be very difficult to troubleshoot.
- A good cable tester is the quickest way to tell if you have exceeded cable length limitations for your logical topology.

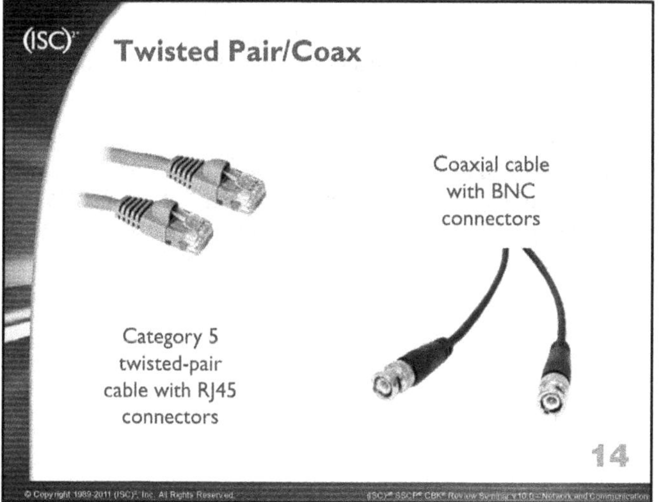
(ISC)²
Twisted Pair/Coax
Coaxial cable with BNC connectors
Category 5 twisted-pair cable with RJ45 connectors
14

- **TWISTED PAIR/COAX –** The electrical pulses used to transmit characters over media such as Cat5 or coax expose your network to a potential security problem: electromagnetic interference (EMI).
  - EMI is a two-way problem: Interference added to the signal is an integrity problem, and interception of signals radiating from the wire is a confidentiality issue.
  - *Tapping* means inserting a device that listens to and possibly repeats the signal. It is a kind of eavesdropping. Twisted pair is easier to tap than coax, which is easier to tap than fiber.
  - A common defense against tapping is to put the cables into a conduit (pipe) and then pressurize the pipe. With the addition of pressure monitors that will send alerts when the conduit is breached, the cables are protected.

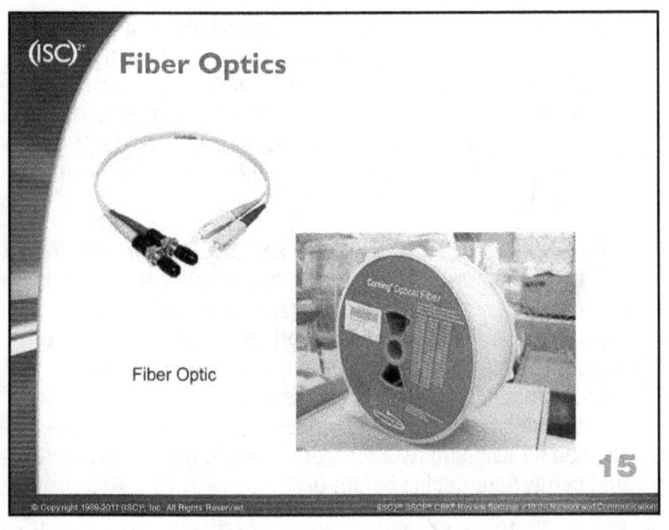


- **FIBER OPTICS –** Transmission across fiber-optic cable uses light rather than electricity, which means that there is no electromagnetic interference (EMI) and that it is not susceptible to the same kind of monitoring as electrical circuits. Single-mode fiber uses laser as the light source, where multimode fiber uses LED.
  - Single mode fiber-optic cable is made of a cylindrical glass thread center core wrapped in cladding that protects the central core. This is then encapsulated in a jacket of tough KEVLAR, which is further sheathed in PVC or Plenum.
  - Multimode fiber-optic cable is made of a plastic core wrapped in cladding, which is then encapsulated in a jacket of tough KEVLAR, which is further sheathed in PVC or Plenum.
  - Fiber signals can radiate if the fiber is bent sharply, but it is difficult to tap. Fiber is resistant to EMI corruption via external interference, which makes it more suitable for industrial/manufacturing environments.

**REFERENCE:**

Understanding Fiber Optics, Second Edition, by Jeff Hecht ISBN: 0-672-30350-7.

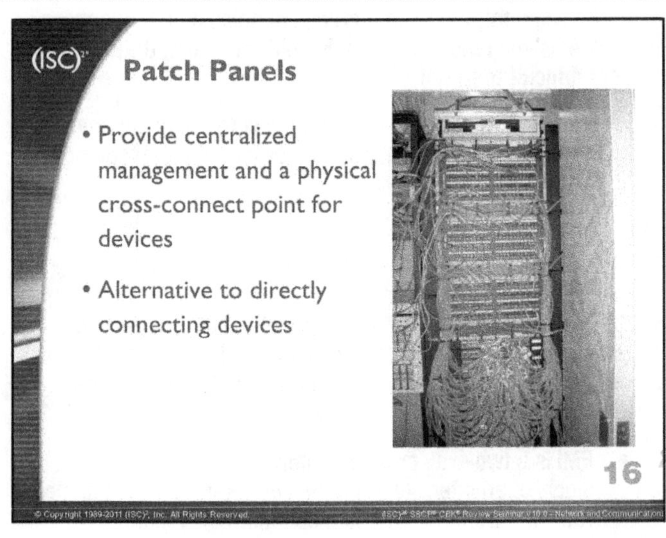

(ISC)²
Patch Panels
• Provide centralized management and a physical cross-connect point for devices
• Alternative to directly connecting devices
16
© Copyright 1989-2011 (ISC)², Inc. All Rights Reserved.


- **PROVIDE CENTRAL MANAGEMENT AND A PHYSICAL CROSS-CONNECT POINT FOR DEVICES –** The advantage of a patch panel is that it allows for many devices located in different places to be managed and connected at one centralized point. This allows the network manager to make quick changes to the network configuration without having to run new cables. Anyone who has ever looked at a patch panel knows that they can be complex and require careful management. Managing a patch panel requires thorough mapping of connections, as even moderately-sized data centers have many interconnected devices such as switches, routers, servers, workstations, and even test equipment. Configuration management and control is important to ensure that unauthorized changes are not made to the cabling layout.
- **ALTERNATIVE TO DIRECTLY CONNECTING DEVICES –** Devices are connected to the patch panel and patch cables are then used to interconnect the devices. "Wireless" patch panels (panels without the connecting wires or patch cords) are also available.

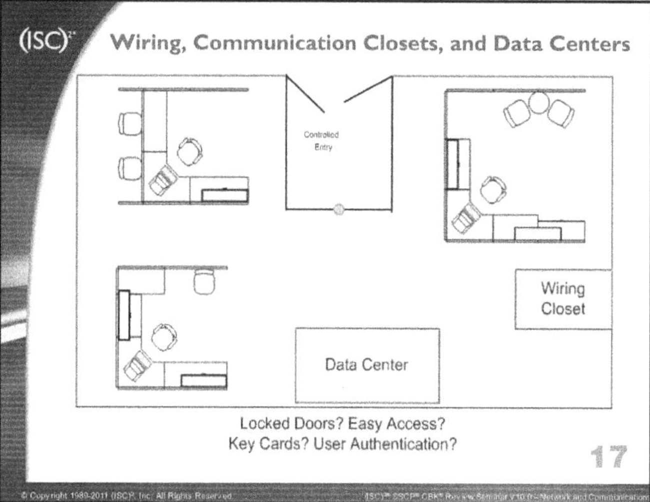


- **WIRING, COMMUNICATION CLOSETS, AND DATA CENTERS** – Physical security may be the most critical element of the security plan with respect to the communication closets, data centers, and wiring.
  - The kind of wiring in our networks today is susceptible only when an attacker gains access to the wires themselves or is within the signal range of a wireless network.
  - Communication closets have a similar physical security risk. If an attacker gains access to the closet, the potential damage that can be done to a corporate network or the corporate resources is enormous. One often-forgotten element to a wiring closet is the lone, modem-connected router used by the IT professional for connection and management purposes. An attacker doing wardialing may encounter this unprotected or poorly-protected modem and use it as an entry to the rest of the corporate network and its resources.
  - Data centers pose the same risk. If an attacker is able to walk around inside of the data center, all corporate resources are at risk.

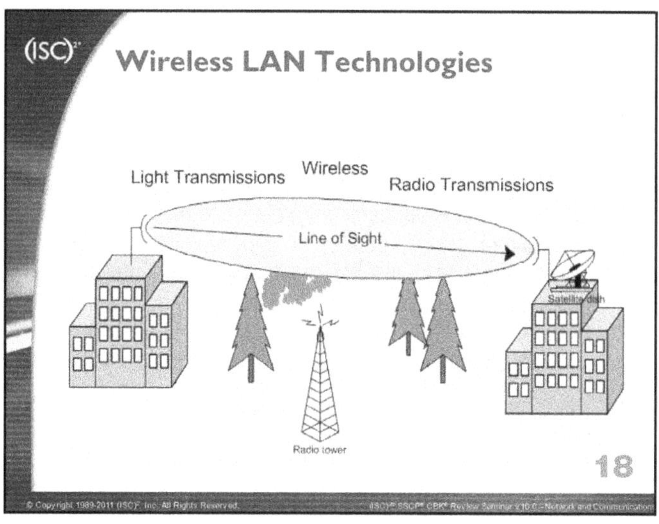


- **WIRELESS LAN TECHNOLOGIES** – Wireless transmissions are not constrained by any formal boundaries and are therefore referred to as "unbound media." Unbound transmissions are more susceptible to undetected interception and monitoring. Some security concerns with line of sight implementations such as microwave and optical transmission include the signal being blocked by buildings, trees, heavy rain, or other interference. Different wireless transmissions include:
  - Light transmissions
  - Radio transmissions
- **FIXED-FREQUENCY SIGNALS** – Traffic is sent over one dedicated channel.
- **SPREAD-SPECTRUM SIGNALS** – The traffic may be sent over several channels and the devices will listen on the channel that has the highest quality signal.

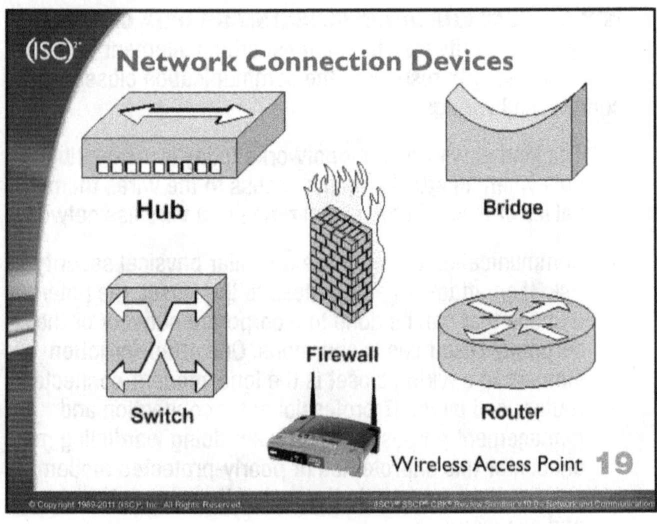


- **NETWORK CONNECTION DEVICES –** The devices involved in network configurations include hubs, bridges, access points, switches, routers, and firewalls. Over the next few pages, we will take a look at each of these devices and discuss their security components as well as their security weaknesses.

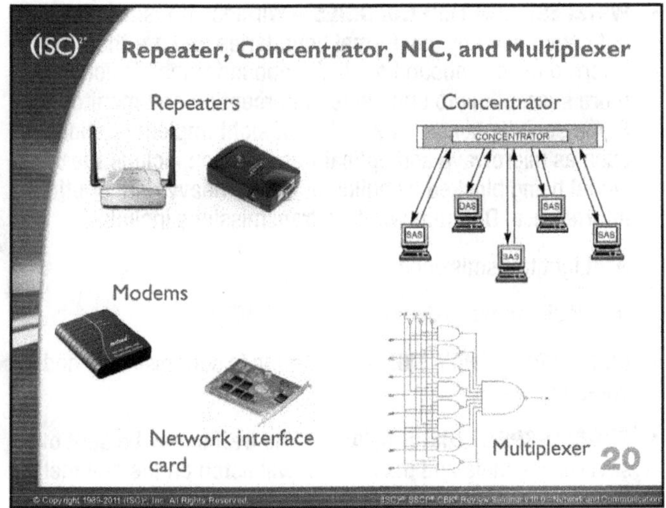


- **REPEATER –** A repeater is a device that receives a low-level signal and retransmits it at a higher strength. This allows the broadcast of a signal over a greater distance. The repeater shown here is the kind used to increase the range of a typical LAN signal, but repeaters can be used to increase the range of many types of wired networks or radio signals.
- **CONCENTRATOR –** Concentrators are used to connect many devices to a single channel. In the diagram above, all of the devices shown are connected through the concentrator onto one channel, which "concentrates" the many devices onto one trunk or communications path. Each device may contend for the use of the medium equally.
- **MULTIPLEXER –** A multiplexer allows many devices to communicate over a shared medium. This can be accomplished through several types of technologies, one of which is frequency-division multiplexing (FDM), wherein the signals from each device are transmitted at different frequencies. Time-division multiplexing (TDM), which is often used in digital communications, separates the traffic from each connected device into individual time slots. Code-division multiplexing (CDM) transmits the signal from each channel as a coded signal. Instead of contending for bandwidth, a multiplexer divides the bandwidth between the various devices (channels) connected to it.
- **NETWORK INTERFACE CARDS (NIC) –** NICs are installed or integrated into end stations (e.g., PCs, servers, etc.) to provide physical and electrical connectivity to the network infrastructure, often through wired connections to a hub, concentrator, or switch. Wireless interface cards permit radio signaling connection to an access point.

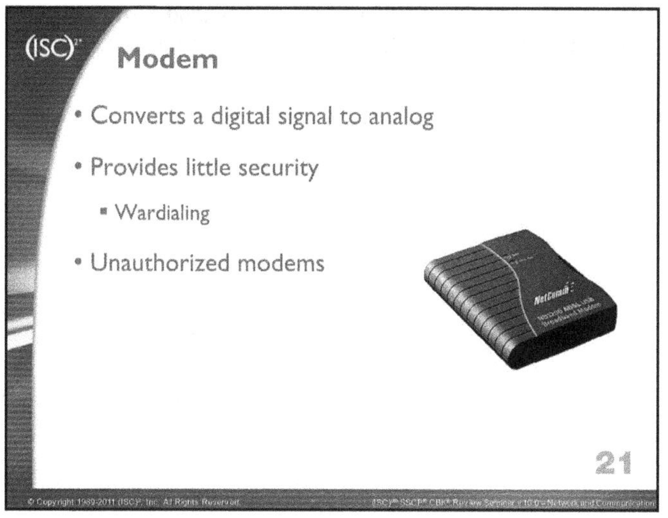
(ISC)²
Modem
• Converts a digital signal to analog
• Provides little security
▪ Wardialing
• Unauthorized modems
21

- **CONVERTS A DIGITAL SIGNAL TO ANALOG –** "Modem" means to "modulate and demodulate" a signal. A modem is connected to the user's computer and converts the digital signal from the computer into an analog signal that can then be carried over a traditional phone line and vice versa.
- **PROVIDES LITTLE SECURITY –** Modems provide little security per se. Modems may use caller recognition to identify an incoming call, but further credentials should be established before the network connection is made. Three basic methods to restrict dial-up remote access are:
  - **RESTRICTED ACCESS –** Only accepts incoming calls from addresses on approved list.
  - **CALLER ID –** Checks each caller's telephone number against an approved list.
  - **CALLBACK –** Callers identify themselves (with pass codes or caller ID, for example), the server terminates the connection and calls the user back at a pre-determined phone number. (Note, that this scheme does not typically require any authentication!)
  - **WARDIALING –** While modems allow an administrator remote access to manage the networks from almost anywhere, they can also be used as a portal into the network by an attacker. Automated dialing software dials a entire range of phone numbers in order to identify modems. If the host to which the modem is attached has a weak password, the attacker can easily gain access to the network. Worse yet, if voice and data share the same network, both voice and data may be compromised.
- **UNAUTHORIZED MODEMS –** Illegitimate modems connected to a network can be used for unauthorized inbound or outbound connections. These pose a special problem because they may be located behind the firewalls and provide access to anyone that discovers the modem's phone number through wardialing or other means.

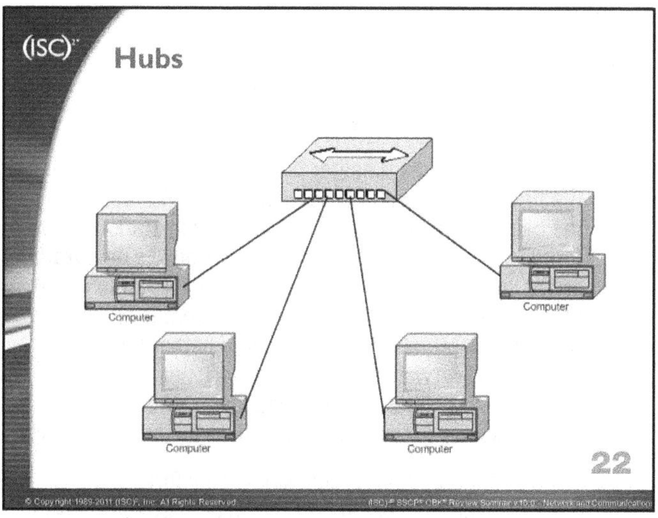
(ISC)²
Hubs
Computer
Computer
Computer
Computer
22

- **HUBS –** A hub is the center device in a star configuration. It is used to connect several twisted-pair connections or fiber optic Ethernet connections. Once connected, the hub will essentially act as a multi-port repeater to take in traffic from one port and forward it to all other ports. It operates at the physical layer of the OSI stack. Logically, the hub acts as a collapsed/concentrated bus (for Ethernet networks) or a collapsed ring (in token ring networks). This physical concentration point allows more efficient placement and management of local hosts.
- **INHERENT SECURITY –** None.
- **ADDED SECURITY FEATURES –** None.
- **SECURITY RISKS –** Any device that can connect to one of the attached cables will be able to see all of the traffic on that segment of the network. One device may monopolize the channel and make it difficult for other devices to communicate.

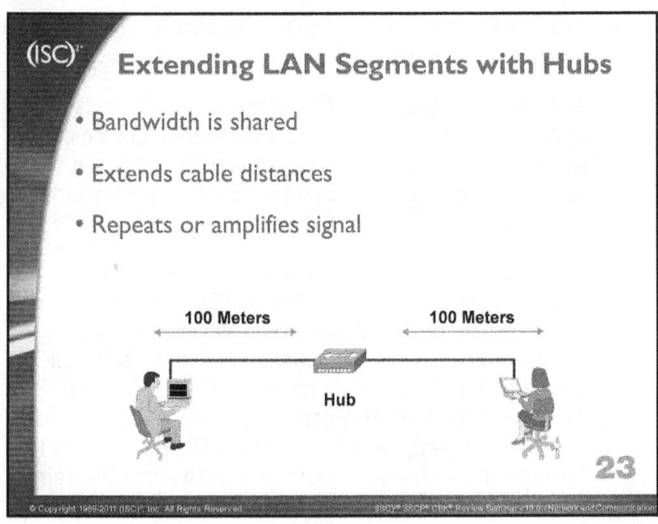


- Example of a traditional flat network extended with a simple hub used to extend range over a greater length than otherwise possible.

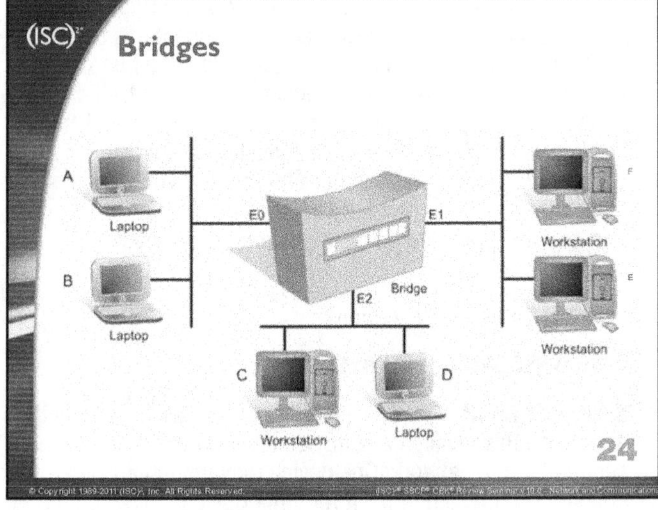


- **BRIDGES –**
  - Bridges connect multiple network segments and allow concurrent conversations within segments, thus extending the capacity of the network.
  - Bridges determine whether host traffic needs to cross the bridge by listening to transmissions and recording the data link-layer address of the sending stations in a forwarding table organized by bridge port. As new traffic arrives on a port, the bridge references this table (sometimes called a MAC address table or content-addressable memory [CAM] table) to determine whether the traffic needs to be forwarded to another port, needs to be suppressed, or is "filtered." All broadcast traffic and most multicasts are forwarded by design to all outbound ports.
- **INHERENT SECURITY –** A bridge selectively forwards traffic to the correct destination port based on hardware (MAC) addresses. Barring some method to defeat normal operations (such as spoofing), bridges add security through higher availability to media. Since it is trivial to force a bridge into forwarding traffic, this feature alone is no longer relied upon for security.
- **SECURITY RISKS –** Broadcast and multicast traffic is still forwarded to all attached network segments. If multiple bridges are interconnected in a meshed configuration, thereby creating multiple paths (traffic loops) between segments, excessive traffic loads (called "storms") can occur. This can quickly result in heavy congestion, and ultimately, complete loss of availability to the network. For this reason, bridges run a standard protocol (IEEE 802.1D, spanning tree protocol) to automatically detect and eliminate traffic loops.

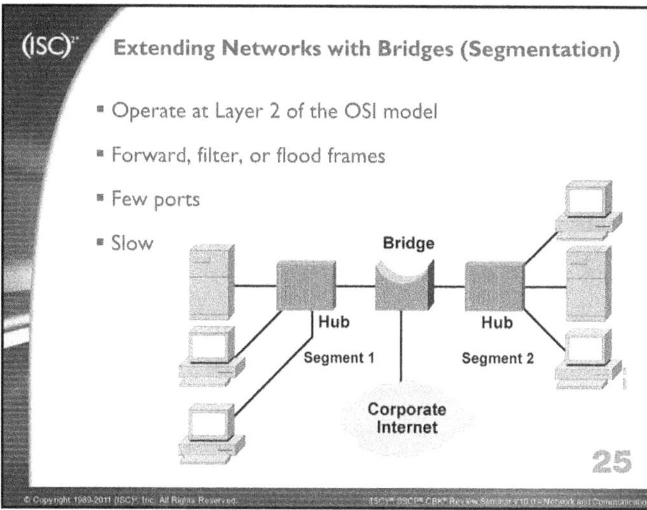

Extending Networks with Bridges (Segmentation)
Operate at Layer 2 of the OSI model
Forward, filter, or flood frames
Few ports
Slow
Bridge
Hub
Hub
Segment 1
Segment 2
Corporate Internet
25


- A typical configuration using a bridge to connect two different networks.

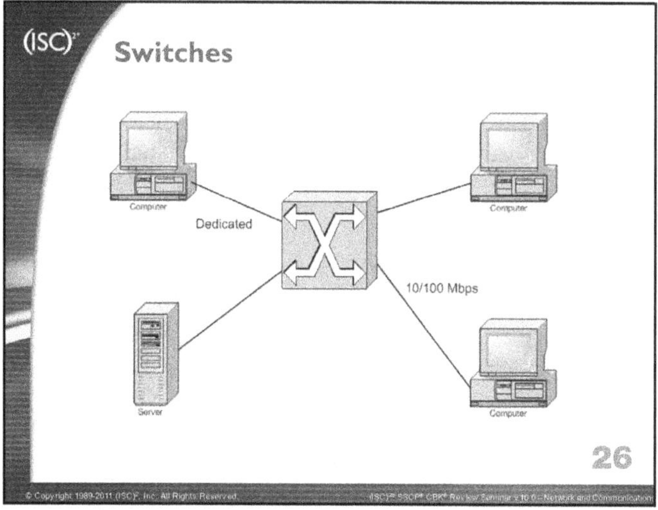


- **SWITCHES –**
  - A switch is essentially a combination of a bridge and a hub, offering end-point connectivity as well as intelligent forwarding. Switches differ from bridges in that the bridging function (logic) is often performed in hardware rather than software, thus permitting much higher performance. Switches also typically offer a much higher density of individually programmable ports. Just like a bridge, the switch will monitor each of the network interfaces and learn the MAC address of attached devices. Because of the higher performance and intelligence capabilities, switches have mostly replaced bridges and hubs in modern networks.
  - There are switches that operate at Layers 2, 3, and 4 of the OSI stack. These are described on the next slides.
- **INHERENT SECURITY –** By design, traffic is only sent to the intended destination.
- **ADDED SECURITY FEATURES –** Most of today's switches can be programmed at the port level, permitting logical isolation of ports using a technique called "virtual LANs," or VLANS. VLANs are logical subnets which act as separate networks. Multiple switches are interconnected via trunk links, which are logical tunnels separating VLAN traffic and extending VLAN capabilities beyond traditional physical LAN deployments. Virtual LANs, like physical LANs, must be interconnected by routers, so at least one switch must either be connected to a router, or must be a Layer 3 switch, which is capable of running internal routing logic.
- **SECURITY RISKS –** A switch port can be configured as a monitoring port and "hear" all traffic passing through. It is also possible to cause the switch to dump its MAC address table and "fail open." Since switches are often deployed in redundant physical arrangements, they have the same potential for traffic loops and broadcast storms as do bridges. Switches can run separate instances of the spanning tree protocol for each programmed virtual LAN.

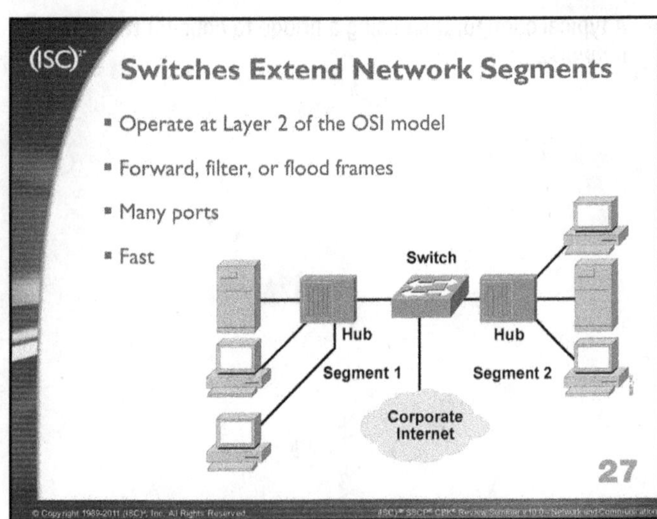


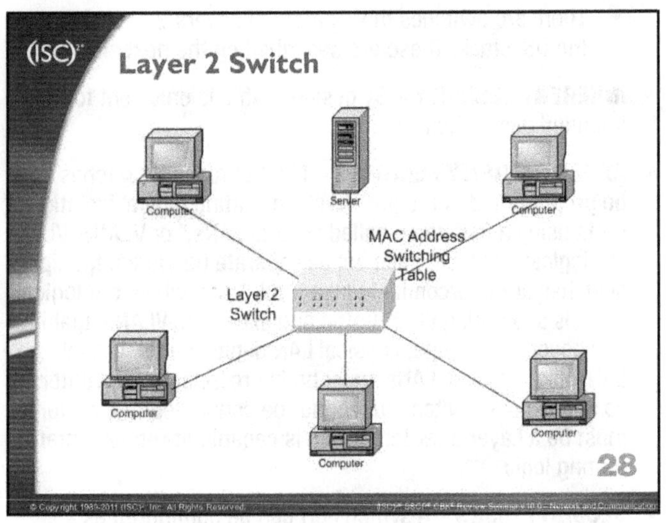


- **LAYER 2 SWITCH –** Layer 2 switches are the most common networking device used to connect PCs, servers, and printers in today's networks and are used to increase the speed and performance of a LAN.
- Most switches have advanced capabilities for transmitting frames as soon as a forwarding decision can be made. This improves throughput but may result in an excessive propagation of errors. Switches can also automatically switch into "store and forward" mode, which means that real-time error checking can be performed before frames are transmitted.
- Because Layer 2 switches are often deployed in wiring closets closest to end-points, it is important to implement additional protection against unauthorized access. Most switches have operating systems permitting enforcement of access through privilege levels. Many can also be configured to enable security at the port level.

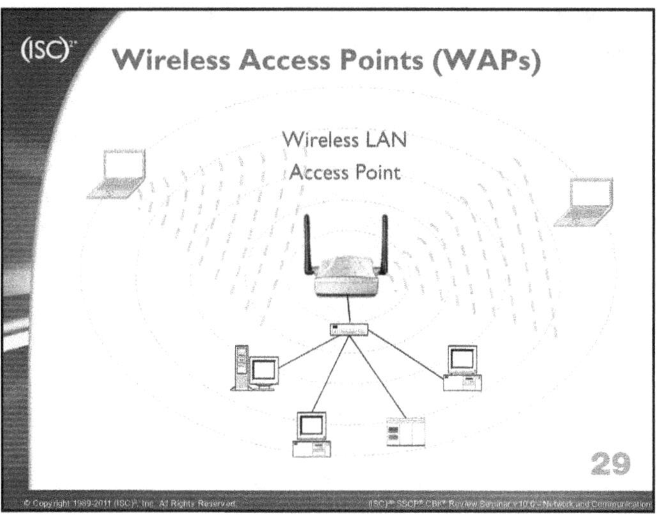


- **WIRELESS ACCESS POINTS (WAPS) –** Wireless access points are where wireless signals are converted into wired signals and transfer from one media type (radio wave) to another (typically copper). Access points started as single input and single output, but through the use of technologies such as multiple frequencies and multiple antennas, MIMO (multiple input, multiple output) has increased the capacity of wireless networks to that of wired networks.
- Because WAPs are the connection points between the wired and wireless networks, they must be properly secured to prevent easy entry into the wired network. WAPs enable the latest recommended security features, including WPA2 and strong authentication. These and other wireless security technologies are discussed in more detail later in this course.

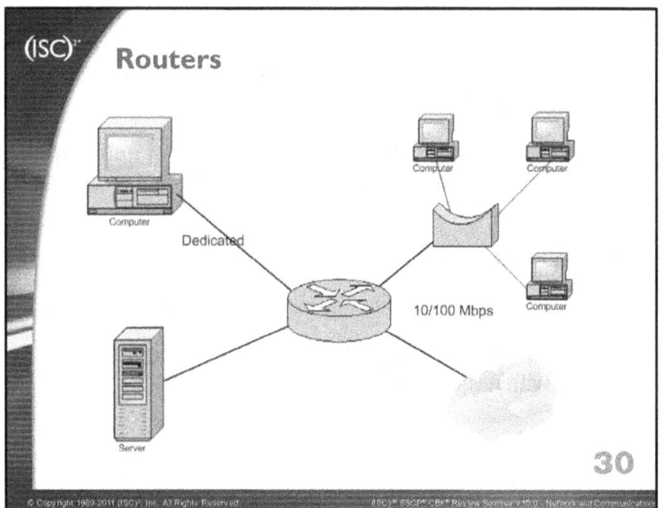


- **ROUTERS –** A router is a media/protocol gateway and a network boundary device that interconnects different networks and allows for implementation of a number of management and control services. Routers handle traffic coming in from multiple ports and forward the traffic based on the network-layer protocol and address. A port on a router may be dedicated to a single device, or it may be shared through the use of a switch or hub. Routers often include interfaces supporting a variety of network standards and architectures and most support multiple protocols.
- **INHERENT SECURITY –** Broadcast traffic is blocked.
- **ADDED SECURITY FEATURES –** Packet filtering, stateful firewall features, network address translation (NAT), and virtual private network (VPN) support.
- **SECURITY RISKS –** One of the primary logic functions of a router is dynamic routing. This enables routers to automatically acquire and disseminate network control information through the use of special routing programs. Properly-tuned routing protocols provide the resiliency necessary for very rapid recovery from changes that may occur in the infrastructure so that end-to-end connectivity is maintained. Due to the dynamic nature of this activity, however, some simple protocols are naturally vulnerable to erroneous information. Latency in dissemination (convergence) can also cause temporary disruptions in communications.
- Routing functions can also be run separately on other appliances such as high-performance Layer 3 switches and even standard hosts. Take care to ensure that no unauthorized routing activities are allowed within the network, and that proper logging of all routing changes is recorded and regularly reviewed. Neighbor authentication is a feature available on most routing protocols, and that ensures a router only receives reliable routing information and from trusted neighbors. That is achieved by certifying the authenticity of each neighbor and the integrity of its routing updates.

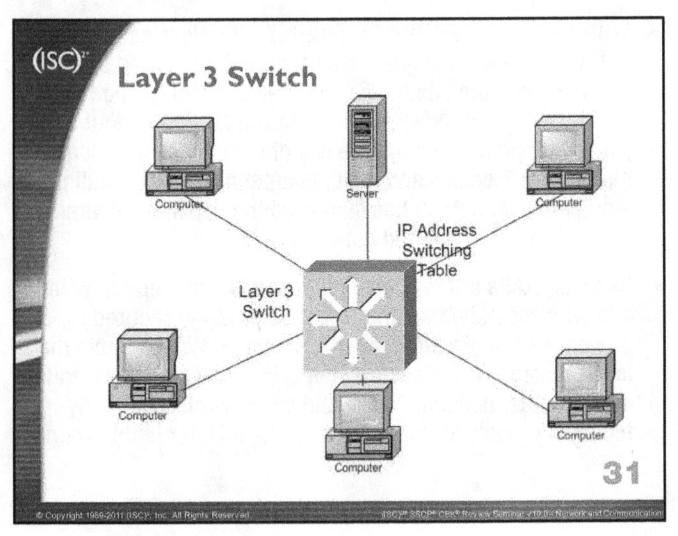


- **LAYER 3 SWITCH –** A Layer 3 switch is essentially a modular Layer 2 switch that includes an additional hardware or embedded Layer 3 routing processor. Layer 3 switches are used to increase transmission speeds between network segments by switching at wire speed (Layer 2) once a forwarding decision is made at Layer 3. The expression "route once, switch many" refers to the dual capability of a Layer 3 switch to pass traffic through the routing function, build a Layer 3-Layer 2 forwarding table, and then use this information to switch similar traffic at Layer 2. The Layer 3 switch will act as a router by reading the network-layer address information and then using switch logic to send the frame on to the correct destination.
- Today, Layer 3 or multi-layer switching is often incorporated into a high performance router which increases the router's throughput capabilities by reducing the amount of processing required per frame. A Layer 3 switch can also fall back to Layer 2 switch mode when necessary.

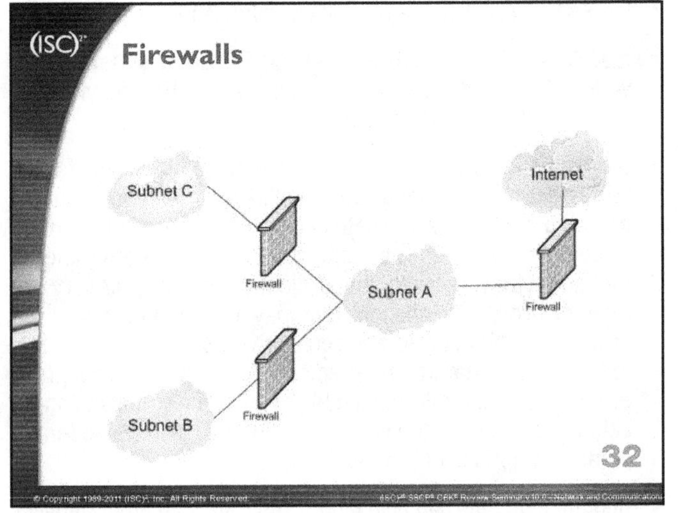


- **FIREWALLS –** Firewalls are a critical element of network security today. But they are just that – a single element. Although they do add some much-needed security, firewalls will not solve all of our security problems.
  - Firewalls are designed to control the flow of traffic by preventing unauthorized traffic from entering or leaving a particular portion of the network.
  - Firewalls can be used:
    - Between corporate networks and the outside world.
    - To allow only authorized access to corporate assets within the corporate network.

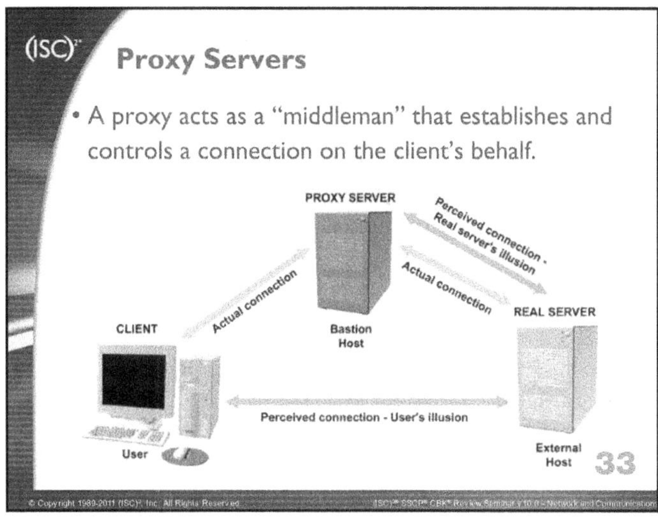


- **PROXY SERVERS –** Proxy servers direct client requests to a dedicated bastion server running a program that interfaces with external hosts (servers) on behalf of internal clients.
- **SECURITY SERVERS –** Proxy servers can isolate trusted (internal) networks from untrusted (external) networks, preventing outside hosts from connecting directly to private hosts. Proxies also examine program code to prevent surreptitious attacks. Proxies hide all internal hosts, which prevents intruders from easily discovering information about the internal network.
- Because firewalls utilizing proxy services make a distinct physical separation between the local network and the Internet, they are a good choice for high security requirements. Because a software program must analyze packets and make decisions about access control, however, these types of firewalls tend to reduce network performance. If an organization plans to use proxy services, it should use the fastest processors available for the computer that will be hosting the proxy.

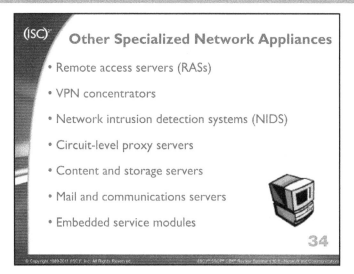

(ISC)²

**Other Specialized Network Appliances**

- Remote access servers (RASs)
- VPN concentrators
- Network intrusion detection systems (NIDS)
- Circuit-level proxy servers
- Content and storage servers
- Mail and communications servers
- Embedded service modules

34

- There are a variety of other network components in today's network infrastructure that offer special services. They may be stand-alone server hosts that are deployed in special network segments, or they may be embedded service modules that are integrated into existing network devices (e.g., encryptor modules or IDS modules installed in enterprise switch platforms).
- While the specifics of IP telephony are discussed later, support for unified communications (e.g., converged data, voice, video, and other collaborative services) is now a feature capability of most vendor offerings and is being exploited by businesses to provide greater levels of service.
- These specialized services, while dramatically increasing business opportunities, also increase the critical importance of protecting the network from disruption and attack.

(ISC)²

## End Systems

- Servers and mainframes
- Operating systems
- Notebooks/laptops
- Workstations
- Smart phones
- Personal digital assistants (PDAs)

35

 (ISC)² SSCP® CBK® Review Seminar v10.0 – Network and Communication

- **END SYSTEMS –** These devices, and the applications they run, are the reason networks exist – to allow these systems to exchange information. Because the information on these devices represents the primary business IT asset, it is imperative that they be well protected.
  - **SERVERS AND MAINFRAMES –** Servers and mainframes are repositories of information, much of which is critical to an organization's mission, its employees, and clients. These computers contain information that supports critical business processes, customer databases, and intellectual property. Further, an ever-growing number of international, national, and local security and privacy regulations demand that the information on these systems be adequately protected.
    - Due to the accessibility of servers and mainframes and the importance of the information stored, servers and mainframes are subject to much risk. The stereotypical intruder is faceless, nameless, and breaking in from an external machine. But, the people who most frequently gain unauthorized access are, in fact, internal personnel. Malicious activity is not always the greatest threat – human error is just as dangerous.
    - Due to the importance of the information kept on servers and mainframes, it is vital that organizations minimize the risk posed by unauthorized access. The following are a few important controls:
      - Owners should only grant the level of access required for personnel to perform their duties, and log all access well enough to support forensic investigations. These logs must be reviewed regularly. Because the failure of an application may increase the risk to other applications on the same host, multiple applications should not run on the same physical or virtual machine. For instance, a compromise of a low-risk application (that may not be rigorously protected) could allow an intruder access to a high-risk application on the same server. Similarly, a failure of a development instance of an application could corrupt production, especially if they share the same database with other applications.
      - Sensitive data should be encrypted with strong encryption algorithms. Encrypt network traffic between client and servers/mainframes.
      - Reduce risks from remote access through ensuring that all remote access is protected by two-factor authentication and encryption.
      - Use controls discussed previously (such as firewalls) to help ensure that only authorized clients are able to access the servers and mainframes.
      - Verify that clients are authorized to access the server (perhaps with digital certificates) and that middleware servers are not an attacker's machine masquerading as such.
  - **OPERATING SYSTEMS –** An operating system is the software interface between applications and the hardware. It services requests for peripherals on behalf of the users and interfaces with the central processing unit. Security is an integral and critical function of the operating system.
    - Operating systems implement access control lists (ACLs) to help ensure that users are only able to access resources for which they are authorized.
    - Operating systems also provide mechanisms to improve the availability of information, such as redundant array of independent disks (RAID) and computer clusters.
    - Regardless of the applications that are running on a computer, the operating system will always be a target of attack because a compromised operating system will allow an intruder to control the computer. Owners should, therefore, remove unnecessary targets of attack (such as dangerous or unused services) and install security patches as it is feasible.
  - **NOTEBOOKS/LAPTOPS –** Notebooks (also known as laptops) have the same problems as workstations, but are subject to additional risks because of their portability.
    - Notebooks can be easily stolen or lost, potentially disclosing sensitive contents.
    - When a user attaches the notebook to another network, such as a home network or wireless hotspot, it is not protected by the organization's firewall. There is a significant danger that the user could unintentionally download malicious code on his or her notebook when attached to another network and unleash it on the organization when the notebook returns to the office. This can be addressed by requiring a scan of all devices when reconnecting a network to ensure antivirus and other controls are up to date.
    - The above issues can be partly mitigated with technical controls, such as ensuring that all notebooks have personal firewalls and antivirus software with current signatures, and by encrypting sensitive files and disks in case the notebook is lost or stolen.
    - Notebook users must be educated on their additional responsibilities, must understand how to use their notebooks when on a different network, and know how to physically protect it from thieves. Cable locks, hard drive encryption, tracing soft-

ware, and not leaving laptops unattended are all good physical security controls.

    - Tablet PCs (notebooks that use a specialized stylus for handwritten input) have the same security risks as regular notebooks. Since tablet PCs are used to take meeting notes, a lost or stolen tablet PC may disclose very sensitive information.

- **WORKSTATIONS –** Workstations are usually desktop computers used by the various users in the organization and typically function as clients. As with all network devices, workstations are potential targets of attack. Some workstation vulnerabilities are similar to those of servers (and some workstation operating systems in fact provide server functionality). Unpatched operating systems and unnecessary network services can, for example, affect both.
    - Workstation user behavior can threaten a network. Some users forget that they do not own "their" workstation, and freely engage in dangerous behavior, such as downloading from untrusted sites, chatting with instant messaging, or leaving their office with their workstation unprotected.
    - It is also common for users to underestimate the sensitivity of the information on their workstation and, therefore, underestimate the importance of protecting it.
    - Organizations should consider NOT granting privileged rights to workstation users. Users should be restricted from having administrator rights on their machines, which would prevent them from installing devices, programs, or downloading materials.
    - As with other end systems, software updates must be installed as soon as possible, unnecessary and dangerous services must be disabled, and antivirus software and personal firewalls should be installed.
- **SMART PHONES –** Smart phones are a combination of a PDA and a cell phone. While smart phones offer the convenience of both devices, they also share the security issues.
    - A smart phone's subscriber identity module (SIM) can be cloned and used to steal personal information that is on the card.
    - A thief can use the cellular capabilities of a smart phone to email stolen information while still on his or her victim's premises.
    - As with PDAs, the best defenses against the issues listed above include encryption, protecting computer ports that might be used to download information, and educating users to recognize and stop a person from using a smart phone to steal corporate data.
- **PERSONAL DIGITAL ASSISTANTS (PDAS) –** PDAs can store confidential and private information, but many models do not include appropriate controls (such as strong encryption) to protect the PDA's contents in the event that the device is stolen or lost. A thief can easily steal information by downloading it to a PDA from an unprotected computer.
    - PDAs with camera attachments can be used to take unauthorized photographs. Because PDAs attach to computers to download information via computer ports, to help reduce the risk of confidential information walking out of the office on a PDA, computer ports should be physically and logically protected.

(ISC)²

## Network Device OSI Layer Positioning

| Devices | Layer | Function |
|---|---|---|
| Application Gateways, Application Layer Firewalls (ALF) | 7 | Ability to examine detail content and context of traffic flows |
| Stateful Inspection Firewalls Circuit Level Proxy, L4Switches/MLS | 4 | Ability to filter on application ports, maintain state of flows |
| Routers, Route Processors Layer 3 (L3) Switches | 3 | Filter on logical IP address, control direction of traffic; provides managed isolation |
| Bridges, Desktop Switches, Access Points | 2 | Filter on MAC addresses, segmentation of traffic flow for higher performance |
| Repeaters, Hubs, Concentrators MAUs, NIC Adaptors, Modems | 1 | Physical connections and signal quality; signal amplification and conversion |

36

(ISC)² SSCP® CBK® Review Seminar v10.0 Network and Communications

- Engineers often describe network devices by the OSI layer at which the device operates.
- While technology has evolved to enhance the performance of most network devices, detailed processing of information often increases latency. Many network designs, therefore, focus on embedding as much network intelligence as possible at the lowest level of processing. This is a primary motivation for the trend toward adopting advanced switching technologies as a core strategy. A multi-station access unit (MSAU) is a hub or concentrator that connects a group of computers ("nodes" in network terminology) to a token ring local area network.

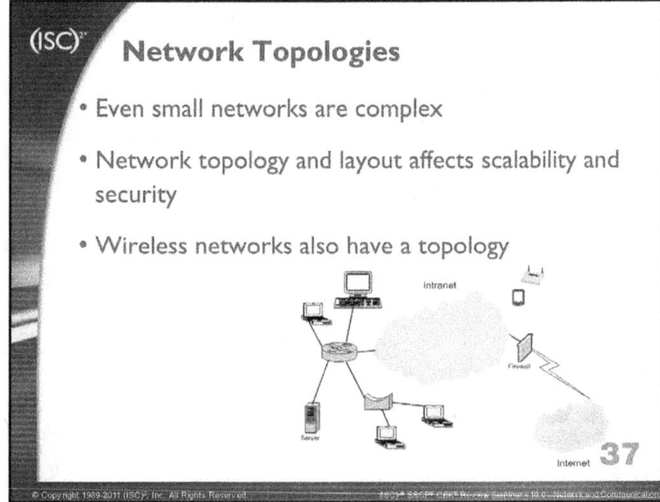
(ISC)²
Network Topologies
• Even small networks are complex
• Network topology and layout affects scalability and security
• Wireless networks also have a topology
Intranet
Internet
37

- **EVEN SMALL NETWORKS ARE COMPLEX –** The network topology defines which devices are crucial to network security, whether there are single points of failure, and whether controls are properly located.
- **NETWORK TOPOLOGY AND LAYOUT AFFECTS SCALABILITY AND SECURITY –** The layout of the physical layer is reflected on the higher layers (starting with the data link layer). Through a secure physical layout, incidents can be isolated, sensitive data segmented, and operating domains established. The physical layout defines how easy it will be for the operators of the network to seal off parts of the network that have been compromised, as well as how easily an attacker might be able to traverse the network. The primary consideration at the physical layer, however, is often the physical parameters, such as the layout of buildings or the distance between them. A network that has to cover a large building (e.g., warehouse, etc.) needs special considerations to avoid exceeding maximum cable lengths and interbuilding network connection requirements.
- **WIRELESS NETWORKS ALSO HAVE A TOPOLOGY –** This becomes more important as more and more office LANs are built in a wireless rather than a wired fashion. (For instance, a peer-to-peer wireless network can be associated with a mesh network. More on this to follow.)

**REFERENCE:**

http://www.ciscopress.com/articles

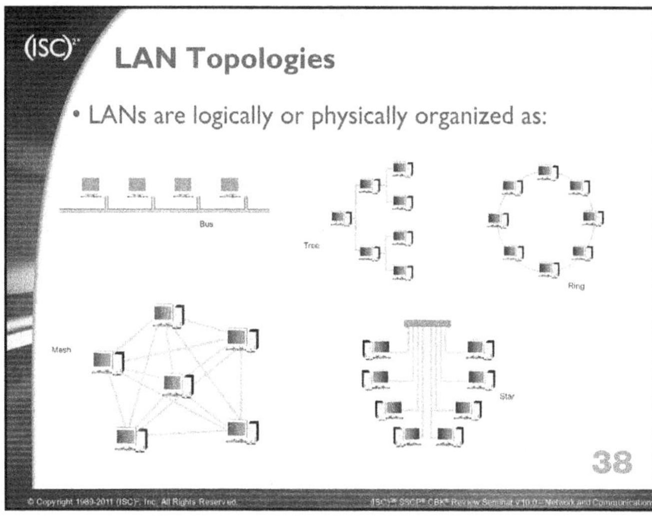


- **LAN TOPOLOGIES –** There are a few commonly implemented network topology schemes. Each scheme has its own native security level and security issues.
- LAN topologies define the manner in which network devices are organized. There are five common LAN topologies: bus, tree, ring, star, and mesh. These topologies are logical architectures, but the actual devices need not be physically organized in these configurations. Logical bus and ring topologies, for example, are commonly organized physically as a star.

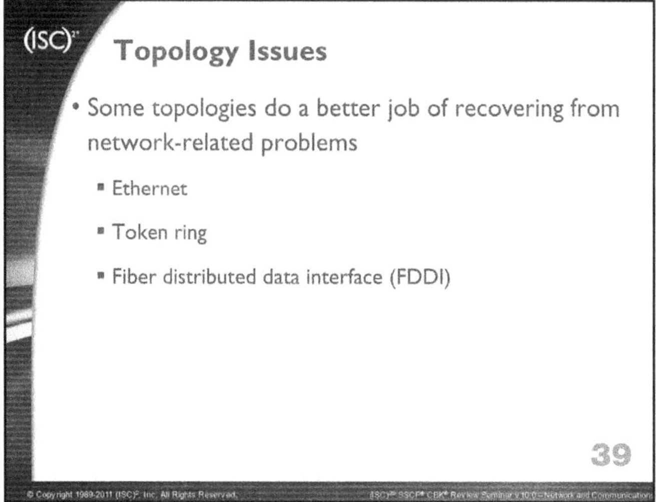


- **SOME TOPOLOGIES DO A BETTER JOB OF RECOVERING FROM NETWORK-RELATED PROBLEMS –** The topology you choose can have a dramatic effect on how resilient your network will be in case of failure. Some topologies do a better job than others of recovering from the day-to-day problems that can happen on any network. Changing your topology may not be an option however.
  - **ETHERNET –** Ethernet is now the topology of choice. When used with twisted-pair cabling, the topology can be extremely resistant to failure from cabling problems on any single segment.
  - **TOKEN RING –** Token ring was designed to be fault tolerant, but it is not without its problems, usually related to faulty NICs (network interface cards).
  - **FIBER DISTRIBUTED DATA INTERFACE (FDDI) –** Is also a ring topology with a second ring added in order to rectify many of the problems found in the traditional token ring. This second ring usually remains dormant until an error condition is detected. When this occurs, the FDDI systems can work together in order to isolate the problem area. FDDI can also be run in full-duplex mode, which allows both rings to be active at all times. This allows the network to continue to run (albeit with lower performance) when it has to wrap around a failure.

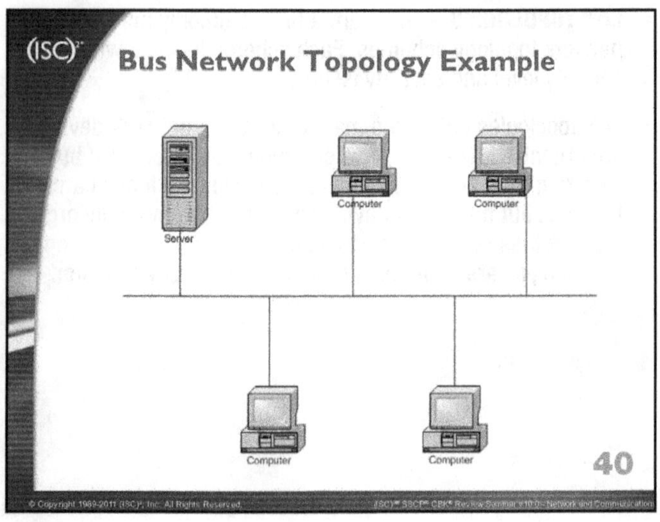


- **BUS NETWORK TOPOLOGY EXAMPLE –** Physical bus topologies have given way to star topologies over the years. The defining characteristic of a bus is that what one station transmits, all stations hear. This means that any traffic transmitted by any user is visible to all other users, which presents an eavesdropping security issue. Also, since only one station can transmit at a time, there will be variable delays before being able to transmit. The solution to both problems is a switched network, which puts one station on each bus.
- Another solution is link-layer encryption. This is often used when it is not possible to have dedicated wires linking stations to switches.
  - Shared buses can be secured using network cards that encrypt and decrypt on the fly.
  - Although wireless access points (WAPs) and their user stations aren't examples of a bus network, they do share an eavesdropping problem with buses. WEP and WPA are link-encryption solutions that we will discuss later on.

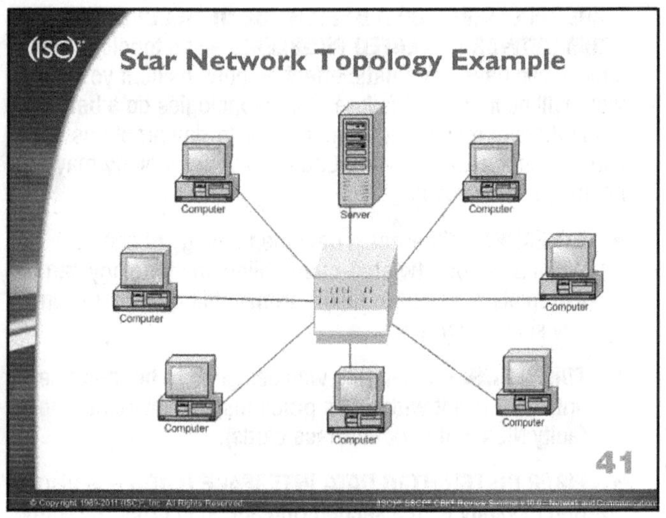


- **STAR NETWORK TOPOLOGY EXAMPLE –** A star topology has a device in the center from which PCs, servers, etc., branch out. As we will discuss below, the device in the center (whether it is a hub, switch, or bridge) will have a great deal to do with the transmission characteristics of the star topology. This configuration is most commonly used for Ethernet LANs and token ring implementations. Even though the network may logically operate as a ring or bus, the topology name is based on its physical layout. Sometimes a qualifier may be added and the topology will be referred to as a star-bus, or star-ring.
- The biggest advantage of a star topology is that a failure in the wiring only affects one station.
- The biggest disadvantage of a star topology is that it needs a lot more cabling. It also introduces a single point of failure, but it is still better than a coax bus or a daisy-chained token ring where a failure at any point means that the entire network (or subnetwork, if configured that way) will fail.

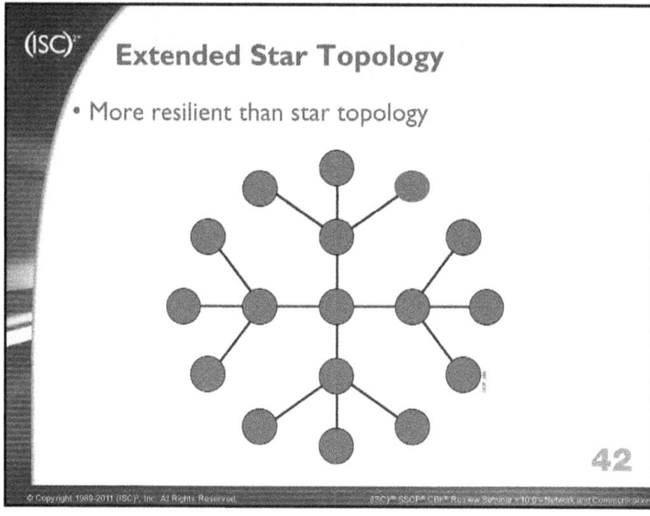


- **EXTENDED STAR TOPOLOGY –** A more complex arrangement of multiple star physical topologies. This example also demonstrates a layered approach to design.
- At the outer edge, the access layer may represent connection points for end-stations (using hubs or layer-2 switches).
- The innermost layer represents the core of the network, which is accessible to all connected devices and typically contains primary business resources, such as servers.
- A separation layer (sometimes called a distribution layer) contains Layer 3 devices such as routers or Layer 3 switches, and is often used to impose control over access to core services.
- Redundancy is critical in this design to ensure that distribution devices have multiple paths into the core. A possible solution is to "mesh" the distribution layer components.

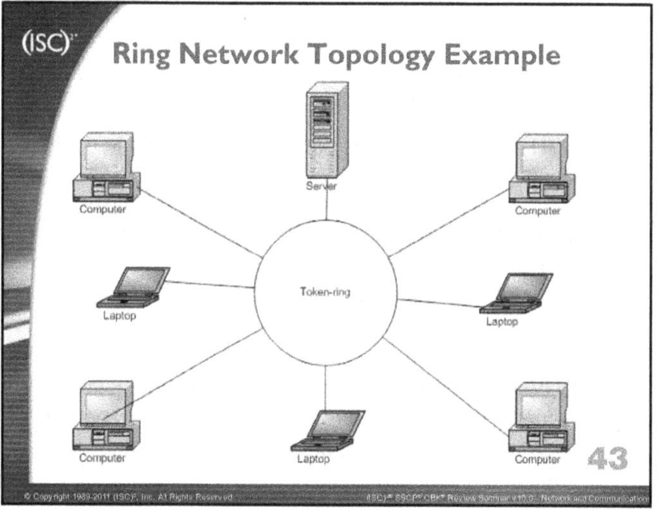


- **RING NETWORK TOPOLOGY EXAMPLE –** A ring topology is similar in nature to the bus topology in distributing information to all users connected to the ring. This has the security disadvantage of not secluding a conversation to the two involved parties. Anyone connected to the ring can view all traffic on the ring.
- Ring topologies are deterministic, which means that it is possible to determine when the station will next get access to the media. For example, in token ring (802.5), every station has a maximum transmission frame size, after which it has to release the token to the next station. Even if all stations wanted to transmit a maximum sized frame (statistically possible, but extremely unlikely), the last station in line would be able to determine the worst-case time at which it would get access again.
- Although the picture doesn't clearly show it, all traffic flows from one station to its neighbor, then to the neighbor's neighbor, etc., until it has completed its traversal of the ring.

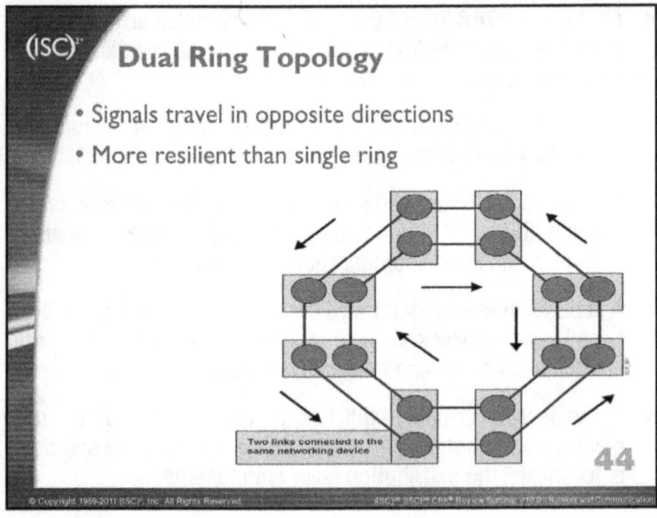

(ISC)²
Dual Ring Topology
• Signals travel in opposite directions
• More resilient than single ring
Two links connected to the same networking device
44


- This dual ring approach is specifically designed for high availability through a self-healing response to a failing link. FDDI backbones are commonly configured as dual-rings to ensure resiliency in the core.

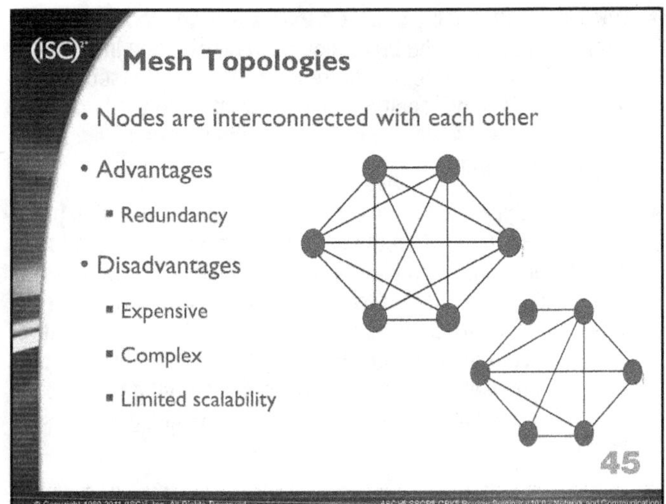

(ISC)²
Mesh Topologies
• Nodes are interconnected with each other
• Advantages
▪ Redundancy
• Disadvantages
▪ Expensive
▪ Complex
▪ Limited scalability
45


- **MESH TOPOLOGIES –** Have many redundant connections between nodes. There are two types of mesh topologies:
  - **FULL MESH –** Every node has a direct connection to every other node in the network. This is very expensive to implement but it provides the greatest amount of throughput and redundancy. Full-mesh topologies are usually reserved for networks with large bandwidth and redundancy needs, such as backbone networks. A full mesh is the fastest type of network topology because there is no routing required; every host is directly attached to every other one. But, on the other hand, it requires many links. You need N*(N-1)/2 links to fully connect N nodes.
  - **PARTIAL MESH –** Some nodes are connected in a full-mesh scheme, while others are only connected to a few other nodes. It is far less expensive than full mesh. Due to the excessive costs of a full mesh, a hybrid arrangement is often used instead. In the hybrid, only critical nodes have redundant paths.
- **ADVANTAGES –**
  - **REDUNDANCY –** Mesh networks provide a high level of redundancy. The failure of any node or combination of nodes or cable links will not affect the operations of the remainder of the network.
- **DISADVANTAGES –**
  - **EXPENSIVE –** A lot of cable is required for a mesh network.
  - **COMPLEX –** It is complex to set up and administer.
  - **LIMITED SCALABILITY –** It is expensive and difficult to connect new nodes, or to remove old ones.

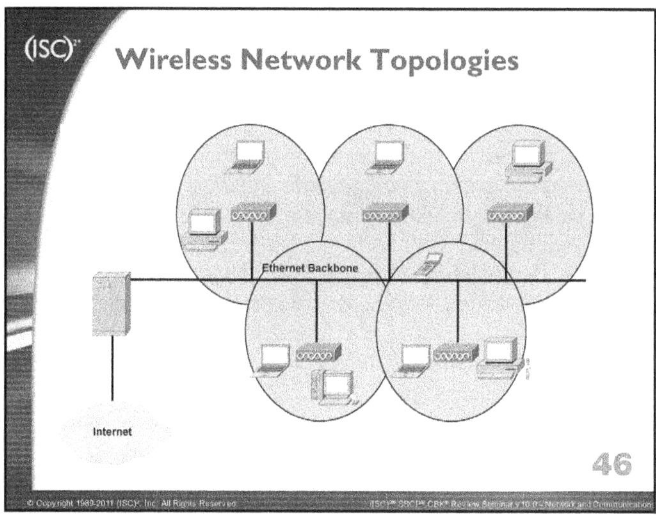


- Wireless portions of a standard network may actually provide a full-mesh capability without requiring physical links. Wireless technologies are most often deployed over traditional physical topologies to extend connectivity and to provide flexibility and mobility.
- Because not all connections are physical, controls must be added to ensure that only authorized end-points are permitted to connect to the wired network. This typically requires security protocol implementations on the access point, as well as some capability to authenticate end-stations.

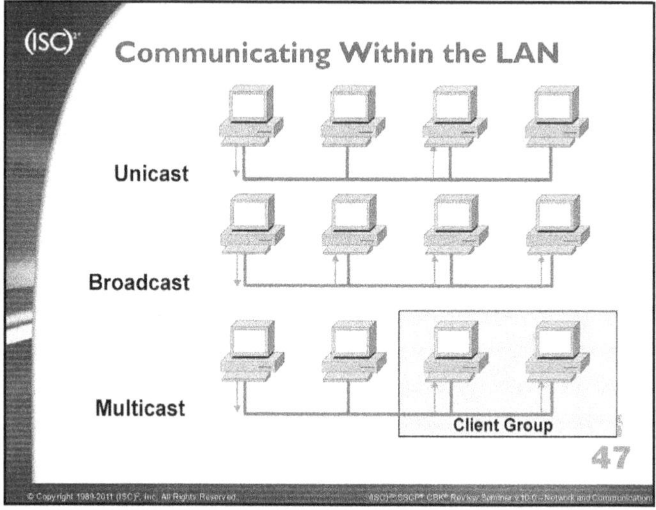


- **COMMUNICATING WITHIN THE LAN –** A transmission sent to one receiving host is called unicast and one sent to several is called multicast. Transmissions sent to an unspecified number of hosts are called Broadcasts.
  - **MULTICASTS –** Are directed to a defined set of recipients. Public and private networks are being used more often than ever for streaming transmissions such as movies, videoconferences, and music. Unless there is a very small audience, unicast delivery is not practical because multiple simultaneous copies of a large stream on the network cause congestion. With broadcasts, every host would receive the transmission whether or not it was interested in the stream. Multicast offers a stream only to hosts interested in receiving it.
    - Multicast agents are used to route multicast traffic over networks and to administer multicast groups. Each network and subnetwork that supports multicasting must have at least one multicast agent.
    - Hosts use the IGMP protocol to tell a local multicast agent that it wants to join a specific multicast group. Multicast agents also route multicasts to local hosts that are members of the multicast's group, and relay multicasts to neighboring agents.
  - **BROADCASTS –** Can have an unlimited number of recipients. A host can send a broadcast to everyone on its network or subnetwork. If a router knows a device's IP address but not its MAC address, it will broadcast an ARP (address resolution protocol) request asking all devices on the network for the single device's MAC address.
    - A broadcast can result in hundreds or even thousands of packets on the network. Intruders often leverage this to launch denial of service attacks.
    - Do not use reliable sessions – There is no guarantee of delivery with multicasts and broadcast transmissions.
  - **UNICAST –** Sending a message from one host to another.

(ISC)²

## LAN Media Access Methods

- Hosts can use three types of methods to access the physical network medium
  - Carrier sense multiple access (CSMA)
    - With collision avoidance (CSMA/CA)
    - With collision detection (CSMA/CD)
  - Token passing
  - Polling

48



(ISC)² SSCP® CBK® Review Seminar v10.0 Networks and Communication

- LAN protocols typically use one of the following methods to access the physical network medium -
  - Ethernet LANs use CSMA-CD.
  - IEEE 802.11 wireless uses CSMA-CA methods.
  - Token-ring LANs and FDDI both use token-passing method.
  - SNA and Bluetooth use the polling scheme.
- CSMA-CD and token passing are by far the most widely used.
- **CARRIER SENSE MULTIPLE ACCESS (CSMA) –** Contention-based media access methods are those in which systems literally compete (or contend) for access to the media. The key word to describe a contention-based system is "shared."' All systems share access to the media and can only transmit data when the wire is clear of signals. Networks using contention methods are, therefore, pretty much "every system for itself."
  - Since systems share the media, any system that has data to transmit must wait until the line is clear. If two systems attempt to communicate at the same time, a collision occurs, corrupting the data. When this happens, systems have to back off from transmitting for a indeterminate period of time. If collisions continue to occur, the back-off time continues to increase. Networks experiencing high rates of collision, therefore, have even poorer performance.
  - A great example of contention in action is when you have multiple systems plugged into an Ethernet hub. Notice the collision light blinking repeatedly? That's a good sign that your network isn't performing nearly as well as it could be. Originally, Ethernet was not thought to be a viable enterprise technology, mainly because of the fact that it is contention based. With the introduction of bridging and especially switching technologies, this has become less of an issue.
- **TOKEN PASSING –** Token passing technologies are referred to as "deterministic" and are a far more orderly way of transmitting data. In deterministic systems, a system gains access to the media in a regular and predictable fashion. In a token passing environment, no system can transmit data unless it has the token. A token is a special frame that continuously circles the network being passed from system to system. When a system has data to send, it waits for the token. Once it has the token, it can then send data to other systems. Once the data has been sent successfully, the system releases the token back onto the network, giving other systems the ability to transmit. Token passing is the media access method used in both token ring and fiber distributed data interface (FDDI) networks.
- **POLLING –** Polling is another media access method, but one that is not terribly popular in LAN environments. As with token passing, polling is deterministic. Unlike token passing where a special frame is passed from system to system polling relies on what is known as a master device. The master device coordinates what system has the ability to transmit at any given point in time. The master device queries (or polls) network systems to see if they have any data to transmit. If they do, they send data. If they don't, the next system is queried, and so on. Polling media access is commonly found in mainframe environments. One major disadvantage of polling is that should the master device fail, all nodes become incapable of sending data. Polling is, therefore, a single point of failure access method.

(ISC)²

## Domain Agenda

- Network protocols and components
- **Wide area and remote access networks**
- Network Security protocols
- Wireless network configuration and protection
- Managing service reliability and quality

49



(ISC)² SSCP® CBK® Review Seminar v 10.0 – Network and Communications

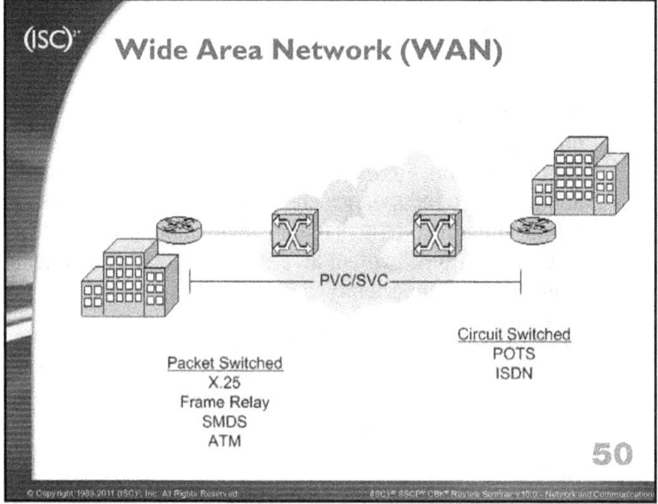


- **WIDE AREA NETWORK (WAN) –** The wide area network (WAN) is a critical element in every corporate network today. Corporations must be able to connect with their offices, their remote users, their customers, and perhaps even with their competition on occasion. The WAN allows access to the corporate resources from almost anywhere in the world. There are several different types of WAN protocols and configurations in use today. As with all other aspects of networking, each configuration has its advantages and disadvantages.

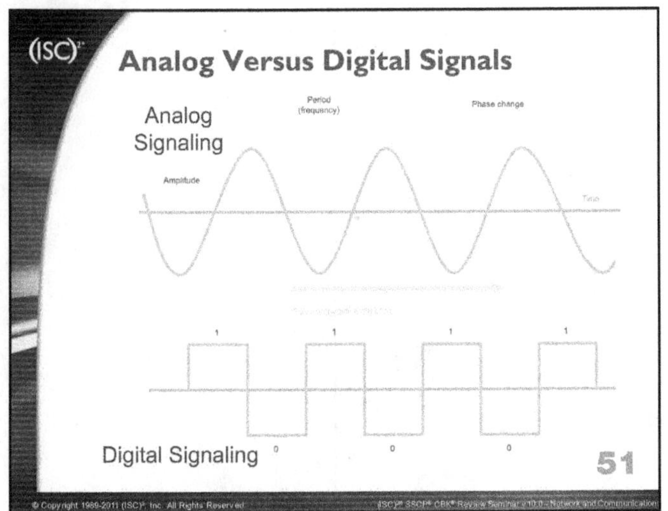


- **ANALOG SIGNALING –** Analog technology is widespread even today. It is implemented in the public switched telephone network (PSTN) and it underlies wireless technologies. Much of today's digital infrastructure is built upon analog components. Analog technology can be implemented in either frequency modulation or amplitude modulation. When frequency modulation (FM) is used the carrier signal is modulated with the information being transmitted. The effect of this is that the sine wave moves closer together and farther apart as it crosses the carrier intermediate frequency (IF). When amplitude modulation (AM) is used the peaks of the phase changes of the carrier signal increase and decrease based on the information that is
    - **TRANSMITTED ON WIRES OR WITH WIRELESS DEVICES –** Analog signals are transmitted on wires, such as twisted pair, or transmitted with a wireless device. In radio communication, for example, the electrical representation of the person's voice is modulated with a carrier signal and broadcasted.
- **DIGITAL SIGNALING –** Brings quantitative and qualitative enhancements. The enhancements from digital technology are a result of higher throughput capability (which in the cases of DSL was accomplished by reusing existing analog infrastructure and removing the frequency filters and other restrictions used in analog communication), a better signal-to-noise ratio and fault tolerant error correction, and the ability to immediately process digital signals in a computer.
    - Packet-switched networks would be difficult to implement using purely analog technology, so the move to digital communication has really enabled a whole new class of telecommunications networks.
    - **USES TWO ELECTRONIC STATES –** Digital communication uses: "on" and "off." By convention, "1" is assigned to the "on" state, and "0" to "off." When a device receives a digital transmission, it can easily determine which digits are 0s and which are 1s.
    - **CAN BE TRANSMITTED OVER MOST MEDIA –** Electrical signals that consist of these two states can be transmitted over cable, converted to light and transmitted over fiber optics, and modulated onto an analog channel with a wired or wireless device.

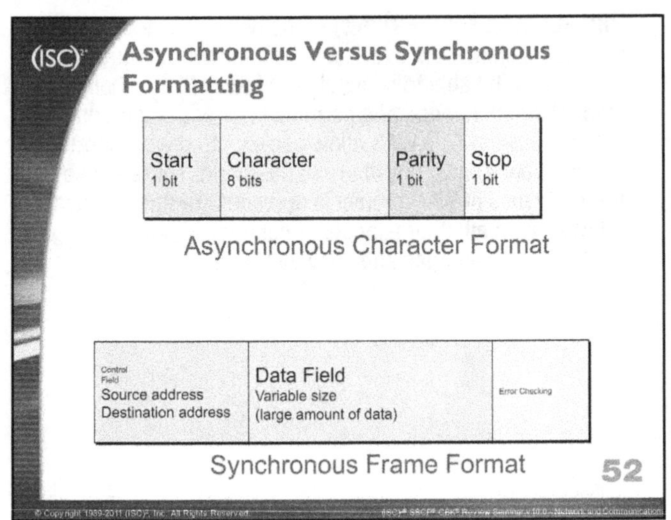


- **SYNCHRONOUS –**
    - **TIMING MECHANISM SYNCHRONIZES DATA TRANSMISSION –** Synchronous communication uses a timing mechanism to synchronize the transmission of data between the two devices. The communicating devices can use a clocking mechanism, or the transmitting device can include timing information in the stream. When devices communicate synchronously, they transmit large frames of data accompanied by synchronizing bit patterns. This is much more efficient than the 3-bit overhead required for every byte in asynchronous transmissions.
    - **ROBUST ERROR CHECKING –** Error checking in synchronous communication is more robust than in asynchronous communication. For instance, the transmitting device can apply a cyclic redundancy checking (CRC) polynomial to a frame, and include the resulting value in the frame. CRC error checking will detect an erroneous transmission with a high degree of certainty.
    - Practical for high-speed, high-volume data because of its minimal use of overhead, synchronous communication is much more practical for high-speed, high-volume data transfer than asynchronous.
- **ASYNCHRONOUS –** Asynchronous communications do not use a clocking mechanism. Instead, the sending device surrounds each byte with bits that mark the beginning and end of each byte as well as one bit for error control. A start bit is sent to signal the start of a transmission for each byte, the data byte is then sent, followed by a parity bit (for error control) and a stop bit to signal the end of transmission. Each byte of data, therefore, requires three bits of overhead. The receiving device strips off the overhead bits before sending the data up the TCP/IP stack. Modems and dumb terminals are examples of devices that use asynchronous communication.

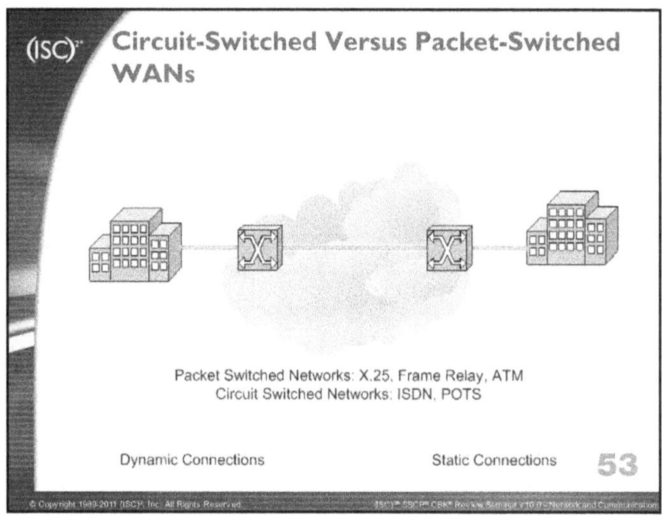


- **CIRCUIT-SWITCHED VERSUS PACKET-SWITCHED WANS –** The first thing to look at is the differing ways in which the WAN can operate. Public networks operate in either a circuit-switched or a packet-switched manner.
  - **CIRCUIT-SWITCHED NETWORKS –** Need dedicated point-to-point connections for the duration of a call. They operate via time-division by allocating time slots to each user's connection. The connection is established between two end points such as between two corporate offices. This connection is either a dynamically-switched virtual circuit (SVC) such as a telephone call, or a statically defined permanent virtual circuit (PVC) created to permanently connect two locations/devices. Examples include the telephone network (plain old telephone system, or POTS), modem access, and ISDN (integrated services digital network).
  - **PACKET-SWITCHED NETWORKS –** Transport data in separate, little blocks called packets with the destination address identified within each packet. When received, packets are reassembled in the proper sequence to make up the message. A packet-switched network operates in a similar fashion to the circuit-switched network in that it establishes either dynamic (SVC) or static (PVC) connections between two end points on the network. The difference is in the bandwidth that is allocated to the connection. The packet-switched connection works on a first-come, first-served basis, allowing users to share all of the available bandwidth. Packet-switched networks include X.25, frame relay, SMDS (switched multi-megabit data service), and ATM (asynchronous transfer mode).
- There is a security risk with dynamically-created connections in either scenario. These connections are created by one end location-dialing the address of the requested destination. The network then places the call across the network – without screening calls for the user.

(ISC)²

WAN Technologies

| Circuit-Switching Networks | Packet-Switching Networks |
|---|---|
| POTS | X.25 |
| 56 Kbps Leased Line | Frame relay |
| T1 | ATM |
| T3 | SMDS |
| ISDN | MPLS (IP) |

54

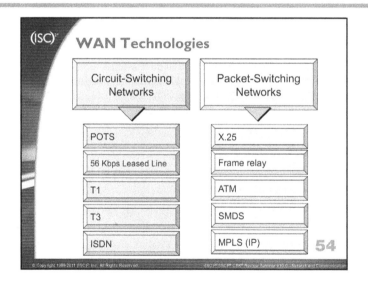

- This Slide provides as overview of the WAN technologies in use today.

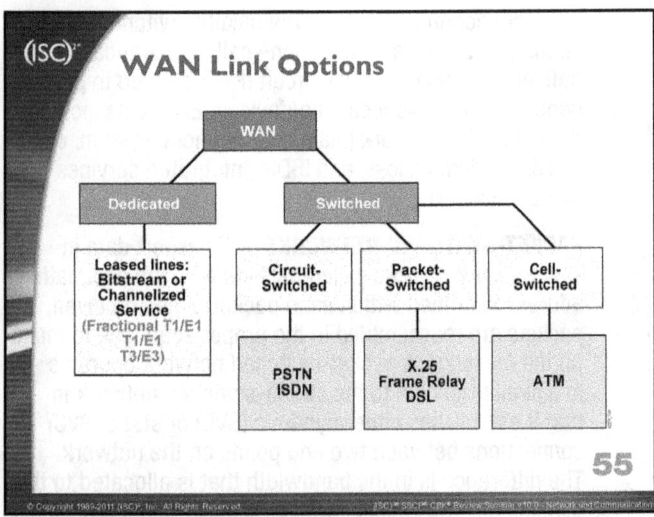


- Please notice in this chart which LANs are switched and which are dedicated.

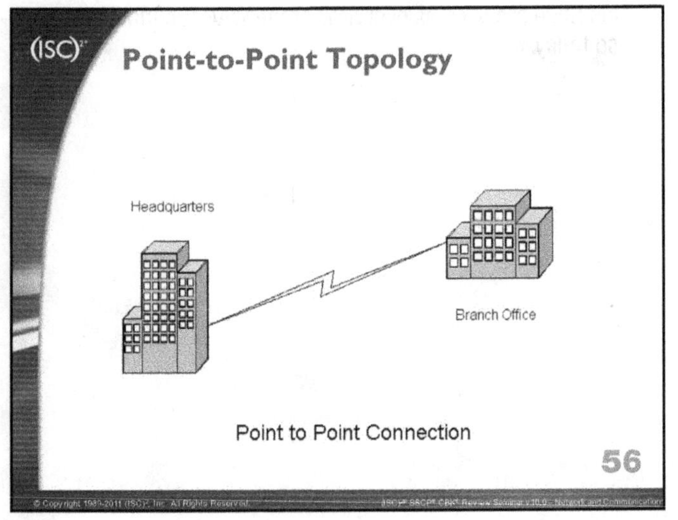


- **POINT-TO-POINT TOPOLOGY –** A point-to-point connection is the most secure of the topologies discussed. Only the sender and the receiver are connected to the line. Although this method is still susceptible to eavesdropping, it is harder to listen in on this connection than with the shared media methods. Point-to-point connections are typically provided via a leased line, ISDN, T1, or microwave.

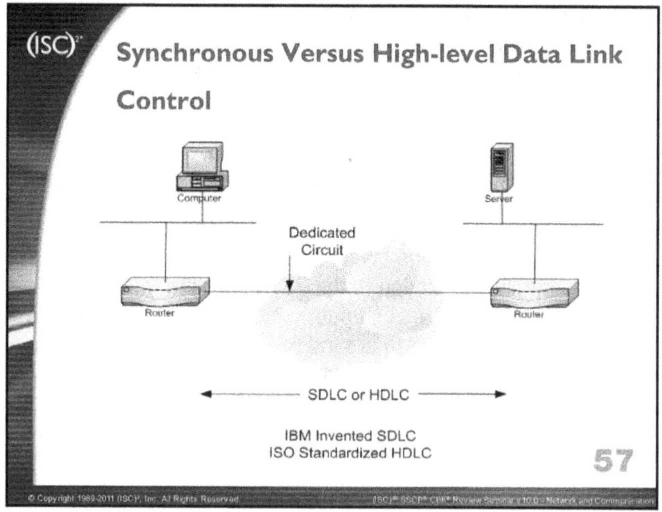


- **SYNCHRONOUS VERSUS HIGH-LEVEL DATA LINK CONTROL –** Synchronous data link control (SDLC) and high-level data link control (HDLC) are two basic, data-link layer protocols that are used to send data across a serial link.
  - HDLC was the International Organization for Standardization's (ISO) revision and standardization of the SDLC protocol created by IBM. SDLC is used primarily in a mainframe environment or in a point-to-point WAN connection with IBM equipment. HDLC is more commonly used than SDLC.
  - There is no authentication or encryption with SDLC or HDLC. In fact, HDLC does not even include information regarding the type of network layer traffic it is carrying. HDLC is a true link-layer protocol.
  - When IBM developed SDLC, transmissions were slow and error prone. SDLC has built-in acknowledgements and retransmissions. The ISO variation, HDLC, came along later, when transmission was more reliable. Most of the changes that were made took advantage of faster and more reliable communications links, retaining SDLC's error-correction capabilities.
- **SECURITY OF SDLC/HDLC –** There is no specific security feature in either protocol since both were primarily designed for use on dedicated leased lines.

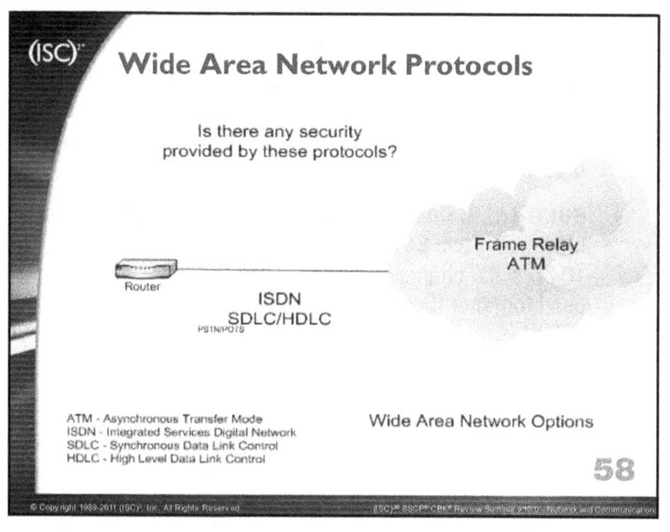

Wide Area Network Protocols
Is there any security provided by these protocols?
Frame Relay
ATM
Router
ISDN
SDLC/HDLC
ATM - Asynchronous Transfer Mode
ISDN - Integrated Services Digital Network
SDLC - Synchronous Data Link Control
HDLC - High Level Data Link Control
Wide Area Network Options
58


- **WIDE AREA NETWORK PROTOCOLS –** Any access to the outside world can open an organization's doors to an intruder – and WAN connections can be that open door. We are going to take a look at a few of the protocols used for these connections to see what level of security each offers.

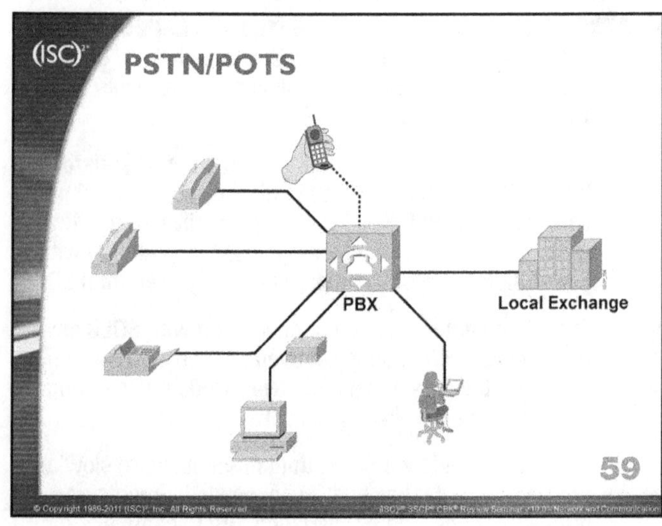


- **PSTN/POTS –** The most common type of circuit-switched WAN communication is packet-switched telephone network (PSTN), also referred to as POTS (plain old telephone system).
- With circuit-switched WAN communication links, a dedicated physical circuit is established, maintained, and terminated through a carrier network for each communication session.
- The physical characteristics of the local loop (the circuit between the telephone switchboard and the end-user instrument) and its connection to the PSTN limit the rate of the signal over the PSTN. The upper limit is around 33 kbps. The rate can be increased to around 56 kbps if the signal is coming directly through a digital connection.
  - **ADVANTAGES:**
    - Simplicity
    - Availability
    - Cost
  - **DISADVANTAGES:**
    - Low data rates
    - Relatively long connection setup time

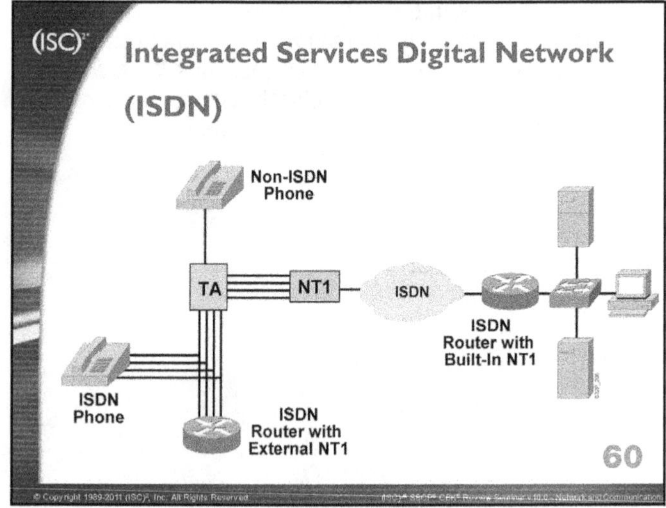


- **ISDN –** Integrated services digital network (ISDN) was designed by the telephone companies to create a method of bringing digital connections all the way to the final end point – the business location. The phone network almost entirely upgraded to digital a long time ago, but the last mile (from the telephone company's equipment building to the office) is still predominantly analog.
- ISDN refers to a set of communication protocols proposed by telephone companies to permit telephone networks to carry data, voice, graphics, music, and video. ISDN was developed to permit faster access over existing telephone systems without the additional call setup time.
- ISDN is a physical layer protocol and, therefore, does not have any built in encryption or authentication. The protocol is similar to SLIP (serial line interface protocol) – one of the oldest protocols used for network communications (and now replaced almost entirely by PPP), in that its job is to send traffic across the interface.
- **BRI – BASIC RATE INTERFACE –** Is the configuration of ISDN using two 64 Kb/s "B'"(bearer) channels and one 16 Kb/s "D" channel (delta). The two "B" channels can be used together (bonded) to provide a transmission rate of 128 Kb/s.
- **PRI – PRIMARY RATE INTERFACE –** Is the rate of transmission described as "DS0." In the U.S. and Japan, this uses 23 B channels of a maximum speed of 64 Kb/s each and one D channel, which has a combined speed of 1.544 Mb/s (T1 line). In Europe, 30 B channels and one D channel are used with a combined speed of 2.048 Mb/s (E1).
- **ADVANTAGES:**
  - Speed.
  - Always available.
- **DISADVANTAGES:**
  - Limited geographic availability.
  - Cost.

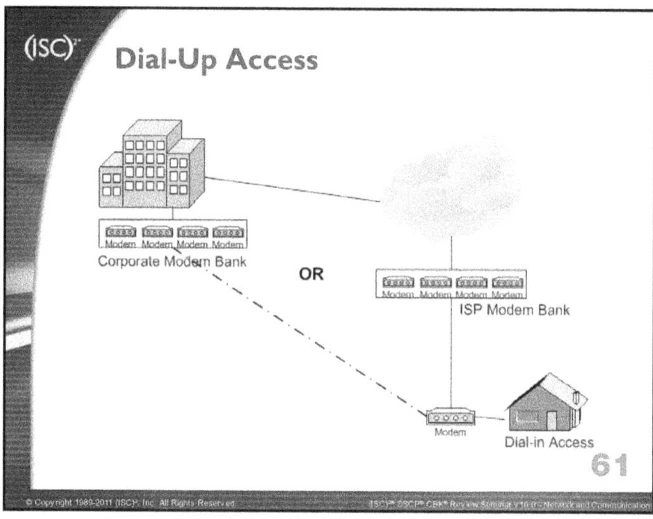


- **DIAL-UP ACCESS –** Dial-up access allows a user with a PC and a modem to access the network over the traditional telephony network. Here, the "modem bank" connection may be maintained either by the Internet service provider (ISP) or by the corporate office itself. This is an economical means of connection from the home, albeit a slow one.
- There is a security issue with this connection type. It leaves both the front door of the home and of the office wide open. Anyone who gains access to the phone number of your computer can call in and connect. Passwords and encryption can help to control these unwanted connections.

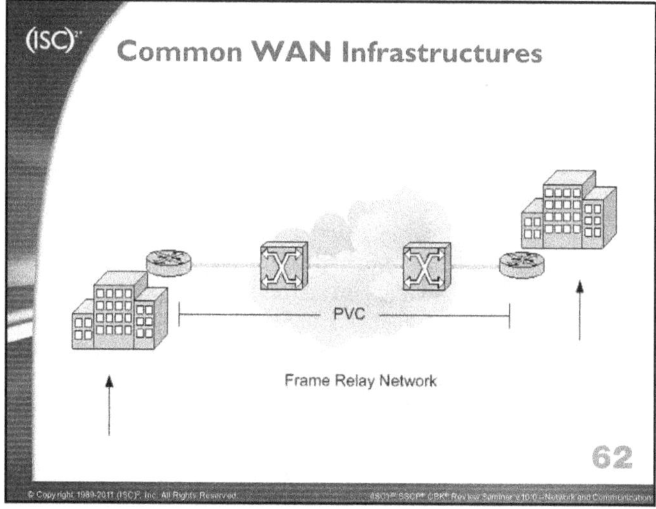


- **COMMON WAN INFRASTRUCTURES –** The most common WAN infrastructure used in enterprise networks at this time is a PVC-based frame relay network. Frame relay currently is the product of choice in the markets and has replaced X.25 in many places.
- Frame relay standards provide for two alternate circuit setup choices: switched and permanent. In a switched virtual circuit (SVC), the provider finds the best path available at that moment and assigns that path for the duration of the connection. (Note that no providers are currently offering this option.) In a permanent virtual circuit (PVC), the provider finds the best path available at that moment and then permanently assigns it to the customer. No additional setup is ever needed. Furthermore, all frames follow the same path every time.
  - The permanent virtual circuit (PVC) used in frame relay adds to the security of the network. A PVC is manually configured by the IT department for the corporation utilizing the frame relay network at the router and by the carrier at the network switches. This manually intensive process makes it harder for an attacker to create an illegal connection to a corporate router.
  - As with all configurations, there is a possible way in for an attacker. If an attacker were to gain access to one of the networks in a corporate office, the frame relay PVC would not protect corporate resources. Remember, an unprotected modem connected to the router in the wiring closet, or an unprotected wireless network, will let an attacker right in. There is also a remote possibility that an attacker could gain access to the carrier's switches and reconfigure the PVC.

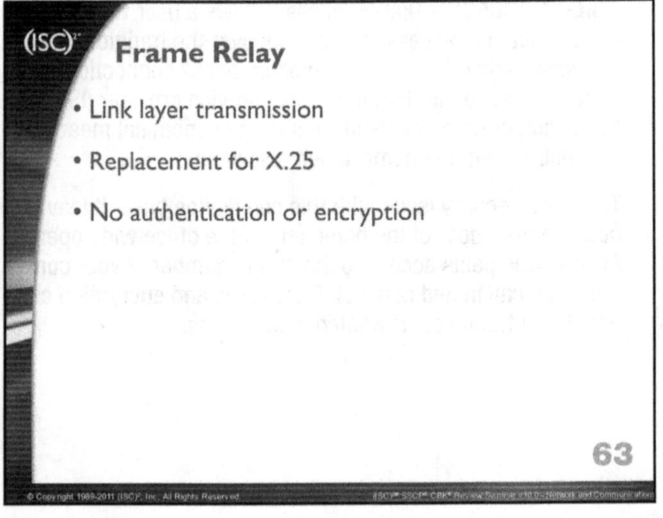


- **FRAME RELAY –** Frame relay is one of the most predominant WAN protocols in use today. Frame relay is a link layer protocol that delivers traffic from one link to the next the entire way across the frame relay network. Frame relay was developed to replace the old X.25 network standard.
  - X.25 has the disadvantage of spending a lot of time checking and rechecking users' traffic for errors because it was designed for low-quality network connections. In the process of building a replacement for X.25, the decision was made to remove all unnecessary functions from frame relay, which essentially left all work possible to the upper layer protocols.
  - Frame relay does not include authentication or encryption. The one advantage of frame relay is its use of permanent virtual circuits (PVC). PVCs are essentially statically built telephone calls across the network. This configuration makes it very difficult for someone to "connect" to you through the frame relay network.

**REFERENCE:**

Frame Relay Principles and Applications, Philip Smith. ISBN: 0-201-62400-1.

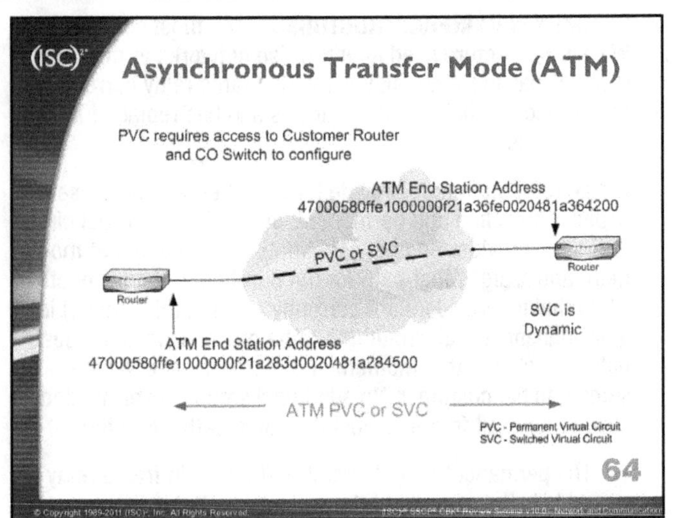


- **ASYNCHRONOUS TRANSFER MODE (ATM) –** Designed to replace frame relay and can also replace the LAN protocols and the telephone network protocols that we use, at least at the data link layer. ATM was scaled down in the design process to make it an even faster data transfer protocol and, therefore, does not include authentication or encryption.
  - At this time, most connections and networks are designed for permanent virtual circuits (PVC), although ATM can and does support switched virtual circuits (SVC). A PVC requires configuration on all routers and switches that the connection traverses. An SVC is created dynamically when an edge device such as a router places a call across the ATM network. In order to place a call, the edge device must know the address of the destination that it is trying to reach. The addressing system that is used in ATM is called the ATM end station address (AESA). The AESA was created based on the network service access point (NSAP) address system from OSI.

**REFERENCE:**

ATM Theory and Applications, Signature Edition, David McDysan and Darren Spohn. ISBN: 0-07-045346-2.

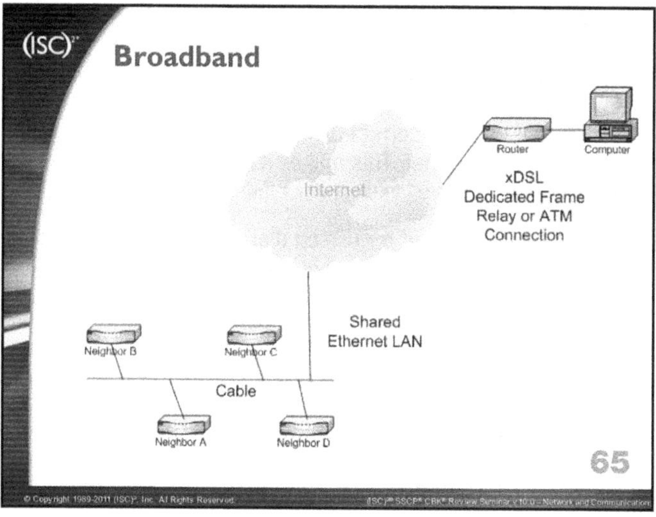


- **BROADBAND –** There are several additional WAN access protocols that are commonly found in the small office/home office (SOHO). These access methods include xDSL* and Cable access.
  - xDSL is a popular method of Internet access from the SOHO. The dedicated, always-on connection provides speeds up to 28 times faster than a 56 kbps modem. The most common xDSL method in use today is ADSL, although there is some SDSL in use as well. Digital subscriber line (DSL) is a physical layer technology that utilizes existing copper lines. DSL is analog. Once the DSL is in place, the user has a dedicated connection to the ISP. The link layer protocol used over DSL is most commonly ATM, although frame relay is also widely used.

* xDSL is used to represent the various forms of DSL. There are several DSL implementations, some of which are proprietary.

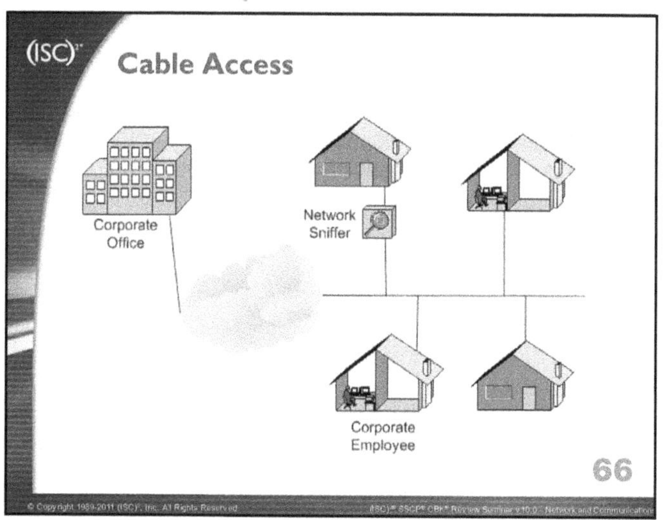


- **CABLE ACCESS –** The speed and low cost of this form of Internet access has made this a very attractive connection method. The downside to this access method is that it shares a medium. The more users connect, the slower your access speed. The other major disadvantage is that it is possible for your neighbors to "listen in" on your network connection. Any computer connected to a cable network should have a personal firewall and VPN. Encryption should be used to access any critical resources, such as the corporate network or banking information.

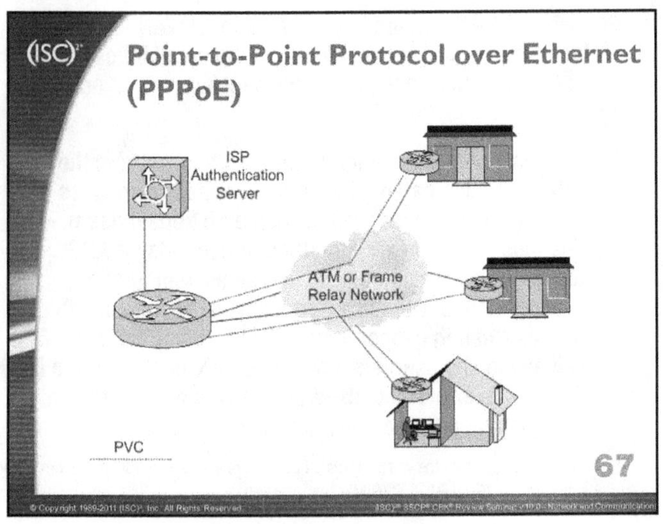


- **POINT-TO-POINT PROTOCOL OVER ETHERNET (PPPOE) –** Adding point-to-point protocol over Ethernet (PPPoE) to a connection such as DSL adds a level of security by insisting on user authentication. The user's PC or router must be configured with the correct username and password to gain access to the Internet. This makes it a little more difficult for someone to "borrow" your access line.
  - PPP was first built for use on dial-up lines. Absent a wiretap, there was no way to eavesdrop, so plain text passwords were the norm. This is known as PAP, or password authentication protocol, within PPP.
  - PPP was later used over shared networks which required some way of obscuring the password. CHAP (challenge-handshake authentication protocol) solved this problem by mixing the password with a one-time random number (the challenge) and then hashing both the password and the random number. Because Ethernet is a shared network, CHAP is the preferred variation.

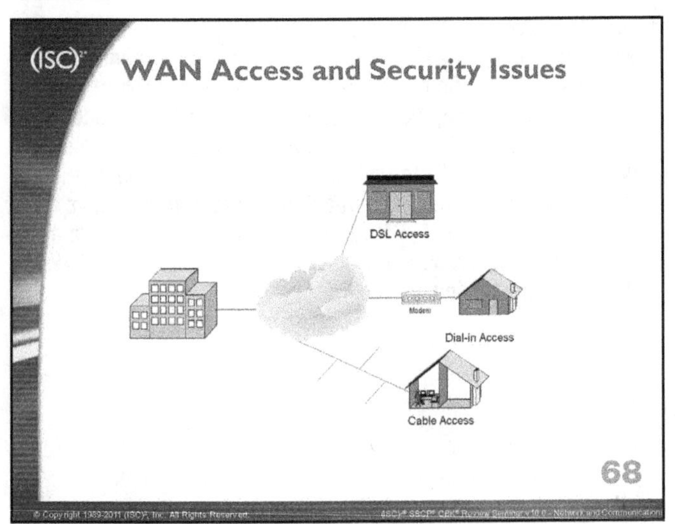


- **WAN ACCESS AND SECURITY ISSUES –** Access to the outside world always has its security risks. The challenge is to add enough security to guard your network assets. In this section, we will look at the physical access methods and security requirements that can be used from the home or the remote office to gain access to the corporate network structure.

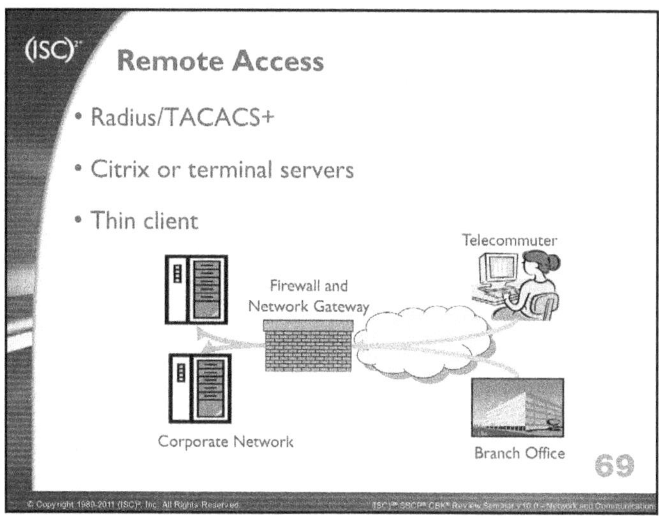


- **REMOTE ACCESS –** Remote access became a common part of many corporate networks with the advent of telecommuting. Many companies today have employees who never or rarely come into the corporate office, but who nonetheless need access to corporate resources. Providing Internet access to more corporate resources increases potential security risks. The challenge is to allow corporate employees to access the systems and files that they need while keeping the attacker out of these potentially open doors.

- **RADIUS/TACACS+ –** RADIUS and TACACS+ are two common methods of authenticating remote users. Both methods of authentication allow centralized management of user logins and passwords. When clients attempt to connect to the network, they are prompted for a username and password combination that the RADIUS or TACACS+ server verifies.

- **CITRIX OR TERMINAL SERVERS –** Microsoft's terminal server and Citrix's server solutions are very common in corporate networks. Both solutions can use thin clients that allow the remote user to log onto a server and operate as if they were sitting in the office, giving them access to the corporate network, printers, and data. The risk is that an attacker who gains access to the terminal or Citrix server may also be able to access other corporate resources.

- **THIN CLIENT –** Thin client describes a system architecture where the computer on the user's desk has very limited functionality. The workstation is usually locked down so that the user cannot run any programs locally, nor use a USB or DVD drive. The concept is similar to the old mainframe implementation of a dumb terminal connected to a central processing unit. This prevents many security problems and virus attacks, and often reduces the cost of equipment deployed on the user's desk.

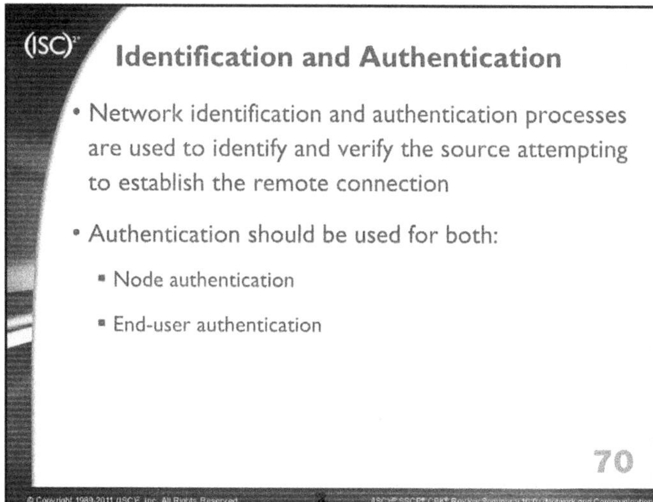

(ISC)²
Identification and Authentication
• Network identification and authentication processes are used to identify and verify the source attempting to establish the remote connection
• Authentication should be used for both:
▪ Node authentication
▪ End-user authentication
70


- **IDENTIFICATION AND AUTHENTICATION –** Authentication protocols that are able to withstand replay attacks (in which the attacker captures and replays a valid authentication handshake) and brute-force attacks are a critical network security technology.
  - **NODE AUTHENTICATION –** It is often desirable to know the source (node) attempting to establish communications. Favorite hacker attacks involve spoofing – pretending to be a trusted node in order to obtain unauthorized access to a target computer. If we can trust the accuracy of a node address, we can use it to identify the location and type of device or data session at both the source and destination addresses and to further authenticate and control other trust relationships. For example, if we wish to allow TCP port 80 (HTTP) sessions between a remote trusted node and a node on our private network, we can create a router access control list entry which enables inbound TCP port 80 traffic from the source IP address (i.e., the trusted remote node) to the destination IP address (i.e., the node on our private network). Also, we can log this activity by date, time, data type (TCP port 80), and source and destination addresses.
    - Note: Network nodes are the point at which terminals and other computers/telecom devices are connected to a data network. Nodes are identified by unique NW addresses. For example, in a TCP/IP NW, nodes are identified by host name (e.g., host1.domainx.com) and IP address (e.g., 204.39.1.123). Whenever data is sent or routed from one address to another, we refer to the address of the originating point as the "source" address and the point to which the data are being sent as the "destination" address.
  - **END-USER AUTHENTICATION –** End-user authentication verifies the identity of the remote user. This is preferable to network node authentication. End-user authentication should be two factor (such as an authentication procedure requiring both a password and token device or smart card).

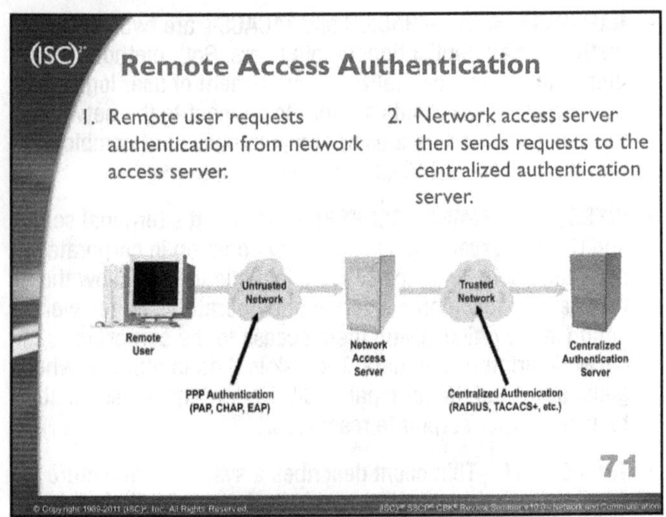


- Replay attacks (wherein an attacker captures credentials off the wire and tries to play them back at a later time) are a major danger to access of networked environments. The two techniques used to catch this are:
  - Timestamps in the credentials (which make them invalid after a period of time), such as with Kerberos.
  - A nonce (a random number which is only used once) in the credentials. Many protocols including parts of Kerberos use this.
- A second major issue with any authentication system is susceptibility to password guessing attacks. As covered in the Access Control domain, all password-based (one factor) authentication systems are vulnerable to a brute force, password-guessing attack. Only two-factor systems can really address this risk. Typically this means using token cards, smart cards with digital certificates, or biometrics in conjunction with a password access control system.

- We will first talk about network authentication protocols used to provide remote access, and then we will talk about the client/server protocols typically used within a LAN. In remote access network authentication, the remote user on the untrusted network connects to the network access server (NAS) using PPP, and one of the PPP authentication methods (PAP, CHAP, or EAP) is used to either authenticate the user or the node. The NAS does not typically have the ability to perform the authentication itself. Instead, the NAS uses a centralized access control protocol to submit a query to a central database, where the user authentication finally takes place. Centralized access control protocols back to the authentication server over the trusted network use server-based access control protocols.
- Definition from SearchSecurity.TechTarget.com of a nonce: In IT, a nonce is a parameter that varies with time. A nonce can be a time stamp, a visit counter on a Web page, or a special marker intended to limit or prevent the unauthorized replay or reproduction of a file. Because a nonce changes with time, it is easy to tell whether or not an attempt at replay or reproduction of a file is legitimate; the current time can be compared with the nonce. If it does not exceed it or if no nonce exists, then the attempt will be authorized. If not, it will not be authorized. Because hashing will always produce the same output if given the same input, the server supplies the nonce as a random value so as to "perturb" the input values to the hash. The same userID/password can be hashed again and again, each time with a different nonce, thus precluding replay attacks.
- In general usage (non-computerese), a nonce is a pronounceable string of characters invented and used only in a given context. The origin of the term goes back to the Middle Ages with "the anes," an expression meaning "for the immediate occasion." This evolved to "the nonce," perhaps based on widespread mispronunciation, on the other hand, Ross Anderson writes in "Security Engineering" that nonce stands for "number used once".

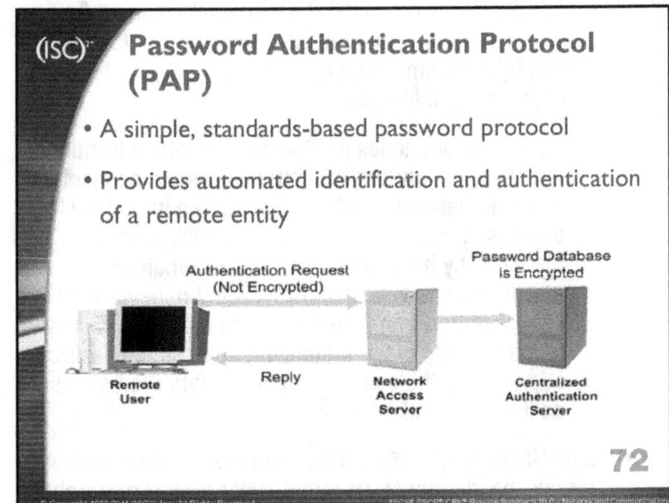

(ISC)²
Password Authentication Protocol (PAP)
• A simple, standards-based password protocol
• Provides automated identification and authentication of a remote entity
Authentication Request (Not Encrypted)
Password Database is Encrypted
Reply
Remote User
Network Access Server
Centralized Authentication Server
72


- **PAP (PASSWORD AUTHENTICATION PROTOCOL) –** PAP is a simple, standards-based password protocol. A user's ID and password are transmitted at the beginning of an incoming call and validated by the receiving equipment using a central PAP database. The PAP password database is encrypted, but PAP does not encrypt the user ID or password on the transmission line.
  - Advantages: A standards-based solution that provides interoperability in a multi-vendor network is inexpensive to install and operate, and has an encrypted database to prevent password snooping.
  - Disadvantages: The password is transmitted in the clear, making it easy to snoop by tapping the line.
- PAP works as in the diagram above. The authentication request includes the user ID and (static) password in clear text and the reply is either an ACK or a NAK. Note that there is no replay protection in PAP.
- PAP is not as secure as CHAP, since it works only to establish the initial link. PAP is also more vulnerable to attack, because it sends authentication packets throughout the network. Nevertheless, PAP is commonly used to log into remote hosts, such as Internet service providers.

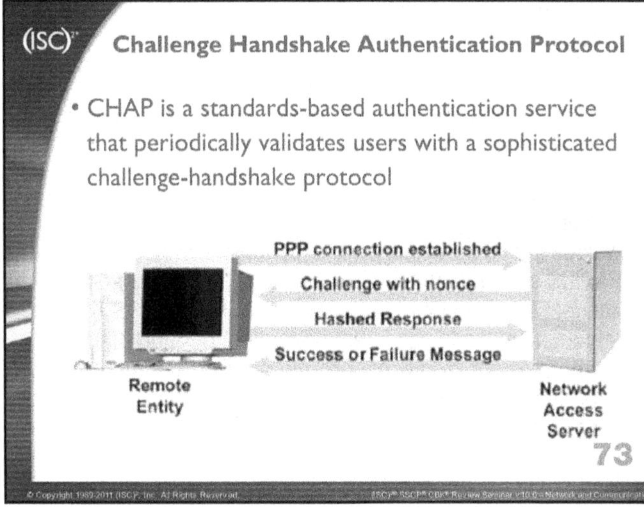

Challenge Handshake Authentication Protocol
• CHAP is a standards-based authentication service that periodically validates users with a sophisticated challenge-handshake protocol
PPP connection established
Challenge with nonce
Hashed Response
Success or Failure Message
Remote Entity
Network Access Server
73


- **CHAP –** Uses "non-replayable" (because of the nonce), challenge/response dialog to verify the identification of the remote entity. Authentication takes place at the initial connection and can be repeated at any time during the session. The standard password database is unencrypted on end nodes.
- **MSCHAP –** Stores one-way encrypted passwords. MSCHAP (Microsoft CHAP) is a variation of the original CHAP standard developed by Microsoft. Unlike the standard CHAP specification, in MSCHAP, the server stores a one-way encrypted hash of the user's password rather than the password itself. This is much better from a security standpoint, but it is not a standard like CHAP.
- Process:
  1. Client connects to the NAS and sets up a PPP link.
  2. The server sends a challenge, including a nonce.
  3. The client sends a response to the challenge, including the user ID, and a one way MD5 hash of the password and the nonce.
  4. The server computes the same hash and compares the value to what the client sent.

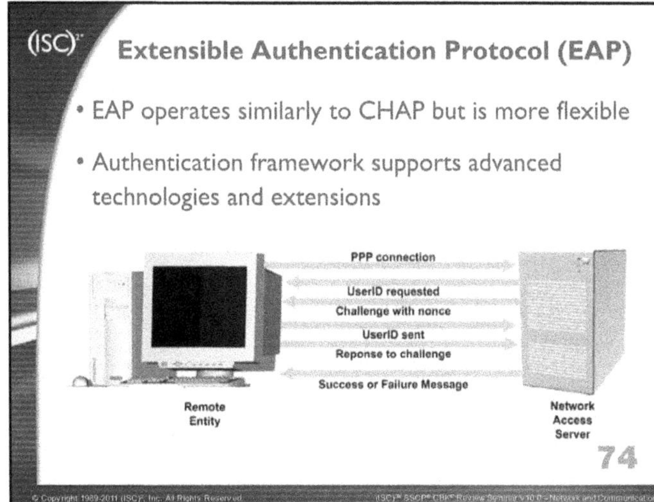

Extensible Authentication Protocol (EAP)
• EAP operates similarly to CHAP but is more flexible
• Authentication framework supports advanced technologies and extensions
PPP connection
UserID requested
Challenge with nonce
UserID sent
Reponse to challenge
Success or Failure Message
Remote Entity
Network Access Server
74


- **EXTENSIBLE AUTHENTICATION PROTOCOL (EAP) –** First work on EAP began in 1998. EAP is in wide use today. Unlike PAP and CHAP, EAP provides the facilities for a general-purpose authentication protocol and can be extended as new authentication methods become available. For example, EAP is the first PPP authentication protocol to provide a standard way to support digital certificates.

- Here are the steps:
  1. Client connects to the NAS and sets up a PPP link.
  2. The server asks for the userID.
  3. The server sends one or more challenges, including a nonce.
  4. The client sends the userID in reply to the request in step 2.
  5. The client sends a response to each of the challenges, using whatever authentication type the NAS requested. If using simple passwords, the challenge is for an MD5 hash of the password and the nonce, much as with CHAP.
  6. The server checks the credentials and either allows the connection, or indicates failure.
- The nonce provides replay protection.
- The use of hash functions for one-time passwords was proposed by Leslie Lamport in 1981. Bellcore devised S/KEY™, based on MD4, and published it in RFC 1760. The latest RFC 2289 is a proposed standard and specifies the use of MD4, MD5, and/or SHA-1.
- EAP is used in new 802.11 wireless LAN security protocols (WPA-WiFi protected access and RSN-robust secure network) to authenticate the end user or device.

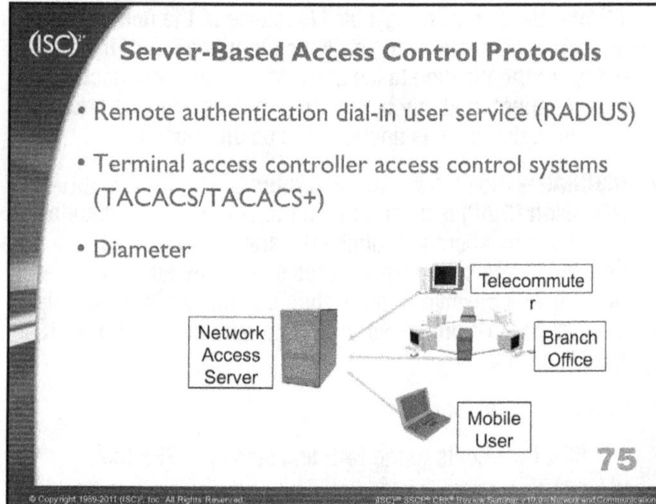
(ISC)²
Server-Based Access Control Protocols
• Remote authentication dial-in user service (RADIUS)
• Terminal access controller access control systems (TACACS/TACACS+)
• Diameter
Telecommute r
Network Access Server
Branch Office
Mobile User
75

- **REMOTE AUTHENTICATION DIAL-IN USER SERVICE (RADIUS)** – RADIUS clients are built into network devices such as routers, firewalls, and remote access servers. When a user dials into the network, the RADIUS client asks its server to begin the authentication process. The server then forwards a challenge to the user's screen, asking for the passcode from the authentication token. When the user is identified, the RADIUS server tells the client device to let the user in. RADIUS is an IETF (Internet Engineering Task Force) standard client-server protocol that uses UDP for transport. RADIUS only encrypts user passwords on the wire.
- **TERMINAL ACCESS CONTROLLER ACCESS CONTROL SYSTEMS (TACACS/TACACS+)** – With TACACS, a local user database is created on the router/device. TACACS+ allows you to create a local database or utilize a central user database established and maintained on a network authentication server. All TACACS+ communications are encrypted. Remember, however, that these protocols are only used between the NAS and the central authentication server. Communication between the end node and the NAS may not be encrypted!
    - Cisco Systems developed TACACS and TACACS+ software and put it in the public domain. Due to Cisco's success in the network market, TACACS+ is a de facto standard.
- **DIAMETER** – Although Diameter uses RADIUS as a base, the two are not strictly compatible with one another. Diameter was designed particularly for situations in which a suitable RADIUS server would not likely be available (e.g., if one has to connect from another company's network). Note as well that although any node can initiate a request through Diameter, Diameter is not strictly peer-to-peer. A typical Diameter implementation involves three different types of entities: clients, agents, and servers. The Diameter client making authentication requests are typically network access servers (NAS) or foreign agents (mobile IP) at the edge of a network. Diameter servers handle authentication, authorization, and accounting requests for a particular realm. Diameter agents do not answer requests, but relay, proxy, redirect, or translate requests and responses to and from clients and servers, particularly between realms. Any node can conceivably play any or all of these roles depending on the application and the implementation.
    - Note as well that Diameter requires both the base protocol and any given application extension. The base protocol cannot run without at least one application extension. The Diameter base protocol assumes that messages are being secured by IPSec or TLS, and offers no native encryption of Diameter traffic. Diameter clients must support IPSec at a minimum, while Diameter servers must support both IPSec and TLS. While it is possible to run Diameter in an insecure manner, it is highly discouraged.

---

**REFERENCE:**

See http://www.ietf.org/Internet-drafts/draft-ietf-aaa-diameter-cms-sec-03.txt for more details.

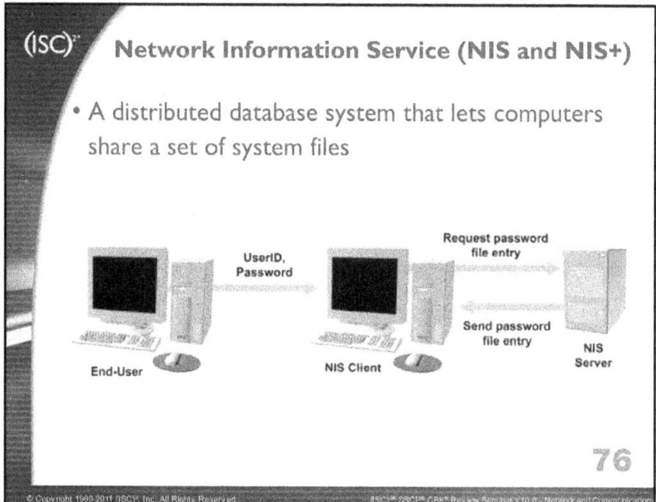
(ISC)²
Network Information Service (NIS and NIS+)
• A distributed database system that lets computers share a set of system files
UserID, Password
Request password file entry
Send password file entry
End-User
NIS Client
NIS Server
76

- **NETWORK INFORMATION SERVICE (NIS AND NIS +) –** Developed by Sun Microsystems to centralize administration of UNIX systems. It is now a de facto industry standard and all major UNIX-like systems support NIS. Its central server stores a shared database with one-way encrypted passwords. Use of these shared files allows users to access any of a set of computers, using credentials stored in a centrally administered database.
- This RPC-based client server system permits a group of machines within an NIS domain to share a common set of configuration files. This allows a system administrator to configure NIS client systems with minimal configuration data and add, remove, or modify configuration data from a single location.
- **NIS** allows users to log on from any machine in the network, as long the machine being used is configured to give that users' password which matches the entry in the NIS password database.
- **NIS+** is a hierarchical and secure NIS implementation.
  - Supports MD5 encryption of passwords.
  - Supports object access restrictions (e.g., NIS allows any user to retrieve the NIS password map, whereas NIS+ supports features restricting access to this type of information).
  - Uses Secure RPC for communication.
  - Supports authentication from the NIS+ client to server.
- **STEPS TO AUTHENTICATE A USER:**
  1. The user presents a user ID and password to the NIS client (the resource server to which the user wants access, such as a file server, database server, etc.).
  2. The NIS client asks for the line out of the password file for the user named "user ID."
  3. The NIS server sends the matching line.
  4. The NIS client computes the password hash based on the password the user gave, and compares it with the value provided by the NIS server. If they match, the user is allowed access.

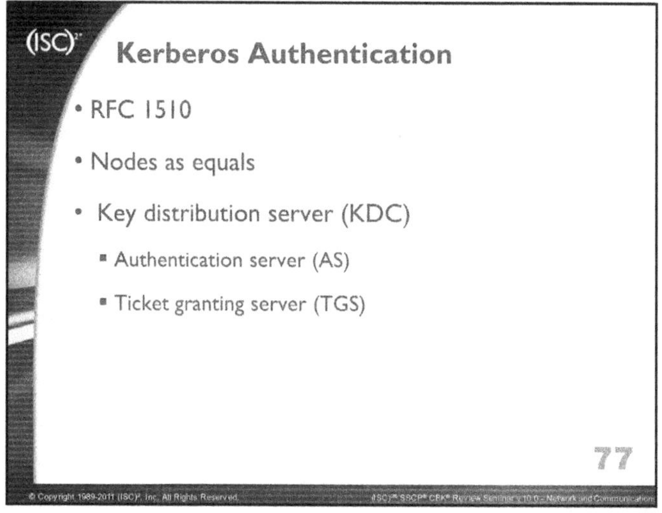
(ISC)²
Kerberos Authentication
• RFC 1510
• Nodes as equals
• Key distribution server (KDC)
▪ Authentication server (AS)
▪ Ticket granting server (TGS)
77

- From the original MIT website: "Kerberos is a network authentication protocol. It is designed to provide strong authentication for client/server applications by using secret-key cryptography. A free implementation of this protocol is available from the Massachusetts Institute of Technology. Kerberos is available in many commercial products as well."
- **RFC 1510 –** Details the current version of Kerberos (v5). Kerberos uses the Needham-Schroeder protocol.
- **NODES AS EQUALS –** Both clients and servers nodes are treated as untrusted by each other. Nodes only trust the 3rd party authenticator, the authentication server. Lack of trust increases security of authentication because it reduces the possibility of impersonation.
- **KEY DISTRIBUTION SERVER (KDS) –** Has two separate logical roles in authentication:
  - Authentication server holds symmetric encryption keys that are shared with only one principle and not between principles.
  - Ticket granting server (TGS) issues symmetric encryption keys for sessions between principles.

**REFERENCES:**

http://web.mit.edu/kerberos/
http://tools.ietf.org/html/rfc1510

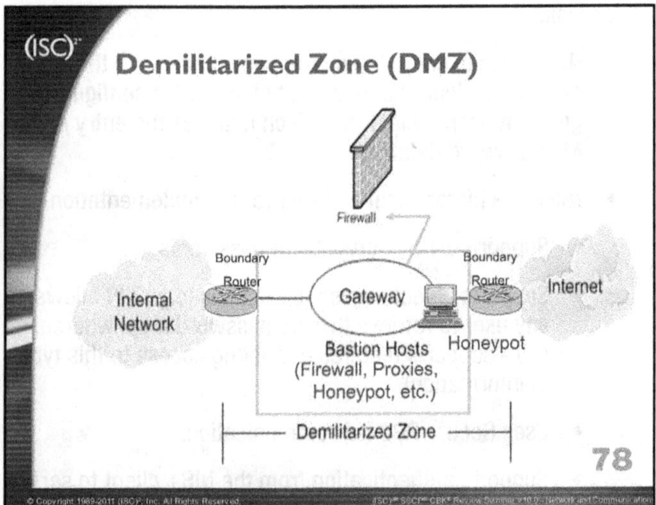


- **DEMILITARIZED ZONE (DMZ) –** The DMZ is a special-purpose isolation network providing physical separation between the internal network and any type of external network, including most wide area network services. The DMZ is sometimes referred to as a screened subnet, as it often contains routers at each end and protects the internal network from direct attack from the Internet.
- The DMZ often contains a number of hosts that provide services for outsiders, most commonly a Web server. It should contain a bastion firewall to impose security rules on all transmissions into and out of the internal network. Many organizations design more complex DMZ configurations to further isolate services such as mail servers, proxies, remote access servers, etc. The objective is to protect any devices on the DMZ from attack and compromise because any server on the DMZ that is compromised may be used to access internal resources.
- A DMZ might also include a server configured to appear normal but which is specifically designed to distract an attacker probing this network area. Such a device, called a honeypot, might provide network security personnel with critical information about a potential or ongoing attack, so that mitigation strategies can be implemented.
- **A CLARIFICATION OF TERMS:**
  - **FILTERS –** Block forwarding of certain classes of traffic.
  - **GATEWAY –** A machine or a set of machines that provide relay services to compensate for the effects of the filter.
  - **DMZ –** (Demilitarized zone). The isolated portion of the network area accessible to outside sources through the gateway. The DMZ is less trusted than the internal network, but more trusted than the Internet. Rules (ACLs) on the gateway will allow Internet traffic to flow into the DMZ, but not into the internal network.
    - Note: this diagram does not show an active DMZ. If it did, there would be a subnet extending off the bottom of the red box.
  - **BASTION HOST –** An exposed gateway machine that is hardened.
  - **PROXY SERVERS –** Used as intermediary devices between a client and a server providing the client transparent access to the resources on the server. Proxies are often a function of a gateway.

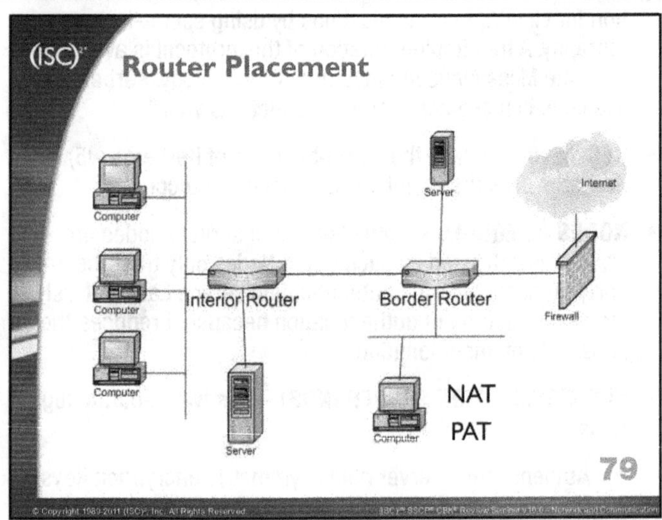


- **ROUTER PLACEMENT –** There are two basic places to put a router: internally, or on the border. The placement of a router within the network architecture is critical.
  - **A BORDER ROUTER** is subject to direct attack from an outside source. When planning the configuration of the router, determine whether the router is the lone defense, or whether it acts in conjunction with other devices such as a firewall. The lone-defense router can protect internal resources but is subject to attack itself.
  - **THE INTERNAL ROUTER** may be configured to allow all traffic to pass through, or it may be configured to protect some internal resources.
  - Other technologies that can be employed by the routers for security purposes are:
    - Network address translation (NAT)
    - Port address translation (PAT)
    - Packet filtering and access control lists
- Network address translation (NAT) was initially implemented to compensate for an inadequate number of available IP addresses. Today, it helps with security by hiding the true IP address of a device. Once communication has been established with a device beyond the router, the router will add it to the translation table. This translation table enables traffic to proceed out of the router to the destination, and it also allows traffic to return. A hacker could exploit the return traffic. Port address translation (PAT) increases the security by also monitoring the port numbers used.

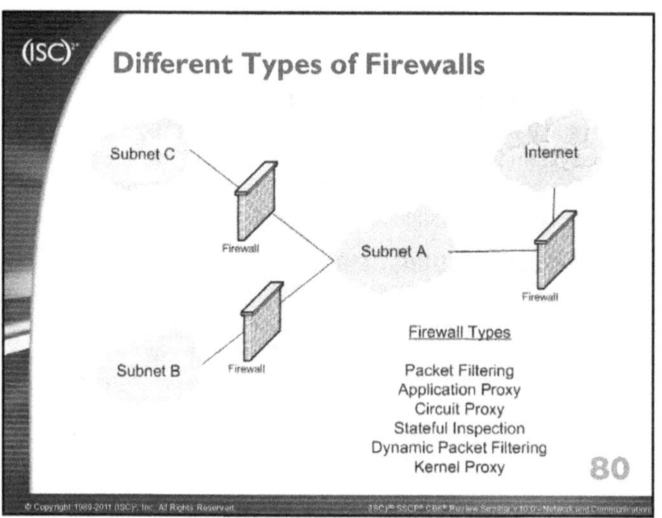


- **DIFFERENT TYPES OF FIREWALLS –** There are six basic types of firewalls:

  1. **PACKET FILTERING –** Packet filtering firewalls are very similar to routers. They compare received packets against a set of rules ("static packet filter") that defines which packets are permitted to pass through the firewall.
  2. **APPLICATION PROXY –** Application proxy firewalls read the entire packet up through the application layer before making a decision as to whether the data is allowed to pass. Here, the client is really communicating with an application proxy that, in turn, communicates with the destination service rather than the allowing the client to communicate with the destination service itself. This allows the application proxy to examine packets in order to protect against known application and data stream attacks. As a result, these firewalls are slower but more effective than packet filtering firewalls.
  3. **CIRCUIT PROXY –** Circuit level firewalls relay TCP connections by reading and tracking header information such as source and destination addresses and ports. The caller connects to a TCP port on the firewall, which connects to some destination on the other side. During the call, the firewall's relay program copies the bytes back and forth, in essence acting as a wire.
  4. **STATEFUL INSPECTION –** Stateful inspection firewalls monitor the state of all connections that pass through it. For example, if a user sends a request to a website, the firewall will allow the return information to pass because it knows that the user's connection is waiting for a response.
  5. **DYNAMIC PACKET FILTERING –** Dynamic packet filtering firewalls function by queuing all of the connectionless packets that have crossed outbound through the firewall and allow responses to pass back through based on the original requests having crossed outbound.
  6. **KERNEL PROXY –** Kernel proxy firewalls are specialized, though nonstandard, firewall services designed to function in the kernel mode of the operating system. This allows for a highly customizable firewall and provides more granular control over the application privileges.

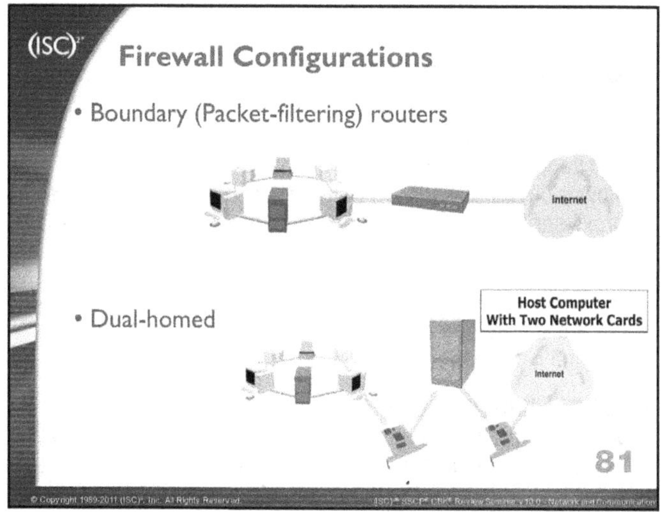


- **FIREWALL CONFIGURATIONS –** There are four types of firewall configuration architectures: boundary or packet-filtering routers, dual-homed host firewalls, screened-host firewalls, and screened-subnet firewalls.
  - **BOUNDARY (PACKET-FILTERING) ROUTERS –** Packet-filtering routers are designed to sit between an internal trusted network and an external non-trusted network. Security is maintained through an ACL which may be time consuming to manage. These firewalls also lack authentication and usually have weak auditing capabilities.
  - **DUAL-HOMED HOST FIREWALL –** Dual-homed host firewall systems have the bastion host connected to one interface on the internal network and one interface on the external network. IP forwarding is disabled in order to prevent hosts on separate networks from communicating with each other because if the bastion host is compromised, the attacker will have access to the internal network.

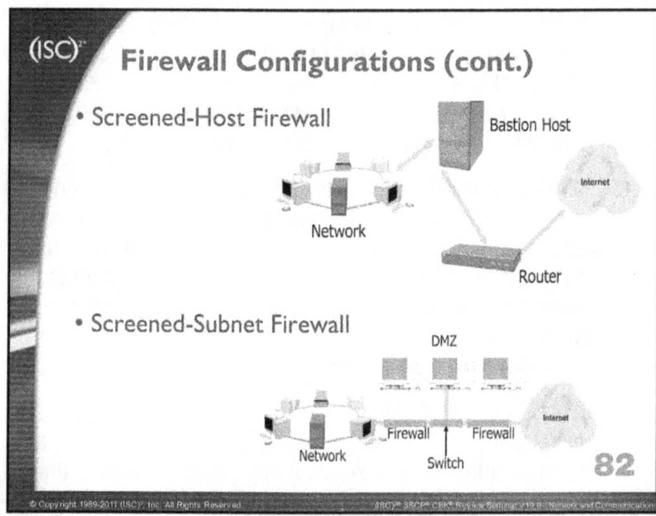


- **FIREWALL CONFIGURATIONS (CONT.) –**
  - **SCREENED-HOST FIREWALL –** Screened-host firewalls are typically a combination of a packet-filtering firewall and a bastion host. A bastion host is an exposed gateway system that has been hardened against attacks. These firewalls are best suited to provide low-risk, limited access for incoming Internet connections.
  - **SCREENED-SUBNET FIREWALL –** Screened-subnet firewalls take the bastion host from the screened-host firewall configuration and place it on a demilitarized zone (DMZ). This requires an attacker to pass through two filtering routers to successfully access the corporate network.

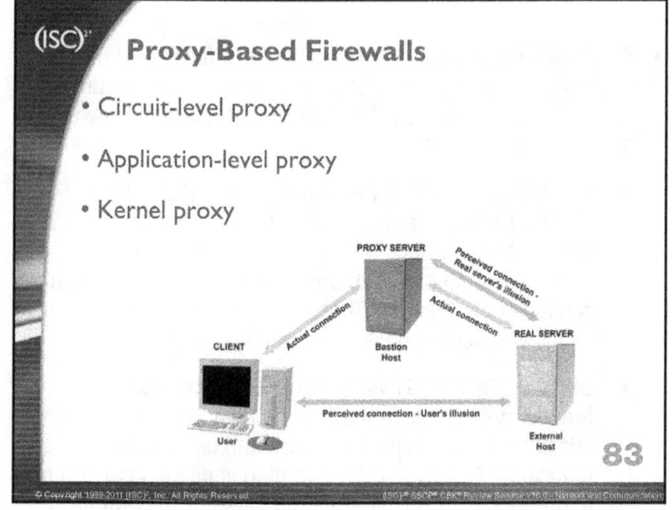


- **PROXY-BASED FIREWALLS –** A proxy firewall communicates with untrusted hosts on behalf of the hosts that it protects. It forwards traffic from trusted hosts, creating the illusion that the traffic originated from the proxy firewall, thus hiding the trusted hosts from potential attackers. Proxy servers are often placed at Internet gateways to hide the internal network behind a single IP address and to prevent direct communication between internal and external hosts. Intruders are, therefore, unable to map the IP addresses and size of your internal network as easily, since the proxy hides all internal hosts behind it. Proxy-based firewalls also allow client requests to be directed to a server running a program that deals with external servers on behalf of internal clients.

- **CIRCUIT-LEVEL PROXY –** A circuit-level proxy creates a conduit through which a trusted host can communicate with an un-trusted one.
- **APPLICATION-LEVEL PROXY –** An application-level proxy relays the traffic from a trusted host running a specific application to an untrusted server. Each application-level proxy can support only one protocol. As a result, these firewalls are slower but more effective than packet-filtering firewalls. Web proxy servers are a very popular example of application-level proxies.
  - The most significant advantage of application-level proxies is that they analyze the traffic for malicious packets and can restrict some of the application's functionality.
- **KERNEL PROXY –** Kernel-proxy firewalls are specialized firewalls designed to function in the kernel mode of the operating system. This technology allows the designing of a firewall to meet individual specifications for speed, reliability, and security. Because an administrator must explicitly permit each user to have access to the firewall's services, a user is unable to start new network services or use new network applications to slip through the firewall server.
- Because firewalls utilizing proxy services make a distinct physical separation between your local network and the Internet, they are a good choice for high security requirements. However, because an actual program must analyze the packets and make decisions about access control, these types of firewalls tend to reduce network performance.

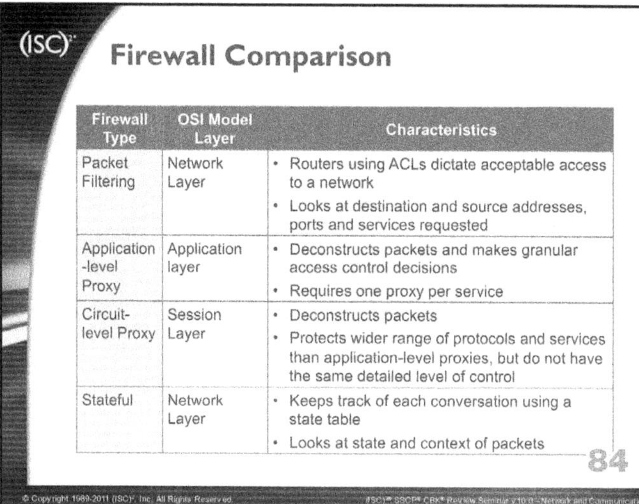

Firewall Comparison

| Firewall Type | OSI Model Layer | Characteristics |
|---|---|---|
| Packet Filtering | Network Layer | • Routers using ACLs dictate acceptable access to a network<br>• Looks at destination and source addresses, ports and services requested |
| Application-level Proxy | Application layer | • Deconstructs packets and makes granular access control decisions<br>• Requires one proxy per service |
| Circuit-level Proxy | Session Layer | • Deconstructs packets<br>• Protects wider range of protocols and services than application-level proxies, but do not have the same detailed level of control |
| Stateful | Network Layer | • Keeps track of each conversation using a state table<br>• Looks at state and context of packets |

84

- Summary Slide of the technologies just discussed.
- Circuit-level proxies are typically implemented as a shim between the application and the transport layer (TCP). In the OSI model, the circuit-level proxy fits the definition of a session layer. But, of course, in TCP/IP there is no session layer, strictly speaking. Remember that models are theoretical and some implementations won't fit perfectly.
- **FIREWALL RULE SETS –** Depending upon the type of firewall chosen, the rule sets may be simple lists or complex logic models which implement the firewall policies. This policy should reflect the intent of network security management and support business requirements. A good practice is to use a restrictive policy which by default prohibits any traffic not explicitly identified as acceptable. This is sometimes referred to as "white listing" where anything NOT listed as acceptable is automatically considered unacceptable.

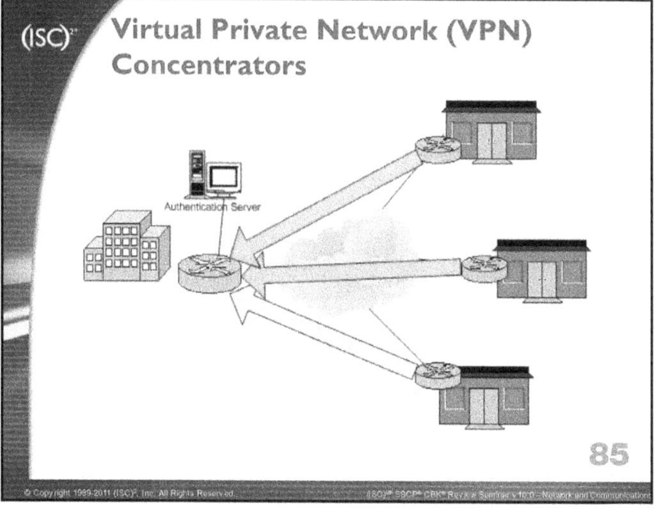


- **VPN CONCENTRATORS –** Virtual private networks (VPNs) are a good way to increase the security of data transmitted across the public data network. Using a VPN for remote network access provides a cost-effective security solution, especially when you compare the cost of using a VPN to communicate securely over a public network to the cost of having a dedicated connection between the same two sites. You can also compare the costs for a user to connect to corporate resources over a locally available Internet connection against dialing into the corporate modem bank from a remote location.
- The security added by the VPN can vary depending on the configuration of the tunnel and the encryption level that is used. This allows a corporation to balance the need of securing data with the cost of slower transmission rates due to encryption.
- One major disadvantage with a VPN is that it requires the use of your gateway equipment processing cycles to handle the encryption algorithms. This increased utilization can be offloaded to another device through the use of a VPN concentrator rather than terminating the VPN at your router or firewall.
- One other security consideration is the potential lack of security on an end user's PC. Once the end user is connected to the corporate network, his or her PC may be an open portal to the corporate resources for an attacker.

(ISC)²

## Network Access (NAP and NAC)

- Network connection enforcement
  - Isolates and verifies compliance before admitting device to connect
- Should be used with additional authentication (802.1x and EAP)
- Requires a compliance audit server and quarantine (remediation) area

86



(ISC)² SSCP® CBK® Review Seminar v10.0 – Network and Communications

- **Microsoft Windows Vista and Windows Server 2008 include network access protection (NAP). This feature allows you to protect your network from unhealthy computers by enforcing compliance with network health policies. This is similar to Cisco's network admission control (NAC), which isolates and denies network access to noncompliant devices. While NAP and NAC play a different role from 802.1X in controlling network connections, they will interoperate.**

(ISC)²

## Domain Agenda

- Network components and topologies
- Wide area and remote access networks
- **Standard network protocols**
- Network security protocols
- Wireless network configuration and protection
- Managing service reliability and quality

87



(ISC)² SSCP® CBK® Review Seminar v10.0 – Network and Communications

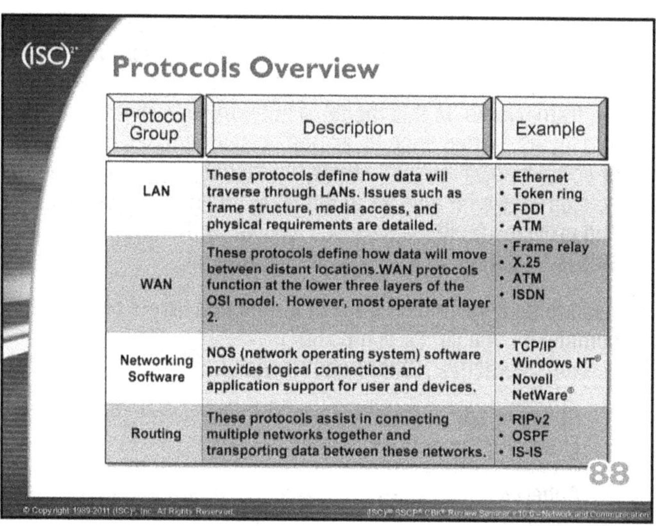

## Protocols Overview

| Protocol Group | Description | Example |
|---|---|---|
| LAN | These protocols define how data will traverse through LANs. Issues such as frame structure, media access, and physical requirements are detailed. | • Ethernet • Token ring • FDDI • ATM |
| WAN | These protocols define how data will move between distant locations.WAN protocols function at the lower three layers of the OSI model. However, most operate at layer 2. | • Frame relay • X.25 • ATM • ISDN |
| Networking Software | NOS (network operating system) software provides logical connections and application support for user and devices. | • TCP/IP • Windows NT® • Novell NetWare® |
| Routing | These protocols assist in connecting multiple networks together and transporting data between these networks. | • RIPv2 • OSPF • IS-IS |

88

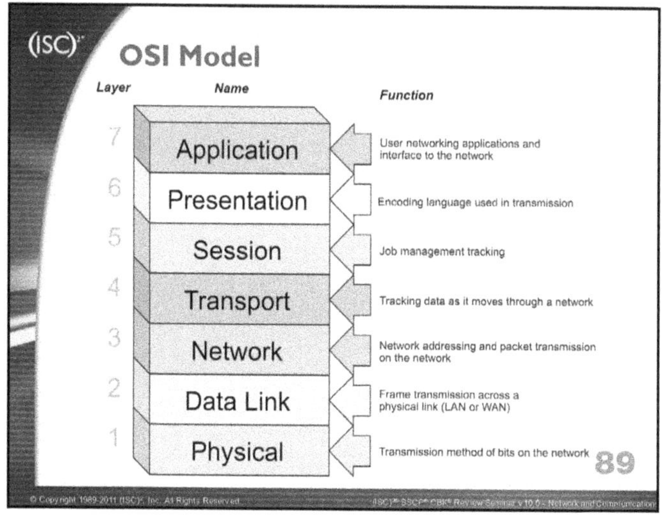
(ISC)²
OSI Model
Layer
Name
Function
7 Application
User networking applications and interface to the network
6 Presentation
Encoding language used in transmission
5 Session
Job management tracking
4 Transport
Tracking data as it moves through a network
3 Network
Network addressing and packet transmission on the network
2 Data Link
Frame transmission across a physical link (LAN or WAN)
1 Physical
Transmission method of bits on the network
89

- **OSI MODEL –** Work on the layered model of network architecture, which was to later to become the OSI model, started in 1977. It became an international standard as ISO 7498. Parts of the OSI have influenced Internet protocol (IP) development, but none more than the concrete operational system model itself, documented in ISO 7498. In this model, a networking system is divided into seven layers. Within each layer, one or more entities implements its functionality. Each entity interacts directly only with the layer immediately beneath it, and provides facilities for use by the layer above it.
- **REMEMBERING THE OSI LAYERS –** Various mnemonics have been created over the years to help remember the order, such as:
  - **A**ll **P**eople **S**eem **T**o **N**eed **D**ata **P**rocessing
  - **P**lease **D**o **N**ot **T**ake **S**ales-**P**eople's **A**dvice
  - **P**lease **D**o **N**ot **T**hrow **S**ausage **P**izza **A**way

**REFERENCES:**

http://standards.iso.org/ittf/PubliclyAvailableStandards/index.html

http://www.itu.int/rec/T-REC-X/en

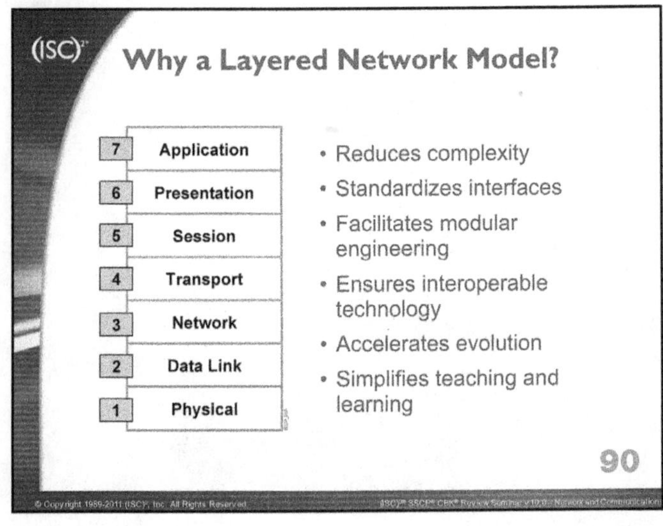


- When OSI was first published (as ISO 7498) in 1978, the concept of a layered model was suggested by Honeywell, based on experiences with ARPANET and several other existing frameworks. In this model, a networking system is divided into layers. Within each layer, one or more entities (processes or components) implements its functionality. Each entity interacts directly with entities in the layer immediately beneath it, and provides facilities/services for use by the layer above it. This is by definition a "client-server" model.
- Describing a system as a set of interacting layers reduces the complexity of a single composite process by dividing it into discrete elements. Other benefits include:
  - Ability to add or modify parts of the system without reengineering the entire system.
  - Adherence to a pre-established set of specifications for how each layer connects (interface standards).
  - Simplification of learning and troubleshooting (each layer can become a point of focus, reference or examination).
  - Provided there is consensus and adherence to specifications, there is better interoperability.

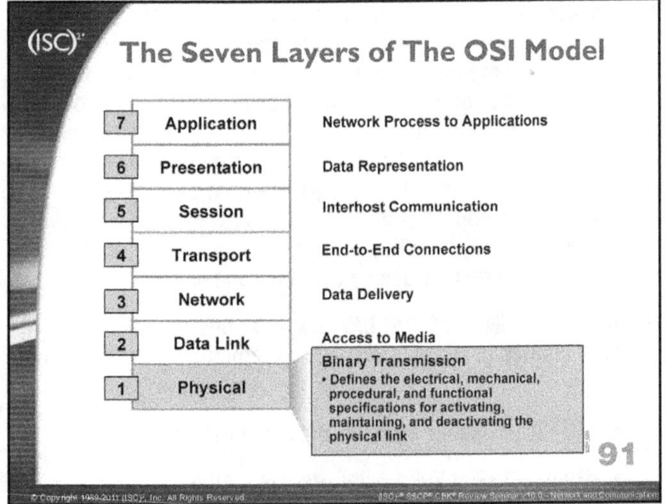

## The Seven Layers of The OSI Model (cont.)

| | Layer | |
|---|---|---|
| 7 | Application | Network Process to Applications |
| 6 | Presentation | Data Representation |
| 5 | Session | Interhost Communication |
| 4 | Transport | End-to-End Connections |
| 3 | Network | Data Delivery |
| 2 | Data Link | Access to Media |
| 1 | Physical | |

**Access to Media**

- Defines how data is formatted for transmission and how access to the network is controlled
- Provides error detection

92

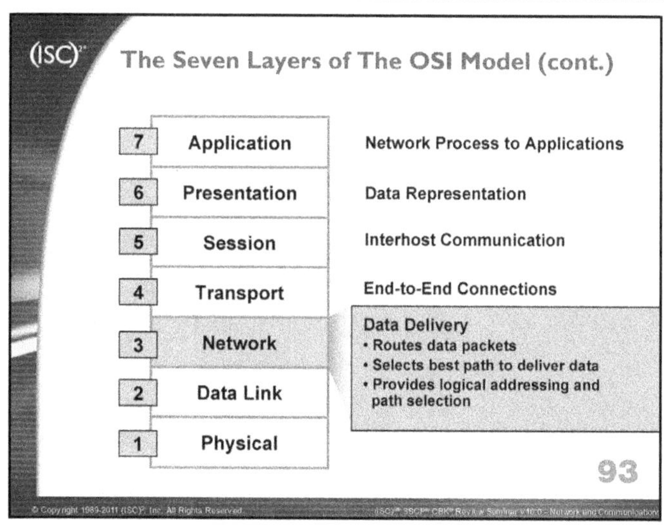

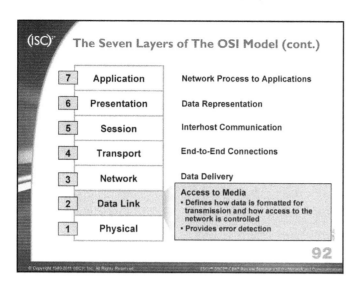

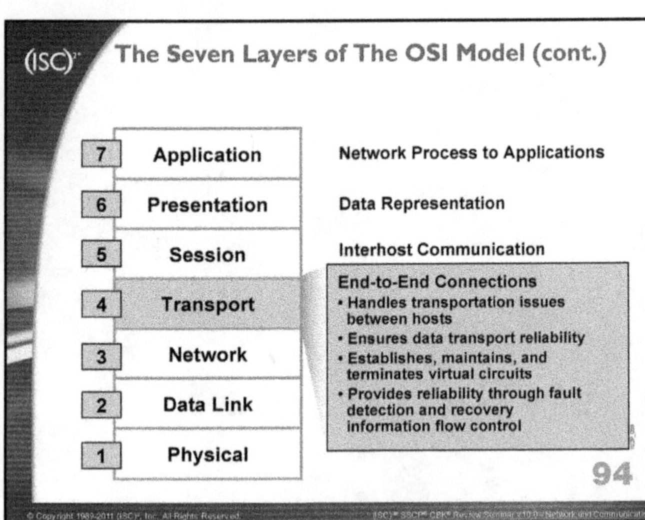
(ISC)²
The Seven Layers of The OSI Model (cont.)
7 Application
6 Presentation
5 Session
4 Transport
3 Network
2 Data Link
1 Physical
Network Process to Applications
Data Representation
Interhost Communication
End-to-End Connections
• Handles transportation issues between hosts
• Ensures data transport reliability
• Establishes, maintains, and terminates virtual circuits
• Provides reliability through fault detection and recovery information flow control
94

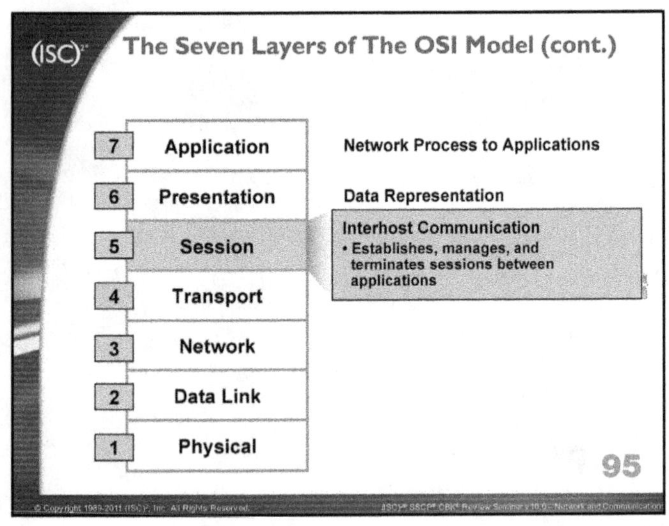
(ISC)²
The Seven Layers of The OSI Model (cont.)
7 Application
6 Presentation
5 Session
4 Transport
3 Network
2 Data Link
1 Physical
Network Process to Applications
Data Representation
Interhost Communication
• Establishes, manages, and terminates sessions between applications
95

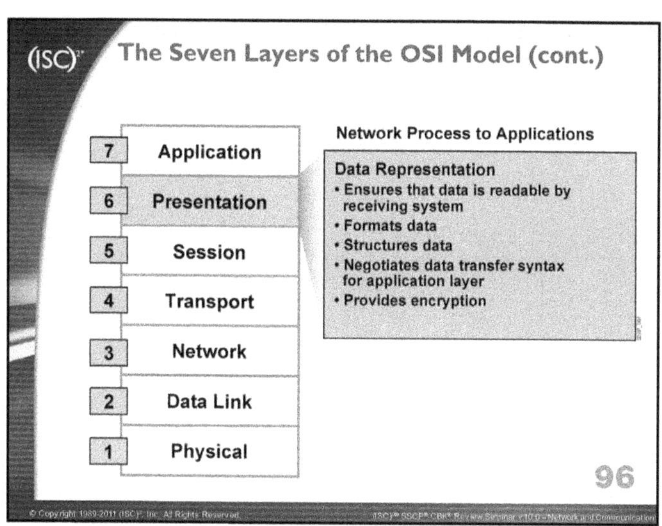
(ISC)²
The Seven Layers of the OSI Model (cont.)
7 Application
6 Presentation
5 Session
4 Transport
3 Network
2 Data Link
1 Physical
Network Process to Applications
Data Representation
• Ensures that data is readable by receiving system
• Formats data
• Structures data
• Negotiates data transfer syntax for application layer
• Provides encryption
96

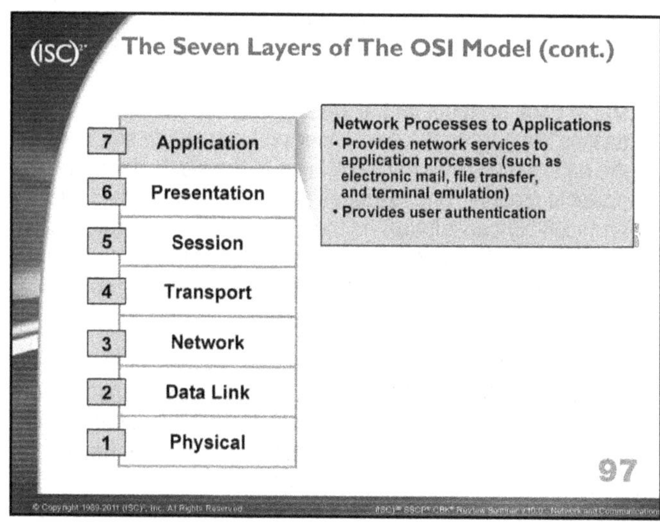
(ISC)²
The Seven Layers of The OSI Model (cont.)
7 Application
6 Presentation
5 Session
4 Transport
3 Network
2 Data Link
1 Physical
Network Processes to Applications
• Provides network services to application processes (such as electronic mail, file transfer, and terminal emulation)
• Provides user authentication
97

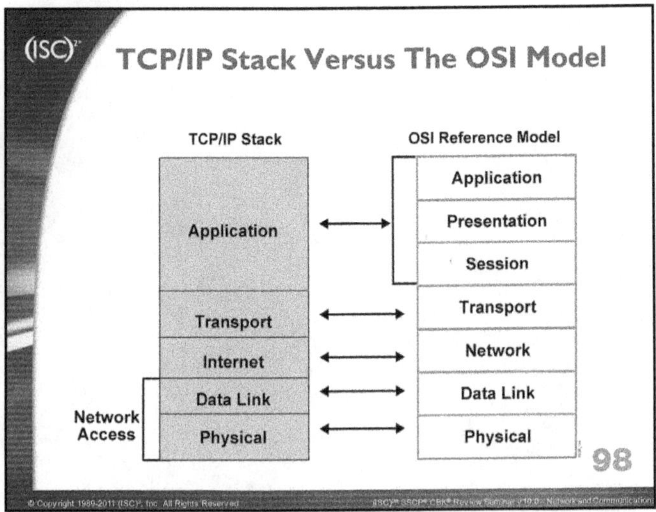


- This diagram shows the relationship between the OSI stack and TCP/IP.

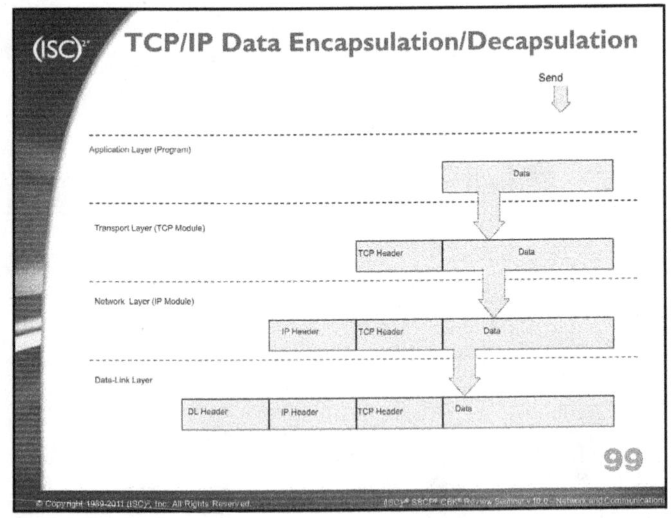


- **TCP/IP DATA ENCAPSULATION/DECAPSULATION –** To transmit data across a layered network, network software passes data from an application to a protocol on the protocol stack. Each protocol on the stack processes the data and then passes the data to the next lower protocol on the stack. As the data passes through each layer of the stack, the network protocol module "encapsulates" the data for the next lower protocol. "Encapsulation" is the process of storing the data in the format that the next lower protocol in the stack requires. As the data flows through the protocol stack, each layer builds on the previous layer's encapsulation.

- Above is a graphical depiction of what happens as the data travels down the TCP/IP stack. Each layer adds its own header information to the data. As it travels up the stack at the other end, the opposite happens. Each layer removes the header information meant for it, reads it, and passes the rest up to the next layer until it gets to the application that can process it properly.

- **THE TCP/IP STACK HAS ITS OWN MODULES THAT DO THE ENCAPSULATION. THIS CHART IS BASICALLY THE ONES WE'VE SEEN BEFORE –** Except that it does not show the physical layer (the network cable). The application layer is the layer on which your programs run.

- IMPORTANT NOTE: Strictly speaking, in TCP/IP, Layer 2 is called the network access layer. Many people still use OSI terminology (as we do here) and call it the data link layer. Also be aware that some references will say that TCP/IP has only the four layers shown here, omitting the physical layer.

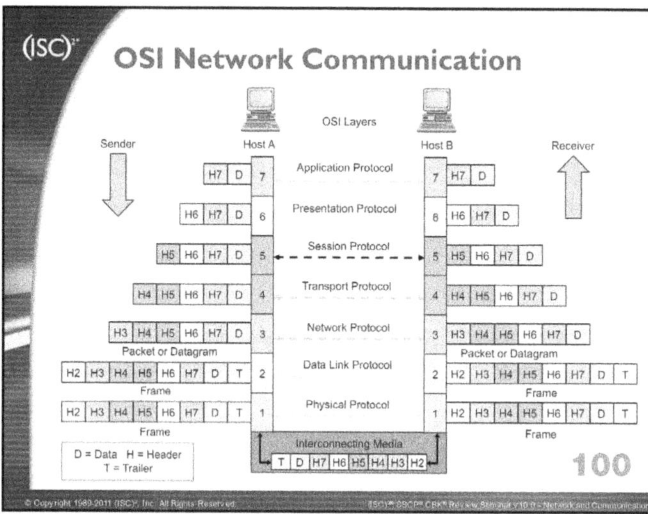


- This diagram shows the encapsulation of the data as it moves down the protocol stack. Each layer puts a header on the front of the packet when necessary. This communicates details about the packet to the remote host.

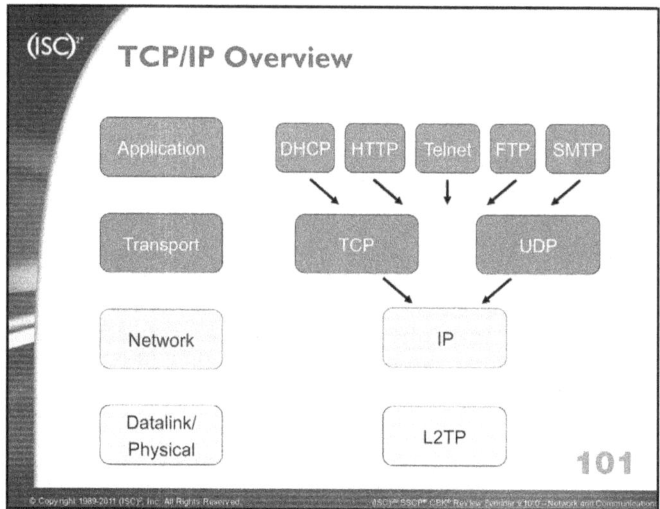


- **TCP/IP OVERVIEW –** Transport control protocol/Internet protocol (TCP/IP) is the primary networking protocol in use at this time. It governs all activity across the Internet and through most organizations and homes. TCP/IP is actually a suite of protocols that was developed for the United States Department of Defense to provide a highly available and fault tolerant network infrastructure. Its focus was reliability rather than security.
  - These protocols are broken up into the TCP/IP application layer, transport layer, network layer, and data link layer.
  - At the application layer, a suite of protocols includes scores of well-known services such as DHCP, FTP, Telnet, SMTP, HTTP, SSL (all TCP based) and TFTP, Syslog, SNMP, DNS-inquiry, and VOIP (all UDP based).
  - At the transport layer, there are two common protocols: TCP is used when error tracking is important, and it will cause retransmission of packets received in error or lost during communications. It will track a session from start to finish. UDP (user datagram protocol) is designed to handle connectionless, or best-efforts delivery. UDP is chosen when error checking is not needed (as in VOIP, where humans can simply say "What?") or when the checking is done at a different layer, such as the built-in error checking done by TFTP.
  - IP is the most common network-layer protocol and is the basis for all the other protocols mentioned in this note. Other network protocols include IPX (used by older versions of Novell's NetWare) and NetBeui, used by DOS and early versions of Windows (and still supported for backward compatibility, much to the joy of many hackers).
- TCP/IP doesn't care how the data is transmitted. Common choices such as bus or ring-based networks were covered earlier. There is even a "humorous" transmission method, RFC (number 1149) called "IP over Avian Carriers." (Its purpose was to point out that there are no timeouts in IP, which gives rise to exploits based on the trust between a logged-in client and server.)

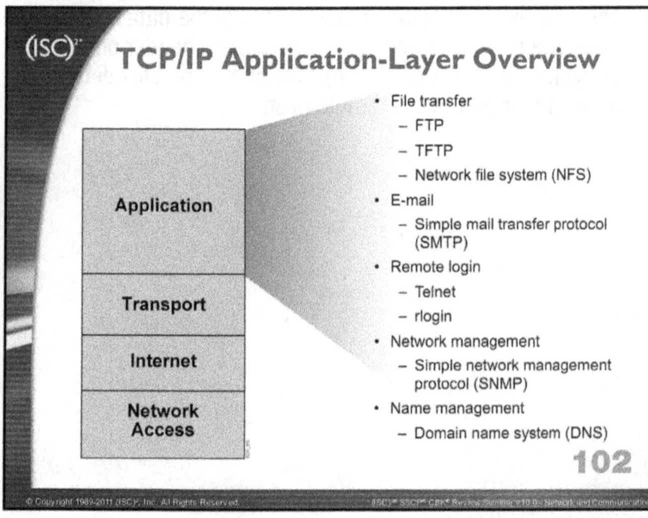


- **TCP/IP APPLICATION-LAYER OVERVIEW –** The common network applications today include file transfer, remote login, network management, and email. We focus on TCP/IP in this course for several reasons:
    - TCP/IP is a universally available protocol and you will use it at work.
    - TCP/IP is a useful reference for understanding other protocols, because it includes elements that are representative of other protocols.
    - TCP/IP is important because the router uses it as a configuration tool. The router uses Telnet for remote configuration, TFTP to transfer configuration files and operating system images, and SNMP for network management.

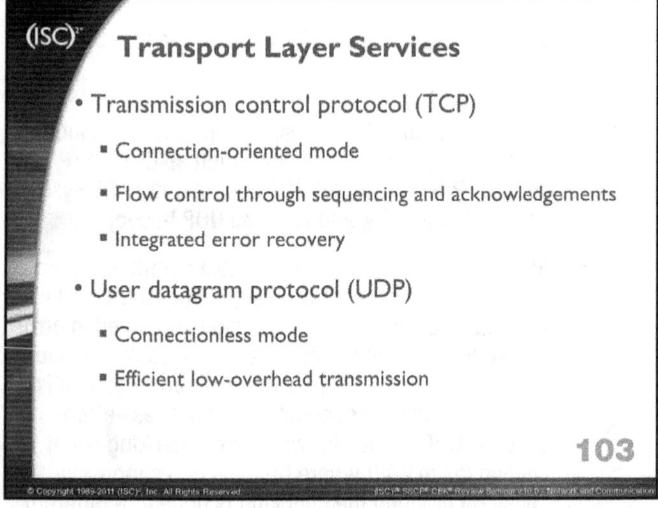

(ISC)²
Transport Layer Services
Transmission control protocol (TCP)
Connection-oriented mode
Flow control through sequencing and acknowledgements
Integrated error recovery
User datagram protocol (UDP)
Connectionless mode
Efficient low-overhead transmission
103


- **TRANSPORT LAYER SERVICES –** The transport layer provides data communication between hosts. It is concerned with the information payload. The transport layer relies on the correct addressing (routing) of information happening on Layer 3, while deferring any process related to handling (starting from authentication) for higher layer protocols. The transport layer is typically implemented as part of an integrated network stack that includes Layer 3 (TCP/IP stack). Layer 4 offers two principal types of communication:
    - A connection mode, where delivery of information is guaranteed and flow control as well as error recovery are provided.
    - A connection-less mode where no such guarantee is required.
    - Attacks on Layer 4 seek to manipulate, disclose, or prevent delivery of the payload as a whole. This can happen by reading the payload (as in a sniffer attack) or by changing it (which could happen in a man-in-the-middle attack). While disruptions of service can be done on other layers as well, the transport layer has become a common target.
- **TRANSMISSION CONTROL PROTOCOL (TCP) –** TCP provides connection-oriented data management and reliable data transfer. Attacks to TCP include sequence number attacks, session hijacking, and SYN floods.
- **USER DATAGRAM PROTOCOL (UDP) –** UDP provides a lightweight service for connection-less data transfer without error detection and correction. Technical advances have allowed a number of protocols within the transport layer to be defined on top of UDP, thereby effectively splitting the transport layer into two. Protocols stacked between Layers 4 and 5 include real-time protocol (RTP) and real-time control protocol (RTCP); MBone, a multicasting protocol; reliable UDP (RUDP); and stream control transmission protocol (SCTP). As a connection-less protocol, UDP services are easy prey for spoofing attacks.
- **SERVICE IDENTIFIERS (PORT NUMBER) –** TCP and UDP map data connections by port numbers. TCP and UDP port numbers are managed by the Internet Assigned Numbers Authority (IANA). There are a total of 65536 ports. These are structured into three ranges:
    - **WELL-KNOWN PORTS –** Ports 0 through 1023 are known as "well-known ports." Ports in this range are assigned by the IANA, and on most systems can only be used by privileged processes and users.
    - **REGISTERED PORTS –** Ports 1024 through 49151 are unassigned, but can be registered with IANA by application developers.
    - **DYNAMIC AND/OR PRIVATE PORTS –** Ports 49152 through 65535 can be freely used by applications. A typical use for these ports is initiation of return connections.

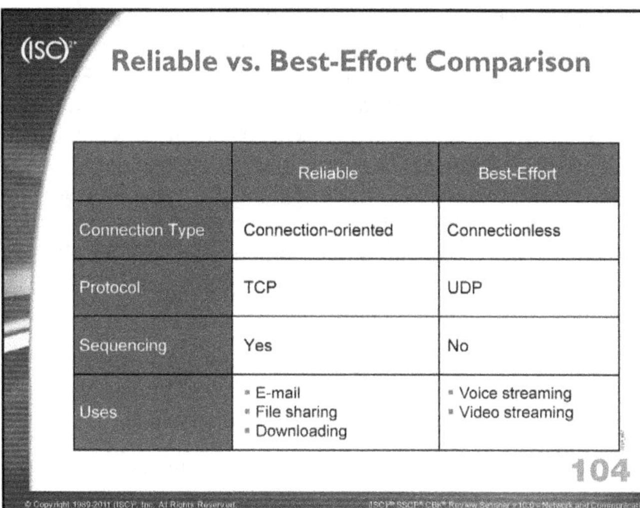


| | Reliable | Best-Effort |
|---|---|---|
| Connection Type | Connection-oriented | Connectionless |
| Protocol | TCP | UDP |
| Sequencing | Yes | No |
| Uses | ▪ E-mail<br>▪ File sharing<br>▪ Downloading | ▪ Voice streaming<br>▪ Video streaming |

- Comparison of the TCP and UDP protocols.

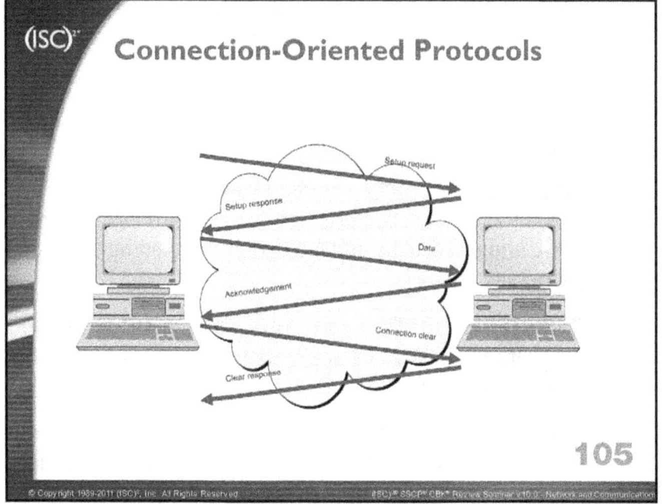


- **TRANSMISSION CONTROL PROTOCOL (TCP) –** The transmission control protocol provides connection oriented data management and reliable data transfer.
- Attacks to TCP include sequence number attacks, session hijacking, and SYN floods. Due to the built in reliability and stateful nature of TCP, attacks on unencrypted sessions can result in corruption of loss of control. The sequence numbers can be used to time an injection of corrupted data segments, which may lead to traffic flow diversion to the attacker's system. Serious service denials are possible, unless filters or proxies are used to validate connection requests. A SYN flood is a repeated, yet unacknowledged connection request which can quickly overflow a server's capacity to accept new requests.
- On the positive side, the stateful nature of TCP connections is that they can be more easily monitored and filtered by firewalls.
- This graphic shows the stages in a connection-oriented protocol communication.

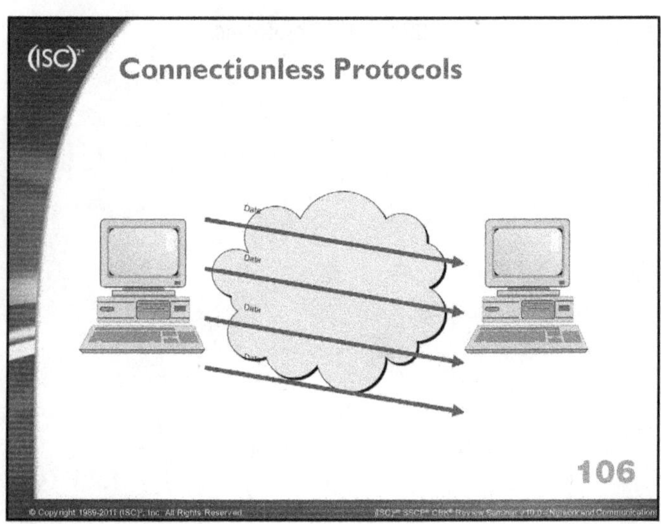


- **USER DATAGRAM PROTOCOL (UDP) –** The user datagram protocol provides a lightweight service for connection-less data transfer without error detection and correction. For UDP, the same considerations for port numbers as described for TCP apply. Responding to technical development, a number of protocols within the transport layer have been defined on top of UDP, thereby, effectively splitting the transport layer into two. Protocols stacked between Layers 4 and 5 include real-time protocol (RTP), real-time control protocol (RTCP), Mbone (a multicasting protocol), reliable UDP (RUDP), and stream control transmission protocol (SCTP).
- Since UDP messages are "stateless" (there is no sequence number and no capability to regulate flow of traffic), there is much less information for a firewall to interrogate.
- This graphic shows a connectionless communication.

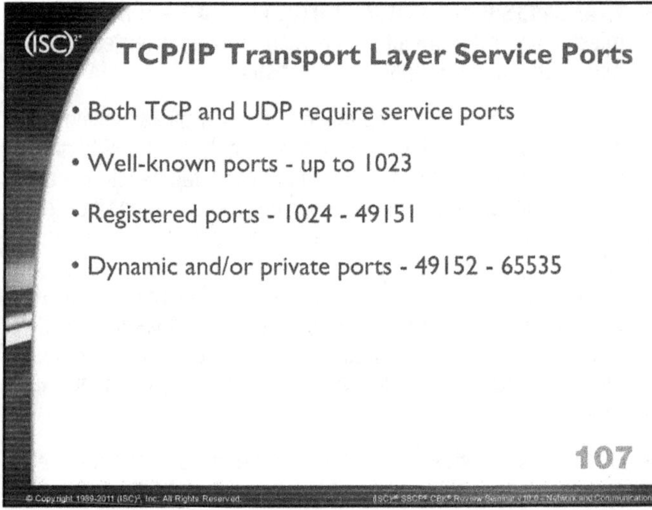

(ISC)²
TCP/IP Transport Layer Service Ports
• Both TCP and UDP require service ports
• Well-known ports - up to 1023
• Registered ports - 1024 - 49151
• Dynamic and/or private ports - 49152 - 65535
107
© Copyright 1989-2011 (ISC)², Inc. All Rights Reserved.


- **TCP/IP TRANSPORT LAYER SERVICE PORTS –** TCP as well as UDP map data connections by so-called port numbers.
- TCP and UDP port numbers are managed by the Internet Assigned Numbers Authority (IANA). A total of 65536 ports exist. These are structured into three ranges:
  - **WELL-KNOWN PORTS –** Ports 0 through 1023 are known as well-known ports. Ports in this range are assigned by IANA, and on most systems can only be used by privileged processes and users.
  - **REGISTERED PORTS –** Ports 1024 through 49151 can be registered with IANA by application developers but are not assigned by them.
  - **DYNAMIC AND/OR PRIVATE PORTS –** Ports 49152 through 65535 can be freely used by applications; one typical use for these ports is initiation of return connections.

**REFERENCE:**

http://www.cs.virginia.edu/~cs458/material/Redbook-ibm-tcpip-Chp5.pdf

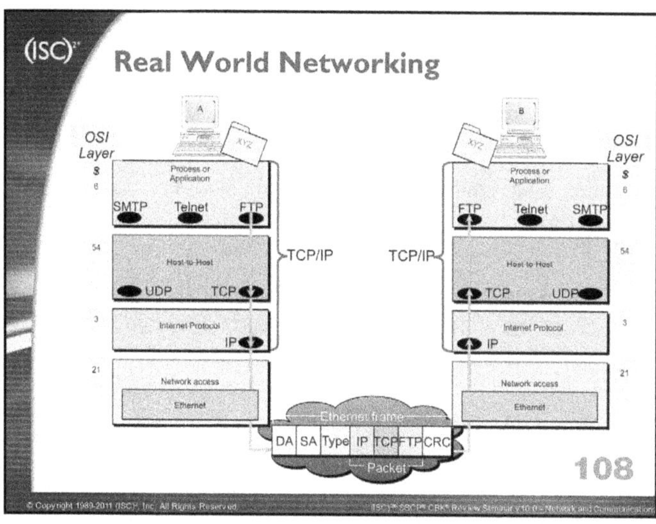


- This graphic shows the development of a communications packet as it traverses down through, and then up through, the TCP/IP protocol stack and the packet is constructed with headers and trailer. In the example above, we are using the FTP protocol. As the information from the sender goes down each layer of the OSI stack, the appropriate headers and footers are added.
- The balloon in the middle of the graphic highlights the difference between an Ethernet frame and a packet.
- On the right side, the graphic show the information going up the OSI stack on the receiving machine.

(ISC)²

NOS Protocol Comparison

OSI
UNIX
Windows NT*
UNIX Application
NFS, TCP/IP Applications, proprietary applications
TCP or UDP
IP
Windows NT Application
Other applications
SMB
NetBIOS
TCP or UDP
SPX
NetBEUI
IP
IPX
AppleTalk stack
109

- The two most common operating systems today are UNIX (or some derivative) and Windows. Both implement the TCP/IP protocol suite and generally conform to the OSI structure as shown.
- Keep in mind that a strict layer-by-layer comparison is not precise and is shown only for illustration of the implementations.

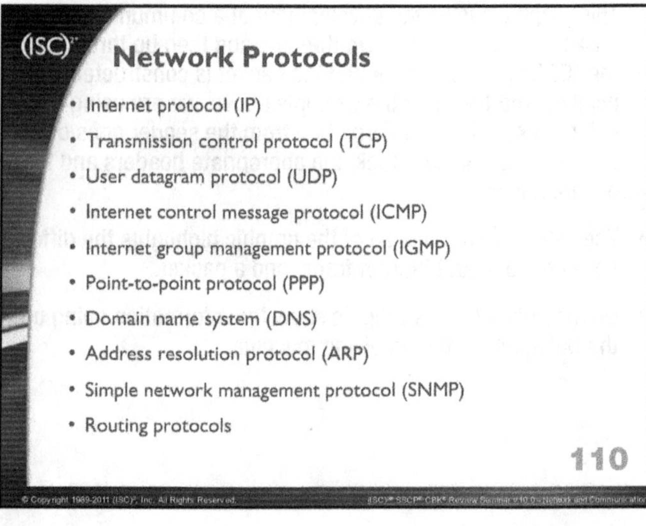


- This Slide shows the protocols within TCP/IP that we describe in this domain. We will provide some information about each protocol, including the weaknesses that make them vulnerable to attacks. We will discuss the security-strengthening protocols later.
- There are a number of standard protocol numbers associated with both network layer and transport layer services. RFC 1700 contains most of the more common numbers.
- Some of the protocols shown on this Slide are considered applications and thus have service ports assigned by IANA (e.g., DNS is port 53, SNMP is port 161, etc.). TCP and UDP are identified in an IP packet by protocol numbers 6 and 17, respectively. ICMP is IP protocol 1.
- Some of the more common routing protocols are identified by protocol number while others are considered applications. For instance, OSPF is IP protocol 89, while BGP is TCP service port 179.

**REFERENCES:**

http://en.wikipedia.org/wiki/List_of_IP_protocol_numbers

http://www.webopedia.com/quick_ref/portnumbers.asp

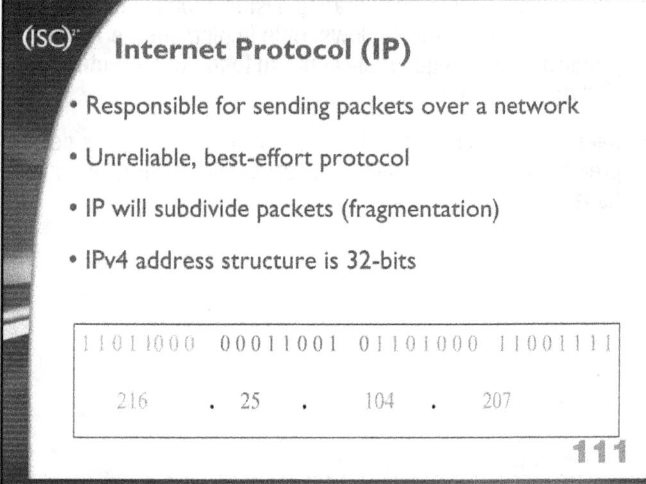


- **INTERNET PROTOCOL (IP) –** For the common user, IP is probably best known for its ability to route information globally.
  - **RESPONSIBLE FOR SENDING PACKETS OVER A NETWORK –** Internet protocol (IP) is responsible for sending packets from the source to the destination hosts over a network.
  - **UNRELIABLE, BEST-EFFORT PROTOCOL –** IP does not guarantee that packets arrive error-free or in the correct order. (That task is left to protocols on higher layers.)
  - **IP WILL SUBDIVIDE PACKETS (FRAGMENTATION) –** Into fragments when a packet is too large for a network.
  - **IPV4 ADDRESS STRUCTURE -**
    - Each octet may have a value between 0 and 255, although 0 and 255 are not used for hosts. The number 0 is usually reserved to refer to the entire subnetwork (see below) and 255 is used for broadcast addresses.
    - Hosts are distinguished by the IP addresses of their network interfaces.
    - The address is expressed as 4 octets separated by a dot ("."), for example: 216.25.104.207.
    - Each address is subdivided into two parts: the network number and the host. The network number assigned by an external organization represents the organization's network. The host represents the network interface within the network.

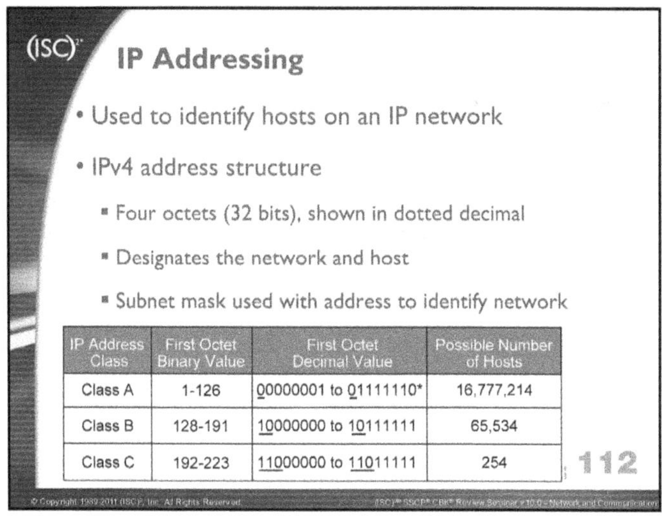


| IP Address Class | First Octet Binary Value | First Octet Decimal Value | Possible Number of Hosts |
|---|---|---|---|
| Class A | 1-126 | 00000001 to 01111110* | 16,777,214 |
| Class B | 128-191 | 10000000 to 10111111 | 65,534 |
| Class C | 192-223 | 11000000 to 11011111 | 254 |

- **IP ADDRESSING –** One of the primary functions of the network layer protocols is to provide an addressing scheme. The addressing scheme in TCP/IP is found at the network layer. IP addressing is a four-byte address, which uniquely identifies every device on the network.
  - Part of the address identifies the site (the network) and part identifies the particular machine (the host). Although it is common for the network/host divisions to occur "at the dots," it is not required.
- Depending on the manner in which addressing is implemented or protected, this addressing system may be a security concern. It is much easier to break through security barriers if you know the location and address of your target.
- Features to add to your network to protect your IP addressing scheme are: NAT (network address translation), PAT (port address translation), or a firewall.
- **SUBNET MASKING –** Networked devices can examine an IP address and identify the part that is specific to the particular device (host) and the part that defines the network on which it can be found.
  - Network masks are a series of binary "1"s, followed by a series of "0" s.
  - 1s represent the bits in the IP address that correspond to the network, while 0s represent the host.
  - Networks sometimes need to be subdivided for efficiency or security. To do this, we use some of the original, default host portion. The network mask is extended (some of the high order 0s are changed to 1s), which turns it into a subnet mask.

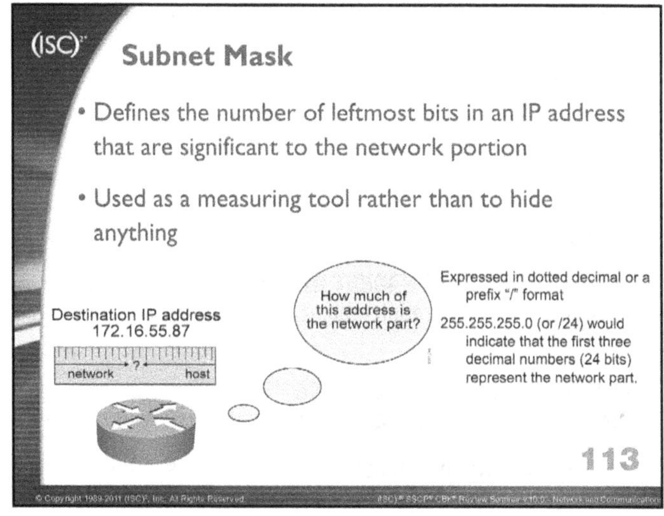


- Subnet masks are 32-bit suffix numbers that are used in conjunction with the actual 32-bit IP address to identify the logical structure of that address.
- The host portion of an IP address identifies the correct source and destination of a message. The network portion (both the default or classful part, as well as any additional subnet part) needs to be determined by network devices (such as routers) in order to forward or route the message to the destination network.
- The network mask is used by routers to organize and identify destination networks by their relative location and distance from the router. These network references are stored in routing or forwarding tables and used to efficiently relay network traffic. Many servers also recognize and use network masks to detect incorrect host addresses.

## Private IP Addresses

| Class | Private Address Range |
|---|---|
| A | 10.0.0.0 to 10.255.255.255 |
| B | 172.16.0.0 to 172.31.255.255 |
| C | 192.168.0.0 to 192.168.255.255 |

114

- Defined by RFC 1918, these three ranges of IP addresses are not registered to individuals or organizations and may be used as private internal addresses for any network, provided that the network is either:
  - Completely isolated from the public Internet, or
  - Network address translation (NAT) is used to convert all private host addresses to public (IANA registered) IP addresses.

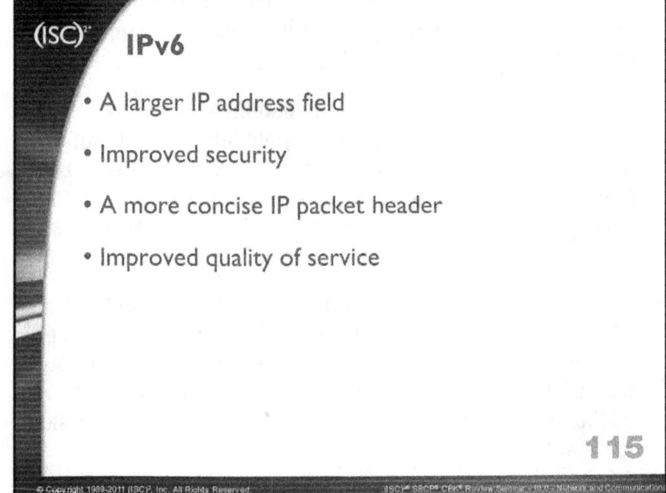
(ISC)²
IPv6
• A larger IP address field
• Improved security
• A more concise IP packet header
• Improved quality of service
115

- **IPV6 –** After the explosion of Internet use in the mid-1990s, IP began to experience serious growing pains. The most obvious problems were a shortage of unallocated IP addresses and serious shortcomings in security. IPv6 is a modernization of the current IP protocol, IPv4 (Version 5 was an experimental real-time streaming protocol).
- **A LARGER IP ADDRESS FIELD –** IPv6 addresses are 128 bits (16 octets), which support approximately 3.4×1038 addresses (or over 10 billion, billion, billion more addresses than IPv4). Suffice it to say that there will never be a shortage of IPv6 addresses. Computing how many hosts will be supported by IPv6 and comparing it to some other large constant (such as the number of grains of sand on a beach) will be left as an exercise for the curious. IPv6 addresses are normally written as eight groups of four hexadecimal digits, where each group is separated by a colon (:). For example, 2001:0db8:85a3:08d3 :1319:8a2e:0370:7334 is a valid IPv6 address.
- **IMPROVED SECURITY –** IPSec must be implemented in IPv6. This will help ensure the integrity and confidentiality of IP packets, and allow communicating partners to authenticate with each other.
- **A MORE CONCISE IP PACKET HEADER –** Hosts will require less time to process each packet, which will result in increased throughput.
- **IMPROVED QUALITY OF SERVICE –** This will help services obtain an appropriate share of a network's bandwidth.
  - The slow process of converting to IPv6 has already begun. Public IPv6 networks (such as 6Net and 6Bone) are accepting additional networks to connect to their IPv6 network. Since there are always stragglers, it will probably take a long time for every network to convert to the new protocol, but if recent history is an indicator, the vast majority of networks will convert in a relatively short period of time.

---

**REFERENCES:**

http://www.ipv6.org/

http://www.faqs.org/rfcs/rfc1884.html

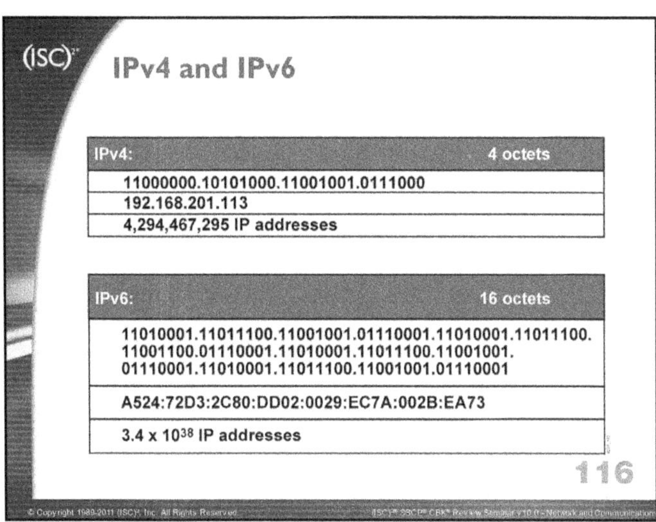


- IPv6 addresses are expressed in hexadecimal format in 8 groups of 4 characters (16 bits) separated by colons (a total of 128 bits).

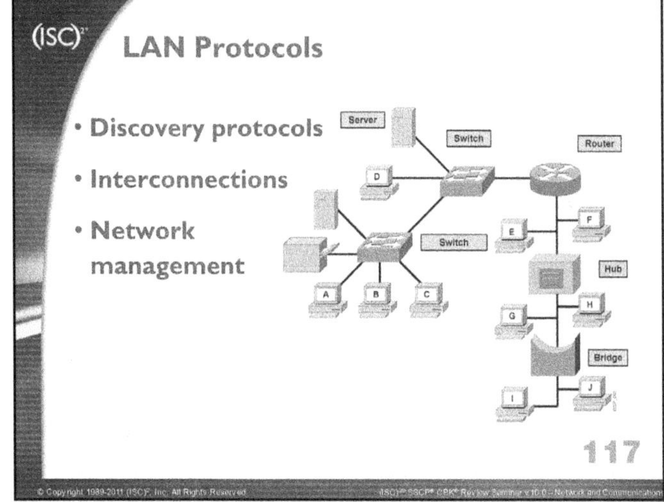


- These are some of the common LAN protocols used in networks to provide information and delivery services.

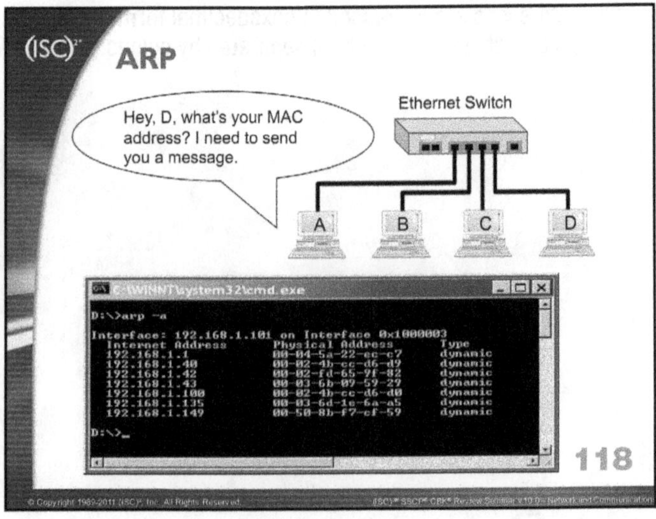


- **ARP** – ARP is used to resolve a Layer 3 IP address of a device with the device's Layer 2 MAC address. ARP tracks IP addresses and their corresponding MAC address in a dynamic table called an ARP cache. To determine a device's address, ARP first looks in its cache to see if the MAC address is already known. If it isn't, ARP sends out a broadcast asking all devices to return the MAC address, if they know it. The returned MAC address is added to the cache.
- Since ARP does not require authentication, an attacker could perform a man-in-the-middle attack by placing bogus entries in the ARP cache. Using our graphic, this would cause our switch to send the information to the attacker's machine. The attacker would then modify or copy the information and then forward it to its original intended destination. This is an example of the man-in-the middle attack using cache poisoning.

(ISC)²

## ARP Security Issues

- ARP is unauthenticated, thus an attacker can poison any host's ARP table (cache) in order to spoof another host by sending unsolicited ARP replies
- An attacker can send an unsolicited (gratuitous) ARP response, mapping the attacker's MAC address to the default router's IP address. The target will then send all traffic destined for the router to the attacker's node instead. The attacker "sniffs" the traffic, then forwards it to the real router
- The information gained by monitoring ARP traffic can be used to set up rogue services, corrupting normal network behavior

119



(ISC)² SSCP® CBK® Review Seminar v10.0 – Network and Communication

- There are also a number of attacks that can be made against the ARP cache itself (where frequently-requested ARP results are stored). If the ARP cache is damaged, ARP itself will not work and network service will not be available until it is fixed. Even unintentional damage of the ARP cache can cause a denial of service.
  - Address resolution protocol (ARP) Redirect
    - Normally, a network switch prevents attackers from eavesdropping on traffic not intended for them to see.
    - ARP traffic is unauthenticated, so an attacker can poison the ARP cache of a target by sending an unsolicited ARP reply.
    - By sending an ARP reply mapping the attacker's MAC address to the default router's IP address, the target will now send all traffic destined for the router to the attacker's node instead.
    - The attacker's node can sniff the traffic and then forward it to the real router. The tool "arpredirect" does exactly this, and it is available as part of the "dsniff" package at http://www.monkey.org/~dugsong/dsniff
    - The attacker must be on the same broadcast segment as the target, so attacks can be made from distant locations.

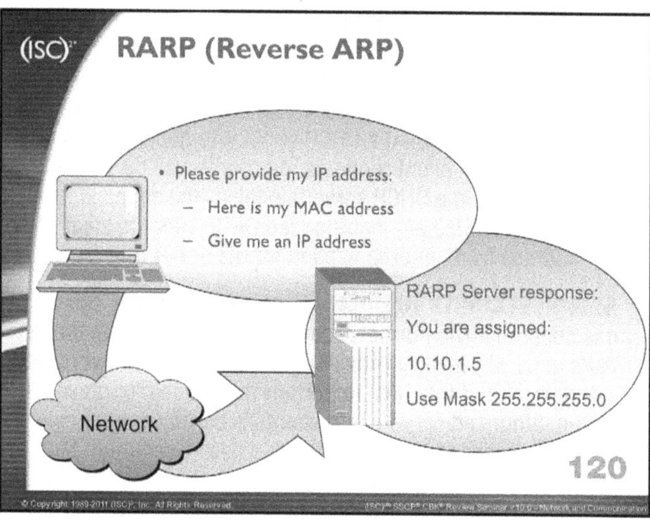


- **RARP (REVERSE ARP) –** Was an early protocol used to map a device's IP address to its MAC address. It is sometimes used by diskless workstations to learn their own IP address.
- **BOOTP (RFC 951) –** Enables a host to locate its assigned IP address and locate a BOOTP server from which to download an executable boot configuration file.
- **DHCP (RFC 2131) –** Extends BOOTP to facilitate dynamic location and binding to an IP address from a dedicated server. Can be static (like BOOTP) or dynamically assigned from a defined "pool" of addresses for a configured finite period of time (called a "lease"), allowing reallocation of addresses. Configuration parameters are built into DHCP.
- These protocols use broadcast IP/UDP packets for discovery with no authentication or confidentiality protection. BOOTP uses a TFTP server to hold the configuration files for every host. TFTP is also an unauthenticated UDP service.

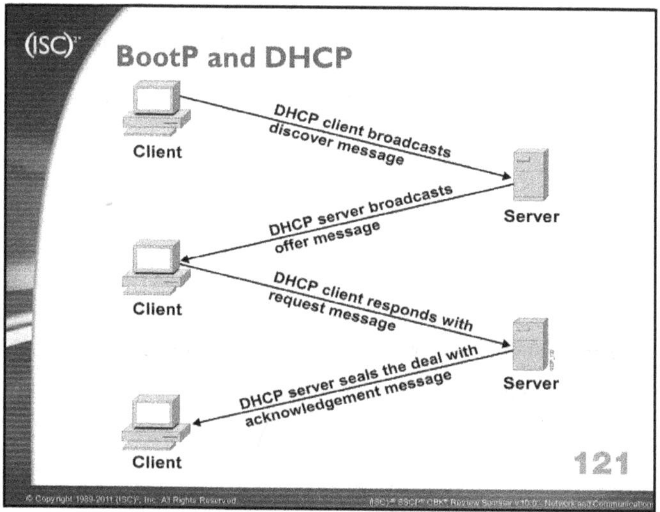


- **DYNAMIC HOST CONFIGURATION PROTOCOL (DHCP) –** System and network administrators are busy people and hardly have the time to assign IP addresses to hosts and track which addresses are allocated to what. To relieve administrators from the burden of manually assigning addresses, many organizations use Dynamic Host Configuration Protocol (DHCP) to automatically assign IP addresses to workstations. (Servers and network devices are usually assigned static addresses.)
- **DHCP DYNAMICALLY ASSIGNS IP ADDRESSES TO HOSTS** – Dynamically assigning hosts configuration is fairly simple. When a workstation boots, it broadcasts a **DHCPDISCOVER** request on the local LAN, which can be forwarded by routers. DHCP servers will respond with a **DHCPOFFER** packet, which contains a proposed configuration, including an IP address. The DHCP selects a configuration from the received **DHCPOFFER** packets and replies with a **DHCPREQUEST**. The DHCP server replies with a **DHCPACK** (DHCP acknowledgement), and the workstation adopts the configuration. Receiving a DHCP-assigned IP address is referred to as "receiving a lease."
- **CLIENT DOES NOT REQUEST A NEW LEASE EVERY TIME –** A client does not request a new lease every time it boots. Part of the negotiation of IP addresses includes establishing a time interval for which the lease is valid and timers that reflect when the client must attempt to renew the lease. As long as the timers have not expired, the client is not required to ask for a new lease. Administrators assign IP addresses within the DHCP servers from which addresses can be dynamically assigned. In addition, they can assign specific hosts to have static (i.e., permanent) addresses.
- Because the DHCP server and client do not authenticate with each other, neither host can be sure that the other is legitimate. For example, in a DHCP network, an attacker can plug his or her workstation into a jack and receive an IP address without having to obtain one by guessing or social engineering. Similarly, a client cannot be certain that a **DHCPOFFER** packet is from a DHCP server rather than from an intruder masquerading as a server.
- Although these vulnerabilities are not trivial, the ease of administration of IP addresses usually makes the risk from the vulnerabilities acceptable, except in very high-security environments.

### Security Issues With RARP, BOOTP, and DHCP

- Can be used for reconnaissance attacks and spoofing attacks
- Rogue servers may disrupt normal bindings
- Denial of service against server may render a network inaccessible
- Available IP addresses can be exhausted through exploits (DHCP gobbler)

122

- **SECURITY ISSUES WITH DHCP –** DHCP was designed in the early 1990s when the number of organizations on the Internet was relatively small. It was based on BOOTP, which was created in the 1980s when the Internet, as we know it today, barely even existed. In those days, Internet security wasn't a big issue, because it was only a relatively small group of research and educational organizations that used TCP/IP. Many protocols of that era do little to address security concerns.
- Not only does DHCP run over IP and UDP, which are inherently insecure, the DHCP protocol itself has no security provisions whatsoever. This is a fairly serious issue in modern networks because of the sheer power of DHCP, which deals with critical configuration information. There are two different classes of potential security problems related to DHCP:
  - **UNAUTHORIZED DHCP SERVERS –** If a malicious person plants a "rogue" DHCP server, this device could respond to client requests and supply them with spurious configuration information. This could be used to make clients unusable on the network, or worse, set them up for further abuse later on. For example, a hacker could exploit a bogus DHCP server to direct a DHCP client to use an erroneous gateway.
  - **UNAUTHORIZED DHCP CLIENTS –** A client could be set up to masquerade as a legitimate DHCP client and thereby obtain configuration information that could then be used to compromise the network. Alternately, a "bad guy" could use software called a DHCP gobbler to generate lots of bogus DHCP client requests in order to use up all the IP addresses in a DHCP server's pool. At the simplest level, a thief could use an unauthorized DHCP client to steal an IP address from an organization for his or her own use.
- **ADDING SECURITY TO DHCP –** These are obviously serious concerns. The normal recommended solutions to these risks generally involve providing security at lower layers. For example, one of the most important techniques for preventing unauthorized servers and clients is careful control over physical access to the network (i.e., Layer 1 security). Security techniques implemented at Layer 2 may also be of use, for example, in the case of wireless LANs. Since DHCP runs over UDP and IP, one could use IPSec at Layer 3 to provide authentication.
- **DHCP AUTHENTICATION –** To try to address some of the more specific security concerns within DHCP itself, in June 2001, the IETF published RFC 3118, Authentication for DHCP Messages. This standard describes an enhancement that replaces the normal DHCP messages with authenticated ones. Clients and servers check the authentication information and reject messages that come from invalid sources. The technology involves the use of a new DHCP option type called "authentication," as well as requiring operating changes to several of the leasing processes. Unfortunately, 2001 was pretty late in the DHCP game, and there are millions of DHCP clients and servers around that don't support this new standard. Both client and server must be programmed to use authentication for this method to have value. A DHCP server that supports authentication could use it for clients that support the feature and skip it for those that do not. However, the fact that this option is not universal means that it is not widely deployed, and most networks must rely on more conventional security measures.

**REFERENCE:**
http://www.tcpipguide.com/free/t_DHCPSecurityIssues.htm

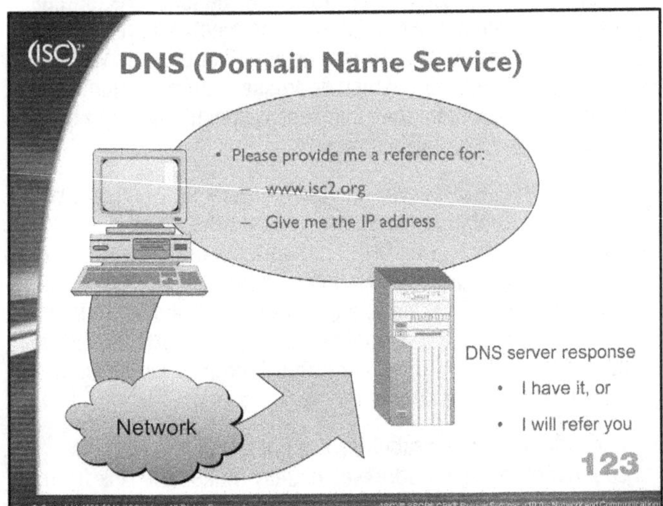
DNS (Domain Name Service)
Please provide me a reference for:
www.isc2.org
Give me the IP address
DNS server response
I have it, or
I will refer you
Network
123

- Hierarchical directory application specified in the TCP/IP suite.
- Translates human-readable names (TLD) into IP addresses.

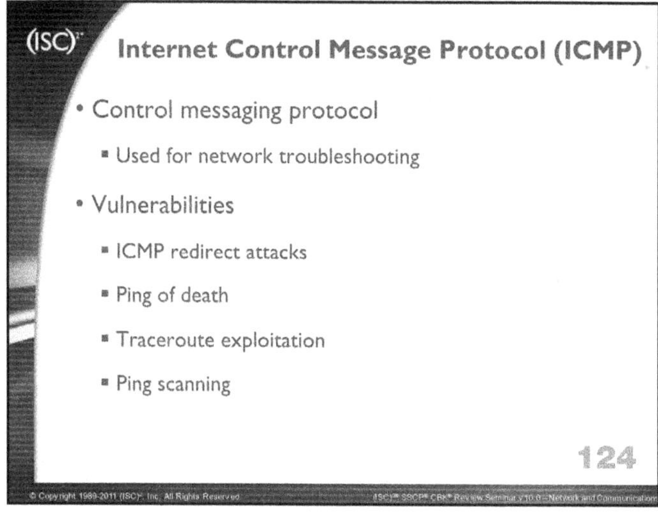

(ISC)²
Internet Control Message Protocol (ICMP)
• Control messaging protocol
▪ Used for network troubleshooting
• Vulnerabilities
▪ ICMP redirect attacks
▪ Ping of death
▪ Traceroute exploitation
▪ Ping scanning
124


- **INTERNET CONTROL MESSAGE PROTOCOL (ICMP) –** Is used for the exchange of control messages between hosts and gateways, as well as for diagnostic tools such as ping and traceroute. ICMP can be leveraged for malicious behavior, including man-in-the-middle and denial of service attacks.
- **VULNERABILITIES –**
  - **ICMP REDIRECT ATTACKS –** A router may send an ICMP redirect to a host to tell to it to use a different, more effective default route, but an attacker can also send a redirect to the host telling it to use the attacker's machine as a default route. The attacker will forward all of the redirected traffic to a router so that the victim will not know that his or her traffic has been intercepted. This is a good example of a man-in-the-middle attack. Some operating systems will crash if they receive a storm of ICMP redirects.
- **PING OF DEATH –** "Ping" is a diagnostic program used to determine whether a specified host is on the network and can be reached from the pinging host. The pinging host sends an ICMP echo packet to the target host and waits for the target to return an ICMP echo reply. Amazingly, an enormous number of operating systems crash or become unstable when receiving an ICMP echo of size greater than the legal packet limit of 65,536 bytes. Before the Ping of death became famous, the source of the attack was difficult to find because many system administrators would ignore a harmless looking ping in their logs.
- **TRACEROUTE EXPLOITATION –** Traceroute is a diagnostic tool that displays the path a packet traverses between the source and destination hosts. Traceroute can be used maliciously to map a victim network and learn about its routing. In addition, there are tools, such as Firewalk, that use techniques similar to traceroute to enumerate a firewall rule set.
- **PING SCANNING –** Ping scanning is a basic network mapping technique that helps to narrow the scope of an attack. An attacker can use one of a number of tools that can be downloaded from the Internet to ping all of the addresses in a range. If a host replies to a ping, the attacker knows that there is a host at that address.

(ISC)²

Other Vulnerabilities on IP Networks

• Distributed denial of service exploits
▪ Smurf attack misuses the ICMP echo request
▪ Fraggle attack uses UDP instead of ICMP
• IP fragmentation attacks
▪ Teardrop
▪ Overlapping fragment
• Spoofing attacks
▪ LAND.c attack

125

- **SMURF ATTACK MISUSES THE ICMP ECHO REQUEST –** To create denial of service attack. The intruder sends an ICMP echo request with a spoofed source address of the victim to a network's broadcast address. The victim will be overwhelmed by the ICMP echo replies.
- **FRAGGLE ATTACK USES UDP INSTEAD OF ICMP –** The attacker sends a UDP packet on port 7 with a spoofed source address of the victim. The victim host will be overwhelmed by the responses from the network.
  - **IP FRAGMENTATION ATTACKS –** Most IP fragmentation attacks were designed to cause some form of denial of service to a system, and have been "fixed" through the deployment of patches. In most cases the attacker was taking advantage of flaws in the Internet protocol related to the fragmentation and reassembly of packets being sent.
  - **TEARDROP ATTACK –** IP packet fragments are constructed so the target host calculates a negative fragment length when it attempts to reconstruct the packet. If the target host's IP stack does not ensure that fragment lengths are reasonable, the host could crash or become unstable. This problem is fixed with a vendor patch.
  - **OVERLAPPING FRAGMENT ATTACKS –** Are used to subvert packet filters that only inspect the first fragment of a fragmented packet. The technique involves sending a harmless first fragment, which will satisfy the packet filter. Other packets follow that overwrite the first fragment with malicious data, resulting in a harmful packet bypassing the packet filter and being accepted by the victim host. A solution to this problem is for TCP/IP stacks not to allow fragments to overwrite each other.
- **SPOOFING ATTACKS –** Because IP does not have imbedded authentication of source addresses, attacks designed to exploit this weakness can have an adverse impact on network security and availability.
  - **LAND.C ATTACK –** Uses the lack of source authentication to cause service denials and other abnormal behavior. In this attack, an IP packet is crafted with identical (spoofed) address values in both the source IP and destination IP address fields (essentially this is a packet which appears to be addressed to the sender). Unless the recipient system is configured to ignore or reject these, or an intermediate router is enforcing split horizon, this could disable a critical service.

(ISC)²

## Simple Network Management Protocol (SNMP)

- Provides for remote administration of network devices
- SNMP is referred to as "simple" because the agent requires minimal software
- Community strings are used to provide read-only or read-write access controls.

126

- RFCs for the different versions of SNMP are: v1 1157, v2 1446, v3 2570.
- SNMP uses TCP and UDP port 161.
- Typically, the read-only community string is "public" and the read-write string is "private." It's a good practice to configure all network devices to only allow SNMP read, not SNMP write. They authenticate messages sent between the SNMP manager and agent. An example of a community string is a password.
- SNMP monitors network and computing devices anywhere. SNMP security issues result from default values that haven't been changed by system and network administrators. These can cause loss of availability due to denial of service attacks.

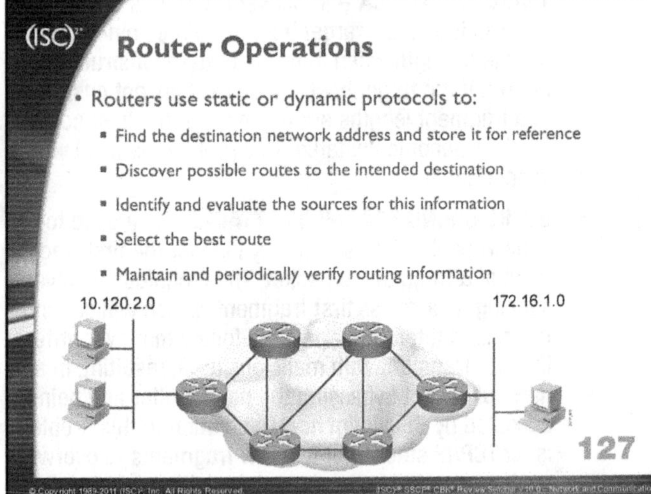

(ISC)²
Router Operations
Routers use static or dynamic protocols to:
Find the destination network address and store it for reference
Discover possible routes to the intended destination
Identify and evaluate the sources for this information
Select the best route
Maintain and periodically verify routing information
10.120.2.0
172.16.1.0
127


- **ROUTER OPERATIONS –**
  - Path determination occurs at Layer 3, the network layer. The path determination function enables a router to evaluate the available paths to a destination and to establish the best path.
  - Routing services use network topology information when evaluating network paths. This information can be configured by the network administrator (static routes) or collected through dynamic processes (routing protocols) running in the network.

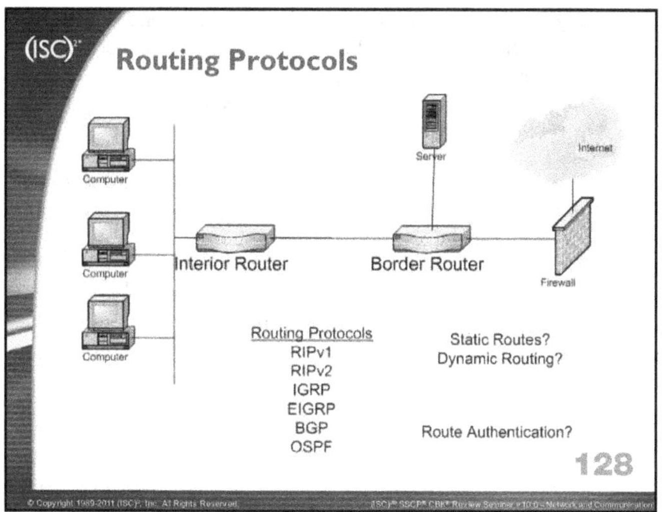


- **ROUTING PROTOCOLS –** Routers are a key element of today's networks. They are a part of our defense structure and if configured poorly, will allow attackers right into our networks.
- A router's main job is to determine the next step along the best path to a packet's destination. It figures this out though a combination of methods. Among them are static routing, dynamic routing, default routing, or a combination of these.
  - Static routing requires a network administrator to configure the router with knowledge of other IP subnets and how they are to be reached.
  - Dynamic routing allows the routers to send routing updates to each other as needed. This is one of the potential security risks of a router. If not carefully controlled, bogus routing updates can be sent by an intruder. Take care to control dynamic routing updates on each router link. Most modern routing protocols provide a method of route update authentication.
  - When a router doesn't have a specific route to follow, it will use a default route. For example, most companies have a default route that says, in English, "if this isn't an internal destination, send the packet to our ISP."
- The IP header supports a function that provides another kind of routing called "source routing." Before routers were invented, the source station had to calculate the path to the destination and place the intermediate station addresses into the header. Each intermediate station along the way would delete its address and pass the packet along to the next station. Although no longer used, source routing is still a part of the standard and is subject to misuse by attackers. Firewalls can delete these source routes and some routers' ACLs can drop packets that contain source route addresses.
- Routers are also used to provide security via access control lists (ACLs). The ACL is the rule set the administrator has established to direct the operation of the router. For example, an ACL can configure a router interface with a range of allowed (or disallowed) destinations or protocols.
- Carefully consider which routing protocol to use. Some routing protocols have the ability to use route authentication, which requires a secret keyword to be programmed into a router. These routing protocols include RIPv2, OSPF, EIGRP, and BGP.
- Three of the protocols listed on this graphic are a bit different from the others: BGP is used by ISPs and large companies to direct Internet traffic. All of the others are used to direct Intranet traffic. IGRP and EIGRP are Cisco proprietary.

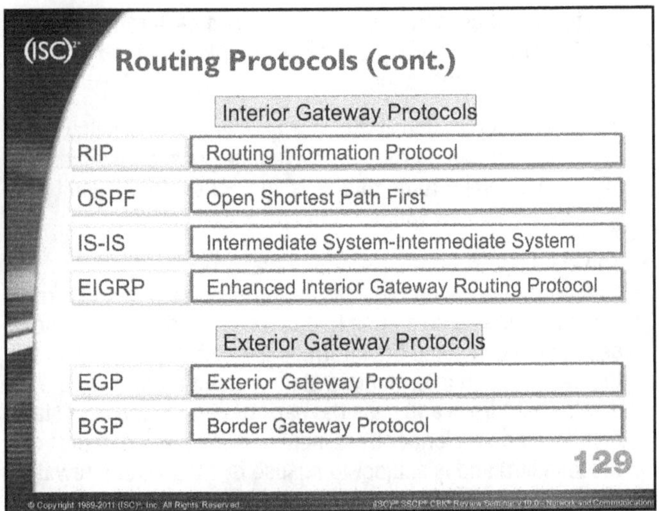

(ISC)²
Routing Protocols (cont.)
Interior Gateway Protocols
RIP
Routing Information Protocol
OSPF
Open Shortest Path First
IS-IS
Intermediate System-Intermediate System
EIGRP
Enhanced Interior Gateway Routing Protocol
Exterior Gateway Protocols
EGP
Exterior Gateway Protocol
BGP
Border Gateway Protocol
129


- **INTERIOR GATEWAY PROTOCOLS -**
- **DISTANCE-VECTOR PROTOCOLS –** Use timers and compute paths based on metrics. They are very simple and may be preferable in smaller networks.
- **LINK-STATE PROTOCOLS –** Use event-based update parameters and must establish persistent relationships (adjacencies) with neighboring routers. These are very complex hierarchical processes which are much more common in larger networks. They generally offer additional features for manageability.
    - **RIP** is a dynamic routing protocol used in local and wide area networks. As such, it is classified as an interior gateway protocol (IGP). It uses the distance-vector routing algorithm. The protocol has since been extended several times, resulting in RIP Version 2. Both versions are still in use today. However, they are considered technically obsolete by more advanced techniques, such as open shortest path first OSPF) and IS-IS.
    - **OSPF** is a dynamic routing protocol for use in Internet protocol (IP) networks. it is a link-state routing protocol.
    - **IS-IS** is an interior gateway protocol (IGP), meaning that it is intended for use within an administrative domain or network. It is not intended for routing between autonomous systems, a job for an exterior gateway protocol, such as border gateway protocol BGP).
    - **EIGRP** is a Cisco Systems proprietary protocol classified as an ADVANCED distance-vector. Metrics are calculated similarly to a simpler DV protocol, but the algorithm used is fast and efficient for larger Cisco-based network designs.
- **EXTERIOR GATEWAY PROTOCOLS -**
    - **EGP** is a now obsolete routing protocol for the Internet originally specified in 1982. EGP is a simple reach-ability protocol, and, unlike modern distance-vector and path-vector protocols, it is limited to tree-like topologies. During the early days of the Internet, an exterior gateway protocol, EGP version 3, was used to interconnect autonomous systems.
    - **BORDER GATEWAY PROTOCOL** is actually a path vector protocol which features policy-based metrics and is most commonly used in the Internet backbone to support inter-domain routing between networks.

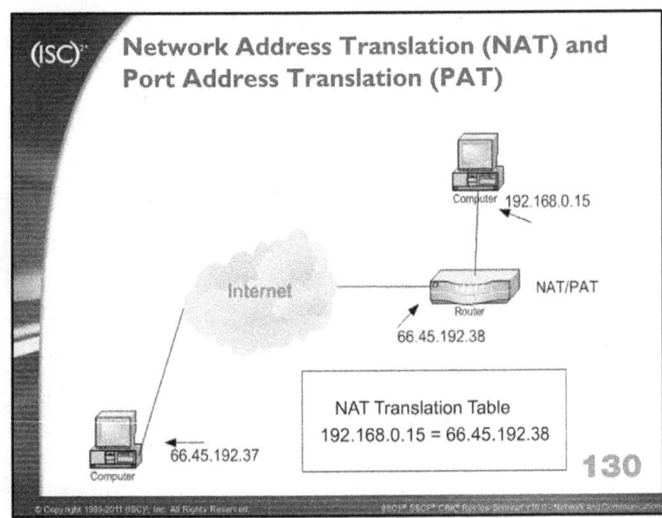


- **NETWORK ADDRESS TRANSLATION (NAT) AND PORT ADDRESS TRANSLATION (PAT) –** NAT and PAT were not designed for security but nonetheless do provide some security benefits.
    - **NAT** was designed to contend with the ever-shrinking number of available IP addresses. It allows a set of computers to be represented on a public network, such as the Internet, as only one IP address. NAT will translate from a hidden internal address to the publically known external address.
    - **PAT –** When the network layer address translation of NAT is combined with the translation of the TCP port number, you arrive at PAT. Because this makes it difficult for the attacker to determine the ports being used on the internal network, it allows for an even greater level of security.

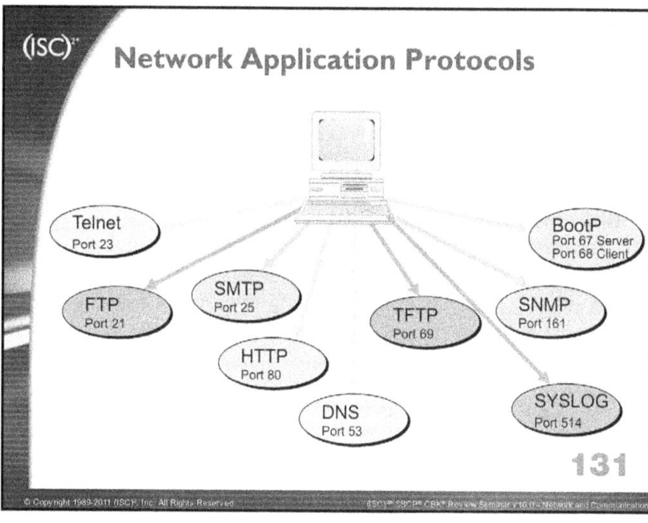


- This slide provides a graphical representation of many of the common protocols in use today and the ports they use.
- **FILE TRANSFER SERVICES:**
    - FTP and TFTP are simple file management services. TFTP does not provide authentication but is often used to store configuration files for quick access on a network.
    - TELNET and HTTP are network communications and data transfer protocols. TELNET is very simply a character transfer protocol between hosts, while HTTP is a formatted information exchange protocol common on web servers.
    - SMTP is a basic mail transfer protocol.
    - DNS and BootP are directory based configuration protocols.
    - SYSLOG is a message logging service often used to capture and track network activity and events from various sources.
- None of these basic services are particularly secure and should always be configured with enhancements or additional protocols to ensure information protection (e.g., DNSSec, HTTP-S, SSH, TLS, etc.).

(ISC)²

## Domain Agenda

- Network components and topologies
- Wide area and remote access networks
- Standard network protocols
- **Network security protocols**
- Wireless network configuration and protection
- Managing service reliability and quality

132

## Securing the Network and Resources

- Physical installations
- Reconnaissance attacks - learning information about a target network by using readily available information and applications
- Access attacks - attacks on networks or systems in order to gain unauthorized entry
- Password attacks - tools used by hackers to compromise passwords

133



- **PHYSICAL INSTALLATIONS –** Physical installations should be secure and prevent unauthorized entry. Use of strong access controls to doors, equipment racks, and other sensitive areas should be monitored and tested on a regular basis. Equipment should be configured with strong restrictions to administrative changes.
- **RECONNAISSANCE ATTACKS –** Learning what is available to identify your network and the services running on it is essential in determining what NOT to expose to an adversary during discovery activities. Changing default settings and suppressing automatic responses without authentication can reduce this visibility.
- **ACCESS ATTACKS –** Use of strong authentication techniques (e.g., two-factor, biometrics, cryptographic factors, etc.) will enhance the resistance of the network to unauthorized access. Hardening critical servers, maintaining a robust patch management program, and user training are good practices.
- **PASSWORD ATTACKS –** Tools used by hackers to compromise passwords depend upon the natural tendency of users to choose simple credentials. Educating users to select strong passwords and adding cryptographic protection for stored credentials, will eliminate or reduce the majority of common password attacks.

## Network/Internet Security Protocols

- Several protocols have been proposed to specifically address security protection in network communications. The most notable is IPSec.
- These protocols can be generically organized by OSI layer (which depends on when and where the service is implemented)
  - Many are designed to support multiple encryption and authentication protocols

134



- Even though most people think that IPSec is fairly new, the idea of having security services in the network is not new. Several protocols have been proposed over the years, but none of them have really become popular.

## Data Link Layer Security Protocols

- Tunneling and VPN protocols are the mechanisms by which transmissions at the data link layer are protected
  - Point-to-point tunneling protocol
  - Layer 2 forwarding
  - Layer 2 tunneling protocol
  - 802.11 wireless LAN security protocols
  - Other Layer 2 solutions

135



- **POINT-TO-POINT TUNNELING PROTOCOL –** PPTP was developed to support a Microsoft VPDN (dial-up VPN) between a Microsoft client and a Microsoft access server. This protocol supports authentication and encryption.
- **LAYER 2 FORWARDING –** Cisco Systems developed Layer 2 forwarding to support multiple upper layer protocols and provides authentication between devices, although no encryption is natively supported.
- **LAYER 2 TUNNELING PROTOCOL –** L2TP was published in 1999 as RFC 2661 and is based on PPTP and L2F, providing encapsulation for multiple protocols, but without encryption. Version 3 of L2TP is RFC 3931. Because of the lack of confidentiality inherent in the L2TP protocol, it is often implemented along with IPSec. This is referred to as L2TP/IPSec, and is standardized in IETF RFC 3193.
- **802.11 WIRELESS LAN SECURITY PROTOCOLS –** There are several Layer 2 protocols to protect wireless networks besides WPA2. One example is "Cranite," which is a FIPS 140-2 compliant VPN solution for Cisco wireless networks using AES (http://www.cisco.com/en/US/products/ps6366/products_tech_note09186a0080987b7c.shtml)
  - IEEE 802.1X will provide initial authentication to prevent unauthorized user from connecting.
- **OTHER LAYER 2 SOLUTIONS –** There are several administrative features which can be used to further enhance security protection at Layer 2. One of the more common protocols at Layer 2 which can be exploited is ARP (address resolution protocol). Modern switches permit administrative security "locking" at the port level so that unauthorized behavior of this protocol can be detected, by placing limits on MAC addresses used.
- Designing VLANs to ensure that secure VLANs are not configured outside firewall boundaries is another administrative design technique that might be used.
- A good discussion of Layer 2 security techniques may be found at: http://www.ciscopress.com/articles/article.asp?p=174313&seqNum=2

## Multi-Protocol Label Switching (MPLS)

- Uses forwarding tables and "labels" to create secure connections
- Does not rely on encapsulation and encryption to maintain a high level of security
  - Service providers create IP tunnels throughout their network without encryption
- Guarantees a certain level of performance, routes around network congestion, and creates IP tunnels for network-based VPNs

136

 (ISC)² SSCP® CBK® Review Seminar v10.0 – Network and Communication

- **MULTI-PROTOCOL LABEL SWITCHING (MPLS) –** MPLS is a new technology that can improve network performance and security. In a typical non-MPLS network, packet paths are determined in real time as routers determine each packet's appropriate next hop. With MPLS, explicit paths for specific types of traffic are predefined (identified by path labels contained within each packet). In other words, the packets are forced to travel a specific "secure" path which can help security and boost network performance.
  - MPLS networks are by default not encrypted, which means a compromise on the carrier network would expose their customer's traffic to interception.
  - If confidentiality is required, use of an additional service would be required (IPSec, for instance). This may pose some additional overhead which will need to be considered when engineering service quality.
- **MPLS BRINGS MANY OTHER BENEFITS TO IP-BASED NETWORKS, INCLUDING:**
  - **TRAFFIC ENGINEERING –** The ability to set the path traffic will take through the network, and the ability to set performance characteristics for a class of traffic.
  - **VPNS –** Using MPLS, service providers can create IP tunnels throughout their network without the need for encryption or end-user applications.
  - Bringing the speed of Layer 2 switches up to that of Layer 3. Because the switches use the contents of a simple label to make forwarding decisions rather than having routers look up routing tables based on the IP destination address, Layer 3 switches are now able to look up routing tables quickly.
  - **ELIMINATION OF MULTIPLE LAYERS –** The majority of carrier networks employ an overlay model. With MPLS, carriers are able to combine many of the functions of the overlay model to Layer 3. This simplifies network complexity and administration. Eventually carriers will be able to use MPLS in place of the commonly used SONET/SDH and ATM controls, eliminating the overhead associated with ATM and IP traffic.
- **HOW IT WORKS –** With MPLS, incoming packets are assigned a "label" by a "label edge router" (LER). Packets are passed along a "label switch path" (LSP). Each "label switch router" (LSR) makes forwarding decisions based on the contents of the label. Each LSR strips off the existing label and creates a new label which tells the next LSR how to pass along the packet.
- **LABEL SWITCH PATH (LSP) –** Guarantees a certain level of performance, routes around network congestion and creates IP tunnels for network based VPNs. LSPs are similar to ATM and frame relay networks' circuit-switched paths, except that they do not rely upon on any particular Layer 2 technology. Because LSPs can be established across multiple Layer 2 transports, MPLS is able to create end-to-end circuits with defined performance. This eliminates the need for overlay networks or Layer-2 only control mechanisms.
- **LAYER 2 TRANSPORT –** New standards being defined by the IETF's PWE3 (pseudo wire emulation edge-to-edge) and PPVPN (provider provisioned virtual private networks) working groups allow service providers to carry Layer 2 services including Ethernet, frame relay and ATM over an IP/MPLS core.

---

**REFERENCE:**

http://www.ietf.org/html.charters/mpls-charter.html

## Network Layer Security Protocols

- Generic route encapsulation (GRE) is designed to support multiple protocols

137

 (ISC)² SSCP® CBK® Review Seminar v10.0 – Network and Communication

- **GENERIC ROUTING ENCAPSULATION –** GRE is a tunneling protocol designed to encapsulate a wide variety of network layer packets inside IP tunneling packets. The original packet is the payload for the final packet. GRE is used to secure VPNs. It was developed by Cisco and was designed to be stateless; the tunnel end-points do not monitor the state or availability of other tunnel end-points. This feature helps service providers support IP tunnels for clients who won't know the service provider's internal tunneling architecture, and it gives clients the flexibility of reconfiguring their IP architectures without worrying about connectivity. GRE creates a virtual point-to-point link with routers at remote points on an IP Internetwork. GRE uses IP Protocol number 47. (See RFCs 2784 and 2890 for details.)

## Network Layer Security Protocols (cont.)

- IPSec is the most common network security protocol
  - It can be implemented with various types of network equipment and provides two basic services for IP transmissions:
    - ESP for privacy
    - AH for integrity

138



(ISC)² SSCP® CBK® Review Seminar v10.0 – Network and Communications

- **IPSEC AUTHENTICATION AND CONFIDENTIALITY FOR VPNS** – IP security (IPSec) is a suite of protocols for communicating securely with IP by providing mechanisms for authenticating and encryption. Implementation of IPSec is mandatory in IPv6, and many organizations are using it over IPv4. Further, IPSec can be implemented in two modes: one that is appropriate for end-to-end protection, and one that safeguards traffic between networks. Standard IPSec only authenticates hosts with each other. If an organization requires users to authenticate, they must employ a non-standard proprietary IPSec implementation, or use IPSec over L2TP (Layer 2 tunneling protocol). The latter approach uses L2TP to authenticate the users and to encapsulate IPSec packets within L2TP. Since IPSec interprets the change of IP address within packet headers as an attack, it does not work well with NATTING. To resolve the incompatibility of the two protocols, NAT-transversal (a.k.a. "NAT-T"), encapsulates IPSec within UDP port 4500. (See RFC 3948 for details.)
- **ONE KEY DIFFERENCE BETWEEN AN ENCRYPTED GRE TUNNEL AND AN IPSEC TUNNEL** – is the ability to make use of multicast protocols over GRE tunnels. An example would be the use of MOSPF over a GRE tunnel.

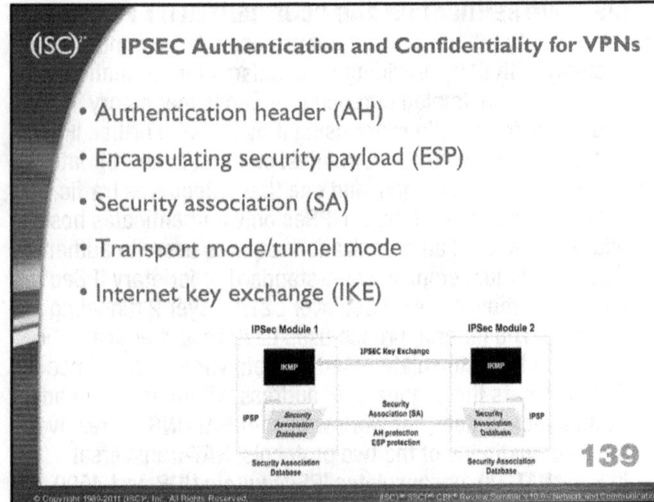


- **AUTHENTICATION HEADER (AH) –** The authentication header is used to prove the identity of the sending node and ensure that the data transmitted have not been tampered with. Before each packet (headers + data) is transmitted, a hash value of the packet's contents (except for the fields that are expected to change when the packet is routed) is inserted in the last field of the AH. The endpoints negotiate the hashing algorithm and the shared secret when they establish their security association. To help thwart replay attacks (in which a legitimate session is retransmitted to gain unauthorized access) each packet transmitted during a security association has a sequence number, which is stored in the AH. In transport mode, the AH is shimmed between the packet's IP and TCP header. Note that the AH helps assure integrity, not confidentiality. Encryption is implemented with the encapsulating security payload.
- **ENCAPSULATING SECURITY PAYLOAD (ESP) –** The encapsulating security payload encrypts IP packets and ensures the packet's integrity. Although AHs and ESPs are both optional, at least one of them must be used. ESP contains four sections:
    - **ESP HEADER –** Contains information showing the security association to use and the packet sequence number. Like the AH, the ESP sequences every packet to thwart replay attacks.
    - **ESP PAYLOAD –** The payload contains the encrypted part of the packet. If the encryption algorithm requires an initialization vector (IV), it is included with the payload. The endpoints negotiate which encryption mode to use when the security association is established. Because packets must be encrypted with as little overhead as possible, ESP typically uses a symmetric encryption algorithm.
    - **ESP TRAILER –** May include padding (filler bytes) if required by the encryption algorithm or to align fields.
    - **AUTHENTICATION –** If authentication is used, this field contains the integrity check value (hash) of the ESP packet. As with the AH, the authentication algorithm is negotiated when the endpoints establish their security association.
- **SECURITY ASSOCIATION (SA) –** A SA is an agreement between the communicating endpoints on factors such as IPSec protocol(s) (AH, ESP), mode of operation of the protocol(s) (transport or tunnel mode), cryptographic algorithms, cryptographic keys, and the lifetime of the keys. SA parameters are stored in security association databases (SADs). SAs cover transmissions in one direction only. A second SA must be defined for two-way communication. Deferring the mechanisms to the SA (as opposed to specifying them in the protocol) allows the communicating partners to use the appropriate mechanisms based on the transmission risks (confidentiality, authenticity, or integrity).
- **TRANSPORT MODE/TUNNEL MODE –** Endpoints communicate with IPSec using either transport mode or tunnel mode. In transport mode, the IP payload is protected. This mode is mostly used for end-to-end protection, for example, between client and server. In tunnel mode, the IP payload AND its IP header are protected. The entire protected IP packet becomes a payload of a new IP packet and header. Tunnel mode is often used between networks, such as with firewall-to-firewall VPNs.
- **INTERNET KEY EXCHANGE (IKE) –** IKE is the IPSec protocol that negotiates and establishes authenticated keying materials for security associations (SAs). IKMP is the module that handles key management, within which IPSec uses IKE (ISAKMP/OAKLEY). IPSP (IP security policy) stipulates the type of traffic (for example, from what source or to what destination) that is allowed to pass through the IPSec system and the security mechanisms that should be applied to the traffic. Internet key exchange allows communicating partners to prove their identity to each other and establish a secure communication channel. IKE uses two phases:
    - **PHASE 1 –** In this phase, the partners authenticate with each other, using one of the following:
        - **SHARED SECRET –** A key that is exchanged by humans via telephone, fax, encrypted e-mail, etc.
        - **PUBLIC KEY ENCRYPTION –** The exchange of digital certificates.
        - **REVISED MODE OF PUBLIC KEY ENCRYPTION –** To reduce the overhead of public key encryption, a nonce is encrypted with the communicating partner's public key, and the peer's identity is encrypted with symmetric encryption using the nonce as the key.
    - **PHASE 2 –** IKE establishes a temporary SA and secure tunnel to protect the rest of the key exchange.

## IPSec Compatible VPN Devices

- The choice should support:
  - Capacity requirements (number of connections)
  - Speed and throughput (and QOS)
  - Ease of use and deployment
- Examples include:
  - Dedicated VPN concentrators
  - IPSEC capable firewalls
  - IPSEC capable routers
  - IPSEC enabled end-stations

140

- While operating systems and purpose-built appliances will support IPSec VPN tunnels, many organizations design solutions that meet operational requirements for maintaining sustained connections and choose the technology that will provide the most flexibility.
- VPN concentrators incorporate the most advanced encryption and authentication techniques available. They are built specifically for creating a remote-access or site-to-site VPN and ideally are deployed where the requirement is for a single device to handle a very large number of VPN tunnels. They were specifically developed to address the requirement for a purpose-built, remote-access VPN device.
- You should already have a good firewall in place before you implement a VPN, but a firewall can also be used to terminate the VPN sessions. A firewall solution may, however, provide fewer sustained connections due to limitations in memory and hardware resources. In addition, the primary purpose of a firewall is to analyze traffic flows and enforce restrictive policies and may sub-optimize performance.
- Routers may also be used in smaller environments where just a few connections are required, or where only one connection must be maintained for all traffic.
- Most operating systems support end-station IPSec connections which enable end-to-end security. This option most often uses transport mode.
- User authentication is not standardized between IPSec implementations. It is either done in a vendor proprietary method, or L2TP is added to provide the authentication segment.

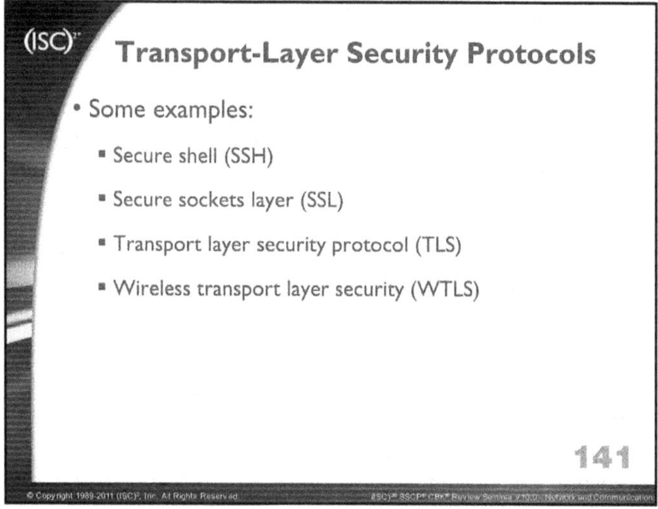
(ISC)²
Transport-Layer Security Protocols
Some examples:
Secure shell (SSH)
Secure sockets layer (SSL)
Transport layer security protocol (TLS)
Wireless transport layer security (WTLS)
141

- There are a number of methods of providing a secure and authenticated channel between hosts on the Internet above the transport layer. The standard protocol specification provides methods for implementing privacy, authentication, and integrity for applications above the transport layer. From a model perspective, SSL and TLS are in the transport layer, but when implemented the software is a "shim" that sits above the transport layer, and below the TCP/IP application layer above it.
- We will discuss secure shell (SSH), secure sockets layer (SSL), transport layer security protocol (TLS), and wireless transport layer security (WTLS) in the slides that follow.

## Secure Sockets Layer (SSL)

- Enables client/server applications to communicate securely, minimizing the risk of eavesdropping, tampering, or message forgery
- Provides data confidentiality, integrity control, server authentication, and optionally, client authentication
- Two layer protocol:
  - SSL handshake protocol - used to establish an SSL connection
  - SSL record protocol - used to pass messages

142



- **SECURE SOCKET LAYER (SSL) –** The SSL handshake protocol was developed by Netscape Communications Corp. to provide security and privacy over the Internet. It supports server and client authentication. The primary goal of the SSL protocol is to provide privacy and reliability between two communicating applications. The protocol is composed of two layers:
  - At the lowest level, layered on top of some reliable transport (e.g., TCP/IP), is the SSL record protocol. The SSL record protocol is used for encapsulation of various higher level protocols. One such encapsulated protocol, the SSL handshake protocol, allows the server and client to authenticate each other and to negotiate an encryption algorithm and cryptographic keys before the application protocol transmits or receives its first byte of data. One advantage of SSL is that it is application protocol independent.
  - A higher-level protocol (such as HTTP, FTP or Telnet) can layer on top of the SSL protocol transparently. SSL is application independent.
- **SSL PROTOCOL PROVIDES CONNECTION SECURITY WITH 3 BASIC PROPERTIES:**
  - The connection is private. Encryption is used after an initial handshake to define a secret key. Symmetric cryptography is used for data encryption (e.g., DES, RC4, etc.).
  - The peer's identity can be authenticated using asymmetric, or public key, cryptography (e.g., RSA, DSS, etc.).
  - The connection is reliable. Message transport includes a message integrity check using a keyed hash. Secure hash functions (e.g., SHA, MD5, etc.) are used for HMAC computations.
- SSL handshake protocol consists of two phases: server authentication and client authentication, with the second phase being optional.
  - In the first phase, the server, in response to a client's request, sends its certificate and its cipher preferences. The client then generates a master key, which it encrypts with the server's public key. It transmits this encrypted master key to the server. The server recovers the master key and authenticates itself to the client by returning a message encrypted with the master key. Subsequent data is encrypted with keys derived from this master key.
  - In the optional second phase, the server sends a challenge to the client. The client authenticates itself to the server by returning the client's digital signature on the challenge, as well as its public-key certificate.
- Secure sockets layer (currently at version 3.0) is a security protocol that provides communications privacy over the Internet. The protocol allows client/server applications to communicate in a way that is designed to prevent eavesdropping, tampering, or message forgery.
- HTTP over SSL typically uses TCP port 443.
- A proposed standard for user authentication is a Kerberos over TLS spec (RFC 2712).

## Transport Layer Security (TLS)

- Based on, and backward compatible with, SSL version 3.0
- Provides for authentication and data protection for communication between two entities
- Supports client authentication as well as server authentication

143



- The TLS Working Group was established in 1996 to standardize a "transport layer" security protocol. TLS is based on, and backward compatible with, SSL version 3.0.
- **TLS VERSION 1 (RFC 2246, 1999) –** Designed as an independent upgrade to SSL version 3. Although they are not interoperable, TLS has a feature permitting downgrading to SSL for compatibility. The basic enhancement is mutual (client and server) authentication.
- **TLS VERSION 1.1 (RFC 4346, 2006) –** This version featured improvements in the cryptographic processes to mitigate several identified attacks, including attacks against internal/implicit IVs, as well as compliance with IANA registration requirements for interoperability.
- **TLS VERSION 1.2 (RFC 5246, 2008) –** Adds support for stronger cryptographic algorithms, including SHA-256 and AES.
- An extensive explanation of each version, as well as the history of the protocol, may be found at: http://en.wikipedia.org/wiki/Transport_Layer_Security. (Although this source is not necessarily authoritative, references to authoritative RFCs and standards are listed for further study.)

### Wireless Transport Layer Security (WTLS)

- Security in the wireless application protocol (WAP) v1.2 uses WTLS instead of standard SSL
- Wireless gateways must use WTLS to secure the channel to the wireless device and SSL to secure the channel from the destination web server
- Security issue: The information on the gateway is unencrypted

144



(ISC)²® SSCP® CBK® Review Seminar v10.0 – Networks and Communications

- **WIRELESS TRANSPORT LAYER SECURITY (WTLS) –** WTLS provides SSL-like transport-level security for wireless devices that use the WAP protocol. WAP is a network protocol that is much like TCP/IP for wireless phones, but much simpler and, therefore, more suitable for situations with limited bandwidth and processing power.
- Like SSL, wireless transport layer security makes user authentication using digital certificates optional. WIM (WAP identity module) modules are smart cards that hold the digital certificate and private key that make the user authentication work and reduce the chance that someone can impersonate someone else with another mobile phone. There are three modes of authentication: Mode 1 is unauthenticated, Mode 2 authenticates the server with a digital certificate, and Mode 3 authenticates both the server and client.
- From a security perspective, the hope is that mobile phones will transition from WWML/WAP/WTLS to the standard HTML/HTTP/SSL, which the rest of the Internet uses as they gain CPU power. Remember, in a hybrid crypto model, the client needs to have the root CA certificate preloaded to be able to verify the digital signature on the server's public key certificate. Public key cryptography provides key distribution and digital signatures (with hash functions) for integrity. Secret keys are used for bulk data encryption.

### Socket Security (SOCKS)

- Circuit-level proxy that contains authentication and encryption features
  - Usually used to allow internal computers access to the external Internet
  - Can be used for tunneling to allow external users access to the internal network
  - Requires client applications to be "SOCKS-ified"

145



(ISC)²® SSCP® CBK® Review Seminar v10.0 – Networks and Communications

- **SOCKET SECURITY (SOCKS) –** SOCKS is not a traditional VPN protocol. It is most often used in a reverse fashion, allowing internal computers access to the external Internet through a firewall. It does contain authentication and encryption features similar to VPN products, however, and can equally be used to allow external access to the internal network. SOCKS is a "unidirectional" protocol, meaning that it allows clients to access servers but does not allow anybody to access the client. Client software is available for non-Windows desktops.
- SOCKS can be proxied, unlike most other tunneling protocols. SOCKS is documented in RFC 1928.

(ISC)²

## Secure Shell (SSH, SSH2)

- SSH
  - Powerful method of performing client authentication
  - Safeguards multiple service sessions between two systems
- Provides support for:
  - Host and user authentication
  - Data compression
  - Data confidentiality and integrity
- Credentials are validated by digital certificate exchange using RSA

146



(ISC)² SSCP® CBK® Review Seminar v10 - Networks and Communications

- **SECURE SHELL (SSH, SSH2) –** Secure shell is a powerful method of performing client authentication and safeguarding multiple service sessions between two systems. Written by a Finnish student, Tatu Ylonen, SSH has received widespread acceptance within the UNIX world. The protocol has been ported to all other operating systems, including Win95/98/2000.
- Systems running SSH listen on port 22 for incoming connection requests. When two systems establish a connection, they validate each other's credentials by performing a digital certificate exchange using RSA. Triple DES is then used to encrypt all information that is exchanged between the two systems. The two hosts will authenticate each other in the course of the communication session and periodically change encryption keys. This helps to ensure that "brute force" or "playback" attacks are not effective.
- SSH is an excellent method of securing protocols that are known to be insecure. For example, Telnet and FTP sessions exchange all authentication information in the clear – but SSH can encapsulate these sessions to ensure that no clear text information is visible.

(ISC)²

## Application Layer Security Protocols

- Secure remote procedure call (S-RPC)
- Domain name system security (DNSSec)
- Secure MIME (S/MIME) email security
- Secure WWW transactions (S-HTTP)
- Electronic payment schemes (SET, Ecash, Netcash, Mondex, Cybercash, etc.)

147



- **APPLICATION LAYER SECURITY PROTOCOLS –** There are two types of application layer security protocols: those that enhance the security of existing protocols such as HTTP, Telnet, etc.,; and those that have been set up for authentication and key distribution systems, such as Kerberos and Sesame.
- **SECURE REMOTE PROCEDURE CALL (S-RPC) –** S-RPC is a security protocol based on DES encryption that is built into the RPC software. Remote programs that use S-RPC expect client users to have a public/secret key entry in a shared master /etc/publickey file. Access to S-RPC programs is controlled by the keyserv daemon that accesses the /etc/publickey file when users invoke keylogin. There is one /etc/publickey database for each S-RPC domain. S-RPC users must be given entries in /etc/publickey by the RPC administrator before they can use S-RPC programs.
- **DOMAIN NAME SYSTEM SECURITY (DNSSEC) –** DNSSec adds security to the domain name system (DNS) used on IP networks. DNSSec is a set of extensions to DNS that provide origin authentication of DNS data, data integrity, and authenticated denial of existence. DNSSEC was designed to protect the Internet from certain attacks such as DNS cache poisoning. All answers in DNSSEC are digitally signed. By checking the signature, a DNS resolver is able to check to see whether the information is identical (correct and complete) to the information on the authoritative DNS server.
  - There are several distinct classes of threats to the DNS, most of which are DNS-related instances of more general problems, but a few of which are specific to peculiarities of the DNS protocol. RFC 3833 attempts to document some of the known threats to the DNS and in doing so, attempts to measure the extent to which DNSSec is a useful tool in defending against these threats. Note that DNSSec does not provide confidentiality of data, nor does it protect against denial of service (DoS) attacks. The DNSSec specifications (called DNSSEC-bis) describe the current DNSSEC protocol in great detail. See RFC 4033, 4034, and 4035. (Note that with the publication of these new RFCs in March 2005, RFC 2535 has become obsolete.)
- **SECURE MULTIPURPOSE INTERNET MAIL EXTENSIONS (S/MIME) –** Originally developed by RSA, S/MIME was heavily backed by most early Internet developers, which may explain some of its success and why it has become the de facto standard for email privacy and authentication services. Building from PEM and MOSS, it is based on public key cryptography standards (PKCS) and focuses strictly on a hierarchical trust model based on certification authorities, although self-signed certificates can be supported. Most commercial implementations use RSA for asymmetric key cryptography, Triple DES for symmetric key, and SHA-1 for hashing. Some will also support other algorithms (for example, AES for confidentiality, elliptic-curve for asymmetric and DSS for signature services). Many implementations are available as plug-ins to common email client software.
  - Typical email offers no security or privacy protection (cleartext).
  - Email security protocols use cryptographic techniques to provide message integrity and encryption services as well as key management and non-repudiation in some cases.
- **SECURE HYPERTEXT TRANSFER PROTOCOL (S-HTTP) –** As opposed to the HTTP over TLS protocol, which relies on an underlying TLS or SSL tunnel to protect its connection, S-HTTP is an enhancement to HTTP 1.1 and aims to manage encryption entirely on the application layer. S-HTTP is designed to coexist with HTTP and can, for instance, use the same port. A server will distinguish an S-HTTP request from an HTTP request by header information. S-HTTP goes hand in hand with security extensions to HTML. S-HTTP is a highly flexible protocol that allows negotiation and re-negotiation of encryption mechanisms and security policies. Through its integration into the client/server requests, S-HTTP is more resilient than HTTP over TLS and in particular less susceptible to man-in-the-middle attacks and known plaintext attacks. An application can be selective in which parts of a request to encrypt and, thereby, enhance performance.
- **ELECTRONIC PAYMENT SCHEMES –** Payment systems developed by the financial industry to enable on-line purchases and transfers of funds. A number of schemes have evolved as proprietary and standard methods of enabling eCommerce, and are sometimes known as a payment mechanisms. Checks and drafts commonly are referred to as the paper-based payment system; electronic fund transfers, such as automated clearing house debits and credits, and Fed Wire transfers, are referred to as the electronic payment system or paperless systems.
  - Among these are systems used by credit card issuers (such as SET and MONDEX), and systems that are integrated into web commerce servers (PayPal, Cybercash, etc.).
  - A current industry issue is the development of 3G and 4G smartphone payment schemes which enable purchasers to use their smartphone for payments. First introduced in Japan and known as electronic wallet applications, users can wirelessly pay for gasoline, groceries, etc., by simply transmitting authorization from their phones. Ecash is an example. An interesting (though nonauthoritative) discussion is at http://en.wikipedia.org/wiki/Digital_wallet

---

**REFERENCE:**

http://www.w3.org/ECommerce/roadmap.html

(ISC)²

## Digital Rights Management

- Digital rights management (DRM) technologies
- Legal protection for intellectual property
  - Enforcement of licensing and use policies
  - Technologies include cryptographic schemes

148

(ISC)² SSCP® CBK® Review Seminar v10.0 – Network and Communications

- **DIGITAL RIGHTS MANAGEMENT (DRM) –** DRM technologies extend digital watermarking to place strict usage conditions on the display and reproduction of digital media.
  - It combines such techniques with emerging hardware and software platforms that strictly enforce the policies they embed into every piece of DRM-protected digital media.
  - They are also known as digital restriction management technologies, and are not without their critics, who argue that these technologies conflict with so-called "fair use" exceptions to the rights of copyright holders.
  - DRM: employs steganography and other techniques to enforce strict usage conditions that will be enforced by DRM hardware/software solutions.

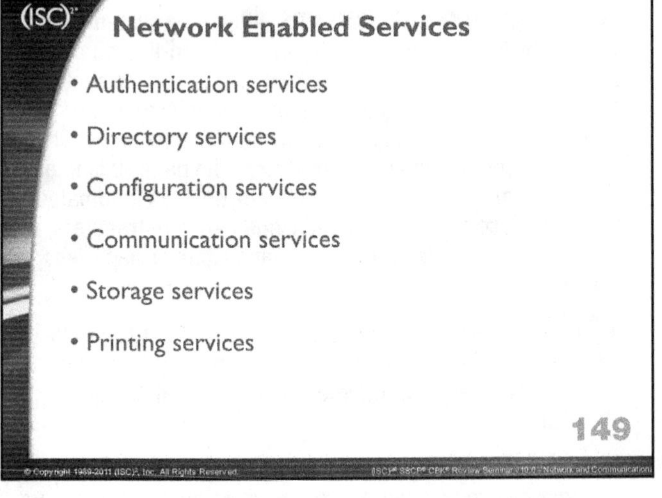
(ISC)²
Network Enabled Services
• Authentication services
• Directory services
• Configuration services
• Communication services
• Storage services
• Printing services
149

- This is a basic categorization of services for this section.

(ISC)²

## Authentication Services

- Centralized authentication
  - Better adherence to policy
  - Generally cheaper to implement
  - Less flexible
  - Examples include Kerberos, TACACS+, and RADIUS
- Decentralized
  - More aligned to business requirements
  - May be more complex/costly
  - Examples include SESAME, certificates, etc.

150



- A major issue with implementing authentication controls in network environments is trying to prevent replay attacks, where an attacker captures credentials off the wire and tries to play them back at a later time. The two techniques used to catch this are:
  - Timestamps in the credentials, to make them invalid after a period of time (Kerberos).
  - A nonce in the credentials, which is a random number which is only used once (many of the other protocols, and parts of Kerberos).
- Another major issue with any authentication system is the susceptibility to password guessing attacks. As we learned in the Access Controls module, any password based (one-factor) authentication system is vulnerable to a brute force password guessing attack. Only two-factor systems can really address this risk. Typically this means token cards, smart cards with digital certificates, or biometrics.
- Here is how the next set of protocols fit together: The remote user connects to our network access server (NAS) using PPP, and one of the PPP authentication methods is used to either authenticate the user, or the node. Typically, the NAS doesn't have the ability to perform the authentication itself. Instead, the NAS uses a centralized access control protocol to submit a query to a central database, where the user authentication finally takes place. The PPP authentication protocols (PAP, CHAP, and EAP) are used to establish the link between the remote user on the untrusted network and the NAS, and the centralized access control protocols (RADIUS, TACACS+, etc.), are used over the trusted network, back from the NAS to the centralized authentication server.
- **REMOTE AUTHENTICATION DIAL-IN USER SERVICE (RADIUS) –** RADIUS is an authentication protocol used mainly in networked environments, such as Internet service providers (ISP); or for similar services requiring single sign-on for Layer 3 network access, for scalable authentication combined with an "acceptable" degree of security. On top of this, RADIUS provides support for consumption measurement such as connection time. RADIUS authentication is based on provision of simple username/password credentials. These credentials are encrypted by the client using a shared secret with the RADIUS server. RADIUS is vulnerable to a number of cryptographic attacks and can be successfully attacked with a replay attack. RADIUS also suffers from a lack of integrity protection due to the fact that just specific fields are transmitted encrypted. Nonetheless, within its usual scope of deployment, RADIUS is generally considered to be sufficiently secure. An ISP in particular will want to balance the risk of unauthorized access (and theft of bandwidth) with deployment cost. As RADIUS is relatively easy to deploy and supported by a large number of devices in the market, its resulting cost reduction will offset the ISP's risk. Conversely, RADIUS may not be sufficiently secure for higher security requirements, such as access to a corporate network. In these cases, the added security offered by VPNs or IPSEC is clearly desirable.

**REFERENCES:**

http://publib.boulder.ibm.com/infocenter/pseries/v5r3/index.jsp?topic=/com.ibm.aix.security/doc/security/radius_server.htm

http://www.untruth.org/~josh/security/radius/radius-auth.html

(ISC)²

## Directory Services

- Domain name service (DNS)
- Lightweight directory access protocol (LDAP)
- Network basic input output system (NetBios)
- Network information service (NIS/NIS+)

151



- **DOMAIN NAME SERVICE (DNS) –** Of the network services below the application layer, the DNS is arguably one of the most prominent and the most visible to the end user. The reason for this is the DNS's role in email and WWW addresses (uniform resource locators [URLs]), which have become an ubiquitous element of everyday life as well as in advertising or private communication. By virtue of this fact, DNS has become a prominent target of attack, aggravating preexistent weaknesses in the protocol. By manipulating DNS, it is easily possible to divert, intercept, or prevent the vast majority of end user communications without having to resort to attacking any end user devices. The DNS as a whole is in fact a distributed, hierarchical database. Through its caching architecture, it possesses a remarkable degree of robustness, flexibility, and scalability.
- Conversely, DNS does not enforce data consistency and integrity, its built-in authentication mechanisms are weak and management of the global DNS infrastructure has become a subject of political and economical controversy. The objects it manages – domain names – are often the subject of local and global trademark disputes. DNS's central element is a set of hierarchical name (domain) trees, starting from a so-called top level domain (TLD). A number of so-called root servers manage the authoritative list of TLD servers. In order to resolve any domain name, each DNS in the world must hold a list of these root servers. Various extensions to DNS have been proposed, in order to enhance its functionality and security.
- **LIGHTWEIGHT DIRECTORY ACCESS PROTOCOL (LDAP) –** LDAP is a client-server based directory query protocol loosely based upon X.500, commonly used for managing user information. As opposed to, for instance, DNS, LDAP is a front-end and not used to manage or synchronize data per se. Back-ends to LDAP can be directory services, such as NIS, Lotus Notes, Microsoft Exchange, etc. LDAP provides only weak authentication based on hostname resolution. It would, therefore, be easy to subvert LDAP security by breaking DNS. LDAP communication is transferred in clear text and, therefore, is trivial to intercept.
- One way to address the issues of weak authentication and clear text communication is the deployment of LDAP over SSL, providing authentication, integrity, and confidentiality. Various other extensions to LDAP have been proposed in order to address these shortcomings; however, they haven't been widely accepted. A reason for this could be that LDAP was meant to be simple. Building a strong authentication and encryption framework around it, could at least to a certain extent defeat that purpose. Note, however, that Microsoft Active Directory does address these through its use of Kerberos. LDAP is also the basis of Microsoft's Active Directory Service (ADS). Applications such as Microsoft NetMeeting are making heavy use of LDAP for this reason. As opposed to its predecessor, NetBIOS, ADS is fully TCP/IP and DNS based. ADS authentication is based on Kerberos.
- **NETWORK BASIC INPUT OUTPUT SYSTEM (NETBIOS) –** The NetBIOS API was developed in 1983 by IBM. NetBIOS was later ported to TCP/IP (NetBIOS over TCP/IP, also known as NetBT). However, implementations running on top of NetBEUI or IPX are still in use. NetBIOS is susceptible to a number of attacks. Exploiting the fact that its credentials are static, a user can inadvertently deliver his credentials through the attacker tricking the user's host by setting up a NetBIOS connection with a host under an attacker's control. NetBIOS services can be used for information collection (they will disclose information on users, hosts and domains). NetBIOS ports have become popular targets of attacks for Internet worms. Circulating exploits rely on weaknesses in the implementation of NetBIOS, not in the protocol itself.
- **NETWORK INFORMATION SERVICE (NIS/NIS+) –** NIS and NIS+ are directory services developed by Sun Microsystems, which are mostly used in Unix environments. They are commonly used for managing user credentials across a group of machines, for instance, a Unix workstation cluster or client/server environment, but can be used for other types of directories. NIS is using a flat name space in so-called domains. It is based on RPC and manages all entities on a server (NIS server). NIS Servers can be set up redundantly through the use of so-called slave servers.
- **NIS –** Is known for a number of security weaknesses.
  - The fact that NIS does not authenticate individual RPC requests can be used to spoof responses to NIS requests from a client. This would, for instance, enable an attacker to inject fake credentials and, thereby, obtain or escalate privileges on the target machine.
  - Retrieval of directory information is possible if the name of an NIS domain has become known or is guessable, as any client can associate themselves with an NIS domain.
  - Conversely, the fact that a NIS server is an attractive target of attacks cannot be considered a weakness of NIS as such; it is in fact an architectural issue with all client/server platforms.
  - A number of guides have been published on how to secure NIS servers. The basic steps here are to secure the platform an NIS server is running on, to isolate the NIS server from traffic outside of a LAN, and to configure it in a way that limits the probability for disclosure of authentication credentials, especially system privileged ones.
- **NIS+ –** Authentication and authorization concepts in NIS+ are more mature, they require authentication for each access of a directory object. However, NIS+ authentication in itself will only be as strong as authentication to one of the clients in a NIS+ environment, as NIS+ builds on a trust relationship between different hosts. The most relevant attacks against a correctly configured NIS+ network comes from attacks against its cryptographic security. NIS+ can be run at different security levels, however, most levels available are irrelevant for an operational network.

**REFERENCE:**

http://www.ehsco.com/reading/19961215ncf1.html

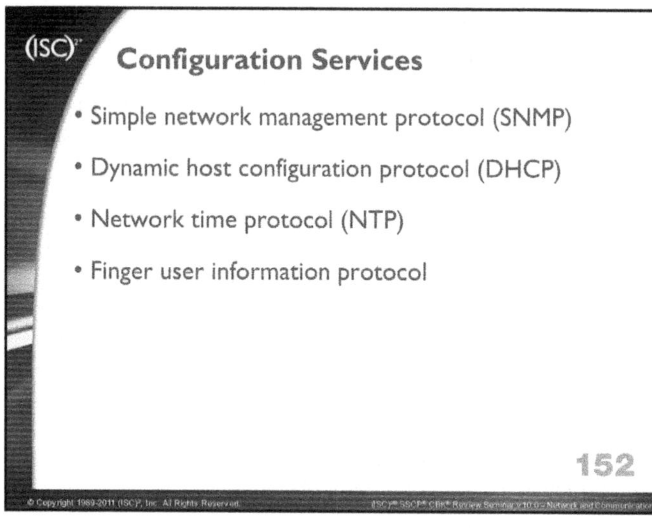


- **SIMPLE NETWORK MANAGEMENT PROTOCOL (SNMP)** – SNMP is a protocol designed to manage network infrastructure. While its basic architecture is a fairly simple client server architecture with a relatively limited set of commands, managing a network via SNMP is anything but "simple," and there are security issues associated with SNMP.
- SNMP architecture consists of a management server (called "manager" in SNMP terminology) and a client, usually installed on network devices (such as routers and switches – called an "agent"). SNMP allows the manager to retrieve ("get") values of variables from the agent as well as "set" variables. Such variables could be routing tables or performance monitoring information.
- While SNMP has proven to be remarkably robust and scalable, and its near omnipresence suggests a high degree of resilience against common attacks, it does have a number of clear weaknesses. Some of them are by design; others are subject to configuration parameters. Probably the most easily exploited SNMP vulnerability is a brute force attack on default or easily guessable passwords. Given the scale of deployment combined, perhaps with the relative inexperience of network administrators, it is certainly a realistic scenario, and a potentially severe but easily mitigated risk.
- **DYNAMIC HOST CONFIGURATION PROTOCOL (DHCP)** – According to RPC 2131: "DHCP provides a framework for passing configuration information to hosts on a TCP/IP network. DHCP is based on the bootstrap protocol (BOOTP), adding the capability of automatic allocation of reusable network addresses and additional configuration options…" It assigns IP address and other configuration information to a host.
- **NETWORK TIME PROTOCOL (NTP)** – NTP is a protocol to synchronize computer clocks in a network. This can be extremely important for operational stability (for instance, under NIS), but also for maintaining consistency and coherence of audit trails (for instance, in log files). A variant of NTP exists in simple network time protocol (SNTP), offering a less resource-consuming, but also less exact, form of synchronization.
- From a security perspective, our main objective with NTP is to prevent an attacker from changing time information on a client or a whole network by manipulating its local time server. NTP can be configured to restrict access based upon IP address. From NTP version 3 onwards, cryptographic authentication has become available, based upon symmetric encryption, but replaced by public key cryptography in NTP version 4. In order to make a network robust against accidental or deliberate timing inaccuracies, a network should have its own time server and possibly a dedicated, highly accurate clock. As a standard precaution, a network should never depend on one external time server alone, but synchronize with several trusted time sources. Manipulation of a single source will have no immediate effect. In order to detect de-synchronization, standard logging mechanisms can be used with NTP to ensure synchronicity of time stamping.
- **FINGER USER INFORMATION PROTOCOL** – "Finger" is an identification service that allows a user to obtain information about the last login time of a user and whether or not he is currently logged into a system. The Fingered user may have information from two files in his home directory displayed (the ".project" and the ".plan" file). Developed as early as 1971, Finger is implemented as a Unix daemon, fingerd. Finger has become less popular, for several reasons:
  - Finger has been the subject of a number of security exploits.
  - Finger is raising privacy and security concerns; it can easily be abused for social engineering attacks.
  - The user's self actuation (an important social aspect in early Unix networks) happens on Web pages today.
  - For all practical purposes, the Finger protocol has become obsolete. Its use should be restricted to situations where no alternatives are available.

---

**REFERENCE:**

http://tools.ietf.org/html/rfc2131

(ISC)²

## Communication Services

- Synchronous messaging
  - Instant messaging
  - Internet relay chat (IRC)
- Asynchronous messaging
  - Simple mail transfer protocol (SMTP)
  - Post office protocol (POP)
  - Internet message access protocol (IMAP)
  - Network news transfer protocol (NNTP)

153



(ISC)² SSCP® CBK® Review Seminar v10.0 – Network and Communication

- **SYNCHRONOUS MESSAGING –**
  - **INSTANT MESSAGING –** Instant messaging systems can generally be categorized in three classes: Peer-to-peer networks, brokered communication, and server-oriented networks. Most chat applications do offer additional services beyond their text messaging capability, such as, screen sharing, remote control, exchange of files, voice and video conversation. Some applications allow command scripting. VOIP is also converging with IM technology.
  - **INTERNET RELAY CHAT (IRC) –** RFC 2810 to 2813 – was developed as a text-based communication. The server's role can be to directly or indirectly send (relay) a message from client to client. Out of the widely deployed chat systems on the Internet, IRC was arguably the first one. IRC is still popular in academia but has lost its dominant position to commercial services. Communication is organized in public discussion groups ("channels") and "private" messaging between individual users. IRC is a client-server based network. IRC is unencrypted, and, therefore, an easy target for sniffing attacks.
- **ASYNCHRONOUS MESSAGING –**
  - **SIMPLE MAIL TRANSFER PROTOCOL (SMTP) –** RFC 2821 – A server-to-server, store-and-forward protocol for electronic mail. SMTP is a protocol to route email on the Internet. SMTP is pervasive and used for practically all mail routing outside of closed application networks (such as Lotus Notes). SMTP is a client-server protocol, using port 25/TCP; information on mail servers for Internet domains are managed through DNS (in so-called mail exchange (MX) records). While SMTP is taking a fairly simple approach towards authentication, it is fairly robust in the way it deals with unavailability; an SMTP server will try to deliver email over a configurable period of time. From a protocol perspective, SMTP's main shortcomings are its nonexistent authentication and its lack of encryption. Identification is performed by sender's email address. A mail server will be able to restrict sending access to certain hosts (which should be on the same network as the mail server) as well as set conditions on the sender's email address (which should be one of a domain served by this particular mail server). Otherwise, the mail server may be configured as an open relay.
  - **POST OFFICE PROTOCOL (POP) –** RFC 1939 – A client-to-server email protocol that operates in a download and delete approach. While SMTP addresses the task of sending and receiving e-mail on a server, POP solves the problem of accessing email on a server from a client. Widely implemented in its current (and probably last) version 3 ("POP3"), POP does, however, only offer basic functionality, such as username/password authentication and unencrypted transmission. Modern email clients, therefore, rely on encryption through TLS to at least provide secure transmission in order to protect the confidentiality and integrity of a message. Once downloaded onto a client, email will be protected only by the client's operating system security.
  - **INTERNET MESSAGE ACCESS PROTOCOL (IMAP) –** RFC 3501 – Functional enhancements over POP are: concurrent access from different clients to different mailboxes, as well as the ability to synchronize email to a client from a server. IMAP offers native support for encrypted authentication as well as encrypted data transfer. IMAP supports plain text transmission if forced by the server.
  - **NETWORK NEWS TRANSFER PROTOCOL (NNTP) –** RFC 3977 – Network news was one of the first discussion systems on the Internet, pre-dating web-based discussion forums and loosely modeled after former dial-up "mailbox" electronic discussion systems. It has been replaced by HTTP thread-based discussion in most cases.

(ISC)²

## Remote Communication Services

- TCP/IP terminal emulation protocol (TELNET)
- Remote login (RLOGIN), remote shell (RSH), remote copy (RCP)
- X window system (X11)

154



- **REMOTE COMMUNICATION SERVICES –** TELNET, RLOGIN, and X11, are present in many Unix operations, and when combined with NFS and NIS they provide the user with seamless remote working capabilities. But, they do in fact form a risky combination if not administrated properly. Conceptually, because they are built on mutual trust, they can be misused to obtain access and to horizontally and vertically escalate privileges in an attack. Their authentication and transmission capabilities are insecure by design; and therefore, had to be retrofitted (as X11) or replaced altogether (TELNET and rlogin by SSH).
- **TCP/IP TERMINAL EMULATION PROTOCOL (TELNET) –** TELNET is a command line protocol designed to give command line access to another host. While implementations for Windows exist, TELNET's original domain was the Unix server world, and a TELNET server is standard equipment for any Unix server (whether it should in fact be enabled is another question, but in small LAN environments, TELNET is still widely used.). Being a fairly low level TCP implementation, a TCP client can be used to emulate other protocols. TELNET offers little security and indeed its use poses serious security risks in untrusted environments. TELNET is limited to username/password authentication and does not offer encryption. Once an attacker has obtained even a normal user's credentials, he has an easy road toward privilege escalation, as he can not just transfer data from and to a machine but also execute commands. As the TELNET server is running under system privileges, it is an attractive target of attack in itself. Exploits in TELNET servers pave the way to system privileges for an attacker. It is, therefore, reasonable to discontinue use of TELNET over the Internet and on Internet facing machines. In fact, the standard hardening procedure for any Internet facing server should include disabling its TELNET service (which under Unix systems would normally run under the name of telnetd).
- **REMOTE LOGIN (RLOGIN), REMOTE SHELL (RSH), REMOTE COPY (RCP) –** In its most generic form, RLOGIN is a protocol used for granting remote access to a machine, normally a Unix server. Similarly, RSH grants direct remote command execution while RCP copies data from or to a remote machine. If an RLOGIN daemon (rlogind) is running on a machine, RLOGIN access can be granted in two ways, by a central configuration file or by a user configuration. By the latter, a user may grant access that was not permitted by the system administrator. The same mechanism applies to RSH and RCP, while they are relying on a different daemon (rshd). Authentication can be considered host/IP address based. While RLOGIN grants access based on user ID, this is not in fact verified, i.e., the ID a remote client claims to possess is taken for granted if the request comes from a trusted host. The RLOGIN protocol transmits data without encryption and is, hence, subject to eavesdropping and interception. The RLOGIN protocol is of limited value – its main benefit can be considered its main drawback, namely remote access without supplying a password. It should only be used in trusted networks, if at all. A drastically more secure replacement is available in the form of SSH for RLOGIN, RSH, and RCP.
- **X WINDOW SYSTEM (X11) –** The X window system is a comprehensive environment for remote control and display of applications. While its original realm is the world of Unix workstations, implementations exist for other operating systems, such as Windows and Mac OSX. X window is composed of a server (which is running on the user's client), used to display graphics and send local events such as mouse clicks back to the client (the remote machine). The X window system's core functionality is also its key risk from a security perspective. X Window allows remote administration and remote display of graphics. If the server is not adequately configured, any client on the Internet can, for instance, use it to display graphics on an attached console. This may sound humorous at first (and in fact has been the subject of many lab pranks). It would, however, be equally possible to use an open X window server for eavesdropping, screen shots and key logging. The X window system is built on unencrypted communication. This can be addressed by using lower layer encryption or by tunneling the X window system (e.g., SSH). Based on its simple security model that can be used to subvert and compromise other, stronger authentication mechanisms, the X window system should only be used in trusted environments, for instance, in a LAN based Unix cluster. Running X11 servers on the Internet bares serious risks and Internet facing servers should never have X11 running.

(ISC)²

## Storage and File Sharing Services

- Common Internet file system (CIFS)/server message block (SMB)
- Network file system (NFS)
- Secure NFS (SNFS)

155

 (ISC)²® SSCP® CBK® Review Seminar v10.0 Networks and Communication

- **COMMON INTERNET FILE SYSTEM (CIFS)/SERVER MESSAGE BLOCK (SMB) –** CIFS/SMB is a file sharing protocol prevalent on Windows systems. A Unix/Linux implementation exists in the free "Samba" project. SMB was originally designed to run on top of the NetBIOS (see section) protocol, it can, however, be run directly over TCP/IP. CIFS is capable of supporting user level and tree/object level (share level) security. Authentication can be performed via challenge/response authentication as well as by transmission of credentials in clear text. This second provision has been added largely for backward compatibility in legacy Windows environments. The main attacks against CIFS are based upon obtaining credentials, by sniffing for clear text authentication, or by cryptographic attacks.
- **NETWORK FILE SYSTEM (NFS) –** NFS is a client server file sharing system common to the Unix platform. It was originally developed by Sun Microsystems but implementations exist on all common Unix platforms including Linux, as well as Microsoft Windows. NFS has been revised several times.
- **SECURE NFS (SNFS) –** NFS offers secure authentication and encryption on the basis of Secure RPC, based on DES encryption. In contrast to standard NFS, Secure NFS (or rather Secure RPC) will authenticate each RPC request. This increases latency for each request as the authentication is being performed and introduces a light performance premium, mainly paid for in terms of computing capacity. Secure NFS uses DES encrypted time stamps as authentication tokens. If servers and clients do not have access to the same time server, this can lead to short-term interruptions until server and client have resynchronized themselves.

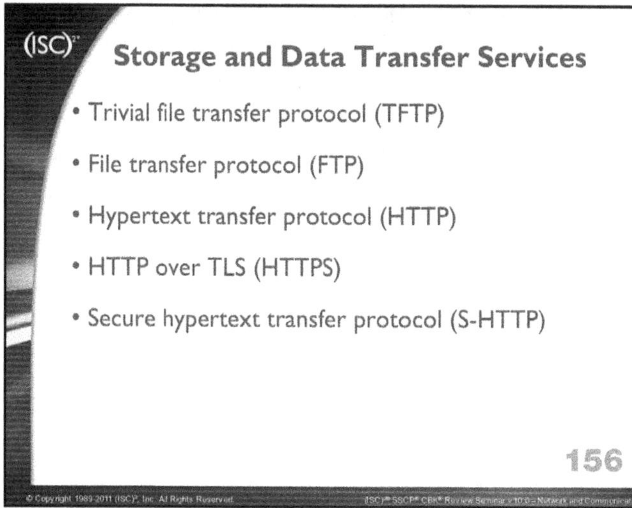
(ISC)²
Storage and Data Transfer Services
• Trivial file transfer protocol (TFTP)
• File transfer protocol (FTP)
• Hypertext transfer protocol (HTTP)
• HTTP over TLS (HTTPS)
• Secure hypertext transfer protocol (S-HTTP)
156

- **TRIVIAL FILE TRANSFER PROTOCOL (TFTP) –** TFTP is a simplified version of FTP, which is used when authentication isn't needed and quality of service is not an issue. TFTP runs on port 69/UDP. It should, therefore, only be used in trusted networks of low latency. In practice, TFTP is used mostly in LANs for the purpose of pulling packages (e.g., in booting up a diskless client).
- **FILE TRANSFER PROTOCOL (FTP) –** Before the advent of the World Wide Web and proliferation of HTTP (which is built on some of its features), FTP was "the" protocol to publish or disseminate data over the Internet. In its early days, the usual way to use FTP was in a non-firewalled environment from a Unix command shell. The protocol reflects some of the early design decisions made to support this environment, even though it is typically being used via dedicated FTP clients or web browsers. As opposed to, for instance, HTTP, FTP is a stateful protocol. FTP requires two communication channels: one control channel on port 21 under TCP, over which state information is exchanged; and a data channel on port 20, through which payload information is transmitted. In its original form, FTP authentication is simple, username/password authentication, and credentials as well as all data are transmitted in clear text. This makes the protocol subject to guessing or stealing of credentials, man-in-the-middle attacks, and sniffing. While this can be addressed by use of encryption on underlying layers, it is a severe drawback as additional effort is required for secure configuration and additional requirements to support encryption have to be met by the client.
- **HYPERTEXT TRANSFER PROTOCOL (HTTP) –** The HTTP protocol, originally conceived as a stateless, stripped-down version of the FTP protocol, was developed at the European Organization for Nuclear Research (CERN) in order to support the exchange of information in hypertext markup language (HTML). As HTTP is transmitting data in clear text and generates a slew of logging information on web servers and proxy servers along the road, resulting information can be readily used for competitor intelligence and illegitimate activities, such as industrial espionage activities or simply in order to satisfy a webmaster's curiosity. As a general rule, HTTP proxy servers should not allow queries from the Internet. It is best practice to separate application gateways (sometimes implemented as reverse proxies) from the proxy for Web browsing as both have very different security levels and business importance. It would be even better to implement the application gateway as an application proxy and not an HTTP proxy, but this isn't always possible.
- **HTTP OVER TLS (HTTPS) –** It is important to note that for most applications, the security offered (and touted) through the use of HTTP over TLS is limited to confidentiality (i.e., HTTP over TLS offers protection against eavesdropping, depending on the strength of encryption jointly supported by both client and server). Common Web browsers, which make for the main share of clients, support DES encryption, which is not a very high degree of protection (reference chapter cryptography). HTTP over TLS is broadly supported, is even recognized in the general public as a "secure" solution and has become a de facto standard for online retailers of all kinds, all of which are offering encrypted connections for their ordering and credit card billing systems. On the other hand, the very popularity of HTTPS can in fact lull the user into a false sense of security. The security offered by TLS is mostly used to protect against eavesdropping, while authentication is still based on username/password credentials. This opens up the possibility of man-in-the-middle attacks, which can be executed, for instance, by DNS spoofing.
- **SECURE HYPERTEXT TRANSFER PROTOCOL (S-HTTP) –** As opposed to the HTTP over TLS protocol, which relies on an underlying TLS or SSL tunnel to protect its connection, S-HTTP is an enhancement to HTTP 1.1 and aims to manage encryption entirely on the application layer. S-HTTP is designed to coexist with HTTP and can, for instance, use the same port. A server will distinguish an S-HTTP request from an HTTP request by header information. S-HTTP goes hand-in-hand with security extensions to HTML. S-HTTP is a highly flexible protocol that allows negotiation and renegotiation of encryption mechanisms and security policies. Through its integration into the client/server requests, S-HTTP is more resilient than HTTP over TLS and in particular less susceptible to man-in-the-middle attacks and known plaintext attacks. An application can be selective in which parts of a request to encrypt and, thereby, enhance performance.

---

**REFERENCE:**

http://www.phptr.com/articles/article.asp?p=169578&rl=1

## Printing Services

- Internet printer protocol (IPP)
- Line printer daemon (LPD)
- Common Unix printing system (CUPS)

157



- **INTERNET PRINTER PROTOCOL (IPP) –** IPP is an application layer protocol that can be used for distributed printing using Internet tools and technologies (RFC 2567).
- **LINE PRINTER DAEMON (LPD) –** The LPD protocol and line printer remote (LPR) were originally known as the Berkeley printing system because they were developed by Berkeley Unix systems. They provide storing or buffering to remote printing services.
- **COMMON UNIX PRINTING SYSTEM (CUPS) –** Is the open source alternative to LPD now maintained by Apple®.

**REFERENCES:**

IPP http://tools.ietf.org/html/rfc2910

LPD: http://tools.ietf.org/html/rfc1179

CUPS: http://www.cups.org/

## Network Monitoring Paradigm

"You can't consider the problem of defense without first understanding the problem of attack."

*- Doug Tygar, Professor of Computer Science and Information Management, University of California, Berkeley*

158

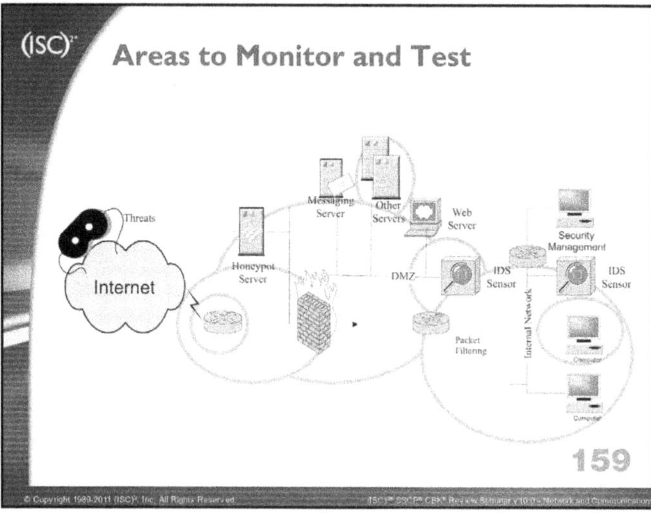


- **AREAS TO MONITOR AND TEST –** Include each major segment of the network infrastructure as well as all critical systems and resources accessible through the network. By using multiple zones of defense, each area can be designed to meet security best practices. They include techniques such as screening routers, firewalls, intrusion detection, antivirus protection, honeypot techniques, and other measures that add layers of protection.
- Note: Specific information about technology and testing activities is covered in the Audit and Monitoring domain.
- Defense-in-depth is the practice of "layering" defenses into defensive zones to increase overall the protection level and provide more reaction time to respond to incidents. It should be designed such that a failure in one safeguard is covered by another. This combines the capabilities of people, operations, and security technologies to establish multiple layers of protection, eliminating single lines of defense and effectively raising the cost of an attack.
- By treating individual countermeasures as part of an integrated suite of protective measures, the IT security practitioner is able to ensure that all vulnerabilities have been addressed. Managers must strengthen these defenses at critical locations and then be able to monitor attacks and react to them quickly.

(ISC)²

**Requirements for Monitoring and Testing**

- Some regulatory requirements specify minimum standards for risk assessments and vulnerability tests
  - PCI - Data Security Standard (PCI-DSS) (Section 6)
  - FISMA
- Requirements often include
  - Frequency of tests
  - Triggering events requiring re-testing
  - Specific types of data or business processes

160

- The common frequency for testing networks is annually. However, any of the following events/changes should include consideration for additional testing and review:
  - Security breaches that are discovered, especially those involving compromise of sensitive data.
  - Significant changes in infrastructure, such as deployment of wireless technologies.
  - Changes in regulations and laws.
  - Major changes in business processes.

(ISC)²

## Domain Agenda

- Network components and topologies
- Wide area and remote access networks
- Network standard protocols
- Network security protocols
- **Wireless network configuration and protection**
- Managing service reliability and quality

161



(ISC)²® SSCP® CBK® Review Seminar v10.0 – Network and Communications

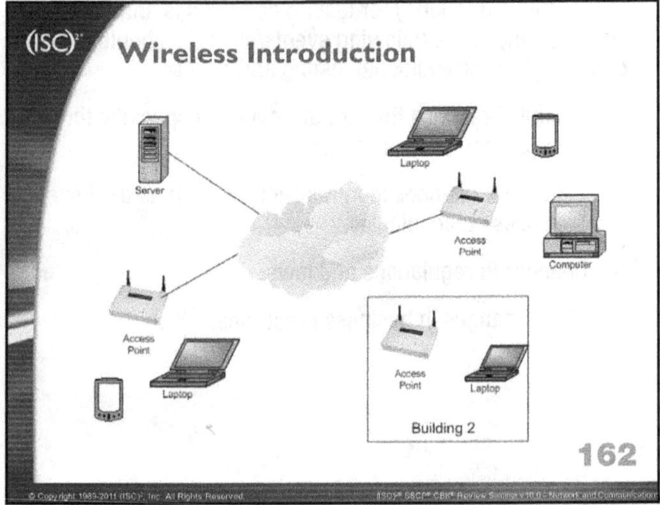


- **WIRELESS INTRODUCTION –** Wireless networks have become very popular for connecting devices within homes, small offices, and even in large office buildings. They are used to connect laptops, desktops, PDAs, and much more. Wireless has added a true feeling of mobility to using laptops and a feeling of freedom with a PDA in hand. Configuring a wireless network has proved to be fairly easy, despite the wide variety of products on the market. The question now is, what does wireless do to the security of a network? Some of the biggest security blunders with wireless networks are:
  - Not enabling encryption.
  - Forgetting that a wireless network can extend outside the perimeter of the building.
  - Broadcasting your wireless networks presence, or SSID (service set identifier). The SSID is the name of the wireless access point. Disabling the SSID broadcast of the SSID makes it more difficult to detect the wireless access point.
  - Treating the wireless network as an integral part of the wired network, rather than an insecure gateway to the wired network.
- Setting up a wireless network that is as secure as any of our wired networks is possible, but requires careful planning, execution, and testing.

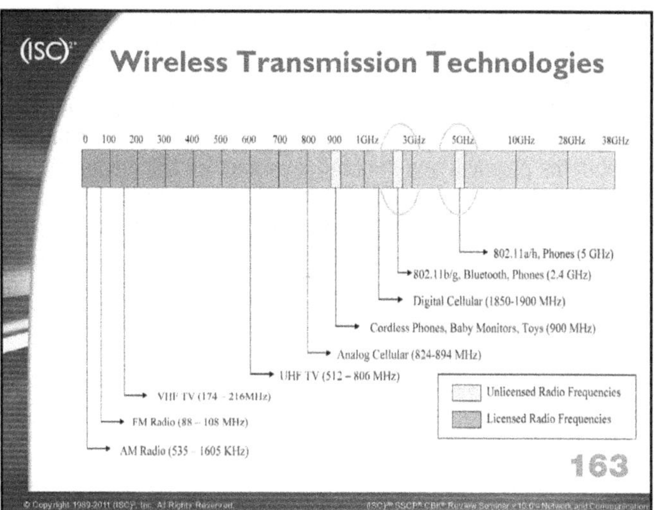


- **WIRELESS TRANSMISSION TECHNOLOGIES** – The electromagnetic spectrum is divided by radio bands. Wireless networks will typically operate on the upper end of the available spectrum.

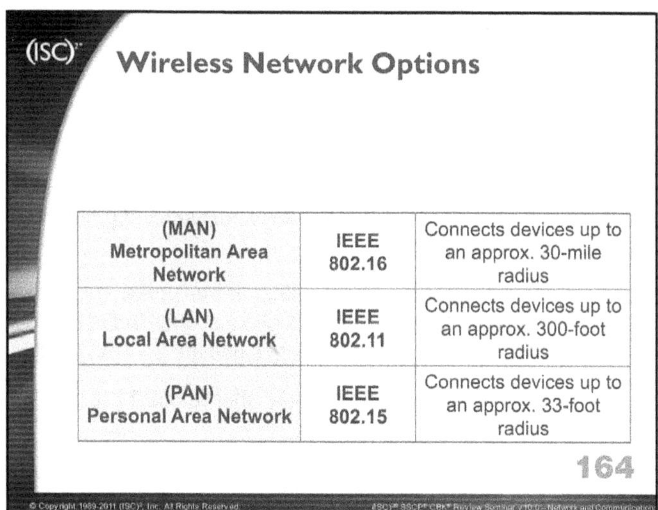


| | | |
|---|---|---|
| (MAN) Metropolitan Area Network | IEEE 802.16 | Connects devices up to an approx. 30-mile radius |
| (LAN) Local Area Network | IEEE 802.11 | Connects devices up to an approx. 300-foot radius |
| (PAN) Personal Area Network | IEEE 802.15 | Connects devices up to an approx. 33-foot radius |

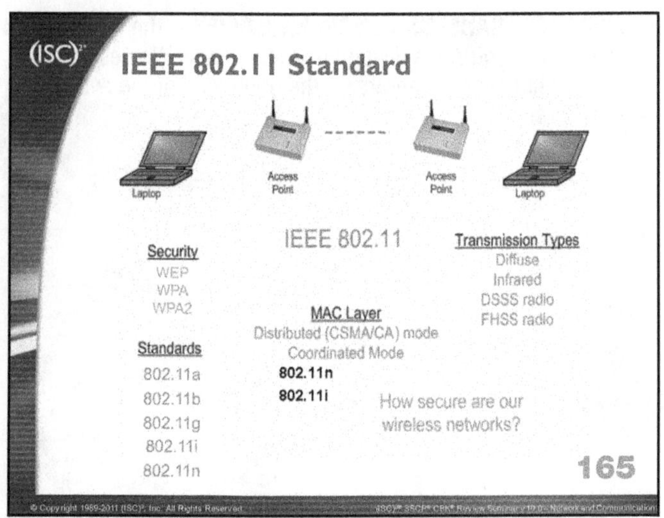


- **IEEE 802.11 STANDARD –** The IEEE committee for Local and Metropolitan Area Network Standards began the 802.11-working group in 1990. The first wireless standard was complete in 1997. 802.11 standards define the interface between wireless clients and their network access points, which includes both the physical and the MAC layers of the OSI model. These standards also define how roaming between access points and the wired equivalent privacy (WEP) security mechanism will work.
  - There are three transmission types defined within the 802.11 standard: infrared, DSSS radio, and FHSS radio.
  - The MAC layer has two main standards of operation: a distributed mode (CSMA/CA) and a coordinated mode.

**REFERENCE:**

www.ieee802.org/11/

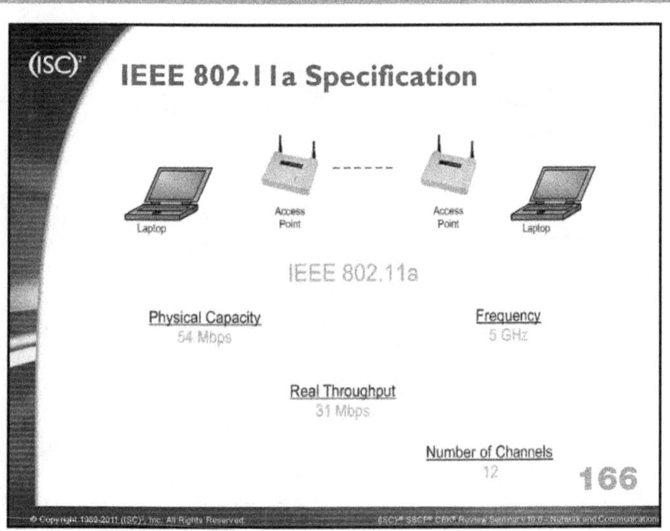


- **IEEE 802.11A SPECIFICATION –** The 802.11a specification was begun before 802.11b, but was completed later. 802.11a uses the 5-GHz band and is designed to send 54 Mbps using the new modulation scheme known as OFDM (orthogonal frequency division multiplexing).
- 802.11a and 802.11b are not compatible because they use different bands. Vendors are, however, making equipment that supports both standards.
- The 5 GHz range should provide cleaner transmissions. Other wireless devices such as cordless phones, microwave ovens, baby monitors, and Bluetooth devices use the 2.4 GHz band.
- The term WiFi is used to collectively refer to 802.11 a, b, g, and n.

**REFERENCE:**

For more info on WiFi, see the WIFI alliance at: www.wi-fi.org

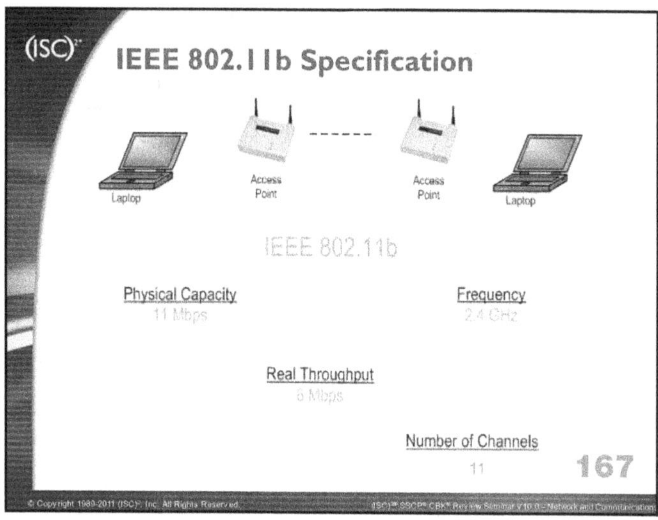


- **IEEE 802.11B SPECIFICATION –** 802.11b is the most widely recognized standard currently in use. This standard was approved in September 1999 and allows for transmission rates of up to 11 Mbps using the 2.4 GHz radio band. Due to media access control (MAC) overhead, errors, and collisions, however, the actual data transfer rate is about 6 Mbps.
- 802.11b uses complimentary code keying (CCK) and direct sequence spread spectrum (DSSS). These allow it to be fully backward compatible with DSSS implementations of 802.11. This standard is also referred to as WiFi.
- The 11 channels statement (or 12 in Europe) is somewhat misleading. All of the channels are individually available for 802.11a, but for 11b, a group of three consecutive channels must be used. This reduces the number to three non-overlapping channels in the US and four in Europe.

**REFERENCE:**

See the IEEE 802.11 working group at: http://grouper.ieee.org/groups/802/11/

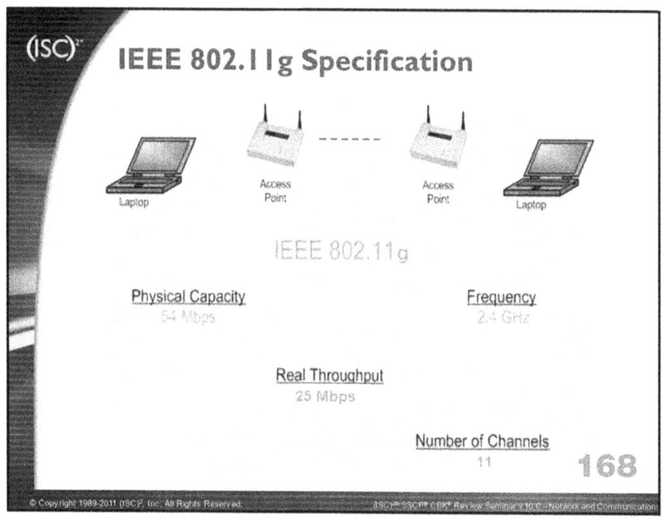


- **IEEE 802.11G SPECIFICATION –** 802.11g was approved by the IEEE on June 12, 2003, although vendors began shipping products well before this date. Like 802.11b, 802.11g is another high-speed extension of the standard. Like 802.11a, 802.11g uses OFDM. The differences, however, allow for transmission rates of up to 54 Mbps.
- 802.11g has backward compatibility and interoperability with 802.11b DSSS-based products, but the presence of an 802.11b device will slow down the operation of the entire network.
- One of the drawbacks of 802.11g is that it uses the same radio frequency as other devices such as wireless phones, microwaves, and Bluetooth devices. This can sometimes cause transmission interference.
- The three consecutive channel requirement of 802.11b also applies to 11g.

**REFERENCE:**

http://www.oreillynet.com/pub/a/wireless/2003/01/23/80211g.html

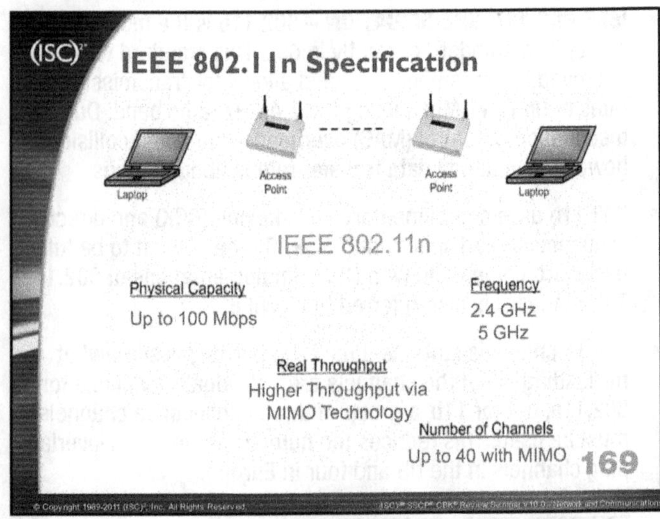


- **IEEE 802.11N SPECIFICATION –** 802.11n is a recent amendment which improves upon the previous 802.11 standards by adding multiple-input multiple-output (MIMO) and many other newer features. The IEEE has approved the amendment and it was published in October 2009. Like 802.11a, 802.11g uses OFDM. The differences, however, allow for much higher transmission rates (up to 150 Mbps) and significantly longer ranges.
- The key feature of 802.11n is MIMO, which supports multiple digital streams simultaneously, vastly improving performance at longer distances.
- 802.11n has backward compatibility and interoperability with 802.11b/g OFDM/DSSS-based products, but the presence of an 802.11b/g device will slow down the operation of the entire network.
- One of the drawbacks of 802.11n is potential transmission interference with other networks due to the increased power.

**REFERENCE:**

http://www.wi-fi.org/files/kc/WFA_802_11n_Consumers_May07.pdf

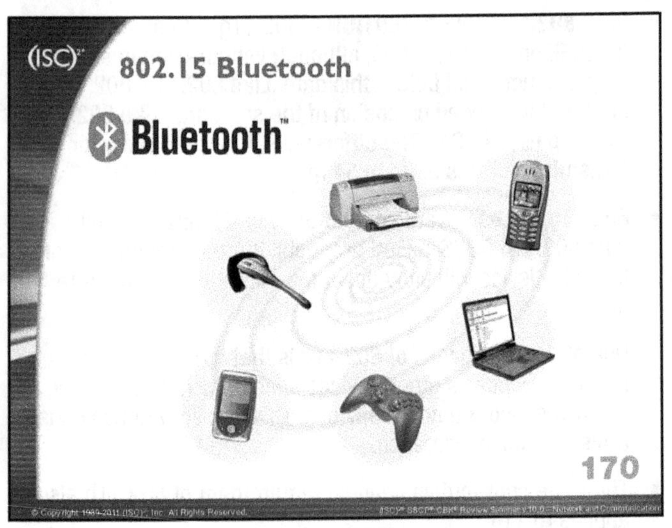


- **802.15 IS MORE COMMONLY KNOWN AS BLUETOOTH –** Bluetooth can be found in cell phones, cars, headsets, and many other very short-range communications devices.
- Although the official distance limitation is 15 meters, the signals can reach beyond that limit under optimal conditions. A Class 1 Bluetooth device, for instance, has a 100mW radio that is rated for 100m range officially, but can be detected from a significantly longer range using a directional antenna on the receiver.
- Like 802.11b/g, it operates in the 2.4 GHz frequency range.

**IMAGES:**

http://cp.home.agilent.com/upload/cmc_upload/Bluetooth_rings_lg.jpg

http://b2b.sony.com/Solutions/pages/BXShowcase/images/large/bluetoothTech.jpg

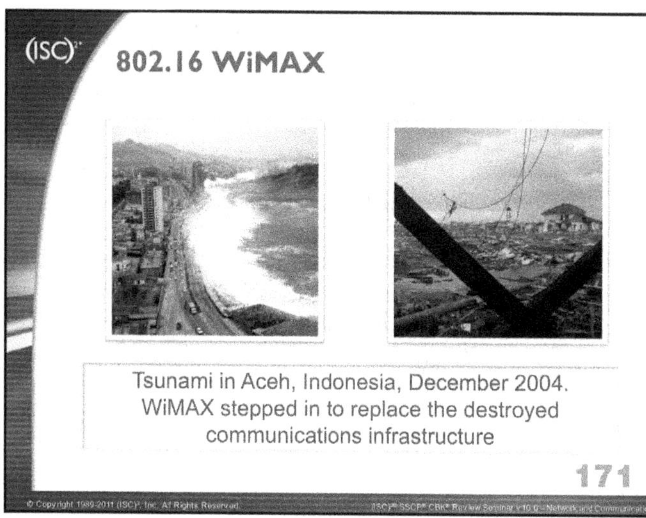

802.16 WiMAX
Tsunami in Aceh, Indonesia, December 2004.
WiMAX stepped in to replace the destroyed communications infrastructure
171


- **802.16 WIMAX** – WiMAX is a wireless access method designed for metropolitan areas. Rather than having isolated hot spots at coffee shops, bookstores, train stations, and the like, major cities are creating wireless zones that allow network communications to operate much the same way that cell service operates for voice communications. Although there are networking solutions that use cell service, the data rates are similar to that of modems. WiMAX data rates are comparable to cable and DSL (and like them, they vary from city to city and country to country).
- **WIMAX VULNERABILITIES** – There are several common vulnerabilities with any IP based technology, including eavesdropping, TCP session hijacking, and denial of service. Rogue base stations can also be deployed (as with any wireless network) to impersonate legitimate WiIMAX connections and compromise sensitive information.
- **WIMAX SECURITY** – The WiMAX Forum has developed support for both DES3 and AES encryption standards, which requires a dedicated security processor be present on base stations. End-to-end authentication is also provided for using PKM-AES, a transport layer security method using public key encryption, adopted from the DOCSIS BPI+ protocol. Since most WiMAX networks may also interconnect to other networks, it is always a good idea to place firewalls and detection technology between any public access infrastructure and internal sensitive infrastructures.

---

**REFERENCE:**

http://voip-facts.net/wimax-security.php

- NOTE OF INTEREST: WiMAX access was used to assist with communications in Aceh, Indonesia, after the tsunami in December 2004. All communication infrastructures in the area other than ham radio were destroyed, preventing survivors from being able to communicate with people outside the disaster area and vice versa. WiMAX provided broadband access that helped regenerate communication to and from Aceh.

---

**IMAGES:**

http://z.about.com/d/urbanlegends/1/0/T/5/tsunami_sm.jpg

http://news.nationalgeographic.com/news/2005/01/photogalleries/tsunami_photos/images/primary/Tsunami1.jpg

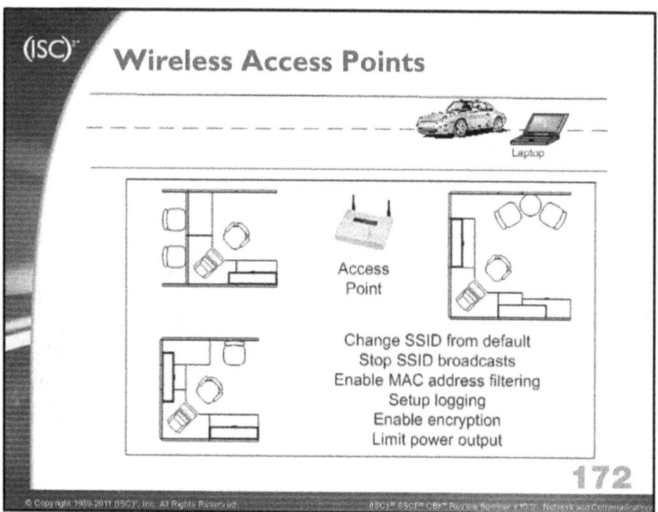


Change SSID from default
Stop SSID broadcasts

Setup logging

Limit power output

- Wireless Access Points (WAPs) – WAPs are the connection points between the wired and wireless networks. If they are not secured properly, they can provide easy entry into your wired network. The recommendations shown on the Slide are very basic steps for limited security. Enabling industry standard encryption technology, such as WPA2, should be required as a policy.
  - Based on the ratified IEEE 802.11i standard, WPA2 implements the National Institute of Standards and Technology (NIST) FIPS 140-2 compliant AES encryption algorithm using the CCMP protocol.
  - NOTE: The actions that you can take for basic security are listed at http://compnetworking.about.com/od/wirelesssecurity/tp/wifisecurity.htm. These recommendations are useful for low value networks which do not interconnect to sensitive infrastructures, and for home office/small office environments using older generation equipment not supporting the newer standards. On any high value wireless network, especially one providing connections to a corporate internal network, these basic recommendations above are of significantly low value, and WPA2 should be a minimum standard. WEP, for instance, has at best about 30 seconds of protection (due to the short IV used with RC-4), and even WPA, using the TKIP protocol, is now considered relatively weak.
  - See also: http://searchnetworking.techtarget.com.au/articles/33055-8-2-11n-security

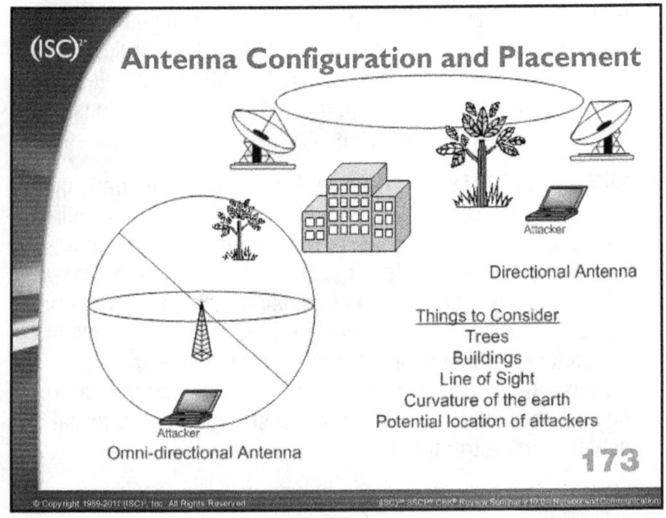


Curvature of the earth

- **ANTENNA CONFIGURATION AND PLACEMENT –** When creating a wireless network for the purpose of a point-to-point connection between two buildings, antennas must be considered. There are two basic types of antennas: omni-directional and directional.
  - Omni-directional antennas pose more of a security concern due to the nature of the horizontal beam width covering a full 360 degrees. If you are using omni-directional antennas, consider terrain masking, or blocking the transmission of the signal in the unwanted direction with a "backstop" such as a roof, stairwell, or a heavily constructed wall.
  - Directional antennas contain the beam within a limited spread and allow for finer control of the area that they cover.
  - Once you choose either an omni-directional or directional antenna, the real work begins with respect to obstructions and signal attenuation when placing and configuring your antenna.

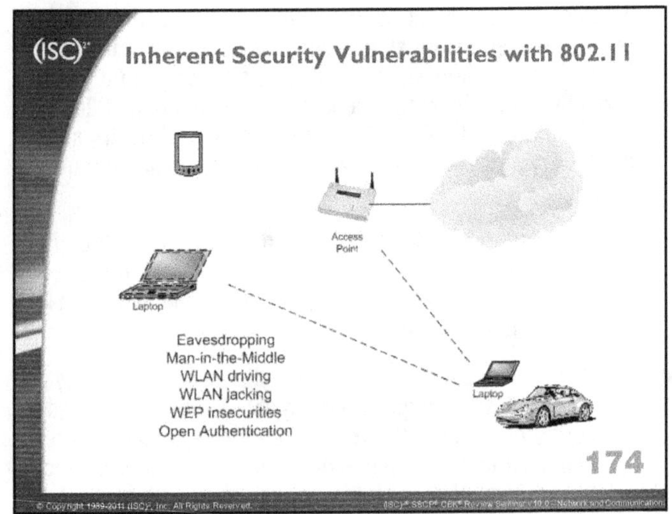

(ISC)²
Things to Consider
Inherent Security Vulnerabilities with 802.11
Access Point
Laptop
Eavesdropping
Man-in-the-Middle
WLAN driving
WLAN jacking
WEP insecurities
Open Authentication
Laptop
174


- **INHERENT SECURITY VULNERABILITIES WITH 802.11 –** There are many inherent security vulnerabilities with IEEE 802.11 variations. The very nature of a wireless network leaves WLANs subject to attacks. Wireless is not bound by the same physical principles as wired networks and are accessible from any location within the antenna's signal beam. The security included with 802.11x is vulnerable to attacks. The first common problem with wireless networks is that security mechanisms are disabled by default and network administrators often do not enable them. This leaves a wireless network susceptible to both passive and active attacks, including everything from simple eavesdropping to "WLAN jacking." Other attacks include data modification, rogue access points, and injection. We will take a look at all of these vulnerabilities and attack techniques over the next few slides.

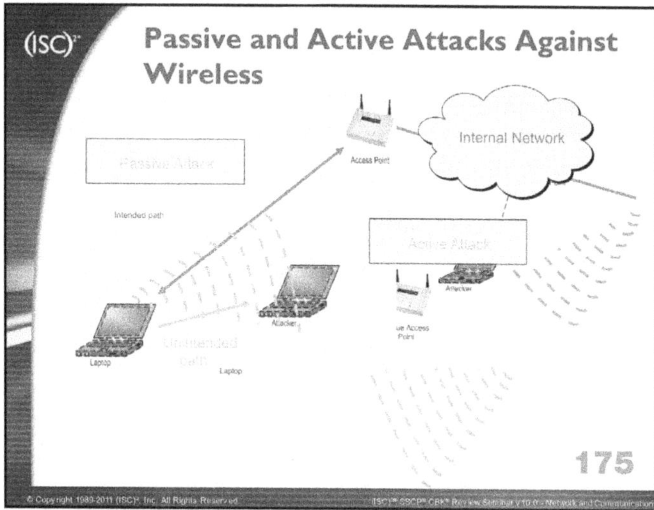


- **PASSIVE NETWORK ATTACKS –** Passive network attacks are relatively easy to implement and are very difficult to detect. An example of a passive attack is eavesdropping.
- **EAVESDROPPING –** The most common problem with wireless technology is that any anonymous attacker could be listening in. Anyone could set up a laptop with relatively little equipment and time invested and start listening in to wireless communications.
  - The equipment needed to listen in on a wireless connection is a computer (laptop, PDA, etc.), a wireless card, and some downloadable software to detect and then eavesdrop on any unsecured wireless network.
  - The purpose of tools like WEPCrack are to enable passive eavesdropping on a poorly secured network.
- **ACTIVE NETWORK ATTACKS –** Active network attacks can take the form of:
  - A rogue client
  - A rogue network access point
  - Client-to-client attacks
  - Infrastructure equipment attacks
  - Denial of service (DOS) attacks
    - Client jamming
    - Base station jamming
- There are many ways that an attacker can gain access to a WLAN. First, an attacker can mimic the identity of a known WLAN client. The attacker could steal an access point or set up a rogue access point to impersonate a valid network resource. He or she can attack another unprotected client on the WLAN to gain authentication information for some other part of the network. The attacker could gain access to the APs through a default login and password or a guessed password such as the company name. It is also possible to attack a switch by using a MAC or ARP table flood causing the switch to fail open.

---

**REFERENCES:**

For information on building a homemade wireless antenna see http://www.turnpoint.net/wireless/has.html

Freeware network discovery tool: www.netstumbler.com

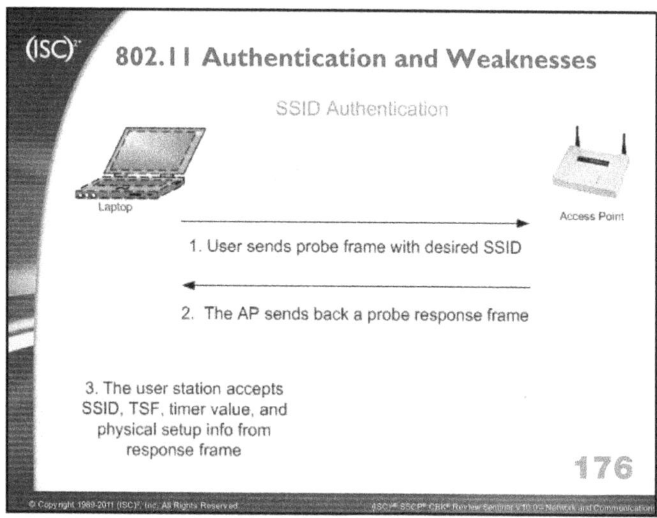


- **802.11 AUTHENTICATION AND WEAKNESSES –** With 802.11, there are few authentication options. 802.11b includes an option called "open authentication," but it is basically no authentication at all. It is certainly not appropriate for corporate environments, but might be suitable for public access points such as libraries or coffee shops.
  - If a company is relying on 802.11b WEP authentication for security, it has missed the boat. The WPA (wireless protected access) and WPA2 standards have reduced this vulnerability significantly.
  - SSID authentication is accomplished as follows:
    - The user's station sends out a probe frame (active scanning) with the desired service set ID (SSID).
    - The AP with that SSID sends back a probe response frame.
    - The user's station accepts the SSID, timing sync function (TSF), timer value, and physical setup values from the AP frame.
  - The SSID is often broadcasted from the AP, making it easy for unauthorized people to detect and log in to unprotected wireless access points and causing a security vulnerability.

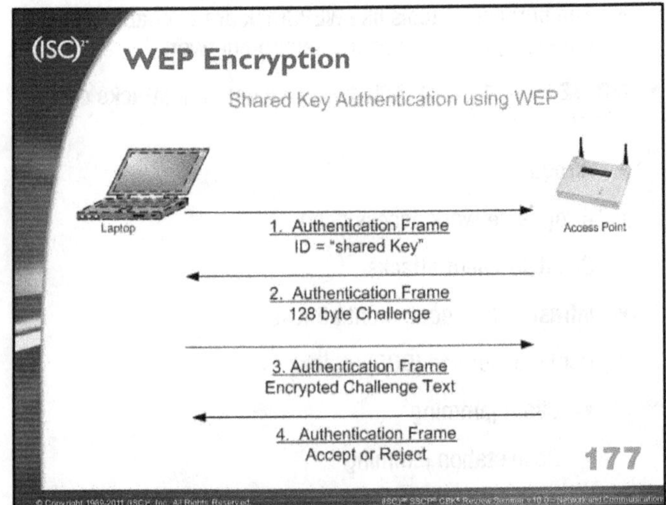


- **WEP DESIGN** – WEP was designed to give the wireless user the equivalent security of a wired user on an Ethernet hub (i.e., although all of the other users on the hub would be able to "hear" (or eavesdrop) on each other, assuming no connection between hubs, users connected to other hubs would not be able to eavesdrop). In a wireless environment, users in radio proximity would normally be able to hear each other, but by obscuring the message using a key known only to your group, they would not.
- **WEP ENCRYPTION** – WEP allows for a standards-based form of encryption on a wireless network. WEP relies on the RC4 encryption algorithm created by Ron Rivest for RSA in the late 1980s. It can be used in either a 64-bit or 128-bit form. Some vendors will advertise a 40-bit or 104-bit WEP encryption method. Note, however, that the 40-bit and 64-bit formats are identical to each other; WEP 64-bit uses 40 bits for the symmetric session key and 24 bits for the initialization vector (IV). Similarly, WEP 128 bits uses 104 bits for the symmetric session key and 24 bits for the IV.
- **WEAKNESSES** – There are several inherent weaknesses with WEP encryption:
  - Authentication is not mutual. The client never has the opportunity to authenticate the WAP and is, therefore, subject to "man-in-the-middle" attacks.
  - The key can be recovered if the attacker gathers enough of the transmission. There are tools available on the Internet that allow an attacker to listen to your wireless transmission, gather the data, and then recover your WEP key within a few hours of beginning. The WEP key will only slow an attacker down. It would be a mistake to rely on WEP alone for security.

**REFERENCES:**

This website contains the results of AT&T Labs and Rice University's attempt at a WEP attack, how they performed the attack and the results. http://www.cs.rice.edu/~astubble/wep/wep_attack.html

Here is a WEP cracking tool for Linux: http://sourceforge.net/projects/wepcrack

Kismet is an 802.11 wireless network sniffer. This is a UNIX based application that also has the capabilities of detecting networks that do not advertise their SSID. http://www.kismetwireless.net

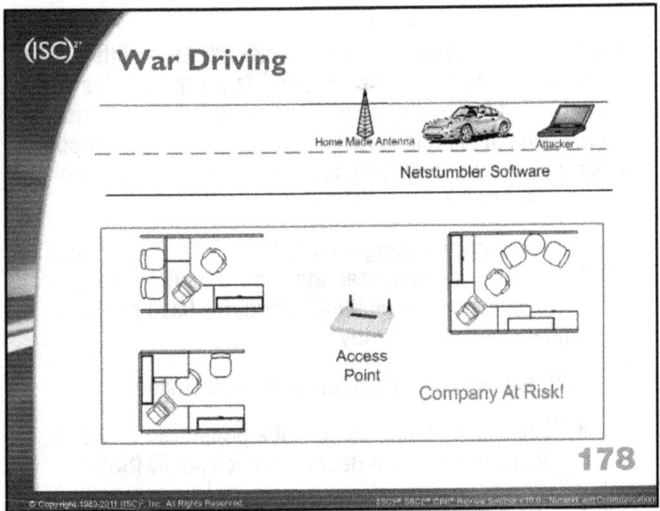


- **WAR DRIVING** – The term "war driving" derives from "war dialing", which is the practice of dialing different phone numbers to locate an open and available modem with which to connect. War dialing can also be used to look for an open PBX that will allow the attacker to place long distance or international calls. In war driving, the laptop attacker drives around in a car equipped with everything that they need to find and then connect to your WLAN.
  - The war driving attacker needs very little equipment to get started. All the attacker needs is a laptop or PDA with a wireless card, the free downloadable software NetStumbler, and a homemade antenna. A GPS will record the location of any discovered networks.
- **WLAN JACKING** – Once an unsecured network has been discovered, it can be exploited. Many attackers are only looking for a way to connect to the Internet, although some are looking for information or resources on your network that they can exploit.
- Take care in setting up a wireless network (or any network for that matter) to avoid potential fines or lawsuits in the event that it is used for malicious intent. The current legal argument is that looking for unsecured WLANs is not a crime, although using it for illegal activity is. There is also an argument that if there is no security turned on at the WAP, anyone logging on might not know that they are not simply logging on to a public access network. Some jurisdictions are placing the responsibility on the owner of the wireless access point to secure it.

**REFERENCES:**

A wireless scanner for purchase http://www.airmagnet.com/products.htm

Some interesting information on war driving http://www.wardriving.com

Freeware network discovery tool http://www.netstumbler.com

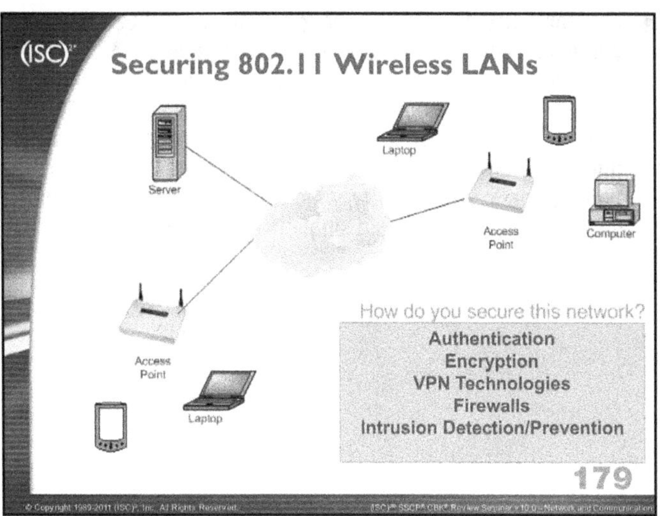


- **SECURING 802.11 WIRELESS LANS –** It is possible to secure your wireless network (relatively speaking) from outside attack. In order to do so, implement:
  - Authentication
  - RADIUS servers using IEEE802.1X
  - Encryption using WPA/WPA2
  - VPN technologies such as WTLS and IPSec
  - Firewalls and intrusion detection/prevention technologies.

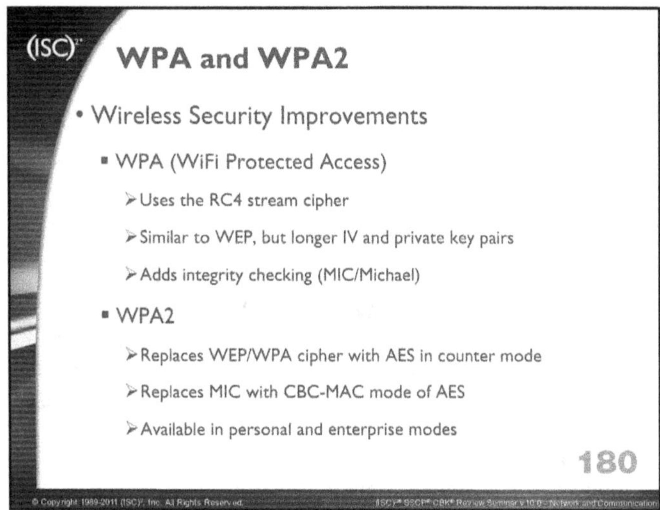


- **WIFI PROTECTED ACCESS (WPA)** was created by the WiFi Alliance as a stopgap measure to address the flaws in WEP until WPA2 would be ready for implementation. The design requirements were: to enhance WEP to make cracking more difficult, to add integrity checking, and to fit all of this into the same firmware space that was dedicated to WEP on existing access points, facilitating a firmware upgrade rather than requiring complete replacement.
  - Cracking was made more difficult by adding part of the station's MAC address to the shared key. This resulted in a separate, private key between each station and the access point rather than a single key shared by all users. The length of the IV was also lengthened. These two changes made the quantity of data that a cracker needed to accumulate significantly greater (days' worth rather than hours, on a busy link) and even then, the attacker would only be able to eavesdrop on a single station rather than all of the stations sharing the key.
    - Integrity checking was introduced via a hash called MIC (message integrity check) and pronounced "Michael".
    - The size requirement was met by lengthening the IV and key.
- **WPA2**
  - While WPA was a big improvement, it was still crackable by a determined intruder. WPA2 provides the advantage of additional integrity and confidentiality controls in an application that would be much more secure and less susceptible to breach. Cracking WPA2 is not technically feasible.
    - Encryption is done using AES in CTR mode, with keys negotiated for each session.
    - Integrity is done using AES based on CBC-MAC.
  - **WPA2 CAN BE ENABLED IN TWO VERSIONS –** WPA2-Personal and WPA2-Enterprise.
    - WPA2-Personal: Designed for small office/home office (SOHO), uses a password to generate a 256-bit AES key (PSK, or pre-shared key).
    - WPA2-Enterprise: Designed for corporate networks and uses IEEE 802.1X to authenticate users through a server (such as RADIUS) and can be configured for strong authentication.
    - WPA2 is backward compatible with WPA.
  - http://www.wi-fi.org/files/wp_9_WPA-WPA2%20Implementation_2-27-05.pdf
  - Note: PSKs are generated based on information that must be administratively configured on the AP and all end-points. If any end-point is compromised, or if the initial parameter exchanges are monitored, the keying materials may be compromised. There are also a number of documented exploits that might compromise the procedures used. See http://archive.cert.uni-stuttgart.de/isn/2003/11/msg00020.html

## Wireless Security Summary

| | 802.11a/b WEP | Wi-Fi Protected Access | Wi-Fi Protected Access 2 |
|---|---|---|---|
| Access Control | Pre-shared keys | 802.1X or Pre-Shared Key | 802.1X or Pre-Shared Key |
| Authentication | Pre-shared keys | EAP methods or Pre-Shared Key | EAP methods or Pre-Shared Key |
| Encryption | WEP | TKIP (RC4) | CCMP (AES Counter Mode) |
| Integrity | None | Michael MIC | CCMP (AES CBC-MAC) |

181

- This table lists the current security options for IEEE 802.11 wireless technology. Please be aware that as the 802.11n standard is fully deployed, WPA2 will be upgraded to a new mode of AES to support the higher, optimized speeds. This new mode is referred to as galois counter mode (GCM) and is published as NIST SP 800-38D. CCMP requires two encryption passes to add integrity, which is not designed for high speed networks. GCM is a single pass solution with very high throughput.

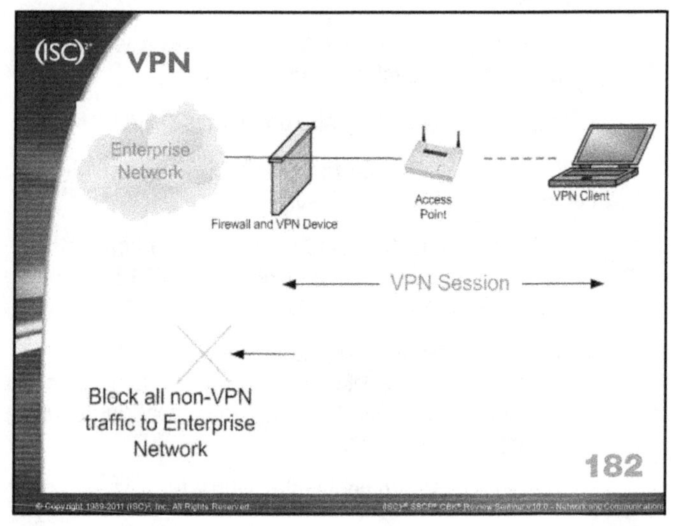


- **VPN –** A virtual private network (VPN) is a valuable addition to a wireless LAN. Best practices here dictate that wireless access users be treated as if they were remote access users, even if they happen to be located on the company premises.

**REFERENCE:**

WLAN/VPN integrated equipment can be found at: www.colubris.com/en/ and www.fortresstech.com

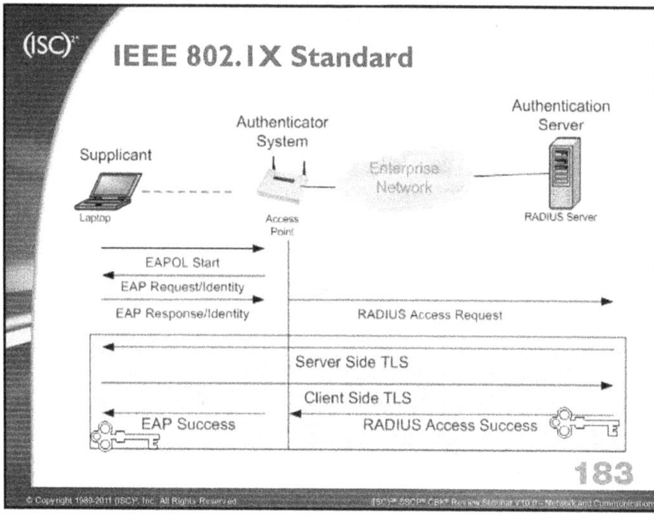


- **IEEE 802.1X STANDARD –** 802.1X was approved in June 2001 as an authentication method that can be used on both wireless and wired networks. This standard uses existing protocols for user authentication such as EAP and RADIUS. Windows XP (as well as some wireless equipment) already has 802.1X capability builtin. 802.1X vendors include Cisco, Agree, and Entrasys.
  - The basic purpose of 802.1X is to authenticate users, although it can also be used to establish encryption keys. Authentication can be performed by any means the vendor chooses, including RADIUS or Kerberos. Until authentication is complete, traffic is not allowed to pass onto the network. The 802.1X standard includes the mandatory use of 128-bit keys for RC4 data encryption, as well as encryption-key rotation.
  - With 802.1X, the user device is referred to as the "supplicant." In wireless, the access point is referred to as the "authenticator system" and the RADIUS server is referred to as the "authentication server."

(ISC)²

## Domain Agenda

- Network components and topologies
- Wide area and remote access networks
- Network standard protocols
- Security network protocols
- Wireless network configuration and protection
- **Managing service reliability and quality**

184



(ISC)²® SSCP® CBK® Review Seminar v10.0 – Network and Communications

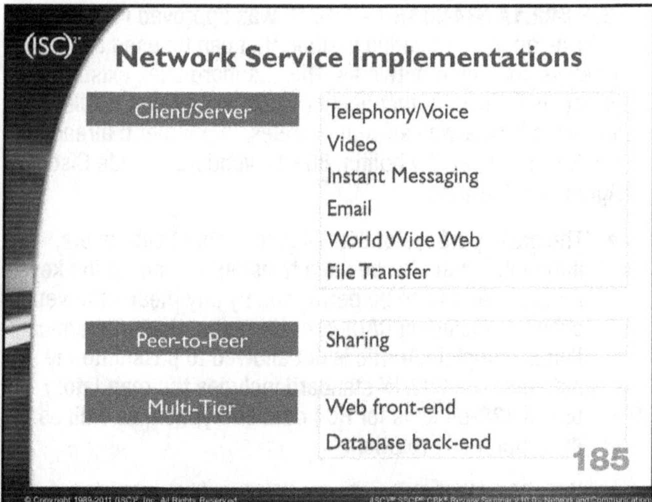

Network Service Implementations
Client/Server
Telephony/Voice
Video
Instant Messaging
Email
World Wide Web
File Transfer
Peer-to-Peer
Sharing
Multi-Tier
Web front-end
Database back-end
185


- **CLIENT/SERVER –** Instead of a single computer or node doing all the work, the bulk of the processing can be completed by a server, freeing the client to do end-user tasks.
  - **TELEPHONY/VOICE –** Today's end users do not need a traditional telephone handset on their desk. Instead, they can use any speakers and microphone connected to the network.
  - **VIDEO –** With the increase in network bandwidth and the decrease in both the size of files and the cost of equipment, face-to-face communication can be done at great distances.
  - **INSTANT MESSAGING –** "Chat" text messaging: Started as an informal method of brief communication between two or more people. Now, however, many organizations use IM for critical business applications.
  - **EMAIL –** Electronic mail is a store-and-forward technology. A client composes a message, sends the message to a server, the server stores the message, forwards the message to another server, and the recipient retrieves the message. Mail can be composed on full-featured clients or text-only clients. Breaking the email process down allows CISSPs to identify actions to be taken at key junctures in the process.
  - **WORLD WIDE WEB –** A way to publish and organize related information so that it can be found quickly. Developed by Tim Berners-Lee, at CERN in March 1989, he famously said, "Hypertext allows documents to be linked into 'live' data so that every time the link is followed, the information is retrieved."
  - **FILE TRANSFER –** Transmission can be done either with no security or with many layers of security.
- **PEER-TO-PEER –** There are many applications that rely on peer-to-peer communications to permit file sharing between several computers. Early networks, for example, were almost all peer-to-peer and allowed users to pass files between each other. Each computer on such a peer-to-peer network could act as either a client or a server. It is the same with many peer-to-peer solutions today – they allow the sharing of files, music, or other downloads and may result in the transmission of malware, unauthorized access to sensitive files, and copyright violations.
  - **SHARING –** In the early days, it was considered wasteful to have each user install a floppy disk or other media reader on a workstation. With the low cost of equipment today, that idea has faded away. Users no longer need to keep a copy of the file when they can get it elsewhere by sharing what they have. This, however, has led to the abuse of intellectual property law. Where organizational property and policy are concerned, users may be overstepping their authority by making these sharing decisions.
- **MULTI-TIER –** Many implementations are designed to spread the workload of a complex process to specialized computers within a subset of computers. For example, millions of clients may want to connect to a single website. The resolution can be done by DNS to many different web servers that act as a front-end. The duplicate web servers connect to groups of database servers that provide the supporting data to the web servers. The process of replying to the clients goes in the reverse order.

**REFERENCE:**

http://www.w3.org/History/1989/proposal.html

**Managing Network Communications Services**

- Examples of management services:
  - High availability services
  - Unified communications services
  - Quality of service
  - Change and configuration management

186

- Managing today's highly complex services requires knowledge and the skills to understand what the business requires so as to implement a comprehensive suite of delivery capabilities that ensure:
  - High availability and redundancy of mission-critical business services.
  - Support for integration of advanced technologies.
  - The maintenance of quality of service.

(ISC)²

## Single Points of Failure Countermeasures

- The best way to minimize disasters is to identify single points of failure and build in redundancy
- Creating single points of failure is a common mistake made in network design
- Be careful of consolidated equipment such as routers or switches
- Deploy redundant equipment

187



(ISC)²® SSCP® CBK® Review Seminar v10.0 – Network and Communications

- **SINGLE POINTS OF FAILURE COUNTERMEASURES –** One of the best ways to eliminate disasters on a network is to identify single points of failure and either build in redundancy or develop a contingency plan. Many network managers make the mistake of unknowingly creating single points of failure such as a single firewall, a single router, or a single leased line or T1 connection.
- **CONSOLIDATED EQUIPMENT –** In the early '90s, chassis hubs became very popular due to their high port density and single point of management. It was not uncommon to have 200 or more systems connected through a single hub. Of course it was also not uncommon to have 200 or more users unable to access network resources because a power supply or management board had failed. Today, there has been a resurgence of interest in consolidated equipment solutions with the release of Cisco's 5000 series switch, as well as multiple product offerings from Cabletron. Like their chassis predecessors, these products claim lower administration costs due to a central point of management, but do not address the financial loss due to a catastrophic failure of a single device.
- **FRAME RELAY –** A frame relay is capable of providing WAN connectivity, but it does so across a shared public switched network. Packet-switching technology allows for traffic to be diverted in cases where a segment goes down. While this may cause a bit of traffic congestion, connectivity will be maintained. It is not impossible, however, for the entire frame relay network to go down. This has happened to several telecommunications suppliers. In most cases, all customers experienced downtime. This varied from a few hours to a few days. While outages are rare, these failures are possible.

(ISC)²

## Single Points of Failure (cont.)

- Take advantage of redundant LAN routes
- Provide on-demand backup for WAN connections
- Build systems that offer:
  - Basic availability – Keep sufficient components to satisfy systems' functional requirements
  - High availability – Keep enough redundancy to support most critical systems
  - Continuous availability – Highest resiliency; also has components to apply to planned outages (i.e., upgrades, backups)

188



(ISC)²® SSCP® CBK® Review Seminar v10.0 – Network and Communications

- **DYNAMIC ROUTING –** Dynamic routing can be used to take advantage of multiple paths between network segments. While static (permanent) routes are your best bet when only a single path is available, for the majority of your internal network you should use a dynamic routing protocol such as OSPF (open shortest path first). If there is only one connection point between each of your routed segments, consider purchasing another router for redundancy or adding more network cards to one of your servers.
- **WAN CONNECTIONS –** WAN connections are prime candidates for providing a single point of failure. Due to the recurrent costs of maintaining a WAN link, most organizations do not build any type of redundancy into their WAN. One solution is to configure your border routers to fail over to a backup circuit if the primary line fails. This backup can be an analog dial-up line along with a couple of modems, or you could choose to implement increased bandwidth by utilizing an ISDN solution. In either case, you will have a lot less available bandwidth if the line that fails is a full T1, but will at least be able to provide a basic availability – a system which is designed, implemented, and deployed with sufficient components to satisfy the system's functional requirements, but no more.
  - **HIGH AVAILABILITY –** A system designed, implemented, and deployed with sufficient components to satisfy the system's functional requirements, but that also has sufficient redundancy in components to mask certain defined faults (a deviation from expected behavior).
  - **CONTINUOUS AVAILABILITY –** Extends the definition of HA and applies it to planned outages (upgrades, backups, etc.) as well.

## Saving Configuration Files

- When network devices fail, local configurations will likely be lost
- Terminal logging - Allows saving of configuration files by logging what appears on the terminal as the device is locally programmed
- Trivial file transfer protocol (TFTP) - Supports saving or retrieving configuration information - a single server can archive configuration files for every device on the network.

189



- Most network disaster solutions deal with availability of service. No disaster recovery solution is complete unless you are able to restore lost information, including the configuration files that you use to program routers, switches, and even hubs along your network. It is also possible that someone may inadvertently change the configuration to an unusable state. In either case, it is a good idea to have a backup of your configuration files.
- **TERMINAL LOGGING –** Allows you to save configuration information by logging what appears on your terminal as you are programming your devices. Recording allows you to save these configuration parameters.
- **TRIVIAL FILE TRANSFER PROTOCOL (TFTP) –** Is similar to FTP except that it uses UDP as transport and does not use any type of authentication. For this reason, it may not be a good idea to allow TFTP through a firewall. Most networking devices support TFTP for saving or retrieving configuration information, however. A single TFTP server can archive configuration files for every device on your network. If a device fails, simply plug it in, assign it an IP address, and use TFTP to retrieve the required configuration file:
  - Secure the TFTP server and put access control lists on TFTP access to network devices.
  - Remember that TFTP does not support user authentication.
  - Configuration files include system passwords and SNMP community strings useful to attackers.

## UPS, Power Generators, and Conditioners

- Uninterruptible power supply (UPS)
  - Provides a source of clean and steady power
- Diesel generators
  - Provide fault tolerance for power blackouts
- Power conditioning and isolation filtering
  - Critical systems should have a dedicated power source
  - By reducing the number of disks that are concurrently active, disk controller costs can be significantly reduced

190



- While all computers need a source of clean and steady power, this is even more important when the computer is acting as a server, because multiple users will be relying on the system. A good power source is not just one that is free from blackout or brownout conditions, but one that is free of surges and spikes as well.
- While a good UPS is an excellent idea for any computer system, it should be considered critical equipment for your servers. An intelligent UPS will include software that can shut the server down if the power is unavailable for a specific amount of time. This ensures that your server does not come crashing down once the battery supply has run dry.
- Larger installations should have an alternate power source for emergencies and extended power outages. Diesel generators are a very common solution.
- The data center and any high availability system should have a dedicated power source that is isolated from the normal infrastructure. This ensures that anomalies affecting the campus or facility do not interfere with critical processing, and that under emergency conditions, the data center can remain operational regardless of the surrounding environment.
- Consolidation of resources, such as utilization of blade server technology, virtualization, clustering, and NAS, may also permit optimization at a reasonable cost and even conserve energy requirements. No matter which solution is chosen, single points of failure should be avoided for high availability systems.

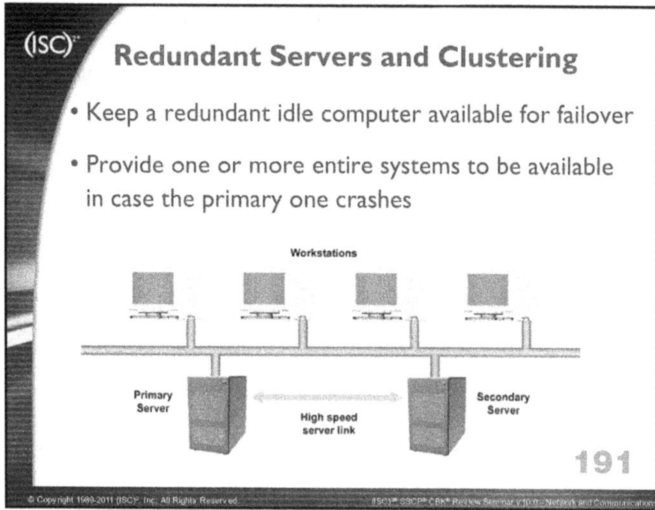

(ISC)²
Redundant Servers and Clustering
• Keep a redundant idle computer available for failover
• Provide one or more entire systems to be available in case the primary one crashes
Workstations
Primary Server
High speed server link
Secondary Server
191


- **REDUNDANT SERVERS –** takes the concept of RAID and applies it to the entire computer. Sometimes referred to as "server fault tolerance," redundant servers provide one or more available systems in case the primary one crashes. It does not matter if the crash is due to a hard disk drive crash, a memory error, or even a motherboard failure. Once the primary server stops responding to requests, the redundant system should take over.
  - As shown in our diagram, redundant servers typically share two communication channels. One is the network connection, while the other is a high-speed link between the two systems. Updates are fed to the secondary server via the high-speed link.
- **CLUSTERING –** Is similar to using redundant servers, except that all systems take part in processing service requests. The cluster acts as an intelligent unit in order to balance traffic load. From a client's perspective, a cluster looks like a single but very fast server. If a server fails, processing continues but with an obvious degradation in performance. What makes clustering more attractive than server redundancy is that your secondary systems are actually providing processing time; they do not sit idle waiting for another system to fail. This ensures that you get the highest level of utilization from your hardware. Clustering is an excellent solution for boosting both fault tolerance (availability) and performance.

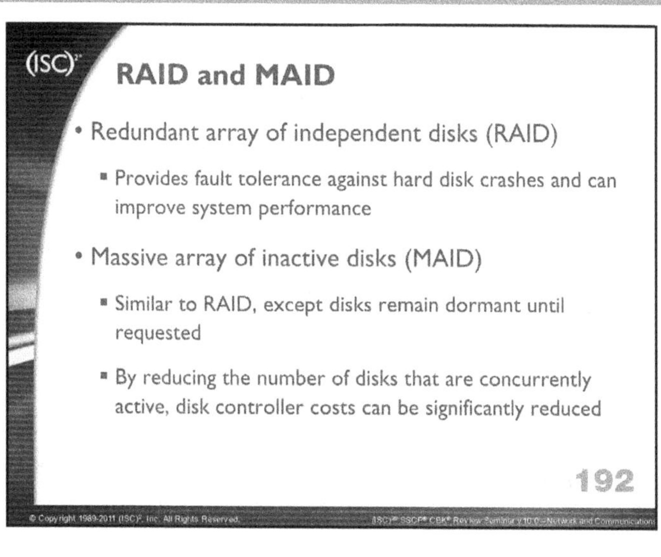

(ISC)²
RAID and MAID
• Redundant array of independent disks (RAID)
▪ Provides fault tolerance against hard disk crashes and can improve system performance
• Massive array of inactive disks (MAID)
▪ Similar to RAID, except disks remain dormant until requested
▪ By reducing the number of disks that are concurrently active, disk controller costs can be significantly reduced
192


- **RAID –** Does not only provide fault tolerance against hard disk crashes, but can also improve system performance. RAID breaks up or copies data you wish to save across multiple hard disks. This prevents a system failure due to the crash of a single drive. It also improves performance, as multiple disks can work together in order to save large files simultaneously. The process of copying data across multiple disks is called "striping."

## Online Storage and Backup: NAS and SAN

- Network attached storage (NAS)
  - Traditional network file server configuration
  - Server and storage are in one platform
- Storage area network (SAN)
  - Shared network that connects multiple servers/hosts to storage devices
  - Often used to implement serverless backups
  - Access is through some common mapping technology

193



- **NETWORK ATTACHED STORAGE (NAS) –** NAS provides storage and backup capabilities over the primary production network. The storage devices are attached to the network and provide service to the servers and other devices also on the network. This contrasts with direct attached storage, in which the storage device is attached to, and directly supports, a server instead of being attached to a network.
- **STORAGE AREA NETWORKS (SAN) –** In SANs, the file-system driver is on the host, and only the storage is remote. SAN can be implemented so that several hosts are able to share a single large RAID system, or more generally, multiple hosts linked to multiple storage systems. SANs offload storage traffic from the general network onto a dedicated network that can have lower latency. They are intended to support serverless backups (direct backup from disk to tape over the SAN without impacting a host). A SAN is typically implemented over a fiber channel, but can also be built over SCSI, SSA, ESCON, or IP. SANs can span tens of kilometers for availability. Access control is implemented by zoning or LUN (logical unit number) masking. Zoning is the creation of logically separated device subsets in the switch fabric that limits which storage devices a host can see. LUN masking logically binds storage volumes within storage devices to specific servers, emulating directly attached storage.

**REFERENCE:**

http://www.storagesearch.com/auspexart.html

## Backups

- Safeguard the information that is stored on the server.
- There are three types of backup:
  - Full backup - complete archive of every file
  - Differential backup - copies only files that have changed since the full backup was last performed
  - Incremental backup - copies only files that have recently been added or changed since the last backup of any kind

194



- **TAPE BACKUPS –** Tape backups are the method of choice for protecting or restoring lost, corrupted, or deleted information. All of the server-based options we have discussed so far have focused on maintaining or restoring the server as a service. None is capable of restoring that proverbial marketing file that was deleted more than three months ago. Here is where tape backups come in: Their strength is in safeguarding the information which actually gets stored on the server.
- Even if you're properly backed up, there are potential backup problems:
  - Slow data-transfer performance.
  - Backup needs to be done during low network traffic or over a dedicated backbone.
  - Backup device performance not keeping up.
  - Amount of data to back up increases.
  - Backup time windows being reduced.
  - Time of last backup was not the time of failure.
  - Lost data to be recreated/entered.

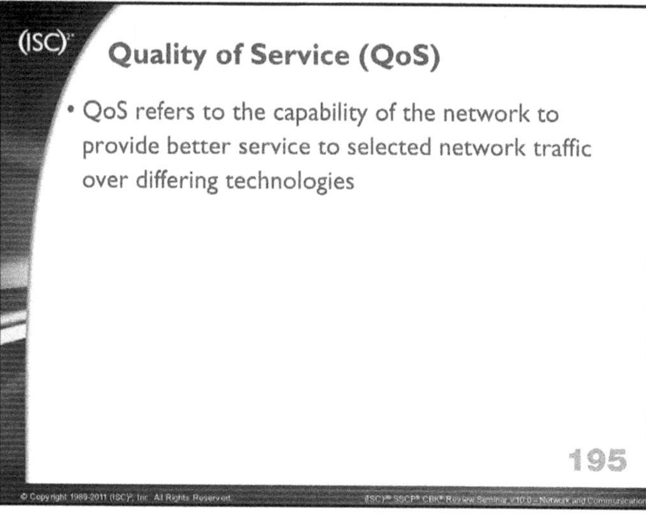

(ISC)²
Quality of Service (QoS)
• QoS refers to the capability of the network to provide better service to selected network traffic over differing technologies
195


- **QUALITY OF SERVICE (QOS) –** Multimedia services such as voice and video traditionally were deployed over circuit-switched networks because of the need for guaranteed bandwidth and predictable latency. Packet-switched data networks have a harder time providing these services. In order to provide service for voice and video, quality of service is key.

(ISC)²

Traffic QoS Needs

- Data (best effort) - bursty, intolerant of errors, and tolerant of jitter
- Audio/video (real time) - constant bandwidth, tolerant of errors, and intolerant of jitter
- Interactive (terminal emulation) - similar to best effort but more impacted by end-to-end latency than by jitter

196

- **TRAFFIC QOS NEEDS –** This lists the type of QoS required to support some different types of data traffic. The primary goals are:
  - Dedicated bandwidth.
  - Controlling jitter and latency.
  - Enabling coexistence of real-time traffic, such as voice/video, with best efforts traffic, such as data.
- **QUALITY OF SERVICE CAN BE CLASSIFIED INTO THE FOLLOWING TYPES -**
  - Best-effort service as basic connectivity with no guarantees.
  - Differentiated service – when some traffic is more important than the rest (i.e., more bandwidth on average, lower loss rate on average).
  - Guaranteed service.
- **DEFINITION OF LATENCY:** arrival times of frames.
- **DEFINITION OF JITTER:** variation in the arrival times of frames, in other words the variation of latency, caused by queuing of routers, problems with routes, etc.

(ISC)²

## Multimedia Security

- Growing concern in competitive global market for confidentiality and privacy
- Increased susceptibility to industrial and economic espionage
- Effective security via encryption - For example, can use virtual private networks with encryption services

197


(ISC)² SSCP® CBK® Review Seminar v10.0 Network and Communication

(ISC)²

## Multimedia Security (cont.)

- Protocols at network level can provide end-to-end security
- Applications can also provide some security
- Use of encryption and security protocols impose a performance penalty
  - Bandwidth overhead
  - Processing time

198


(ISC)² SSCP® CBK® Review Seminar v10.0 Network and Communication

- **MULTIMEDIA SECURITY (CONT.) –** Use of VLANs can isolate VoIP traffic away from data traffic to limit the exposure to eavesdropping on voice traffic by users with packet sniffers, and improve availability and quality of service. To provide security for multimedia transmissions, protocols can be used at the network level. Other security services provided by the application itself can also be used. The drawback here is that the use of encryption and security protocols can impose a performance penalty both in terms of bandwidth overhead and processing time.
  - **CONFIDENTIALITY –** A sender can encrypt media streams to provide confidentiality. Only authorized receivers with access to the cryptographic key will be able to decrypt the contents of those streams.
  - **AUTHENTICATION AND INTEGRITY –** A sender can use either digital signatures or message authentication codes to provide authentication and integrity. The receiver can determine the origin of a media stream and verify that its contents have not been modified in transit. Digital signatures are required for authentication in a group setting. Messages are signed with a private key unique to each individual participant and verified with a corresponding public key.

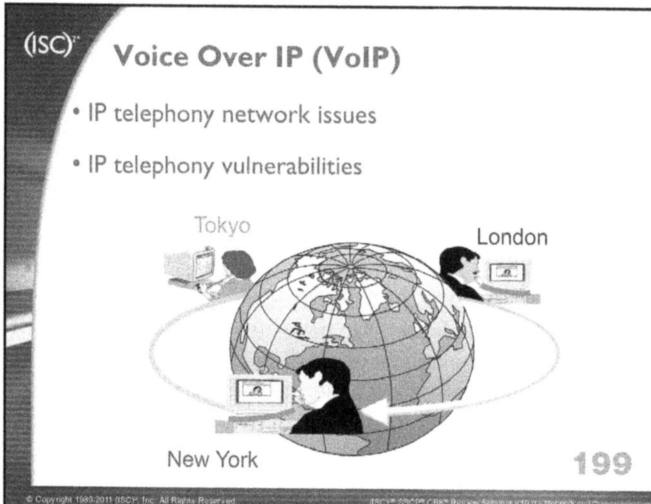

Voice Over IP (VoIP)
• IP telephony network issues
• IP telephony vulnerabilities
Tokyo
London
New York
199


- **VOICE OVER IP (VOIP) –** Concept of a "merged" IP telephony network, where we've combined the traditional IP network with the traditional analog phone network. Here, we show some of the typical devices that can be connected: telephony servers, wireless IP phones, etc.
  - Again, the advantages of IP telephony do not stop at low cost or free "voice." Along with audio, users have the capability of sending video and other data. By installing a "video phone" rather than a regular voice phone, users can send and receive video signals.
  - It is also possible to send files, chat in a text window, and work together to edit a document – just to name a few benefits. Imagine sitting at your computer talking to a colleague and simultaneously taking turns editing a presentation that you must give the next day to 500 people. Now, imagine that you give that presentation to 500 people who are all sitting at their desks in offices all over the world and are able to hear you, see you, and watch your presentation – all on their computers or video phones.
- **IP TELEPHONY NETWORK ISSUES –** Inherits security issues of traditional IP networks -
  - Uses non-secure operating systems.
  - IP/Web based administration.
  - Susceptible to denial of service (DoS).
  - Connected to an untrusted IP network.
  - Note, however, that IP Telephony intelligence is advancing rapidly.
- **IP TELEPHONY VULNERABILITIES -**
  - Voice system.
    - Operating system/support software implementation
    - Application implementation
    - Application manipulation (e.g., toll fraud, blocking, etc.)
    - Unauthorized administrative access.
  - Network and media.
    - DoS on media and signaling
    - DoS against media gateway/TDM sites
    - DoS against any shared network resource
    - Eavesdropping on conversations
    - Media tunneling.
- The vulnerabilities listed under "voice system" all deal with vulnerabilities inherent to the operating systems, software, and applications that drive IP telephony. Since IP telephony relies on similar technologies as TCP/IP, the vulnerabilities are very similar. Operating systems, software, applications, administrative userIDs, etc., all have to be secured.
- The same is true for the vulnerabilities listed under "network and media." VoIP is susceptible to DoS attacks, because there are many devices involved in VoIP including media, gateways, network resources such as routers, etc., that are vulnerable to DoS. We also need to watch out for eavesdropping, since everything is sent in clear text (unless encrypted – in which case we cannot look at the contents of the data packets. With media tunneling, IP telephony traffic is sent through a tunnel and may or may not include encryption. The issues here have to do with the added overhead of encapsulation of each packet and the fact that anytime you use tunneling, there is the chance that malicious traffic will be able to disguise itself as legitimate.
- **DANGERS -**
  - IP phone attacks
  - "Rogue" softphones (an unauthorized IP phone that is connected to the IP telephony network)
  - Implementation attacks (DoS and access controls)
  - Remote access attacks
  - Local access attacks
  - Unauthorized firmware/applications
  - Protocol attacks

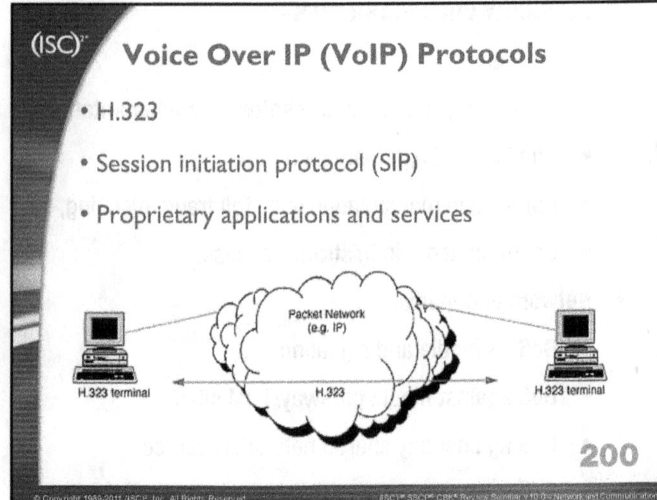
(ISC)²
Voice Over IP (VoIP) Protocols
• H.323
• Session initiation protocol (SIP)
• Proprietary applications and services
Packet Network
(e.g. IP)
H.323 terminal
H.323
H.323 terminal
200

- **VOICE OVER IP (VOIP) PROTOCOLS –** While it has long been possible to transmit voice over an Internet connection, the widespread acceptance of broadband home-access has only recently created a large market for voice over IP solutions. In essence, Internet and telephony are switching roles: Previously, the telephone network was a ubiquitous commodity that would carry Internet dial-up traffic. Increasingly, the Internet is taking over the role of the principal commodity and VoIP is replacing corporate telephony networks.
- While the benefits (such as negligible connection cost at a comparable initial investment and a larger degree of configurability) are obvious, VoIP networks are impacted by security risks in ways that would have left traditional telephony systems unaffected. VoIP is assailable by viruses, hacking, and dependence on electric power at all communication endpoints. In addition, VoIP systems are significantly more complex and need higher expertise to operate. For public services, questions of interconnectivity and interoperability with emergency services (such as calling 911 or 112 in the event of an emergency) come into focus. Traditional phone systems identify the address of the calling phone number to emergency services, but VOIP systems do not inherently provide that capability. From a legal perspective, it is still unclear whether VoIP networks should be regulated in the same way as the public switched telephone network (PSTN).
- One common requirement is the availability of gateways to public emergency services. Another one is access for lawful interception, which while legitimate from a public policy perspective, raises concerns from a security perspective, because of the potential design of backdoors into existing systems that could then be exploited by third parties.
- Deployment of VoIP services may raise security concerns for its carrier network, such as enabling interconnectivity with other VoIP applications in a secure manner. Finally, it is important that a form of backup communication channel is available with any VoIP installation, in order to have independent communication channels available in case of a disaster or network outage. Familiarity with protocols such as H.323 is also recommended.
- **H.323 –** The H.323 standard is a cornerstone technology for the transmission of real-time audio, video, and data communications over packet-based networks. It specifies the components, protocols, and procedures providing multimedia communication over packet-based networks. H.323 can also be applied to multipoint-multimedia communications. H.323 provides a myriad of services and can, therefore, be applied in a wide variety of areas including consumer, business, and entertainment applications.
- **SESSION INITIATION PROTOCOL (SIP) –** As its name implies, SIP is a protocol designed to manage multimedia connections. It is not a comprehensive protocol suite and leaves much of the actual payload data transfer to other protocols (e.g., real time transport protocol [RTP]). A number of phone companies have begun offering SIP services to end users.
    - SIP has been included in applications such as Microsoft Windows Messenger. Open source clients have been developed as well. SIP is designed to support digest authentication structured by "realms," similar to HTTP (although basic username/password authentication has been removed from the protocol as of RFC 3261).
    - SIP also provides integrity protection through MD5 hash functions. SIP supports a variety of encryption mechanisms such as TLS. Privacy extensions to SIP, including encryption and caller ID suppression, have been defined in extensions to the original session initiation protocol, as defined in RFC 3325. While SIP, which has been closely modeled after HTTP, is a peer-to-peer application by design, it is possible to proxy SIP and thereby build a scalable and manageable public infrastructure.
    - Conversely, SIP does not work with network address translation (NAT) as it is impossible for at least one client to address the other. This results in a target conflict between network security and VoIP operation that must be resolved in a secure manner, for instance by building a gateway in the form of a session controller. This controller can act as a proxy for SIP sessions (although not necessarily for some of the streaming protocols carrying the actual voice information). On a related note, a SIP client is also a server that can receive requests from another machine. This may be considered a general risk for the machine on which software is deployed – as with any server software, there is a risk of security gaps such as buffer overflows that can be exploited over the network.
- **PROPRIETARY APPLICATIONS AND SERVICES –** e.g., Skype, which is an online telephony/voice over IP application that offers clearing points with the public switched telephony network (PSTN). While the protocol is proprietary, its basic architecture has been published by the vendor as well as by independent analysis. From a security perspective, Skype's peer-to-peer architecture is its most important feature. Any Skype client can turn into a so-called "super node," i.e., is able to serve as a gateway for communication from other clients.

---

**REFERENCE**

for Comparison between H.323 and SIP: http://www.packetizer.com/ipmc/h323_vs_sip/

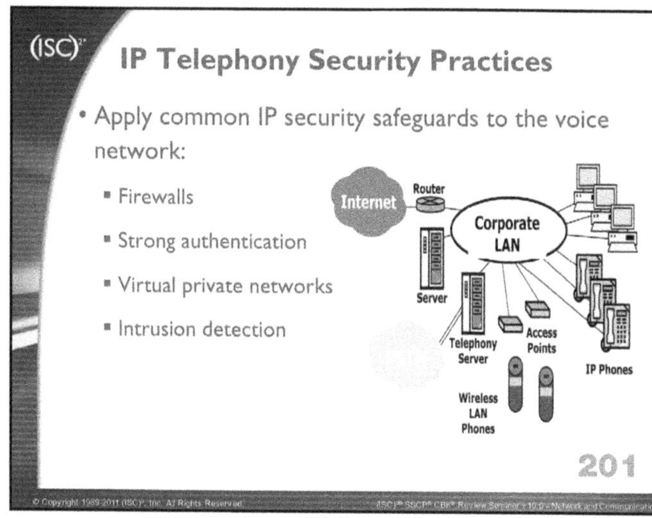

IP Telephony Security Practices
Apply common IP security safeguards to the voice network:
Firewalls
Strong authentication
Virtual private networks
Intrusion detection
Internet
Router
Corporate LAN
Server
Telephony Server
Access Points
IP Phones
Wireless LAN Phones
201


- **IP TELEPHONY SECURITY PRACTICES –** Your IP telephony network requires the same security controls that a regular IP network needs as the technology is the same. With VoIP, we have simply expanded regular IP technologies to be able to support voice applications.
- IP phones become end points for attacks, just like workstations in a regular network. The security controls are, therefore, much the same as you would implement in your workstations.
- **BEST PRACTICES FOR SECURITY –** Engineer the network to have proper security.
  - Deploy IP Telephony-aware perimeter devices for end-to-end security.
  - Maintain strong security on all networking components.
  - Limit the number of calls over media gateways.
- Infrastructure requirements:
  - Switched networks
  - Firewalls and NIDS
  - Perimeter firewalls to block unauthorized IP telephony
  - VLANs to isolate voice traffic
- Encryption:
  - Encrypting phones
  - Un-trusted parts of the network

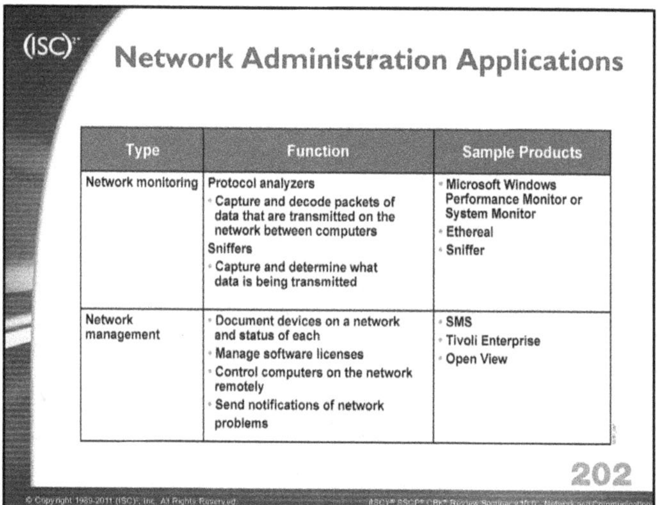

Network Administration Applications

| Type | Function | Sample Products |
|---|---|---|
| Network monitoring | Protocol analyzers<br>· Capture and decode packets of data that are transmitted on the network between computers<br>Sniffers<br>· Capture and determine what data is being transmitted | · Microsoft Windows Performance Monitor or System Monitor<br>· Ethereal<br>· Sniffer |
| Network management | · Document devices on a network and status of each<br>· Manage software licenses<br>· Control computers on the network remotely<br>· Send notifications of network problems | · SMS<br>· Tivoli Enterprise<br>· Open View |

202

(ISC)²

## Domain Summary

- The SSCP should
  - Fully understand network security principles and strategies
  - Understand network models and components
  - Be able to describe network layouts
  - Understand network protection techniques
  - Describe network protocols
  - Understand wireless telecommunications security
  - Describe advanced service reliability and quality

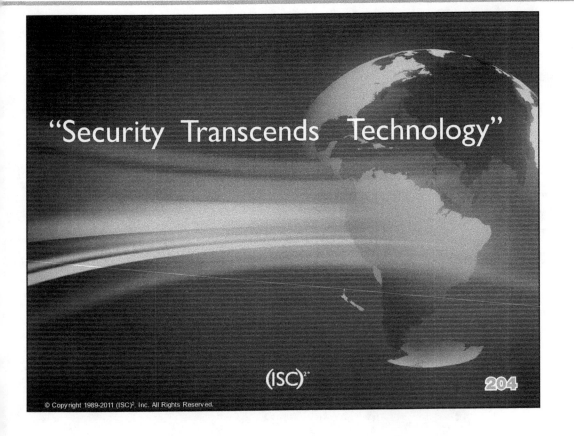

203



“Security Transcends Technology”

(ISC)²

204

# Review Questions

## NETWORKS AND COMMUNICATIONS

**1. What is the correct sequence of the open system interconnect (OSI) model structure from the bottom up?**

a. Physical, network, data link, transport, session, presentation, and application
b. Physical, data link, network, session, transport, presentation, and application
c. Physical, data link, network, transport, presentation, session, and application
d. Physical, data link, network, transport, session, presentation, and application

**2. What is the basic job of an access point?**

a. To act as a bridge for a wireless network between the wireless computer and the other devices, whether wired or wireless.
b. To enforce an access control policy at the access points of a network.
c. To generate random wireless encryption protocol (WEP) keys.
d. To generate random media access control (MAC) addresses.

**3. What is the most common security risk involved with firewalls?**

a. Hackers
b. Misconfigurations
c. Dial-up configuration ports
d. Malware

**4. When using an electrical cable such as category 5 (CAT5) twisted pair or coaxial (coax), your network is opened up to what potential security problem?**

a. Electrical magnetic interference (EMI) radiation
b. Cable tapping
c. EMI monitoring
d. Radio frequency interference (RFI)

**5. If an organization is using a physical star configuration with a hub as the center device, it is possible to add security to the physical transmission of the network by**

a. creating exclusion lists.
b. switching the hub out for a switch.
c. adding encryption at the application layer.
d. adding access controls to the server.

**6. What security technique can assist with securing a physical bus topology local area network?**

a. Change the hub out and replace it with a switch.
b. Add encryption to the transmission.
c. There is nothing that can secure a physical bus topology.
d. Add access controls to all computers.

**7. What layer of the open system interconnect (OSI) model is Internet protocol (IP) found at?**

a. Data link
b. Network
c. Transport
d. Session

**8. The addressing scheme in the transport control protocol/internet protocol (TCP/IP) is found where?**

a. Physical layer
b. Transport layer
c. Data link layer
d. Network layer

**9. Internet control message protocol (ICMP) is susceptible to which of the following attacks?**

a. Smurf
b. Replay
c. Spoofing
d. Man-in-the-middle

**10. Simple mail transfer protocol (SMTP) servers are susceptible to which of the following attacks?**

a. Smurf
b. Buffer overflow
c. Replay
d. Spoofing

**11. The Secure socket layer (SSL) is an option for providing security that is often associated what?**

a. Hypertext transport protocol (HTTP) browsers
b. Terminal emulation protocol (TELNET)
c. File transfer protocol (FTP)
d. Simple mail transport protocol (SMTP)

**12. The two basic methods of intrusion detection are:**

a. Stateful inspection and packet filtering.
b. Packet filtering and anomaly detection.
c. Signature matching and packet screening.
d. Signature matching and anomaly detection.

**13. Which of the following steps is the least likely action to be taken on an access point when turning on the security features?**

a. Change the Station Set Identifier (SSID).
b. Disable SSID broadcasts.
c. Enable Wired Equivalent Privacy (WEP) encryption.
d. Enable media access control (MAC) address filtering.

**14. Which of the following is a vulnerability of the Institute of Electrical and Electronics Engineers (IEEE) 802.11x standard?**

a. Crashing
b. Hammering
c. Cracking
d. Eavesdropping

**15. What is the PRIMARY weakness of wired equivalent privacy (WEP) encryption?**

a. It can be cracked in a matter of minutes.
b. The client is not authenticated to the access point so it is subject to the man in the middle attacks.
c. The encryption key is too short compared to other methods.
d. You cannot change the encryption key once established.

**16. The 802.11b standard allows for what transmission rate (in megabits per second (Mbps)) and utilizes what frequency band (in gigahertz (GHz))?**

a. 31Mbps and 5GHz
b. 54Mbps and 2.4GHz
c. 54Mbps and 5GHz
d. 11Mbps and 2.4GHz

**17. Wired equivalent privacy (WEP) relies on the which encryption algorithm?**

a. RSA
b. RC4
c. RC5
d. Advanced Encryption standard (AES)

**18. Which domain defines the roles, responsibilities, and accountabilities for employees and non-employees that access corporate owned resources and systems?**

a. Workstation domain
b. Local area network (LAN) domain
c. Wide area network (WAN) domain
d. User domain

**19. Why does fiber optic communication technology have a significant security advantage over other transmission technology?**

a. Higher data rates can be transmitted.
b. Interception of data traffic is more difficult.
c. Traffic analysis is prevented by multiplexing.
d. Single and double-bit errors are correctable.

**20. Which one of the following is the PRIMARY objective of a firewall?**

a. To protect networks from each other.
b. To prevent Internet protocol (IP) traffic from going out of the network.
c. To block Internet control message protocol (ICMP) and user datagram protocol (UDP) traffic.
d. To monitor network traffic.

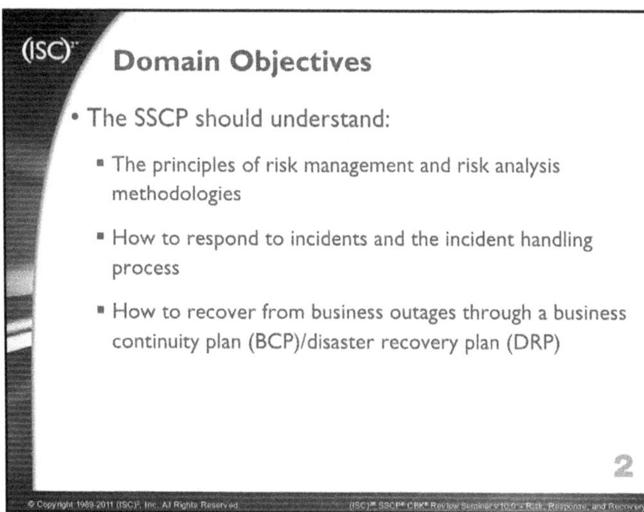


- **RISK MANAGEMENT –**
  - The information security industry is about risk management. Every action we take, or fail to take, involves some degree of risk. In the business world, successfully managing risk is the difference between operating a successful business and gambling.
  - As an SSCP, you work with others to identify risks and to implement risk management solutions. You need to remember two key facts in support of risk management:

    1. Never spend more to protect an asset than the asset is worth.

    2. A countermeasure, without a corresponding risk, is a solution seeking a problem. It is never cost justified.
- **INCIDENT RESPONSE –**
  - You may at some point be assigned to an incident response team. You will need to be able to handle the tasks described while maintaining the security of the evidence, including the integrity of the investigation and preserving the confidentiality and availability of the evidence gathered.
- **BUSINESS CONTINUITY PLANNING (BCP)/DISASTER RECOVERY PLANNING (DRP) –**
  - The role of the SSCP is to help identify serious risks, some of which might even put the company out of business, and to assist in creating or maintaining a plan that will help the business survive.
  - BCP and DRP are mostly concerned with availability, but maintaining the integrity of processes and data is an important concern during a recovery.

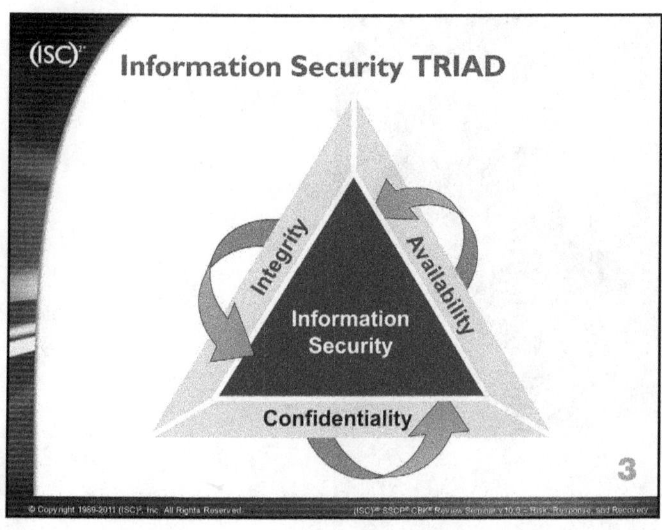


- The three disciplines discussed in this domain are primarily focused on protection of assets.
- Risk management addresses all risks to assets, and seeks to ensure the availability, integrity, and confidentiality of business information and physical assets.
- Incident response is a management control focused on timely response to threats, that are exposed during operations, which can impact the entire AIC triad.
- Recovery and BCP/DRP focus primarily on ensuring continued availability of business and IT operations in the event of an unplanned outage or emergency.

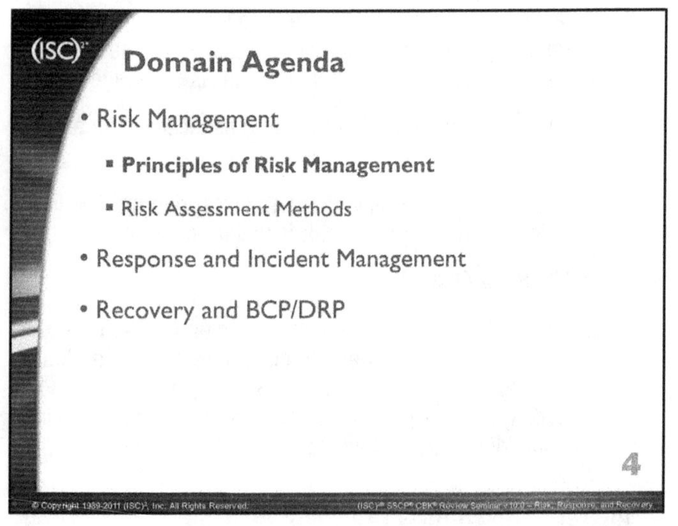

(ISC)²
Domain Agenda
• Risk Management
▪ Principles of Risk Management
▪ Risk Assessment Methods
• Response and Incident Management
• Recovery and BCP/DRP
4


- In this section, we discuss risk to the business. Definitions and key terms are defined, as well as the importance of managing risks. The common approaches to analyzing risks (quantitative and qualitative) are explored, and then choosing options for treating or mitigating risks are discussed.
- This is an important section and provides the basis for many other activities with which the SSCP needs to be familiar.

- **TODAY'S RISK LANDSCAPE –** Is influenced by many external and internal factors. It is a balance between meeting the expectations and regulations of customers and governments, and protecting the assets of the shareholders in a cost effective manner. Information security is rapidly changing and must understand the needs and directions of the organizations. Every organization today requires professional security staff with a wide ranging level of expertise and knowledge. This is critical in order to maintain the stable networking and computing platform that nearly every business process relies on for operation.

- **RISK, RESPONSE, AND RECOVERY IN CONTEXT –** Organizations exist within changing environments. They need to be compliant with legislation and standards. They need to maintain the supply chain between the organization and its suppliers and customers. These needs are driven by various stakeholders.

  - Business strategies are developed to meet the organization's mission and business goals, and to gain and sustain competitive advantage. Changes to the organizational structure may include changes to personnel, to the IT organization, and to procedural operations and logistics. All of these changes can cause changes in the risk environment. The structure of the organization also reflects the culture of the organization, which in turn has an impact on the organization's level of commitment with respect to protecting the information systems and the people, processes, data, and technology of the organization. The risks, and the response to those risks, will also be determined by the value the organization places on the assets held, and the financial constraints of the organization.

  - If the culture of the organization is one of *disposability (a culture that only seeks short-term gains and will readily be abandoned in adversity),* it is possible that only essential measures will be implemented to meet any legislation.

  - If the culture of the organization is one of *sustainability (a culture that seeks long-term success and the willingness to battle through adversity),* then all cost-effective measures will probably be implemented.

  - Either strategy might be correct for a particular organization. The only clear error is to mismatch – to require sustainable countermeasures in a company with a disposable culture.

- **IDENTIFY RISKS, PROTECT, AND RECOVER –** The core principles of information security relate to the need to identify the risks to the organization to prevent damage (insofar as possible) from these risks through the implementation of controls, and to have plans and procedures to react to incidents that are not preventable. These principles and controls are expressed in terms of people, processes, technology, and data.

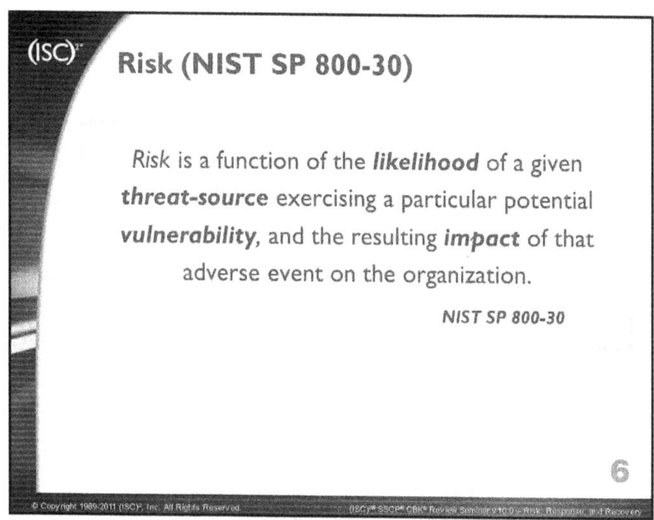


- **RISK DEFINITIONS –** This excerpt is the classic definition of risk. It comes from NIST SP 800-30, the Risk Management Guide for Information Technology Systems. It is a good roadmap to an effective risk-management program in IT.

  - The words in italics are a definition that you are expected to know as an SSCP.

  - It is worth looking at and monitoring the NIST SP 800 series of security practices. Most of the basics are part of the SSCP's knowledge base. Some of the more detailed items are more closely aligned with the (ISC)² CISSP, ISSMP, and ISSAP credentials.

- **DEFINITIONS FROM NIST SP 800-30 –**

  - **LIKELIHOOD –** The probability that a potential vulnerability may be exercised within the construct of an associated threat environment.

  - **THREAT-SOURCE –** A threat-source is either an intent and method targeted at the intentional exploitation of a vulnerability, or a situation and method that may accidentally trigger a vulnerability. Common threat sources are natural, human, or environmental. NOTE: The "threat source" is also called the "threat agent."

  - **THREAT –** The potential for a threat-source to exercise (accidentally trigger or intentionally exploit) a specific vulnerability.

  - **VULNERABILITY –** A flaw or weakness in system security procedures, design, implementation, or internal controls that could be accidentally or intentionally exploited that would result in a security breach or a violation of a system's security policy.

  - **IMPACT –** The magnitude of harm that could be caused by a threat's exercise of a vulnerability.

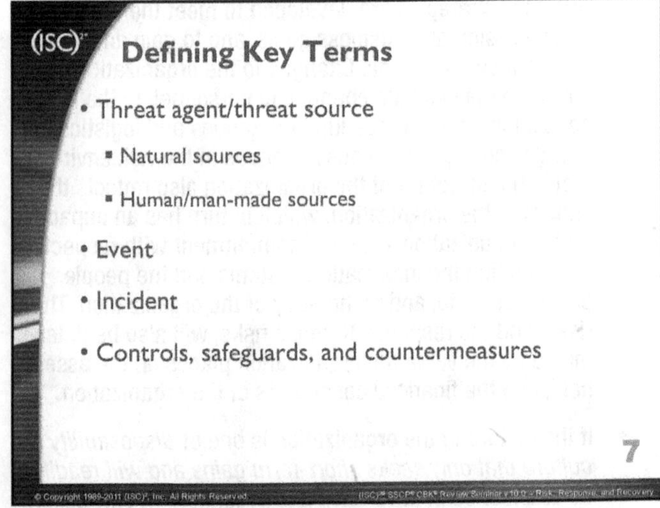

(ISC)²
Defining Key Terms
• Threat agent/threat source
▪ Natural sources
▪ Human/man-made sources
• Event
• Incident
• Controls, safeguards, and countermeasures
7


- **THREAT AGENT/THREAT SOURCE –** The underlying root cause of a threat to an asset which may result in loss or damage. The threat itself may be an event that occurs which triggers an undesirable outcome. The activity that causes the event is the source of that threat. Threat sources may be naturally occurring events or they may be intentionally or unintentionally caused by the actions of a person.
    - **NATURAL SOURCES –** Natural events, such as floods, storms, earthquakes, power failures, etc., cannot necessarily be prevented, but they can be mitigated through preparation, planning, and provisioning for the event.
    - **HUMAN/MAN-MADE SOURCES –** Human sources are sometimes referred to as threat agents. Malicious hacking, sabotage, theft, etc., are attacks against an organization's assets (both tangible and intangible) and can often be prevented by implementing strong access controls and authentication schemes. Accidental damage through errors or misuse can generally be reduced by proper training and supervision.
- **EVENT –** A measurable occurrence that has an impact on the business. Some events are fairly benign, whereas others may escalate into incidents.
- **INCIDENT –** An incident is an event that has a negative impact on operations. Incidents are events that justify the implementation of a control.
- **CONTROLS, COUNTERMEASURES, AND SAFEGUARDS –** We discuss the difference between these three terms later on. However, note that the three terms are not synonymous, and that a control is the higher-level category that includes both safeguards and countermeasures. Controls are actions taken to limit or constrain behavior. Safeguards are built in or used in a system to address gaps or weaknesses in the controls that could otherwise lead to an exploit, whereas countermeasures are installed to "counter" or address a specific threat (such as a fire sprinkler system).

**REFERENCE:**

Whitman, M. E. and Matford, H. J. (2007) Principles of Incident Response and Disaster Recovery, p. 492.

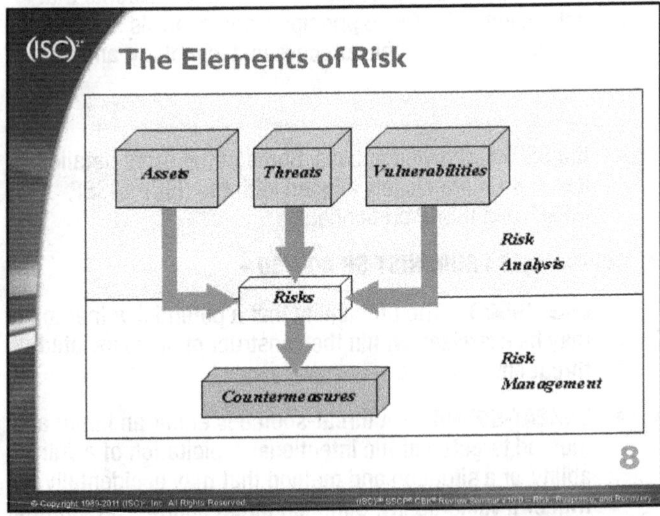


- **THE ELEMENTS OF RISK –** Risk is made up of assets, vulnerabilities, and threats. These are component parts rather than a formula. Assets increase or decline in value. Vulnerabilities get discovered and patched. New threats emerge and old ones dissipate. As these factors change over time, risk changes as well. Risk reassessments need to be performed periodically in order to identify new risks.
    - **ASSETS –** What we are trying to protect, or anything requiring protection.
    - **THREATS –** The forces or activities that may exploit a vulnerability (referred to as a threat/vulnerability pairing) and which lead to a successful attack.
    - **VULNERABILITIES –** Weaknesses or faults in our systems or processes. A lack of awareness and monitoring which could allow an attack to be successful.
- Don't assume that all threats come from the outside. In July 2007, Sophos released a report saying that 80% of malware caught by its products came from company insiders who were themselves victims of hackers as a result of their having visited inappropriate or corrupted websites. (A common term for this kind of threat is "drive-by downloading.")
- New threats appear all the time. An example of a new threat occurred in the spring of 2008 with the discovery of "phishing piers." A phishing pier is a standard phishing site that has been placed into a subdirectory of an otherwise respected and legitimate site, usually via an unpatched vulnerability on the target site. Victims of the phishing emails linked to the pier and saw a legitimate looking site with a working and valid certificate. At that time, this exploit represented a new vulnerability for commercial website administrators, who had previously believed that phishing sites were external to their protected servers.

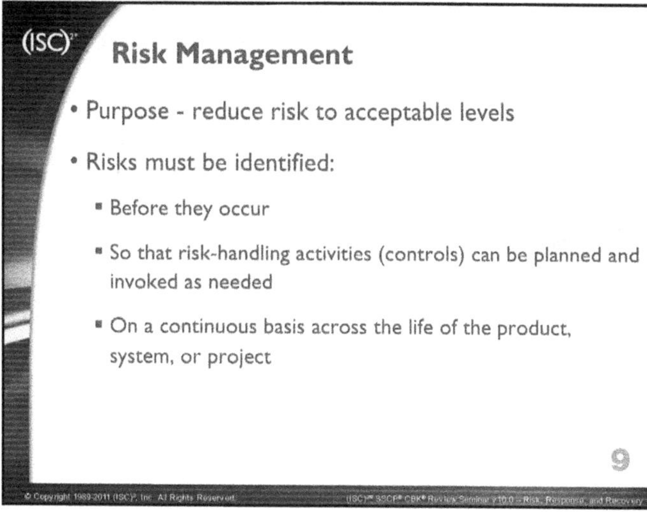

(ISC)²
Risk Management
• Purpose - reduce risk to acceptable levels
• Risks must be identified:
▪ Before they occur
▪ So that risk-handling activities (controls) can be planned and invoked as needed
▪ On a continuous basis across the life of the product, system, or project
9


- **PURPOSE –** It is rarely, if ever, possible to reduce risk levels to zero. After identifying the risk culture (or appetite) of an organization, the SSCP needs to participate in evaluating risks and then work toward reducing the ones that have a significant effect on the organization. Risk reduction methods must always be cost justified. In many cases, incremental reductions in risk have significantly high costs. Part of the SSCP's job is to help identify the tolerable risk level and implement the controls to reduce risks to that level.
- **RISKS MUST BE IDENTIFIED –** Some risk management efforts need to be allocated to identify new risks so that they can be managed prior to an event. Part of this process includes continually re-evaluating risks to make sure that the proper countermeasures are in place.

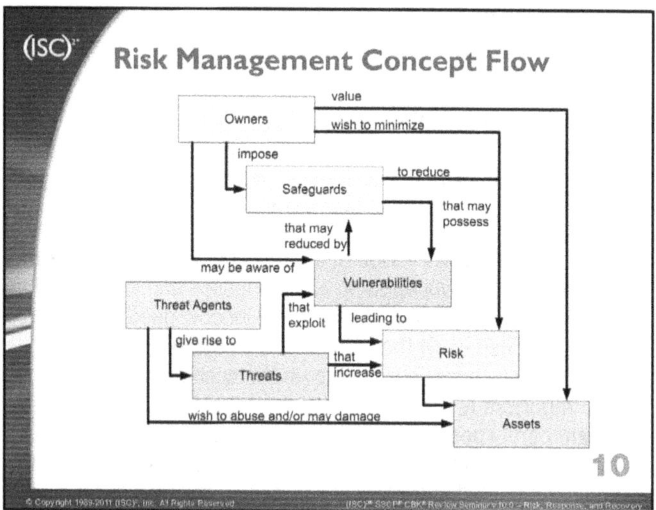


- This is a valuable outline of the concepts of risk management as described in the Common Criteria standard.

**REFERENCE**

http://www.commoncriteriaportal.org/public/files/CCPART1V3.1R1.pdf

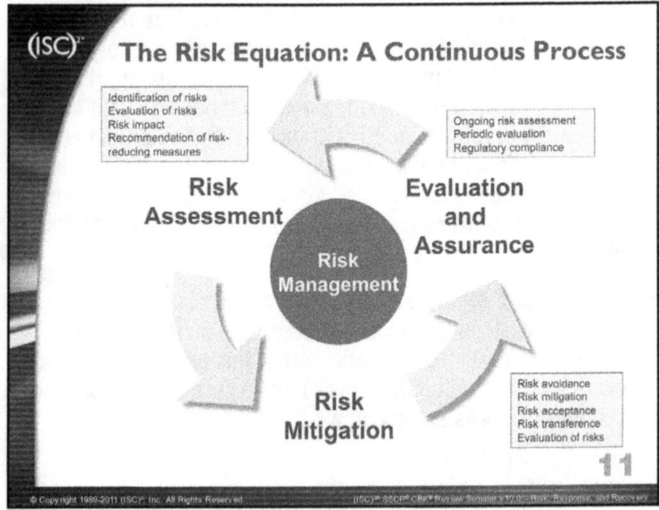


- **THE RISK EQUATION: A CONTINUOUS PROCESS –** Risk management comprises risk assessment, risk mitigation, and risk evaluation and assurance.
- Note that risk management is a continuous, ongoing effort and includes the periodic re-evaluation of risk and risk assessment in all three phases of the risk management effort.

---

**REFERENCE:**

NIST SP 800-30.

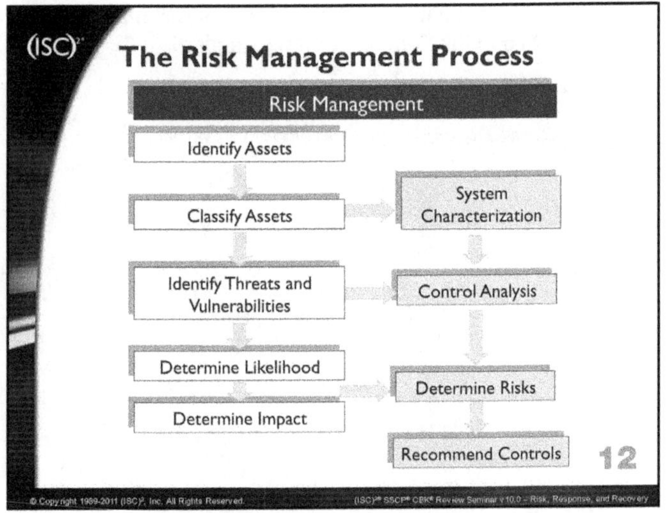


- **THE RISK MANAGEMENT PROCESS –** This flowchart outlines the steps in a risk management effort.
  - The left column outlines the assessment and monitoring of risk. The right column addresses some of the details of the risk assessment step.
  - Create an inventory of assets so that loss assessment can be added to the risk assessment equation.
  - Classify assets according to their value to the business.
  - Identify the threats and vulnerabilities to each asset and compare them to the proposed controls in order to determine if the controls are (still) appropriate.
- **RISK IDENTIFICATION –** What could go wrong? Fire, flood, earthquake, lightning, loss of electric or other utility, transportation unavailability (for workers or supplies), etc. Scenarios will have to be developed in order to be assessed.
- **RISK ASSESSMENT –** Not all identified risks will be measurable, and not all will apply to all businesses and locations. For example, businesses in Montana or Moscow need not worry about hurricanes. Of the risks that are possible, impact will be more or less severe depending on the scenario and location. It is important to avoid "movie plot" risks. Scriptwriters can create barely possible or impossible scenarios and make them look possible or even likely. Spending money to protect against these false threats is a waste of money and resources.
- **RISK CONTROLS –** Once a risk is identified, various types of controls can be evaluated.
- **CONTROL SELECTION STRATEGY –** Factors to be considered include reliability, scalability, cost, ease of use, and safety. Doing so will eliminate some of the potential choices, while moving others to the forefront.
- **CONTROL JUSTIFICATION –** The cost of all controls must be compared with the associated risk. It is not appropriate to spend $100 to protect $10.

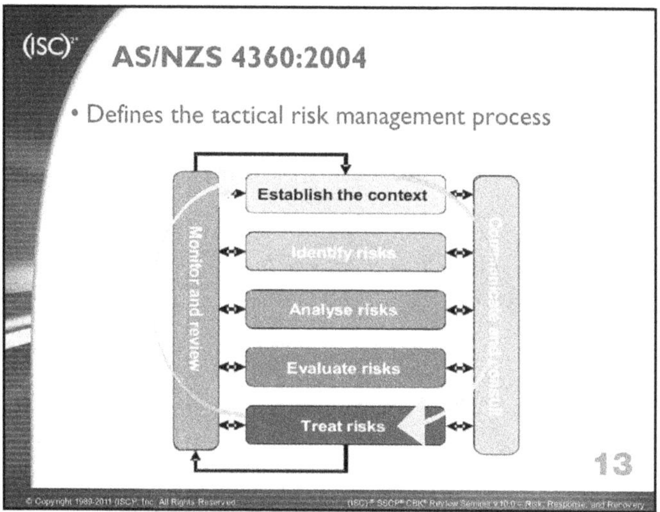


- **DEFINES THE TACTICAL RISK MANAGEMENT PROCESS –** "This Standard specifies the elements of the risk management process, but it is not the purpose of this Standard to enforce uniformity of risk management systems. It is generic and independent of any specific industry or economic sector. The design and implementation of the risk management system will be influenced by the varying needs of an organization, its particular objectives, its products and services, and the processes and specific practices employed."
- Each element of the process flows into each other making ANZ 4360 a continual flow in business.

**REFERENCE**

From pages 11 and 25 of ANZ4360:2004.

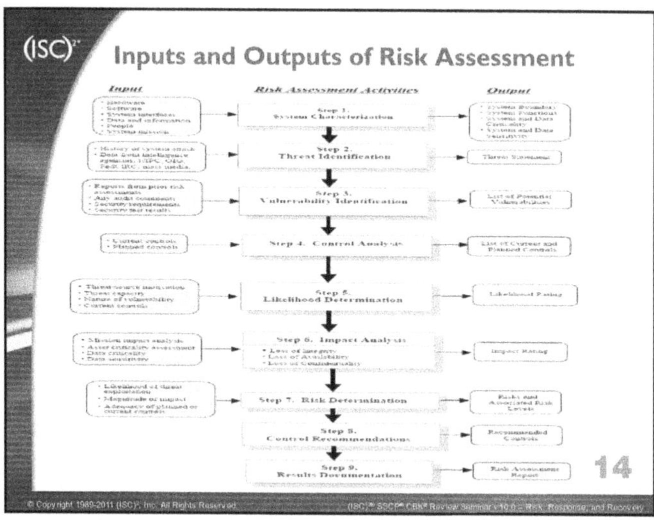


- According to NIST SP 800-30, there are nine steps to the risk assessment process. The output of the ninth step gives management the options for mitigation. The cycle is started again by evaluation. A good risk analysis should provide data to explain the company's risk environment to management in terms they understand. The process of risk analysis should remain focused on the objectives set on "what does this mean to the company?" and "what is the value of this to the company?"
- A brief description of each step directly from the NIST publication:

1. In assessing risks for an IT system, the first step is to define the scope of the effort. In this step, the boundaries of the IT system are identified, along with the resources and the information that constitute the system. Characterizing an IT system establishes the scope of the risk assessment effort, delineates the operational authorization (or accreditation) boundaries, and provides information (e.g., hardware, software, system connectivity, and responsible division or support personnel) essential to defining the risk.
2. The goal of this step is to identify the potential threat-sources and compile a threat statement listing potential threat-sources that are applicable to the IT system being evaluated.
3. The goal of this step is to develop a list of system vulnerabilities (flaws or weaknesses) that could be exploited by the potential threat-sources.
4. The goal of this step is to analyze the controls that have been implemented, or are planned for implementation, by the organization to minimize or eliminate the likelihood (or probability) of a threat's exercising a system vulnerability.
5. The likelihood that a potential vulnerability could be exercised by a given threat-source can be described as high, medium, or low.
6. A Business impact analysis (BIA) prioritizes the impact levels associated with the compromise of an organization's information assets based on a qualitative or quantitative assessment of the sensitivity and criticality of those assets.
7. The purpose of this step is to assess the level of risk to the IT system.
8. The goal of the recommended controls is to reduce the level of risk to the IT system and its data to an acceptable level.
9. A risk assessment report is a management report that helps senior management, the mission owners, make decisions on policy, procedural, budget, and system operational and management changes.

**REFERENCE**

http://csrc.nist.gov/publications/nistpubs/800-30/sp800-30.pdf.

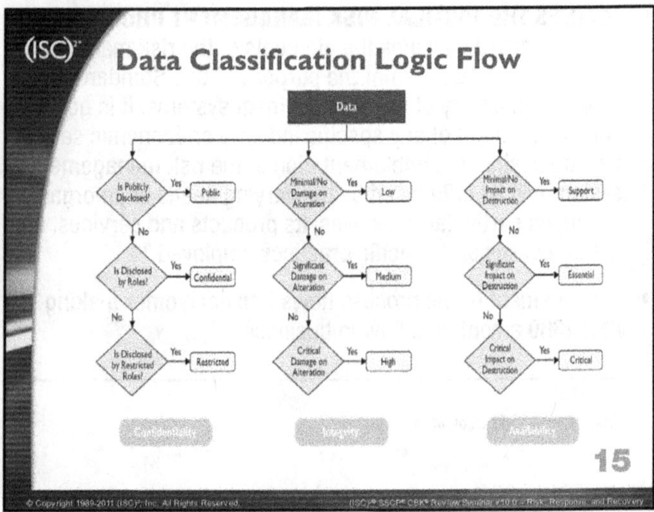


- Data classification can be performed for confidentiality, and also to determine business sensitivity to unauthorized alteration or loss of service.

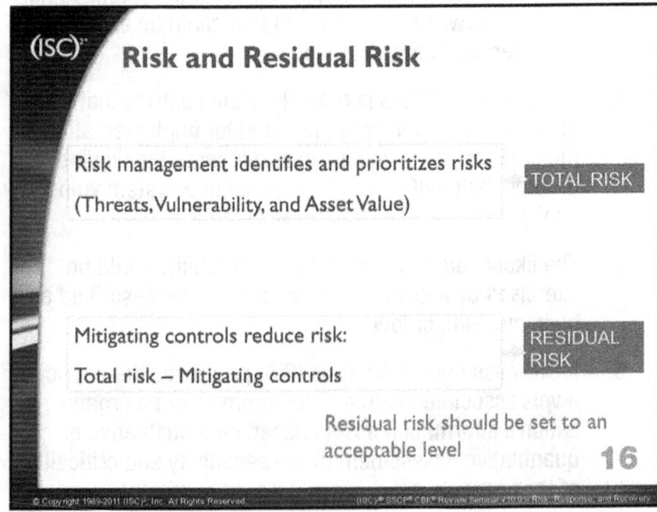


- **RISK MANAGEMENT IDENTIFIES AND PRIORITIZES RISKS –** As stated previously, risk is made up of threats, vulnerabilities, and asset value.
  - **TOTAL RISK** is the combined risk to all business assets.
- **RESIDUAL RISK –** Applying countermeasures and controls reduces risk. An example would be insurance on a car. When risk is not reduced to zero (either because it is impossible or because it is too expensive), the risk that remains is known as "residual risk" (Risk – Mitigating Controls = Residual Risk).
- A company must always be prepared to accept the cost of the residual risk. If the cost of the residual risk is too great, either a different or new countermeasure must be put into place, or the risky behavior should not be undertaken.

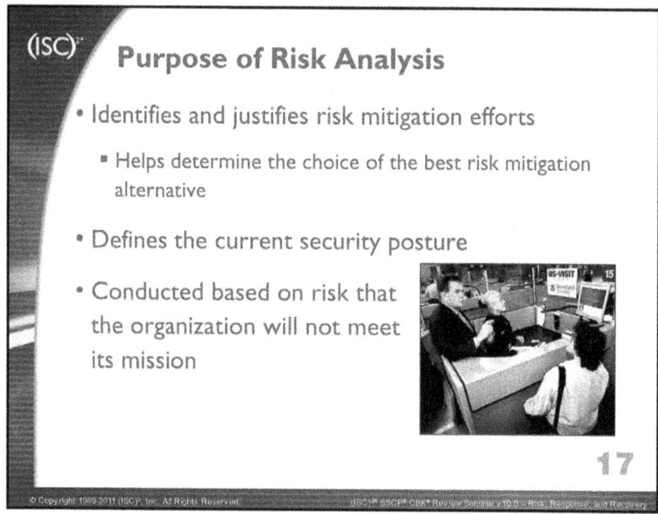
(ISC)²
Purpose of Risk Analysis
• Identifies and justifies risk mitigation efforts
▪ Helps determine the choice of the best risk mitigation alternative
• Defines the current security posture
• Conducted based on risk that the organization will not meet its mission
17

- **PURPOSE OF RISK ANALYSIS –** A good risk analysis does much for an organization, including providing relevant data to explain the company's risk environment to management in terms they understand. Risk analysis is based on the risks to the company that might prevent it from being able to accomplish its objectives. Sometimes, IT professionals make the mistake of getting so emotional about protecting their IT infrastructure that they forget that their systems are actually there to enable the company to accomplish its goals and objectives. During the risk analysis process, remain focused on "what does this mean to the company?" and "what is the value of this to the company?", rather than what does this mean for my systems and infrastructure.
- **IDENTIFIES AND JUSTIFIES RISK MITIGATION EFFORTS –**
  - Risk analysis identifies the threats to business processes and information systems.
  - Justifies the implementation of specific countermeasures to mitigate risk.
  - While there may be many choices with respect to mitigating an identified risk, a key reason for risk assessment and analysis is to provide the data necessary to determine the best risk mitigation alternative depending on elements such as cost, impact on productivity, user acceptance, etc.
- **DEFINES THE CURRENT SECURITY POSTURE –** Risk analysis helps us explain the current security posture to management in terms that they understand.
- **CONDUCTED BASED ON RISK THAT THE ORGANIZATION WILL NOT MEET ITS MISSION –** Risk analysis is more than risk to the IT system. It is about the risk to the entire organization's ability to conduct operations.
- **INCIDENTS WILL OCCUR –** Risk analysis, countermeasures, and mitigations, coupled with disaster planning (covered later in this domain), often make the difference between a company surviving or failing in the event of a disaster.

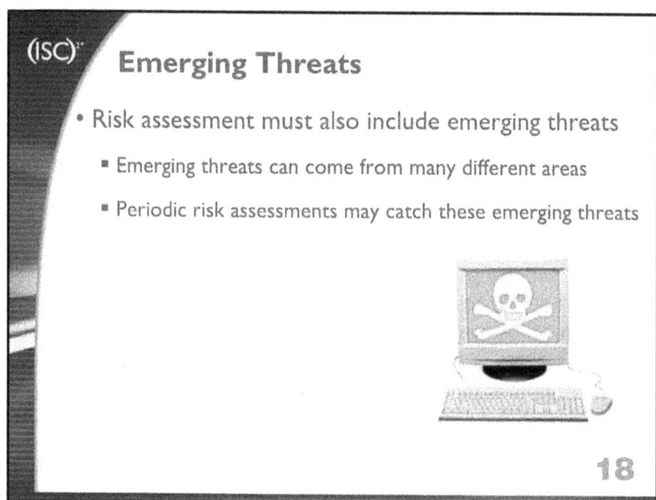
(ISC)²
Emerging Threats
• Risk assessment must also include emerging threats
▪ Emerging threats can come from many different areas
▪ Periodic risk assessments may catch these emerging threats
18

- **EMERGING THREATS CAN COME FROM MANY DIFFERENT AREAS –** Both internal and external sources:
  - New technology.
  - A change in the culture of the organization or environment.
  - Unauthorized use of technology (i.e., wireless technologies, rogue modems, PDAs, unlicensed software, iPods, etc.).
  - The threat from PDAs includes theft of corporate data, poor controls over wireless transmission and traffic, as well as the risk of having multiple copies or versions of data when different versions of files are kept on several devices.
  - Changes in regulations and laws.
  - Changes in business practices (i.e., outsourcing, globalization, etc.).
- **PERIODIC RISK ASSESSMENTS MAY CATCH THESE EMERGING THREATS –** Properly done, a new risk assessment continues to pick up these new threats as they appear. Emerging threats and vulnerabilities are the reason for periodic risk analysis and the reason that risk analysis is a continuous process. A pro-active SSCP watches for new threats that might trigger the need for a renewed risk review.

(ISC)²

## Domain Agenda

- Risk Management
  - Principles of Risk Management
  - **Risk Assessment Methods**
    - Quantitative
    - Qualitative
- Response and Incident Management
- Recovery and BCP/DRP

19


(ISC)²® SSCP® CBK® Review Seminar v 10.0 – Risk, Response, and Recovery

(ISC)²

## Two Approaches to Risk Analysis

- Quantitative versus qualitative risk analysis

| | | |
|---|---|---|
| Quantitative | • Numerically-based<br>• (Hard) data | • Financial data<br>• Objective |
| Qualitative | • Scenario-based<br>• (Soft) data | • Scenario-oriented<br>• Subjective |

- Most organizations will use a hybrid of both approaches to risk assessment

20


(ISC)²® SSCP® CBK® Review Seminar v 10.0 – Risk, Response, and Recovery

- **TWO APPROACHES TO RISK ANALYSIS –** There are two main approaches to risk analysis. Quantitative analysis puts a monetary value on risk. Qualitative analysis defines risk through the application of a scenario that describes the risk. A good risk assessment will combine both techniques.
- **QUALITATIVE RISK ASSESSMENT** is the process of describing a risk scenario and then determining the degree of impact that event would have on business operations. This is usually done through discussion with the business units and experts who understand what the effect of that adverse event would be on the primary mission of that business unit. It also allows the business units and technical experts to understand how the events cause ripple effects through other departments or operations. The process of discussion used to gather information from the experts is sometimes called the "Delphi technique" of risk assessment.
- **QUANTITATIVE RISK ANALYSIS** describes risk in numerical terms and assigns a monetary value to risk. This analysis has a limitation in financially assessing intangible assets, such as reputation, proprietary information and methods, goodwill, trade secrets, and research information, to name a few. This limitation is especially relevant in determining or predicting the impact of future events.
- **IT IS USUALLY DESIRABLE TO USE A HYBRID OF THE TWO METHODOLOGIES –** An advantage of qualitative risk analysis is the ability to consider risk from the perspective of a complete scenario and thereby gain a better understanding of the overall impact as it might spread through an organization. A qualitative risk analysis often leads to better communication between departments particularly with respect to interdependencies and downstream liabilities. However, it lacks some of the solid financial data that can be required to justify the adoption of countermeasures. It is usually necessary to provide financial data in order to justify a security program. This requires the combination of both techniques.

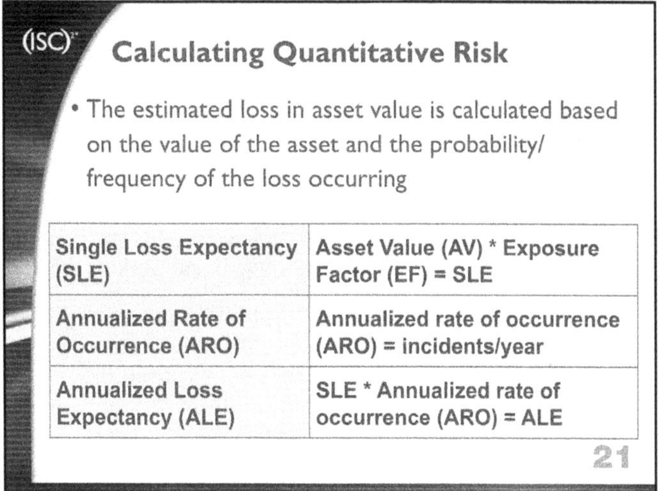


| | |
|---|---|
| Single Loss Expectancy (SLE) | Asset Value (AV) * Exposure Factor (EF) = SLE |
| Annualized Rate of Occurrence (ARO) | Annualized rate of occurrence (ARO) = incidents/year |
| Annualized Loss Expectancy (ALE) | SLE * Annualized rate of occurrence (ARO) = ALE |



- **CALCULATING QUANTITATIVE RISK –** This is a multistep process.
  1. **CALCULATE THE ASSET VALUE (AV) –** An asset can be described as anything of value to an organization. Therefore, assets can be tangible (buildings) or intangible (reputation). A first step in risk assessment is to determine all the assets of the organization and their value. The asset value can be measured as the importance of that asset to the organization's ability to achieve its mission. Asset values should consider the replacement value of equipment or systems, but should also include factors such as lost productivity, loss of reputation, or customer confidence.
  2. **CALCULATE THE EXPOSURE FACTOR (EF) –** This represents the percentage of the asset value that will be lost if an incident were to occur. As an example, not every car accident is a total loss. Insurance companies have actuaries who accurately calculate the likely percentage loss for every claim. They know the cost of repairs for every individual claim and can predict the exposure factor per claim. Their prediction won't be right for any single claim (except by chance) but will be right when grouped by the hundreds or thousands.
  3. **CALCULATE THE SINGLE LOSS EXPECTANCY (SLE) –** The value of a single loss can be calculated using the above two factors. If the actuaries calculate that the EF of a late model SUV is 20%, then every time the phone rings all they need to do is look up the asset value, multiply by the EF, and they'll have a very good prediction of the payout. This allows them to calculate insurance premiums accurately and mitigate the risk of the insurance company losing money by ensuring enough revenue is being gathered to offset the payout of claims.
  4. **DETERMINE HOW OFTEN A LOSS IS LIKELY TO OCCUR EVERY YEAR (ANNUALIZED RATE OF OCCURRENCE (ARO) –** Some AROs will be greater than one (e.g., a snowstorm in Buffalo or Berlin will happen many times per year) while others are likely to happen far less (e.g., a warehouse fire might happen once every 20 years). It is often difficult to estimate how often an incident will happen, and sometimes internal or external factors can affect that assessment. Historical data does not always predict the future, and incidents such as internal threats are far more likely during times of employee unrest or contract negotiations than they are at other times.
  5. **DETERMINE ANNUALIZED LOSS EXPOSURE (ALE) –** The ALE is the SLE (the loss when an incident happens) times the ARO. For infrequent events, the ALE will be much less than the SLE.
- The purpose of this exercise is to determine the maximum amount that should be spent on a countermeasure. The cost of the countermeasure should always be less than the ALE.

| | POTENTIAL IMPACT | | |
|---|---|---|---|
| *Security Objective* | LOW | MODERATE | HIGH |
| Confidentiality<br>Preserving authorized restrictions on information access and disclosure, including means for protecting personal privacy and proprietary information.<br>[44 U.S.C., SEC. 3542] | The unauthorized disclosure of information could be expected to have a **limited** adverse effect on organizational operations, organizational assets, or individuals. | The unauthorized disclosure of information could be expected to have a **serious** adverse effect on organizational operations, organizational assets, or individuals. | The unauthorized disclosure of information could be expected to have a **severe or catastrophic** adverse effect on organizational operations, organizational assets, or individuals. |
| Integrity<br>Guarding against improper information modification or destruction, and includes ensuring information non-repudiation and authenticity.<br>[44 U.S.C., SEC. 3542] | The unauthorized modification or destruction of information could be expected to have a **limited** adverse effect on organizational operations, organizational assets, or individuals. | The unauthorized modification or destruction of information could be expected to have a **serious** adverse effect on organizational operations, organizational assets, or individuals. | The unauthorized modification or destruction of information could be expected to have a **severe or catastrophic** adverse effect on organizational operations, organizational assets, or individuals. |
| Availability<br>Ensuring timely and reliable access to and use of information.<br>[44 U.S.C., SEC. 3542] | The disruption of access to or use of information or an information system could be expected to have a **limited** adverse effect on organizational operations, organizational assets, or individuals. | The disruption of access to or use of information or an information system could be expected to have a **serious** adverse effect on organizational operations, organizational assets, or individuals. | The disruption of access to or use of information or an information system could be expected to have a **severe or catastrophic** adverse effect on organizational operations, organizational assets, or individuals. |



- FIPS Publication 199 addresses the first task cited under Title III of Public Law 107-347 (The E-Government Act of 2002) — To develop standards for categorizing information and information systems. Security categorization standards for information and information systems provide a common framework and understanding for expressing security impacts and requirements in information systems. Title III of this law, known as the Federal Information Security Management Act (FISMA), requires all information and information systems to be categorized, based on the objectives of providing appropriate levels of information security according to a range of risk levels, as shown above.
- While this is US legislation, the principles of establishing a common basis for ensuring the confidentiality, integrity, and availability of information assets can be applied to any organization worldwide.
- This can serve as a template for classification of any information asset to determine reasonable protection levels and the business impact due to loss or compromise of protection.

**REFERENCE**

http://csrc.nist.gov/publications/fips/fips199/FIPS-PUB-199-final.pdf

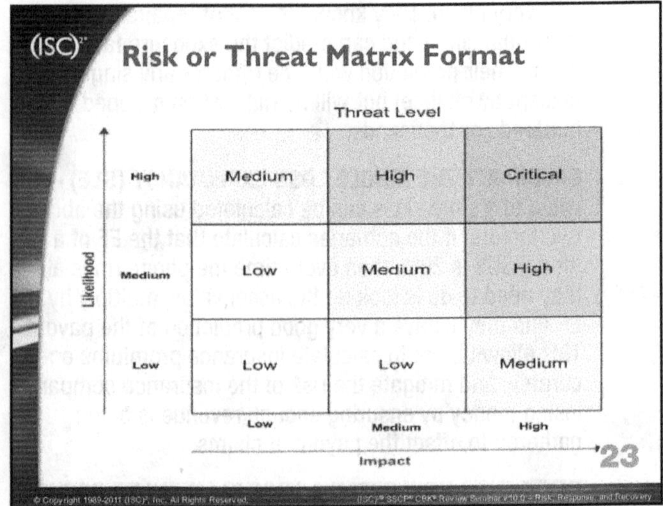


- Every risk can be judged on two scales: the likelihood of it occurring, and the impact it will have.
  - **LIKELIHOOD** – Some things will seldom happen (for example, a badge reader on the employee entrance malfunctioning) and some things will almost certainly happen (for example, employees calling in sick).
  - **IMPACT** – Some things will have an insignificant impact (for example, a workstation that fails to boot up) and others will have a major impact on the organization (for example, a production system breaking down and the inability to produce products).
- Events should be evaluated with respect to both scales and then placed on the chart. Those on the right side of the median are candidates for countermeasures, starting from the top right (highest probability and impact) and working down.
- It often takes the opinion of many experts to determine the placement of an event on either or both scales. When those experts disagree, it is important to reach a consensus. The benefit of this kind of analysis is that it takes into account intangible factors such as reputation or public interest.
- Risk management is not conducted solely in the upper right quadrant, but this is where risk mitigation is focused. Risk mitigation, transference, or avoidance are most likely for risks in the upper right quadrant. Risk acceptance is most likely for those in the other quadrants.

**REFERENCE**

http://www.emergencyriskmanagement.com/site/711336/page/248974

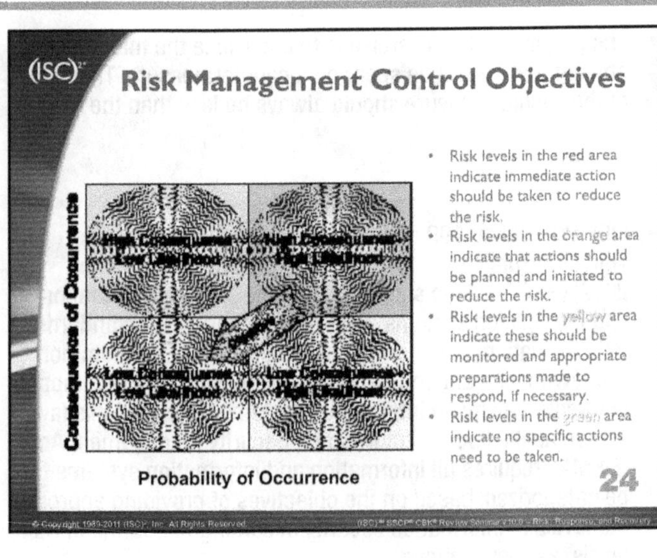

(ISC)²
Risk Management Control Objectives
Consequence of Occurrence
High Consequence Low Likelihood
High Consequence High Likelihood
Low Consequence Low Likelihood
Low Consequence High Likelihood
Probability of Occurrence
Risk levels in the red area indicate immediate action should be taken to reduce the risk.
Risk levels in the orange area indicate that actions should be planned and initiated to reduce the risk.
Risk levels in the yellow area indicate these should be monitored and appropriate preparations made to respond, if necessary.
Risk levels in the green area indicate no specific actions need to be taken.
24
© Copyright 1989-2011 (ISC)², Inc. All Rights Reserved.


- The overall objective in risk management is to reduce the consequences or likelihood of adverse events to an acceptable level. The higher the impact to the organization, the more aggressive the actions should be to reduce it. Note that the primary focus for risks in the upper left quadrant is on emergency and disaster planning, while risks in the other quadrants are the focus of ongoing risk management activities.

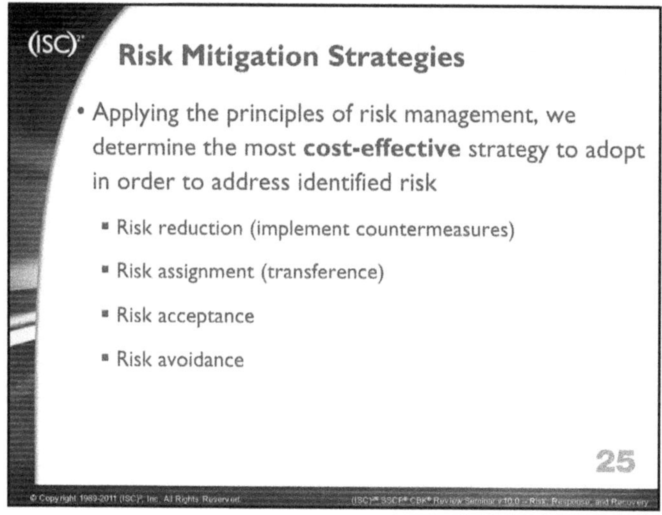

(ISC)²
Risk Mitigation Strategies
• Applying the principles of risk management, we determine the most **cost-effective** strategy to adopt in order to address identified risk
▪ Risk reduction (implement countermeasures)
▪ Risk assignment (transference)
▪ Risk acceptance
▪ Risk avoidance
25


- **RISK MITIGATION STRATEGIES –** These are the most commonly accepted responses to risk:
  - **RISK REDUCTION (IMPLEMENT COUNTERMEASURES) –** Is accomplished through the implementation of various controls that mitigate identified risks. These controls may be administrative in nature, technical, or physical controls. (These are covered in the Analysis and Monitoring Domain.)
  - **RISK ASSIGNMENT (TRANSFERENCE) –** The most frequently used method of reducing risk is by insuring it, and thereby "selling" it to another organization that is willing to accept the risk in return for a premium. Other times, transference is done to insulate an organization from excessive liability, such as a hotel that engages a separate car parking corporation to manage its parking facility. Losses are the responsibility of the car-parking corporation, not the hotel, and an incident in the car park is less likely to put the entire hotel in jeopardy of a lawsuit.
  - **RISK ACCEPTANCE –** Is where the organization is willing to accept the risk. It knowingly accepts that the risk exists and have decided that the cost of implementing a control to reduce the risk is higher than the loss would be. This can include self-insuring or using a deductible. The level of risk an organization is willing to accept is dependent on the risk appetite of senior management.
  - **RISK AVOIDANCE –** Is the decision to avoid the risk by discontinuing or not entering into a line of business or a situation that would pose an unacceptable level of risk.

(ISC)²

**Risk Mitigation (Treatment) Options**

| Treatment Option | Examples |
|---|---|
| Avoid the risk if the risk is high, is unmanageable, too costly to manage or an alternative is readily available. | • Cease the activity affected by the risk<br>• Change a hazardous material to a non-hazardous one. |
| Accept the risk if the likelihood and consequence are both low. | • Manage the risk using existing procedures. |
| Transfer the risk to another party (or share the risk). | • Introduce contract conditions such as rise and fall, inclement weather, latent conditions.<br>• Develop agreements with other agencies.<br>• Contract to an expert, e.g., handling hazardous materials.<br>• Require insurances to be in place. |
| Reduce the likelihood of the risk occurring. | • Provide training/ implement quality management<br>• Review contract conditions/ maintenance procedures.<br>• Increase supervision/ audit/ compliance requirements.<br>• Install warning devices/ alarms<br>• Regularly analyse the project environment.<br>• Conduct further project analysis.<br>• Develop partnering agreements. |
| Reduce the consequence if the risk does occur. | • Prepare contingency plans.<br>• Provide greater cost and time contingencies.<br>• Store copies of project documentation off site.<br>• Separate or duplicate resources/ provide barriers.<br>• Develop fraud control plans.<br>• Develop public relations processes. |

26

 (ISC)²® SSCP® CBK® Review Seminar v10.0 – Risk, Response, and Recovery

- This table includes some of the more common mitigation (or risk treatment) options available to management.

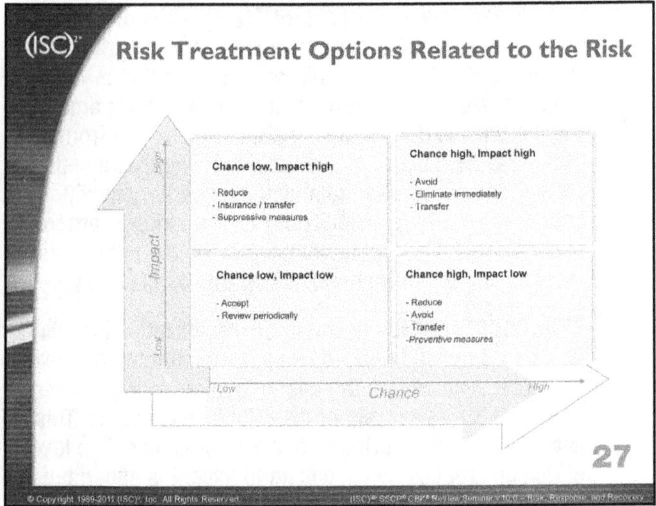


- This graphic highlights when the risk treatment choices are most commonly applied. Keep in mind that cost-benefit will still be the primary driver of any decision.

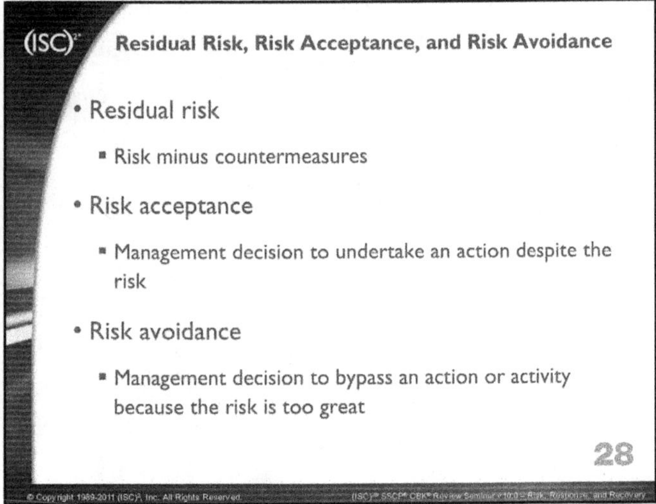


- **RESIDUAL RISK –** Is the risk that remains, even after risk-mitigation efforts have been implemented. An example might be a deductible on insurance, or the remaining (but decreased) chance of fire after installation of alarms, sprinkler systems, and training sessions.
- **RISK ACCEPTANCE AND RISK AVOIDANCE –** These are management decisions dealing with what to do when faced with residual risk.
  - **ACCEPTANCE –** Management decides that the cost of undertaking some further risk mitigation control would be more than the reduction in loss that would be realized by installing the control. Therefore, it decides to accept the level of risk rather than try to mitigate it further. Example: A physician buys malpractice insurance and accepts the residual risk of loss in the amount of the deductible. He must decide whether to pay an even higher premium in order to reduce his deductible, but may decide that the higher premium would not be worth the cost, since he would rarely need to make a claim.
  - **AVOIDANCE –** Management decides that the loss to the company exceeds the potential value to be gained by continuing the risky activity. Example: A company decides not to open a branch in a country where it is not likely to make a profit.
- A common mistake is to consider only the lower level risk (e.g., the deductible). Suppose you have homeowner's (or tenants') insurance. If someone trips over your couch, you'll remember that you'll be responsible for the deductible. You might not remember that you're also responsible for any claim in excess of the upper limit of the policy. That's residual risk, too.

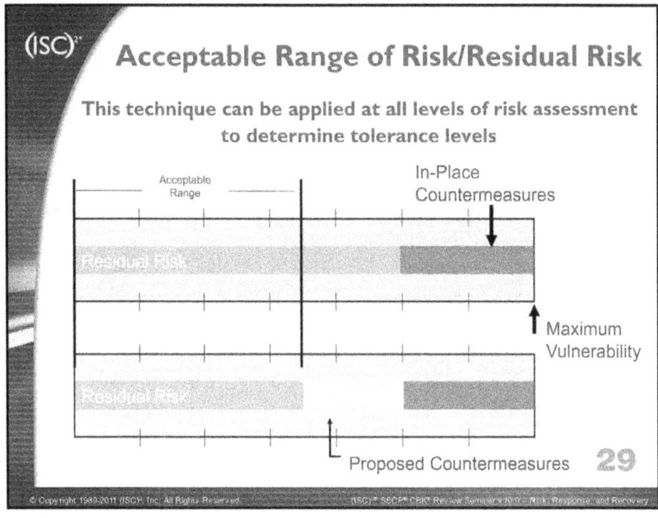


- **ACCEPTABLE RANGE OF RISK/RESIDUAL RISK –** The "acceptable range" of risk is bounded on the upper side by the amount of risk that would be too great for the organization to bear and on the lower range by the increased cost of the countermeasures compared with the remaining (residual) risk. The goal of risk management is to stay inside the acceptable range. Since it is not usually possible to eliminate risk entirely, the organization must, therefore, select (define) a level of risk it is willing to accept. The acceptable range is sometimes referred to as the organization's "risk appetite" or simply "risk tolerance."
- The top graph represents the total risk to an organization due to an individual vulnerability. If the "in-place countermeasures" are not adequate to reduce the risk from unacceptable residual risk levels into the acceptable range, then additional proposed countermeasures should be implemented to reduce the risk levels down into the acceptable (as seen on the lower graph).

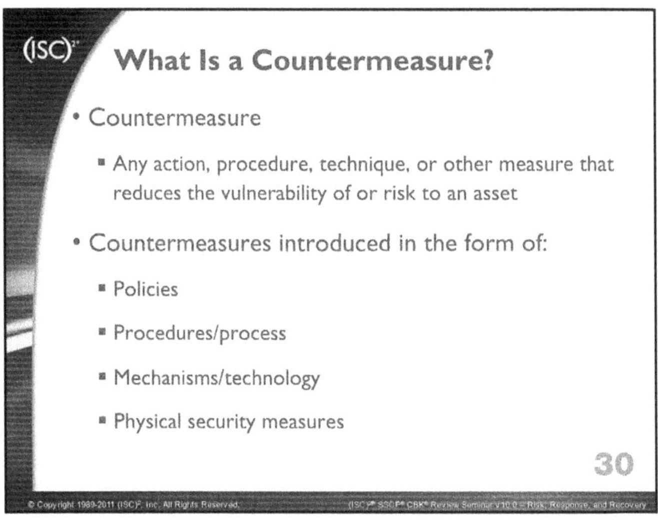

(ISC)²
This technique can be applied at all levels of risk assessment to determine tolerance levels
What Is a Countermeasure?
Countermeasure
Any action, procedure, technique, or other measure that reduces the vulnerability of or risk to an asset
Countermeasures introduced in the form of:
Policies
Procedures/process
Mechanisms/technology
Physical security measures
30


- **CONTROLS, SAFEGUARDS, AND COUNTERMEASURES ARE NOT INTERCHANGEABLE TERMS.**
- A **CONTROL** is any action taken to limit or constrain behavior. A **CONTROL IS THE TOP-LEVEL TERM**. Safeguards and countermeasures are subsets of the term "control."
- **SAFEGUARDS AND COUNTERMEASURES** are both controls that exercise restraint on, or the management of, activity.
  - Examples:
    - A safe for storage of valuables is a **CONTROL**.
    - A guard to monitor the safe is a **SAFEGUARD**.
    - Insurance against loss of their value, if stolen, is a **COUNTERMEASURE**. It will "counter," or address, the loss from a specific incident.

**REFERENCE**

Whitman, M. E. and Matford, H. J. (2007) Principles of Incident Response and Disaster Recovery, p. 492.

(ISC)²

## Pricing/Costing a Countermeasure

- The following should be considered before a countermeasure is implemented:
  - Cost of product
  - Design/planning/implementation costs
  - Environmental and compatibility costs
  - Testing requirements (time, frequency, and duration)
  - Impact on productivity

31



(ISC)² SSCP® CBK® Review Seminar v10.0 – Risk, Response, and Recovery

- **PRICING/COSTING A COUNTERMEASURE** – Factors to consider when evaluating countermeasures:
  - **COST OF PRODUCT** – The price of the product includes its base price, additional features, and the service level agreement (or annual maintenance) costs.
  - **DESIGN/PLANNING/IMPLEMENTATION COSTS** – This involves the costs associated with changes to the infrastructure, construction, design, training costs, etc. An example would be the cost to train people to operate a new piece of machinery with improved safety features.
  - **COMPATIBILITY COST** – The countermeasure must fit within the overall structure. For example, a Windows-only organization would have to carefully consider the additional costs related to training and interoperability of a Linux-based countermeasure.
  - **ENVIRONMENTAL COST** – For example, if the countermeasure is a large consumer of energy, one would need to consider whether the physical infrastructure will be able to provide it (and to cool the increased waste heat it will generate).
  - **TESTING REQUIREMENTS (TIME, FREQUENCY, AND DURATION)** – Requires time and money to perform and can lead to disruptions. All of these are costs that must be considered.
  - **IMPACT ON PRODUCTIVITY** – The impact may generate more calls to the helpdesk, increasing response times and decreasing productivity.
- **REMEMBER** – The cost of a countermeasure is more than just the purchase price of a piece of technology.

(ISC)²

## Countermeasure Examples

- Fix known exploitable software flaws
- Develop and enforce operational procedures and access controls (data and system)
- Provide encryption capability
- Improve physical security
- Disconnect unreliable networks

32



(ISC)² SSCP® CBK® Review Seminar v10.0 – Risk, Response, and Recovery

- There are an infinite number of possible countermeasures. The main rule is that a countermeasure must have a clearly defined purpose. It must address a risk and mitigate the vulnerability. A countermeasure (or control) without an exposure (risk) is a solution seeking a problem.

(ISC)²

## Countermeasure Examples (cont.)

- Delete redundant/guest accounts
- Train system administrators (specific training)
- Train everybody (security awareness)
- Install virus scanning software
- Install IDS/IPS and network scanning tools

33



(ISC)²® SSCP® CBK® Review Seminar v10.0 – Risk, Response, and Recovery

- Everyone needs to be aware of his or her security responsibilities. Security is a full-time job for some people, whereas others have only minor responsibilities (e.g., locking the door on the way out).

(ISC)²

## Countermeasure Evaluation

- Ensure that countermeasures will address the risks identified
- Note that countermeasures may themselves pose new risks to the organization
  - False sense of security
  - New point of failure
- Perform certification and accreditation of countermeasure programs to prove their effectiveness
- Assurance of best practices and "due diligence"

34



(ISC)²® SSCP® CBK® Review Seminar v10.0 – Risk, Response, and Recovery

- **COUNTERMEASURE EVALUATION –** The most important part of putting any control or countermeasure into place is to ensure that it is effectively meeting the objectives for which it was chosen. A countermeasure is of no value if it does not actually accomplish the benefit for which it was designed.
  - When evaluating a countermeasure, first ask "What problem is this countermeasure designed to solve?" Then ask, "Does this countermeasure solve this problem?"
- **NOTE THAT THE COUNTERMEASURES MAY THEMSELVES POSE A NEW RISK TO THE ORGANIZATION –** A countermeasure may create a false sense of security, or it may itself be a new point of failure on a critical system. Make sure that the countermeasure is continuously monitored, check it for compliance and good design, and perform regular maintenance. There is an inherent risk in control measures. The control may not address the underlying risk, or the control may not achieve the objective desired. This is sometimes referred to as "control risk."
- **PERFORM CERTIFICATION AND ACCREDITATION OF COUNTERMEASURE PROGRAMS TO PROVE THEIR EFFECTIVENESS –** No system, control, or application should go into production without first going through a change control process. This also applies to changes to existing production systems. Controls and countermeasures must be properly reviewed before installation or changes so that administrators do not make inadvertent or misconfiguration errors. The certification process is designed to prove that the control achieves the desired goal of reducing risk to an acceptable level.
- **ASSURANCE OF BEST PRACTICES AND "DUE DILIGENCE" –** A good risk management program indicates to auditors that the company is taking a prudent and diligent approach to security risks. Due diligence is exercised by frequently evaluating that the countermeasures are performing as expected.

(ISC)²

## Domain Agenda

- Risk Management
- **Response and Incident Management**
  - Incident Handling and Analysis
- Recovery and BCP/DRP

35



(ISC)® SSCP® CBK® Review Seminar v.10.0 – Risk, Response, and Recovery

(ISC)²

### Incident Response Objectives

- Incident response is the practice of:
  - Detecting a problem
  - Determining its cause
  - Minimizing the damage it causes
  - Resolving the problem
  - Documenting each step of the response for future reference in improving the process

36



(ISC)® SSCP® CBK® Review Seminar v.10.0 – Risk, Response, and Recovery

- **These objectives are self-explanatory. The key to incident response is maintaining a capability to effectively address all threats to security.**

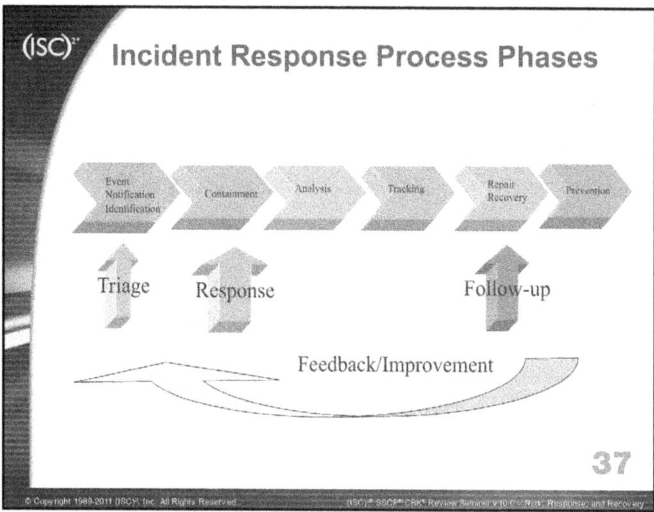


- These are the typical process phases of incident response, organized into three primary activities: Triage, response, and follow-up.

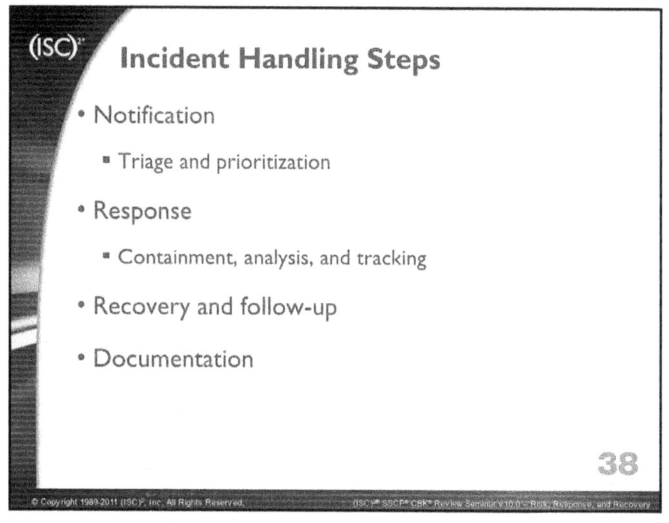


- **INCIDENT HANDLING STEPS –** This is an overview of the incident handling process that will be detailed on the following slides.

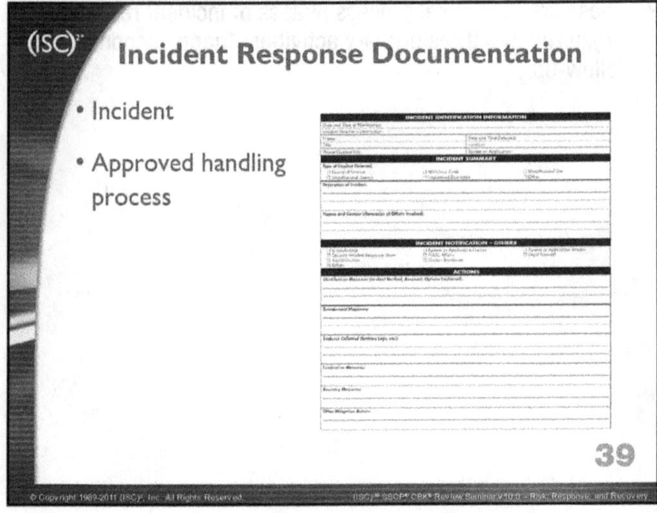


- **INCIDENT –** Any event that has the potential to negatively impact the business or its assets. It is up to the organization to categorize events that warrant the activation of the incident response escalation process.
- **APPROVED HANDLING PROCESS –** When an event becomes an incident, it is essential that a methodical approach be followed.
  - A methodical approach allows for the proper documentation and collection of information that may be of importance to the latter stages or phases of the response.
  - If you get to the phase of discovery (let alone testimony) in a case that goes to trial, you will be asked if you followed standard procedure and if you are sure you didn't leave out any steps (or if you did, why?). Having and following a checklist will help maintain admissibility.

**REFERENCE**

The definition of incident is taken from Incident Response and Computer Forensics, 2nd Edition – Prosise, Mandia & Pepe (2004).

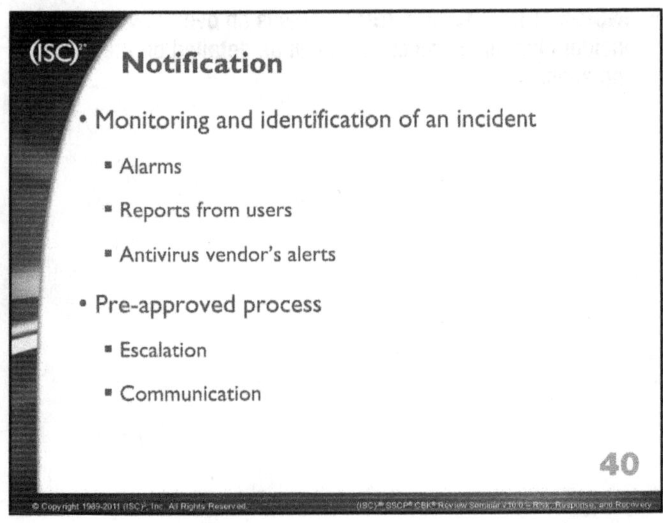

(ISC)²
Notification
• Monitoring and identification of an incident
▪ Alarms
▪ Reports from users
▪ Antivirus vendor's alerts
• Pre-approved process
▪ Escalation
▪ Communication
40
© Copyright 1989-2011 (ISC)², Inc. All Rights Reserved.


- **NOTIFICATION –** The first step in an incident response program is to determine whether an incident has in fact taken place. Not all events are incidents. A determination has to be made as to whether the incident is serious, or whether it is a common, benign occurrence.
- **MONITORING AND IDENTIFICATION OF AN INCIDENT –** The initial notification may come via an alarm, a complaint from a user, an alert from a security vendor, or from log analysis.
- **PRE-APPROVED PROCESS –** The SSCP is often one of the first people aware of an event and must know how to react. The goal is to contain the incident and, if possible, improve the situation. (Take care not to make the situation worse!) The SSCP must determine whether or not the event is a false positive. Be careful to ensure that several false positives do not cause you to become "desensitized" to real events. Keep in mind that although a series of seemingly individual events taken independently might not justify a response, when taken collectively, they may be very important.
  - A major part of an incident response process is to know how and when to escalate. And, who to notify in the event of a problem.
  - This works best when response scenarios are planned in advance and incident response team members are trained.

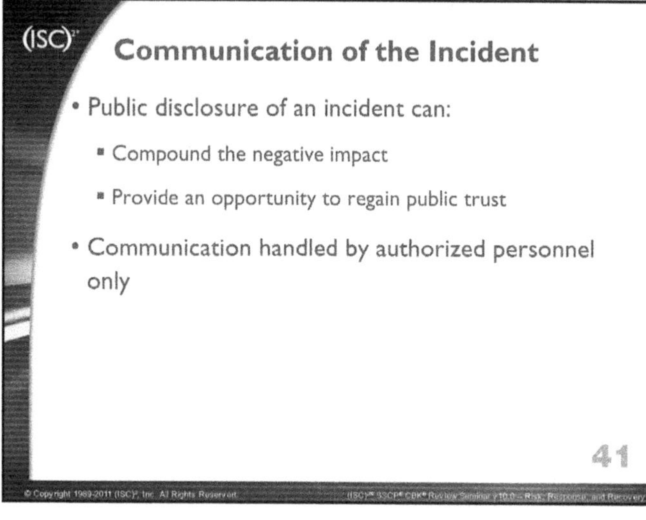


- **PUBLIC DISCLOSURE OF AN INCIDENT –** Two possible outcomes.
  - **COMPOUND THE NEGATIVE IMPACT –** May result in a very negative impact on the organization if not handled correctly.
  - **PROVIDE AN OPPORTUNITY TO REGAIN PUBLIC TRUST –** Public disclosure properly handled may create confidence in the organization, if the organization is perceived as being open and forthright.
  - In some countries/jurisdictions, legislation which requires disclosure of suspected or successful security breaches (especially of personally identifiable information) exists or is being contemplated.
- **COMMUNICATION HANDLED BY AUTHORIZED PERSONNEL ONLY.**
  - Only trained communications, human resources, and other authorized individuals should handle the communications and external notifications.
  - Denial and "no comment" are not an effective public relations strategy in today's information culture!

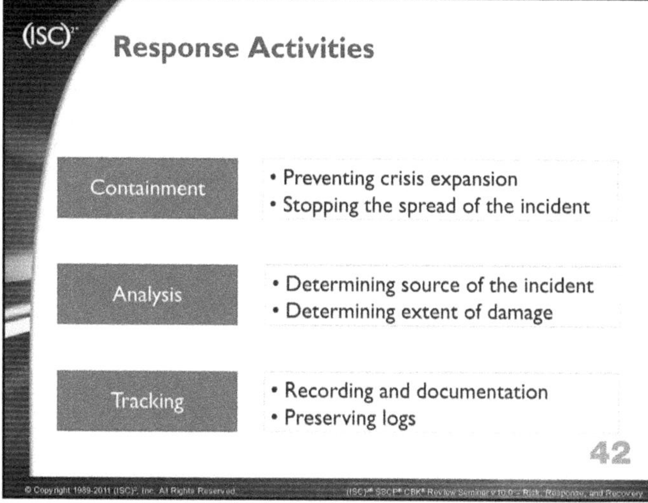


- **RESPONSE ACTIVITIES –** Once an incident has been identified, the next phase is to limit the damage.
- **CONTAINMENT –** Many incidents grow and expand rapidly, possibly affecting other systems, departments, and even business partners. The incident response plan must outline the steps that need to be taken to stop the spread of the incident without causing unnecessary outage.
  - It is essential to have a plan. The odds of guessing correctly at the best course of action during the pressures of the ongoing incident are slim.
  - Remember, the evaluation of what the "best" thing to have done will be done afterward, with the benefit of time and hindsight. A pre-approved response plan leads to better, more effective response, while also providing you with blame reduction.
- **ANALYSIS –** It is essential to correctly identify the source and type of incident so that proper recovery procedures can be enacted. Fixing symptoms doesn't solve problems. The responders must determine the extent of the damage and possibly recommend the initiation of the disaster recovery plan if the damage is too severe.
- **TRACKING –** A key component of incident management is to prevent future incidents. The logs and documentation gathered during the incident must be protected and available for future analysis.

## Computer Forensics and the Law

- The inclusion of the "law" introduces concepts that may be foreign to many information security professionals
  - Crime scene
  - Chain of custody
  - Best evidence
  - Admissibility requirements
  - Rules of evidence

43

 (ISC)² SSCP® CBK® Review Seminar v10.0 – Risk, Response, and Recovery

- These legal concepts are discussed at greater length in the following slides. Keep in mind that the prevailing "laws" may be interpreted and applied differently depending upon the country or jurisdiction in which an issue must be handled.

## Crime Scenes

- The principles of criminalistics apply to both digital and physical crime scenes
  - Identify the scene
  - Protect the environment
  - Identify evidence and potential sources of evidence
  - Collect evidence
  - Minimize the degree of contamination

44

 (ISC)² SSCP® CBK® Review Seminar v10.0 – Risk, Response, and Recovery

- Most criminal activity occurs in the physical world at some level. So, there will be some characteristics that are generally easy to distinguish. Electronic criminal activity occurs "virtually" and is not easily discovered or measured. An investigator must have a good sense of purpose and know the correct procedures to ensure that the "scene," however diverse, is identified and protected throughout an investigation.

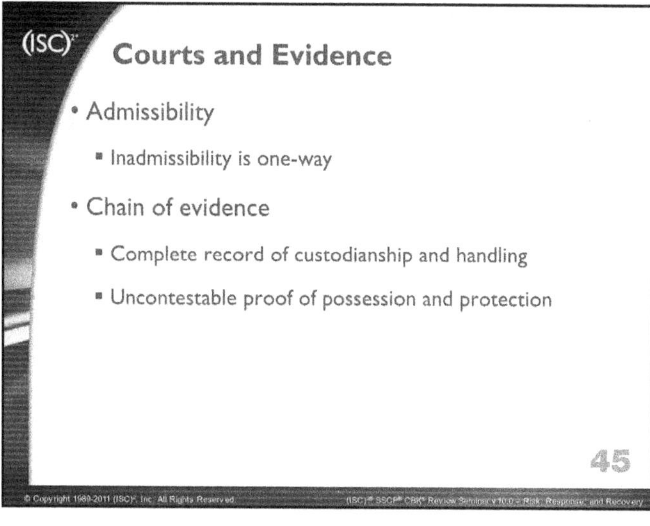

(ISC)²
Courts and Evidence
• Admissibility
▪ Inadmissibility is one-way
• Chain of evidence
▪ Complete record of custodianship and handling
▪ Uncontestable proof of possession and protection
45


- **ADMISSIBILITY –** From time to time, an incident will be the grounds for a civil or even a criminal case. Because of this, all investigations need to be handled with care to ensure that evidence is not tainted or made inadmissible. Note that even if an incident does not end up in court, the threat of court action may be enough to meet the needs of the company. For example, rather than prosecuting someone, the company may choose to force a resignation.
- **CHAIN OF EVIDENCE –** The laws of individual countries may vary. The following is true nearly everywhere – once something is done to make evidence inadmissible, there is no way to fix it (it cannot be "decontaminated").
  - In all common law countries (generally, the English-speaking countries) and many countries that follow civil law (generally, mainland Europe and South America) evidence must be shown to be authentic. In other words, it must be proven that the evidence was not altered after the incident. The "chain of custody" under which the evidence is gathered and documented is created to show this. This document lists everyone who had contact with the evidence from the moment it was first discovered. It shows how it was handled, what was done to it, and that it was protected from alteration.

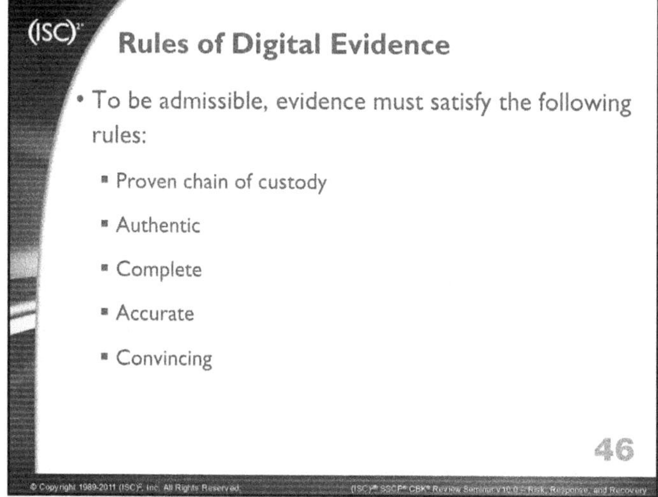

(ISC)²
Rules of Digital Evidence
• To be admissible, evidence must satisfy the following rules:
▪ Proven chain of custody
▪ Authentic
▪ Complete
▪ Accurate
▪ Convincing
46


- **RULES OF DIGITAL EVIDENCE –** These five rules are based on legal principles and should be representative of most legal systems. Digital or electronic evidence, while more fragile and volatile, must meet these criteria as well.
- **PROVEN CHAIN OF CUSTODY –** Admissible (fragile) – If at any time during an investigation, evidence is mishandled or contaminated, it cannot later be revised or "decontaminated." Once evidence is considered or judged to be inadmissible, the decision cannot be reversed. This requires extreme care to avoid making or allowing any undocumented changes to the evidence. Therefore, a complete and provable record (chain) of custody must be established and maintained at all times.
- **AUTHENTIC –** To be admissible, evidence must be provably authentic (an original, not a copy or summary) and be relevant to the issue being addressed. Generally, if there is a choice between an original and a duplicate, the original is considered best evidence. This becomes especially important when digital evidence, such as electronic records, is involved. Special techniques are usually required to ensure that tampering, modification, or loss is prevented. This usually requires trained experts.
- **COMPLETE –** Truth, whole truth, etc. Exculpatory evidence may not be hidden. It must be turned over in response to discovery.
- **ACCURATE (RELIABLE) –** Your evidence collection and analysis procedures must not cast doubt on the evidence's authenticity and veracity.
- **CONVINCING (BELIEVABLE) –** The evidence you present should be clear, easy to understand, and believable by a jury.
- **COMMENT ABOUT THE AUTHENTICITY RULE:** Ordinarily, copies or other non-direct evidence are considered "hearsay" and would not be admissible. There is commonly a business record exception rule which allows computer-generated business records to be admitted, providing it can be proven that such records are created in the normal course of business (transaction journals, audit log files, etc.). There is often a requirement that experts demonstrate the veracity of this material by recreating it or providing evidence of the underlying business procedures related to these records to show that no fabrication/falsification could have occurred.

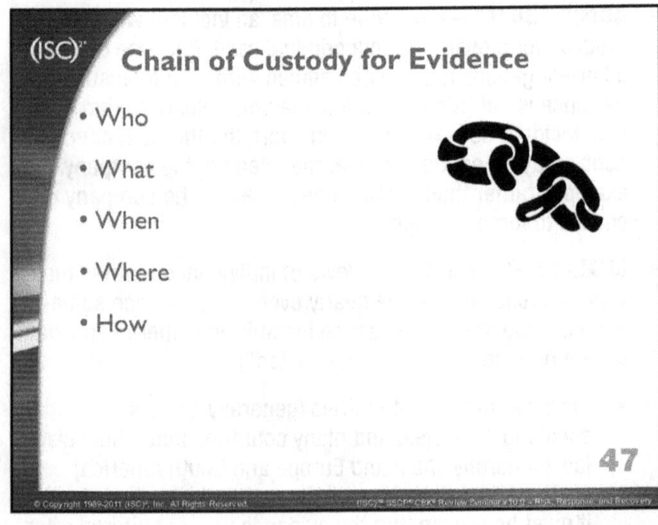
(ISC)²
Chain of Custody for Evidence
• Who
• What
• When
• Where
• How
47

- At the heart of dealing effectively with any digital/electronic evidence, is the **CHAIN OF CUSTODY** for **ACCURACY/INTEGRITY.**
- **THE CHAIN OF CUSTODY REFERS TO EVIDENCE HANDLING, AND FOLLOWS EVIDENCE THROUGH SEVERAL LIFE CYCLES** – Identification to destruction, return to the owner, or permanent archiving. Treating evidence properly requires following a formal and well-documented process. **ANY BREAK IN THIS CHAIN CAN CAST DOUBT ON THE INTEGRITY OF THE EVIDENCE** and on the professionalism of those directly involved in either the investigation or the collection and handling of the evidence.
- Documentation tracks who, what, when, where, and how … and forms part of a standard operating procedure that is used in all cases.
- One of the ways that the "when" element of the chain of custody is addressed is via a timestamp showing when the evidence was collected and in what order. For this reason it is important to record the time on any system or network that is the source of evidence.

(ISC)²

## Computer Forensics: Evidence

- Identification of evidence
- Collecting of evidence
  - Use appropriate collection techniques
  - Reduce contamination
  - Protect scene
  - Maintain the chain of custody and authentication
- Analysis of evidence
- Documenting and presenting evidence

48



- **IDENTIFICATION OF EVIDENCE –** The identification process refers to discovering the location of all data that you may have to potentially disclose in a possible legal proceeding. While the legal issue at hand may not necessarily be classified as "criminal," the same collection methods and care should be taken regardless of the nature of the investigation.
  - **COMPUTER FORENSICS: EVIDENCE –** In the past, identification was fairly trivial – you seized the "thing" that the monitor was sitting on. In most cases, the "thing" had a keyboard and mouse attached to it as well. Today, identifying containers or potential containers of digital evidence is very difficult. Small scale digital devices (i.e., cell phones, PDAs, thumb drives, USB watches, GPS devices, iPods, Xboxs, TiVos, etc.) can all store data, may be network-able, and are, therefore, potential sources of digital evidence.
- **COLLECTING OF EVIDENCE:** Adhere to principles appropriate to a criminal investigation.
  - Use sound, repeatable, collection techniques that allow for the demonstration of the accuracy and integrity of evidence or copies of evidence. The generally accepted method today is to use some kind of "hardware write-blocking device" between the suspect's hard drive and the forensic examination system. This allows an examiner or first responder to conduct a field preview on the hard drive and then make forensic bit stream copies for later archiving and analysis. A forensic bit stream image captures every sector on the drive from 0 until the last sector. Backups (or merely copying) do not capture the unallocated or residual data on a drive (i.e., deleted files). Examples of imaging software are FTK Imager, DD, EnCase, and Safeback. These are good for Windows/Linux, but not for cell phones, Palm, BlackBerry, etc. – though there are some specialized tools available for these as well.
  - A critical component of evidence gathering is to keep contamination and destruction of the scene to a minimum.
  - The acquisition process becomes more complicated with live systems and systems utilizing network storage, such as a SAN (storage area network). In some cases, you cannot turn a system off in order to make a copy of the hard drive (try Helix for live forensics). Most corporate environments would be upset if you shut down their primary database system or exchange mail system because you wanted to make a forensic image of its contents. Systems that have on-the-fly encryption enabled would also need to be imaged while running, or the investigator would have to try and break the encryption on the data only after the system was shut down. (Note that we have already discussed issues with RAM and losing the potential evidence stored there.)
  - Protect the "crime scene" from unauthorized individuals: Once a scene has been contaminated, there is no "undo" or "redo" button to push. The damage is done! Only those individuals with knowledge of basic crime scene analysis should  be allowed to deal with the scene. If the scene does become contaminated, it is vital that proper documentation is done. While contaminating a crime scene does not necessarily negate the derived evidence, it does make it harder for the investigator, since all kinds of avenues for attack and questions by the opposition/suspect are now available.
- **ANALYSIS OF EVIDENCE:** Using the scientific methods for analysis -
  - Determine the characteristics of both primary and secondary evidence, including source, reliability, and permanence.
  - Compare evidence from the various sources, determining timelines and chronology of events.
  - Reconstruct the event by recovering deleted files, sequences of events, and system activity.
  - NOTE:  This is usually conducted in a controlled environment such as a lab, but field triage is now also possible thanks to advances in hardware write-blockers and forensic software.
- **DOCUMENTING AND PRESENTING EVIDENCE:**
  - When evidence is lacking, well-trained, experienced investigators will often be called upon to give their opinion, or interpret and analyze the examination and present these findings in nontechnical terms. It can be very difficult to explain technical concepts to nontechnical audiences. Most judges, lawyers, CEOs, or board members are not technical. It is imperative that SSCPs are able to explain things using nontechnical terms, analogies, and metaphors (e.g., a computer stores information like a filing cabinet).
  - Findings may be considered secret or as confidential information. If done under the auspices of a legal department or outside counsel, they're also likely to be privileged.

(ISC)[2] **Types of Digital Evidence Analysis**

- There are at least three distinct types of analysis:
  - Media analysis (i.e., computer forensics)
    - Examining physical media for evidence
  - Software analysis
    - Review of software for malicious signatures and identity of author
  - Network analysis
    - Scrutinize network traffic and logs to identify and locate source or destination characteristics

49




- **MEDIA ANALYSIS:** Media analysis is commonly termed computer forensics.
  - Media analysis is the disciplined and detailed process of searching a drive for information. The analyst needs to understand and be able to explain several aspects of the operating system and its file system. This process includes:
    1. Recognizing operating system artifacts (i.e., the types of files created as the system runs, where they should be, and what their contents are likely to be).
    2. Understanding, analyzing, and possibly reconstructing the file system itself based on the state that it is in at the point of collection.
    3. Being able to construct a likely timeline analysis based on the three file times – modified, accessed, and created.
    4. Searching through data files that applications create and being able to interpret that data.
- **SOFTWARE ANALYSIS:** Software analysis is also used in software development (i.e., the identification of an author out of a group, reverse engineering, porting, and source code salvage).
  - There are two broad categories involved in software analysis:
    - First, the software itself must be analyzed in order to see what it does when it executes. In the case of potentially malicious software, the analyst needs to monitor disk and network activity in order to determine the software's activity. It may very well be that the computer user had no idea that this software was running.
    - Second, software must be analyzed in order to determine what types of files it creates, where it creates them, and how data is arranged in those files. Cases often hinge on proving "someone did something" such as accessing a website or sending an email. An analyst may be asked to duplicate or prove that the evidence collected actually comes from a given software application and the analyst may, therefore, need to reproduce the same information in order to show that he or she recovered what he or she claims to have recovered.
- **NETWORK ANALYSIS:** Network analysis is **COLLECTING DATA ON THE WIRE**, dissecting the data based on the protocol being used, and then being able to read the data in the network stream.
  - As discussed previously, clients and servers communicate over known and designated ports. Based on the traffic analysis and data presentation, the analyst should be able to determine what type of communication is taking place.
  - Data collected on the network should be compared with **NETWORK PORTS** in use on either end of the communication. The ports used on the systems should be visible – not hidden from someone running commands that show network status on either system. If administrators on the systems cannot see the network ports that are in use from network analysis on the system itself, there may be rootkit software on the system **HIDING TRAFFIC** flow.

(ISC)[2] **Recovery and Follow-Up**

- Repair damage
  - Backups
  - Clean systems
  - Close vulnerability to prevent reoccurrence
- Follow-up
  - New procedures
  - Better monitoring
  - Improved response plan

50




- **RECOVERY AND FOLLOW-UP –** After the incident has been contained and its source eliminated or blocked, it will be time to recover to a normal state.
- **REPAIR DAMAGE –** Before turning the system over to its normal use, the vulnerability that was exploited must be dealt with in order to stop an immediate reoccurrence. Systems may need to be rebuilt using uninfected backups of applications and data. Malicious content may also have to be cleaned off of the system to prevent reinfection.
- **FOLLOW-UP –** Learning from the incident will let management establish new procedures and controls designed to prevent or react to an incident more effectively in the future.

## Guidelines: IOCE/SWGDE Principles

1. When dealing with digital evidence, all of the general forensic and procedural principles must be applied
2. Upon seizing digital evidence, actions taken should not change that evidence
3. When it is necessary for a person to access original digital evidence, that person should be trained for the purpose

51

 (ISC)² SSCP® CBK® Review Seminar v10.0 – Risk, Response, and Recovery

- **GENERAL GUIDELINES –** Most seasoned computer forensics investigators have mixed emotions regarding detailed guidelines for dealing with an investigation.
- These principles form the foundation for the current international models most prominent today.
  - IOCE = International Organization on Computer Evidence
  - SWGDE = Scientific Working Group on Digital Evidence (USA)

**REFERENCES:**

http://www.ioce.org/core.php?ID=5

http://www.swgde.org/

## Guidelines: IOCE/SWGDE Principles (cont.)

4. All activity relating to the seizure, access, storage, or transfer of digital evidence must be fully documented, preserved, and available for review
5. An individual is responsible for all actions taken with respect to digital evidence while the digital evidence is in his or her possession
6. Any agency, which is responsible for seizing, accessing, storing, or transferring digital evidence is responsible for compliance with these principles

52

 (ISC)² SSCP® CBK® Review Seminar v10.0 – Risk, Response, and Recovery

- The six principles of the IOCE/SWGDE continued.

(ISC)²

## Domain Agenda

- Risk Management
- Response and Incident Management
- **Recovery and BCP/DRP**
  - **Business Continuity Planning**
  - Disaster Recovery Planning
  - Backup/Redundancy Alternatives

53



(ISC)²® SSCP® CBK® Review Seminar v10.0 – Risk, Response, and Recovery

(ISC)²

## Business Continuity Management

- Business continuity management includes both:
  - Business continuity planning (BCP) - Keeping critical business processes operational in the event of a disaster
  - Disaster recovery planning (DRP) - Recovering the infrastructure necessary for normal business operations

54



(ISC)²® SSCP® CBK® Review Seminar v10.0 – Risk, Response, and Recovery

- **BUSINESS CONTINUITY MANAGEMENT –** How an organization responds to a disaster may well determine whether the organization can continue to operate. Lack of planning greatly increases the risk that the organization will not be able to respond appropriately and, therefore, be unable to return to normal operations. Business continuity management (BCM) will not only include BCP and DRP, but also crisis management, incident response management, and risk management.
  - Examples of disasters include:
    - Extreme weather – Hurricanes, tornados, etc.
    - Criminal activity – Theft of credit card numbers at e-commerce sites.
    - Civil unrest/terrorist acts.
    - Operational – Electric blackout – For example, northeastern United States, summer of 2005.
    - Application failure – For example, London Stock Exchange down one day in April 2000.
- The purpose of BCP is to mitigate incidents. But, in the event of an incident, the first priority must always be to ensure the safety of people. Mitigation or containment of the damage is secondary.

**REFERENCE**

http://www.adrc.or.jp/publications/TDRM2005/TDRM_Good_Practices/PDF/Chapter1_1.2.pdf

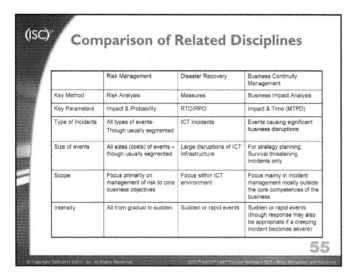

## Comparison of Related Disciplines

| | Risk Management | Disaster Recovery | Business Continuity Management |
|---|---|---|---|
| Key Method | Risk Analysis | Measures | Business Impact Analysis |
| Key Parameters | Impact & Probability | RTO/RPO | Impact & Time (MTPD) |
| Type of Incidents | All types of events-Though usually segmented | ICT Incidents | Events causing significant business disruptions |
| Size of events | All sizes (costs) of events – though usually segmented | Large disruptions of ICT Infrastructure | For strategy planning: Survival threatening incidents only |
| Scope | Focus primarily on management of risk to core business objectives | Focus within ICT environment | Focus mainly in incident management mostly outside the core competences of the business |
| Intensity | All from gradual to sudden | Sudden or rapid events | Sudden or rapid events (though response may also be appropriate if a creeping incident becomes severe) |

55



(ISC)² SSCP® CBK® Review Seminar v 10.0 – Risk, Response, and Recovery

- This graphic outlines the differences between risk management, disaster recovery, and business continuity management factors and processes.

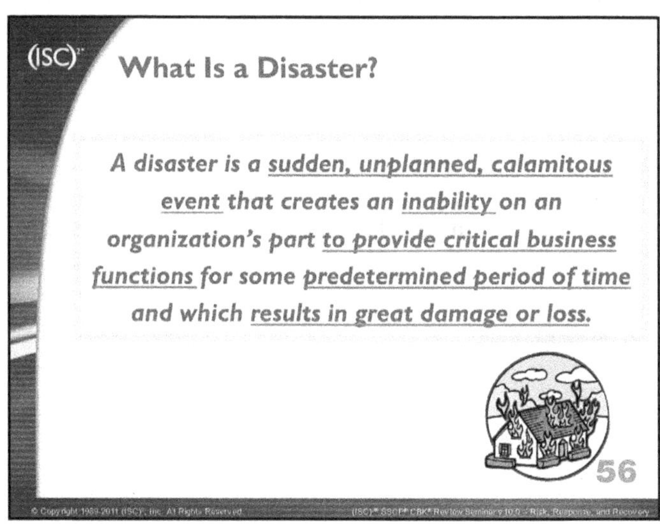

(ISC)²
What Is a Disaster?
A disaster is a sudden, unplanned, calamitous event that creates an inability on an organization's part to provide critical business functions for some predetermined period of time and which results in great damage or loss.
56


- Or a simpler definition: A disaster is any event that makes a critical business function (CBF) unavailable for longer than its maximum tolerable downtime (MTD).

**REFERENCE**

http://www.adrc.or.jp/publications/TDRM2005/TDRM_Good_Practices/PDF/Chapter1_1.2.pdf

**Key Business Continuity Terminology**

- BIA: business impact analysis
- CBF: critical business function
- MTD: maximum tolerable downtime
- RTO: recovery time objective
- RPO: recovery point objective
- EOC: emergency operations center

57



- **BIA: BUSINESS IMPACT ANALYSIS –** An analysis of the business to determine what kinds of events will have an impact on what systems.
  - Do not limit the focus of the BIA to the information systems department and infrastructure! A business with a supply chain disaster (e.g., warehouse fire, trucking strike, etc.) could easily suffer a major impact that is not related to technology at all.
  - Some scenarios affect some departments, some affect others, and a critical few affect the entire business.
- **CBF: CRITICAL BUSINESS FUNCTION –** Once the BIA has identified the business systems that are affected by an incident, the affected systems must be ranked in terms of most to least critical. The ranking of the critical business functions have to do with whether the business can survive, and for how long, in the absence of a critical function.
- **MTD: MAXIMUM TOLERABLE DOWNTIME –** MTD is the maximum time that a business can survive without a particular critical system. Each of the disaster planning and mitigation solutions must be able to recover CBFs within their MTDs. Clearly, those with the shortest MTDs are the most critical.
- **RTO: RECOVERY TIME OBJECTIVE –** The time frame for restoring a CBF. RTO must be shorter than or equal to the MTD.
- **RPO: RECOVERY POINT OBJECTIVE –** Incidents can cause loss of data. The amount of tolerable data loss must be calculated for each business function. Recovery procedures must be able to meet the minimums defined here. If the business can afford to lose up to one day's data, then nightly backups may be an acceptable solution. However, if the business must prevent all data loss, a redundant server or storage solution will be required.
- **EOC: EMERGENCY OPERATIONS CENTER –** The place in which the recovery team meets and works during a disaster. Many businesses will have more than one EOC. One might be nearby (to handle a building fire, for example) and another might be a significant distance away (to handle an earthquake or regional power outage, for example).
- Here is how MTD and RTO work together. Power goes out in the data center. It takes six hours to move to the alternate site (RTO). The business can survive for nine hours without a functioning data center. At this moment, there is an event, but not yet an incident that can be defined as a disaster. If power is expected to return within three hours (MTD – RTO) the business may not declare a disaster in anticipation that the business will resume normally. However, if power is still out at the three hour mark, it is time to declare a disaster.

**The Business Continuity Processes**

- Appoint an owner
- Define the objectives and scope
- Get Executive approval
- Develop and approve a planning process and timetable
- Create a planning team
- Decide the structure, format, components and content
- Determine the strategies and integration with other plans
- Determine circumstances beyond the scope
- Gather information about critical business processes
- Assess information and set priorities and requirements
- Write and review the plan
- Test the plan and measure results
- Revise and improve the plan
- Schedule ongoing testing and maintenance
- Periodically assess readiness (awareness) of constituents

58



- **THE BUSINESS CONTINUITY PROCESS –** This is a brief overview of the primary activities involved in the performance of a BCP project. These activities are arranged into a series of phases that are reviewed in detail throughout the course.

## Business Impact Analysis (BIA)

- Describes the impact that a disaster has on a critical business function
- We primarily ask two questions:
  - What can affect the business?
  - How will it affect the business?
- A successful BIA will map the critical business functions to the processes on which they rely
- All impacts should be considered, including those that are difficult and less obvious

59



- **BUSINESS IMPACT ANALYSIS –** What is a business impact analysis (BIA)? A BIA is the determination of the extent of the impact that a particular incident would have on business operations over time. The determination of the BIA drives the selection of the recovery strategy and the CBFs.
- Different incidents require different recovery strategies. A fire in the accounting department might call for some outsourcing and temporary quarters, a flood in the basement might activate a service bureau plan, while an earthquake or hurricane might cause a permanent move to a new facility.
- Business impact analyses are done for three key reasons:
  - To establish the organizational value of each business unit or resource as it relates to the functioning of the overall organization.
  - To provide the basis for identifying the critical resources required to develop a business recovery strategy.
  - To establish the timely order or priority for restoring the functions of the organization in the event of a disruption.

---

REFERENCE

http://www.continuitycentral.com/HazardIdentificationBusinessImpactAnalysis.pdf

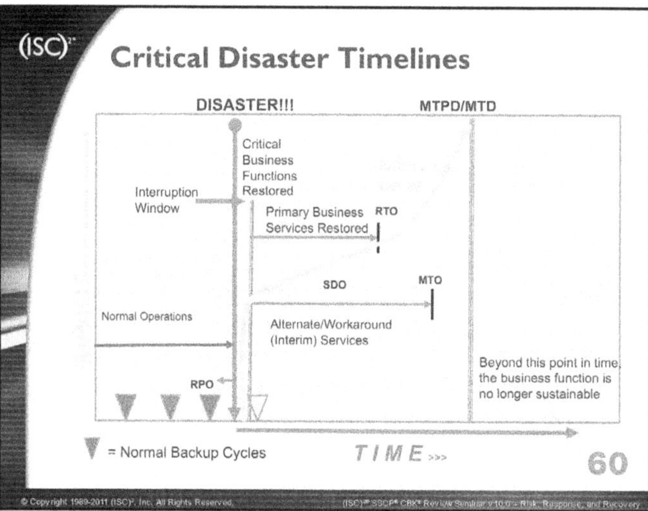


- **CRITICAL DISASTER TIMELINES –** This diagram is an example of a planned recovery effort. The first area on the left represents normal operations including regular backups. The left-most line represents the occurrence of a disaster. This begins a period of disruption known as the interruption window. Service is not available during this time period. The second line from the left represents the establishment of minimal service levels – perhaps a manual workaround or other process that provides at least partial service. The length of the interruption window is the time between the disaster and the establishment of critical services. After critical functions are restored, additional, alternate services may be required while recovery activities continue. This reduced level of service should be measured by the SDO – Service delivery objective.
- Once the critical business functions/services **(CBF)** are properly re-established, the interim services may be turned down. This should be accomplished within the period defined as RTO – Recovery time objective. Depending on the severity of the disaster, the organization may need to continue operating in this condition for an extended period of time.
- It is important that the RTO is less than the MTPD. If service is not restored prior to the point in time declared to be the MTPD, the business is not likely to recover.
- The next major step is the restoration of the business to normal and the closure of the incident.
- **LOSS OF DATA –** Since the last known data backup was generally performed at a time prior to the disaster, the data that changed between the time of the backup and the time of the disaster is usually lost. This is a criterion for the RPO, recovery point objective, that the organization had set. It represents the most current level of data that can be recovered following a disaster.
- **KEY DEFINITIONS:**
  - **MAXIMUM TOLERABLE PERIOD OF DISRUPTION/MAXIMUM TOLERABLE DOWNTIME (MTPD/MTD) –** The maximum period of significant loss or disruption of primary (critical) services that can be sustained before PERMANENT, unrecoverable conditions are encountered.
  - **RECOVERY POINT OBJECTIVE (RPO) -**
    - Based on acceptable data loss.
    - Indicates latest point in time in which it is acceptable to recover the data.
  - **RECOVERY TIME OBJECTIVE (RTO) -**
    - Based on acceptable downtime.
    - Indicates the desired point in time at which the business operations will resume after a disaster.
  - Additional parameters important in defining recovery strategies:
    - **INTERRUPTION WINDOW –** Time between point of failure and restoration of critical services (CBF).
    - **SERVICE DELIVERY OBJECTIVE (SDO) –** Interim level of alternate services until normal services are restored.
    - **MAXIMUM TOLERABLE OUTAGE (MTO) –** Maximum duration of interim services.

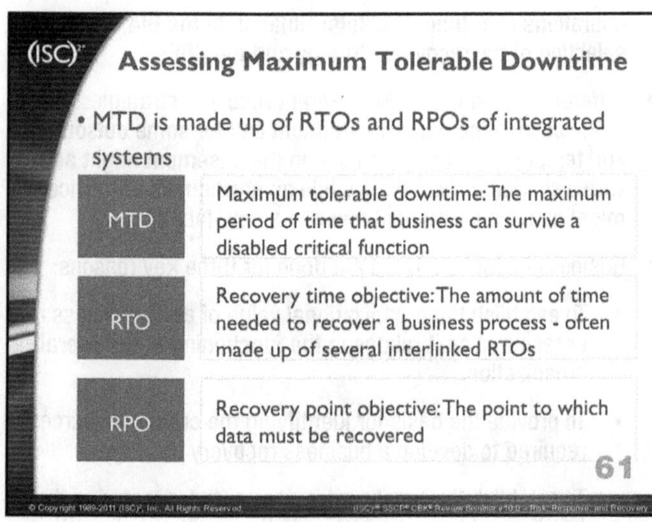


- **MTD –** Comprises the RTOs of several integrated functions. For example, e-commerce Web servers depend on network services, ISP availability, and electricity. Each of these has its own incident-dependent RTO. Parts of the recovery are able to take place in parallel, but some may have to be sequential.
- **RPO –** Defines the amount of tolerable data loss. The RPO can come from the business impact analysis or sometimes from a government mandate (e.g., banking laws, pharmaceutical research data retention regulations, etc.).

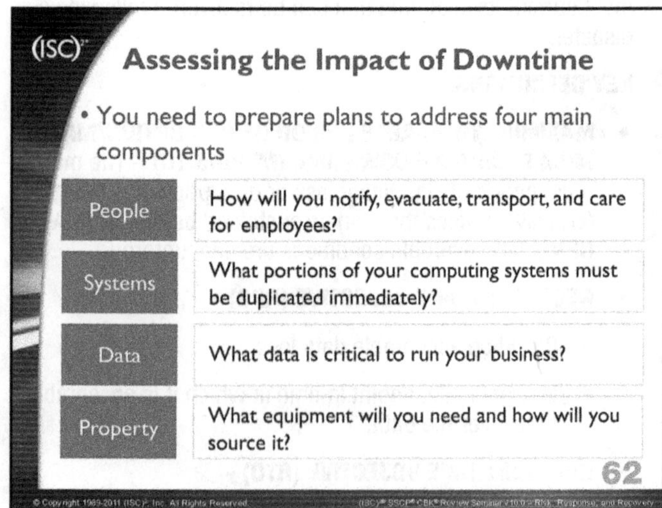


- **ASSESSING THE IMPACT OF DOWNTIME –** The BIA identifies critical data and systems. Note that the criticality of systems and the criticality of data are not always the same. A system may be more critical than the data it contains and vice versa. Criticality describes the extent to which the business relies on the availability of those systems and/or data.
- **ISSUES TO BE CONSIDERED DURING THE BIA INCLUDE –**
  - **PEOPLE –** How will you notify them of the incident and the impact? How will you evacuate, transport, and care for employees (including, for example, paying them)?
  - **SYSTEMS –** What portions of your computing and telecommunications infrastructure must be duplicated immediately? How long do you have? A minute, an hour, or a day?
  - **DATA –** What data is critical if you are to run your business? How will you recover critical data that is lost?
  - **PROPERTY –** What items are essential to your business? Things such as tools, supplies, and special forms all must be recoverable or easily replaced.
- Assessing the impact of downtime is a planning step in the BIA. You are helping to determine what must be done and in what order so as to accomplish the goals described in these four categories. Figuring out how to do this is the main thrust of BCP.

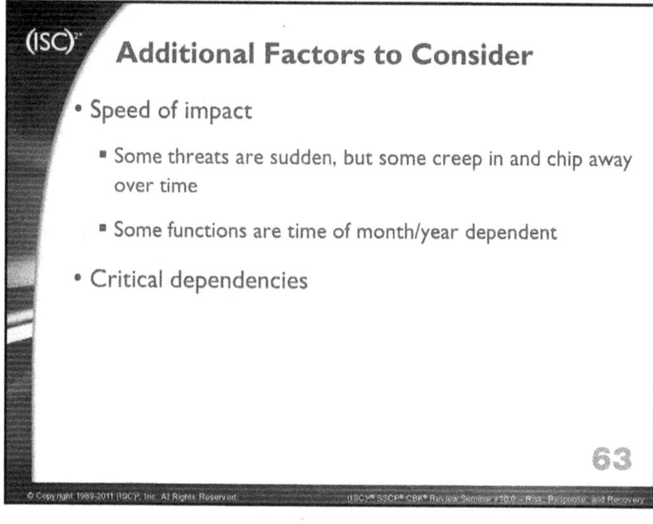

(ISC)²
Additional Factors to Consider
• Speed of impact
▪ Some threats are sudden, but some creep in and chip away over time
▪ Some functions are time of month/year dependent
• Critical dependencies
63


- **IMPACTS FROM DISRUPTIONS OVER TIME –** Some incidents may become more significant over time. The slow deterioration of a critical processing facility might generate a disaster, or continuous installation of new devices in a computer room might overtax the electric supply capacity and eventually cause a blackout or a fire.
- **SPEED OF IMPACT –** Some systems are more important during certain times of the year. A company that supplies heating oil will be taxed to its limits in the winter and will have service level agreements that will be jeopardized with even the smallest outage. That same company might easily withstand far more severe incidents (longer MTDs) in the summer when load is minimal.
- **CRITICAL DEPENDENCIES –** The BIA must also identify what supporting elements critical operations need in order to function:
  - Information processing.
  - Personnel.
  - Communications.
  - Equipment.
  - Facilities.
  - Other organizational functions.
  - Vendors.
  - Suppliers.

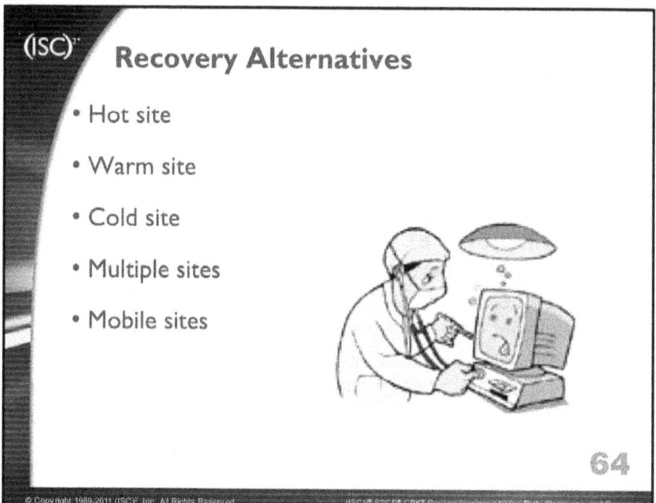


- **RECOVERY ALTERNATIVES –** A business continuity (BC) coordinator considers each alternative's ability to support critical business functions, its operational readiness compared with RTO, and the associated cost. He or she examines specifications for workspace, security requirements, IT, and telecommunications.
- If the business (or some part of it) has to be moved for recovery, there are typically three choices:
  - The first is a dedicated site operated by the organization, such as a multiple processing center.
  - The second is likely to be a commercially leased facility, such as a hot site or mobile facility.
  - The third is likely to be an agreement with an internal or external facility. These are all addressed on the next slide.
- When contracting with external commercial providers, understand that they offer services to numerous organizations. Keep in mind that disasters can affect many customers. What priority will you have if this happens? Know your options (along with prices) for things such as test time, declaration fees, and minimum/maximum recovery days. Make sure that the specifications for workspace, security requirements, IT, and telecommunications are suitable for your critical business functions. Ensure that there are suitable accommodations for staff including rest, showering, and catering.
- Regardless of the alternative chosen by the organization, it is the responsibility of the IT department to ensure that all the equipment and data identified as necessary is in place at the alternate site. This includes the documentation and other items identified in the recovery categories.

(ISC)²

## Interim or Alternate Site Strategies

| Feature | Hot Site | Warm Site | Cold Site | Multiple Sites |
|---|---|---|---|---|
| Cost | High | Medium | Low | No direct costs |
| Computer equipped | Yes | Yes | No | Yes |
| Connectivity equipped | Yes | Yes | No | Yes |
| Data equipped | Yes | No | No | Yes |
| Staffed | Yes | No | No | Yes |
| Typical lead time to readiness | Hours | Hours to days | Days to weeks | Moments to minutes |

65

- **MULTIPLE SITES –** A multiple processing center or mirrored site supports 100% availability. It is always ready and under the organization's control. It is the most expensive option because it requires fully redundant or duplicate operations and synchronized data and it is continuously operated by the organization. Its additional costs might be justified by business needs (such as having a duplicate support staff) other than recovery planning, however, making cost allocation a complex process.
- **HOT SITE –** There are two kinds of hot sites. One is company owned and dedicated, and the other is a commercial hot site. The advantage of a hot site is the rapid availability of alternate computing facilities and a fairly rapid recovery timeframe. An internally-owned hot site is more expensive than some other alternatives, but there is no competition for its facilities in the event of a regional disaster.
- **WARM SITE –** A warm site has some common IT, communications, power, and HVAC, but IT equipment, such as servers, and communications will have to be procured and transferred there. Data will also have to be retrieved and loaded as well. A warm site is often owned by the organization and used for their offsite storage of data.
- **COLD SITE –** A cold site is an empty data center with HVAC and power. It is the least expensive option, but it needs substantial time to get into running order because all equipment and telecommunications must be procured, delivered, and configured. Some organizations begin recovery in a hot site and transfer over to a warm site or cold site in the case of a lengthy interruption.
- **MOBILE SITE –** Not mentioned on this Slide are mobile sites. Mobile sites are trailers that have been converted to self-contained portable data centers with power generators. Note that there is a time delay while the trailer is driven to the recovery location, set up, configured, and data loaded. They are also relatively small, and their primary use is to handle a single department that has to be relocated on an emergency basis (small fire, hazardous materials spill, etc.).

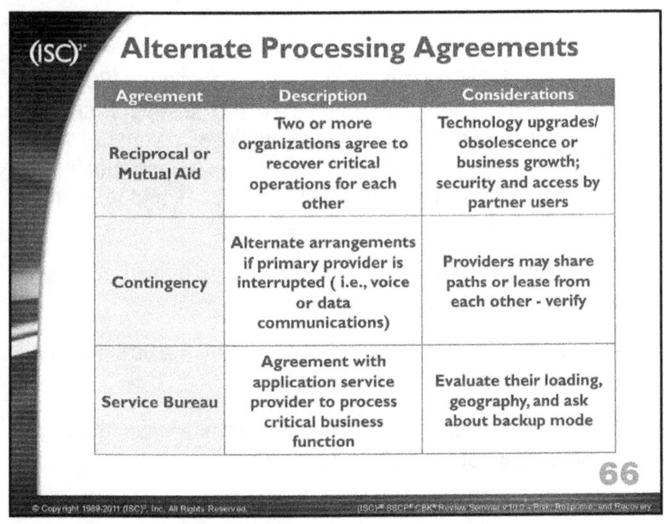

(ISC)²

## Alternate Processing Agreements

| Agreement | Description | Considerations |
|---|---|---|
| Reciprocal or Mutual Aid | Two or more organizations agree to recover critical operations for each other | Technology upgrades/ obsolescence or business growth; security and access by partner users |
| Contingency | Alternate arrangements if primary provider is interrupted ( i.e., voice or data communications) | Providers may share paths or lease from each other - verify |
| Service Bureau | Agreement with application service provider to process critical business function | Evaluate their loading, geography, and ask about backup mode |

66

- **ALTERNATE PROCESSING AGREEMENTS –** Another approach to recovery alternatives is to identify organizations with equivalent IT configurations and backup technologies, such as another company, a contingent carrier, or a service bureau. In this approach, a formal agreement is established between these organizations for support should there be an interruption. Draft agreements should be carefully reviewed by IT, security, and legal departments.
- **RECIPROCAL OR MUTUAL AID –** The organization may enter into a reciprocal agreement, also known as mutual aid or a consortium agreement, with a company that has similar technology. A consortium agreement is one in which a number of companies agree to support the other members. Careful consideration must be given before committing to this approach. For example, can each organization continue its primary business while supporting the agreement partner? Can the equipment and infrastructure support both organizations? Testing is strongly encouraged to confirm technical and extra-load processing compatibility. Another concern is the sensitivity of the information and any regulations that might surround that information because it may be accessible by the agreement partner's administrators or users. Ensure that neither partner upgrades nor retires technology (making processing incompatible) without notice or review.
    - **RECIPROCAL CENTERS** are often businesses that are in the same line of business but are not direct competitors, such as cross-town hospitals, or a paperback book publisher paired with a hardcover publisher. There are advantages of familiarity and commonality– things such as sharing of special codes, industry jargon, and special forms needed in the industry being on hand already, etc.
    - For example, hospitals use the term "DRG code" to refer to a number that corresponds, in a common database, to a diagnosis, procedure, or disease.
- **CONTINGENCY –** An organization may contract for contingency carriers or contingent suppliers should their primary supplier experience an interruption. Considerations are maintenance fees and activation time. Another concern is that carriers (especially communications carriers) may share the same cable or routing paths. It is prudent to question them.
- **SERVICE BUREAU –** A service bureau is an application service provider that has extra capacity (such as a call center to handle incoming calls) and the organization contracts for emergency use of it. Concerns with this arrangement are similar to those with a reciprocal agreement arrangement. The vendor might increase its business and consume its extra capacity, or the vendor might modify its hardware or configurations.

## Plan Review

- Plan review
  - At least annually
  - Following regular tests
  - As part of incident review process
- Inventory and configuration lists
  - Review current inventory of systems, processes, and network connections periodically

67

- **PLAN REVIEW –** The business continuity plan (BCP) must be regularly updated and maintained. Some firms do this annually, other firms choose different periods. In addition to the scheduled reviews, any major changes such as a merger or acquisition or adding or abandoning a line of business or facility should trigger a plan review. In addition to the obvious benefit of having an up-to-date plan, testing and plan revision is an excellent way of training new employees as they are added to the team.
- **INVENTORY AND CONFIGURATION LISTS –** The inventory and configuration lists for the systems and applications must also be regularly updated and maintained. This action should occur on a periodic basis, as appropriate for the individual organization. In addition to the scheduled reviews, any major changes -- such as a merger or acquisition, or adding or abandoning a line of business or facility -- should trigger a plan review.

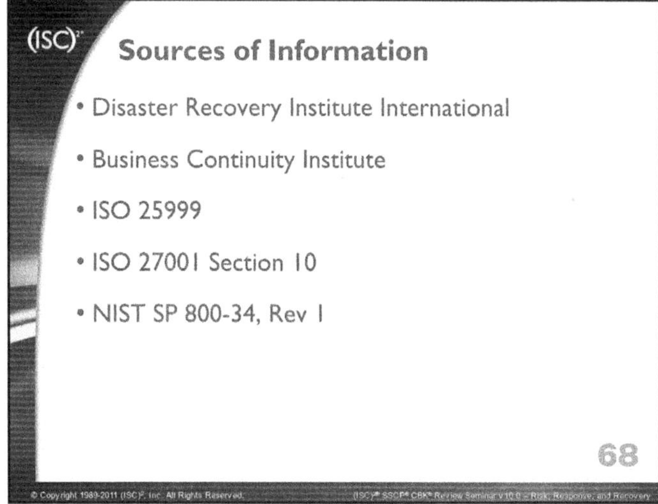

(ISC)²
Sources of Information
Disaster Recovery Institute International
Business Continuity Institute
ISO 25999
ISO 27001 Section 10
NIST SP 800-34, Rev 1
68


- Two organizations that are the thought leaders in continuity planning joined together in 2003 to create The Professional Practices for the Business Continuity Planner. "This body of knowledge is accepted by both DRI International (headquartered in the United States) and by the Business Continuity Institute (BCI) (headquartered in the United Kingdom)." This document's information is mirrored in many other documents, for example:
  - BS 25999-1.
  - ISO 17799-section 10.
  - NIST Special Publication 800-34, Rev 1, Contingency Planning Guide for Federal Information Systems.
- The BCI Good Practices Guideline (GPG) is an extension/improvement to the professional practices document and is available from the Business Continuity Institute.
- One other source bears special mention for deep details: www.disasterrecoverybooks.com is a website dedicated to disaster recovery books and software.

**REFERENCES:**

http://www.thebci.org/gpgdownloadpage.htm

http://www.drj.com/GAP/

http://www.disasterrecoverybooks.com/data/index.htm

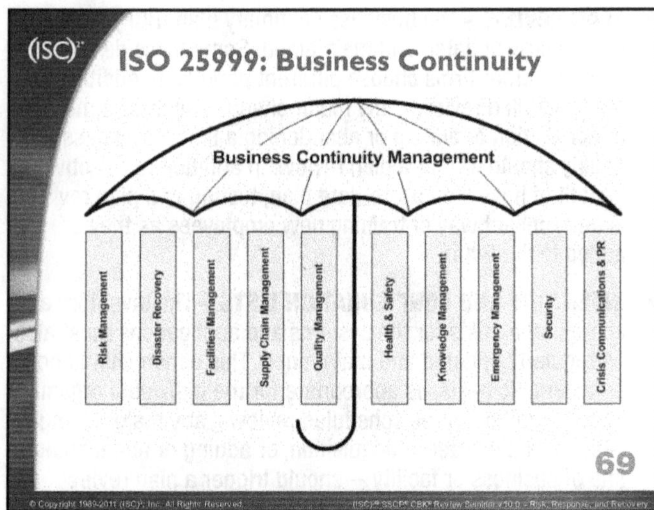


- **BS 25999** is a standard in the field of business continuity management (BCM), published in 2006-2007. This standard replaces PAS 56, a publicly available specification, published in 2003 on the same subject. The standard addresses a business continuity management system (BCMS) and is published in two parts. The first part provides general guidance for establishing processes and covers principles and terminology. The second part can be independently verified through audit and specifies the requirements for implementing, operating, and improving a BCMS. It is based on the PDCA model for continuous improvement (PLAN-DO-CHECK-ACT).
- A useful means of understanding the difference between the two is that Part 1 is a guidance document and uses the term "should," while Part 2 is an independently verifiable specification that uses the word "shall."
- Certification (independent verification) to this standard is available from several accredited certification bodies (LRQA and BSI) and is a multistage process involving assessments by a BCMS professional.
- The BCMS Code of Practice (BS 25999-1) covers: Scope, terminology, and definitions, and an overview of what a BCMS covers. The business continuity life cycle is described, which includes:
  - Establishing a policy.
  - Program management.
  - Understanding the organization.
  - Determining strategies.
  - Developing and implementing a response plan.
  - Exercising, maintaining, and assessing the BCM culture.
  - Embedding the BCM into organizational culture.
- *The specification (BS 25999-2) defines the scope of the BCMS and addresses requirements for implementation:*
  - **PLAN** the BCMS, establishing and embedding the BCMS within the organization.
  - **DO –** Implementing and operating the BCMS, the actual work process of the BIA, determining BC strategies, developing and implementing a response capability, and finally verification (e.g., exercise, maintenance, and review).
  - **CHECK –** Monitoring and reviewing the BCMS covers internal audit and management review of the BCMS.
  - **ACT –** Maintaining and improving the BCMS preventative and corrective action.
- There are a number of similar worldwide standards:
  - **NORTH AMERICA –** National Fire Protection Association NFPA 1600: Standard on Disaster/Emergency Management and Business Continuity Programs.
  - **AUSTRALIA –** Standards Australia HB 292-2006: A practitioner's guide to business continuity management HB 293-2006: Executive guide to business continuity management.
  - **WORLDWIDE –** (ISO) ISO/PAS 22399:2007 Guideline for incident preparedness and operational continuity management.

(ISC)²

## Domain Agenda

- Risk Management
- Response and Incident Management
- **Recovery and BCP/DRP**
  - Business Continuity Planning
  - **Disaster Recovery Planning**
  - Backup/Redundancy Alternatives

70




(ISC)²

## Disaster Recovery Planning

- Disaster recovery planning is the recovery of information processing functionality
  - Advance planning
  - Benefits
- Emergency operations center
  - Emergency operations manager

71




- The disaster recovery plan defines an emergency operations center (an alternate location from which the BCP/DRP is coordinated and implemented) as well as an EOC manager and a determination of when that manager should declare an incident a disaster. Remember, a disaster is an event that prevents a critical business function (CBF) from operating for a period of time greater than the maximum tolerable downtime (MTD).
- **DISASTER RECOVERY PLANNING –** Having a disaster recovery plan in place allows critical decision making to take place ahead of time when it can be managed and reviewed, without the urgency and pressure of an actual disaster. Failure to create these plans in advance results in managers making best-guess decisions under a great deal of pressure.
  - DRPs are long-term, time-consuming, and expensive projects. Eight figure budgets are not uncommon. It is essential that senior management not only support, but mandate an effective, well-tested DRP.
  - The process starts with a business analysis, identifying critical functions and their maximum tolerable downtimes, and then identifying strategies for dealing with a wide variety of scenarios that might call the plan into action. The SSCP's most likely participation in this process is as a member of the disaster planning and disaster recovery teams.
  - Note that DRPs can be used to lower insurance rates and the preparation of a DRP can assist in risk management efforts.
- **EMERGENCY OPERATIONS CENTER –** The hub for command, coordination, and control of the incident. This should be set up with all necessary equipment, including copies of plans, communications services, and office supplies.
- Example of an EOC manager in action:
  - Electricity is out in your building.
  - Your generators have six hours capacity, which matches your MTD for loss of power.
  - It takes three hours to bring the alternate site up to operational state, but costs tens of thousands of dollars to activate.
  - The electric utility company is promising that power will be restored in "half an hour."
  - For the first three hours, the EOC manager takes reports from the utility company, and if power is restored, no disaster is declared.
  - As the elapsed time reaches three hours (the time it takes to recover and still be within the MTD), the EOC manager declares a disaster and activates the alternate site and DRP.
  - If power is restored before the site is active, the EOC manager cancels the declaration and processing resumes at the primary site. Otherwise, processing begins at the alternate site.

(ISC)²

## Steps in a Disaster

- The first priority in a disaster is the safety of individuals
- The second priority is to contain the damage
- The third is to assess the damage, and begin recovery operations according to the disaster recovery plans and business continuity plans

72

(ISC)² SSCP® CBK® Review Seminar v10.0 – Risk, Response, and Recovery

- This Slide lists some of the priorities in the event of a disaster.

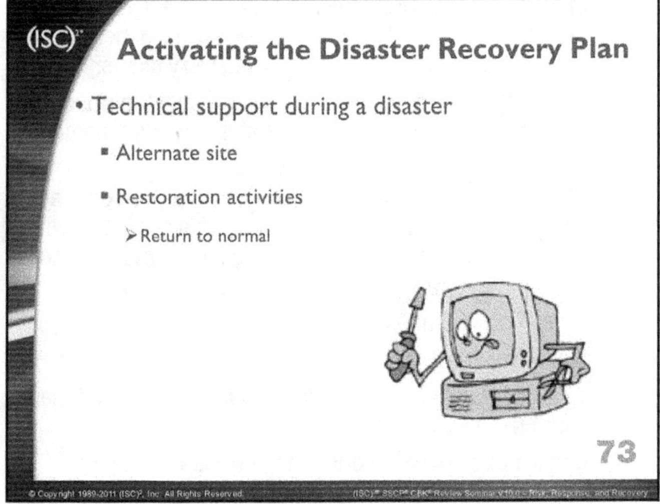
(ISC)²
Activating the Disaster Recovery Plan
• Technical support during a disaster
▪ Alternate site
▪ Restoration activities
➢ Return to normal
73

- **ACTIVATING THE DISASTER RECOVERY PLAN –** The SSCP plays a key role in re-establishing business operations in a crisis by rebuilding the networks and systems that the business requires.
- **ALTERNATE SITE –** In many cases, the recovery may be at an alternate site and requires the SSCP to build a network rapidly from available backup data, equipment, and any equipment that may be available from vendors.
- **RESTORATION ACTIVITIES –** This is the return to normal operations by rebuilding the primary site. The transition back to the normal site and the closure of the alternate site should be part of the "return to home site" portion of the BCP/DRP.
  - Salvage and repair teams are activated and do their work before people and data can return to the primary site. SSCPs are often on the repair team in order to rebuild the damaged parts of the network infrastructure with an eye to matching or increasing the previous level of security. If new equipment is needed, use this opportunity to implement security improvements.

(ISC)²

## Sequencing of Activities After Disaster

- Respond to the disaster and assess damage (emergency response team-EOC)
- Recover (recovery team)
  - Most critical functions take priority
  - Least critical functions last
- Restore (salvage or resumption team)
  - Salvage and repair as necessary
  - Non- or least-critical functions first
  - Most-critical functions last
- Reset and reverify all emergency resources
- Resume normal operations

74

 (ISC)² SSCP® CBK® Review Seminar v10.0 – Risk, Response, and Recovery

(ISC)²

## Operating at a Reduced/Modified Level

- Absence or reduction of normal controls
  - Loss of separation of duties
- Combined services on fewer servers
- Backups during alternate processing

75

 (ISC)² SSCP® CBK® Review Seminar v10.0 – Risk, Response, and Recovery

- **OPERATING AT A REDUCED/MODIFIED LEVEL –** During a crisis, many of the normal conditions such as controls, support, processes, etc., may not be available. The SSCP may need to adapt very quickly in order to ensure the secure operation of systems, including backups and reconciliation of errors.
- **ABSENCE OR REDUCTION OF NORMAL CONTROLS –** Normal processes such as separation of duties or spending limits might need to be suspended. This should be handled by instituting compensating controls such as additional auditing after the fact. The disaster recovery plan should predesignate certain personnel/roles with escalated privileges or spending authority.
  - If a number of systems are unavailable, users may require additional technical support or guidance on how to use alternate systems or access. The minimum recovery resources should have been initially identified in the BIA as part of the recovery requirements.
- **COMBINED SERVICES ON FEWER SERVERS –** During a disaster and business recovery effort, it may be expedient to combine services that were formerly on different hardware platforms onto common servers. This may speed up recovery, but must be done carefully to ensure that the movement and recovery goes smoothly.
- **BACKUPS DURING ALTERNATE PROCESSING –** During the period of running at the alternate site, it is important to continue to take backups of data and systems. This may prevent further disasters that might otherwise occur in the event of a failure at the recovery site.

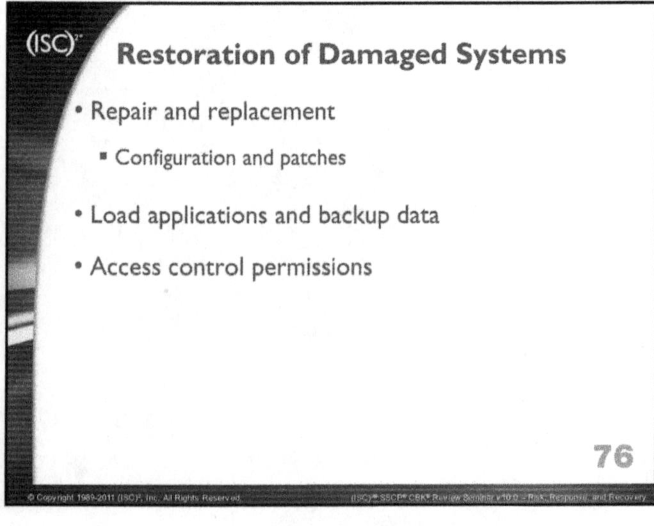


- **RESTORATION OF DAMAGED SYSTEMS –** Rebuilding of damaged systems requires preplanning. Configuration charts and inventory lists must be available and backup applications and data accessible. Access control lists must be provided to ensure that only legitimate users are allowed on the system.
- **LOAD APPLICATIONS AND BACKUP DATA –** Once the rebuilding starts, the administrator must ensure that the operating systems and applications are updated with the most current patches. Backups or installation disks often contain older versions that do not have the latest patches and updates.
    - After the system is rebuilt, data must be restored to the RPO. This includes reconciliation of books and records and making sure that the operating systems and applications are current and secure.
- **ACCESS CONTROL PERMISSIONS –** This is often overlooked in recovery plans. The access control rules, directories, and remote access systems must be activated to permit the users to access the new systems. This can also be a problem to be addressed when making the plan to ensure that any vendor software will run on alternate processors. Some vendor products are licensed to only operate on a certain CPU.

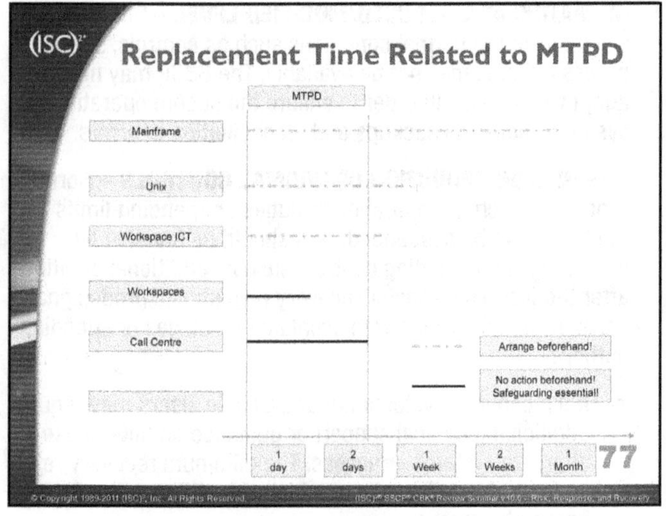


- This graphic summarizes the various potential technology impacts on the maximum tolerable downtime determination. Strategy and planning must be accomplished beforehand for equipment replacement indicated by "red dashed line" in the graphic.

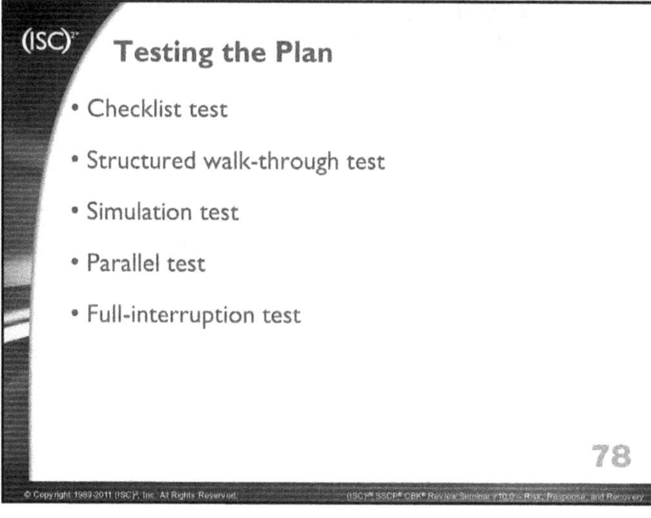
(ISC)²
Testing the Plan
• Checklist test
• Structured walk-through test
• Simulation test
• Parallel test
• Full-interruption test
78

- **TESTING THE PLAN –** No BCP or DRP is complete or should be accepted without having been thoroughly tested. Testing may help ensure that the plan works and that the objectives of the CBFs, MTDs, RPOs, and RTOs will be met.
  - Each stage of the testing process must consider the continued need for security and the technical resources required both to perform the test and to handle an actual disaster.
- **CHECKLIST TEST –** A checklist test is a simple review of the plan by managers and the business continuity team in order to ensure that contact numbers are current, and that the plan reflects the priorities and structure of the organization. This kind of check is also called a "desk check" because each member of the team checks his or her portion of the plan while sitting at his or her desk. As well as checking their contact lists, team members will determine whether there have been changes in the functions of their departments that might make the current plan obsolete or even partially invalid. They also look at the near-term (one or two years) plan for their departments and make sure that the plan will cover those needs too, insofar as they can be predicted.
- **STRUCTURED WALK-THROUGH TEST –** (also known as a "table top exercise") – Have a team of representatives from each department.
  - Each team should present its portion of the plan to the other teams.
  - Review objectives of the plan for completeness and correctness.
  - Affirm the scope of the plan, as well as any assumptions made.
  - Look for overlaps and gaps.
  - Review the structure of the organization as well as the reporting/communications structure.
  - Evaluate the testing, maintenance, and training requirements.
  - Conduct a number of scenario-based exercises to evaluate the effectiveness of the plan.
  - Participants in this test meet (usually in a board or meeting room) to step through the plan together in a structured manner, as if they were executing the plan for a certain type of incident. The goal of the structured walk-through is to identify errors in individual departments' plans such as gaps or overlaps. (Gaps are where one department is under the impression a critical task was to be handled by a different department. Overlaps are where two departments thought they'd have exclusive (or majority) use of the same resource (e.g., two departments each thinking they'd have 2/3rds of the replacement desktops.))
- **SIMULATION TEST -**
  - More than a paper exercise and requires more planning than a walk-through.
  - All of the members of staff involved in the operations/procedures participate in the test.
  - The test identifies:
    - Reaction and response times of staff.
    - Inefficiencies or previously unidentified vulnerabilities.
  - The simulation is conducted onsite using only countermeasures defined in the plan.
  - The simulation test involves many of the employees who have not otherwise participated in plan development. They are often asked to come in on an otherwise off day (such as a weekend).
  - The simulation test is intended to identify shortcomings. The test should be carried through as far as possible. If, for example, a critical file is missing, the file should be generated or obtained from the main site, and the test should then continue. On-the-spot corrections must be logged for evaluation and plan update later, but the test should only be terminated when it completes or if it becomes impossible to continue.
- **PARALLEL TEST –**
  - This test is usually conducted at the alternate site. It is the same as the full-interruption test (below), except that processing does not stop at the primary site.
  - It is an operational test, so it will not include the representatives from HR, PR, Purchasing, Facilities, etc.
  - Since a parallel test means activating the alternate site, there is usually a significant cost involved. The test **MUST** have senior management approval before it is carried out.
  - The results of the test are compared with the processing at the original site.
  - A gap analysis exposes any weaknesses (or under-performance issues) that require attention.
  - The auditors are usually involved at every step in order to monitor the success of the test and to ensure that the parallel run data does not get mixed into the normal operational data.
- **FULL-INTERRUPTION TEST –** This test is conducted at the alternate site. During the test, the original system is shut down for the duration. Only those processes that exist at the alternate site are used to continue the business operations. **THIS IS HIGH RISK: running a full-interruption test runs the risk of actually creating a disaster! A full-interruption test should only be conducted when all other types of tests have been undertaken successfully. SENIOR MANAGEMENT APPROVAL MUST BE OBTAINED *PRIOR* TO THE TEST.**

(ISC)²

**Disaster Recovery Issues**

- Safety/security of damaged site
- Availability of resources
  - Generators/UPS
    - Fuel supplies
    - Capacity
- Transportation of equipment and backups
- Communications and networks

79

 (ISC)²® SSCP® CBK® Review Seminar v 10.0 – Risk, Response, and Recovery

- **DISASTER RECOVERY ISSUES –** This is a short list of disaster recovery issues that are often overlooked in the maintenance and execution of a disaster recovery plan.
- **AVAILABILITY OF RESOURCES**
  - **GENERATORS/UPS –**
    - **FUEL SUPPLIES –** Fuel must be fresh and contracts should be in place to guarantee a supply of fuel in a crisis.
    - **CAPACITY –** The generators must receive routine maintenance and should be run periodically to ensure that they are ready to operate and capable of carrying the expected system load.
  - **SAFETY OF DAMAGED SITE –** The primary (damaged) site must be protected from further damage or looting.
  - **RE-ENTRY –** The damaged site must be examined by people qualified to determine whether it is safe for people to re-enter.
- **TRANSPORTATION OF EQUIPMENT AND BACKUPS –** The plan must also provide safe transportation of people, equipment, and backup data to and from the alternate site.
- **COMMUNICATIONS AND NETWORKS –** Regular telephone service often fails in a crisis and it may be necessary to have an alternate method of communication available, especially between key team members.

(ISC)²

**Domain Agenda**

- Risk Management
- Response and Incident Management
- **Recovery and BCP/DRP**
  - Business Continuity Planning
  - Disaster Recovery Planning
  - **Backup/Redundancy Alternatives**

80

 (ISC)²® SSCP® CBK® Review Seminar v 10.0 – Risk, Response, and Recovery

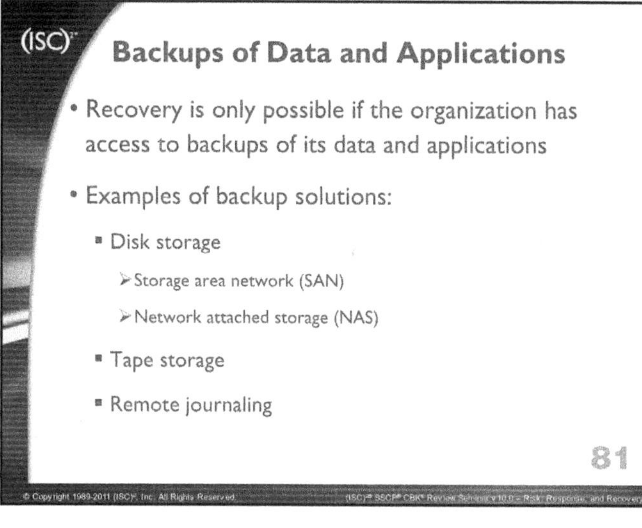

(ISC)²
Backups of Data and Applications
• Recovery is only possible if the organization has access to backups of its data and applications
• Examples of backup solutions:
▪ Disk storage
➢Storage area network (SAN)
➢Network attached storage (NAS)
▪ Tape storage
▪ Remote journaling
81


- Plans must include dealing with backup storage media, location, and access. Tape backup is traditional and still the most common. However, restoration from tape is slow and many systems have RTOs that are shorter than the tape restore time. These kinds of sites often use disk-based solutions such as a SAN, NAS, or even offsite network-based storage such as remote journaling. (In remote journaling, a log of online transactions is made at an offsite location. The log is used to update a copy of the database. Should the primary site become unavailable, the offsite copy will be very current.)
- Backups provide extra copies of needed resources (data, documentation, equipment, etc.). A backup site can be activated should a primary site become unavailable. Similarly, a backup tape can be restored, possibly at an alternate site, and then processing can resume.
- Redundancy options provide for the availability of alternate resources. For example, RAID1 mirroring writes data to two disks instead of just one. Should one disk fail, the other will carry the load. Similarly, standby or clustered servers are set up so that standby servers will take over should the other fail, or just absorb the extra load (clustered).
- When a second server takes over from a failed primary, it needs access to the data. SANs and NASs (described on the next pages) are designed to attach to the network rather than to a particular machine, thus enabling server/data redundancy options.

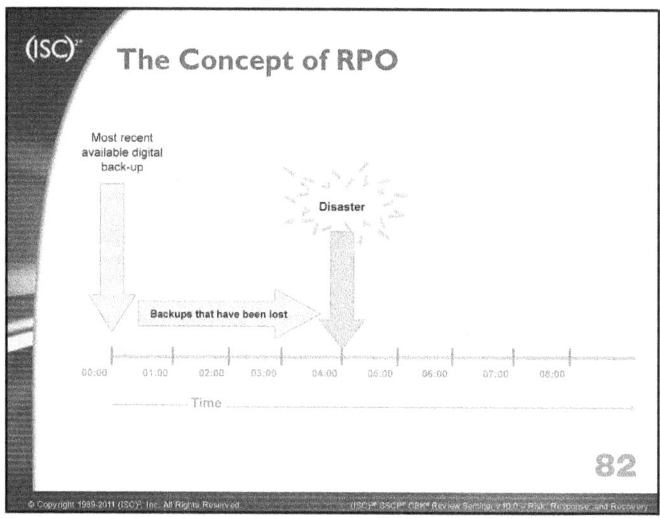


- The recovery point objective (RPO) is that point in time when all data must be recovered. RPO is based on acceptable data loss. It indicates the latest point in time in which it is acceptable to recover the data.

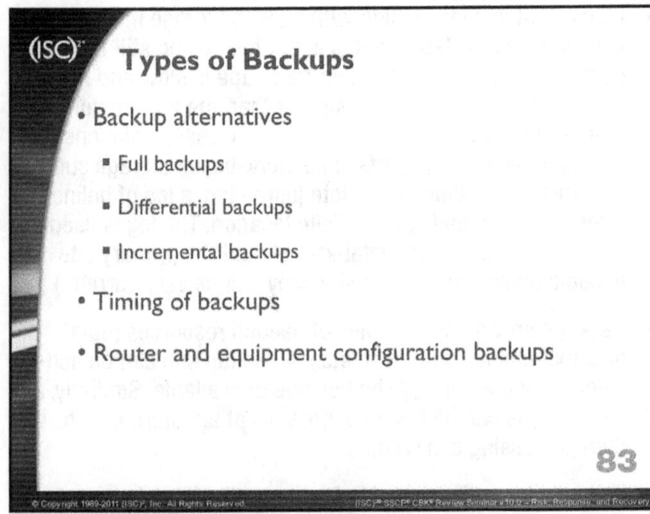
(ISC)²
Types of Backups
• Backup alternatives
▪ Full backups
▪ Differential backups
▪ Incremental backups
• Timing of backups
• Router and equipment configuration backups
83

- **BACKUP ALTERNATIVES –** Backups and restores are slow. Businesses have three alternatives for processing them:
  1. **FULL BACKUP –** As its name implies, everything is copied to a backup media (usually tape, sometimes CD, DVD, or disk).
  2. **DIFFERENTIAL BACKUP –** A full backup is made, perhaps on Sunday when traffic is lightest. On Monday through Saturday, daily changes since Sunday's full backup are also copied to backup. As the week progresses, each night's backup (the differential) will take a little longer.
  3. **INCREMENTAL BACKUP –** Again, a full backup is made when traffic is light. Then, each night, only that day's changes are recorded. As the week progresses, the nightly (incremental) backup takes about the same amount of time.
- **TIMING OF BACKUPS –** It is faster to create the incremental weekday backups than the differential backups. This comes at a price, however. Should a restore be needed, systems using differential backups would only need to restore the full backup and then the latest differential, while those using incremental backups would need to restore the full backup and then each day's incremental backups in order to complete the restore.
- **ROUTER AND EQUIPMENT CONFIGURATION BACKUPS –** Items such as router and switch configurations, user access permissions and configurations (e.g., active directory), and server/workstation operating systems and configurations must also be backed up. To make this more manageable, most large companies have a standard base configuration for workstations that can be reloaded on demand. As long as these are kept up to date (patched and fixed) this is an attractive solution.

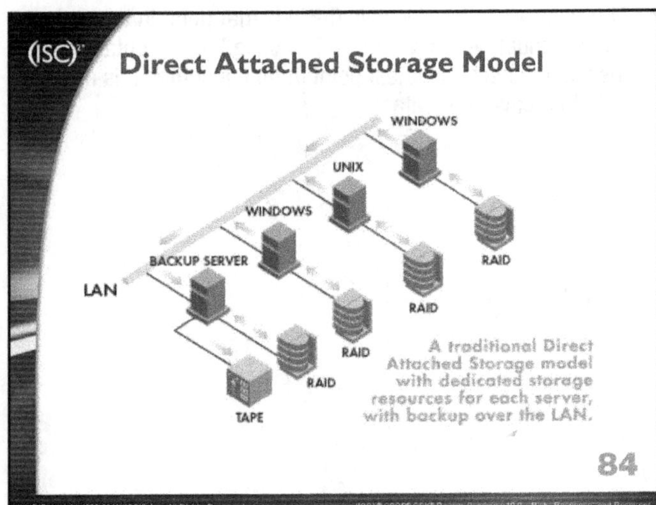
(ISC)²
Direct Attached Storage Model
WINDOWS
UNIX
WINDOWS
BACKUP SERVER
LAN
RAID
RAID
RAID
RAID
RAID
TAPE
A traditional Direct Attached Storage model with dedicated storage resources for each server, with backup over the LAN.
84

- The most basic method of attaching storage to a network is a one-to-one direct connection to a network server. Disk arrays are typically connected to a server using SCSI connectors and then shared out to network users.
- Although this method is certainly the easiest to implement, it does not scale very well as storage needs grow.
- It also does not provide system redundancy. If the computer fails, access to the data will be lost even if the data is otherwise intact.

**REFERENCE**

http://www.brocade.com/san/evaluate/compare_san.jsp

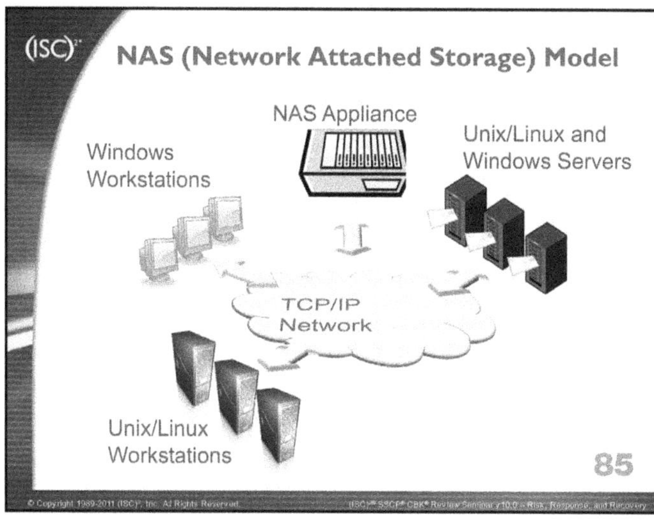


- **NETWORK ATTACHED STORAGE (NAS) –** Is a self-contained storage appliance. It connects to the existing network infrastructure and communicates using network protocols such as TCP/IP. NAS devices are typically capable of communicating with multiple file system implementations.
- From the point of view of the user, the data will still appear to be attached to a server. The servers can be set up in "standby" or "redundant" mode, wherein the primary server is monitored by a secondary server and jumps in if the primary fails to respond to probes, or it can be set up in "clustered" mode, wherein multiple servers all share the load and absorb the extra work if one of them fails.

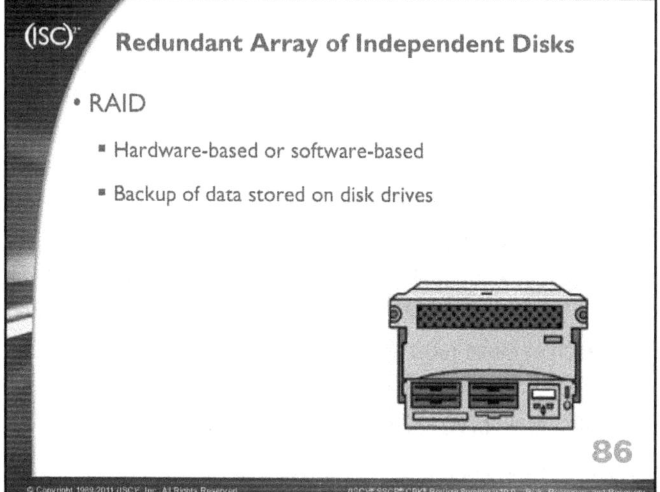


- **RAID –** RAID uses two or more hard disks to store data. There are various forms of RAID, some of which provide speed, some of which provide redundancy, and some of which (at greater cost) provide both.
  - **HARDWARE-BASED RAID –** Requires a RAID controller (often a PCI expansion card or motherboard capability) that interfaces the host with the storage disks. (The interface may be as a high-speed SCSI, a network attached storage or fiber channel.) The controller is responsible for the management of the disks as well as the calculation of parity bits where needed. A hardware implementation often includes hot-swappable disks to allow for data recovery with no system downtime.
- **SOFTWARE-BASED RAID –** Is handled by the operating system through the normal drive controller. It can be faster than hardware-based RAID but it does pose a penalty on CPU performance. This option is often used for high-transaction volume systems and OLTP (online transaction processing). A drawback to software-based RAID is that the system must be rebooted after a failure.

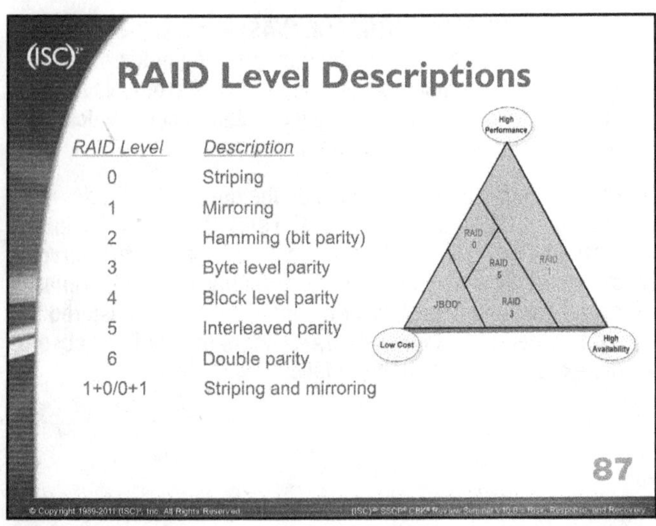

RAID Level Descriptions
RAID Level
Description
0
Striping
1
Mirroring
2
Hamming (bit parity)
3
Byte level parity
4
Block level parity
5
Interleaved parity
6
Double parity
1+0/0+1
Striping and mirroring
High Performance
Low Cost
High Availability
JBOD
87


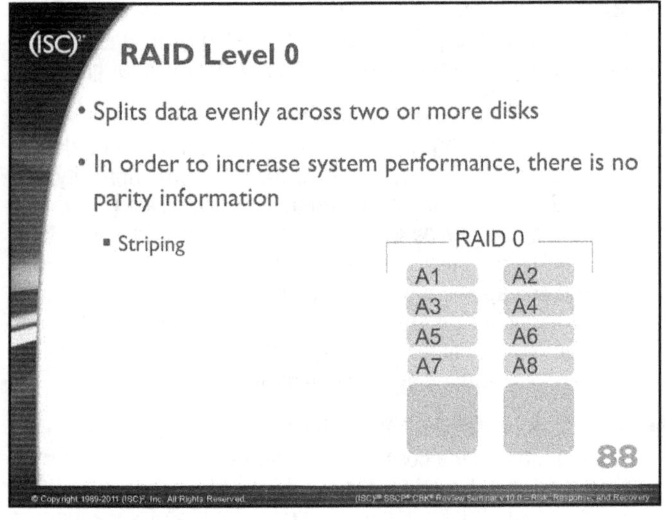

RAID Level 0
Splits data evenly across two or more disks
In order to increase system performance, there is no parity information
Striping
RAID 0
A1
A2
A3
A4
A5
A6
A7
A8
88


- **RAID LEVEL 0 –** Stripes the data across several disks allowing for a faster read and write speed. It does not provide backup or redundancy, so it is not useful for high-integrity systems or high-availability applications.
    - The data is broken into blocks which are then written to separate disks. Ideally, there will be a separate disk controller for each disk.
    - Since RAID 0 does not provide any redundancy or parity bits, it is not fault-tolerant and should not be used on mission-critical systems.
- In each of these RAID options, assume that the disks are 1TB (terabyte) drives (for easy math). Then ask several questions:
    1. If a drive fails, how much data is lost?
    2. For RAID options that have spare or recovery drives, what is the overhead percentage?
    3. What impact will each configuration have on read speed? On write speed?

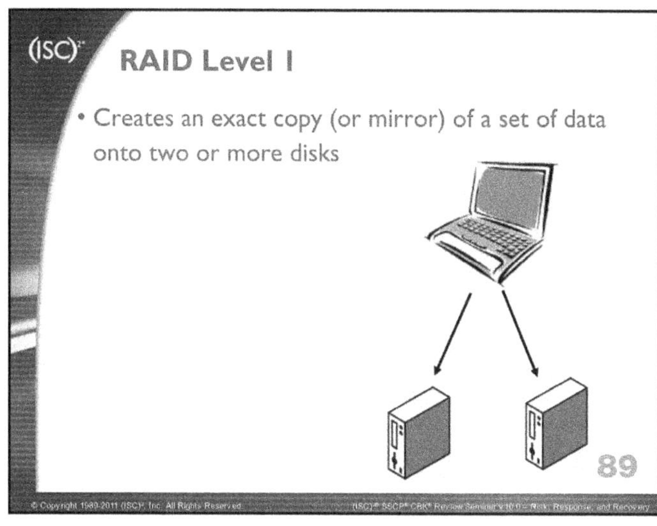

RAID Level I
• Creates an exact copy (or mirror) of a set of data onto two or more disks
89


- **RAID LEVEL 1 –** Also called mirroring, is popular because of its simplicity and high level of reliability and availability. Mirrored arrays consist of two or more disks. Each disk in a mirrored array holds an identical image of the user data. A RAID Level 1 array may use parallel access for a high transfer rate when reading, but more commonly, RAID Level 1 array members operate independently and improve performance for read-intensive applications, albeit at relatively high inherent cost. This is a good entry-level redundant system, since it only requires two drives.
- RAID 1 provides 100% redundancy of data, so data can just be copied onto a replacement disk in the event of a disk failure.
- There are two alternative RAID 1 configurations:
  - One uses two controller cards, each connected to a single drive.
  - One uses a single controller card attached to two drives.

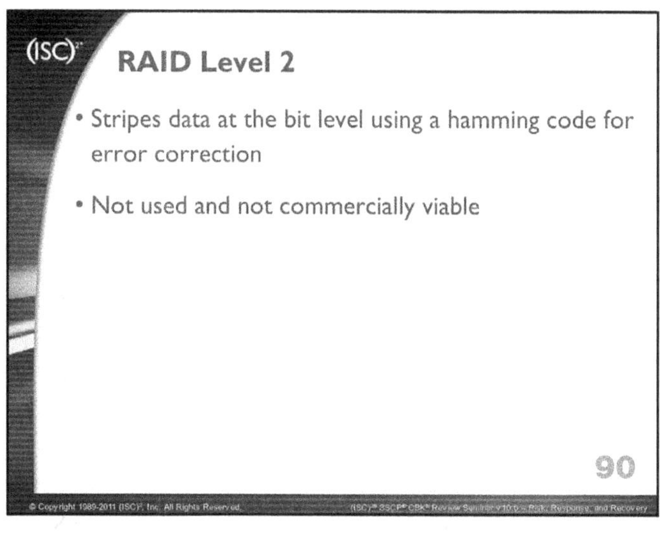

RAID Level 2
• Stripes data at the bit level using a hamming code for error correction
• Not used and not commercially viable
90


- **RAID LEVEL 2 –** This form of RAID is not used and is not commercially viable. It creates a hamming code for error correction and was designed for very high data transfer rates with simultaneous error correction.

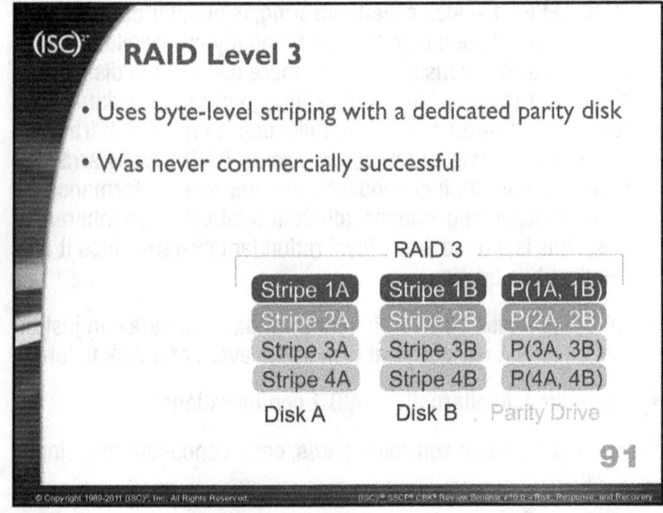


- **RAID LEVEL 3 –** Adds redundancy of information in the form of storing parity to a parallel access striped array, permitting regeneration and rebuilding in the event of a disk failure. One stripe of parity protects corresponding stripes of data on the remaining disks. RAID Level 3 provides for a high transfer rate and high availability at an inherently lower cost than mirroring. Its transaction performance is poor, however, because all RAID Level 3 array-member disks operate in lockstep.
  - RAID 3 has very high read and write data transfer rates. Any disk failure has an insignificant impact on throughput. RAID 3 ensures that if one of the disks in the striped set (other than the parity disk) fails, its contents can be recalculated using the information on the parity disk and the remaining functioning disks. If the parity disk itself fails, then the RAID array is not affected in terms of I/O throughput but it no longer has protection from additional disk failures. A RAID 3 array can also improve the throughput of read operations by allowing reads to be performed concurrently on multiple disks in the set.
  - Even though it is "byte" level, it must be remembered that disk hardware only does reads and writes a sector (512 bytes) at a time. In byte-level striping (in a three disk set), the odd bytes go to the first disk, the even ones to the second, and parity to the third.
  - RAID Level 3 added overhead without an offsetting gain, and so was never commercially successful.

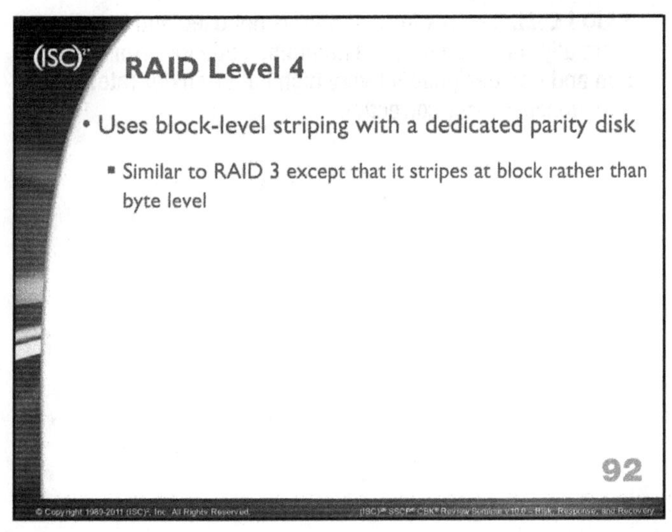

(ISC)²
RAID Level 4
• Uses block-level striping with a dedicated parity disk
▪ Similar to RAID 3 except that it stripes at block rather than byte level
92


- **RAID LEVEL 4 –** Is similar to RAID 3 in that it uses parity bits stored on a single disk to protect data. RAID Level 4 array's member disks are independently accessible and its performance is more suited to transaction I/O than to large file transfers.
- RAID 4 has a very high read data transaction rate. Its low ratio of ECC (parity) disks to data disks results in a higher level efficiency. It also has a high aggregate read-transfer rate.
- RAID 4 eases the burden of sorting bytes that RAID 3 imposes. Its only drawback is that the first disk is used more heavily than the second, the second more heavily than the third, and so on.
  - In a three disk system, one is parity, two are data.
  - Some files use an even number of sectors, some don't.
  - In files that have an odd number of sectors, the system pads as necessary with 0s so as to fill both the even and odd sector for the last block, thereby writing both.
  - The padded sector need not be read back in when reading. As a result, the first disk is read more often than the second. In most computer systems, a file is read far more often than it is written.

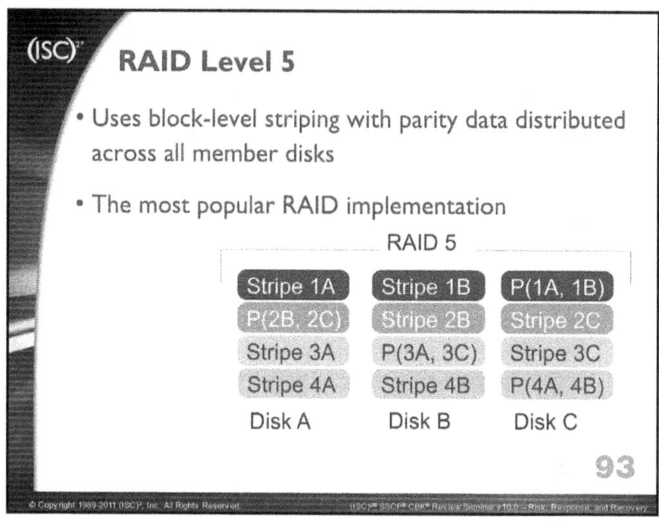


- **RAID LEVEL 5 –** Stripes the data and the parity bits across the entire disk array. It provides redundancy and the ability to recover lost data due to disk failure through the calculation of the parity bit. It provides low cost redundancy and has, therefore, become the most popular RAID implementation.
- RAID 5 has much the same benefits of RAID 4 when compared with RAID 3. But, RAID 5 also balances the workload across all the disks by spreading the parity around.
- When writing files, the first file starts on disk A, then continues on disk B (parity on C), then the next two sectors are written to A and C with parity on B and so on.

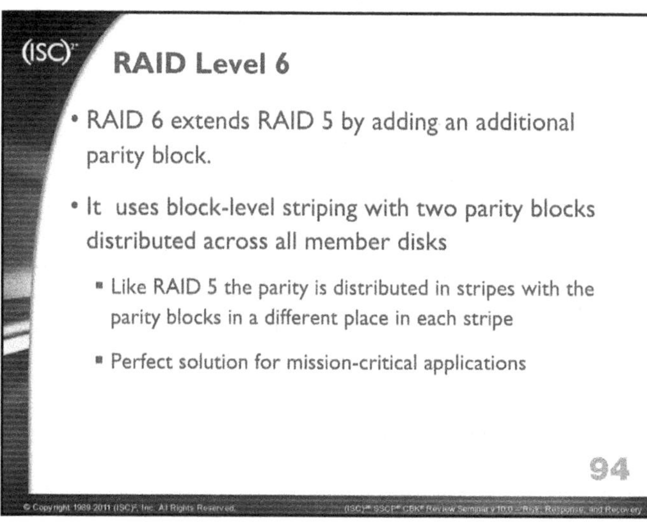


- **RAID LEVEL 6 –** Provides protection against double disk failures and failures while a single disk is rebuilding.
  - RAID 6 does not have a performance penalty for read operations, but it does have a performance penalty on write operations due to the overhead associated with the additional parity calculations.
  - RAID 6 is essentially an extension of RAID Level 5 that allows for additional fault tolerance by using a second independent distributed parity scheme (two-dimensional parity). Data is striped on a block level across a set of drives, just as in RAID 5, and a second set of parity is calculated and written across all the drives. RAID 6 provides for extremely high data fault-tolerance and can sustain multiple simultaneous drive failures. Perfect solution for mission-critical applications.
  - RAID 6 has a very complex controller design. Controller overhead to compute parity addresses is extremely high. It yields very poor write performance.

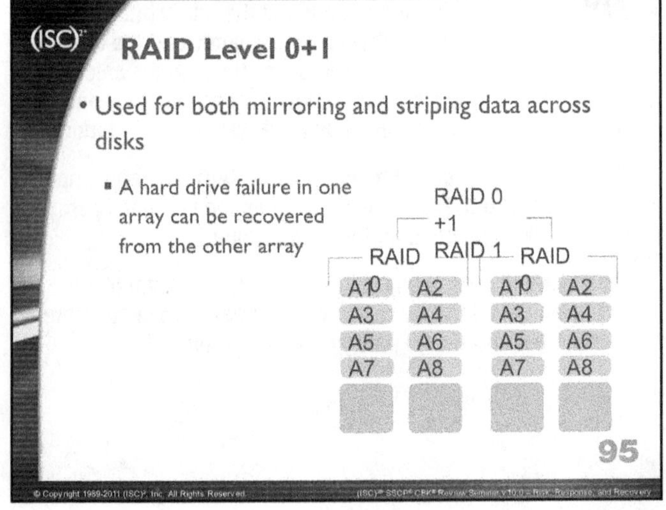

RAID Level 0+1
Used for both mirroring and striping data across disks
A hard drive failure in one array can be recovered from the other array
RAID 0 +1
RAID 1
RAID
RAID
A1
A2
A3
A4
A5
A6
A7
A8
95


- **RAID LEVEL 0+1 –** Used for both replicating and sharing data across disks.
  - The advantage of RAID 0+1 is that when a hard drive fails in one of the Level 0 arrays, the missing data can be transferred from the other array. However, adding an extra hard drive to one stripe means that you have to add an additional hard drive to the other stripes to balance out storage among the arrays.
  - RAID 0+1 is not as robust as RAID 10 (covered on the next slide) and cannot tolerate two simultaneous disk failures from the same stripe. That is, once a single disk fails, each of the mechanisms in the other stripe becomes single point of failure. Note that once the single failed mechanism is replaced, all the disks in the array must participate in the rebuild.
  - **ADVANTAGES –** RAID 0+1 is implemented as a mirrored array the segments of which are RAID 0 arrays. RAID 0+1 has the same fault tolerance as RAID Level 5 and the same overhead for fault-tolerance as mirroring alone. High I/O rates are achieved thanks to multiple stripe segments. This is an excellent solution for sites that need high performance but are not concerned with achieving maximum reliability.
  - **DISADVANTAGES –** A single drive failure will cause the whole array to become, in essence, a RAID Level 0 array. RAID 0+1 is very expensive and yields a high overhead. All drives must move in parallel to the proper track, thereby lowering sustained performance. It has very limited scalability at a very high inherent cost.

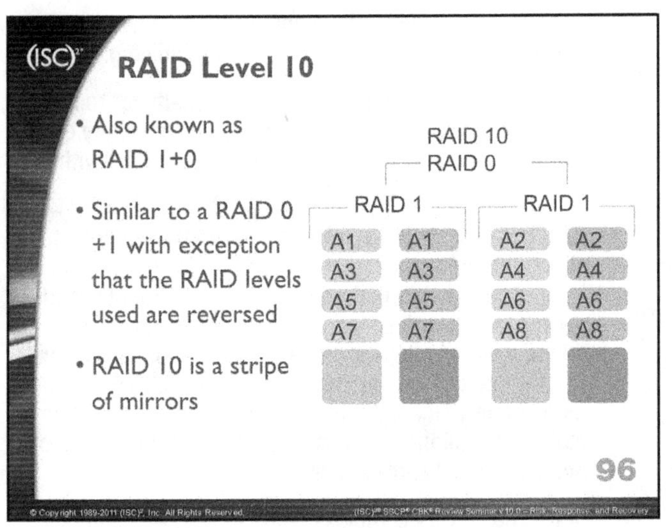


- **RAID LEVEL 10 –** Sometimes called RAID 1+0, or RAID 1&0, RAID Level 10 is similar to a RAID 0+1 with the exception that the RAID levels used are reversed: RAID 10 is a stripe of mirrors, whereas RAID 1+0 is a mirror of stripes. All but one drive from each RAID 1 set can fail without damaging the data.
  - RAID 10 is implemented as a striped array the segments of which are RAID 1 arrays that have the same fault tolerance as RAID Level 1. RAID 10 has the same overhead for fault-tolerance as mirroring alone. The high I/O rates are achieved by striping RAID 1 segments. It provides an excellent solution for sites that would otherwise have gone with RAID 1 but need additional performance.
  - RAID 10 is very expensive with a high overhead. It has very limited scalability at a very high inherent cost.

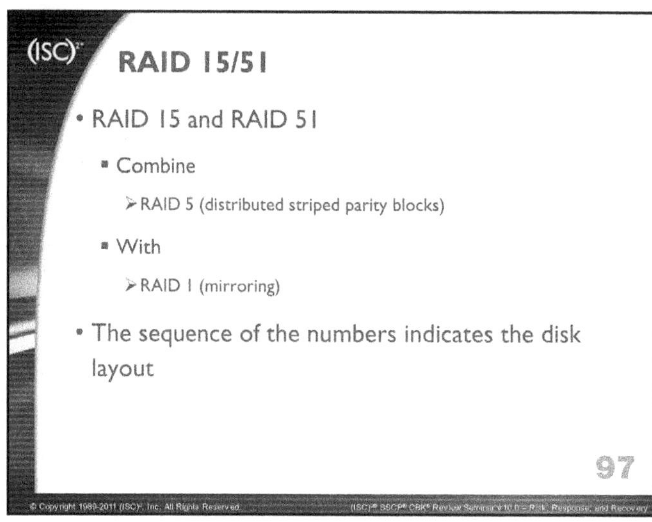


- RAID 1 (mirroring) had the advantage of being very fast, but introduced the risk of loss of all data should a single disk fail.
- RAID 5 brought data protection in that the failure of a single disk would not introduce data loss. It was often not fast enough, however, nor could it survive multiple disk loss.
- The combination of these two solutions brought speed and redundancy. The system could read from one array while writing to the other, thus improving speed by eliminating the write queue. It could also handle multiple disk loss as many combinations of disks from the mirrored arrays could combine to provide intact data.

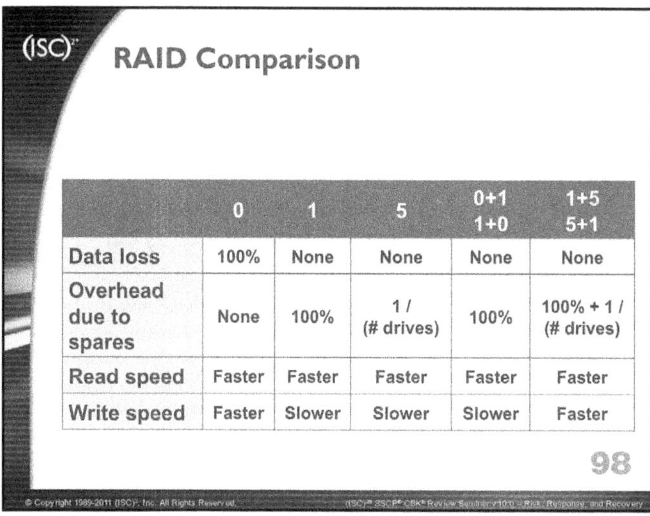


| | 0 | 1 | 5 | 0+1<br>1+0 | 1+5<br>5+1 |
|---|---|---|---|---|---|
| Data loss | 100% | None | None | None | None |
| Overhead due to spares | None | 100% | 1 / (# drives) | 100% | 100% + 1 / (# drives) |
| Read speed | Faster | Faster | Faster | Faster | Faster |
| Write speed | Faster | Slower | Slower | Slower | Faster |

- When the data is shared across multiple drives, read speed is always faster. Write speed depends on how the RAID array is structured. If there is delay due to additional copies being made, or for parity calculations, it will be slower. However, if the structure allows one array to be read while the other is written, it will be faster.
- RAID types 2, 3, 4, and 6 are not used and are, therefore, not included in the table.

(ISC)²

## Single Points of Failure

- Server clustering
  - Multiple physical servers managed as one
  - Provides transparent management
- Virtualization
  - Multiple services hosted on single hardware platforms
  - Provides optimization of resources
  - Can be quickly reimaged for redundancy

99

 (ISC)² SSCP® CBK® Review Seminar v10.0 – Risk, Response, and Recovery

- Redundancy in hardware and software, particularly for critical business servers, must be designed in to avoid single points of failure.
- **SERVER CLUSTERING –** May provide load-balancing of resources and enable transparent maintenance of high volume services. Multiple physical servers are managed as if they are a single server providing high availability.
- **VIRTUALIZATION (E.G., VMWARE SERVICES) –** Allows exploitation and optimization of high-performance/high-capacity hardware platforms available today and has become a popular technology in many client-server environments. While a single host supporting many virtual services can become a single point of failure, backups and recovery can be performed quickly from stored images.

(ISC)²

## Other Considerations for Resiliency

- Inventories of equipment
  - Locations
  - Configurations (software and hardware)
- Availability of documentation
  - Maintenance and error handling procedures
  - Media handling and protection procedures
- Regular training and reviews
- Periodic testing of procedures

100

 (ISC)² SSCP® CBK® Review Seminar v10.0 – Risk, Response, and Recovery

- **INVENTORIES OF EQUIPMENT –** Equipment inventory is an important resiliency-related consideration. The specific location and hardware/software configurations must always be documented. This becomes important if the systems have to be located or reconstituted.
- **AVAILABILITY OF DOCUMENTATION –** Documentation must be backed up and stored along with other critical files and data. Documentation which addresses issues such as maintenance and error handling procedures, media handling and protection procedures, and other contingency situations must be updated and maintained, as appropriate.
- **REGULAR TRAINING AND REVIEWS –** Personnel (e.g., security, information technology, operations staff, etc.) must be trained on a regular basis on current policies and proper procedures for dealing with contingency operations.
- **PERIODIC TESTING OF PROCEDURES –** Along with regular training, it is important to periodically review and test all contingency procedures, and update as appropriate.

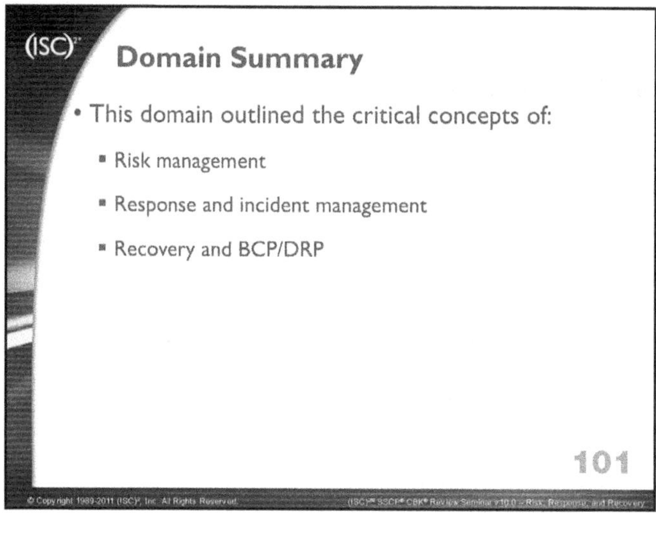

(ISC)²
Domain Summary
• This domain outlined the critical concepts of:
▪ Risk management
▪ Response and incident management
▪ Recovery and BCP/DRP
101


- We have now covered three of the critical areas of focus for SSCPs who are involved in protecting assets.
- It is important to understand the concepts and approaches to understanding and managing risks. We discussed the elements of risk (assets, vulnerabilities, and threats), key terms that are used in describing and assessing risks, and the two main approaches to analyzing risks (quantitative and qualitative).
- Incident response represents the first line of defense when an event occurs which may jeopardize assets. Proper handling of the incident is critical to timely resolution of any problems that may have occurred. When a legal issue is involved, it is important that the handling process be methodical so that any evidence gathered and any information shared does not compromise the investigation process.
- Disasters are often sudden and potentially devastating to an organization and its people. Preparedness is vital to survival of the business. Developing, testing, and maintaining a business continuity plan and a disaster recovery plan often makes the difference between successful recovery and catastrophe.
- The SSCP should now have a much better understanding of his or her role in participating in these activities.

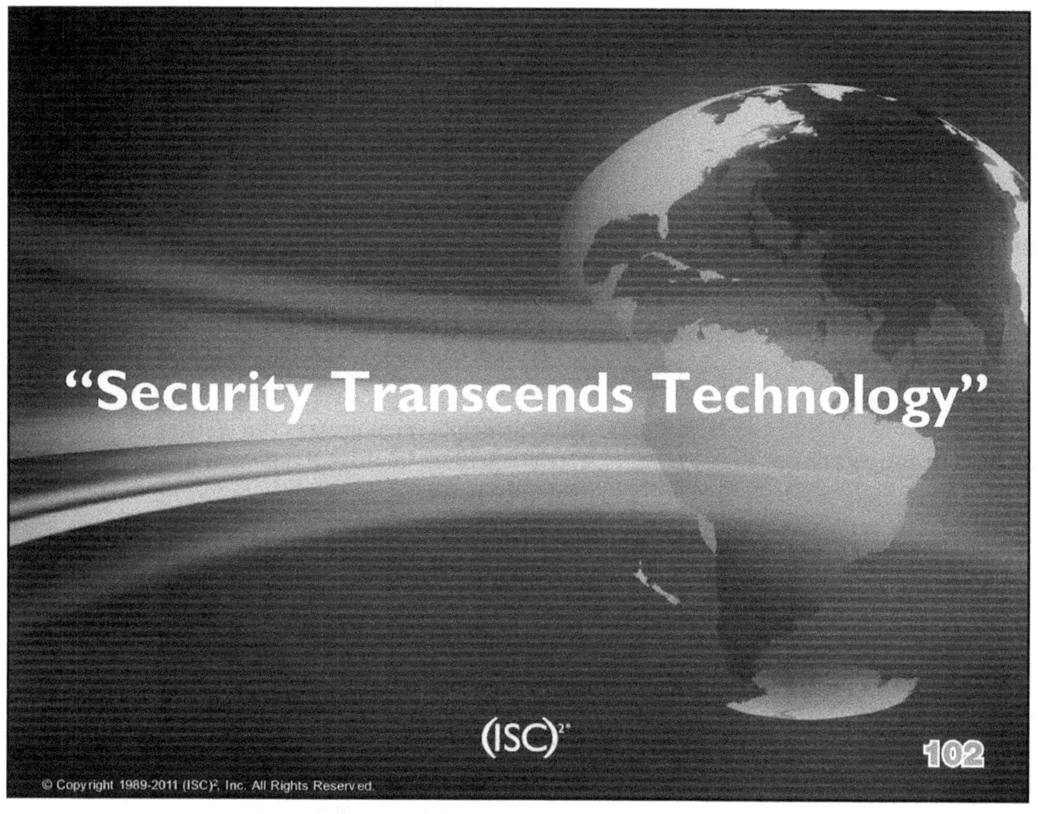

# Review Questions

## RISK, RESPONSE, AND RECOVERY

**1. Emergency actions are taken at the beginning stage of a disaster with the objectives of preventing injuries, loss of life, and**

a. determining damage.
b. protecting evidence.
c. relocating operations.
d. mitigating damage.

**2. A fully equipped backup center with external interfaces and communications BEST defines what type of backup site?**

a. Cold site
b. Warm site
c. Hot site
d. Mobile site

**3. Which of the following represents an annual loss expectancy (ALE) calculation?**

a. ALE = GLE * ARO (gross loss expectancy multiplied by annual rate of occurrence)
b. ALE = AV * EF (asset value multiplied by the exposure factor)
c. ALE = Risk (AV, threat, vulnerability) minus the countermeasure effectiveness (residual risk)
d. ALE = SLE * ARO (single loss expectancy multiplied by the annual rate of occurrence)

**4. A contingency plan should be written to**

a. address all possible risks.
b. remediate all vulnerabilities.
c. prepare for all reasonable threats.
d. recover all operations.

**5. Step-by-step instructions used to satisfy control requirements are called**

a. policies.
b. standards.
c. guidelines.
d. procedures.

**6. Separation of duties should be**

a. enforced in all organizational areas.
b. cost justified for the potential for loss.
c. enforced in the program testing phase of application development.
d. determined by the availability of trained staff.

**7. A timely review of system access audit records would be an example of which basic security function?**

a. Avoidance
b. Deterrence
c. Prevention
d. Detection

**8. How does closed-circuit television (CCTV) help management and security forces MINIMIZE loss during a disaster or emergency?**

a. Facilitates direction of resources to hardest hit areas.
b. Records instances of looting and other criminal activities.
c. Documents shortcomings of plans and procedures.
d. Captures the exposure of assets to physical risk.

**9. Which one of the following is the MOST effective method for reducing security risks associated with building entrances?**

a. Minimize the number of entrances.
b. Use solid metal doors and frames.
c. Brightly illuminate the entrances.
d. Install tamperproof hinges and glass.

**10. What is the BEST definition of a countermeasure?**

a. Control which helps mitigate potential risks.
b. Measure taken to counteract with something else.
c. An action taken in order to relieve a certain cause.
d. Threats to a system with vulnerabilities.

**11. What principle recommends the division of responsibilities to prevent a person from committing fraud?**

a. Separation of duties
b. Mutual exclusion
c. Need to know
d. Least privilege

**12. In what two ways can asset valuation BEST be approached?**

a. Qualitatively and quantitatively
b. Meticulously and quantitatively
c. Properly and qualitatively
d. Analytically and specifically

**13. What is a quantitative risk analysis?**

a. Examination of the numerical value of a computer's chance of crashing.
b. Analysis of the hard disk and all its components.
c. Tools that allow "What if?" scenarios.
d. A program that checks the integrity of the hard disk.

**14. Which of these events should get the least attention from the information security staff?**

a. Extreme weather
b. Application failure
c. Terrorist attack
d. Virus released "in-the-wild"

**15. Accurate identification of the maximum tolerable downtime (MTD) is a part of which phase?**

a. Testing, verification, validation, and maintenance
b. Business impact analysis
c. Recovery strategies
d. BCP development

**16. What do the recovery time objective (RTO) and the maximum tolerable downtime (MTD) have in common?**

a. The RTO is not related to the MTD.
b. The MTD is a superset of the RTO.
c. The RTO is a component of the MTD.
d. The MTD describes the RTO.

**17. What process identifies the business continuity requirements for the organization's assets?**

a. Risk analysis
b. Business impact analysis
c. Threat analysis
d. Asset classification

**18. A contingency plan should be written to**

a. address all possible risk scenarios.
b. address all likely risk scenarios.
c. remediate all vulnerabilities.
d. recover all operations.

**19. Which sentence best describes the main goal of business continuity?**

a. To ensure the confidentiality, integrity and availability of business assets.
b. To ensure the business is able to continue operations throughout different incidents.
c. To ensure the business maintains sensitive assets at their required protection level.
d. To ensure the business is able to continue operations throughout different disasters.

**20. Which of the following is not typically a part of business continuity management documentation?**

a. Business impact analysis
b. Risk and threat assessment
c. Response plans
d. Certification and accreditation plan (CAP)

# Notes

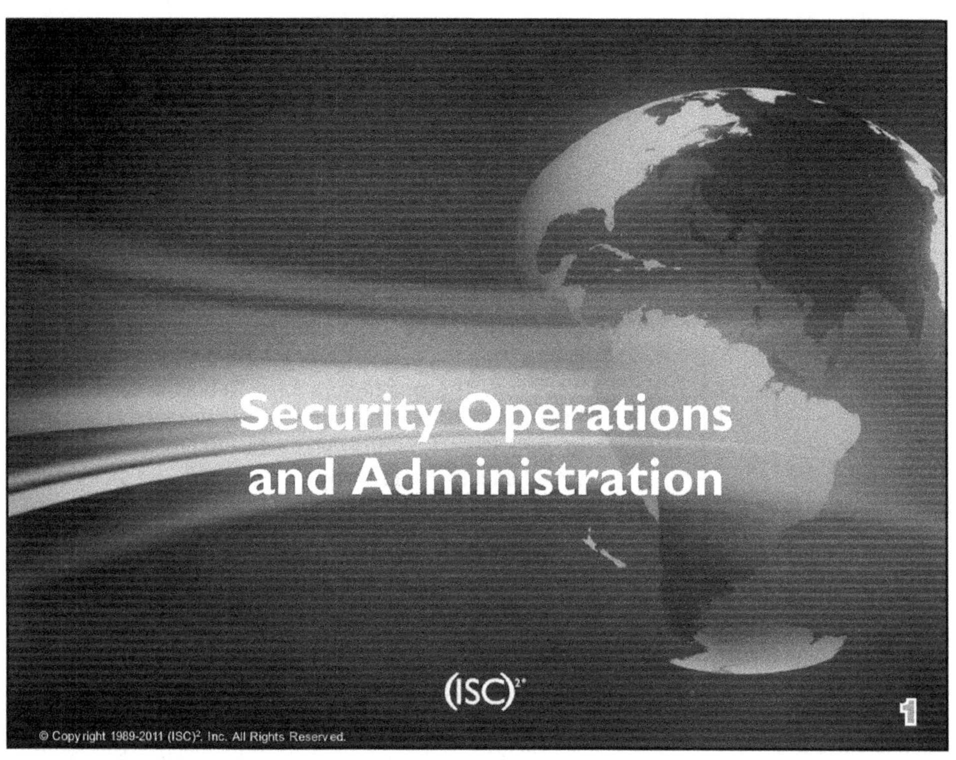


- Security Operations and Administration covers important information security concepts and information for the SSCP to understand and apply, beginning with an overview of the development and alignment of business goals to security requirements. Key among these activities is the creation of security strategies and the implementation of a policy framework to ensure attainment.
- We will discuss a number of other areas of involvement for the SSCP to ensure the protection of assets, including identifying and classifying assets, development and implementation of a security program, managing changes to the environment, and encouraging responsible behavior among constituents (ethical and security-aware behavior).
- Paramount is the cost-effective management of risks (we will discuss this in much more detail in the Risk, Response, and Recovery domain) throughout the organization, focusing on people, processes, and technology.

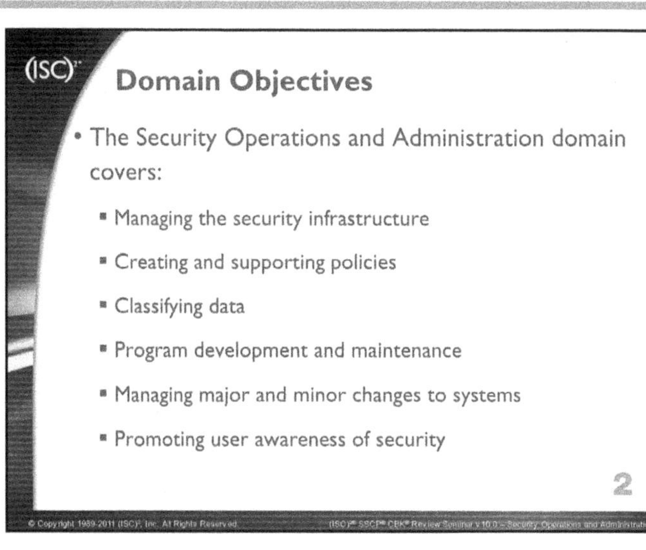


- The Security Operations and Administration domain covers:
  - Managing the security infrastructure
  - Creating and supporting policies
  - Classifying data
  - Program development and maintenance
  - Managing major and minor changes to systems
  - Promoting user awareness of security

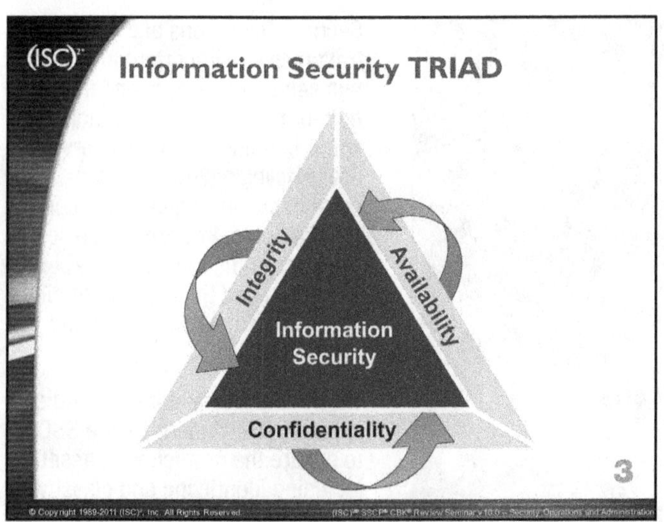


- **INFORMATION SECURITY TRIAD –** Information security begins with the core principles:
  - **AVAILABILITY –** The design of the security architecture must consider the needs of the organization both from a current as well as a strategic perspective. The architecture must address the growth and technologies that the organization expects to experience over the next months and years.
    - **UNAVAILABILITY –** Denial of service is a classic example of unavailability. Another example might be a fixed log-file space that is constantly being overwritten due to increased volume. This is easily prevented by allocating more space.
  - **INTEGRITY –** Every organization has different requirements for integrity of information and processes. The architecture must address those requirements and ensure that the organization can properly control modifications to data in a stable and reliable manner.
    - **UNAUTHORIZED ALTERATION (IMPACTS INTEGRITY) –** Inadvertent or intentional mis-keying of data into a spreadsheet is a good example of this. As new systems are developed and new access points are introduced (e.g., kiosks, web-enabling, or telecommuting), so too are new ways to intentionally or accidentally alter data improperly.
  - **CONFIDENTIALITY –** The architecture will play a key role in enforcing the protection of information from improper disclosure. The architecture must be built in accord with the regulations and laws that the organization is subject to, particularly from the perspective of privacy and protection of intellectual property.
    - **IMPROPER DISCLOSURE (COMPROMISES CONFIDENTIALITY) –** New privacy laws and regulations often provide for fines (and at minimum, public embarrassment) for unauthorized disclosure.
- Full implementation of the AIC TRIAD does not come easily or inexpensively. Many systems and applications were designed without security in mind. As a result, some systems never had built-in security, while in others, security mechanisms were added as an afterthought. Furthermore, many users will have become accustomed to working on their systems in a certain way. It will take a commitment from everyone involved to change their habits to ensure good future security.
- You should be able to identify the AIC Triad concepts and requirements for each of the domains.

**REFERENCE**

"Integrity in Automated Information Systems," National Computer Security Center Technical Report 79-91, Sept. 1991

(ISC)²

## Domain Agenda

- **Security Administration**
- Policies and Supporting Documents
- Information Classification
- System Life Cycle and System Development Life Cycle
- Change and Configuration Management
- User Security Awareness

4



(ISC)²® SSCP® CBK® Review Seminar v 10.0 – Security Operations and Administration

## Why Have a Security Framework?

- The organization takes risk reduction seriously and takes responsibility for it
- The organization is proactive about reducing risk to employees
- The organization is proactive about reducing risk to organizational assets
- The organization periodically tests its risk reduction processes through auditing

5

(ISC)² SSCP® CBK® Review Seminar v10.0 – Security Operations and Administration

- **FIRST, WHAT IS A "SECURITY FRAMEWORK"?** According to Rahaju Pal and Dhawal Thacker of PriceWaterhouseCoopers (http://www.networkmagazineindia.com/200211/guest.shtml), an "…Information Security Framework provides a model for developing comprehensive security programs." It can provide a template or guide to illustrate the approach to be taken for good security practices. It begins with a strong commitment from senior management, along with a long-term vision and strategy, and a structured approach to design and implementation. We will discuss some of the other key elements later in this domain.
- **WHY HAVE A SECURITY FRAMEWORK? –** Security does not happen by accident or automatically. Preventing, detecting and responding to all possible security threats requires everyone in the organization to work together.
    - **THE ORGANIZATION TAKES RISK REDUCTION SERIOUSLY AND TAKES RESPONSIBILITY FOR IT –** In a world of increasing regulation and possible litigation, each organization must take a closer look at their security responsibilities and demonstrate that they are exercising due care in the protection of their assets, confidential information, and sensitive personal data.
    - **THE ORGANIZATION IS PROACTIVE ABOUT REDUCING RISK TO EMPLOYEES –** Through security measures intended to prevent incidents, and incidence response plans designed to minimize the impact of any incident. Proper security programs protect employees and customers from risk of identity theft, illegal activities, accidental errors, malicious code, and other threats.
    - **THE ORGANIZATION IS PROACTIVE ABOUT REDUCING THE RISK TO ORGANIZATIONAL ASSETS –** For example protecting trade secrets, physical infrastructure, and the reputation of the organization.
    - **THE ORGANIZATION PERIODICALLY TESTS ITS RISK REDUCTION PROCESSES THROUGH AUDITING –** We look in more detail at auditing in the analysis and monitoring domain, but the essence here is that risk is an ever-moving target and requires continuous monitoring and review. The audit must ensure that the organization has adequate controls to address risk.
- **SECURITY FRAMEWORK –** Security is not a natural function in an organization. The organization should not imagine that everyone by nature will work in a secure manner, understand what makes a good information security program, understand how it works and the benefits it provides. All organizations, therefore, need a security framework that includes accountability and structure. Someone must be responsible for the security program and the elements needed to support the program including managerial concerns, technology, and processes that need to be developed, implemented, and maintained. The audit process provides the due diligence component to the security framework.

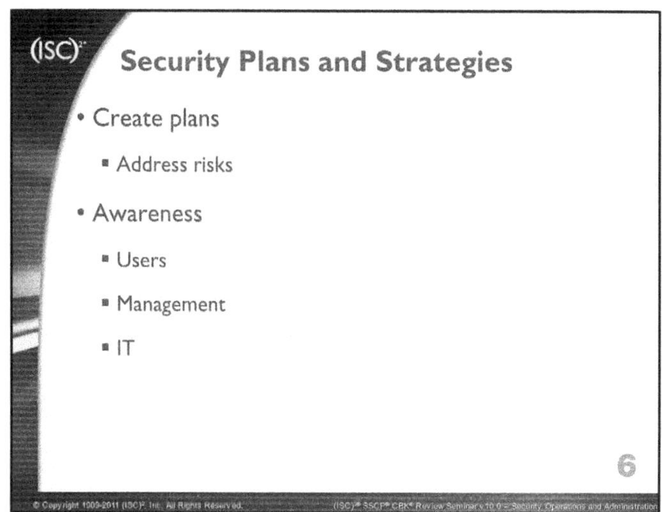
(ISC)²
Security Plans and Strategies
• Create plans
▪ Address risks
• Awareness
▪ Users
▪ Management
▪ IT
6

- **SECURITY PLANS AND STRATEGIES –** A security program consists of plans and strategies to address risks and security requirements. A plan should be based on the priorities of the organization as well as resource and budget availability.
- **CREATE PLANS –** The organization's strategies should be tied to a security framework to ensure alignment of IT with, first, the business, and then with security goals. Each plan should be supported with milestones to track progress and detect deviations from the plan. Senior management should be directly involved in formulating security strategies and considering all relevant security recommendations which provide cost-effective solutions to reducing business risks to an acceptable level.
- Security strategies are then used to formulate a security policy, and, if properly aligned to business requirements, become the foundation for asset protection.
- **AWARENESS –** The plan should be communicated to users, management, and IT in order to ensure that everyone knows the security strategy and can integrate security objectives into their projects and activities.

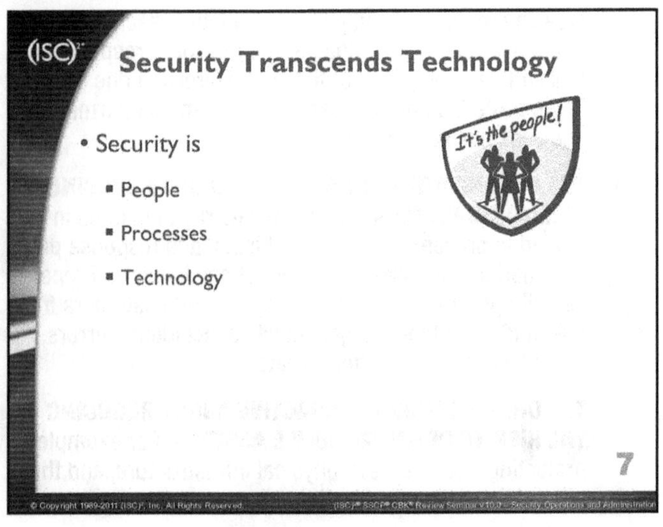

(ISC)²
Security Transcends Technology
• Security is
▪ People
▪ Processes
▪ Technology
It's the people!
7


- **SECURITY TRANSCENDS TECHNOLOGY –** Security has to do with more than just installing more firewalls, access control devices, or other technologies. A complete security solution comprises good management and administration, the right technologies installed in the right locations, and the processes and procedures that will enable the technologies to be used in an effective manner.
- "Those who think that technology will solve their problems don't understand technology and they don't understand their problems" (Bruce Schneier, Secrets and Lies).

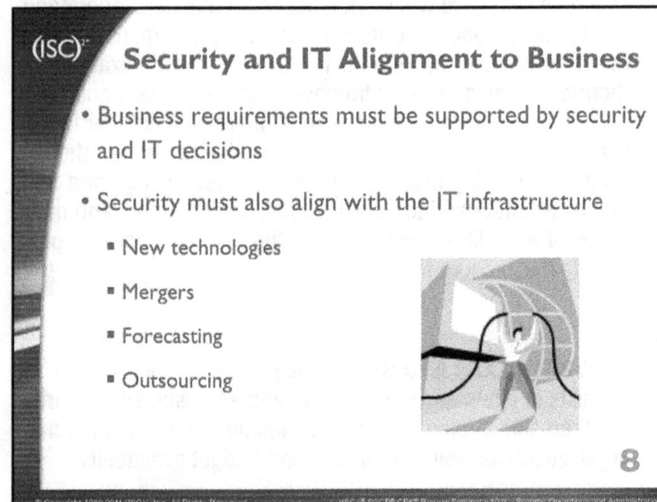

(ISC)²
Security and IT Alignment to Business
• Business requirements must be supported by security and IT decisions
• Security must also align with the IT infrastructure
▪ New technologies
▪ Mergers
▪ Forecasting
▪ Outsourcing
8


- **BUSINESS REQUIREMENTS MUST BE SUPPORTED BY SECURITY AND IT DECISIONS –** Today's business environment is dynamic, global, and interdependent. Organizations often develop unique strategies for a variety of reasons (profitability, competitive advantage, exploitation of new technology, etc.); however, they share a common theme: Protection of assets and assurance that business processes achieve defined goals. This is a governance issue which compels senior management to support and enforce good security practices throughout the organization. There is an expectation that skilled security practitioners will have a clear understanding of not only the security and IT issues, but most important, the underlying business drivers.
- **SECURITY MUST ALSO ALIGN WITH THE IT INFRASTRUCTURE –** Adequate security is often limited by the IT infrastructure of the organization. Legacy systems, poorly designed networks, lack of consistency in equipment, lack of policy, baselines, and procedures all make security an elusive target. Alignment today often means building security in from the start, whether as part of the specifications for new development, or for purchasing commercial products. Senior managers have long since learned that it is cheaper and more effective to build security in than it is to graft it on.
  - **NEW TECHNOLOGIES –** Are a constant challenge. Each new technology brings new risks and yet the business may well be forced into adopting the new technologies by competitive forces and the constant need for gains in productivity.
  - **MERGERS –** Cause a lot of stress in an organization and this stress affects the security posture as well. Staff may fear losing their jobs and not be as security conscious; there may be pressure to piece together networks that are not easily interoperable and may lead to security gaps; and there may be a lack of coherent and consistent policy.
  - **FORECASTING –** An important role for the security practitioner is to know the current state of the business and to be able to forecast what the requirements for new services, bandwidth, technologies, and security components will be in order to properly present the business case for procuring these components.
  - **OUTSOURCING –** With the growing trend to outsource, the SSCP will increasingly be required to assist with vendor compliance monitoring. Keep in mind that whereas work can be delegated, responsibility cannot. While the decision to outsource and the choice of vendor will be made by senior managers, it often falls to the SSCP to manage the contract and to assure management that the various negotiated security service levels are being met.

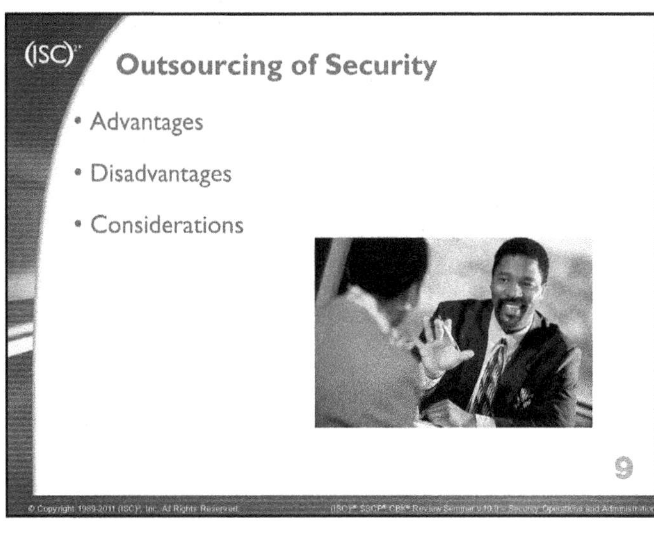
(ISC)²
Outsourcing of Security
• Advantages
• Disadvantages
• Considerations
9

- **OUTSOURCING OF SECURITY –** Many organizations rely on outsource firms to handle their security monitoring and analysis. This requires the SSCP to either monitor the performance of the outsource firm or be involved in handling incidents on behalf of another organization.
- **ADVANTAGES –** The advantage of an outsourced, managed security contract is the higher level of expertise that should be available with a company that focuses on security every day.
- **DISADVANTAGES –** The outsourcing firm will not gain the expertise in-house to deal with incidents and analysis. The contract will require monitoring to ensure that the vendor delivers according to their contract.
- **OUTSOURCING CONSIDERATIONS –** Any outsourcing contract should have explicit terms addressing security requirements, service level agreements, immediate communication of a potential breach, log and event reporting, as well as handling requirements of confidential data.

(ISC)²

## Domain Agenda

- Security Administration
- **Policies and Supporting Documents**
- Information Classification
- System Life Cycle and System Development Life Cycle
- Change and Configuration Management
- User Security Awareness

10

(ISC)²® SSCP® CBK® Review Seminar v.10.0 – Security Operations and Administration

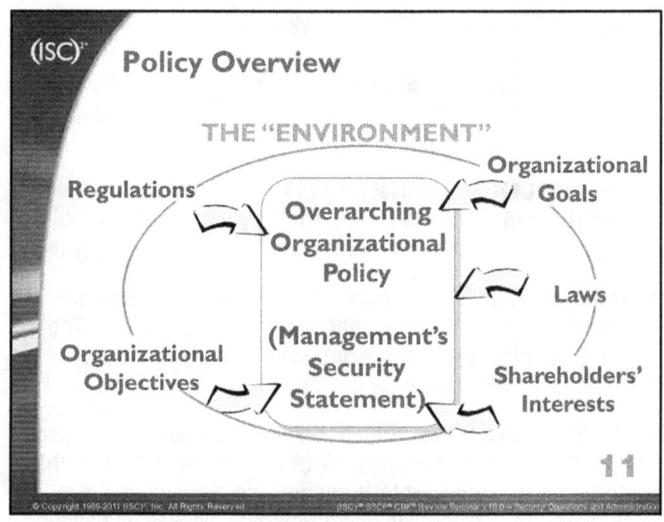


- **POLICY OVERVIEW –** The environment within which every company operates is a complex web of laws, regulations, requirements, competitors, and partners. In addition to these forces, senior management must consider those within the organization such as morale, labor relations, productivity, cost, cash flow, and many others. Within this environment, management must develop and publish the overall security statement and directives. From the security team perspective, proper implementation of a security program will address these directives through security policies and their supporting elements such as standards, procedures, baselines, and guidelines.
- **SSCP TASKS –** Each of these items has its specific tasks for SSCPs. For example, the SSCP may be involved with compliance monitoring, security awareness, training, access control, privacy, incident response, log analysis, and so on.

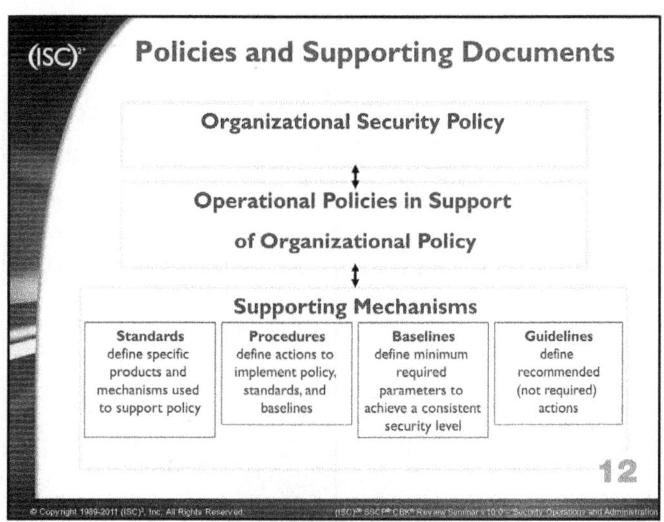


- **POLICY OVERVIEW –** Policy sets the tone and culture of the organization. Because the SSCP is often required to implement policy, an understanding of the structure is essential.
    - The organizational security policy is overarching and very high level; in fact, it is often very brief and reflects the overall intent of the organization to support and enforce security.
    - Operational policies are sometimes called "functional policies" and carry the force of directives. They address specific functional areas of the business; such as remote access, use of internet resources, ethics statements/policies, etc.
- The supporting mechanisms describe how policy will be implemented and what is minimally acceptable.
- While policy is the high-level statement of values and direction, a policy is enacted through standards, baselines, procedures, and guidelines.
    - The role the SSCP is typically responsible for implementing the controls to support policies, standards, procedures, etc.
    - This means distribution/communication of policies, security awareness training, enforcement, and input toward updating/modification.

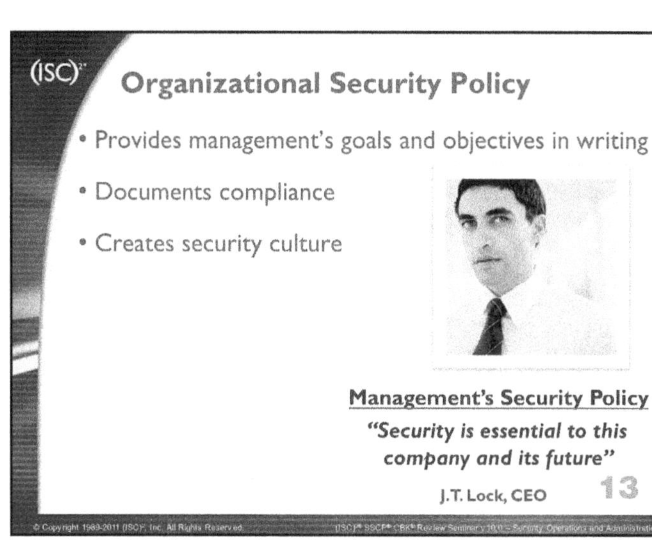


- **PROVIDES MANAGEMENT'S GOALS AND OBJECTIVES IN WRITING –** The organizational policy mandates the security needs within the company. The overarching security policy should be kept "high-level" and short. If it is too complex, it will be difficult to get approved and it may not be read or understood.
  - A sample organizational security policy statement might be, "Security is essential to the future of our organization" or "Security in our products is our most important task." With statements like these to rely on, the rest of the organization's management is given guidance for their decision making processes.
- **DOCUMENTS COMPLIANCE –** Policy documents the company's intent to comply with laws, regulations, and standards of due care and due diligence.
  - Policies are of no value if not read, available, enforced, and current. Policies must be posted where they are available to every employee for review. They must be current, and reflect new laws and regulations. All employees must be kept aware of the policies through annual reviews. A record of this review with each employee should be maintained.
- **CREATES SECURITY CULTURE –** Policy establishes the internal environment for the security program by explaining what assets and principles the organization considers valuable.

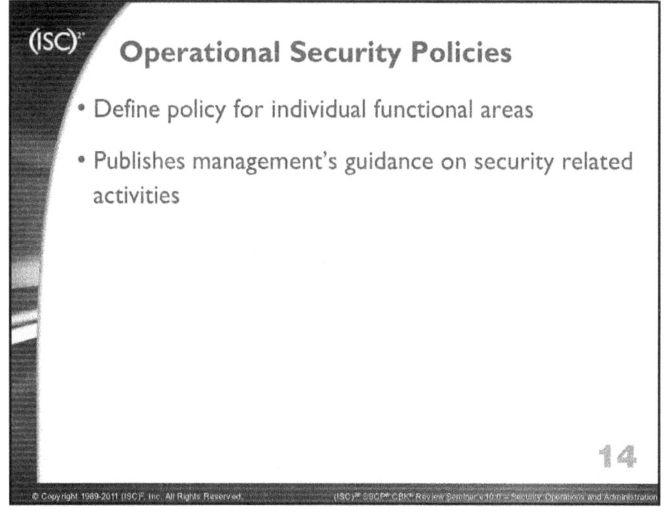


- **OPERATIONAL SECURITY POLICIES –** An operational or functional policy sets forth management's direction for various functional areas such as email, remote access, or Internet surfing. The functional areas to develop implementing policies are the organizational functions, such as HR, IT, Operations, etc. Also, a policy uses positive terms like "will" and "must", not "should", because policies are mandatory.
  - An example of an access control functional policy statement would be, "All authorized users must be allowed to do only their authorized tasks. Unauthorized users must not have access to the company systems or resources."
  - Note that this statement says **WHAT** to do, not **HOW** to do it.

(ISC)²

## Common Operational Policies

- Acceptable use policy
- Identification and authentication policy
- Internet usage policy
- Campus and remote access policy
- Incident handling policy
- Software use and misuse policy

15

 (ISC)² SSCP® CBK® Review Seminar v10.0 – Security Operations and Administration

- One of the most common operational (functional) security policy components is an acceptable use policy (AUP). This component defines what users shall and shall not do on the various components of the system, including the type of traffic allowed on the networks. The AUP should be as explicit as possible to avoid ambiguity or misunderstanding. For example, an AUP might list any prohibited USENET newsgroups.
- Other typical operational policies address more specific functional activities to support the organization's mission and business objectives, such as:
  - Identification and authentication policy
  - Internet usage policy
  - Campus/facility and remote access policy
  - Incident response handling policy
  - Software use and misuse policy
- All of these should be aligned with good practices and be supported by standards and procedures to ensure consistency.
- The security policy and all of the supporting elements should have the acceptance and support of all levels of employees in the organization. Representatives of all key stakeholders and affected management should be involved in creating and revising the security policy. A statement of authority and scope should be an integral component of all operational policies. User security awareness educational programs should be used to ensure that all personnel are informed.

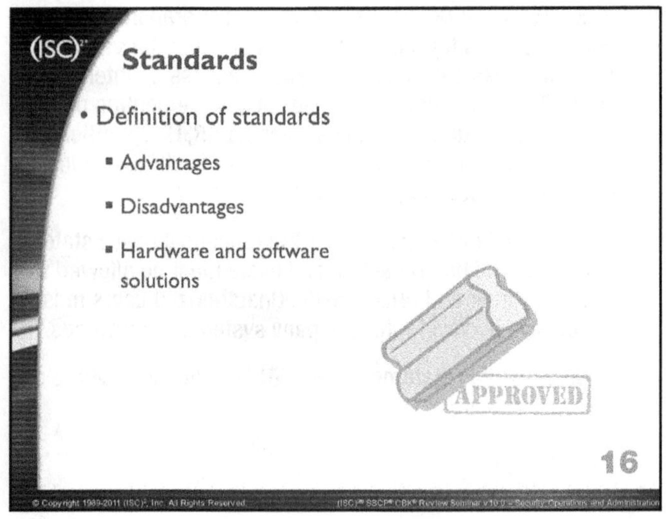
(ISC)²
Standards
• Definition of standards
▪ Advantages
▪ Disadvantages
▪ Hardware and software solutions
APPROVED
16

- **DEFINITION OF STANDARDS –** These refer to standardization of the hardware and software solutions that are selected to address a security risk throughout the enterprise. They might refer to a specific antivirus product or password generation token that has been chosen for use throughout the organization.
  - **ADVANTAGES –** This often reduces cost of ownership by allowing for large bulk purchase agreements with vendors as well as standardized training. Standards can also be guidelines created by government, industry, or other organizations that have been formally adopted by the organization as an organizational standard.
    - Standards are essential so that a common baseline can be established and implemented. Having a common basis for the overall organization is better than having each individual department operating under its own separate (and in some cases noncompliant) environment. This helps reduce the seams that can develop between sections, departments, and subordinate organizations.
  - **DISADVANTAGES –** A vulnerability in the selected product can place the entire organization at risk. There is also the risk of a vendor not supporting the product, or it becoming too expensive to maintain and license.

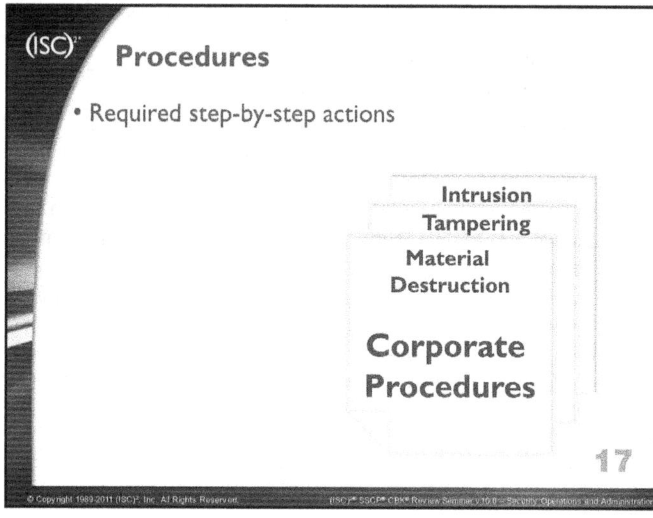


- **PROCEDURES –** Are the way to ensure that the intent of policy is enforced through a mandated series of steps that must be followed to accomplish a task.
  - **REQUIRED STEP-BY-STEP ACTIONS –** Procedures are statements of step-by-step actions to be performed in order to accomplish a security requirement, process, or objective. They are one of the most powerful tools available in the security arsenal and must be used wisely. Procedures cover such matters as password changing, incident response, implementing antivirus software, etc.
  - Procedures:
    - Reduce mistakes in a crisis
    - Ensure that important steps are not missed
    - Provide for places within the process to conduct assurance checks
  - Like policies and standards, procedures are mandatory requirements.

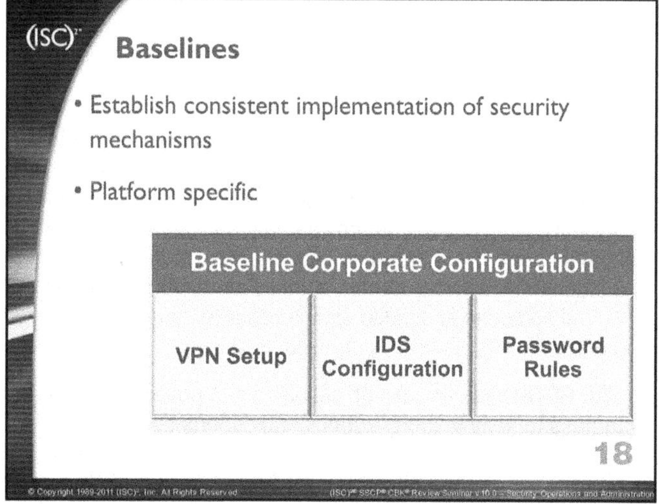


- **BASELINES –** Are the benchmarks used to ensure that a minimum level of security configuration is provided across multiple implementations of the systems and across different products.
- **ESTABLISH CONSISTENT IMPLEMENTATION OF SECURITY MECHANISMS –** Baselines are descriptions of how to implement security mechanisms to ensure that implementations result in a consistent level of security throughout the organization. Different systems (platforms) have different methods of handling security issues. Baselines are created to inform user groups and system administrators about how to set up the security for each platform so that the desired level of security is achieved consistently.
- **PLATFORM SPECIFIC –** Baselines are the great "leveler" of security options between different security products, including those from different vendors. This is becoming more important as more and more "hybrid" products are entering the security market, combining services into "multifunctional" devices, and defying many of our old definitions, such as the original roles of a switch and router.

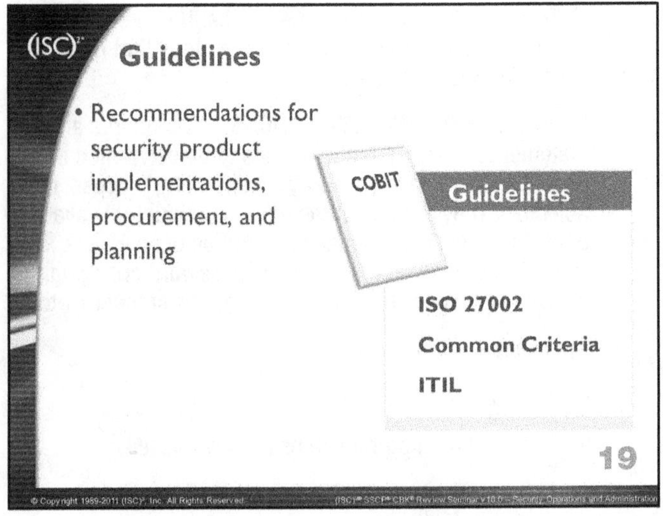


- **GUIDELINES –** Guidelines are recommendations!!!
  - Guidelines are simply recommended actions unless mandated by company policy and adopted as a standard, baseline, or procedure. They are often white papers, best practices, or formats for a security program that may be used by an organization. However, care must be used to ensure that careless use of words in policies doesn't move a guideline from a best practice into the realm of a company standard unless that is the intent. For example, an overarching statement in a security policy signed by the CEO stating that "this company will follow the recommendations of the ISO 27002 guideline" makes implementation of ISO 27001 mandatory within that organization.
  - Guidelines are often used to help provide structure to a security program and to outline recommendations for the procurement and deployment of acceptable products and systems.

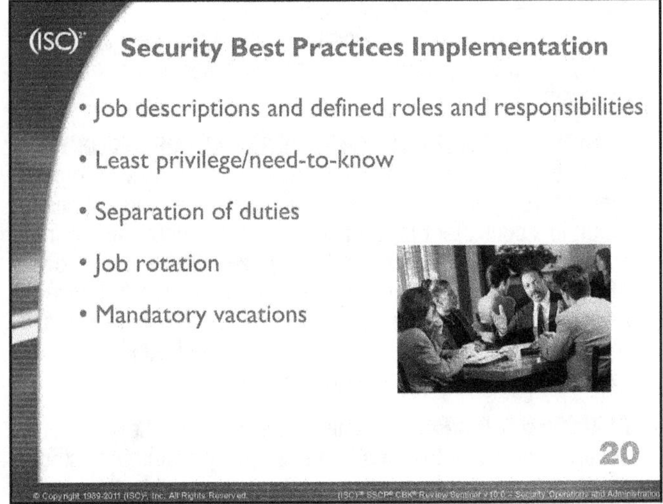


- **PERSONNEL GOOD PRACTICES –** This was mentioned earlier in several places, most prominently in risk, response, and recovery.
- **JOB DESCRIPTIONS AND DEFINED ROLES AND RESPONSIBILITIES –** Clearly defined job descriptions and defined roles and responsibilities help ensure that everyone knows what an individual should be doing and can aid in detecting unusual behavior.
- **LEAST PRIVILEGE/NEED-TO-KNOW –** The principle of least privilege and the requirement for need-to-know should always be executed to minimize access to information and assets. Least privilege is concerned with granting a user or process only the level of permissions that he or she require to perform their duties. Need-to-know is similar in that it restricts the access by an individual (or process) to the data required for their duties. These concepts are addressed in more detail in the Access Control domain.
- **SEPARATION OF DUTIES –** Separation of duties break a task into subtasks that are to be executed by different people. This restricts any person from making changes to a system without the assistance and approval of another person. This can help prevent errors, fraud, or lack of approval for changes. As a side effect, it forces someone intent on breaking the rules to find someone to collude with in order to manipulate the system for unauthorized purposes.
- **JOB ROTATION –** Breaks up collusion and provides opportunities to review authorizations and actions taken by the individual. If our other security measures have failed, this gives us an opportunity to find the breach in security before it gets worse or goes on for too long. Job rotation also provides trained backup.
- **MANDATORY VACATIONS –** Much like job rotation, mandatory vacations provide the opportunity to detect fraud. When people are on vacation, their access to the site should be suspended. This prevents working from home (possibly covering their tracks) and provides them with the much needed vacation they have earned. Under U.S. banking rules, employees of retail banks (those with savings or checking accounts) must take two consecutive weeks of vacation. Until recently, they were forbidden from contact with work-related matters. That rule has been relaxed to allow for read-only content so they can keep up on emails and such, but they are still not allowed to participate.

(ISC)²

## Domain Agenda

- Security Administration
- Policies and Supporting Documents
- **Information Classification**
- System Life Cycle and System Development Life Cycle
- Change and Configuration Management
- User Security Awareness

21

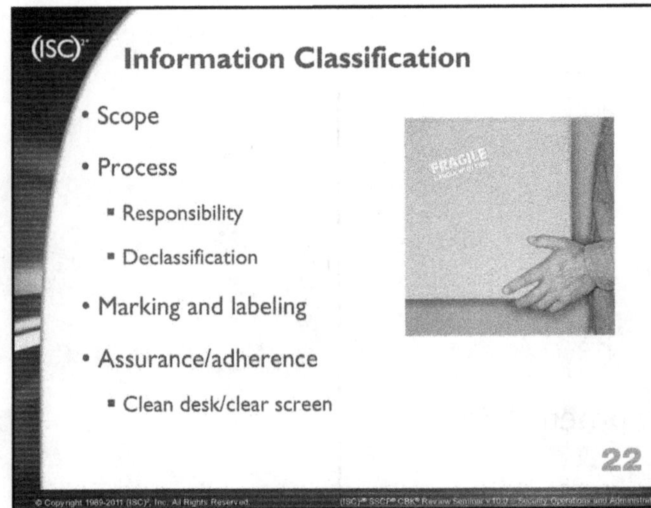
(ISC)²
Information Classification
• Scope
• Process
▪ Responsibility
▪ Declassification
• Marking and labeling
• Assurance/adherence
▪ Clean desk/clear screen
FRAGILE
22

- **SCOPE –** A business impact analysis should be completed that evaluates all of the data handled by the organization in order to determine its value and criticality to the operations of the organization. Points to consider include: exclusive possession (trade secret, etc.), utility (usefulness), cost to create or recreate the data, liability (protection regulations), convertibility/negotiability (financial, etc.), operational impact (if data is unavailable), threats to the information, and risks.
- **PROCESS –** Based on the results of the business impact analysis, identify the number of levels of classification necessary to appropriately control access to the information and standardize their titles for use throughout the organization. Develop and promulgate policy and procedures addressing information classification. The information owner or delegate is then responsible for assigning the initial classification. Classifiers must understand the related regulations, customer expectations, and business concerns. The goal is to achieve a consistent approach to the handling of classified information. It may be useful to create a training program to help classifiers achieve the desired consistency. The owner is also responsible for a periodic review of classifications to ensure that they are still current, particularly in light of any new government regulations. Finally, the owner is responsible for declassifying information that no longer requires special handling. Government organizations often declare information automatically declassified after a certain number of years.
- **MARKING AND LABELING –** It is important that all media containing sensitive and critical information be marked in accordance with classification policy and procedures, because that is the only way personnel will be able to know what special handling measures to employ. Magnetic and optical media are normally labeled both electronically and by easily read visual labels. Documents in hard copy form are labeled externally on the cover and internally on the pages.
- **ASSURANCE/ADHERENCE –** Internal and external auditors should include a review of the information classification status within the organization as a component of their regular audit process. This should include an evaluation of the level of compliance with the classification policy and procedures to ensure that all parts of the organization are properly adhering to the process. Part of this review may detect cases where information is over-classified – a situation that often detracts from the purposes of classification when noncompliance is observed. Information security staff personnel should regularly visit workstations and other areas where classified materials may be left unprotected and ensure that appropriate reports are made to supervisors and managers. Ideally, employee performance evaluations should include records of mishandling classified information in order to bring to their attention the importance of this process. One of the requirements an organization may enforce is the clean desk/clear screen policy, which stipulates that an unattended desk or workstation should never have sensitive information sitting in open view.

**REFERENCE**

"Guideline for Information Valuation," ISSA, 1993

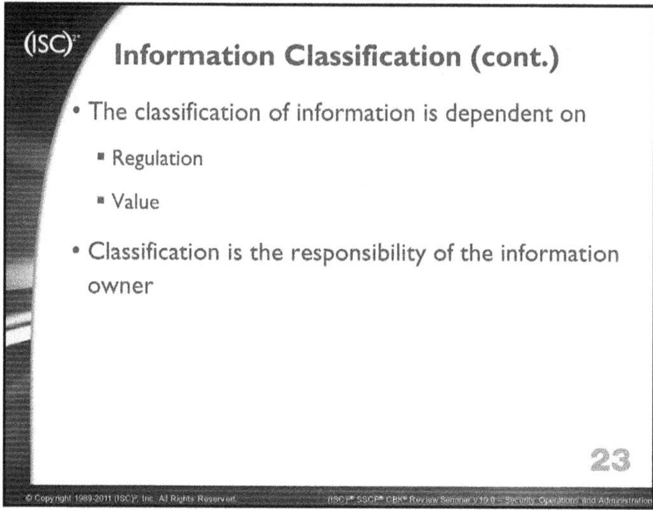
(ISC)²
Information Classification (cont.)
The classification of information is dependent on
Regulation
Value
Classification is the responsibility of the information owner
23

- **INFORMATION CLASSIFICATION (CONT.) –** is the process of assigning a value or label to an asset to signify its importance to the organization and to establish a requirement for protection. The value may be determined externally by government doctrine or regulation, or internally based on its tangible or intangible worth to the organization. Classification is commonly associated with a level of confidentiality, but it may also reflect the potential impact on the organization if the asset became unavailable (a critical resource) or became corrupted or unreliable. The values assigned become the justification for selecting controls to protecting the asset and managing associated risks.

- **REGULATION –** The classification of information is often dependent on the regulations that apply, such as the protection of personal information, financial information (that may affect share price, etc.), health information, etc.

- **VALUE –** The value of information is subject to numerous influences such as the value to the organization, the value to competitors, the cost of replacement or loss, and the value to reputation.
  - **SENSITIVITY –** Is the measure of the effect that a breach of the integrity or disclosure of the information would have on the organization. This may be measured in many ways – liability or fines, reputation, credibility, loss of market share, etc.
  - **CRITICALITY –** The measure of the importance of the information to the mission of the organization. How much would the organization be impacted if the information was not available?

- **CLASSIFICATION IS THE RESPONSIBILITY OF THE INFORMATION OWNER –** Or the designate of the information owner. This person is also sometimes called the data owner. A similar term, "system owner," refers to the person or group that manages the infrastructure. System owners are often in control of change/configuration management (a topic discussed later in this domain) but not classification.

**REFERENCE**

There is more information on classification in the Access Control Domain, which focuses on how classification is used and enforced. These pages focus on how and by whom decisions are made.

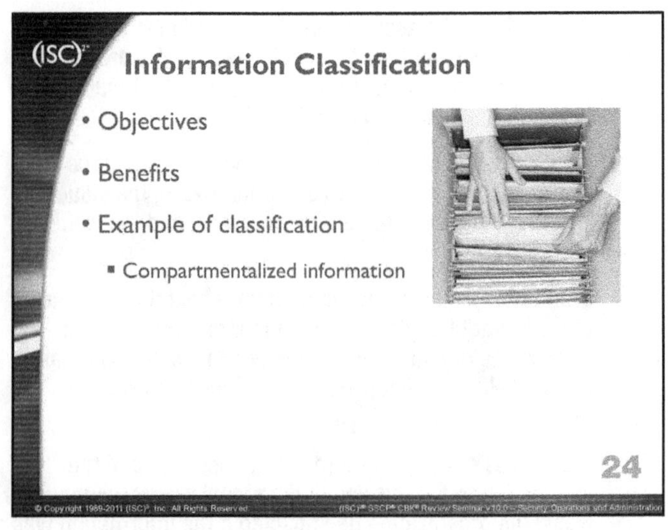
(ISC)²
Information Classification
• Objectives
• Benefits
• Example of classification
▪ Compartmentalized information
24

- **OBJECTIVES –**
  - Identify information protection requirements based on business risk related to unauthorized disclosure or data/ system corruption.
  - Identify data value in accordance with organization policy.
  - Ensure sensitive and/or critical information is provided appropriate protection/controls.
  - Lower costs by only protecting sensitive information.
  - Standardize classification labeling throughout the organization.
  - Alert employees and other authorized personnel to protection requirements.
  - Comply with privacy law, regulations, etc.
- **BENEFITS –**
  - Data that is classified as sensitive or critical is afforded a level of protection commensurate with its classification.
  - Cost/benefit accrues to the organization because increased controls are applied only where they are needed most. Compare, for example, the costs of the physical security infrastructure that you can observe in an expensive jewelry store, an inexpensive jewelry store, and a costume jewelry store. None of those stores would be properly served by the security infrastructure of one of the others. Similarly, a business will have data that is of high, medium, and low value. Business Impact Analysis will suggest the appropriate value of the controls to be placed on those data.
  - Appropriate markings will enable employees to recognize the need to protect classified data.
- **EXAMPLE OF CLASSIFICATION –** The U.S. Government classification employs a hierarchical series of classification schemes that include: unclassified, confidential, secret, and top secret. The private sector uses various categories such as: public, internal use only, and company confidential.
  - One of the problems we face is that while government classifications are well known and standardized, companies lack similar consistency.
    - It makes matters difficult when someone changes jobs and the new company values "internal use" above "company confidential" while the old company had it the other way around.
    - It is worse when different divisions of the same company have varying definitions.
    - Part of an SSCP's job is to identify these exposures and make appropriate recommendations in order to get them corrected.
- **COMPARTMENTALIZED INFORMATION –** Is that which has been determined to require a special authorization beyond the normal classification system.

---

**REFERENCES**

"Information Security Management Handbook," Tipton & Krause, 5th Edition, 2004.

"Glossary of Infosec and Infosec Related Terms," Corey Schou PhD, Idaho State University, 1996.

(ISC)²

**Clearance vs. Classification**

- People are granted clearances
- Data is classified
- Systems enforce access control through determining that a subject has the appropriate clearance to access a classified object
- Access is usually enforced along the principles of "least privilege" or "need-to-know"

25

- This topic is discussed in detail in the Access Control domain.
- Data classification occurs in both discretionary and mandatory systems, but mandatory access control systems require labels as well.

(ISC)²

## Domain Agenda

- Security Administration
- Policies and Supporting Documents
- Information Classification
- **System Life Cycle and System Development Life Cycle**
- Change and Configuration Management
- User Security Awareness

26



(ISC)²® SSCP® CBK® Review Seminar v 10.0 – Security Operations and Administration

(ISC)²

**System Life Cycle/System Development Life Cycle (SLC/SDLC)**

- It is a project management technique used to plan, execute, and control the system throughout its existence
  - It includes all needed personnel in the development process
  - It provides a framework for the development and maintenance of a system

27

 (ISC)² SSCP® CBK® Review Seminar v10.2 – Security Operations and Administration

- **SYSTEM LIFE CYCLE –** The security practitioner should be familiar with the systems life cycle (SLC)/systems development life cycle (SDLC). The steps are complementary, and in most instances, SLC and SDLC are used interchangeably (see the definition in the glossary of the Information Security Management Handbook, 6th edition). Generally, the SLC includes operations, maintenance and disposal, while SDLC ends with the transition to production.
  - For some organizations, maintenance is done by the developers (making it part of SDLC), while for others it is done by specialized maintenance teams (and is thus part of SLC). We are seeing more and more organizations now just using the terms SDLC to describe the entire change and maintenance process for applications.
- There are a number of major initiatives today focused on engendering the practice of "building security in" as a critical element of secure systems development, including the US Department of Homeland Security initiative "Build Security In" (http://www. buildsecurityin.us-cert.gov/ ), The Open Web Application Security Project (http://www.owasp.org/index.php/Main_Page), and the Common Weakness Enumeration (http://cwe.mitre.org/), among many others. It is therefore imperative that security practitioners become skilled in participating in SLC/SDLC activities to provide security recommendations as inputs early enough in the design phase to ensure that systems are built and maintained efficiently and securely.
- Bruce Schneier wrote an essay on his blog, "Schneier on Security," in July 2008, just after a major DNS flaw was publicized and a fix was in the news. His blog is well worth reading for all of us in the security industry. Here's a quote from that day that explains what secure system design is all about:

  *"The real lesson is that the patch treadmill doesn't work, and it hasn't for years. This cycle of finding security holes and rushing to patch them before the bad guys exploit those vulnerabilities is expensive, inefficient and incomplete. We need to design security into our systems right from the beginning. We need assurance. We need security engineers involved in system design. This process won't prevent every vulnerability, but it's much more secure — and cheaper — than the patch treadmill we're all on now.*

  *What a security engineer brings to the problem is a particular mindset. He thinks about systems from a security perspective. It's not that he discovers all possible attacks before the bad guys do; it's more that he anticipates potential types of attacks, and defends against them even if he doesn't know their details. I see this all the time in good cryptographic designs. It's over-engineering based on intuition, but if the security engineer has good intuition, it generally works.*

  *Kaminsky's vulnerability is a perfect example of this. Years ago, cryptographer Daniel J. Bernstein looked at DNS security and decided that Source Port Randomization was a smart design choice. That's exactly the work-around being rolled out now following Kaminsky's discovery. Bernstein didn't discover Kaminsky's attack; instead, he saw a general class of attacks and realized that this enhancement could protect against them. Consequently, the DNS program he wrote in 2000,djbdns, doesn't need to be patched; it's already immune to Kaminsky's attack.*

  *That's what a good design looks like. It's not just secure against known attacks; it's also secure against unknown attacks. We need more of this, not just on the internet but in voting machines, ID cards, transportation payment cards ... everywhere. Stop assuming that systems are secure unless demonstrated insecure; start assuming that systems are insecure unless designed securely."*

---

**REFERENCE**

http://www.schneier.com/blog/archives/2008/07/the_dns_vulnera.html

(ISC)²

## System Life Cycle/System Development Life Cycle (SLC/SDLC)

**Basic phases:**

- Project initiation and planning
- Functional requirements definition
- System design specifications
- Build (develop) and document
- Acceptance testing
- Implementation (transition to production)
- Operations and maintenance support
- Disposal

28



(ISC)²® SSCP® CBK® Review Seminar v.10.0 – Security Operations and Administration

- **SYSTEM LIFE CYCLE –** These are common steps used in the SLC. The more the security practitioner can be involved in each step, the more likely it is that the needed security will be built into the system.
  - The main justification for a SLC, and for building security in at the start, is cost avoidance or cost reduction.
  - Consumers of commercial software products will see cost avoidance in that there will be fewer patches and fixes and fewer losses due to inadequate security.
  - Vendors of commercial software will see cost reduction because they require smaller support staffs and have lower warranty and product maintenance costs.
- **PROJECT INITIATION AND PLANNING –** One of the secrets to a successful project is to have all the necessary resources available to represent the areas that need to be considered and integrated into the project. The security practitioner role here is providing advice on building security into the project, including the project budgets, design of the system, ongoing maintenance of the system, and project timeline. Threats, vulnerabilities, risks, and controls are all issues that should be addressed here first.
- **FUNCTIONAL REQUIREMENTS AND DEFINITION –** This is the "what if" phase. Requirements are always stated in the positive: The program must handle some data or perform some function. The SSCP will need to think about what the program should or will do when the data does not meet its specifications (too many characters, missing fields, delays in transmission, etc). Failure to consider these "negatives" is the cause of a great number of program and security mishaps.
- **SYSTEM DESIGN SPECIFICATIONS –** In this phase a project is broken into functions and modules and the nature of the hardware it is going to run on is considered. Security issues here are physical security of the hardware and network and must account for all the possible platforms. It isn't enough to say the project is limited to Linux or Windows for example, because each has a wide variety of versions and runs on an almost infinite combination of peripherals, chipsets, and drivers.
- **BUILD (DEVELOP) AND DOCUMENT –** Coding standards should include standard libraries of function calls and industry-standard solutions for items such as cryptography, hashing, and access control. Code in development should be secured such that only the developers have access, and under the practice of need-to-know, even if they only have access to the parts they need to see. Copies should not be left lying around in printed or machine readable form (e.g., CDs or USB memory sticks).
  - One of the main causes of buffer overflows is the use of insecure read functions. For example, there are functions that read as many characters as the user enters and secure variations of those functions that set a maximum number of input characters allowed. Secure programming techniques include inspecting code to make sure that only the latter are used. This, combined with similar safeguards for other buffer overflow causes, will result in significantly reducing and perhaps even eliminating this risk from a company's systems.
- **ACCEPTANCE TESTING –** A defined test plan must be created during the functional design stage. This plan must include testing to make sure that the new programs provide necessary security and, where applicable, privacy. The people responsible for the tests should not be the developers, nor should past-due delivery dates for developers impact the time allotted for testing.
- **IMPLEMENTATION (TRANSITION TO PRODUCTION) –** During this transition, the developers will be working on the delivery of training and assistance to the users and help desk personnel. Security features need to be carefully explained to both groups. In some organizations, developers will also help manage a turnover of the code to maintenance staff.
- **OPERATIONS AND MAINTENANCE SUPPORT –** When problems with the system arise, the maintenance, operations, and help desk people will be the first to know. They need to track the issues that come in and be ready to report their results to management in order to fuel the change-management process. These personnel need training in order to understand the differences between a request for change, a malfunction in the software, or a security weakness or breach, and they need to know how to properly handle each of those cases.
- **DISPOSAL –** After a period of time, component parts will reach end-of-life (backup system upgrade, larger disk replacing smaller one, etc). Procedures should be in place to sanitize the media and then dispose of it in a cost-effective manner. In years past, it was common to wipe a disk and then resell it. Today, the value of a small used disk is often less than the cost to securely wipe it. As a result, destruction is the most common form of secure disposal today.

## Security During Software Development

- Importance of security in applications
  - Controlling access to data in applications
  - Maintaining integrity of data within applications, processes, and databases
- Design, test, and review of security components
- Cost-benefit analysis and feasibility of security methodologies
- Manage and protect software libraries

29




- **SSCP DURING SOFTWARE DEVELOPMENT –** Software development requires special attention from a security perspective.
  - **APPLICATIONS ARE THE MOST COMMON WAY FOR USERS AND CUSTOMERS (AND ATTACKERS) TO ACCESS DATA –** which means the software must be built to enforce the security policy and ensure compliance with regulations (i.e., privacy) and integrity of both data and systems processes.
- As examples:
  - The security practitioner should ensure that the application does the following tasks properly:
    - Checks user authentication to the application.
    - Checks user authorization (privilege level).
    - Has edit checks, range checks, validity checks, and other similar controls to prevent the contamination of databases or production data.
    - Has procedures for recovering database integrity in the event of system failure.
- Manage and Protect libraries:
  - Software developed in house will have source code, object code, and runtime executables. These need to be managed and protected by policies, standards, and procedures. For example:
    - Source code should be protected from access by unauthorized users.
    - Changes to source should be tracked by version control systems so that rollback to a previous version is error free.
    - Programmers should not be able to update production systems directly.

## Testing and Development of Systems

- Test all possible contingencies
  - Permissible value ranges
  - Out of range values
  - Load tests
  - Error handling
- Do not expose sensitive data during tests

30




- **TESTING AND DEVELOPMENT OF SYSTEMS –** The SSCP will often assist in testing new systems or upgrades to existing systems. The tests should be thorough enough to ensure that all expected and unexpected actions are tested and that error handling is done correctly. Tests should also be done that test the maximum load on the system, including transaction volume, memory allocation, network bandwidth, and response times.
- **DO NOT EXPOSE SENSITIVE DATA DURING TESTS –** If production or sensitive data is used in testing, care must be taken to avoid the exposure of sensitive data.

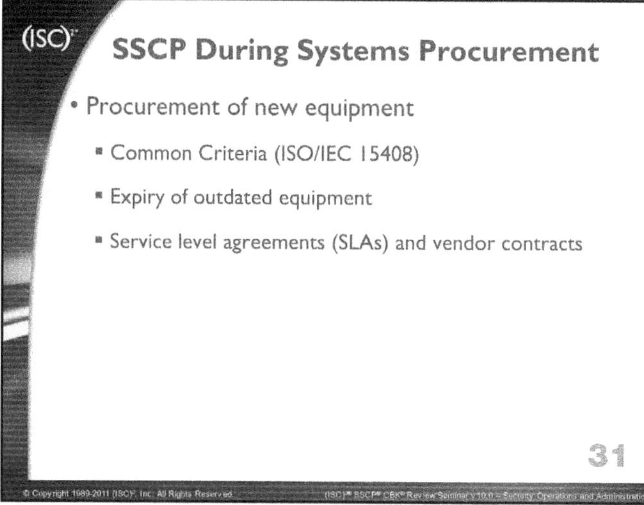

(ISC)²
SSCP During Systems Procurement
• Procurement of new equipment
▪ Common Criteria (ISO/IEC 15408)
▪ Expiry of outdated equipment
▪ Service level agreements (SLAs) and vendor contracts
31


- **SSCP DURING SYSTEMS PROCUREMENT –** Procurement of new equipment is a critical part of the role of the security practitioner. This requires:
  - Evaluation of the various solutions available.
  - Evaluation of the vendors in terms of ongoing maintenance, support, training.
    - Evaluation is made simpler via the Common Criteria. (See notes below.)
  - Monitoring of vendor contracts and service level agreements.
  - Correct implementation of equipment and formal acceptance of the equipment at the conclusion of the project.
  - Following the procurement procedures of the organization to ensure a fair purchasing process.
  - Monitoring of systems and equipment to identify equipment that is reaching the end of its lifespan so that it can be scheduled for replacement.
- **COMMON CRITERIA -**
  - The U.S. government created a series of documents known as the "rainbow series" (because of the bold colors on their covers). The red book described the components of a trusted network infrastructure (TNI) and the orange book talked about maintaining access control and confidentiality in a classified system. Both used a series of evaluative levels (C2, B3, etc.) and vendors had their products evaluated. This was known as TCSEC.
  - Other governments created their own equivalents (some started with TCSEC and made modifications) and eventually these were merged into ITSEC.
  - The governments of the U.S., UK, Canada, Germany, France, and the Netherlands used ITSEC as a starting point, then redeveloped a new procurement standard called "Common Criteria".
    - It has a series of increasingly more difficult evaluation assurance levels (EALs) numbered from one (lowest) to seven (highest). There are evaluation labs scattered all over the world. Leading vendors within an industry (e.g., vendors of firewalls) collectively create a standard, ideal, perfect solution, after which any individual vendor can have its product evaluated against the standard.
    - An EAL rating provisdes assurance that the vendor's claims match, to a defined level of testing, the collective standard, and that the product's documentation, development, and performance match the claims.
- Common Criteria is more formally known as ISO 15408.

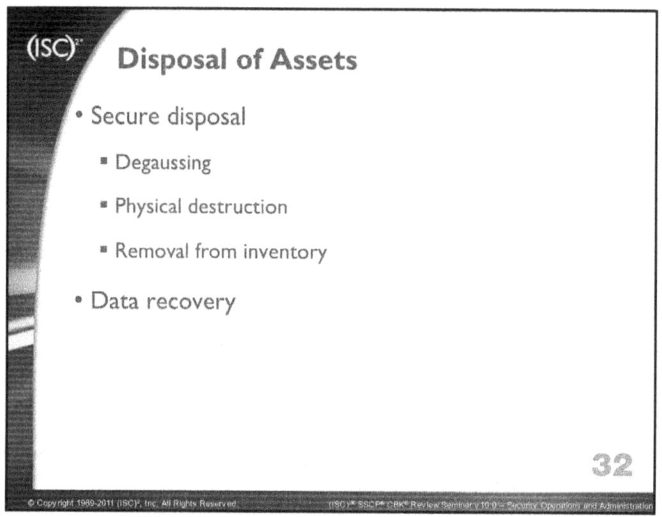


- **SECURE DISPOSAL –** The SSCP ensures that outdated equipment is disposed of in a secure manner so that no confidential data is exposed.
  - **DEGAUSSING –** the deletion of data through applying a coercive magnetic force to magnetic media. Usually renders all electronics unusable.
  - **PHYSICAL DESTRUCTION –** The only safe way to discard magnetic or optical storage devices that have contained classified data.
  - **REMOVAL FROM INVENTORY –** In order to maintain control over hardware assets it is important to show discarded equipment removed from inventory and service.
- **DATA RECOVERY –** Care must be taken to ensure that all data on discarded media has been backed up to alternate storage and that it is possible to access or read the data with new equipment.

## Certification and Accreditation Process

- The process to approve systems for implementation into production and ensure that the risk to the organization's mission, assets, and individuals is acceptable
- Authorizing official
- Certifier
- System owner

33



- **CERTIFICATION AND ACCREDITATION PROCESS** – Is the process to review a system throughout its lifecycle to ensure that it meets, and continues to meet, its specified security requirements. Accreditation is the formal acceptance by the authorizing official to accept the risk of implementing the system.
- **AUTHORIZING OFFICIAL** – Is the senior manager, also known as designated approving authority, who must review the certification report and make the decision to approve the system for implementation. The AO who approves the implementation of the system officially acknowledges and accepts the risk that the system would pose to the organization's mission, assets, or individuals.
- **CERTIFIER** – Is the individual or team responsible for performing the security test and evaluation (ST+E) for the system and preparing the report for the AO regarding the risk of operating the system.
- **SYSTEM OWNER** – Is the person who is responsible for the daily operations of the system and ensuring that the system continues to operate in compliance with the conditions set out by the AO.

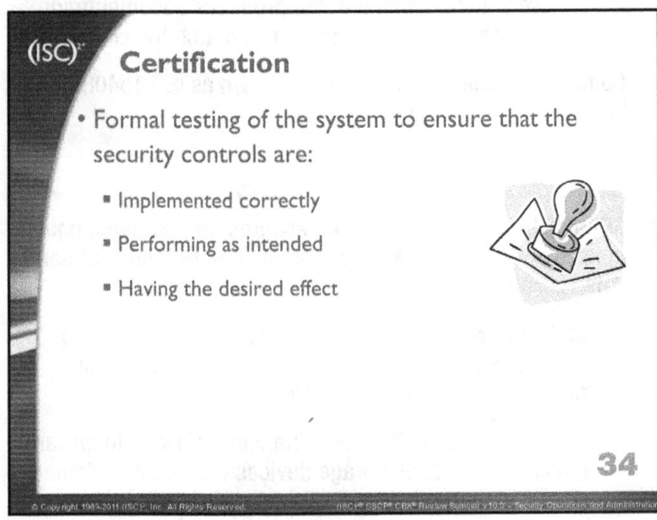

(ISC)²
Certification
Formal testing of the system to ensure that the security controls are:
Implemented correctly
Performing as intended
Having the desired effect
34


- **CERTIFICATION** – Certification is the technical evaluation of a project to provide assurance that the system is implemented correctly, meeting the initial design requirements, and that the security controls are working effectively to limit the risks to the system. This task is performed by a "certifier" or team of certifiers that have the skills needed to perform the verification process and the tests needed to prove compliance.
- Certification of a system means:
  - It meets the technical requirements.
  - It meets the functional requirements.
  - It provides assurance of proper operation.
- In order to certify, those involved in the process must first know the technical and functional requirements. They must also know the capabilities of the system that they are recommending for purchase or for approval to move into production.
  - These may be software or hardware requirements. They may be in terms of quantity or quality (able to authenticate 100 users a minute, 99.99% uptime, etc). They may be based on non-IT factors such as weight or energy consumption. The accreditors must examine all of the requirements called for. Many of these testing tasks (whether conducting them or managing them) will fall to SSCPs.
- Finally, they must match these lists to make sure that the system to be implemented meets or exceeds each and every one of the specifications. When they're sure that it does, they issue a recommendation for management approval.
- This doesn't mean that the system is right for your organization or that it is the best solution available. Certification only means that the product meets its technical and functional promises and operates as promised.

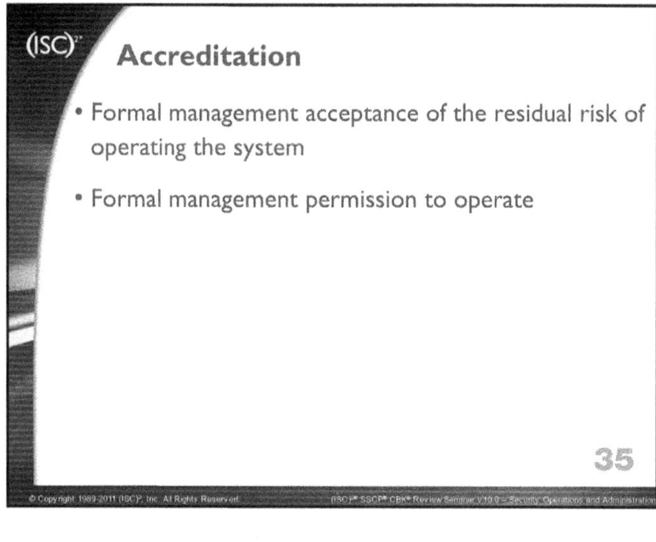


- **ACCREDITATION –** Once a system has been certified, the accreditation process provides the official management acceptance of the system.
  - The authorizing official or designated approving authority reviews the certification reports and, based on the operational environment, accepts the system for operation. This process can be defined in two ways:
    - Accreditation is management's formal acceptance of risk.
    - Accreditation is management's permission to implement.

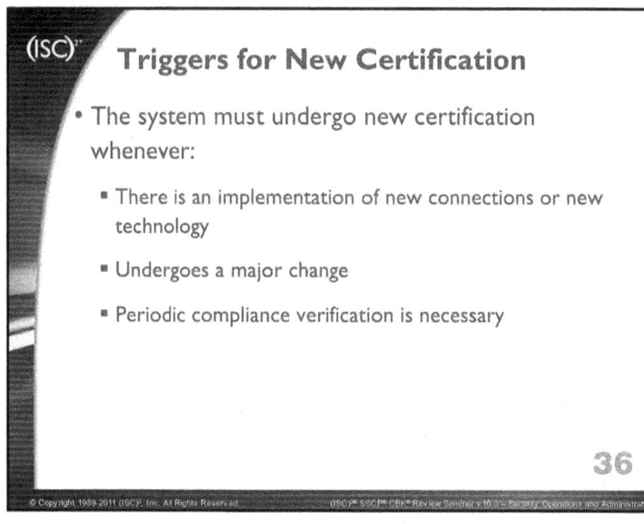


- **TRIGGERS FOR NEW CERTIFICATION –** The certification and accreditation process ensures that a system not only meets the security requirements today, but that it continues to meet the security requirements through the operations and maintenance phases of its life cycle.
  - The post-accreditation phase lists the activities required to continue to operate and manage the system so that it will maintain an acceptable level of risk.
  - In order to meet this requirement, continued risk assessments must be made.
    - Business needs change due to new products, new processes, mergers, or divestitures.
    - Products (solutions) that were once accredited might no longer meet the needs of the business.
    - Products are often updated or replaced by their vendors and these replacements need to be recertified and reaccredited.

# Domain Agenda

- Security Administration
- Policies and Supporting Documents
- Information Classification
- System Life Cycle and System Development Life Cycle
- **Change and Configuration Management**
- User Security Awareness

37

(ISC)²® SSCP® CBK® Review Seminar v 10.0 – Security Operations and Administration

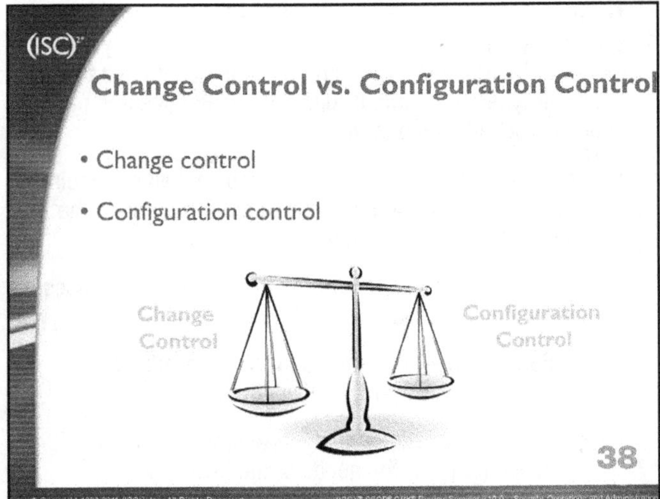
Change Control vs. Configuration Control
• Change control
• Configuration control
Change Control
Configuration Control
38

- While change and configuration control are often discussed as a pair, they are really two ends of a spectrum. The confusion, of course, is where a particular activity crosses from one to the other. Part of the reason it is so hard to define a sharp line between the two concepts is that different organizations of different complexities will, rightfully, draw the line in different places.
- Configuration control can be described as the management of the baseline settings for a system device. Those settings are designed to meet security requirements and require careful implementation and approval.
- Change control is the management of changes to the configuration. This is a time of risk since a change may affect the security operations or controls and an improper change could even disable the system or equipment being changed. The purpose of change control is to ensure that any changes to a production system are adequately tested, documented, and approved. The change itself must follow a change control process that ensures the change is made correctly and reported to management.

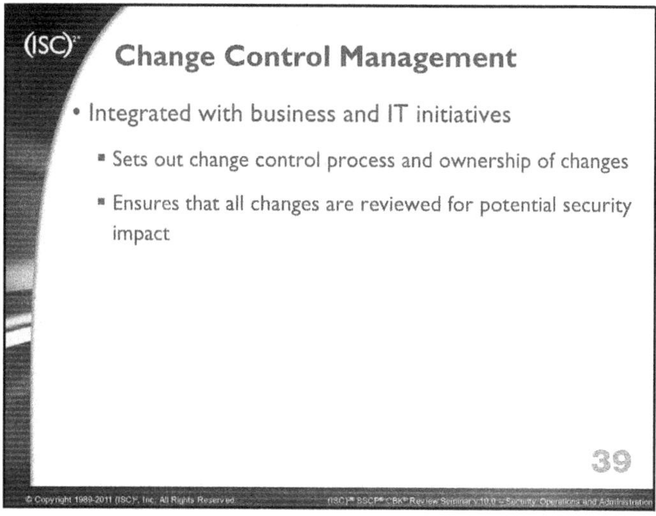


- **CHANGE CONTROL MANAGEMENT –** Is the process of developing a planned approach to controlling change in an environment by involving all pertinent departments (including the security department). Typically, the objective is to maximize the collective benefits for all people involved in the change and minimize the risk of failure in implementing the change.
  - **INTEGRATED WITH BUSINESS AND IT INITIATIVES –** To be effective, change management should be multidisciplinary, touching all aspects of the organization. It should also allow the business to change as needed. A business should not be constrained to the point of being inflexible and unable to change as needed to adopt new technologies, improvements, and modifications.
  - **SETS OUT CHANGE CONTROL PROCESS AND OWNERSHIP OF CHANGES –** Change management requires a written policy approved by the CIO/IT director, and the business information security manager that defines all roles, responsibilities, and procedures related to change management.
    - Change management procedures and standards are communicated and define the techniques and technologies to be used throughout the enterprise in support of the above policy.
    - Change management can be either "reactive," in which case management is responding to changes in the business environment (when, the source of the change is external – i.e., changes in regulations, customer expectations, supply chain) or "proactive," in which case management is initiating the change in order to achieve a desired goal. In this case, the source of the change will be internal – e.g., the adoption of new technology.
    - Change management can be conducted on a continuous basis, on a regularly scheduled basis (such as an annual review), on a "release" basis (where many small changes are incorporated into one larger change), or when deemed necessary on a program-by-program basis.
  - **ENSURES THAT ALL CHANGES ARE REVIEWED FOR POTENTIAL SECURITY IMPACT –** A change is a time of risk for a business. It may circumvent security features previously built into a system, it may result in an outage or system failure, and it may require extensive retraining in order for employees to learn how to use the new systems. The involvement of security is, therefore, particularly important in the change control process.
- The objectives of the formal change control process are to protect the integrity of the IT systems and ensure that all changes to the production environment are properly tested, scheduled, and communicated. Members of this group attend various meetings and forums estimating, planning, reviewing, and preparing for the organization's production environment.
- In cooperation with IT, the change control committee (in some cases called a change control board) provides heightened sensitivity to protect the computing resources and the information contained within those applications and databases. As part of the change process, the key members meet with counterparts from the IT organizations to review upcoming plans and ensure that all changes have been properly evaluated. They also ensure that the necessary security controls have been implemented correctly and tested, and that all changes are documented and communicated throughout the organization. In the event of a production problem, we should be able to easily identify recent changes that should be considered in the problem resolution process.

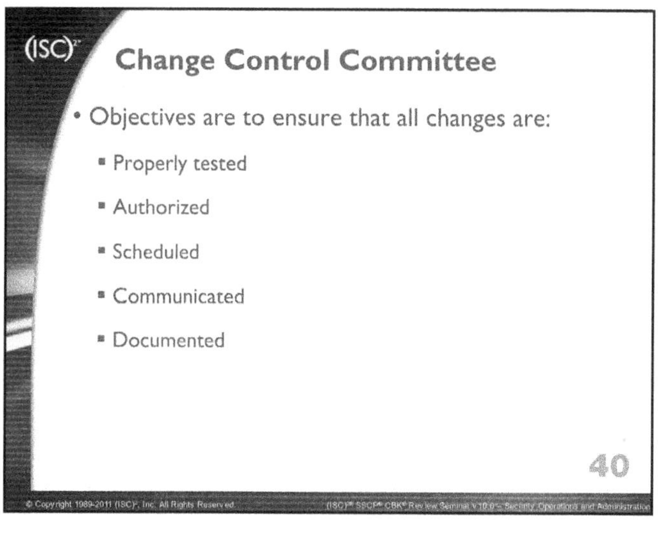


- **CHANGE CONTROL COMMITTEE –** Led by a senior manager or business process owner, the change control committee oversees all proposed changes to systems and networks and approves those changes and the change schedule that it deems appropriate. In this manner, changes cannot be made to a system, application, or network without the proper review, funding, and documentation being supplied.

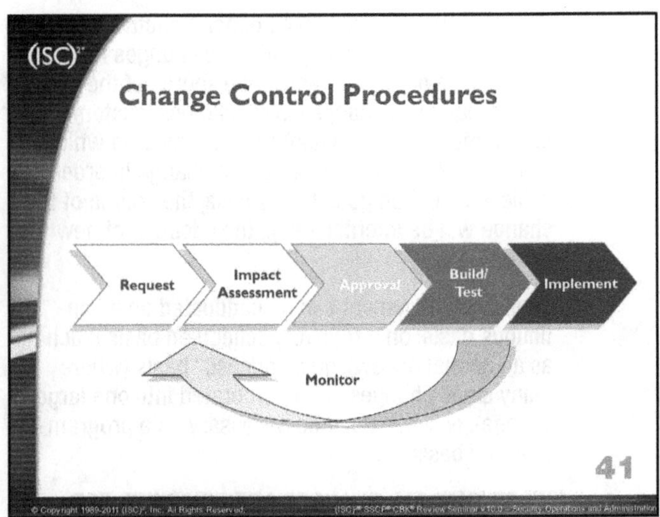


- **CHANGE CONTROL PROCEDURES –** These are the steps in a change control process to ensure that a change does not happen without going through the correct steps. This will avoid problems such as "scope creep," where unauthorized changes sneak into a project. It will also avoid problems with lack of oversight or testing, or of changes being implemented without proper authorization.
  - **REQUEST –** All proposed changes should be made formally (in writing) and submitted to the change control committee for review. A change should never be made to a project without having gone through the proper approval process.
  - **IMPACT ASSESSMENT –** This step evaluates the effect of the change on the project, budget, resources, and the security of the system or project.
  - **APPROVAL –** Or in some cases disapproval. Approval is the formal review and acceptance of the change by the change control committee.
  - **BUILD/TEST –** This step is the actual development or building of the change according to the approved change document. The change must then be tested to ensure that it does not impact other systems or programs in an unexpected manner. This testing may include regression testing and an in-depth review of the security of the modified product.
  - **IMPLEMENT –** Once the change has been tested and approved for release, the change is scheduled for implementation. This is where adequate separation of duties is important to ensure that no person can implement the change on his or her own without proper review and oversight. The final step in the implementation is the notification of management that the change has been made successfully.
  - **MONITOR –** All systems must be monitored following any implementation to ensure that the system, program, network, etc., is working correctly and to address any user complaints or problems. Ongoing monitoring may identify areas that require future changes, thus restarting the change control process.

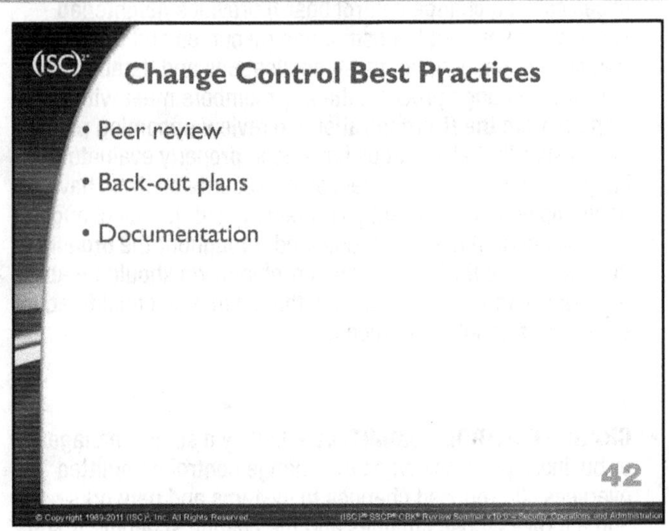


- **CHANGE CONTROL BEST PRACTICES –** A successful change control program will include the following:
  - **PEER REVIEW –** Ensure all changes are double checked by a peer or other expert before being put into production.
  - **BACK-OUT PLANS –** Ensure that if the change does not work properly, there is a plan to restore to a "known good" condition.
  - **DOCUMENTATION –** Must be kept current to reflect the true design of the system. Backup copies should be kept off-site as well.

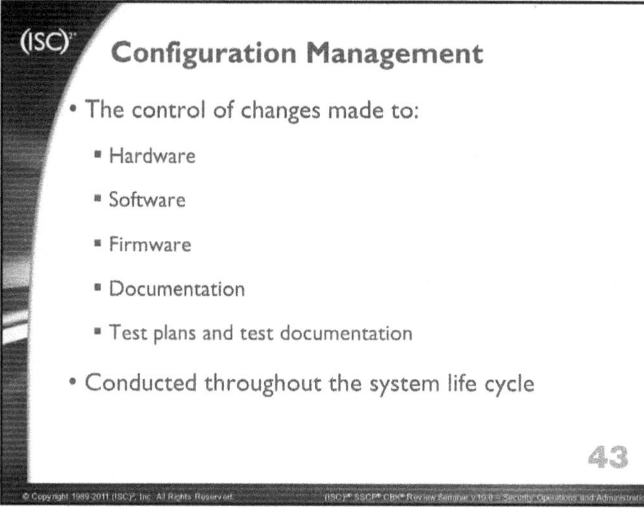


- **CONFIGURATION MANAGEMENT –** The control and documentation of modifications that are made to the hardware, software, firmware, and documentation of an automated system throughout the system life cycle.
  - From the perspective of a security professional, configuration management is concerned with evaluating the impact that a modification may have on the security (availability, confidentiality, integrity) of the system, application, or documentation, to ensure that all changes to a system are adequately reviewed and that the change to the configuration will not negatively impact the security in an unexpected manner.
  - All modifications must be controlled so that there is a level of assurance that the change will operate as authorized.
- **DEFINITION –** The management of security features and the supporting assurances through control of modifications made to hardware, software, firmware, documentation, test plans, and test documentation of an automated system commencing with the development and conducted throughout the operational life of a system.
  - Ensures that changes will not lead to a weakness or fault in the system.

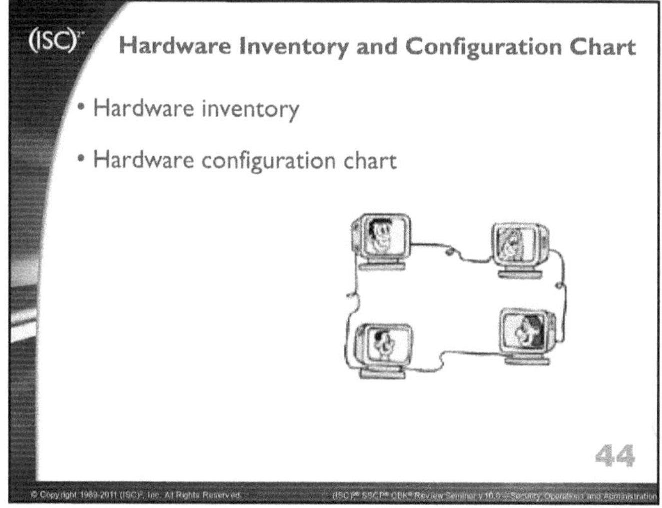

(ISC)²
Hardware Inventory and Configuration Chart
Hardware inventory
Hardware configuration chart
44


- **HARDWARE INVENTORY –** Most organizations lack a hardware inventory of what equipment they have, who has ownership or possession of it, and which departments or systems are using that equipment. This is a serious gap in their security program. In the event of a fire, equipment failure, or theft, this lack of documentation may result in extended loss of operations and poor response.
  - It also makes proper configuration management impossible. A decision to roll out a patch or fix (or even a new service pack or release) will be limited by the ability to positively locate, update, and test every affected device.
- **HARDWARE CONFIGURATION CHART –** To ensure that all systems are configured according to the baseline, and that work on a system or network is properly reviewed to ensure that the correct changes are made and will not bypass security features, it is important to have an up-to-date map or layout of the configuration of the hardware components.
  - This includes an as-built diagram of the network in order to plan the sequence of a change and see the ripple effects a change might generate.
  - This also includes copies of all software configurations; such as router, switch, and firewall configurations; so that changes and updates planned for one device can be examined for their impact on other devices.

## Patch and Service Pack Management

- Regular check for vendor upgrades
- Review for impact on system operations
- Patch rollout plan

45

 (ISC)²® SSCP® CBK® Review Seminar v10.0 – Security Operations and Administration

- **PATCH AND SERVICE PACK MANAGEMENT –** regular checks must be made for all upgrades and service packs from vendors.
- **REVIEW FOR IMPACT ON SYSTEM OPERATIONS –** Patches should be tested prior to rollout to ensure that the patch will not disable other systems or functionality.
- **PATCH ROLLOUT PLAN –** The organization must have a patch management process to ensure that patches are rolled out to all machines without causing system outages.

## Domain Agenda

- Security Administration
- Policies and Supporting Documents
- Information Classification
- System Life Cycle and System Development Life Cycle
- Change and Configuration Management
- **User Security Awareness**

46

 (ISC)²® SSCP® CBK® Review Seminar v10.0 – Security Operations and Administration

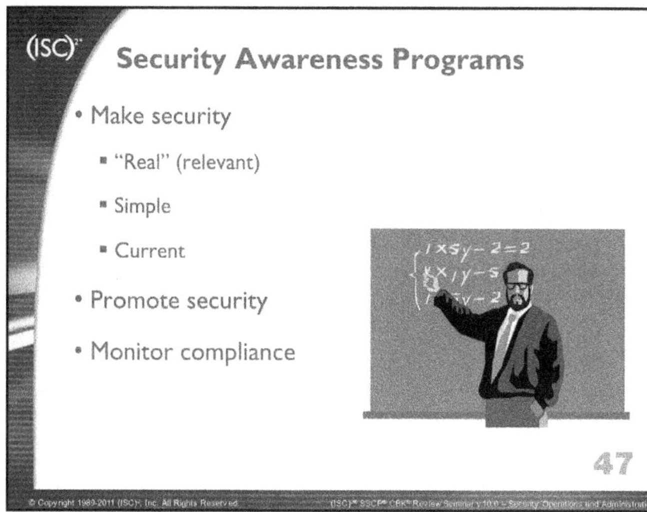
(ISC)²
Security Awareness Programs
• Make security
▪ "Real" (relevant)
▪ Simple
▪ Current
• Promote security
• Monitor compliance
47

- **SECURITY AWARENESS PROGRAMS –** Raising security awareness is an important part of the role of a security practitioner. Most people do not really understand what security is and what it is trying to accomplish. The security practitioner can use security awareness programs to deliver the message of the security objectives of the organization, and the current trends and threats in security, and to motivate personnel to comply with security policies.

- Users generally want to do "what's best" for the company. But, when security seems to be a stumbling block to productivity, they'll assist in bypassing it. You can remind them every day to keep passwords private, but one phone call to them at home on the weekend is all it takes for them to divulge it so someone else can finish a project on time. It is our job to teach the value of maintaining security and that there are alternate but still secure ways to solve productivity problems.

- Awareness programs can both teach users about security and measure their adherence to the security policies.
  - These sessions can provide practical advice on addressing or minimizing security incidents, and impress upon them the need for all users to see security as their personal responsibility.
  - **PROMOTE SECURITY –** Awareness will increase the inclusion of security into projects, processes, and daily activities.
  - **MONITOR COMPLIANCE –** A security awareness program is most effective when it is related to real-world issues. This can be achieved by monitoring employees for adherence to policy and then tailoring the awareness program according to the gaps found. The training sessions themselves can identify gaps by asking "what would you do" questions in response to company-tailored scenarios.

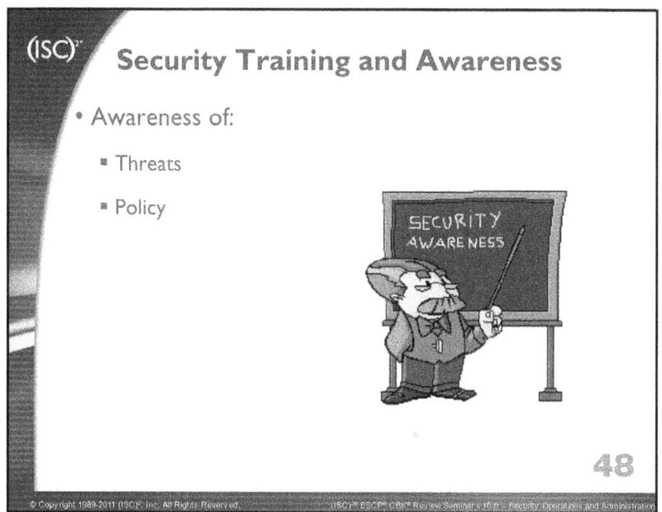
(ISC)²
Security Training and Awareness
• Awareness of:
▪ Threats
▪ Policy
SECURITY
AWARENESS
48

- **SECURITY TRAINING AND AWARENESS –** Perhaps one of the best security controls available is a strong awareness program. Awareness gains the support of all employees and assists in the effectiveness of the security program. Each person becomes a security advocate and is motivated to comply with policy, and to take care not to do something that could lead to a security breach.
  - **THREATS –** Employees should be aware of the threats that face an organization (especially from human factors) including the installation of rogue technologies, the poor selection of passwords, the risk of a phishing attack, etc.
  - **POLICY –** Policy is one of the best security tools we have. It mandates actions and provides authority for security controls. In many cases, employees will be more apt to comply with a security control if they realize that it is mandated by policy. A security awareness program should address the requirements and expectations of policy and the provisions included in the policy for lack of compliance.

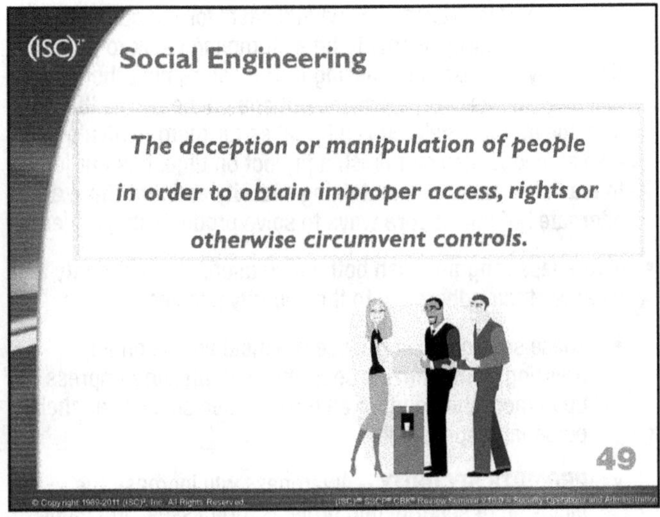

(ISC)²
Social Engineering
The deception or manipulation of people in order to obtain improper access, rights or otherwise circumvent controls.
49


- **SOCIAL ENGINEERING –** Social engineering is one of the most critical areas of security. As more and more people within an organization are granted electronic access to systems and data, the threat of improper release or modification of information increases. Social engineering in all its forms should be addressed in security awareness programs.
- Since the awareness and behavior of individuals is critical to mitigating social engineering exploits, there is no technical solution to the problem. An authorized user may be viewing sensitive data on a secure computer screen, and then read it aloud over the phone to a caller who sounds authoritative.

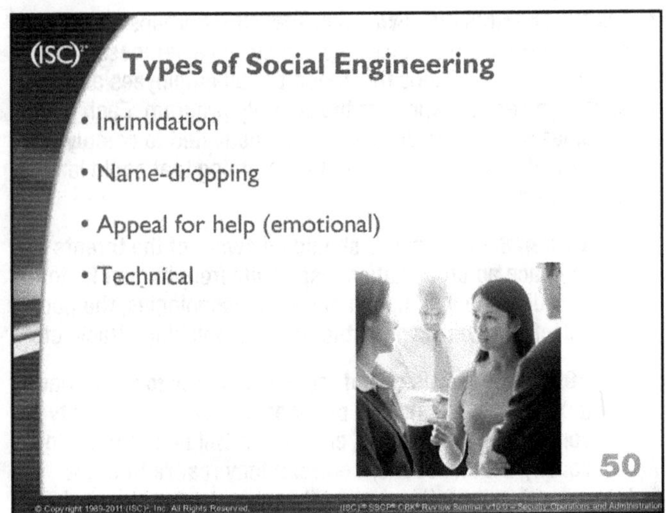

(ISC)²
Types of Social Engineering
• Intimidation
• Name-dropping
• Appeal for help (emotional)
• Technical
50


- **INTIMIDATION –** "Bullying" someone for information through threats or harassment.
- **NAME-DROPPING –** The use of names of other managers or persons of responsibility to convince another person that approval has been given by a higher authority or other party for the access request.
- **APPEAL FOR HELP (EMOTIONAL) –** Appeals to a person's sense of compassion or understanding of a difficult and maybe unreasonable situation are used to bypass normal procedures, or get special consideration. When combined with an incentive such as a reward, this type of engineering is very effective. For example, the "419" scam promise of monetary award for assistance with illegal transfer of money for a disadvantaged person – fools many people every year.
- **TECHNICAL –** The use of technology such as phishing attacks or illicit surveys to capture a person's or organization's data.

## Ethical Responsibilities

- "Set the example"
- Encourage the adoption of ethical guidelines and standards
- Inform users through security awareness training

51

- **ETHICAL RESPONSIBILITIES –** (ISC)² has provided us with good ethical guidelines to provide direction, but we must adopt them and encourage others to do the same. Our awareness training is a great place to conduct initial ethics training and refresher training for our users.
- **"SET THE EXAMPLE" –** By demonstrating strong ethical principles in our daily activities.
- **ENCOURAGE THE ADOPTION OF ETHICAL GUIDELINES AND STANDARDS –** Security professionals and practitioners not only know where the ethical boundaries are, but also must set the example for others to follow. This often means making hard decisions and setting a good example, as well as encouraging the organization to define its code of ethics so that its staff will operate in an ethical and responsible manner.
- **INFORM USERS THROUGH SECURITY AWARENESS TRAINING –** About ethical responsibilities.

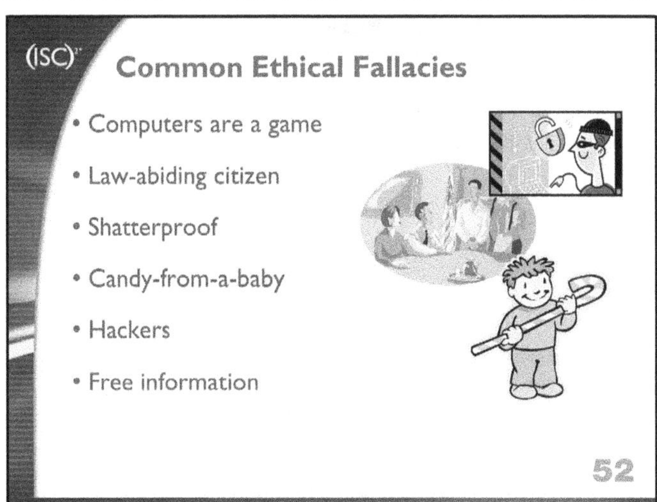
(ISC)²
Common Ethical Fallacies
• Computers are a game
• Law-abiding citizen
• Shatterproof
• Candy-from-a-baby
• Hackers
• Free information
52

- **COMMON ETHICAL FALLACIES –** Here are some of the common ethical fallacies we see almost daily:
- **COMPUTERS ARE A GAME –** Computers should prevent abuse, if you don't keep me out, it's your fault.
- **LAW-ABIDING CITIZEN –** In some legal systems, you may have the right to write viruses as a form of free speech/expression.
- **SHATTERPROOF –** Action could only hurt a few files, a little damage won't bother anyone.
- **CANDY-FROM-A-BABY –** If it's easy to break in, it must be all right.
- **HACKERS –** Learning motives makes nonprofit hacking OK. If I gain experience and more knowledge about computers, I'm not guilty of a crime.
- **FREE INFORMATION –** Information should be free; therefore, it must be OK to look through somebody's system to obtain information.

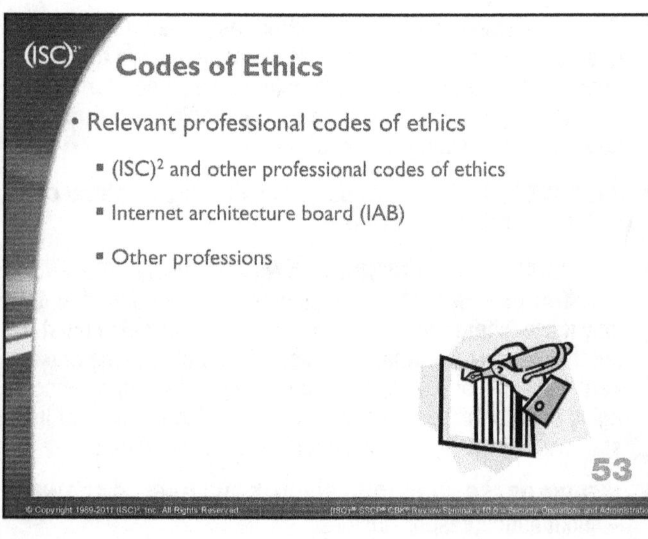

(ISC)²
Codes of Ethics
• Relevant professional codes of ethics
▪ (ISC)² and other professional codes of ethics
▪ Internet architecture board (IAB)
▪ Other professions
53


- **RELEVANT PROFESSIONAL CODES OF ETHICS –** One of the marks of professional status is a code of ethics.
- There are several codes of ethics that apply to information security, however, we will focus on the (ISC)² code of ethics over the next few slides. We will also note the published statements from the Internet architecture board (IAB) explaining what the IAB considers ethical and appropriate behavior.
  - Other organizations and professions have ethical codes that bind their members.
- Examples from other professions include:
  - Auditors: www.iso.org/tc176/ISO9001AuditingPractices-Group
  - Lawyers, U.S.: www.abanet.org/cpr/mrpc/model_rules.html
  - Lawyers, Japan: www.nichibenren.or.jp/en/
  - Physicians, worldwide: The Hippocratic Oath:
    - Classic: http://www.pbs.org/wgbh/nova/doctors/oath_classical.html
    - Modern: http://www.pbs.org/wgbh/nova/doctors/oath_modern.html
  - Physicians U.S. (Guidance on following the law within the Oath)
    - www.ama-assn.org/ama/pub/category/2512.html

(ISC)²

## (ISC)² Code of Ethics Preamble

*"Safety of the commonwealth, duty to our principals, and to each other requires that we adhere, and be seen to adhere, to the highest ethical standards of behavior"*

*"Therefore, strict adherence to this code is a condition of certification"*

54



(ISC)² SSCP® CBK® Review Seminar v.10.0 – Security Operations and Administration

- **(ISC)² CODE OF ETHICS PREAMBLE –** You will be asked to sign a statement agreeing to follow this code before you will be allowed to take the exam. It is wise to understand it as you will likely be asked to apply it in situations as you go through your daily activities.

## (ISC)² Code of Ethics Canons

- "Protect society, the commonwealth, and the infrastructure"
- "Act honorably, honestly, justly, responsibly, and legally"
- "Provide diligent and competent service to principals"
- "Advance and protect the profession"

55

- **(ISC)² CODE OF ETHICS CANONS –** These canons are expressed in the priority that they should be followed. Sometimes it becomes impossible to apply all of the canons, as they may conflict in a particular situation. To work through difficult ethical challenges, carefully note the order in which the canons are applied.

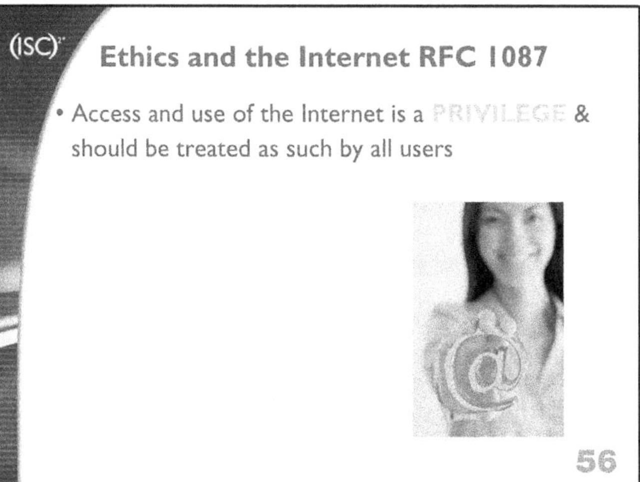

Ethics and the Internet RFC 1087
Access and use of the Internet is a PRIVILEGE & should be treated as such by all users
56


- **REQUEST FOR COMMENT (RFC) 1087 –** From the Internet architecture board (IAB). Provides recommendations concerning the proper use of the resources of the Internet. It highlights that access to the Internet is a PRIVILEGE, not a right.

(ISC)²

## Internet Architecture Board (IAB)

**Any activity is unethical and unacceptable that purposely:**

- Seeks to gain unauthorized access to Internet resources
- Disrupts the intended use of the Internet
- Wastes resources (people, capacity, computer) through such actions
- Destroys the integrity of computer-based information
- Compromises the privacy of users
- Involves negligence in the conduct of Internet-wide experiments

57

 (ISC)²® SSCP® CBK® Review Seminar v10.0 – Security Operations and Administration

- **INTERNET ARCHITECTURE BOARD (IAB) –** The IAB has provided this list of unethical and unacceptable practices. Although it was one of the first ethical statements for Internet use, it is still applicable today.

(ISC)²

## Professional Requirements

- Required behavior
- Professions
  - (ISC)²
  - Lawyers
  - Accountants
- Legislated
  - HIPAA/PIPEDA
  - SOX
  - OECD guidelines

58

 (ISC)²® SSCP® CBK® Review Seminar v10.0 – Security Operations and Administration

- Professional ethics are often the subject of rules and regulations. Those rules might come from the certifying agencies in any profession and violation of them could cause loss of certification or license.
- In other contexts, legislatures have created laws or regulations that require ethical behavior. The examples on this page are U.S. and Canadian privacy laws and U.S. corporate accounting laws. The OECD (Organization for Economic Cooperation and Development) is an organization of 30 countries whose goal is economic cooperation and growth. In 1980, it created eight privacy principles that have formed the basis for much of the international privacy legislation (http://www.privacilla.org/government/oecdguidelines.html). The essence is that an organization should collect only what it needs, not share it, keep it up to date, use it only for the purpose collected, and destroy it when done.

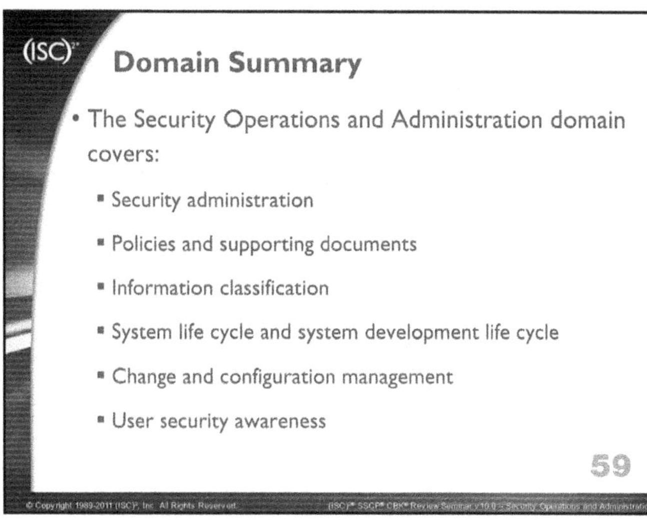

(ISC)²
Domain Summary
• The Security Operations and Administration domain covers:
▪ Security administration
▪ Policies and supporting documents
▪ Information classification
▪ System life cycle and system development life cycle
▪ Change and configuration management
▪ User security awareness
59


- The SSCP should now have a good understanding of the essential security practices which all organizations require and are responsible for. Key among these are the development of security strategies necessary for adequate protection of assets, and administering the various tools available to ensure success.
- The elements in administering an effective security program depend upon planning, developing, designing, implementing and managing the operational controls to ensure availability, integrity, and confidentiality of business assets (people, processes and information, and technology).

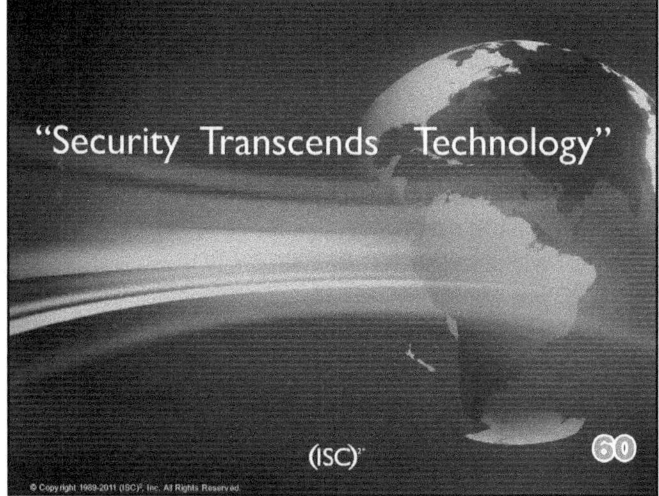

# Review Questions

## SECURITY OPERATIONS AND ADMINISTRATION

1. **At what stage of the application development process should the security department first become involved?**
   a. Prior to the implementation.
   b. Prior to user acceptance testing.
   c. During unit testing.
   d. During requirements development.

2. **Security of an automated information system is most effective and economical if the system is**
   a. optimized prior to addition of security.
   b. customized to meet a specific security threat.
   c. subjected to intense security testing.
   d. designed originally to provide the necessary security.

3. **Programmed procedures which ensure that valid transactions are processed accurately and only once are referred to as**
   a. data installation controls.
   b. application controls.
   c. operation controls.
   d. physical controls.

4. **What common attack can be used against passwords if a copy of the password file can be obtained?**
   a. Birthday attack
   b. Dictionary attack
   c. Plaintext attack
   d. Smurf attack

5. **What is the BEST method of storing user passwords for a system?**
   a. Password-protected file
   b. File restricted to one individual
   c. One-way encrypted file
   d. Two-way encrypted file

6. **The concept that all accesses must be mediated, protected from modification, and verifiable as correct is the concept of**
   a. a secure model.
   b. security locking.
   c. a reference monitor.
   d. a secure state.

7. **The MAIN goal of an annual security awareness program designed for senior management is to provide**
   a. a way to communicate security procedures.
   b. a clear understanding of potential risk and exposure.
   c. an opportunity to disclose exposures and risk analysis.
   d. a forum to communicate user responsibilities.

8. **Key elements of an information security program include**
   a. business continuity and disaster recovery planning, definition of access control requirements, and human resources policies.
   b. business impact, threat and vulnerability analysis, delivery of an information security awareness program, and physical security of key installations.
   c. security policy implementation, assignment of roles and responsibilities, and information asset classification.
   d. senior management organizational structure, message distribution standards, and procedures for the operation of security management systems.

9. **Authentication that can be determined as genuine and in which those involved cannot deny their participation is referred to as**
   a. identification.
   b. authorization.
   c. non-repudiation.
   d. auditability.

10. **A chronological record of system activities that is saved to a file to potentially identify actions and processes on a system is known as**
    a. an audit trail.
    b. data mining.
    c. an algorithmic computation.
    d. a non-repudiated list.

11. **Controlling levels of access to a network or an information system is accomplished through the use of**
    a. password changes.
    b. directory permissions.
    c. biometrics.
    d. identification.

**12. When users are given only the minimum levels of permission to perform their tasks, it is referred to as**

a. limited authority.
b. restricted privileges.
c. separation of responsibilities.
d. least privilege.

**13. When each process has distinct address space for application code and data, it is called**

a. a reference model.
b. process isolation.
c. least privilege.
d. system high.

**14. In the initial phases of the system development life cycle (SDLC), what must be performed?**

a. Cost justification
b. Performance analysis
c. Software patches
d. Application coding

**15. The MOST common method of indicating the protection requirements of information is via**

a. separation of duties.
b. auditing.
c. need to know.
d. classification.

**16. In a multi-level security (MLS) system, access to information at a particular security classification is based upon a**

a. user'sjob title.
b. security clearance.
c. user identification (Userld).
d. Job function.

**17. The principle of least privilege restricts a user according to**

a. job duties.
b. time of day.
c. mandatory access controls.
d. dual control.

**18. Which access control model requires the owner of data to specify who can access the data?**

a. Mandatory access control (MAC)
b. Discretionary access control (DAC)
c. Non-discretionary access control (NDAC)
d. Owner access control (OAC)

**19. Which of the following encompasses conceptual definitions, functional requirements, design reviews, and software development?**

a. Configuration management process
b. Software development life cycle (SDLC)
c. Change control process (CCP)
d. System security plan (SSP)

**20. When a system operates at the same classification level as the data housed within, it is referred to as**

a. isolated.
b. compartmented.
c. multi-level.
d. system high.

# Notes

# Index

## B



## C

## E



## F



## G



## H

## J



## K



## L

## M

## N

## Q



## R

## S

## T

## X



## Y



## Z

# SSCP Review Seminar Questions, Answer Key

**ACCESS CONTROL**

1. C
2. B
3. A
4. C
5. D
6. A
7. C
8. B
9. D
10. A
11. B
12. A
13. B
14. D
15. A
16. B
17. C
18. D
19. C
20. A

**CRYPTOGRAPHY**

1. D
2. C
3. B
4. A
5. A
6. D
7. B
8. A
9. C
10. C
11. D
12. B
13. A
14. D
15. C
16. B
17. D
18. B
19. B
20. C

**NETWORKS AND COMMUNICATIONS**

1. D
2. A
3. B
4. B
5. B
6. B
7. B
8. D
9. D
10. C
11. A
12. D
13. B
14. C
15. A
16. D
17. B
18. D
19. B
20. D

**SECURITY OPERATIONS AND ADMINISTRATION**

1. D
2. D
3. B
4. B
5. C
6. C
7. B
8. C
9. C
10. A
11. B
12. D
13. B
14. A
15. D
16. B
17. A
18. B
19. B
20. D

**ANALYSIS AND MONITORING**

1. D
2. B.
3. A
4. A
5. B
6. B
7. D
8. D
9. A
10. D
11. B
12. C
13. A
14. B
15. B
16. C
17. B
18. B
19. C
20. C

**MALICIOUS CODE AND ACTIVITY**

1. D
2. D
3. A
4. A
5. B
6. B
7. D
8. B
9. D
10. B
11. C
12. D
13. A
14. A
15. C
16. B
17. B
18. B
19. B
20. C

**RISK, RESPONSE, AND RECOVERY**

1. D
2. C
3. D
4. C
5. D
6. B
7. D
8. A
9. A
10. A
11. A
12. A
13. A
14. D
15. B
16. C
17. B
18. B
19. D
20. D